READINGS IN PHILOSOPHY OF ART AND AESTHETICS

READINGS IN PHILOSOPHY OF ART AND AESTHETICS

Milton C. Nahm
Bryn Mawr College

PRENTICE-HALL, INC.
Englewood Cliffs, N.J.

Library of Congress Cataloging in Publication Data

Nahm, Milton Charles, 1903– comp.
Readings in philosophy of art and aesthetics.

(The Century philosophy series)
Includes bibliographical references.

1. Aesthetics—Collected works. 2. Art—Philosophy —Collected works. I. Title.
BH21.N33 1974 700'.1 72–11659
ISBN. 0–13–760892–6

FOR ELINOR

Printed in the United States of America

10 9 8 7 6 5 4 3 2 1

PRENTICE-HALL INTERNATIONAL, INC., LONDON
PRENTICE-HALL OF AUSTRALIA, PTY. LTD., SYDNEY
PRENTICE-HALL OF CANADA, LTD., TORONTO
PRENTICE-HALL OF INDIA PRIVATE LIMITED, NEW DELHI
PRENTICE-HALL OF JAPAN, INC., TOKYO

Contents

To the Reader

Among the motley crew of academics who grace the pages of Robert Lewis Taylor's *Professor Fodorski*[1] is one Hugo Van Dusen, "an anthologist . . . considered to have no peer, even north of the Mason Dixon line." This "eroded man in a shaggy tweed jacket" occupies the scene but for a brief moment, a moment long enough, however, for one of his colleagues to express his admiration. "It's a pleasure to watch the fellow work . . . By gad, the way he stepped around that room! Picking out a book here, slapping down a magazine there, shaking his head—analyzing, rejecting, choosing . . . When the fever's on him, Van Dusen swings the sledge."

I quote this passage for a variety of reasons, principally because it amuses me but also because it reflects, as in a distorting mirror, what might be supposed to be the activities of all collectors of writings. Moreover, it hints at the truth—namely, that all editors of essays are prone to occupational infirmities. Van Dusen's stem from the fact that he is getting along in years: "His legs are giving out—the legs go first in collecting, you understand."

It may well be that it is the legs that give out if you are an anthologist who collects the little flowers of literature, but it is not the legs that are adversely affected in the construction of such a book as *Readings in Philosophy of Art and Aesthetics,* despite the fact that here one deals with the deep roots and heavy timbers upon which colossal superstructures have been erected during two and a half millenia. There are, if not infirmities, at least moments of acute discomfort that occur in the process of editing a book in this area of speculation. One may solace oneself with the hope expressed by Aristotle that while the roots are bitter, the fruits are sweet. But no book that includes material written from the middle of the sixth century B.C. down to the present merits much attention if it is merely an *omnium gatherum,* and it may be of some value to indicate to the reader some of the methods by which the contents were chosen from the enormous bulk of a truly noble literature.

When, years ago, I first planned a book of readings in Philosophy of Art and Aesthetics, it seemed obvious that I should follow several—to me—well-marked lines of procedure. I wanted to present essays of sufficient length to give as much of the context of the sustaining argument as possible. I resolved at the same time that the skeletal structure of the book would consist in the classical writings in Philosophy of Art and Aesthetics. It seemed to me then, and I am no less certain of it now, that a book of readings that did not include the principal contributions

[1] From *Professor Fodorski (A Politico-Sporting Romance),* p. 41. Copyright 1950 by Robert Lewis Taylor. Reprinted by permission of Doubleday & Company, Inc.

of writers such as Plato, Aristotle, Plotinus, Longinus, Kant, Hegel, and Croce would be of little value. It seemed to me also that were it possible to include, among others, Leonardo da Vinci, Leone Ebreo, Alexander Gerard, David Hume, Friedrich Schiller, and E. M. Forster, I should achieve my goal insofar as classical Philosophy of Art is concerned. This appeared to me to be a desirable end in terms of my own interpretation of "classical," which has less to do with the fact that a writing has endured than that it has endured because it has exerted a profound and fruitful influence upon speculation. This suggested the third primary point of departure for this book. If one were to consider the classical philosophies as the spine of the book, the remainder of the structure of the volume should be closely bound to that spine and yet at the same time remain self-sufficient. If one were to take care to show how, for example, Plato's theory that art is play recurs in Schiller's *On the Aesthetic Education of Man,* both in terms of Platonic and Kantian theory, and yet is elaborated and so moves beyond both Plato and Kant in its author's interpretation of what the object of art is and how the imagination is employed in aesthetic experience, the relation of ancient and modern speculation should come clear. Themes recur in an extraordinary way in speculation upon art and beauty, a fact that provides a fascinating spectacle in the history of the subject.

With this I return to the "infirmities" of the editor of a book in Philosophy of Art and Aesthetics. He suffers not because his legs give out, as does Mr. Taylor's anthologist—rather, because he must choose and decide. It is easy enough to decide to include Aristotle's *Poetics* in its entirety; it is painful to choose from among the riches of a Plotinus, a Kant, a Hegel, or a Croce. Nor is this the sole problem. For, if I may revert to my early survey of the book I intended to produce, it was clear to me then and it is clearer to me now that I have observed with some interest various books published in this field, that there is a tendency among collectors to re-collect material which is somewhat readily available. If, as I have suggested, one does provide the spine of a book of collections from the "classical" writers, some such repetition is inevitable. But there is also much valuable material that is not so readily accessible. In the present volume, the reader will come upon selections from a number of the writings by extraordinary men and these, so far as I know, are not as well known nor as readily available as they might be. I have included some of Descartes' letters on music; Philostratus on imagination; Feijóo—the Spanish monk—on taste; Dionysius the Areopagite on beauty; Leone Ebreo on creativity; George Puttenham on the Augustinean conception of the artist; Edward Young on the genius, and others who repay reading.

One final remark on my original plan for this book. I had then and I have now neither profound interest nor great competence in the contemporary methods of approach to Aesthetics. I should have regarded the omission of this material years ago as a greater fault in a book of readings than I do now. The spate of collections devoted solely to this technique and its results has relieved me of the responsibility to include this material here, valuable though it may be.

Let me now return to the problems of choice and decision. I have mentioned that they must be exercised, even though one decide at the outset to include both the classical and the comparatively novel. It is noticeable, however, that the recurrence of theme I have mentioned comes to the assistance of the collector. Moreover, the recurring themes are the great themes of Philosophy of Art and Aesthetics. The theory of imitation, dominant in Greek speculation, holds the field until late in the eighteenth century, whereupon imagination supplants it in the interest of philosophers of art and of aestheticians. The need for Aesthetics as a central theme begins to exclude Philosophy of Art, once Baumgarten's *Aesthetica* exerts the influence of its title. In the course of history, the divergence of artist and critic widens, with its beginnings in Plato's *Laws* and its denial in Aristotle's *Poetics* serving later speculation as points of departure. Taste and criticism vie for the center of the aesthetic stage. Almost wholly divergent theories of the genius illustrate the conflict between philosophers and critics who maintain that art is wholly intelligible and those who believe that the *sine qua non* of beauty and aesthetic value is inexplicable originality. I have tried to show the relation of these themes by the use of footnotes that refer to what is to come and what has been written, and I have avoided, insofar as I could do so, burdening this book with additional footnotes that might well have doubled its size.

These are all techniques available to the editor of a book of readings in Aesthetics and Philosophy of Art, and I have used them as my experience in this subject has suggested that I needed them. Still, the problems of choice and decision are, in my estimation, insoluble without one device that is in fact so much more than a device that it proved to be integral to the conception and completion of this book. This is the pattern into which the collected materials fit, the systematic philosophy of art that permits emphasis to be placed upon writings that may otherwise be of lesser significance but serve to interrelate the major traditions of aesthetic speculation. I discovered what this pattern might be shortly after my introduction to Philosophy of Art and Aesthetics. Imitation and imagination, making and creating, taste and criticism, "art for art's sake" and expression—all, it seemed to me, were primarily assumptions and arguments concerning freedom in art and fine art. Freedom for the artist and for the man who experiences art is liberation from criteria and judgment in nonaesthetic terms. Such nonaesthetic criteria are alien to freedom. They subordinate the subject to such values as mathematicians, political theorists, theologians, moralists and the like have brought to art in its long history. More important, still, is that freedom as the pattern for Philosophy of Art and Aesthetics, in manifesting itself in freedom to make and create and criticize, presents in the long history of speculation conflicting claims. Interpreted as making, it is freedom to make what is intelligible and therefore open to rational criticism. The primary criterion is accuracy. Freedom has also been interpreted as the freedom to create what is original. Here the role of accuracy is reduced to a minimum, and the criteria of novelty and individuality serve as the marks of value.

Presupposed by the bifurcated interpretations of Philosophy of Art and Aesthetics in terms of freedom as making and of freedom as creating is the basic pattern for the readings in this book. In 1947 I published in *The Journal of the*

History of Ideas an article entitled "The Theological Background of the Theory of the Artist as Creator." This I have used as the concluding portion of the introductory chapter of this book of *Readings in Philosophy of Art and Aesthetics,* and it serves as its encompassing pattern. In my opinion, no aspect of art—its production, its experience, and its criticism—has remained outside the influence of what I have called "the great analogy" of the artist to God. The analogy is in fact a double one. The artist as maker is argued by analogy to the Greek demiurgic artisan or architect of the universe, as in Plato's dialogue *Timaeus.* The artist as creator is argued by analogy to God the Creator in *Genesis.* Within the tradition of these analogies, the theories of making and creating, of imitation and imagination, of genius and artisan have taken on meaning for me and have illuminated many otherwise obscure passages in the history of speculation.

I add only a brief note concerning more technical matters. In presenting this material, I have used footnotes sparsely and provided introductions varying in length according to need. In my *Selections from Early Greek Philosophy* I found valuable the method of brief introductions and biographies following upon longer and more detailed introductions to sections of the book. The reader of this book will find himself comparatively free to make his own interpretations and draw his own conclusions from the readings themselves.

Many choices I have made have been difficult, but I console myself that no book of readings in this field could ever claim to be exhaustive. There is also the greater consolation in having brought together materials that may serve to illuminate one of the great themes of speculation, that of freedom as creativity. Schiller is correct in holding that "Beauty . . . is our second Creator." Kant's comment—"Productive imagination is a powerful faculty for creating another nature out of the material which actual nature gives"—is much more than an aesthetic dictum.

M.C.N.

READINGS IN PHILOSOPHY OF ART AND AESTHETICS

INTRODUCTION

Chapter 1

Philosophy of Art and Aesthetics

A. On the Emergence of the term "Aesthetic"

In her illuminating study of Philosophy of Art, Katherine E. Gilbert draws a sharp contrast between the Renaissance interpretation of the artist as one who creates a work of art and the classical philosophy of the artist as a maker. She writes that in the period of the rebirth of learning the conception of the artist's "invention" is one of "creating . . . a mental image by human strength alone," whereas for the Greek speculative mind the artistic process is one of finding "what is already there, though hidden. . . ."

This summary contrast between making and creating serves admirably to place before us the pattern of *Readings in Philosophy of Art and Aesthetics*. It is the more admirable once it is realized that the contrast between originating or finding what is already there holds in speculation upon art from the earliest period of philosophy, the Pre-Socratic, to the present. The quotation from *A History of Esthetics*[1] is acute and succinct. It is, however, neither inclusive nor conclusive. One of its merits is precisely the fact that, beyond being a starting point, it touches not only upon what the artist does but also illuminates speculation concerning the experience, judgment, criticism, and evaluation of fine art and of aesthetic objects and events. No period of either Philosophy of Art or of Aesthetics fails to present the identical puzzles concerning the nature of the activity that produces and the nature of the experience that judges an object or event made by an artist who occupies a space and persists in a time separate from the spatial locus and the temporal duration of the object he produces.

We are interested in this Introduction to the book of *Readings* to delineate the central pattern into which the selections fall. It is evident that the extension of the application of "creating" and "finding" into speculation concerning experience and judgment might suggest that we are embarked upon a project that gathers together all problems in Aesthetics. If, however, we quote Mrs. Gilbert's sentence entire, we come at once upon emphases in theme that prove helpful in limiting our task to the consideration of certain central problems in Philosophy of Art and Aesthetics. "The artist's invention," she writes, "has subtly shifted from finding what is already there, though hidden, to selecting or creating or

[1] K. E. Gilbert and H. Kuhn, *A History of Esthetics* p. 186. See also Mrs. Gilbert's "The Relation between Aesthetics and Art-Criticism," (pp. 569 et seq.) in Chapter 13.

fashioning a mental image by human strength alone." We get to the nerve of the statement in the phrase "by human strength alone." The basic issue between art as creating and art as making is one between two conceptions of human freedom. It is clear from the context of the quotation that what Mrs. Gilbert has in mind is the increased independence of the artist, won at least conceptually from the assumption of an actual or a metaphorical control by, or influence of, the Muses or the Gods to which classical speculation sometimes attributed the artist's powers to transcend in art the limitation of "minute correctness." As Mrs. Gilbert interprets it, "Art is no longer cosmic energy but human power." To the implications of this statement, we shall shortly come. There is evidently some doubt in Mrs. Gilbert's mind that writers in the Renaissance make the distinction with precision: "In this period the line between the human contribution and the divine infusion in the composition of genius was lightly drawn and shifting in its position."

The doubt is well grounded, as will be evident in the second portion of this Chapter. Still, we have now come upon the conceptions in art that serve to guide interpretations of human freedom. What is made explicit by Mrs. Gilbert is that the freedom attained by the artist is gained because he is a "genius" and what remains implicit is that the "genius" is "inspired." The two words and the beliefs that lie behind them have persisted from the Greek period to the present, and they have been used in artistic and aesthetic discourse in connection with "invention." Some of our difficulties both in Philosophy of Art and Aesthetics arise precisely because "invention" is a free process presumed to apply both to "human strength alone" and to "cosmic energy."

If the framework of reference for both "human strength alone" and "cosmic energy" is freedom, it is freedom manifested, at any rate at the outset, in making and creating. Implicit in making is the argument that the artist makes actual what is potential in a material, as a sculptor "discovers" the statue in the marble and carves out what he finds. Implicit in creating is the argument that no such statue exists in the marble but is originated by the sculptor. The shift from making to creating is in fact from one conception of freedom to quite a different but no less radical one. The theory of making is presupposed by the conception of an artist free to choose or to select, the theory of creating by that of an artist free to originate. When, for example, Aristotle tells us that "the poet should work out his play to the best of his power, with appropriate gestures," he is arguing, as he does with considerable consistency throughout the *Poetics*, that the artist is free to select this alternative from among various possibilities and that he makes his choice in the process of constructing the drama. By way of contrast, when Kant writes that the fine artist, who is the genius, uses that powerful faculty, the productive imagination, "for originating a new nature out of the material that actual nature gives it," his concern is less with choice or selection than with accounting for the new, for what is not commonplace, for what marks off fine art from art and with what is only remotely related to what "actual nature" provides.

Mrs. Gilbert is correct in directing attention to this shift from "finding what is already there, though hidden," to "creating a mental image by human strength alone" as it occurred and to the extent that it occurred in the Renaissance. It should be noticed, however, that such writers as Marsilio Ficino and Leone Ebreo wrote of artistic creation within a Platonic tradition and that for them the artist was not yet regarded as free of some of the restrictive metaphysical and theological implications they had inherited not only from Greek speculation but also from the Hebraic–Christian tradition of deity. This fact—as well as the fact that the entire history of Philosophy of Art and Aesthetics is necessarily to be understood in part in terms of the analogy of the artist to God—makes of the eighteenth century a period in which the issues are more clearly drawn than in the period of the rebirth of knowledge. The theory of the genius emerged in the eighteenth century in such a way that its meaning for art is clearly discernible. This is the more evident in the convergence in the eighteenth century of two speculatively separate and separable conceptions of human freedom in creativity—that creativity is an intelligible process and that it is indefinable.

The convergence of the problems of making and creating, of freedom to choose and freedom to originate, is furthered and its significance made more evident by the publication that gave Aesthetics its name. The book was called *Aesthetica,* and it was written by the rationalist philosopher, Alexander Gottlieb Baumgarten. In *Aesthetica,* published in 1750, this follower of Leibnizian speculation elaborated upon a view he had expressed in 1735 in *Reflections on Poetry*. In the earlier work, Baumgarten had tried to distinguish what he called the science of sensuous knowledge (*αἰεθητά*) from logic, the science of knowledge, the objects of which were traditionally known as *νοητά*.

Once we try, however, to determine accurately what it is that lends importance to Baumgarten's writings, we encounter a variety of problems. The *Reflections on Poetry* and the *Aesthetica* are not of preeminent value, if we measure them by the standard of Aristotle's *Poetics,* Longinus' *de Sublimitate,* Kant's *Critique of Judgment,* or Hegel's *The Philosophy of Fine Art*. Moreover, the *Aesthetica* is a seminal book only because of its title, not of its argument. Its title did, however, make a difference. Within a half century of the publication of the *Aesthetica,* two eminent men, the philosopher Immanuel Kant and the poet Friedrich Schiller, had adopted "Aesthetics" and used it in the titles of their own writings on the subject. It is an important question to ask why this occurred.

The answer is not that Baumgarten either invented the word, "Aesthetics," or that he created the field of speculation to which he applied the name. He adopted the name from classical philosophy, and he adapted it to an area of speculation in which the issues had been clear and significant from ancient times. That he did in his use of the word, *Aesthetica,* perform an important task is an assumption that led to the use in the title of the present book of readings of both "Philosophy of Art" and "Aesthetics." To use both terms is not redundant, despite the fact that by the year 1750 the major problems of speculation upon the artist, art, the experience of art, and the judgment of art had been investigated thoroughly by philosophers, critics, and artists beginning in classical times and proceeding through the Graeco–Roman period, the Middle Ages, the Renaissance, and the seventeenth and eighteenth centuries. It has been asserted—and much has been made of the point—that an entire area of speculation—the Aesthetic—had been closed to the Greeks because they not only lacked that word but because they had no word for "fine art." They did not have the term and, as we shall see, this is an important lack. They did, however, know the problems. Plato writes of the Idea of Beauty and of the beauty of mathematical forms. But, most interestingly, he writes of the art of the painter and the sculptor as an imitation of an imitation, and he draws a distinction between what the artisan produces and what the mimetic artist produces in copying that copy. Imitations of imitations may not be fine art, but they differ and are intended to differ from what they imitate. This is not the difference between art and fine art; it does indicate, however, why the word "Aesthetic" was needed.

One might go further, not only in order to clarify the point concerning Baumgarten but to suggest in a brief survey some of the material the reader will encounter in this book of readings. We discover, in fact, as the material is presented, that the Greeks set the pattern for subsequent speculation in Philosophy of Art and in Aesthetics. They weighed the value or disvalue of profoundly moving music and of great tragedy. They studied the work of art as a something analogous to an organism and anticipated the conception of the life of forms in art. Aristotle discusses not only criticism but taste as well and so anticipates one of the great controversies of modern times. Plato's theory of mathematical beauty anticipates not only a Vitruvius and a Leonardo da Vinci but a Hambidge and a Le Corbusier as well. Plato asks whether beauty may be limited to objects seen and heard, and Hegel repeats the question. Plato asks whether art and play may not be identical and whether both may not have value as pedagogical techniques, questions also investigated by Schiller. Longinus writes of sublimity, and the word serves not only to subordinate "minute correctness" as one of the criteria of works of art, but its implications are of singular importance for Hegel, Kant, and Bradley. Heraclitus brings the problem of the relativism of judgments into the area of beauty; Democritus argues that madness is essential to the production of beautiful poetry. The ancient theory of inspiration is put forward by Socrates, Plato, Plotinus, Dionysius the Areopagite, Leone Ebreo—and it reappears in the writings of Schopenhauer, Nietzsche, and Croce.

This is not at all to deny that there are basic differences between ancient and modern speculation, between Philosophy of Art and Aesthetics. On the whole, ancient theory assumes that the work of art is a stimulus to a response, the modern that it is an image proceeding from the artist. Still, modern speculation ordinarily buttresses the theory of imagination with one of media or symbols or forms, elaborations of the ancient interpretation of the stimuli that induce the experience. Moreover, Philostratus formulated a theory of imagination in opposition to that of imitation, and he did so in the third century A.D.

What, then, did Baumgarten accomplish that made the title of his book so signal an event in the history of speculation? In my opinion, it is plausible to explain his contribution in terms of several sentences in Baumgarten's books. In the first,[2] he draws a hard-and-fast distinction between things known by the superior faculty as the object of knowledge and things perceived by the science of perception or aesthetics. Baumgarten is in pursuit of what we should now call a universe of discourse in which aesthetic objects are unique. It is not unimportant to notice that history has interpreted Aesthetics as the science of perception to mean Aesthetics as the science of "feeling" or "imagination" or both. In the other pertinent sentences,[3] we learn that *Aesthetica,* the science of sensuous knowledge and the science that has as its end the perfection of sensuous knowledge, includes not only that end—beauty—but also the theory of the fine arts, the theory of the lower kind of knowledge, the art of thinking beautifully, and the art of analogical reasoning. This is the more immediately important. What it implies is evident from the fact that Baumgarten calls the criticism of poetry "philosophical poetics," whereas for the criticism of all arts he coins the word "Aesthetics."

What Baumgarten does is to try to delineate a separate and unique universe of discourse for what had hitherto been a field of objects and events susceptible not only to evaluation in terms of beauty or sublimity or tragedy or comedy or taste or art or of fact but to interpretation in terms of metaphysics, epistemology, religion, morality, mathematics, and theology. He is in search of what is common to all of the arts and eventually to what is

[2] A. G. Baumgarten, *Reflections on Poetry,* Sect. 116.

[3] A. G. Baumgarten, *Aesthetica,* Sections 1 and 14.

common to the fine arts. Moreover, and scarcely less important, he is writing at the height of speculation in a period in which enormous energy was being directed and had been directed to the basic questions of what is now called "Aesthetics." Voltaire, Feijóo, Hume, Kant concerned themselves, as did myriad others, with the problems of criticism and the claims of the superiority of taste over criticism. The Platonic conception of sublimity challenged the Aristotelian conception of formal beauty. The proponents of imitation were in combat with theorists of imagination and fancy. Judgment was weighed against direct experience. Men urged that art is definable, others that it was inexplicable. Men asserted that originality should be used as the basic criterion for judging art, others that intelligibility lay at the core of all artistic techniques. Men devoted their talents to explaining great art in terms of primitivism, of the theory of the great man unhampered by civilization, and they were speculating concerning play, both of art and of imagination. The diversity of the problems and the complexity of the answers called for simplification in a single science, so constructed as to be all-inclusive. A common principle of explanation was needed for the arts, the artists, and the experience of works of art and of fine art.

Once Aesthetics is established and accepted as such a science, another important point becomes evident. It is then possible to distinguish objects that are solely within the province of Aesthetics and those that, while they are works of art, are not within its province. What Baumgarten deepened was the conviction that Aesthetics is a unique and separate field of speculation. The issue then becomes one of determining whether or not there are unique objects in that universe of discourse and how their aesthetic character could be determined and established. There had been profound speculation before 1750 and it was still relevant to Aesthetics, but Philosophy of Art, which included both non-aesthetic and aesthetic subject-matter, came more and more to yield to Aesthetics, from which the non-aesthetic could be excluded. And that Philosophy of Art was adulterated is evident. Before Baumgarten's writings, no such *systematic* distinction had been drawn, and as we glance at even the greatest of the earlier philosophers of art we discover the difficulties they encounter in consequence of their failure to make essential distinctions. Even though Plato separates imitations and imitations of imitations, a point that, as has been pointed out, argues that a hard and fast distinction was drawn between the artisan and, let us say, the painter, had not brought the Athenian to the point at which systematically he could free the Idea of Beauty from the implications of theory of knowledge and morality. Similarly, Aristotle offers a superb analysis of Art and of making, but the *Poetics* leads one to suppose that tragedies are in some sense interpretable in medicinal terms and that art in general is valuable because it increases knowledge or improves morals. The relativism of Heraclitus' philosophy and that of its Sophist followers is integral to a theory of the flux of things in this world. Plotinus writes of art and beauty in terms of a metaphysic of emanations. Longinus formulates his theory of sublime poetry but tends to interpret art as a means by which man realizes his superiority in the universe. The Platonic tradition of Plato and Plotinus is continued in the writings of Dionysius the Areopagite and in some degree in the writings of Albertus Magnus and Thomas Aquinas. But here theology intrudes and what is ultimately argued is a theory of beauty as a transcendental. The Platonist tradition continues in the writings of Leone Ebreo, the Aristotelian–realist–Anaxagorean in Leonardo da Vinci. Descartes writes of music in terms of the physics of vibrating strings; Leibniz of music in mathematical terms; Spinoza in terms of nominal universals.

Briefly, then, thinking on art and beauty

prior to the middle of the eighteenth century was profound and illuminating, but it was neither specified nor naturalized to art and fine art, nor were its various branches allocated to a single discipline. At the beginning of the eighteenth century, however, men began to doubt the efficacy of multiplying the criteria of criticism and began seriously to consider taste as a substitute for the critical technique. The impressive conquests made by men who preferred imagination to imitation began to multiply in number, and the faculty of imagination itself, investigated by Huarte, Bacon, Descartes, Hobbes, and Addison, began to display its peculiar and unique adaptability for explaining the experience and the creation of art. Then, too, in order to account for that comparatively new concept—fine art in contrast to art—there began to develop an intense interest in the ancient conception of the original genius, as is evident in writings as different as Edward Young's *Conjectures on Original Composition* and Alexander Gerard's *An Essay on Genius.*

It is perhaps fair to summarize what occurred in the last half of the eighteenth century by mentioning four issues that emerged and whose emergence was hastened by the gradual adoption of Baumgarten's terminology. In the first place, it became clear that it was possible to rid Art of non-aesthetic definitions and objects. Secondly, there occurred an increased specification of the differences between art and fine or free art. Thirdly, there emerged more precise ways of defining and systematizing, as well as of bringing within the scope of a single systematic philosophy, of such hitherto but loosely related terms as taste, genius, art, fine art, imagination, making, creating, sublimity, beauty, tragedy, comedy, existence, and media. Finally, the issue of the problem of the relation of fine art to feeling began to be faced.

Once the gradual systematization of aesthetic theories and of philosophies of fine art occurs, many of the non-aesthetic problems drop out of Aesthetics. A significant one remains, and to it we shall come shortly. It is well, however, to illustrate what we have just mentioned concerning the systematization of Aesthetics and the closer relating of problems in art and its experience as a result of Baumgarten's use of the word "Aesthetics" by a brief mention of the classical instance of what occurred. Immanuel Kant's *Critique of Judgment* is, perhaps, the most powerful and influential treatment of Aesthetics ever written. Kant at first had rejected the use made by "that admirable thinker, Baumgarten" of the word "aesthetics," principally because he believed that the subject could be treated only empirically. That was in 1781. By 1787, is is clear from his correspondence that Kant was moving towards the acceptance of the word to replace "taste," and it has been thought that he did so principally because he was contemplating a *Critique of Judgment* that would include not only the problem of the beautiful but also that of teleology. There may be doubt concerning the precise chronology of the change; there is no doubt that in 1790 Kant published the third critique as the *Critique of Judgment* and that in it he had gathered together and systematized the principal "aggregates" of Philosophy of Art into an "architectonic" called "The Critique of Aesthetic Judgment." Roughly, the *Critique* limits the universe of discourse to the beautiful and the sublime and explains the experience of forms unique to Aesthetic in terms of the harmonious interplay of the faculties of Imagination and Understanding. The sublime is treated in terms of its dynamical and mathematical specifications, and in its discussion Reason and Imagination are related in terms of feeling. The state of mind is sublime; objects and events are occasions for this state of mind. Kant excludes mathematical, teleological, and ideal entities as objects of the judgment of taste. He denies the validity of the canon of the human form. He relates art and fine art. He argues that fine art is the product of Spirit and mechanisms. He classifies the arts and formulates a brilliant theory of laughter.

Kant's is a classical example of the efficacy of a word, "Aesthetics," that at once permits a philosopher of art to gather together the issues of Philosophy of Art under one head and to produce a separate and distinct discipline. It is now of importance both speculatively and historically to observe what in addition Kant succeeds in doing, once he has adopted Baumgarten's term "Aesthetics." Kant's third Critique tends to dominate nineteenth century Aesthetic theory, as well as to influence critics of Coleridge's stature. First, then, Kant systematized the vigorous and extensive literature of criticism and Philosophy of Art as it appeared in such diverse writers as David Hume, Lord Shaftesbury, Alexander Pope, Edward Young, Alexander Gerard, William Duff, Lord Kames, Edmund Burke, as well as Baumgarten. Moreover, he transformed what they had written by examining under the general title "Aesthetics," their material and his own. For Kant, the judgment of taste—the aesthetic judgment—is not conceptual; it is a priori; it is related to pleasure and pain. The most important point is that it is distinguishable from moral judgments and judgments of gratification because it is the sole free and disinterested judgment. Kan't quest for freedom in Aesthetics does not end with beautiful forms that are objects of the judgment of taste. Sublimity is a state of mind free of all external objects. Kant succeeds in bringing into Aesthetics in natural terms two ancient ingredients of philosophy of art—the genius and inspiration. These are in fact functions of freedom as creativity and originality. The genius is free to produce what is new, although what is produced must also be intelligible. The genius is inspired, and his productive imagination is an originative faculty—but the fine artist must display taste as well.

What is of especial interest as illustrative of the influence upon Kant's speculation of Baumgarten's program in Aesthetics is a point that has proved puzzling to aestheticians. Kant limits the use of the term "genius" to the fine artist and offers reasons for this procedure. Here it suffices to point out that the limitations implicit in Baumgarten's effort to define precisely what Aesthetics is leads Kant—mistakenly—to exclude from the category, genius, men of the stature of Newton and to regard only those gifted with productive imagination. This is perhaps the best proof that the word "Aesthetics" leads to an effort to delimit its field.

With Kant, the issue of freedom as making and creating comes clear. It also becomes a central problem in nineteenth and twentieth century Aesthetics. Schiller's *On the Aesthetic Education of Man* is a work notable for many reasons, but for none more so than the theme that "Beauty . . . is our second creator" and for the conversion of play into free imagination. Hegel believes that the genius is a rational artist whose imagination works in sensuous media and who produces works of art that are manifestations of Spirit in Symbolical, Classical, or Romantic forms. Schopenhauer holds of the genius that he is the man most sensitive to delicate stimuli and one who is able to free us from the force of the Will. Nietzsche's writing offers a fine description of inspiration. Croce argues art as expression and imagination, holding that the primitive stage of spirit is the intuitive one. It is a stage free of economic, practical, scientific implications, as it is free from such philosophical requirements as truth or falsity, validity or invalidity, and for the same reason: the stage of art is the primitive one in which these issues have not yet arisen. This is, indeed, to be a theory of Aesthetics, in contrast to a Philosophy of Art.

It is notable, however, that Croce's argument is not only a statement concerning art as free expression; it is also one in which the artist's image is wholly original and incomparable. This means explicitly that the work of art may not be criticised or classified. At this point, it is no less notable that into Croce's theory of art as expression have entered the words "genius" and "inspiration." With them, it becomes clear that the unique universe of discourse, implicit in Baumgarten's *"Aesthetica,"* has not been achieved. These terms bring with them the echoes of an ancient speculative conflict. To it we shall turn in the next section of this Introduction. By way of advancing toward that Section, however, let us recall that Mrs. Gilbert commented upon the shift in the artist's invention from finding what is already there, although hidden, to creating a mental image by human strength alone. We may recall as well, however, that she also added, in the same paragraph, that in the Renaissance "Art is no longer cosmic energy but human power." In the theory of art as expression, the most powerful statement of a limited, aesthetic universe of discourse, of "art for art's sake," the conception of the genius brings with it the theological and nonaesthetic implication that an artist is endowed with godlike power to produce without the need to resort to means camparable to those used in the production of artifacts. The conception of inspiration brings with it the nonaesthetic connotation of an artist endowed with the godlike power to produce what is wholly original. Such attributions of omnipotence and omniscience argue the persistence of the analogy of the artist to God the creator and God the maker. To this analogy we turn in the following portion of this Introduction.[4]

B. The Theological Background of the Theory of the Artist as Creator

The arts bear upon few philosophical issues more significant than that of freedom, although Aesthetic does not compare to Ethics as a battleground for controversy concerning free will or determinism. Rather, the issue of freedom has been an implicit, if pervasive, presupposition of theories of artistic creativity, of aesthetic perception, and, indeed, of the nature of the fine arts themselves. It is the purpose of the present paper to examine the theory of the artist as creator, which I take to be the ground for this omnipresent attribution of freedom in the aesthetic realm. Theology, which has frequently provided religion with the numerous arguments it has employed to restrain the artist, is in its turn curiously enough, if not the ultimate, at least the conserving source for the western world's theory of the almost unlimited freedom of the artist as creator.

The lack of precision in current theories of the artist as creator suggests the truth of Robert Frost's remark that "the best way out is always through." It is interesting to speculate whether or not centuries of dialectical controvery would have helped to clarify the issue—just as such discussion brought the Aristotelian practical wisdom into the vexed realms of freewill, foreknowledge, and predestination. In this paper, however, I should like only to point out what did in fact occur and to examine some consequences of that occurrence. I should like, first, to consider the heritage of aesthetic from an earlier theological and metaphysical conflict

[4] Milton C. Nahm, "The Theological Background of the Theory of the Artist as Creator," *The Journal of the History of Ideas,* Vol. VIII, No. 3, (June, 1947), pp. 363-372. I have indicated such additions to this article as refer to more extensive material in the present volume by the use of square brackets.

in the theory of creation. I should like then to evaluate the consequences of this inheritance, principally the assumption that the artist has power to transcend natural laws, as well as the related hypotheses that he can produce unique individuals and cause novelty to emerge.

The early theological and metaphysical conflict to which I refer is well known in the historical differences between the Greek and the Hebraic-Christian theories of the making and creation of the world, and to its brief consideration I shall shortly come. But it is well at the outset to make clear that the implications of this conflict for aesthetic are not merely what the western tradition once drew upon for guidance, but are, as well, what that tradition still draws upon. By way of illustration, Robert Browning writes of Abt Vogler's extemporization upon music:

> . . . For think, had I painted the whole,
> Why, there it had stood, to see, nor the process so wonder-worth:
> Had I written the same, made verse—still, effect proceeds from cause,
> Ye know why the forms are fair, ye hear how the tale is told:
> It is all triumphant art, but art in obedience to laws,
> Painter and poet are proud in the artist-list enrolled:—
> But here is the finger of God, a flash of the will that can,
> Existent behind all laws, that made them and, lo, they are!
> And I know not if, save in this, such gift be allowed to man,
> That out of three sounds he frame, not a fourth sound, but a star.
> Consider it well: each tone of our scale in itself is naught:
> It is everywhere in the world—loud, soft, and all is said:
> Give it to me to use! I mix it with two in my thought:
> And there! Ye have heard and seen: consider and bow the head!

In suggesting that the musician has powers identical with the "Existent behind all laws that made them," the poem discloses a clear discernment of two significant facts, namely, that to the artist are attributed miraculous powers, and that his divine freedom consists precisely in a capacity to transcend "art in obedience to laws."

Let us glance in turn at a philosophical statement of the theory. Benedetto Croce urges that "expression is free inspiration."[1] At the particular point at which this proposition is presented, Croce has been analyzing "the search for the *end of art*," a search which he calls "ridiculous": "To fix an end," he writes, "is to choose. . . . A selection among impressions and sensations implies that these are already expressions, . . . To choose is to will: to will this and not to will that: and this and that must be before us, expressed. Practice follows, it does not precede theory; expression is free inspiration."

Croce undercuts the problem of free will or determinism of will for aesthetic by asserting the logical priority of intuition to willing, by identifying intuition, art and expression, and by associating practice and making. The artist is freed in this fashion both from the limitations placed upon his will and from those imposed upon art by the requirements of material and end. In a sense, too, the artist is freed from causal laws, because Croce never considers them to be applicable at the level of expression, but only within the scope of technique and its products. It in no less significant that on this hypothesis the artist is not only free but is free to produce novelty, i.e., to intuit individuals and to express "the individual expressive fact."[2] The mode of attack permits Croce to hold that "individual expressive facts are so many individuals, not one of which is interchangeable with another,"[3] to assert that every impression or "content differs

[1] *Aesthetic,* D. Ainslie translation, 51. [See below, pp. 537 et seq. and 559 et seq.]
[2] *Ibid.,* 35.
[3] *Ibid.,* 67–68.

from every other content,"[4] and to regard "expression" as "a species which cannot function in its turn as a genus."[5]

I believe that Croce is in error, for reasons which I have put forward elsewhere, and with consequences to which I shall later allude. It is true, nonetheless, that he has delineated a fundamental problem for Aesthetic in his efforts to provide freedom for the artist and to establish the work of art's unique individuality. What has occurred is clear: Croce has inherited the spirit of a tradition but has doffed the trappings. The poet-philosopher, Coleridge, in suggesting that poetry is "a dim analogue to creation," is wholly within that tradition. Moreover, it is only within the tradition that we may discern plainly the full implications of the key word, "creation." Coleridge, in fact, echoes Athanasius[6]—probably through Schelling:

> For God creates, and to create (Τὸ κτίζειν) is also ascribed to men; . . . Yet does God create as men do? . . . Perish the thought; we understand the terms in one sense of God, and in another of men. For God creates, in that He calls what is not into being, needing nothing thereunto; but men work some existing material (ὑποκειμένη ὕλη).

The western tradition of creation in aesthetic reflects the spirit of this denial to man of God's miraculous power. It is significant, however, that the use of the word "analogous" has sufficed to endow the artist with freedom commensurate with that attributed to Deity, in that as maker he has power to produce by his art unique individuals and to transcend natural laws.[7] In this respect, aesthetic theory is heir to one of the great theological and metaphysical controversies of history. To account for the artist's presumed capacity to produce unique individuals, a specification of the general theory of the emergence of novelty in essences and immortal souls has been employed. The presumption that the artist is capable of transcending natural law is but a specification of the theory that God has power to perform miracles. And these two general issues are among the principal points of differentiation between the Hebraic-Christian theory of God's creativity and the classical view of "making" put forward by Plato.

A glance at that historical conflict will suffice to make explicit much that is merely implicit in present day assertions concerning the artist as creator. The classical theory is found in Plato's *Timaeus*,[8] where, in Shorey's words,[9] "A demiurgos or supreme artisan does not precisely create the universe out of nothing but reduces a vaguely visioned pre-existent chaos to a cosmos." This demiurgos, which Cornford identifies with the World-Soul,[10] imposes upon uncreated matter the eternally existing "forms," to make after their model the structure of the universe. The theory put forward in *Timaeus* is one of making, not of creation. The demiurge works upon already existent material, which, in turn, provides necessity and limitation, and serves as the *principium individuationis*.[11]

4 *Ibid.*, 68.

5 *Ibid.*, 68.

6 "De Decretis, or Defence of the Nicene Definition," *A Select Library of Nicene and Post-Nicene Fathers of the Christian Church*, IV, 11. Cf. *ibid.*, 19; and "de Orat.," II, 22. [Compare St. Augustine, below p. 233.]

7 It should be noted, however, that Browning's musician does not create *ex nihilo*. Compare Croce, *op. cit.*, 5–6, on the "passivity" of matter, and "the notion of it as a mere limit." [See below p. 539.]

8 *Timaeus*, 28 B ff. [See below, p. 93.]

9 *What Plato Said* 332.

10 *Plato's Cosmology*, 176–177.

11 *Timaeus* 51E, A. E. Taylor's translation. "The form is one thing, self-same, never born, never perishing, neither receiving anything else into itself from without nor entering anywhere into anything else, invisible and imperceptible to any sense; it is that, in fact, which it is the function of thinking to contemplate. A second thing is that which bears the same name and is like the first, but is perceptible to sense, is born, is continually in motion, comes to be in a place and again vanishes out of it, is apprehended by opinion based on sense. Our third term, once more, is, in every case, *space* which never perishes but provides an emplacement for all that is born. . . ." [See below, p. 95.]

Concerning the latter point, Constantin Ritter remarks[12] that "whatever appears as extended is in space (the various positions in space are all different) and as such an object appears only once, as something individual." However sound may be this interpretation of Plato's place, space or receptacle, it still is true that no one of the many problems implicit in Plato's account of the making of the world has exercised history more than that which concerns the adequacy of the account of the means of individuating. Nor need we search far for the reason, since what we are here primarily concerned with is the possibility, validity, and process of the emergence of novelty. Plato, no doubt, held that the essence is archetypal, and his search for a canon of beauty, his praise for the conservatism of Egyptian art, and his dislike of artistic novelty in art appear to be aesthetic consequences of this fundamental doctrine. Still, I believe that Ritter is correct in interpreting the Platonic theory to mean[13] that "Each Idea indicates the essence of the individual appearance in so far as that is knowable." Implicit in Platonic and Aristotelian theories of universals, however, is the interpretation developed by the realists of the Middle Ages, who urged that universals[14] "are *the more Real in proportion as they are the more universal*." We need not here trace the significant view which endows matter with greater self-subsistency and reality. It is necessary only to mention the Stoic, Hebrew, and Christian interest in the personality and individuality of man to suggest the difficulties inherent in any view that subordinates the value of the individual to that of the form, or which interprets the significance of the individual substance in terms only of its capacity to manifest the type.

[12] *The Essence of Plato's Philosophy,* 210.

[13] *Op. cit.,* 210.

[14] W. Windelband, *A History of Philosophy,* English Translation, 290. Compare *ibid.,* 232–33, 252–55, and 287 ff. [See below, pp. 96, 97, and 104 et seq. for Plato's attitude toward novelty and "rational" art.]

Whatever Plato's theory may have been, the predilection to make the typical the essential is one scarcely in accord with the Hebraic-Christian conception of unique individuals endowed with personality and granted individual immortality. The issue is the more complex because the problem of personality is integral, in the western tradition, to that of human freedom.[15] To those, therefore, who have followed the course of the controversy concerning creating or making, it is not strange that, as Erich Frank points out,[16] St. Augustine, in contrast to Plato, maintains that "the world was created by God out of nothing and this creation was due to God's absolute free will, not to any logical or other necessity, or to any Idea outside himself."[17] This notion of St. Augustine's is true "creation," not only because specifically it is the bringing into being of something from nothing, but also and more significantly for a general reason implicit in the Alexandrian philosophy intermediate between Plato and the Church Father. In a brilliant paper,[18] Professor Wolfson, writing upon Philo's conception of free will, calls attention to the fundamental difference between Plato's and Philo's evaluation of God's power over the "laws of nature." Both believe that these laws "were implanted by God in the universe as an act of good will." Plato held, however, that once implanted, they could "never be upset," while

[15] Windelband, *op. cit.,* 251 et seq.

[16] E. Frank, "St. Augustine and Greek Thought," 5 (The Augustinian Society, 1942). See also Professor Frank's *Philosophical Understanding and Religious Truth,* Chapter 3, note 19.

[17] The validity of this type of interpretation of Plato is denied by implication by A. E. Taylor. See, for example, *Plato: The Man and His Work,* 443–44: "It seems plain that the *Timaeus* knows of no external limitations imposed on God's will by conditions independent of God himself." Taylor maintains that the Demiurge is a true "Creator" and that "everything sensible has 'emerged' as a result of a process . . . the world is always in 'evolution,' even if the evolution never begins and will never come to an end." [For St. Augustine, see below, p. 233.]

[18] Harry Austryn Wolfson, "Philo on Free Will," *Harvard Theological Review,* XXXV, No. 2 (1942), 138–40. [See below, pp. 193, 200.]

Philo thought that "God may change the order of natural events when it serves some good purpose."

The reason for this historical divergence in the evaluation of God's power to change "the order of natural events" is of crucial importance for any consideration of creation, cosmological or artistic. As Professor Wolfson points out,[19] "There is no room for miracles in the philosophy of Plato." Although Philo's God "is philosophically the Demiurge of Plato," there is room in the Alexandrian's system of thought "for miracles." Philo's God retains "the essential characteristics of the miracle-working Jehovah of the Hebrew Scriptures . . . Philo held that God may change the order of natural events."

This moment in Alexandrian speculation is crucial for the unfolding theory of creation throughout later centuries. It was then that the aura of the miraculous emanated, and first reformed and later largely supplanted the classical theory of making. And it is this aura of the miraculous which, in my estimation, has enveloped the thought of the West upon the subject of artistic creation. Moreover, here at its beginning is that conjunction of the miracle of creation and of limitless freedom which makes of human freedom one function of the creative power. The crucial point is that both Plato and Philo regard man as a microcosm of the macrocosm. Plato maintains, however, that man makes under the laws of nature and by necessity, while Philo, whose God "has reserved for himself the power of freedom to upset the laws of nature which He established in the world at the time of its creation," has "endowed man with similar power of freedom to upset the laws of nature to which he is subject."[20] Acts of the will are "absolutely of man's free choice," determined neither by God nor "by any of the natural causes" by means of which His purpose is effected in the universe.[21]

I have labored this historical distinction between creating and making because in the emergence and evolution of the theory that man possesses miraculous powers to transcend the laws of nature we discover as well the prototype and sustaining source for much in contemporary thinking concerning the artist's powers. Moreover, precisely as one of theology's miracles is the existence of unique and individual souls, free and endowed with personality, so the aesthetic miracle is the production of unique and individual works of art, created by an artist liberated from the technique of making. Again this is manifest in Croce's theory:[22] "The true artist, in fact, finds himself big with his theme, he knows not how; he feels the moment of birth draw near, but he cannot will it or not will it . . . The impossibility of choice of content completes the theorem of the *independence of art*." The analogy, in turn, is complete: one recalls that this "*independence of art*" completes the theorem of the uniqueness and individuality of all impressions.

With this small portion of the available evidence before us, we may well inquire concerning the validity or invalidity of such a theory of creation. A more immediate question arises, however: why has a theory of this character been insulated from contact with the currents that flow in the field of the determined or undetermined will? I believe that our proximate answer to the question, which turns on the western tradition's acceptance of views similar to those put forward by Croce as to the artist's freedom, has its philosophical ground in the Aristotelian distinction between making and acting.[23] That distinction, which in itself has had enormous influence on the bearing of the philo-

[19] *Ibid.*, 139–40. Cf. F. M. Cornford, *Plato's Cosmology*, 176: "This last instance [i.e., Reason must be content to sacrifice the less important advantage and achieve the best result attainable] illustrates the truth of Galen's observation that the Demiurge is not strictly omnipotent. In arranging the world he could not group physical qualities in such a way as to secure all the ends he desired." Cf. *ibid.*, 209 ff.

[20] Wolfson, *op. cit.*, 163.

[21] *Ibid.*, 138.

[22] *Op., cit.*, 51-52. [See below, pp. 536–37.]

[23] [For Aristotle's philosophy of art, see below, Chapter 4.]

sophy of art upon philosophic issues in general, has proved to be of considerable value for the critical approach to art. Implicit in Aristotle's judgment that "making has an end other than itself" has been history's intepretation that the object made is not only separate from the maker but is likewise subject to laws different from those governing the maker. On this interpretation, the work of art is freed from the willing agent. It is nonetheless true, however, that the distinction and its value conceal a difficulty for the analysis of the maker. It is clear that making is a form of acting and, insofar as acting comes within the framework of natural law, so likewise does making fall under its rules. The "freedom" of the work of art does not warrant the ascription of unlimited freedom to the artist, if by creative power is meant an escape from laws either of cause and effect or of will.

What compulsion leads to the maintenance of a theory that disregards the inclusion of making within acting, and leaves aesthetic theory in a state comparable to that of the classical atomic hypothesis, once Epicurus had succumbed to the urgent demand that the human will be endowed with unlimited freedom in a world of atoms and the void, for which Leucippus had stated the law: "Nothing occurs at random, but everything for a reason and by necessity"?[24] Here is a factor far less abstract than the distinction between making and acting. The will is a mysterious and imperceptible entity. The process of making is thoroughly concrete. Cornford remarks[25] of Plato's account in *Timaeus* that "the image of the craftsman is employed as the most simple and vivid means of making us realize that the world was not a chance product born of aimless natural powers but exhibits evidences of rational design, like a product of human art." If we think, not of the abstract phrase, *ex nihilo*, but of the image in *Genesis*, we have ample evidence of tremendous imaginative powers and extraordinary poetic gifts. Small wonder, indeed, that Philo treats the story of creation[26] "as in a class by itself throughout the history of the philosophic interpretation of Scripture."

The fact of the matter is that man's control of nature is, for the imagination, far less a function of abstract rational powers than of rational powers in process of making or constructing something. It is in fact a function of the power Bergson regards[27] as distinguishing "the two main lines of evolution of animal life . . . the Arthropods and the Vertebrates." For while instinct and intelligence "have each as their essential object the utilization of implements," the implements of instinct are "organs supplied by nature and hence immutable," whereas those of intelligence are "invented tools, and therefore varied and unforeseen." Instruments and tools as means to the control of nature appear to be unlimited in variety and infinite in power. If we think, then, of the artist, whose production of beauty presupposes technical skill but who transcends the realm of mere technique, we seem to have come upon the supreme artificer. With the tremendous image of God's creation in *Genesis* before us, it is almost inevitable that the fine artist should come to be called a creator.

But this, in effect, renders the position of the artist as creator paradoxical, since the freedom attributed to him in terms of such hypothesis as Croce's "free inspiration" would appear to be available only if it be denied that true artistry is or even presupposes technique. This means the denial and abrogation of the Greek theory of making for some reinterpretation of the Hebraic-Christian doctrine of creation. The alternative may be put in the form of a question: Can aesthetic theory explain unique and individual works of fine art, that is, can it account for the emergence of novelty, without converting freedom into caprice or worse? My answer is that it

[24] Fr. 2, translated by Cyril Bailey, *The Greek Atomists and Epicurus,* 85.

[25] *Op. cit.,* 176.

[26] Wolfson, *op. cit.,* 143.

[27] Henri Bergson, *The Two Sources of Morality and Religion,* 19.

not only can but must do so. But for the effort to succeed, we must first recognize that Kant's statement of the third antinomy concerning freedom holds for the artist as well as for other men: "Freedom [independence] from the laws of nature is no doubt a *deliverance* from restraint, but also from the *guidance* of all rules." Once having examined the implications of this dictum and learned that the laws of nature applicable in this field are those of technique, signs, and material, the theorist must search for the guidance contained therein and consider facts running counter to the analogy of the artist to the creator. Plato, in theory, is correct. The artist is one who works upon material. As Aristotle suggests, things made fall within the scope of the variable, "where all such things might actually be otherwise." The material upon which the artist works is infinite in potentialities, but those potentialities are offered within severely definable limits. Productivity is creative, but it is creative only in the sense that the artist is free, within the limits of his technique, materials, and symbols, to produce images, not to effect miracles.

How profoundly this affects some derivative aspects of our problem of artistic creativity may be but briefly suggested. Were it true that the artist works a miracle, he could probably "utter wisdom from the central deep." It would appear doubtful, however, that he could listen "to the inner flow of things." It is certain that another miracle would be required to permit him to

> . . . utter wisdom from the central deep,
> And, listening to the inner flow of things,
> Speak to an age out of an eternity.[28]

For the theory of creativity, stated on the analogy of God's miraculous powers, presents the most formidable problems for an intelligible account of the structure either of fine art or of aesthetic experience. The work of art is an instrument by which the artist communicates something to the aesthetic percipient, and the task of the fine artist is fulfilled only if the maker expresses a communicable datum and if we, the perceivers, make that potentially communicable datum one that actually communicates. But if the theory of creation is carried to its logical conclusion in the philosophy of art—as it has been by Croce—we discover that the postulation of "free inspiration" for the artist results, first, in the purchase of individuality and uniqueness at the expense of intelligibility; for, as Croce[29] argues, "expressions considered directly or positively are not divisible into classes," and "likenesses such as are observed among individuals . . . can never be rendered with abstract determinations."[30] But this is to deny the relevance to fine art of the theory of classes or types, a theory which Plato's philosophy of making correctly presupposes—if only because one must know what kind of thing a thing or event is before we know whether or not it is good or bad of its kind—and which on the theory of generic symbols makes the individual an intelligible member of a class. And, secondly, the theory of creation leads to nominalism, since, to quote again Croce,[31] "the sublime (or comic, tragic, humorous, etc.) is *everything* that is or shall be so *called* by those who . . . shall employ these *words*." The consequence, it appears to me, is that the theory of the artist as creator would entail not one but two events which pass the bounds of rational explanation, the first, that the artist could effect the work of art, the second, that we, the aesthetic percipients, could make it intelligible and re-effect it.

The alternative, I suggest, is a sound theory of artistic productivity which will account for the emergence of novelty through the reconciliation of the Greek theory of making, concerned as it is with the typical and the necessary, with the Hebraic-Christian doctrine of creating, con-

[28] James Russell Lowell, "Columbus."

[29] Croce, *Aesthetic*, 70.
[30] *Ibid.*, 73.
[31] *Ibid.*, 90.

cerned as it is with the individual and the free.[32] A reconciliation of the two traditions in art is a task of formidable proportions, impossible on such simple grounds as the identification of the two theories in question. For no sensible man will maintain that such a reconciliation occurs in writings like George Puttenham's *The Arte of English Poesie*,[33] where we are told in successive paragraphs that "the very Poet makes" like God "who without any trauell to his diuine imagination, made the world out of nought, nor also by any patterne or mould"; and that "a Poet may in some sort be said a follower or imitator, because he can expresse the true and liuely of everything is set before him, and which he taketh in hand to describe: and so in that respect is both a maker and a counterfaitor." The reconciliation I have in mind is possible if to it is brought knowledge of technical processes, of iconology, and of materials. From the perspective of such a reconciliation, the value of the theory of unlimited and unrestricted creative power with which we have been concerned may be discerned. As philosophic issues, the ideas of pure creativity, the unique individual, and absolute freedom are for the artist and for the aesthetic percipient limiting conceptions. By using them in this way, man may at once measure his present achievement in terms of perfection and give himself a goal of value, definable, unattainable, but progressively approachable without limit. By means of such limiting conceptions, the artist adjusts the infinitely variable and flexible instruments of art to the artistic structure and to the aesthetic end. In so doing, he is at once creative and free, as the discerning eye of the poet[34] perceives, because

How exquisitely the individual Mind
(And the progressive powers perhaps no less
Of the whole species) to the external World
Is fitted :—and how exquisitely, too—
Theme this but little heard of among men—
The external World is fitted to the Mind ;
And the creation (by no lower name
Can it be called) which they with blended might
Accomplish :—this is our high argument.

[32] The artist is heir to the ages in style and design, in tools and symbols. He is free to individualize each aspect of his heritage. Similarly, the ancient doctrine of the "typical" is essential for our recognition of the class to which the object of art belongs and within which it is individualized. The modern doctrine is strong in that it demands that the work of art be accounted for in terms of the emergence of novelty and by the substantiation of the work's individuality. [See below, Chapters 9 and 10 for discussions of the work of art and of criticism.]

[33] *Op. cit.*, 19–20. [See below, p. 385 and pp. 391 et. seq.]

[34] William Wordsworth, "The Recluse."

PART ONE

GREEK PHILOSOPHIES OF ART

Chapter 2

Heraclitus to Socrates

Diogenes Laertius, an inveterate gossip but nonetheless a source for much sound information concerning early Greek philosophy, reports[1] that someone once asked Aristotle, "Why do we spend time with the beautiful?" To this question the man whom Dante was to call 'the Master of them that know,' replied "That is a blind man's question."

It is doubtful that any early Greek philosopher would have asked the question that evoked Aristotle's reply. Among the fragments of the earliest speculation, once the science that began in "wonder" had migrated from Miletus, there is ample evidence that beauty and art received their due of speculation and that, because of its close relation to the problem of accurate definition, Art as a technique was paid the closest attention. Not only are the problems of philosophy of art pervasive in the fragments of philosophy that have survived, but it is also quite clear that the philosophers expressed at an early period the most diverse and often contrary opinions concerning the nature of art, the character of judgments concerning works of art, and the puzzling problem of what beauty is. Heraclitus of Ephesus brought judgments of works of art within the pattern of his philosophy of a universe undergoing ceaseless transformation, one in which all judgments of natural and artistic objects are held to be relative.[2] In contrast, Pythagoras formulated a theory that has served for millenia as the pattern for the explanation of beauty in objective and mathematical terms. The most deeply rooted and widely received Greek interpretation is that art is mimetic or imitative. This is expressed as early as the middle of the sixth century B.C. by Xenophanes. Only less pervasive than the theory of imitation is the Greek conclusion that the artist, and more particularly the poet, is inspired. It is startling to learn that Democritus, a contemporary of Socrates and a thorough-going mechanist, believes that beautiful poetry is produced only if the poet is mad and this despite the fact that his general philosophy is based upon the assumption that everything occurs of necessity and not at random. The Greek interest in Art as making or producing according to rule leads in Plato's philosophy to the search for the definition of specific arts in terms of their unique subject matter and techniques. It also leads Plato to exile the poet from the ideal state, because his is one of the imitative arts that borrow their subject matter and because the imitative artist does no more as a technician than to hold a mirror up to reflect the cosmos and himself. Finally, the growth and extra-

[1] Diogenes Laertius, *The Lives of the Eminent Philosophers*, V. 20.

[2] See M. C. Nahm, *Selections from Early Greek Philosophy*, 4th ed. (New York, Appleton-Century-Crofts, 1964), pp. 62–78. Except where specifically indicated, all references to the early Greek thinkers are quoted from that book.

ordinary development of medical centers in Hellas and Magna Graecia provide Philosophy of Art with the ground for the assumption that tragedy and some kinds of music effect, as Aristotle argues, a purgation of pity and terror and "such like emotions." The Greeks use the theory of purgation in a variety of ways, but precisely what Aristotle means remains perhaps the most notable ground for controversy in the history of speculation concerning art.[3]

The emergence—and perhaps even more, the recurrence—of these early Greek hypotheses provide some of the most fascinating aspects of the selections from Philosophy of Art and Aesthetics that we include in this book. Overshadowing them all in importance, if we consider the entire sweep of speculation on these subjects, are the core and central problems of the artist's creativity; of the originality of the work of art and of the compatibility of the work of art's originality with intelligibility; of the function of criticism in a theory of artistic inspiration; and of the end of art and the end a specific work of art subserves. We shall come to these central problems shortly. In the meantime, it is well to remind ourselves that abstract as some of the speculation upon art and beauty may be, yet in conjunction with the magnificence of Greek art itself it has exerted an enormous impact upon philosophers, artists and critics throughout the millenia that stretch from the sixth century B.C. to our own times.

Let us glance briefly at some of the more notable influences.

We begin with Heraclitus,[4] for whom "The fairest ape is ugly compared with anything of another kind, and the fairest pot is ugly compared with the fairest maiden." This for "the dark thinker" of Ephesus is but one illustration for the philosophy in which he insists that everything flows. For T. S. Eliot, however, the Heraclitean theory leads in *Burnt Norton* to

At the still point of the turning world. Neither
  flesh nor fleshless;
Neither from nor towards; at the still point, there
  the dance is,
But neither arrest nor movement. And do not
  call it fixity,
Where past and future are gathered. Neither
  movement from or towards,
Neither ascent nor decline. . . . [5]

Pythagoras explained[6] *harmonia* [the musical scale] in terms of the "qualities of numbers"; Plato sought to explain[7] the beauty of the human head as a microcosmic copy of the beautiful cosmic sphere; Polycleitus formulated a canon of proportions, to be followed by Vitruvius in *de Architectura*, Leonardo da Vinci in *Paragone*, and Le Corbusier in his study of architectural designs. The poetess might as aptly have sung of Pythagoras and Plato when she wrote that Euclid "alone had looked on beauty bare." Aristotle explains [8] that tragedy and some kinds of music produce a catharsis of emotions and John Milton writes in *Samson Agonistes* that

Nothing is here for tears, nothing to wail
Or knock the breast, no weakness, no contempt
And what may quiet us in a death so noble. . . .

Similarly, Aristotle repeatedly describes[9] the process by means of which a material is made into a work of art. Michelangelo Buonnaroti writes in Sonnet XVI that

The best of artists hath no thought to show
which the rough stone in its superfluous shell
doth not include; to break the marble spell
is all the hand that serves the brain can do. . . .

and in doing so brings over into a work of art that remarkable insight of Aristotle's that a

[3] See below, Chapter 5.

[4] Nahm, *op. cit.*, fr.99, p. 74. See below, pp. 30 and 31 et seq.

[5] T. S. Eliot, "Burnt Norton," FOUR QUARTETS, by permission of Harcourt Brace Jovanovich, Inc., publishers. Also reprinted by permission of Faber & Faber Ltd. from THE COMPLETE POEMS AND PLAYS OF T. S. ELIOT.

[6] *Ibid.*, p. 54. 2.

[7] Plato, *Timaeus*, 44 D.

[8] Aristotle, *Poetics* 1449 b 24 and *Politics* 1337 b 40 et seq. See below, Chapter 5.

[9] See below, pp. 292 et seq. (*E.N.* VI.)

man's hand, with its retractable thumb, is a tool for the making of tools and, by implication, the means by which the form in the mind of the artist is imposed upon the material to be made into a work of art. Albrecht Dürer depicts the Platonic solid geometrical bodies in his *Melencolia I*, a work of art which has in itself been interpreted as an illustration of the Aristotelian hypothesis that genius results from "black bile." Again, John Milton writes in *Areopagitica* that "As good kill a man as kill a good book; who kills a man kills a reasonable creature, God's image; but he who destroys a good book, kills reason itself, kills the image of God, as it were, in the eye." The analogy to a living organism appears in Plato's *Phaedrus*: ". . . Every discourse ought to be a living creature, having a body of its own and a head and feet; there should be a middle, beginning, and end, adapted to one another and to the whole. . . ." Again, Plato writes that the poet is "a slight, winged and holy thing," who says many fine things but does not know the meaning of what he says. The modern poet, Robert Bridges, echoes Plato but also widens the scope of the judgment:

How in its naked self
Reason were powerless showeth when philosophers
will treat of Art, the which they are fully read to
 do,
having good intuition that their master-key
may lie therein; but since they must lack vision
 of Art,
(for elsewhere they had been artists, not
 philosophers)
they miss the way. . . . [10]

Bridges expresses the deep-seated conviction, suggested in our earlier mention of Democritus, held by the most rationalist philosophers that beauty and great art transcend explanation. Plato provides in the *Laws*[11] an enduring image of the inspired imitative poet: "The poet," he writes, "according to the tradition which has ever prevailed among us, and is accepted of all men, when he sits down on the tripod of the muse, is not in his right mind; like a fountain, he allows to flow out freely whatever comes in, and . . . he is often compelled to represent men of opposite dispositions, and thus to contradict himself; neither can he tell whether there is more truth in one thing that he has said than in another . . ." This is not the only description Plato gives of the inspired poet; it is, however, the one which influenced one of the important writers in the eighteenth century in the examination of criticism. Daniel Webb, writing in *Letters on Literature*, uses the Platonic figure of the "fountain" in this denial to the critic of originality: ". . . The best critic considered merely as such, is but a dependent, a sort of planet to his original; he does no more than receive and reflect that light of which the poet is a fountain."

The philosophical point of the theory of artistic inspiration is a complicated and difficult one.[12] It is integrally related in Plato's *Symposium* and *Phaedrus* to the experience of the Idea of beauty, an Idea that exists in the suprasensible world. The spirit of Plato's writing, as well as its philosophical point, invades Shelley, who in the *Defense of Poetry* writes that he is one who "participates in the eternal, the infinite, and the one" and so far as relates to his conceptions, "time and place and number are not." Here Shelley offers an interesting interpretation of Plato's suprasensible world. Uncounted other poets and artists have followed Plato, although it is often difficult to distinguish his influence from that of his followers, notably Plotinus. It is probably the author of the *Enneads*, however, who so notably influenced the thinking of Michelangelo and so brought Neo-Platonism to the Medici Chapel.

It is clearly of more consequence in this book of readings to indicate the history of ideas in Philosophy of Art and Aesthetics than to encroach on the fields of the iconologist and historian of art and literature. It was briefly mentioned above that the Greeks believed basically

[10] From *The Testament of Beauty* by Robert Bridges (1930), by permission of the Clarendon Press, Oxford.

[11] Plato, *Laws* 719C.

[12] See below, Chapter 9.

that art is imitative and, by implication, that to escape the toils of *mimesis,* they judged that the poet was a man possessed. It is natural that their theory, based on the assumption that the artist copies either nature or another work of art, should bring to bear upon what we should now regard as aesthetic questions or problems of taste issues which may appear to the modern mind to be wholly pragmatic or concerned with utility to a degree not likely to be encountered in the period after Kant. The reasons for this have already been hinted at in the suggestion that Art is taken to be productive. In the hands of Aristotle,[13] making is defined in terms of a reasoned state of capacity to make and concerns the thing made, as well as the maker and the process by means of which something becomes. It is natural, also, to ask what the function of the object made is and for the Greek this is clearly a problem for the speculative mind, more particularly because it relates the object made to the end of art. This in turn suggests use and it is in the course of considering what the function or use of an imitation could conceivably be that Plato raises one of the significant systematic questions in his Philosophy of Art. "The real artist," Plato tells us, "would be interested in realities and not in imitations." In plainer terms, the painter "will paint reins, and he will paint a bridle," the worker in leather and brass will make them, but "it is only the horseman who knows how to use them and therefore knows their right form."

Among the ingenious ways in which the work of art is treated so that its complete identification with what its maker has copied is avoided, Plato argues that there are absolutely beautiful mathematical forms. To this widely accepted and powerful argument,[14] we shall come, but it is of interest here to point out that an earlier philosophical writer, Xenophanes,[15] attacks the imitative artist—and indeed all men who formulate anthropomorphic images of the gods—who if they were Ethiopeans "make their gods black and snub-nosed," if they are Thracians make them "red-haired and with blue eyes." But, says Xenophanes, "if cattle or lions had hands, so as to paint with their hands and produce works of art as men do, they would paint their gods and give them bodies in form like their own—horses like horses, cattle like cattle." Xenophanes attack is directed primarily to what he believes are malpractices in religion rather than to the realism of imitation. It is interesting, however, that this Eleatic wanderer is no less severe on an activity in which many Greeks engaged and one the theory of which was developed into a notable systematic philosophy of art. When the German poet Friedrich Schiller wrote that 'beauty . . . is our second creator,' he returned[16] to Plato for the hypothesis that art is play.[17] For Plato[18] and Aristotle, the activity of children at play and of men in playful activities provide a kind of preparation for later serious activities and, the alleviation of past toil—in Aristotle's words, for refreshment and "recreation."[19] Xenophanes holds no such view. For him, the glorification of the runner, the wrestler, the boxer, the horseman in their victories is "indeed a wrong custom," because men should not prefer "strength to excellent wisdom."

As was suggested earlier, Plato's examination of the arts is clearly integral to his search for sound definitions. He argues that if a philosopher can display the unique subject matter of an art and its unique technique, we know what the art is. "When the subject of knowledge is different, the art is different, too," he tells us in *Ion.*[20] It is not easy, however, to argue the nature of Art in terms of function and use, and to offer a distinguishing explanation for the mimetic art.

[13] Aristotle, *E.N.*, 1140 a 1. See below, pp. 136 et seq.

[14] See below, pp. 96 and 74 et seq. for passages from *Philebus* and *Hippias Major.*

[15] See below, p. 39, fr. 15.

[16] See below, pp. 437 et seq.

[17] See below, pp. 121–3.

[18] See below, pp. 120–21 for Plato, *Laws* 660.

[19] See below, p. 143, for Aristotle, *Politics* 1341b.

[20] See below, *Ion* 538, pp. 57 et seq.

Imitative arts by definition borrow their subject matter from what is copied. But the attack upon the artist, "who is the maker of all the works of all other workmen" and who is likened to the man who is a creator only in the sense that he resembles one who turns a mirror round and round, "catching the sun of the heavens, and the earth and yourself, and all other creations of art as well as of nature, in the mirror . . ." leads Plato himself to argue that the artist is like the cosmic artisan, the *Demiurgos*. With this introduction of theology into philosophy of art, we are launched upon a central problem of this book of selections. The issue becomes that of the nature of freedom as creativity. In the two and a half millenia of speculation, two theories concerning the artist, the work of art, the experience of the work of art, have been dominant. In the first, both the artist and the demiurgic artisan are held to possess freedom of choice. Their creativity is conditioned by Ideas and matter. In the second, the artist is regarded as analogous to God the creator, wholly free to create, conditioned by neither external ideas nor matter which he doesn't create.

The theory of the artist as maker awaits for its most powerful statement Plato's systematic philosophy.[21] The theory of the artist as creator awaits the development of commentary upon *Genesis*.[22] An illuminating foreshadowing of the demiurgic theory, with its implications concerning the freedom of the artist and of the cosmic artisan, appears in Empedocles' poem, *On Nature*, and to this we turn.

Empedocles[23] principal interest is to present his pluralist philosophy of elements and compounds and to indicate the function performed by the two forces, Love and Strife, which later came to be known as "efficient causes." Love, as a cosmic force, mixes together the elements, earth, air, fire, and water. Strife separates the compounds that Love brings together. In this four-fold set of cycles of being and becoming, there occurs "the generation of mortal things/ Born visible, /a countless host," because generation and corruption occur for "unspeakable numbers" of things. It seems clear that an earlier becoming ended in the production of all varieties of monsters and abortions and that the present part of the cycle of becoming persists because there is at least some vestige of harmony. What is interesting for the philosopher of art is that Empedocles draws an analogy between the artist, in this case painter, and Love as a cause that brings together the elements, for all things come together in Love. The elements are the source of "all things that are or have been or shall be." What we perceive are compounds of the elements brought together by Love or separated by Strife. The cosmic process is compared to the way in which painters of votive offerings proceed, selecting many-colored pigments to work with and blending them harmoniously together until a likeness of things is produced.

The passage is complex and difficult. It is evident, however, that Empedocles adopts the accepted theory of painting as a mimetic art. It is more important that the conception of an anthropomorphic cosmic efficient cause is made specific by analogy to the votive-painter, and that the cosmic artisan and the painter are tacitly free to choose and select. Such freedom is a function of the art or τεχνή the painter and the cosmic artist employ, for these painters are men "well taught in the wisdom of their art," i.e., they know the right procedure. They are, moreover, "quick of hand," i.e., they are able to apply their wisdom. Not only do they practice an art, but they practice it in such a way that they blend the colors harmoniously, knowing the quantity to be used.

As we shall see, the analogy Empedocles draws between the painters and the cosmic artisan is an anticipation of the *Demiurgos* in Plato's *Timaeus*.[24] A more immediate issue is raised,

[21] See above, Introduction, pp. 12 et seq.

[22] See above, pp. 12 et seq. and below, St. Augustine, pp. 233 et seq.

[23] See below, pp. 34 et seq. for Empedocles' life and for lines from his poem.

[24] See below, pp. 93 et seq.

however, by Empedocles' mention of the harmonious blending of colors. Here we come upon an echo of Pythagorean philosophy and on a second echo of a radically different thinking, that of Heraclitus. To these contrasting views we shall now turn.

The rigor of Greek mathematical speculation is most evident in Greek philosophy of art in the Pythagorean theory of "harmonia"[25] and in the applications of that theory not only to the pleasing sounds made by striking tautened cords but also in a cosmology that endowed the language with the phrase "the music of the spheres." In the speculation of Pythagoras and that of his followers[26] the search for a beauty definable in mathematical terms without reference to end or purpose begins. This speculation in ateleological terms leads directly to Plato's conception[27] of a beauty, the essence of which is in itself and not in another. The Idea of Beauty in the *Symposium* and the absolutely beautiful objects and events of the *Philebus* are not, therefore, regarded by Plato as mimetic,[28] since mimetic objects have their essences in another. The promise held forth by the Pythagorean philosophy of art and the rigor of the mathematical defining upon which they laid stress is also one of the great influences upon such theorists and artists as Vitruvius, Leonardo da Vinci, Dürer, and others who formulate canons of proportions for the human figure.

It is the later Pythagoreans and Plato in the Pythagorean dialogue, *Timaeus,* who introduce the figure of the cosmic artisan. Hippolytus, in his ***Refutatio Omnium Haeresium,*** tells us[29] that number is "undefined, incomprehensible" and contains within it all numbers. He adds that the first principle is "a male monad," which he describes as "begetting as a father all other numbers." Hippolytus goes on to mention the female number, as well, but his point is sufficiently clear. The "begetter" of all numbers is a conception based on analogy to organic generation. It is intended to account for becoming, i.e., change, growth and motion in a world defined in terms of solid geometrical figures. Plato merely hints at such generation, preferring the theory that making will account for change.

It is not strange that Plato, after whom the five geometrical solids are named and over the gateway of whose Academy was written "Let no one enter who is not versed in mathematics," should have been radically influenced by the Pythagoreans. It is interesting, however, that Aristotle, who prefers the biological to the mathematical sciences, should display in his *Metaphysics* a fascination for these early philosophers. It could be argued that he was primarily interested to refute their doctrines and there is without a doubt much truth in this. Still, this does not account for the fact that Aristotle's own definition of beauty is basically Pythagorean: "The chief forms of beauty," Aristotle writes,[30] "are order and symmetry and definiteness, which the mathematical sciences demonstrate in a special degree."

The resemblance of Aristotle's definition of beauty to what we know of the "mathematical" philosophers' speculation does not necessarily mean that he wholly understood it. As a matter of fact, his failure to grasp what one Pythagorean attempted to do has led to some confusion in speculation concerning the School's philosophy of art. To this issue we shall come as we examine the Pythagorean Eurytus. More immediately, it is well to indicate the main outlines of Pythagorean Philosophy of Art.

It is important to mention the fact that the Pythagorean number theory did have relations to the belief that knowledge and rationality are valuable for the purification of souls, a general point mentioned earlier.[31] It is this theory of

[25] The lives of the Pythagorean philosophers who contributed to speculation on art, and selections from the fragments of Pythagorean philosophy are given below, pp. 35 et seq.

[26] See below, pp. 37 et seq.

[27] See below, pp. 87 et seq.

[28] See below, pp. 96 et seq.

[29] See M. C. Nahm, *op. cit.,* pp. 56–7.

[30] Aristotle, *Metaphysics* 1078 b l. See below, p. 37.

[31] See above, pp. 7 and 24.

catharsis or purgation that plays such an important role in the history of the drama. It is, however, less with the therapeutic intent than with the strictly mathematical formulae and their extensions to man and the cosmos that we are here concerned. One of the most brilliant creative acts in the history of ideas was accomplished by Pythagoras in reducing "woodland notes wild" to an intelligible and demonstrable formula. Experimenting with different lengths of taut cords or with varying lengths of the same tautened cord, Pythagoras discovered[32] that the concordant intervals of the scale could be related in terms of the ratio 6 : 8 : : 9 : 12. In extending the conception of harmony as the basic principle explanatory of the cosmos, he created[33] the image of "the harmony of the spheres." The image of a universe in which the heavenly bodies move in a circle and so produce harmonious sounds has seized upon the creative and artistic imaginations of musicians, poets, and scientists.

Although he devotes much attention to Pythagorean philosophy, Aristotle clearly had the gravest doubts concerning the argument attributed to Eurytus,[34] one member of the School. Aristotle's own doubts have led many commentators into absurdity in their "explanations" of what Eurytus meant. Properly understood, however, the remarks attributed to this presumed pupil of Archytas are integral to one of the extraordinary and long-lived efforts to make painting and sculpture arts wholly intelligible in mathematical terms. They throw light on the Greek indebtedness to Egyptian painting and sculpture and provide us with a clearer understanding both of the Egyptian canon of proportions and the Polycleitean *Doryphorus*. Properly understood, what Eurytus said goes far to clarify much in succeeding attempts to provide formulae for making or creating works of beauty. What Eurytus intended is part of the tradition embodied in the Canon of Proportions formulated by Polycleitus.[35] For Polycleitus, "Beauty . . . arises . . . in the commensurability of the parts, such as that of the finger, not in the commensurability of the constituent elements (of the body), but in the commensurability (i.e., *symmetria*,) of the parts, such as that of finger to finger, and of all the fingers to the palm and the wrist, and of these to the forearm, and of the forearm to the upper arm, and, in fact, of everything to everything else, just as it is written in the Canon of Polycleitus . . . ."

Concerning the method Eurytus adopted in order to reduce painting to mathematical formulae, we turn to Aristotle and Alexander of Aphrodisias.[36] Aristotle tells us that Eurytus decided what the number of man or of horse is by imitating the figures of living things. Aristotle adds that Eurytus did this with pebbles, . . . "the method used by Pythagoreans to indicate the termini of the spatial figures which were their numbers, as," writes Aristotle, "some people bring numbers into the forms of triangles and squares." Aristotle professes to be puzzled by Eurytus' statement, asserting that it has not been determined whether the Pythagoreans use numbers "as causes of substances or of being—whether . . . as boundaries (as points are of spatial magnitudes) . . ." or because "harmony is a ratio of numbers, and so is man and everything else . . . ." The ambiguity disappears, however, once we recall that the pebbles or calculi were the means of defining the spaces within the terms and that a square or triangular number was so called because of its shape. What Eurytus did *was* to give what for him was the essence of man, that is, the essential number of pebbles that would define him in contrast to the number of pebbles needed to define for instance, a plant. Thus, 250 is the number that defines man, 360 the number that defines plant. It is clear that Eurytus was indicating the number of pebbles needed to provide the *outline* or *delineation* of a man for

32 See below, p. 36.
33 See below, p. 37.
34 See below, p. 37 et seq.

35 Galen, *de Placititis Hippocratis et Platonis,* V.
36 See below, pp. 28 et seq.

as Alexander tells us,[37] Eurytus proceeded ". . . to fix some of the counters in the *outline* of the man he had imaged by the number of counters equal in number to the unities he said defined man." This is no more than to say, however, that in the depiction of a man the Pythagorean took the outline or the delineation to be the form and, in the depiction of a man, implies that outline or delineation is not only the form but that it is also the common, the intelligible and the essential aspect of man.

Not only does Eurytus' suggestion fit into the tradition in which the essence of the work of art is believed to be an abstract "form," but it falls within the line of speculation in which the origins of Greek painting—and sculpture—are traced to Egypt.[38]

Eurytus' mention of *delineation*—i.e., outline—takes us to Pliny,[39] who tells us that either Philokles of Egypt or Cleanthes of Corinth invented painting. Pliny speculates on the possibility that the art originated "with the outlining of a man's shadow" *(omnes umbra hominis lineis circumducta)*. We also learn from Pliny[40] that Boutades, a potter of Sikyon, discovered with the help of his daughter how to model portraits in clay. It is of less consequence whether or not this is sound history than that in the history of ideas the "outline" or "form" is the essential and permanent factor to be considered in the creation and criticism of art. We are on the path from the Egyptian canon of proportions to the Platonic theory of mathematical forms that Plato held to be "absolutely and eternally beautiful."

It is well to point out that, while there is no evidence that Eurytus was arguing that a work of art constructed in terms of the number of pebbles needed to provide the outline of what is to be defined is beautiful, there is ample evidence that the brief passage quoted by Aristotle brings the Pythagorean's speculation well within the scope of the Greek conception of art as imitation. As we have noted, Aristotle,[41] concerned to explain the Pythagorean metaphysic of visible numbers in Book XIII of the *Metaphysics*, professes not to know whether Eurytus meant by the use of points as the boundaries of spatial magnitudes "boundaries" in fact or whether he meant the phrase to indicate that "harmony is a ratio of numbers, and so too is man and everything else." Still, Aristotle himself suggests that Eurytus meant the imitation of "the shape of natural objects." Things "embody or represent numbers" and a "ratio of numbers" is a relation of numbers, not a number. The figures or delineations of which Eurytus wrote were "likenesses" or "imitations" of numbers. Aristotle himself remarks in *Metaphysics* 985 b 35 that "The Pythagoreans say that things exist by imitation of number" and adds that "all other things seemed to be modelled on numbers . . ."

What, precisely, is implied for the history of art and for speculation concerning the making of art becomes evident in the passage quoted below from Alexander's *Metaphysics*.[42] What Eurytus suggested was a method for making the imitation. Not only is the number of "counters" or pebbles specified, i.e., 250 pebbles are needed to define man, but we learn also that the counters were green, black, red, and "all sorts of other colors." We are told more. Eurytus wrote that the wall is to be plastered, a sketch of a man or plant is to be made on it, and some of the colors are to be fixed in the outline of the face, some in that of hands and some in that of other parts. "And so he completed the *outline* of the man he had imaged by a number of counters equal in number to the units which he said defined the man."

The word used here is δκιαγραφία or outline-drawing. Eurytus evidently believed that he had

[37] pp. 28 et seq.

[38] See below, pp. 105–06 et seq. for Plato's reasons for accepting Egyptian art as the Canon.

[39] *The Elder Pliny's Chapters on the History of Art*, Chs. XXXV–XXXVI, trans. K. Jex-Blake. (London, Macmillan and Co.), 1896.

[40] *Ibid.*, XXXV.151.

[41] Cf. below, p. 37. (Aristotle, *Met.* 1092 b 8.)

[42] Alexander of Aphrodisias, *Met.* 827.1.

defined the essence of man by imitating or outlining the external shape of a man. Once we realize that the colors mentioned in the passage in Alexander's *Metaphysics* are intended to give an impression of three dimensions to a two-dimensional drawing, we may properly conclude that Eurytus is in fact forging an important link in the chain of one of the longest-lived and most important theories of creativity in art. Aristotle had observed that orderly arrangement and definiteness are obviously causes of many things and that the mathematical sciences must treat "this sort of causative principle also ((i.e., the beautiful) as in some sense a cause." Pliny, as we have observed, takes us back in this speculation upon delineation and outline to the Egyptians. We do not know whether the Egyptians believed that the canon of proportions was the "cause" of beauty. Certainly, the practice of the Greeks more than suggests that they and later theorists did believe that could they but discover the correct set of proportions from which to work, beauty would result from its application. If we ask what the speculative philosophers sought in the canon of Eurytus the Pythagorean, it is to Plato that we are well advised to turn for an answer. The rigor of the mathematical sciences would appear to have held promise for him of a solution to the difficulties raised by art as imitation.[43] Moreover, it would appear that Plato believed that a canon would permit the production of a beauty independent of time and place. Of the Egyptians he remarks[44] that "their ancient paintings and sculptures are not a whit better or worse than the work of today, but are made with just the same skill." If what is made into a beautiful work of art may be made so without reference to the particular circumstances in which the artist finds himself, the canon of proportions provides a demonstrable technique not only for the intelligibility of the object made but also a ground for general agreement in judgment. The Egyptians, Plato believes, habituated their young citizens "to forms and strains of virtue" in music and dancing. Of painting and other art, no painter or other representative artist is allowed to innovate upon the forms they fixed and exhibited "in the patterns of them in their temples, or to leave the traditional forms and invent new ones." Plato believes that the forms were the same for works of art painted or moulded ten thousand years ago.

In a sense, the canon of proportions implicit in Pythagorean theory and made more explicit in Eurytus' brief statement and in Plato's philosophy of art suggests that creativity is to be sought in the use of the most rational of techniques. To be free in art means here a function of the power to make one's art intelligible regardless of particular circumstances, specific periods of time, or geographical locations.

We turn now to the antithesis to Pythagorean mathematical theory in its application to art. This appears in the philosophy of Heraclitus and of his Sophist follower, the anonymous author of *The Arguments on Both Sides*.

Men are led to search in the area of mathematics for the key to art and to the mysteries that surround its creation and judgment for many reasons, not the least important of which is the fascination implicit in speculation. Pythagorean speculation, concerning the changeless Egyptian technique and the "fact" that works of art produced "ten thousand years ago" are not inferior to those of the present day, provided an eagerly sought clue to human freedom in the means for accomplishing the same thing, i.e., producing beautiful objects whatever the circumstances in which one found oneself. Some credence is given this assumption by the oft-repeated story told by Diodorus of Sicily. Diodorus tells us that two brothers, Telecles and Theodorus each made half a statue, Telecles in Samos and Theodorus in Ephesus. ". . . When the two parts were brought together," writes Diodorus, "they fitted so perfectly that the whole work had the appearance of having been made by one man. . . ."

43 See below, pp. 92 et seq. and 109 et seq.

44 Plato, *Laws* 656 D–657 B. Quoted below, p. 105 et seq.

The implication that the work is wholly intelligible, that the creative process is duplicable, and that the form of the statues is demonstrable is not far removed from our present-day theory concerning the assembly line. It provides a goal, as we have observed, that millenia of artists have adopted as their own. It is, however, diametrically opposed to the view of art maintained by the formidable philosopher of Ephesus, Heraclitus,[45] and by the argument of his follower, the Sophist who wrote *The Arguments on Both Sides*. This is one of the more striking instances of contrast to be found in Philosophy of Art, and it suggests how powerful systematic speculation had come to be early in speculation on works of art.

If the germ of ateleological and mathematical defining of art in Pythagorean philosophy exercises an enormous influence upon succeeding philosophies of art, Heraclitean relativism and subjectivism does so with little less force.[46] The nerve of Heraclitus' argument is the fragment that argues[47] that "In the same rivers we step and we do not step. We are and we are not." In this fragment, the philosophy of eternal and ceaseless change implies not only ceaseless flux in the external world but also relativism of judgment—for we are and we are not—and subjectivity. The cosmos is in balanced process. What we take to be fixed and stable is in fact in process of change from what it was to what it will be—the present—the "ever-present now"—is an obvious consequence of Heraclitus' relativism. But the main thrust of the argument is the relativism expressed in fragment 99, "The fairest ape is ugly compared with anything of another kind and the fairest pot is ugly compared with any maiden."

The full impact of Heraclitus' thinking as it concerns subjectivity in philosophy of art awaits the development of Sophist philosophy.[48] The nerve of the Sophist argument is Protagoras' famous statement[49] that "Man is the measure of all things, of existing things that they exist and of nonexisting things that they exist not." Concerning art and judgment, the ablest expression we have inherited from a Sophist is *The Arguments of Both Sides*,[50] in the portion in which the anonymous author writes, "On the Relation of the Fair and Ugly." He gives a vigorous statement of an argument that in the course of centuries has become the cliché, *de gustibus non est disputandum*. It is important to emphasize how radically the implications concerning the freedom of the judge of art differ from those implicit in Pythagorean mathematical philosophy. "Some say," the Sophist writes, "that the fair is one thing and the ugly another as the name differs . . . . If anyone bade all men to bring together into a single place the things that each thought were ugly, and then bade them take from this gathering the things each considered fair, nothing would have been left, and all would have taken every last thing. . . ." The correlative to the story of Telecles and Theodorus[51]—since both sculptors must not only have been artists but critics as well—is that their creativity consisted in the freedom to do the same thing irrespective of the circumstances and surroundings in which they found themselves. The creativity of judgment for the anonymous author of *The Argument on Both Sides* is no less clearly conceived to be the ability of each individual, according to his subjective taste, to do anything he wishes to do in any circumstance and to justify the deed. This is the first statement concerning the judgment of art in which it is implied that a man may make a wholly free, i.e., unconditioned judgment. It

[45] See below, pp. 40 et seq. for Heraclitus' life and teaching and pp. 42 et seq. for mention of the anonymous author of the two-sided argument.

[46] See above, p. 22 for Eliot's remarks on the dance and below, Chapter 8, pp. 323–24, 332–33 for Voltaire.

[47] Nahm, *op. cit.*, p. 73, fr. 81.

[48] See Nahm, *op. cit.*, pp. 208–248, for the various Sophists' doctrines.

[49] *Ibid.*, pp. 224–25.

[50] See below, pp. 42 et seq. for selection from text.

[51] See above, p. 29.

should be noted that such theory makes judgment meaningless. As Aristotle puts it,[52] if man is the measure of all things, "... It follows that the same thing both is and is not ... and that the contents of all other opposite statements are true, because often a particular thing appears beautiful to some and the contrary of beautiful to others, and that which appears to each man is the measure." It need be added only that each man in these circumstances could have the right to insist upon correctness of his judgment, even though he might utter contrary judgments or even contradictory ones in successive moments.

The influence of Sophist philosophy upon Plato's theory of art will be examined in the next chapter. It is noteworthy, however, that we possess Heraclitus' comparison of the ape and the maiden because Plato quotes[53] it in the *Hippias Major*. Before turning to Plato, however, we shall mention briefly some additional implications of a remark made by the Atomist, Democritus, upon which we have already commented[54] and suggest the importance of Socrates' remarks concerning inspiration, painting and sculpture.

In both Democritean and Socratic philosophy of art we come upon the third markedly important aspect of early Greek philosophy of art—the conviction that the poet and many of his fellow artists are inspired. This is a theory no less subjective than that formulated by Heraclitus and elaborated upon by the author of *The Arguments on Both Sides*. It should be noted, however, that it is the other side of the coin of theories in which there are well-defined statements concerning art as technique and, as we shall see, in Plato's hands,[55] inspiration becomes a device used to insure the artist's escape from the rigors of technique and by Plato specifically to provide a second necessary theory of knowledge.[56]

As was suggested earlier, it is the most notable aspect of Democritus' mention of inspiration that it is the correlative to the strictest theory of mechanism formulated in early Greek philosophy. The Atomists, Leucippus and Democritus, reduced nature's dimensions to a minimum—atoms and void. In their cosmos, nothing occurs at random, "but everything for a reason . . . and by necessity."[57] Yet, it is said, it is precisely the mad and irrational poet who writes with enthusiasm and divine inspiration who makes what is most beautiful. Whereas technique is rational, inspiration moves beyond reason and, as history shows, produces what transcends intelligibility because it is made by an artist for whom neither the technique nor the purpose of art is meaningful. Here we have the beginnings of the later assumption that it is owing to inspiration that the fine artist may produce what is in fact original.[58]

In the philosophy of art attributed by Plato and Xenophon to that extraordinary genius, Socrates, many of the themes that the early philosophers "lisped" in the tradition of speculation come clear and are transformed by one of the most powerful minds and skillful dialecticians who ever lived.[59] The theory of art as imitation oppears, as does that of inspiration, both interesting in themselves, and as anticipations of Platonic Philosophy of Art.

In his discussion of more general philosophical and moral problems, Socrates devotes his dialectical skill to the task of "beating out"

[52] Quoted, Nahm, *op. cit.*, p. 226, no. 19.

[53] See below, pp. 71–2.

[54] See above, p. 21.

[55] See below, pp. 52–3. See also below, Chapters 6 and 9 for later developments of the theory of inspiration.

[56] See below, pp. 63 et seq. and 84 for *Symposium* 201 et seq.

[57] See below, pp. 45 et seq. for Democritus' life and teaching.

[58] See below, pp. 394 et seq. for Edward Young's statement concerning the original genius.

[59] See below, pp. 47 et seq. for a brief life of Socrates and for selections from what is reported concerning his teachings on art. See also Nahm, *op. cit.*, pp. 251–294 for a fuller study of Socrates' life and philosophy.

concepts. These, he believes, may be secured by sound definition and are the objects of knowledge. This is in contrast to the Sophists' emphasis upon percepts and their insistence that perception is the sole mode of knowing available to us. It is clear, in such a dialogue as Plato's *Hippias Major*[60] that the perfecting of dialectic was in fact primarily directed to beat out the answer to problems arising from the effort to say "What beauty is" and to answer the question, "What is beautiful?" For Socrates wants the concept, the connotation, not the denotation, the denoted percept. Still, the Socrates of Plato's dialogues and of Xenophon's *Memorabilia* is a myriad-minded man. He sought conceptual knowledge. It is also true that he sought to define Art as a technique[61] and that his concern with his own *daimon* is not alien to a similar concern for an understanding of the inspiration[62] that he believed permitted the tragic poets to utter many profound things but did not permit them to explain what they wrote.

With these evidences of Socrates' diverse interests in mind, it is surprising to discover that despite his interest in concepts, this gadfly of the Athenian steed is more Heraclitean and Sophist than Pythagorean in the accounts we have of his discussions of painting and sculpture with the artists themselves. Socrates is a man of extraordinary perception. More significantly, his view is in contrast to that of the Pythagorean philosophers—and of Plato—in which the object of art tends to disappear into the ratio formulated to account for objective beauty. Where the canon is formulated in terms of freedom, we have the freedom to do the same thing regardless of differences in circumstances. Where Socrates is concerned, to inquire[63] concerning the art of Parrhasius, the painter, or Cleiton, the sculptor, we encounter an individual and inquiring mind determined to discover the answer to the question, How can the artist contrive "to make the whole figure look beautiful" when there are variations in the figures represented—in the light and in shadow and in the difficulty presented in finding "a perfect model." Socrates poses the question, whether the painter is not in fact portraying the "character of the soul" and asks whether it is possible to "imitate" it. This suggests how much even in the fifth century B.C. the meaning of *mimesis* was being widened. Even more interesting, perhaps, is that Socrates hazards the opinion to Cleiton, the sculptor, that the illusion of life is given by accurate representation—but not representation by formula but of "the different parts of the body as they are affected by the pose. . . ." In other words, Socrates supposes that the sculptor is free in precisely the sense that he may choose and is not bound by formula. The suggestion that the sculptor must represent in his figures the activities of "the soul" is diametrically opposed to the view put forward by Plato[64] that the sculptor makes a likeness (imitation) "by producing a copy which is executed according to the proportions of the original," and that if he does not do so he is deceiving the spectator. We know that Pheidias was willing to make "proportions which appear to be beautiful, disregarding the real ones," and we learn from Xenophon that Socrates approved. Plato inveighs against the creative freedom of the painter who believes that he has absolute power of making whatever he likes. Socrates sees the need to permit the artist to be free to portray not what he sees, but an "imitation" of the feelings.

It may be that Socrates' interest in the individual object and his attention to variations in technique required in sculpting and painting specific models in order to produce "the whole" are systematically related to his

60 See below, pp. 66 et seq. where the dialogue is given.

61 See Plato, *Ion* 532, below pp. 51 et seq.

62 See below, pp. 49 et seq. (*Apology* 22) and p. 51 (*Ion* 534).

63 See below, pp. 50 et seq.

64 See below, pp. 104–05 for Plato's attack on the use of proportion in sculpture, (*Sophist* 235D–236E.)

denial to the tragic poet of mastery of technique, while at the same time the tragedians are lauded for the fine things they write but cannot explain. The point is speculative. What is not speculative is the contrast drawn in the Platonic dialogues of the early, Socratic period, between art and inspiration. For Socrates,[65] art is a technique that is master of a whole art. If the subject of knowledge is different, the art is different and if we are not dealing with the product of art there is no possible validation of judgment. In contrast,[66] the inspired poets "say many fine things, but do not understand the meaning of them." Poets write by a sort of genius and inspiration. The inspired poet is a "slight wing'd, and holy thing," carried out of himself in the process of creating. Inspiration is likened to a chain of rings[67] and a magnet, imparting the "power" to attract and so "one man hangs down from another" in the chain.

Ion differs radically from *Hippias Major*.[68] Both are Platonic dialogues but what marks the latter off from the former is that in it we come upon the Platonic theory of an absolute beauty, which is not relative to person, time or place. *Ion* would seem, on the other hand, to be compatible with what we know elsewhere of Socrates as a thinker, e.g., in Plato's early dialogues and in Xenophon's *Memorabilia*. As we turn to Plato and Aristotle, we turn from fragments of philosophy to systematic philosophies, from profound thinkers to two of the preeminent of all philosophers.

65 See below, Plato, *Ion*, pp. 53 et seq.

66 See below, pp. 52–3 et seq. (Plato, *Apology* 22.)

67 See below, Plato, *Ion*, 533D pp. 54 et seq.

68 See below, pp. 66 et seq. for Plato's *Hippias Major*.

Empedocles

Ca. 494–434 B.C.

A. Life

Empedocles,[67] the first philosopher to formulate the theory of elements, was the son of Meton and a native of Akrages or Agrigentum in Sicily. It is said that Empedocles, born to a distinguished family, opposed tyranny, refused the rule of Agrigentum and was exiled from his native city. To him were attributed powers of magic. "Once, when the Etesian gales were blowing violently, so as to injure the crops, he ordered some asses to be flayed, and some bladders to be made of their hides, and these he placed on the hills and high places to catch the wind. . . ." He is reported to have leapt into the crater of Mt. Etna in order "to confirm," by his disappearance, "the report that he had become a god." However, one of his slippers was thrown up by the volcano and his effort to deceive was thwarted.

Empedocles wrote two poems, one called *On Nature,* the second entitled *Purifications.* The passage which follows is from *On Nature.*

[67] See pp. 111–133 of Nahm, *op. cit.,* for introduction to and fragments of Empedocles' philosophy. I have retained throughout this Chapter the enumeration of fragments and selections I have used in the above work.

On Nature 104–121[68] *(arranged)*

And as when painters are preparing elaborate votive offerings—men well taught by wisdom in their art—they take many-colored pigments to work with, and blend together harmoniously more of one and less of another till they produce likenesses of all things, making trees and men and women, wild beasts and birds and water-nourished fishes, and the very gods, long-lived, highest in honor. So let not error overcome thy mind to make thee think there is any other source of mortal things that have likewise come into distinct existence in unspeakable numbers; but know these [elements], for thou didst hear from a god the account of them.

[68] This fragment is 104 and 121 of H. Stein's enumeration of lines in *Empedoclis Agrigentini Fragmenta* (London, A. Marcum, 1852.)

Pythagoras and the Pythagoreans[69]

The Pythagoreans

A. Lives

The Pythagoreans are the "Italian School" of early Greek Philosophy. Pythagoras, a great mathematician and religious teacher, was born in Samos and went from Greece to Croton, in southern Italy, in 532 B.C. He was the son of Mnesarchus, a seal engraver. Before going to Italy, Pythagoras is said to have traveled to Egypt and learned the language of that country. Returning from Egypt, he fled the tyranny of Polycrates. He died at the age of eighty years in a conflagration in Croton, in which his disciples also perished. Heraclitus tells us that Pythagoras "prosecuted scientific investigations beyond all other men." He worked out the theory of the length of the hypotenuse, as well the mathematical expression of a right-angled triangle and of the octave. Pythagoras held the belief that the soul is immortal and that it transmigrated at death from one body to another.

Eurytus, whom Aristotle mentions in the 12th Book of the Metaphysics as having "decided what was the number of what . . . by imitating the figures of living things with pebbles. . . ." is said to have been the pupil of the famous Pythagorean, Archytas. So little is known of Eurytus, however, that he has been thought to have been only a symbolic person into whose mouth Aristotle placed the words of Archytas. Whoever he is or whether he existed or not, his are among the most important words on art spoken by a Pythagorean. To Aristotle's remarks on Eurytus, are to be noted those of Alexander of Aphrodisias and Theophrastus, Aristotle's successor as head of the Lyceum.

[69] See Nahm, *op. cit.*, pp. 46–61.

B. Thought

Aristotle, *Metaphysics* I. 5. 985 b–986 b 8. . . . And since of these [sciences] numbers are by nature the first, in numbers rather than in fire and earth and water they thought they saw many likenesses to things that are and that are coming to be. . . . And further, discerning in numbers the conditions and reasons of harmonies also, since, moreover, other things seemed to be like numbers in their entire nature, and numbers were the first of every nature, they assumed that the elements of numbers were the elements of all things, and that the whole heavens were harmony and number.

——I. 8. 989 b 32–990 a 32. . . . Now those who are called Pythagoreans use principles and elements yet stranger than those of the physicists, in that they do not take them from the sphere of sense, for mathematical objects are without motion, except in the case of astronomy. . . . In what manner motion will take place when limited and unlimited, odd and even, are the only underlying realities, they do not say; nor how it is possible for genesis and destruction to take place without motion and change, or for heavenly bodies to revolve. . . .

Hippolytus, *Philosophumena,* 2, *Dox.* 555. And he [Pythagoras,] in his studies of nature mingled astronomy and geometry and music [and arithmetic]. And thus he asserted that god is a monad, and examining the nature of number with especial care, he said that the universe produces melody and is put together with harmony, and he first proved the motion of the seven stars to be rhythm and melody. . . .

Aristotle, *Metaphysics* XII. 6. 1080 b 16. But the Pythagoreans, because they see many qualities of numbers in bodies perceived by sense, regard objects as numbers, not as separate numbers, but as derived numbers. And why? Because the qualities of numbers exist in a musical scale (*harmonia*), in the heavens and in many other things.

——*de Caelo* II. 9. 290 b 15. Some think it necessary that noise should arise when so great bodies are in motion, since sound does arise from bodies among us which are not so large and do not move so swiftly; and from the sun and moon and from the stars in so great number, and of so great size, moving so swiftly, there must necessarily arise a sound inconceivably great. Assuming these things and that the swiftness has the principle of harmony by reason of the intervals, they say that the sound of the stars moving on in a circle becomes musical. And since it seems unreasonable that we also do not hear this sound, they say that the reason for this is that the noise exists in the very nature of things, so as not to be distinguishable from the opposite silence; for the distinction of sound and silence lies in their contrast with each other, so that as blacksmiths think there is no difference between them because they are accustomed to the sound, so the same things happen to men.

——II. 9. 291 a 7. What occasions the difficulty and makes the Pythagoreans say that there is a harmony of the bodies as they move, is a proof. For whatever things move themselves make a sound and noise; but whatever things are fastened in what moves or exists in it as the parts in a ship, cannot make a noise, nor yet does the ship if it moves in a river.

Aristotle, *Metaphysics* I. 985 b 35.[70] . . . Since, again, they saw that the modifications and the ratios of the musical scales were expressible in numbers, and numbers seemed to be the first things in the whole of nature, they supposed the elements of numbers to be the elements of all things, and the whole heaven to be a musical scale and a number. And all the properties of numbers and scales which they could show to agree with the attributes and parts and the whole arrangement of the heavens, they collected and fitted into their scheme; and if there was a gap anywhere, they readily made additions so as to make their whole theory coherent. . . .

——987 b 10. . . . The Pythagoreans say that things exist by 'imitation' of numbers, and Plato says they exist by participation, changing the name. But what the participation of the Forms could be they left an open question.

——1078 b 1. The chief forms of beauty are order and symmetry and definiteness, which the mathematical sciences demonstrate in a special degree. . . .

Eurytus

Aristotle, *Met.* 1092 b 8.* Once more, it has in no sense been determined in which way numbers are causes of substances and of being —whether (1) as limits (as points are of spatial magnitudes); this is how Eurytus decided what was the number of what (e.g., of man, or of horse), viz., by imitating the figures of living things with pebbles, as some people bring numbers into the forms of triangle and square; or (2) is it because harmony is a relations of numbers. . . . ?

Theophrastus,[71] *Met.* II, 6 a 14. . . . But at any rate, starting from this first principle or these first principles, one might demand (and presumably also from any other first principles that may be assumed) that they should go straight on to give an account of the successive derivatives, and not proceed to a certain point and then stop; for this is the part of a competent and sensible man, to do what Archytas once said Eurytus did as he arranged certain pebbles; he said (according to Archytas) that this is in fact the number of man, and this of horse, and this of something else. But now *most* people go to a certain point and then stop, as those do also who set up the One and the indefinite dyad; for after generating numbers and planes and solids they leave out almost everything else, except to the extent of just touching on them and making this much, and only this much plain, that some things proceed from the indefinite dyad, e.g., place, the void, and the infinite, and others from the numbers and the one, e.g., soul and certain other things; and they generate simultaneously time and the heavens and several other things, but of the heavens and the remaining things in the universe they make no further mention. . . .

* See M. C. Nahm, *op. cit.*, p. 57.

[70] The following three passages from Aristotle's *Metaphysics* are translated by W. D. Ross. *The Works of Aristotle Translated into English by J. A. Smith and W. D. Ross.* Oxford, The Clarendon Press, 1908–31.

[71] Translated by W. D. Ross and F. H. Forbes, Theophrastus, *Metaphysics* (Oxford, Clarendon Press, 1929), p. 13.

Xenophanes

565 B.C.

A. Life

Xenophanes[72] was a wandering poet and maker of satires and elegies. He believed that God is not correctly described in anthropomorphic terms and argued as well that "Ethiopians make their gods black and snub-nosed, Thracians red-haired and with blue eyes."

Xenophanes was born in 565 B.C., a date fixed by his statement that he had wandered over Hellas for 67 years after the conquest of Ionia by the Persians. He was born in Ionia but lived in Elea in Italy and his thought is usually interpreted in Eleatic terms. He is said by Diogenes Laertius to have been a native of Colophon and the son of Dexius. "He used to recite his poems," Diogenes tells us.

B. Thought[73]

2. But if one wins a victory by swiftness of foot, or in the pentathlon, where the grove of Zeus lies by Pisas' stream at Olympia, or as a wrestler, or in painful boxing, or in that severe contest called the pancration, he would be more glorious in the eyes of the citizens, he would win a front seat at assemblies, and would be entertained by the city at the public table, and he would receive a gift which would be a keepsake for him. If he won by means of horses he would get all these things although he did not deserve them, as I deserve them, for our wisdom is better than the strength of men or of horses. This is indeed a very wrong custom, nor is it right to prefer strength to excellent wisdom. For if there should be in the city a man good at boxing, or in the pentathlon, or in wrestling, or in swiftness of foot, which is honored more than strength (among the contests men enter into at the games), the city would not on that account be any better governed. Small joy would it be to any city in this case if a citizen conquers at

[72] See Nahm, *op. cit.*, pp. 79–87.

[73] The enumeration of the fragments accords with the order given in Nahm, *op. cit.*

the games on the banks of the Pisas, for this does not fill with wealth the secret chambers.

14. But mortals suppose that the gods are born (as they themselves are), and that they wear man's clothing and have human voice and body.

15. But if cattle or lions had hands, so as to paint with their hands and produce works of art as men do, they would paint their gods and give them bodies in form like their own—horses like horses, cattle like cattle.

16. Ethiopians make their gods black and snub-nosed, Thracians red-haired and with blue eyes.

Heraclitus

d. 378–370 B.C.

A. Life

Heraclitus[74] was called "the dark" philosopher owing to the obscurity of his writings. Socrates is said to have remarked of one of Heraclitus' works that "the book requires a Delian diver to get at the meaning of it." Heraclitus was born in Ephesus, on the coast of Asia Minor. He was a descendant of the royal line of his native city. He probably exercised priestly as well as temporal duties, although his attacks on the mysteries and the sacrifices suggest that he abandoned any role in the religious rites of his native city.

Heraclitus' conceptions of art are integral to his philosophy of constant change and of relations between aspects of fire, rather than on what is related. In Heraclitean thought, judgments are relative, although a hidden law of harmony governs the constant change, the process we observe as phenomena. "Everything flows" except the law of change itself. "Wisdom[75] is a single thing. It is to understand the mind by which all things are steered through all things."

B. Philosophy of Art

56. The harmony of the world is of tensions, like that of the bow and the lyre.

59. You should combine things whole and not whole, what is drawn together and what is drawn apart, the harmonious and the discordant; from all one, and from one all.

61. All things are fair and good and right to God; but men think of some as wrong and others as right.

98. The wisest of men shows like an ape beside God, in wisdom, beauty, and everything else.

99. The fairest ape is ugly compared with anything of another kind, and the fairest pot is ugly compared with any maiden.

130. They are purified by defilement with blood, as if one were to step into mud and wash it off with mud.

[74] See Nahm, *op. cit., pp.* 62–77 for introduction to and fragments of Heraclitus' philosophy.

[75] *Ibid,* Heraclitus, fr. 19.

The Sophists

A. General Introduction

The Sophists[76] were the great professional teachers of ancient Greece. Their methods of teaching were in sharp contrast to those traditional practices in which the young man was permitted to study with a friend of the family, concentrating upon the subjects of music and gymnastic. The Sophists taught rhetoric, instructed their pupils in the best ways to present set-speeches, and in the defense of skeptical doubts concerning laws and customs. They charged fees for this instruction and to this professionalism both Plato and Socrates object. The principal thrust of the Socratic and Platonic attacks upon the Sophists, however, was directed against the relativism that pervaded sophistic thought, against the skepticism with which they sought to imbue their hearers. The basis for the criticism was, however, the subjectivity to which they reduced all processes of knowing.

Protagoras (born ca. 432 B.C.), the greatest of the Sophists, argued that "Man is the measure of all things, of existing things that they exist, and of non-existing things that they exist not." This is an application of the Heraclitean theory of constant change, and it leads to the denial of absolutes and constants in politics, morals, and knowledge. Each man is the judge or criterion of truth.

Gorgias (ca. 483–375 B.C.), held that nothing is; that if anything did exist, no one could know it; and finally, that if anyone did find it out, he could not communicate it to another. This relativism and subjectivism of the fifth century B.C. was enormously important and influential and had a permanent echo in the recurrent arguments concerning the subjectivity or objectivity of judgments of art and beauty. Gorgias in fact carried his dialectical methods over into the area of speech. He held that speech is the means by which we indicate and "is not the real and existent things." He argued that "the visible things are apprehensible by sight and the audible by hearing. . . ." He concluded, therefore, that ". . . we do not indicate to our neighbors the existent things," but, rather, we indicate speech, "which is other than the existing realities. . . ."

We know nothing concerning the author of *The Arguments on Both Sides.* Whoever he was, he provides us with a strong argument in favor of the view that judgments of the fair and the ugly are relative. It is clear, too, that the author applies to art such arguments as those put forward by Gorgias. The result is that a succinct but well-rounded theory of the subjectivity of taste is put before us.

[76] For a general account of the Sophists and for the remaining material attributed to others of the school, see Nahm, *op. cit.*, pp. 204–248.

B. Thought

Anonymous

The arguments on both sides

1. (1) Two-fold arguments are uttered by the philosophers in Greece about the good and the bad. For some say that the good is one thing and the bad another. Others say they are the same thing and for some, it is good, for others bad, and for the same man at one time good at another bad. (2) And I also apply myself to these (following) matters, and I shall consider (them) in terms of man's life and its concern with food, drink and love. For these are things which are bad for the sick but good for the healthy and him who needs them. . . . (11) And there is another view given, that the good is one thing but the bad another, as the name differs, in the same way the thing differs. And I myself too make this kind of distinction. (17) This and all the others are the points which have been stated in our prior discussion. And I am not saying, what is the good? But I am trying to teach this, that the bad and the good are not the same thing but each different.

ON FAIR AND UGLY

2. (1) There are two-fold arguments about the fair and the ugly. For some say that the fair is one thing and the ugly another, as the name differs, in the same way the body differs. Others say that the same thing is fair and ugly. (2) And I shall make the trial working it out in this manner. For example, it is fair for a youth to gratify a lover who is decent, but it is ugly to gratify a lover who is not fair and good. . . . (18) And I believe if anyone bade all men bring together into a single place the things that each thought were ugly, and then bade them take from this gathering the things each considered fair, nothing would have been left, but all would have taken every last thing. For everybody does not think alike. (19) And I shall cite also a poem: "For if you distinguish you will see the other law for mortals thus: nothing was every way fair, nor ugly, but occasion took the same things and made them ugly, and with a change made them fair." (20) In short, all is fair with timeliness, but in untimeliness ugly. . . .

ON JUST AND UNJUST

3. . . . (17) And they bring in skills in which there is no justice and injustice. And the

Translated by Alister Cameron, Department of Classics, University of Cincinnati. The text is from H. Diels' *Die Fragmente der Vorsokratiker* (Berlin, 1906–10), II. 407 et seq. Permission to print granted by Alister Cameron.

poets do not compose their poems with regard to truths but with regard to the pleasures of men. . . .

ON WISDOM AND VIRTUE, ARE THEY TEACHABLE?

4. (1) A certain argument is made that is neither true nor novel: that wisdom and virtue are neither teachable nor can be learned. Those who say this use the following proofs: (2) That if you should hand anything on to anybody one would not continue to have it. For it, wisdom or virtue they say, is one. (3) Secondly, if it were teachable, that the teachers would have professed it as they have music. (4) And third that those who became the wise men of Hellas would have taught their art to their intimates. (5) And fourth that some people have gone to the Sophists and had no benefit. (6) And fifth that many who have not gone to school to the Sophists have become famous. (7) I think this a very silly argument. For I know that the teachers teach letters, which indeed is what he happens to know himself, and the lyre-players teach people to play the lyre. And with regard to the second proof, that teachers have not professed, what is it the Sophists teach if it isn't wisdom and virtue? (8) Or what Anaxagoreans and Pythagoreans? And for the third, Polycleitus taught his son to make statues. (9) And if somebody has not taught it doesn't signify. Whereas if some one did teach it is evidence that it is possible to teach. (10) And fourth, suppose they did not become wise having gone to the Sophists; surely many people having learned their letters don't know them. (11) And nature enters in also, by which indeed one though he has not learned from the Sophists becomes able, at least if he has the natural endowment, to grasp the majority of things easily, having learned a few things from those from whom we learn our words. One man learns more or less of these from his father, the other from his mother (12) And if some one does not believe that I learn the words but am born knowing them, let him see from this: if someone sends a child to Persia as soon as it is born and rears it there, out of hearing of the Greek tongue, he would speak Persian. If someone bring one from there he would speak Greek. Thus we do learn the words and our teachers we do not know. (13) Such is my argument. It has a beginning, an end and a middle. And I am not saying that it is teachable but those proofs do not satisfy me.

5. (1) Some haranguers say that it is right for offices to come by lot. In this they think far from right. (2) For if anyone should ask the person who says this, Why don't you assign your slaves their duties by lot so that your coachman would cook, if that were his lot, and the cook drive your horses and, in the same way with other things? . . . (3) And why don't we bring the bronze-smiths and tanners together, and the builders and goldsmiths, and make the distribution of lots and force each to work at the allotted craft instead of the one he knows? (4) And similarly at the musical contests, assign the contestants by lot and force them to contend in the allotted thing. The flautist will play the lyre since it so fell out and the lyre-player will blow the flute. And in war archer and infantryman will be mounted, and cavalryman will shoot the bow, so that everybody will do what he neither knows how to do nor can do. And they say it is both good and very democratic. I think it least of all democratic. For in the states are men who hate the people and if the lot ever falls to them they will destroy the people. (6) Rather the people itself must choose with foresight all those well-disposed to them, and those equipped to command, and others to be guardians of the law, and so with other things.

6. (1) It is in the range of the same man and the same art, I believe, to be able to discuss

briefly, to know the truth of things, to know how to judge correctly and to be able to speak in public, to know the arts of words and to teach about the nature of all things, both how they are and how they were. (2) And first, the man who knows about the nature of all things, how shall he not be able to teach the city too to manage properly? (3) And further he who knows the arts of speech will understand how to speak properly also about all things. (4) For it is necessary for him who means to speak properly to speak about the things he knows. Indeed, he will know all things. (5) For he knows the arts of all the words while the words are, all of them, about all the things there are. (6) And the one who means to speak correctly must understand the affairs about which he may speak, both how to teach the city correctly to do the good and to prevent them from doing the bad. (7) And if he knows these things he will also know the things that are different. For he will know everything. For this is the case with everything, and in the particular case he will do what is fitting, if he must. (8) And if he knows how to play the flute he will always be able to play the flute, if ever he must do this. (9) The man who knows how to plead a case must understand justice correctly. For the trials are about this, and knowing he will know also the opposite to it and the different. (10) And it is necessary for him also to know all the laws. If in turn he shall not know the practise neither shall he know the laws. (11) The same man knows the law in music who also knows music, and who does not know music does not know the law. Who then knows the truth of the practise of things it follows easily that he knows all things. (13) Thus he is able to discuss in brief responses on all matters, if being questioned he should require to answer. Thus he must know all things.

7. (1) The greatest [and] noblest discovery is memory, useful for everything, for wisdom and life both.

Democritus

Ca. 470–360 B.C.

A. Life

Democritus[77] was born in Abdera, in Thrace. He was a pupil of Leucippus, the founder of Atomism, a philosophy that has served from its beginnings as the basis for many of the most significant scientific theories formulated in the West. The Atomists' most fundamental assumption is that "Nothing occurs at random, but everything for a reason . . . and by necessity." The passages given in the following selections are of primary interest because, despite the rigor of Atomist doctrine and the extraordinary range of application of its principles, we discover how pervasive in Greek speculation is the notion that the poet is "mad," that he creates while experiencing the "furor poeticus." The extraordinary power and strength of the notion of inspiration leads even the philosopher who constructed the most rational of mechanist systems expressed in ancient times to accept the possibility that beauty is produced in a non-rational state and while the poet is "taken out of himself," occupied by the gods, and that he speaks divine words.[78]

According to Diogenes Laertius, Democritus was the son of Hegesistratus. He is said to have traveled in Egypt to learn geometry and to have associated with the Gymnosophists in India.

B. Thought: On Art

Golden maxims

17. There is no poetry without madness.

18. What a poet writes with enthusiasm and divine inspiration is most beautiful.

21. Homer, having been gifted with a divine nature, built an ordered structure of many verses.

"Golden Maxims" translated by William Romaine Newbold. See Nahm, *op. cit.*, pp. 200 et seq.

[77] See Nahm, *op. cit.*, pp. 148–207.

[78] See below, pp. 55 et seq. and 53 et seq. for Socrates' statements concerning inspiration. See also, above, pp. 4, 32.

72–3. Excessive desires for anything blind the soul to anything else. Excessively to pursue the beautiful is righteous love.

102. In everything the fair is right; excess and deficiency please me not.

105. The beauty of the body is merely animal unless there be intelligence beneath.

112. It is characteristic of a divine mind always to think on something beautiful.

154. We are pupils of animals in the most important things: the spider for spinning and mending, the swallow for building, and the songbirds, swan and nightingale, for singing, by way of imitation.[79]

194. The great pleasures are got from the contemplation of beautiful works.

[79] In this fragment of Democritus' philosophy, we have the source of one of the great nonaesthetic genetic theories of art. In the passage that follows, Lucretius develops the Democritean theory that art originates in imitation of birds' songs. Compare Lucretius, *De Rerum Natura,* V.1379 et seq. "But imitating with the mouth the liquid notes of birds came long before men were able to sing in melody right through smooth songs and please the ear. And the whistling of the zephyr through the hollows of reeds first taught the men of the countryside to breathe into hollowed hemlock-stalks. Then little by little they learned the sweet lament, which the pipe pours forth, stopped by the players' fingers, the pipe invented amid the pathless woods and forests and glades, among the desolate haunts of shepherds, and the divine places of their rest. These tunes would soothe their minds and please them when sated with food; for then all things win the heart. And so often, lying in friendly groups on the soft grass near some stream under the branches of a tall tree, at no great cost they would give pleasure to their bodies, above all when the weather smiled and the season of the year painted the green grass with flowers. Then were there wont to be jests, and talk, and merry laughter. For then the rustic muse was at its best; then glad mirth would prompt to wreathe head and shoulders with garlands twined of flowers and foliage, and to dance all out of step, moving their limbs heavily, and with heavy foot to strike mother earth; whence arose smiles and merry laughter, for all these things then were strong in freshness and wonder. . . ." (Translated by Cyril Bailey, *Lucretius on the Nature of Things* (Oxford 1910), pp. 231–232.)

Socrates

469–399 B.C.

A. Life

Socrates[80] was one of the most remarkable human beings of whom we have record. He was an original genius in philosophy, a master of the technique of argumentation to which the name, "Socratic dialetic," has been given, a dangerous foe in war and in philosophical dialogue. In argument, he used the ironical mode again named after him and is an extraordinary instance of hard-headed rationalist who on occasion listened to the words of his inner *daimon.* All of Socrates' gifts are made evident by Plato in his brilliant and profound dialogues and in Xenophon's straight-forward *Memorabilia of Socrates.*[81] There can be little doubt that Plato is the greater systematic philosopher, yet it is evident that Socrates, at least in the area of art and its examination, is his disciple's superior. As is clear from what we read in Xenophon's memoirs of him, Socrates is an acute observer. More significantly, he is one not interested in insisting on the validity of fixed concepts in the face of the diversity, variety, and individuality in a work of art.[82] Plato, as we shall see, is primarily concerned, after *Hippias Major,*[83] with the search for and the philosophy of Ideas, the Idea of beauty, and in the establishment of the mathematical formulae derived from the Pythagoreans.[84]

Socrates was born in Athens, the son of Sophroniscus, a stonemason, and of Phaenarete, a midwife. He regarded himself as a midwife of men's ideas and a gadfly devoted to stirring the steed—Athens—to life. His wife, Xantippe, has become the by-word for "shrew." When asked why he continued to live "with a wife who is the hardest to get along with of all the women there are," Socrates replied that by living with Xantippe he was "well assured that if I can endure her, I shall have no difficulty in my relations with all the rest of human kind."

Socrates fought at Potidaea, Delium, and Amphipolis and proved himself so formidable a soldier that Alcibiades maintained that the philosopher should have been awarded the honors he, the military leader, had been given. Alcibiades offers in the *Symposium* a brilliant picture of Socrates on the battlefield and in the same Platonic dialogue describes Socrates' "outer mask" as like the carved head of a Silenus. "When I opened him, and looked

[80] See Nahm, *op. cit.,* pp. 251 et seq.

[81] See below, pp. 51 et seq. for *Ion* and pp. 66 et seq. for *Hippias Major.*

[82] See below, pp. 50 et seq.

[83] See Plato, *Republic* X, below, pp. 109 et seq.

[84] See above, pp. 37 et seq.

within at his serious purpose, I saw in him divine and golden images of such fascinating beauty that I was ready to do in a moment whatever Socrates commanded. . . ."

In 399 B.C., Socrates was charged with a capital crime. He was accused of having introduced into Athens alien gods, of having corrupted the young, and of having made the worse appear the better reason. His trial, described by Plato in the *Apology,* gives a portrait of Socrates exercising his dialectical skill in "beating out" the truth or falsehood of his accusers' statements. Socrates was condemned to drink the hemlock. Plato's *Phaedo* is a moving and powerful description of the man's death, following upon a profound discussion of immortality. *Crito* and *Euthyphro* round out the Platonic dialogues devoted to the trial and death of Socrates. To the Platonic portrait, Xenophon's *Memorabilia of Socrates* and Aristophanes' *Clouds* add memorable details. The fact that Plato has made Socrates the central figure in all but two of his *Dialogues* has provided Platonic scholars with one of their most difficult problem—that of determining what in Plato's philosophy is Socratic and what his own.

The Selections begin with Socrates' report of the question he asked of the poets and the artisans.

Plato: Apology

. . . You must[85] have known Chaerephon; he was early a friend of mine, and also a friend of yours, for he shared in the recent exile of the people, and returned with you. Well, Chaerephon, as you know, was very impetuous in all his doings, and he went to Delphi and boldly asked the oracle to tell him whether—as I was saying, I must beg to you not to interrupt—he actually asked the oracle to tell him whether anyone was wiser than I was, and the Pythian prophetess answered that there was no man wiser. Chaerephon is dead himself; but his brother, who is in court, will confirm the truth of what I am saying.

Why do I mention this? Because I am going to explain to you why I have such an evil name. When I heard the answer, I said to myself, What can the god mean? and what is the interpretation of his riddle? for I know that I have no wisdom, small or great. What then can he mean when he says that I am the wisest of men? And yet he is a god, and cannot lie; that would be against his nature. After long perplexity, I thought of a method of trying the question. I reflected that if I could only find a man wiser than myself, then I might go to the god with a refutation in my hand. I should say to him, 'Here is a man who is wiser than I am; but you said that I was the wisest.' Accordingly I went to one who had the reputation of wisdom, and observed him—his name I need not mention, he was a politician; and in the process of examining him and talking with him, this, men of Athens, was what I found. I could not help thinking that he was not really wise, although he was thought wise by many, and still wiser by himself; and thereupon I tried to explain to him that he thought himself wise, but was not really wise; and the consequence was that he hated me, and his enmity was shared by several who were present and heard me. So I left him, saying to myself as I went away: Well, although I do not suppose that either of us knows anything really worth knowing, I am at least wiser than this fellow—for he knows nothing, and thinks that he knows; I neither know nor think that I know. In this one little point, then, I seem to have the advantage of him. Then I went to

[85] Unless otherwise indicated, all quotations from Plato in this book are from *The Dialogues of Plato,* translated by Benjamin Jowett, fourth ed., 1953. By permission of the Clarendon Press, Oxford. I have used capital letters in all references to the text.

another who had still higher pretensions to wisdom, and my conclusion was exactly the same. Whereupon I made another enemy of him, and of many others besides him.

Then I went to one man after another, being not unconscious of the enmity which I provoked, and I lamented and feared this: but necessity was laid upon me,—the word of God, I thought, ought to be considered first. And I said to myself, Go I must to all who appear to know, and find out the meaning of the oracle. And I swear to you, Athenians,—for I must tell you the truth—the result of my mission was just this: I found that the men most in repute were nearly the most foolish; and that others less esteemed were really closer to wisdom. I will tell you the tale of my wanderings and of the 'Herculean' labours, as I may call them, which I endured only to find at last the oracle irrefutable. After the politicians, I went to the poets; tragic, dithyrambic, and all sorts. And there, I said to myself, you will be instantly defeated; now you will find out that you are more ignorant than they are. Accordingly, I took them some of the most elaborate passages in their own writings, and asked what was the meaning of them—thinking that they would teach me something. Will you believe me? I am ashamed to confess the truth, but I must say that there is hardly a person present who would not have talked better about their poetry than they did themselves. So I learnt that not by wisdom do poets write poetry, but by a sort of genius and inspiration; they are like diviners or soothsayers who also say many fine things, but do not understand the meaning of them. The poets appeared to me to be much in the same case; and I further observed that upon the strength of their poetry they believed themselves to be the wisest of men in other things in which they were not wise. So I departed, conceiving myself to be superior to them for the same reason that I was superior to the politicians.

At last I went to the artisans, for I was conscious that I knew nothing at all, as I may say, and I was sure that they knew many fine things; and here I was not mistaken, for they did know many things of which I was ignorant, and in this they certainly were wiser than I was. But I observed that even the good artisans fell into the same error as the poets;—because they were good workmen they thought that they also knew all sorts of high matters, and this defect in them overshadowed their wisdom. . . . This inquisition has led to my having many enemies of the worst and most dangerous kind, and has given rise also to many imputations. . . .

On the Subjects of Socrates' Conversation

Xenophon, *Memorabilia of Socrates,* I. 1. 16–17[86]

His own conversation was ever of human things. The problems he discussed were, What is godly, what is ungodly; what is beautiful, what is ugly; what is just, what is unjust; what is prudence, what is madness; what is courage, what is cowardice; what is a state, what is a statesman; what is government, what is a governor. . . .

ON THE BEAUTIFUL

III. 8. 4. Again, Aristippus asked him whether he knew of anything beautiful: "Yes, many things," he replied. "All like one another?" "On the contrary, some are as unlike as they

[86] Reprinted by permission of the publishers and The Loeb Classical Library from E. C. Marchant's translation of Xenophon, *Memorabilia of Socrates,* Cambridge, Mass.: Harvard University Press; London: W. Heinemann, 1923.

can be." "How then can that which is unlike the beautiful be beautiful?" "The reason, of course, is that a beautiful wrestler is unlike a beautiful runner, a shield beautiful for defense is utterly unlike a javelin beautiful for swift and powerful hurling." 5.] ". . . Men . . . are called 'beautiful and good' in the same respect and in relation to the same things: it is in relation to the same things that men's bodies look beautiful and good and that all other things men use are thought beautiful and good, in relation to those things for which they are useful." 6.] "Is a dung basket beautiful then?" "Of course, and a golden shield is ugly, if the one is well made for its special work and the other badly." "Do you mean that the same things are both beautiful and ugly?" 7.] "Of course—and both good and bad. For what is good for hunger is often bad for fever, and what is good for fever bad for hunger. . . . For all things are good and beautiful in relation to those purposes for which they are well adapted, bad and ugly in relation to those for which they are ill adapted. . . ."

CONVERSATIONS ON PAINTING, SCULPTURE, AND ARMOR

III. 10. 1. . . . On entering the house of Parrhasius the painter one day, he asked in the course of conversation with him: "Is painting a representation of things seen, Parrhasius? Anyhow, you painters with your colors represent and reproduce figures high and low, in light and in shadow, hard and soft, rough and smooth, young and old. . . . 2. And further, when you copy types of beauty, it is so difficult to find a perfect model that you combine the most beautiful details of several, and thus contrive to make the whole figure look beautiful. . . . 3. . . . Do you also reproduce the character of the soul, the character that is in the highest degree captivating, delightful, friendly, fascinating, lovable? Or is it impossible to imitate that?" . . . 4. "Do human beings commonly express the feelings of sympathy and aversion by their looks?" . . . "Then cannot thus much be imitated in the eyes?" . . . 6. On another occasion he visited Cleiton the sculptor, and while conversing with him said: "Cleiton, that your statues of runners, wrestlers, boxers, and fighters are beautiful I see and know. But how do you produce in them that illusion of life which is their most alluring charm to the beholder?" . . . 7. "Is it," he added, "by faithfully representing the form of living beings that you make your statues look as if they lived?" . . . "Then is it not by accurately representing the different parts of the body as they are affected by the pose—the flesh wrinkled or tense, the limbs compressed or outstretched, the muscles taut or loose—that you make them look more like real members and more convincing?" . . . 8. "Does not the exact imitation of the feelings that affect bodies in action also produce a sense of satisfaction in the spectator?" . . . "Then must not the threatening look in the eyes of fighters be accurately represented, and the triumphant expression on the face of conquerors be imitated?" . . . "It follows, then, that the sculptor must represent in his figures the activities of the soul."

9. On visiting Pistias the armourer, who showed him some well-made breastplates, Socrates exclaimed: "Upon my word, Pistias, it's a beautiful invention, for the breastplate covers the parts that need protection without impeding the use of the hands. But tell me, Pistias," he added, "why do you charge more for your breastplates than any other maker, though they are no stronger and cost no more to make?"

"Because the proportions of mine are better, Socrates."

"And how do you show their proportions when you ask a higher price—by weight or measure? For I presume you don't make them all of the same weight or the same size, that is, if you make them to fit."

"Fit? Why, of course! a breastplate is of no use without that!"

"Then are not some human bodies well, others ill proportioned?"

"Certainly."

"Then if a breastplate is to fit an ill-proportioned body, how do you make it well-proportioned?"

"By making it fit; for if it is a good fit it is well-proportioned."

"Apparently you mean well-proportioned not absolutely, but in relation to the wearer, as you might call a shield well-proportioned for the man whom it fits, or a military cape—and this seems to apply to everything according to you. And perhaps there is another important advantage in a good fit."

"Tell it me, if you know, Socrates."

"The good fit is less heavy to wear than the misfit, though both are of the same weight. For the misfit, hanging entirely from the shoulders, or pressing on some other part of the body, proves uncomfortable and irksome; but the good fit, with its weight distributed over the collar-bone and shoulder-blades, the shoulders, chest, back and belly, may almost be called an accessory rather than an encumbrance."

"The advantage you speak of is the very one which I think makes my work worth a big price. Some, however, prefer to buy the ornamented and the gold-plated breastplates."

"Still, if the consequence is that they buy misfits, it seems to me that they buy ornamented and gold-plated trash. However, as the body is not rigid, but now bent, now straight, how can tight breastplates fit?"

"They can't."

"You mean that the good fits are not the tight ones, but those that don't chafe the wearer?"

"That is your own meaning, Socrates, and you have hit the right nail on the head."

Plato: ION

Persons of the Dialogue

SOCRATES ION

SOCRATES. Welcome, Ion. Are you from your native city of Ephesus?

ION. No, Socrates; but from Epidaurus, where I attended the festival of Aesculapius.

SOC. Indeed! Do the Epidaurians have a contest of rhapsodes in his honour?

ION. O yes; and of other kinds of music.

SOC. And were you one of the competitors—and did you succeed?

ION. I—we—obtained the first prize of all, Socrates.

SOC. Well done; now we must win another victory, at the Panathenaea.

ION. It shall be so, please heaven.

SOC. I have often envied the profession of a rhapsode, Ion; for it is a part of your art to wear fine clothes and to look as beautiful as you can, while at the same time you are obliged to be continually in the company of many good poets, and especially of Homer, who is the best and most divine of them, and to understand his mind, and not merely learn his words by rote; all this is a thing greatly to be envied. I am sure that no man can become a good rhapsode who does not understand the meaning of the poet. For the rhapsode ought to interpret the mind of the poet to his hearers, but how can he interpret him well unless he knows what he means? All this is much to be envied, I repeat.

ION. Very true, Socrates; interpretation has certainly been the most laborious part of my art; and I believe myself able to speak about Homer better than any man; and that neither

From *The Dialogues of Plato,* translated by Benjamin Jowett, fourth ed., 1953. By permission of the Clarendon Press, Oxford.

Metrodorus of Lampsacus, nor Stesimbrotus of Thasos, nor Glaucon, nor anyone else who ever was, had as good ideas about Homer as I have, or as many.

SOC. I am glad to hear you say so, Ion; I see that you will not refuse to acquaint me with them.

ION. Certainly, Socrates; and you really ought to hear how exquisitely I display the beauties of Homer. I think that the Homeridae should give me a golden crown.

SOC. I shall take an opportunity of hearing your embellishments of him at some other time. But just now I should like to ask you a question: Does your art extend to Hesiod and Archilochus, or to Homer only?

ION. To Homer only; he is in himself quite enough.

SOC. Are there any things about which Homer and Hesiod agree?

ION. Yes; in my opinion there are a good many.

SOC. And can you interpret what Homer says about these matters better than what Hesiod says?

ION. I can interpret them equally well, Socrates, where they agree.

SOC. But what about matters in which they do not agree? for example, about divination of which both Homer and Hesiod have something to say,—

ION. Very true.

SOC. Would you or a good prophet be a better interpreter of what these two poets say about divination, not only when they agree, but when they disagree?

ION. A prophet.

SOC. And if you were a prophet, and could interpret them where they agree, would you not know how to interpret them also where they disagree?

ION. Clearly.

SOC. But how did you come to have this skill about Homer only, and not about Hesiod or the other poets? Does not Homer speak of the same themes which all other poets handle? Is not war his argument? and does he not speak of human society and of intercourse of men, good and bad, skilled and unskilled, and of the gods conversing with one another and with mankind, and about what happens in heaven and in the world below, and the generations of gods and heroes? Are not these the themes of which Homer sings?

ION. Very true, Socrates.

SOC. And do not the other poets sing of the same?

ION. Yes, Socrates; but not in the same way as Homer.

SOC. What, in a worse way?

ION. Yes, in a far worse.

SOC. And Homer in a better way?

ION. He is incomparably better.

SOC. And yet surely, my dear friend Ion, where many people are discussing numbers, and one speaks better than the rest, there is somebody who can judge which of them is the good speaker?

ION. Yes.

SOC. And he who judges of the good will be the same as he who judges of the bad speakers?

ION. The same.

SOC. One who knows the science of arithmetic?

ION. Yes.

SOC. Or again, if many persons are discussing the wholesomeness of food, and one speaks better than the rest, will he who recognizes the better speaker be a different person from him who recognizes the worse, or the same?

ION. Clearly the same.

SOC. And who is he, and what is his name?

ION. The physician.

SOC. And speaking generally, in all discussions in which the subject is the same and many men are speaking, will not he who knows the good know the bad speaker also? For obviously if he does not know the bad, neither will he know the good, when the same topic is being discussed.

ION. True.

SOC. We find, in fact, that the same person is skilful in both?

ION. Yes.

SOC. And you say that Homer and the other poets, such as Hesiod and Archilochus, speak of the same things, although not in the same way; but the one speaks well and the other not so well?

ION. Yes; and I am right in saying so.

SOC. And if you know the good speaker, you ought also to know the inferior speakers to be inferior?

ION. It would seem so.

SOC. Then, my dear friend, can I be mistaken in saying that Ion is equally skilled in Homer and in other poets, since he himself acknowledges that the same person will be a good judge of all those who speak of the same things; and that almost all poets do speak of the same things?

ION. Why then, Socrates, do I lose attention and have absolutely no ideas of the least value and practically fall asleep when anyone speaks of any other poet; but when Homer is mentioned, I wake up at once and am all attention and have plenty to say?

SOC. The reason, my friend, is not hard to guess. No one can fail to see that you speak of Homer without any art of knowledge. If you were able to speak of him by rules of art, you would have been able to speak of all other poets; for poetry is a whole.

ION. Yes.

SOC. And when anyone acquires any other art as a whole, the same may be said of them. Would you like me to explain my meaning, Ion?

ION. Yes, indeed, Socrates; I very much wish that you would: for I love to hear you wise men talk.

SOC. O that we were wise, Ion, and that you could truly call us so; but you rhapsodes and actors, and the poets whose verses you sing, are wise; whereas I am a common man, who only speak the truth. For consider what a very commonplace and trivial thing is this which I have said—a thing which any man might say: that when a man has acquired a knowledge of a whole art, the inquiry into good and bad is one and the same. Let us consider this matter; is not the art of painting a whole?

ION. Yes.

SOC. And there are and have been many painters good and bad?

ION. Yes.

SOC. And did you ever know anyone who was skilful in pointing out the excellences and defects of Polygnotus the son of Aglaophon, but incapable of criticizing other painters; and when the work of any other painter was produced, went to sleep and was at a loss, and had no ideas; but when he had to give his opinion about Polygnotus, or whoever the painter might be, and about him only, woke up and was attentive and had plenty to say?

ION. No indeed, I have never known such a person.

SOC. Or take sculpture—did you ever know of anyone who was skilful in expounding the merits of Daedalus the son of Metion, or of Epeius the son of Panopeus, or of Theodorus the Samian, or of any individual sculptor; but when the works of sculptors in general were produced, was at a loss and went to sleep and had nothing to say?

ION. No indeed; no more than the other.

SOC. And if I am not mistaken, you never met with anyone among flute-players or harp-players or singers to the harp or rhapsodes who was able to discourse of Olympus or Thamyras or Orpheus, or Phemius the rhapsode of Ithaca, but was at a loss when he came to speak of Ion of Ephesus, and had no notion of his merits or defects?

ION. I cannot deny what you say, Socrates. Nevertheless I am conscious in my own self, and the world agrees with me, that I do speak better and have more to say about Homer than any other man; but I do not speak equally well about others. After all, there must be some reason for this; what is it?

SOC. I see the reason, Ion; and I will proceed to explain to you what I imagine it to be. The gift which you possess of speaking excellently about Homer is not an art, but, as I was just saying, an inspiration; there is a divinity moving you, like that contained in the stone which Euripides calls a magnet, but which is commonly known as the stone of Heraclea. This stone not only attracts iron rings but also imparts to them a similar power of attracting other rings; and sometimes you may see a number of pieces of iron and rings suspended from one another so as to form quite a long chain: and all of them derive their power of suspension from the original stone. In like manner the Muse first of all inspires men herself; and from these inspired persons a chain of other persons is suspended, who take the inspiration. For all good poets, epic as well as lyric, compose their beautiful poems not by art, but because they are inspired and possessed. And as the Corybantian revellers when they dance are not in their right mind, so the lyric poets are not in their right mind when they are composing their beautiful strains; but when falling under the power of music and metre they are inspired and possessed; like Bacchic maidens who draw milk and honey from the rivers when they are under the influence of Dionysus but not when they are in their right mind. And the soul of the lyric poet does the same, as they themselves say; for they tell us that they bring songs from honeyed fountains, culling them out of the gardens and dells of the Muses; they, like the bees, winging their way from flower to flower. And this is true. For the poet is a light and winged and holy thing, and there is no invention in him until he has been inspired and is out of his senses, and reason is no longer with him: no man, while he retains that faculty, has the oracular gift of poetry.

Many are the noble words in which poets speak concerning the actions of men; but like yourself when speaking about Homer, they do not speak of them by any rules of art: they are simply inspired to utter that to which the Muse impels them, and that only; and when inspired, one of them will make dithyrambs, another hymns of praise, another choral strains, another epic or iambic verses, but not one of them is of any account in the other kinds. For not by art does the poet sing, but by power divine; had he learned by rules of art, he would have known how to speak not of one theme only, but of all; and therefore God takes away reason from poets, and uses them as his ministers, as he also uses the pronouncers of oracles and holy prophets, in order that we who hear them may know them to be speaking not of themselves, who utter these priceless words while bereft of reason, but that God himself is the speaker, and that through them he is addressing us. And Tynnichus the Chalcidian affords a striking instance of what I am saying: he wrote no poem that anyone would care to remember but the famous paean which is in everyone's mouth, one of the finest lyric poems ever written, simply an invention of the Muses, as he himself says. For in this way God would seem to demonstrate to us and not to allow us to doubt that these beautiful poems are not human, nor the work of man, but divine and the work of God; and that the poets are only the interpreters of the gods by whom they are severally possessed. Was not this the lesson which God intended to teach when by the mouth of the worst of poets he sang the best of songs? Am I not right, Ion?

ION. Yes, indeed, Socrates, I feel that you are; for your words touch my soul, and I am persuaded that in these works the good poets, under divine inspiration, interpret to us the voice of the Gods.

SOC. And you rhapsodists are the interpreters of the poets?

ION. There again you are right.

SOC. Then you are the interpreters of interpreters?

ION. Precisely.

SOC. I wish you would frankly tell me, Ion, what I am going to ask of you: When you produce the greatest effect upon the audience in the recitation of some striking passage, such as the apparition of Odysseus leaping forth on the floor, recognized by the suitors and shaking out his arrows at his feet, or the description of Achilles springing upon Hector, or the sorrows of Andromache, Hecuba, or Priam,—are you in your right mind? Are you not carried out of yourself, and does not your soul in an ecstasy seem to be among the persons or places of which you are speaking, whether they are in Ithaca or in Troy or whatever may be the scene of the poem?

ION. That proof strikes home to me, Socrates. For I must frankly confess that at the tale of pity my eyes are filled with tears, and when I speak of horrors, my hair stands on end and my heart throbs.

SOC. Well, Ion, and what are we to say of a man who at a sacrifice or festival, when he is dressed in an embroidered robe, and has golden crowns upon his head, of which nobody has robbed him, appears weeping or panic-stricken in the presence of more than twenty thousand friendly faces, when there is no one despoiling or wronging him;—is he in his right mind or is he not?

ION. No indeed, Socrates, I must say that, strictly speaking, he is not in his right mind.

SOC. And are you aware that you produce similar effects on most of the spectators?

ION. Only too well; for I look down upon them from the stage, and behold the various emotions of pity, wonder, sternness, stamped upon their countenances when I am speaking: and I am obliged to give my very best attention to them; for if I make them cry I myself shall laugh, and if I make them laugh I myself shall cry, when the time of payment arrives.

SOC. Do you know that the spectator is the last of the rings which, as I am saying, receive the power of the original magnet from one another? The rhapsode like yourself and the actor are intermediate links, and the poet himself is the first of them. Through all these God sways the souls of men in any direction which He pleases, causing each link to communicate the power to the next. Thus there is a vast chain of dancers and masters and under-masters of choruses, who are suspended, as if from the stone, at the side of the rings which hang down from the Muse. And every poet has some Muse from whom he is suspended, and by whom he is said to be possessed, which is nearly the same thing; for he is taken hold of. And from these first rings, which are the poets, depend others, some deriving their inspiration from Orpheus, others from Musaeus; but the greater number are possessed and held by Homer. Of whom, Ion, you are one, and are possessed by Homer; and when anyone repeats the words of another poet you go to sleep, and know not what to say; but when anyone recites a strain of Homer you wake up in a moment, and your soul leaps within you, and you have plenty to say; for not by art or knowledge about Homer do you say what you say, but by divine inspiration and by possession; just as the Corybantian revellers too have a quick perception of that strain only which is appropriated to the god by whom they are possessed, and have plenty of dances and words for that, but take no heed of any other. And you, Ion, when the name of Homer is mentioned have plenty to say, and have nothing to say of others. You ask, 'Why is this?' The answer is that your skill in the praise of Homer comes not from art but from divine inspiration.

ION. That is good, Socrates; and yet I doubt whether you will ever have eloquence enough to persuade me that I praise Homer only when I am mad and possessed; and if you could hear me speak of him I am sure you would never think this to be the case.

SOC. I should like very much to hear you, but not until you have answered a question which I have to ask. On what part of Homer do you speak well?—not surely about every part?

ION. There is no part, Socrates, about which I do not speak well: of that I can assure you.

SOC. Surely not about things in Homer of which you have no knowledge?

ION. And what is there in Homer of which I have no knowledge?

SOC. Why, does not Homer speak in many passages about arts? For example, about driving; if I can only remember the lines I will repeat them.

ION. I remember, and will repeat them.

SOC. Tell me then, what Nestor says to Antilochus, his son, where he bids him be careful of the turn at the horse-race in honour of Patroclus.

> ION. 'Bend gently,' he says, 'in the polished chariot to the left of them, and urge the horse on the right hand with whip and voice; and slacken the rein. And when you are at the goal, let the left horse draw near, so that the nave of the well-wrought wheel may appear to graze the extremity; but have care not to touch the stone."[87]

SOC. Enough. Now, Ion, will the charioteer or the physician be the better judge of the propriety of these lines?

ION. The charioteer, clearly.

SOC. And will the reason be that this is his art, or will there be any other reason?

ION. No, that will be the reason.

SOC. And every art is appointed by God to have knowledge of a certain work; for that which we know by the art of the pilot we shall not succeed in knowing also by the art of medicine?

ION. Certainly not.

SOC. Nor shall we know by the art of the carpenter that which we know by the art of medicine?

ION. Certainly not.

SOC. And this is true of all the arts;—that which we know with one art we shall not know with the other? But let me ask a prior question: You admit that there are differences of arts?

ION. Yes.

SOC. You would argue, as I would, that if there are two kinds of knowledge, dealing with different things, these can be called different arts?

ION. Yes.

SOC. Yes, surely; for if the object of knowledge were the same, there would be no meaning in saying that the arts were different,—since they both gave the same knowledge. For example, I know that here are five fingers, and you know the same. And if I were to ask whether I and you became acquainted with this fact by the help of the same art of arithmetic, you would acknowledge that we did?

ION. Yes.

SOC. Tell me, then, what I was intending to ask you,—whether in your opinion this holds universally? If two arts are the same, must not they necessarily have the same objects? And if one differs from another, must it not be because the object is different?

ION. That is my opinion, Socrates.

SOC. Then he who has no knowledge of a particular art will have no right judgement of the precepts and practice of that art?

ION. Very true.

SOC. Then which will be the better judge of the lines which you were reciting from Homer, you or the charioteer?

ION. The charioteer.

SOC. Why, yes, because you are a rhapsode and not a charioteer.

ION. Yes.

SOC. And the art of the rhapsode is different from that of the charioteer?

[87] *Il.* xxiii. 335.

ION. Yes.

SOC. And if a different knowledge, then a knowledge of different matters?

ION. True.

SOC. You know the passage in which Hecamede, the concubine of Nestor, is described as giving to the wounded Machaon a posset, as he says,

'Made with Pramnian wine; and she grated cheese of goat's milk with a grater of bronze, and at his side placed an onion which gives a relish to drink.'[88]

Now would you say that the art of the rhapsode or the art of medicine was better able to judge of the propriety of these lines?

ION. The art of medicine.

SOC. And when Homer says,

'And she descended into the deep like a leaden plummet, which, set in the horn of ox that ranges the fields, rushes along carrying death among the ravenous fishes',[89]

will the art of the fisherman or of the rhapsode be better able to judge what these lines mean, and whether they are accurate or not?

ION. Clearly, Socrates, the art of the fisherman.

SOC. Come now, suppose that you were to say to me: 'Since you, Socrates, are able to assign different passages in Homer to their corresponding arts, I wish that you would tell me what are the passages of which the excellence ought to be judged by the prophet and prophetic art;' and you will see how readily and truly I shall answer you. For there are many such passages, particularly in the Odyssey; as, for example, the passage in which Theoclymenus the prophet of the house of Melampus says to the suitors:—

'Wretched men! what is happening to you? Your heads and your faces and your limbs underneath are shrouded in night; and the voice of lamentation bursts forth, and your cheeks are wet with tears. And the vestibule is full, and the court is full, of ghosts descending into the darkness of Erebus, and the sun has perished out of heaven, and an evil mist is spread abroad.'[90]

And there are many such passages in the Iliad also; as for example in the description of the battle near the rampart, where he says:—

'As they were eager to pass the ditch, there came to them an omen: a soaring eagle, skirting the people on his left, bore a huge blood-red dragon in his talons, still living and panting; nor had he yet resigned the strife, for he bent back and smote the bird which carried him on the breast by the neck, and he in pain let him fall from him to the ground into the midst of the multitude. And the eagle, with a cry, was borne afar on the wings of the wind.'[91]

These are the sorts of things which I should say that the prophet ought to consider and determine.

ION. And you are quite right, Socrates, in saying so.

SOC. Yes, Ion, and you are right also. And as I have selected from the Iliad and Odyssey for you passages which describe the office of the prophet and the physician and the fisherman, do you, who know Homer so much better than I do, Ion, select for me passages which relate to the rhapsode and the rhapsode's art, and which the rhapsode ought to examine and judge of better than other men.

ION. All passages, I should say, Socrates.

SOC. Not all, Ion, surely. Have you already forgotten what you were saying? A rhapsode ought to have a better memory.

ION. Why, what am I forgetting?

SOC. Do you not remember that you

[88] *Il.* xi. 639, 640.
[89] *Il.* xxiv. 80.
[90] *Od.* xx. 351.
[91] *Il.* xii. 200.

declared the art of the rhapsode to be different from the art of the charioteer?

ION. Yes, I remember.

SOC. And you admitted that being different they would know different objects?

ION. Yes.

SOC. Then upon your own showing the rhapsode, and the art of the rhapsode, will not know everything?

ION. I should exclude such things as you mention, Socrates.

SOC. You mean to say that you would exclude pretty much the subjects of the other arts. As he does not know all of them, which of them will he know?

ION. He will know what a man and what a woman ought to say, and what a freeman and what a slave ought to say, and what a ruler and what a subject.

SOC. Do you mean that a rhapsode will know better than the pilot what the ruler of a sea-tossed vessel ought to say?

ION. No; the pilot will know best.

SOC. Or will the rhapsode know better than the physician what the ruler of a sick man ought to say?

ION. Again, no.

SOC. But he will know what a slave ought to say?

ION. Yes.

SOC. Suppose the slave to be a cowherd; the rhapsode will know better than the cowherd what he ought to say in order to soothe infuriated cows?

ION. No, he will not.

SOC. But he will know what a spinning-woman ought to say about the working of wool?

ION. No.

SOC. At any rate he will know what a general ought to say when exhorting his soldiers?

ION. Yes, that is the sort of thing which the rhapsode will be sure to know.

SOC. What! Is the art of the rhapsode the art of the general?

ION. I am sure that I should know what a general ought to say.

SOC. Why, yes. Ion, because you may possibly have the knowledge of a general as well as that of a rhapsode; and you might also have a knowledge of horsemanship as well as of the lyre, and then you would know when horses were well or ill managed. But suppose I were to ask you: By the help of which art, Ion, do you know whether horses are well managed, by your skill as a horseman or as a performer on the lyre—what would you answer?

ION. I should reply, by my skill as a horseman.

SOC. And if you judged of performers on the lyre, you would admit that you judged of them as a performer on the lyre, and not as a horseman?

ION. Yes.

SOC. And in judging of the general's art, do you judge as a general, or as a good rhapsode?

ION. To me there appears to be no difference between them.

SOC. What do you mean? Do you mean to say that the art of the rhapsode and of the general is the same?

ION. Yes, one and the same.

SOC. Then he who is a good rhapsode is also a good general?

ION. Certainly, Socrates.

SOC. And he who is a good general is also a good rhapsode?

ION. No; I do not agree to that.

SOC. But you do agree that he who is a good rhapsode is also a good general.

ION. Certainly.

SOC. And you are the best of Hellenic rhapsodes?

ION. Far the best, Socrates.

SOC. And are you the best general, Ion?

ION. To be sure, Socrates; and Homer was my master.

SOC. But then, Ion, why in the name of goodness do you, who are the best of generals as well as the best of rhapsodes in all Hellas, go about reciting rhapsodies when you might be a general? Do you think that the Hellenes are in grave need of a rhapsode with his golden crown, and have no need at all of a general?

ION. Why, Socrates, the reason is that my countrymen, the Ephesians, are the servants and soldiers of Athens, and do not need a general; and that you and Sparta are not likely to appoint me, for you think that you have enough generals of your own.

SOC. My good Ion, did you never hear of Apollodorus of Cyzicus?

ION. Who may he be?

SOC. One who, though a foreigner, has often been chosen their general by the Athenians: and there is Phanosthenes of Andros, and Heraclides of Clazomenae, whom they have also appointed to the command of their armies and to other offices, although aliens, after they had shown their merit. And will they not choose Ion the Ephesian to be their general, and honour him, if they deem him qualified? Were not the Ephesians originally Athenians, and Ephesus is no mean city? But, indeed, Ion, if you are correct in saying that by art and knowledge you are able to praise Homer, you do not deal fairly with me, and after all your professions of knowing many glorious things about Homer, and promises that you would exhibit them, you only deceive me, and so far from exhibiting the art of which you are a master, will not, even after my repeated entreaties, explain to me the nature of it. You literally assume as many forms as Proteus, twisting and turning up and down, until at last you slip away from me in the disguise of a general, in order that you may escape exhibiting your Homeric love. And if you have art, then, as I was saying, in falsifying your promise that you would exhibit Homer, you are not dealing fairly with me. But if, as I believe, you have no art, but speak all these beautiful words about Homer unconsciously under his inspiring influence, then I acquit you of dishonesty, and shall only say that you are inspired. Which do you prefer to be thought, dishonest or inspired?

ION. There is a great difference, Socrates, between the two alternatives; and inspiration is by far the nobler.

SOC. Then, Ion, I shall assume the nobler alternative; and attribute to you in your praises of Homer inspiration, and not art.

Chapter 3

Plato

Plato[1] establishes the theory of Ideas, elaborates, defends, and alters it. He, like Empedocles and Xenophanes, writes of art in terms of imitation[2]; like Heraclitus[3] and the anonymous author[4] of *The Arguments on Both Sides,* he assumes the judgments of works of art are both subjective and relative. Like Democritus[5] and Socrates,[6] Plato believes that great art occurs because its maker is inspired. None the less, an art is "master of its own subject-matter." Like Socrates, Plato sharply distinguishes percepts and concepts, but unlike his master, the head of the Academy affirms the separate existence of concepts as universals or ideas, as well as asserting that ideas are the ground for truth. The latter point is both important and instructive. Plato's is not merely a combination of various speculative hypotheses taken over from his predecessors. Rather, it is a systematic philosophy of infinite variety and complexity. It is not to be explained either genetically or by reduction to the social conditions of Plato's time, as various distinguished sociologists have frequently argued.[7]

Imitation is an integral part of Plato's mature metaphysic of beauty and art. One direct approach to an interpretation of the Platonic Philosophy of Art and theory of beauty consists in examining in Plato's reiterated assertions that art is mimetic, this in contrast to the frequently expressed conviction that creativity in art is at least conditioned by inspiration;[8] that the experience of beauty is a communion with the Idea of beauty;[9] that in contrast, an imitation is an imitation of an imitation;[10] i.e., a copy of what is produced by such an artisan, as a carpenter or maker of chariots, and that in turn the artisan copies the idea. In contrast, beauty has no external relations. Its essence is in itself[11] and not in another.

To these matters we shall come shortly. It is of value, however, to point out that while it is true that Plato exiled the poet from his ideal commonwealth,[12] he is at pains to point out that "if they can show that they ought to exist in a well-constituted state," poets will be welcomed back. The point should be kept in mind as we observe that Plato's search for

[1] The selections from Plato's writings begin below, p. 66.

[2] See above, pp. 24, 27, 34 and 39.

[3] See above, pp. 30, 40.

[4] See above, pp. 30 and 42 et seq.

[5] See above, p. 45.

[6] See above, p. 49.

[7] See, for example, Arnold Houser's *The Social History of Art,* I, p. 99.

[8] See above, pp. 7, 23–24, 45, 49, 54 et seq.; below, pp. 87–88.

[9] See Plato, *Symposium* 210, below, p. 87.

[10] *Republic X,* quoted below, p. 110.

[11] *Symposium* 211A, below, p. 87.

[12] Plato, *Republic* III 398A. See below, p. 97.

absolute beauty leads him to assert[13] that there is not only an Idea of Beauty but that there are absolutely beautiful, non-mimetic mathematical forms. For Plato has justly been called the "progenitor" of speculation on Philosophy of Art, the producer of speculation which "contained the seed of all within its loins." Here, then, are some of the ingredients of his philosophy and a hint of some of his achievement in formulating an integrated system of speculation on art and beauty. The Pythagorean mathematical theory and the implication that the beauty of art consists in the work of art's form and is to be understood in terms of its intelligibility receives systematization in his philosophy. As a correlative to this mathematical hypothesis, Plato argued[14] that the experience of such forms is without precedent desire and is one of "pure pleasure" unmixed with pain. Alternatively, it may be that the experience is preceded by desire but of this we are not aware. Plato formulated[15] the theory that art is play and so provided not only a continuation and application of Xenophanes' attack upon sports but also laid the ground for Aristotle's argument[16] that play refreshes after toil and for Schiller's[17] famous suggestion that man is only man when he plays and only plays when he is a man. Moreover, following upon other suggestions by Kant[18] concerning the play of the imagination, Schiller at last identified art and play and argued that "Beauty is our second creator." In the *Symposium,*[19] Plato provides millenia of philosophers with the pattern of an ascent to beauty,[20] for the conception of an absolute beauty, and for an experience that is basically creative. In *Phaedrus* too, he draws the hard-and-fast distinction between the artisan and the inspired artist, between the product of art and the product of inspiration. Plato offers[21] in *Philebus* the first classification of the arts in terms of the criterion of accuracy and in the same dialogue provides[22] an account of non-mimetic objects and events. He offers grounds[23] for the censorship of art for the young and balances this with the theory that the souls of the young surrounded by beauty will become beautiful. He anticipates[24] the famous argument made by Aristotle[25] that the experience of tragedy involves a purgation of the emotions, only to deny its validity. His philosophy is the great fount[26] of the tradition that the artist is inspired and that the products of inspiration are neither true nor false, whereas works produced by art may be judged to be either correct or erroneous.[27] His was the first argument[28] in philosophy of art that maintains that vision and hearing are the "aesthetic" senses. He is the first to apply[29] the theory that perspective involves deception. He argues[30] plausibly that beauty makes things beautiful. His dialogue, *Timaeus,* systematizes[31] the analogy between the artist and the world artisan in a theory[32] that has occupied a place in men's thinking concerning both the artist and God for millenia.

For the modern philosopher of art, the

[13] See below, pp. 95–96 for Plato, *Philebus* 11, 51B. For Pythagoreans, see above, pp. 26 et seq.

[14] See below, p. 96 for *Philebus* 51B.

[15] *Laws* 654D. See below, pp. 119 et seq.

[16] See below, p. 143, *Politics* 1371 b.

[17] See below, pp. 438–39 et seq.

[18] See below, pp. 368 et seq., *Kritik of Judgment.*

[19] See below, p. 87, *Symposium* 210.

[20] Cf., for example, Plotinus, *Enneads,* 6th Tractate. See below, p. 226.

[21] *Philebus* 55E–56C. See below, p. 128.

[22] *Philebus* 51, see below, pp. 96 et seq.

[23] See below, pp. 97, 99, *Republic* III.

[24] See below, p. 116, *Republic X* 606.

[25] For discussion of catharsis, see below, Chapter 5.

[26] See below, pp. 87–88 et seq.

[27] See *Ion* 538. See above, p. 56. Cf. below, pp. 124 et seq.

[28] See *Hippias Major* 290. Quoted below, p. 79.

[29] See *Sophist* 235D. Quoted below, pp. 104-05.

[30] See *Hippias Major* 291D. Quoted below, p. 72.

[31] See below, *Timaeus* 27A, p. 93 et seq.

[32] See above, pp. 10 et seq.

most notable lack in Plato's speculation concerning art is any inkling that in artistic productivity and in the experience of art there is need for imagination. It remains for a lesser writer, Philostratus,[33] to deny that sculptors use imitation and to assert that they rely on imagination. Both Plato and Aristotle write of art in terms of *mimesis*. The term leads us to the core of Plato's speculation on art. Having no theory of imagination, yet convinced that there are basic differences between technical and beautiful works of art, Plato writes at length concerning inspiration. This is a state in which the artist is carried out of himself and beyond the restrictions of technique.[34] The value of such art as the inspired man produces, Plato asserts, derives from God. Curiously enough, how the poet—that "light, wingéd and holy thing"—moves from the inspired state to embody God's word in the work of art is a problem left largely unexplored. Plato merely tells us that the inspired artist is an imitator.[35]

Plato's speculation leads to two conclusions concerning imitation. The first is that he regards painting, sculpture, and other arts as imitations of imitations and the second is that inspiration provides an epistemological basis for knowledge of the idea of beauty in the experience called "communion." To both of these conclusions, we shall come in due course. It is, however, important at this juncture to point out that the model for the artisan and for the mimetic artist is Plato's *Demiurge*, the world artisan and architect which served as a model for Philonic speculation[36] and for some writings in the Renaissance.[37] Plato's *Demiurgos* makes the cosmos; he does not create it. The cosmos is made after the pattern of already existing ideas,[38] out of material which is also pre-existent.

It is against this background of a cosmic craftsman and of Ideas which are eternal and transcendent that we may best understand Plato's conception of making and imitating. It is evident, first of all, that for Plato, no object made by technique can equal much less excel the value of the absolute beauty of which he writes in *Hippias Major*[39] and *Symposium*.[40] It should also be noted that the objects he does permit entrance into the good life are non-imitative.[41] It is also clear that in contrast to inspiration, the artist practises an art that is master of its own subject matter, i.e., he knows what he is doing. The product of such an art is open to judgment in terms of truth or falsity.[42]

We have observed[43] that both Xenophanes and Empedocles are committed to theories of art as imitation. It is important to note, however, that Plato's interpretation of *mimesis* differs in one major respect from that of his predecessors. For him, the imitative artist is thrice removed from truth and being. "The shoemaker," Plato writes (*Alcibiades* I, 125A), "is wise in respect of making shoes. The art of the cobbler and other craftsmen is knowledge." The imitative artist, in contrast, neither knows the subject matter he copies nor does he practice an intelligible technique. The shoemaker and his fellow-artisans copy the Idea. The carpenter and the cobbler copy this copy, but they make a particular bed or pair of shoes. Plato, writing in the *Republic*,[44] argues that

[33] See below, pp. 191, 192 et seq.

[34] See *Ion* 535 and *Phaedrus* 245, quoted below, p. 88. See, in contrast, below, pp. 383 et seq.

[35] *Laws* 668 and 654D. Quoted below, pp. 124 et seq. and 119 et seq.

[36] For Philo, see below, pp. 203 et seq.

[37] By way of illustration, see below, pp. 257 et seq. in Leone Ebreo's *Dialogues of Love*.

[38] See *Timaeus* 28 B et seq. Quoted below, pp. 93 et seq. See also George Puttenham, quoted below, pp. 385 et seq.

[39] See below, pp. 71 et seq. and 73.

[40] See below, pp. 83 et seq. (*Symposium* 202); and *Phaedrus* 250 et seq. below, pp. 91 et seq.

[41] See *Philebus* 39, 48, 56.

[42] *Ion* 532. Cf. *Laws* 719, below, p. 128.

[43] See above, pp. 25, 38.

[44] *Op. cit.*, Book X, 597. See below, pp. 110 et seq.

there are three kinds of beds: the first is made by the painter, and the second is made by the carpenter; the third and real bed exists in nature. It is made by God.[45] It is the sole real bed. If we want to know what a thing is, we must know what its function is and to ascertain this we should scarcely go to the vase painter. We go to the artisan who makes the bed to learn what its function is, precisely as, in Plato's opinion, the artisan must go to the man who uses the bed to discover what it is good for. Inspiration, Plato concludes, is a mode of deception.

Plato carries his argument to such length that monumental sculpture is said to require what is distorted and deceptive.[46] The mimetic artist struggles not only with falsehood, however, but his lot is worse than that of the men who dwell in the underground cave.[47] The life of the imitative artist is a form of bondage, a life spent in search of "images of beauty," a beauty "infected with the pollutions of the flesh and all the colors and vanities of mortal life."[48] Sound art and sound classification[49] are beyond his reach and so too is the only genuine happiness which comes from the highest kind of knowledge.

There is a possible salvation for us and for the man who judges shadows to be real. Such salvation is possible provided we undertake the arduous ascent[50] to the world of Ideas and only on this condition can we attain to truth and reality. This, however, raises the issue of inspiration, which for Plato appears to be the precondition for the production of beauty. The mere technician is not permitted into the temple of beauty.[51] In the *Ion*, we are told[52] that there is no invention in the poet until he is inspired and out of his senses. The state of inspiration, essential to the production of beauty, is the end of the climb to the world of Ideas, the suprasensible world of universal. "The true order of going . . . is to begin with the beauties of earth as steps and mount upwards . . . for the sake of that other beauty." He who searches for beauty proceeds from all fair forms to fair actions to fair notions until he arrives at absolute beauty and knows what its essence is.[53] Until beauty is reached, the procedure is a rational one, but the experience of beauty itself is non-rational.

Men who have experienced the Idea of Beauty have achieved immortality. They possess creative souls.[54] Their souls are pregnant with Ideas and they practice creative arts, arts that are inventive in contrast to those available to the technician. Men who have been inspired and have experienced beauty produce processes by means of which non-being passed to being. By implication, the experience of beauty is creative of creativity.

The idea of Beauty, to which men aspire and which they experience in an inspired state, is a universal. It is without external relations. The experience of it is a union of the subject with the object. In consequence, Plato holds that the inspired man does not know what he produces. Rational knowledge is predicated upon the separation of subject and object. The imitative artist, as we have observed, is caught up in a set of double external relations. For he can know only the product of the artisan's art that is externally related to the idea.

Many conclude that Plato's theory of the transcendence of the idea of beauty imposes an insuperable obstacle to the explanation of beautiful objects in terms of the universal beauty. It may be argued, on the contrary, that the transcendence of the world of images and

45 *Ibid.* This is the only instance in Plato's *Dialogues* in which an Idea is said to be created.

46 *Sophist* 235 D–236C. Quoted below, p. 105.

47 *Republic* VII.

48 *Symposium* 211 E–212 A. Quoted below, p. 87.

49 See *Philebus* 56. Quoted below, p. 128.

50 *Symposium* 211–12. See below, p. 86–87.

51 *Phaedrus* 245. Quoted below, p. 88.

52 See above, *Ion* 533 B; above, p. 54.

53 See *Symposium* 211. Quoted below, p. 87.

54 *Ibid.* 212A.

of images twice removed from truth and reality is valuable precisely for the establishment of the grounds for a technique that will produce objects and events which are not mimetic. The main thrust of Plato's attack is against *mimesis*. He is in search of a guarantee that the painter or the sculptor can provide his art its own autonomous subject matter. It is no less clear that any imitative art will force the artist to depend upon either another art or upon nature. Or, to put the matter otherwise, Plato wants a free artist and he wants an art in which the objects are not relatively but absolutely free—within the severe limits of spatial and temporal conditions. It should not be forgotten in this context that Plato is a mathematician and that solid geometrical figures are not mimetic in the sense that, let us say, the drawing of a warrior is or the representation of either a bed or a pair of shoes is. Plato believes that the absolutely beautiful forms of *Philebus*[55] are beautiful because they are not copies of living things or of nature. They are not, however, mathematical figures. In the *Phaedrus*,[56] Plato tells us that the beauty which shone bright in the world of forms is apprehended in this world through sight, "the most piercing of our bodily senses" and that coming to earth from the world of ideas we find beauty here, too, for it is the "privilege of beauty," that being the loveliest she is also the most palpable to sight. The "vision" of absolute beauty is "communion" with the supreme value, beauty. It is also the presupposition of the experience of the mathematical forms in *Philebus* as beautiful forms. Plato argues that neither they nor the Idea of beauty are relatively beautiful; nor are they imitative of man or animals.[57]

Plato's exclusion of objects of mimetic art from the good life of man in *Philebus* shows him in his most rigorous mood. The exposition is brilliant but the argument excludes too much.

[55] *Philebus* 51. Quoted below, p. 96.
[56] *Phaedrus* 250 C–D. Quoted below, p. 92.
[57] Plato, *Philebus* 51 B–C. See below, p. 96.

It is of interest, nonetheless, that the fertility of Plato's speculation in Philosophy of Art provides for the possibility that art other than the mathematical is available for our experience. The ascent to the Idea of beauty implies a progress from fair bodies to fair institutions to fair forms. Once the idea of beauty is experienced, the identical objects are experienced, in the descent to the world from the suprasensible realm, but they are experienced on the return in terms of beauty and no longer simply in non-aesthetic terms. The mathematical objects of *Philebus* are not only geometrical figures; they are also beautiful.

Plato's earlier examination of art and works of art bears the imprint of the same powerful mind that produced the later speculation. Moreover, there is a fascination in following his casting about for some justification for art, although it is always treated as inferior to beauty. The selections from Plato's writings on philosophy of art that are given below begin with the *Hippias Major*, in which the disjunction between art and beauty emerges clearly. There is no reconciliation in the dialogue between "What is beautiful" and "What beauty is" but in the course of the discussion between Socrates and the extravagantly proud Hippias we are offered suggestions that have become integral to the tradition of speculation in Philosophy of Art. Among the more important are the following: (1) the beautiful is the appropriate and it is the appropriate that makes objects either appear or be beautiful; (2) the beautiful is useful; (3) what has power is useful for the beautiful; (4) sight and hearing are senses especially appropriate to the experience of beautiful objects because they are harmless; (5) the beautiful is that which makes us feel joy.

The nerve of the argument in *Hippias Major* remains, however, the assertion of the existence of an absolute beauty which is never ugly anywhere or to anyone and which makes what is beautiful to be what is beautiful.

Plato

427–347 B.C.

A. Life

Plato, the most fruitful mind and one of the most powerful influences in the history of the philosophy of art, was born in Athens, the son of Ariston and Perictione. His parents were members of distinguished families, his father tracing his descent to Codrus, his mother to Solon and Dropides, Archon for the year 644 B.C. Through his mother, Plato was related to Critias and Charmides, friends of Socrates and members of the oligarchy of 404 B.C.

As a young man, Plato was ambitious both for a political career and for the laurels of a tragic poet. He became a disciple of Socrates and after his master's trial and death determined to devote his life to philosophy. In his *Dialogues,* Plato produces not only an immortal portrait of Socrates but appears also to have tried to embody philosophy itself in that portrayal of the superb dialectician and powerful thinker in his efforts to know himself and other men.

After Socrates' death in 399 B.C., Plato and other of Socrates' friends left Athens for a brief self-exile in Megara. At the age of 40 years or thereabouts, Plato traveled to Syracuse, in Sicily, intending to instruct the tyrant, Dionysius I, in philosophy. The luxury of the court and the incapacity of the tyrant to submit to the discipline Plato held to be essential to the training of a philosopher made the philosopher's position untenable. The tyrant first planned to execute Plato and in fact ordered that he be put on the slave-block. Plato was bought by an Athenian merchant. The sojourn in Syracuse had ended in near-catastrophe, but while in Sicily Plato had become fast friends with Dion, nephew of Syracuse's tyrant.

On his return to Athens, ca. 387 B.C., Plato founded the Academy, the great philosophical school and center for research that remained a center of studies until 529 A.D., when it was closed by order of Justinian. Plato visited Syracuse at the invitation of his friend Dion but returned to Athens in 361–360 after the ruler fell in disgrace. He is said to have made a third journey to Syracuse, but the place was in turmoil, assailed by external enemies. Plato returned to the Academy, to which Aristotle came as a student ca. 367 B.C. Plato died at a wedding feast in 347 B.C.

The selections that follow the section on Plato's thought are best understood in terms of the theory of universals called the theory of Ideas. On Plato's view, Ideas exist in a suprasensible world, in separation from the world of becoming.

The general theory of arts

Hippias Major: On the beautiful

Characters, SOCRATES, HIPPIAS[58]

SOC. Hippias, beautiful and wise, what a long time it is since you have put in at the port of Athens!

HIPP. I am too busy, Socrates. For whenever Elis needs to have any business transacted with any of the states, she always comes to me first of her citizens and chooses me as envoy, thinking that I am the ablest judge and messenger of the words that are spoken by the several states. So I have often gone as envoy to other states, but most often and concerning the most numerous and important matters to Lacedaemon. For that reason, then, since you ask me, I do not often come to this neighbourhood.

SOC. That's what it is, Hippias, to be a truly wise and perfect man! For you are both in your private capacity able to earn much money from the young and to confer upon them still greater benefits than you receive, and in public affairs you are able to benefit your own state, as a man must who is to be not despised but held in high repute among the many. And yet, Hippias, what in the world is the reason why those men of old whose names are called great in respect to wisdom—Pittacus, and Bias, and the Milesian Thales with his followers—and also the later ones, down to Anaxagoras, are all, or most of them, found to refrain from affairs of state?

HIPP. What else do you suppose, Socrates, than that they were not able to compass by their wisdom both public and private matters?

SOC. Then for Heaven's sake, just as the other arts have progressed, and the ancients are of no account in comparison with the artisans of to-day, shall we say that your art also has progressed and those of the ancients who were concerned with wisdom are of no account in comparison with you?

HIPP. Yes, you are quite right.

SOC. Then, Hippias, if Bias were to come to life again now, he would be a laughing-stock in comparison with you, just as the sculptors say that Daedalus,[59] if he were to be born now and were to create such works as those from which he got his reputation, would be ridiculous.

HIPP. That, Socrates, is exactly as you say. I, however, am in the habit of praising the ancients and our predecessors rather than the men of the present day, and more greatly, as a precaution against the envy of the living and through fear of the wrath of those who are dead.

SOC. Yours, Hippias, is a most excellent way, at any rate, of speaking about them and of thinking, it seems to me; and I can bear you witness that you speak the truth, and that your art really has progressed in the direction of ability to carry on public together with private affairs. For this man Gorgias, the sophist from Leontini, came here from home in the public capacity of envoy, as being best able of all the citizens of Leontini to attend to the interests of the community, and it was the general opinion that he spoke excellently in the public assembly, and in his private capacity, by giving exhibitions

[58] Reprinted by permission of the publishers and The Loeb Classical Library from H. N. Fowler's translation of Plato, *Greater Hippias*, Cambridge, Mass.: Harvard University Press; London: W. Heinemann, 1926.

[59] Daedalus, the traditional inventor of sculpture.

and associating with the young, he earned and received a great deal of money from this city; or, if you like, our friend here, Prodicus, often went to other places in a public capacity, and the last time, just lately, when he came here in a public capacity from Ceos, he gained great reputation by his speaking before the Council, and in his private capacity, by giving exhibitions and associating with the young, he received a marvellous sum of money; but none of those ancients ever thought fit to exact the money as payment for his wisdom or to give exhibitions among people of various places; so simple-minded were they, and so unconscious of the fact that money is of the greatest value. But either of these two has earned more money from his wisdom than any artisan from his art. And even before these Protagoras did so.

HIPP. Why, Socrates, you know nothing of the beauties of this. For if you were to know how much money I have made, you would be amazed. I won't mention the rest, but once, when I went to Sicily, although Protagoras was staying there and had a great reputation and was the older, I, who was much younger, made in a very short time more than one hundred and fifty minas, and in one very small place, Inycus, more than twenty minas; and when I came home, I took this and gave it to my father, so that he and the other citizens were overwhelmed with amazement. And I pretty well think I have made more money than any other two sophists together.

SOC. That's a fine thing you say, Hippias, and strong testimony to your wisdom and that of the men of to-day and to their great superiority to the ancients. For the earlier sophists of the school of Anaxagoras must have been very ignorant to judge from what is said, according to your view; for they say that what happened to Anaxagoras was the opposite of what happens to you; for though much money was left him, he neglected it and lost it all; so senseless was his wisdom. And they tell similar tales about others among the ancients. So this seems to me fine testimony that you adduce for the wisdom of the men of to-day as compared with the earlier men, and many people agree with me that the wise man must be wise for himself especially[60]; and the test of this is, who makes the most money. Well, so much for that. But tell me this: at which of the cities that you go to did you make the most money? Or are we to take it that it was at Lacedaemon, where your visits have been most frequent?

HIPP. No, by Zeus, it was not, Socrates.

SOC. What's that you say? But did you make least there?

HIPP. Why, I never made anything at all.

SOC. That is a prodigious marvel that you tell, Hippias; and say now: is not your wisdom such as to make those who are in contact with it and learn it, better men in respect to virtue?

HIPP. Yes, much better, Socrates.

SOC. But you were able to make the sons of the Inycenes better, and had no power to improve the sons of the Spartans?

HIPP. That is far from true.

SOC. Well, then, the Siceliotes desire to become better, and the Lacedaemonians do not?

HIPP. No certainly, Socrates, the Lacedaemonians also desire it.

SOC. Then it was for lack of money that they avoided intercourse with you?

HIPP. Not at all, since they have plenty of money.

SOC. What, then, could be the reason, that when they desired it and had money, and you had power to confer upon them the greatest benefits, they did not send you away loaded with money? But I see; perhaps the Lacedaemonians might educate their own children better than you? Shall we state it so, and do you agree?

HIPP. Not in the least.

[60] Apparently a proverbial expression, like "physician, heal thyself" or "look out for number one."

SOC. Then were you not able to persuade the young men at Lacedaemon that they would make more progress towards virtue by associating with you than with their own people, or were you powerless to persuade their fathers that they ought rather to hand them over to you than to care for them themselves, if they are at all concerned for their sons? For surely they did not begrudge it to their children to become as good as possible.

HIPP. I do not think they begrudged it.

SOC. But certainly Lacedaemon is well governed.

HIPP. Of course it is.

SOC. And in well-governed states virtue is most highly honoured.

HIPP. Certainly.

SOC. And you know best of all men how to transmit that to another.

HIPP. Much best, Socrates.

SOC. Well, he who knows best how to transmit horsemanship would be most honoured in Thessaly of all parts of Greece and would receive most money—and anywhere else where horsemanship is a serious interest, would he not?

HIPP. Very likely.

SOC. Then will not he who is able to transmit the doctrines that are of most value for the acquisition of virtue be most highly honoured in Lacedaemon and make most money, if he so wishes, and in any other of the Greek states that is well governed? But do you, my friend, think he will fare better in Sicily and at Inycus? Are we to believe that, Hippias? For if you tell us to do so, we must believe it.

HIPP. Yes, for it is not the inherited usage of the Lacedaemonians to change their laws or to educate their children differently from what is customary.

SOC. What? For the Lacedaemonians is it the hereditary usage not to act rightly, but to commit errors?

HIPP. I wouldn't say so, Socrates.

SOC. Would they, then, not act rightly in educating the young men better, but not in educating them worse?

HIPP. Yes, they would; but it is not lawful for them to give them a foreign education; for you may be sure that if anybody had ever received money there in payment for education, I should have received by far the most; they certainly enjoy hearing me and they applaud me; but, as I say, it is not the law.

SOC. But, Hippias, do you say that law is an injury to the state, or a benefit?

HIPP. It is made, I think, with benefit in view, but sometimes, if the law is badly made, it is injurious.

SOC. Well, then, is it not true that those who make the law make it as the greatest good to the state, and that without this it is impossible to enjoy good government?

HIPP. What you say is true.

SOC. Then, when those who make the laws miss the good, they have missed the lawful and the law; or what do you say?

HIPP. Speaking accurately, Socrates, that is true; however, men are not accustomed to think so.

SOC. The men who know, Hippias, or those who do not know?

HIPP. The many.

SOC. Are these, the many, those who know the truth?

HIPP. Certainly not.

SOC. But surely those who know, think that in truth for all men that which is more beneficial is more lawful than that which is less beneficial; or do you not agree?

HIPP. Yes, I agree that they think it is so in truth.

SOC. Well, it actually is as those who know think it is, is it not?

HIPP. Certainly.

SOC. But for the Lacedaemonians, as you say, it is more beneficial to be educated in your education, which is foreign than in the local education.

HIPP. Yes, and what I say is true.

SOC. And do you say this also, Hippias, that beneficial things are more lawful?

HIPP. Yes, I said so.

SOC. Then, according to what you say, it is more lawful for the sons of the Lacedaemonians to be educated by Hippias and less lawful for them to be educated by their fathers, if in reality they will be more benefited by you.

HIPP. But certainly they will be benefited, Socrates.

SOC. Then the Lacedaemonians in not giving you money and entrusting their sons to you, act contrary to law.

HIPP. I agree to that; for you seem to be making your argument in my favour, and there is no need of my opposing it.

SOC. Then, my friends, we find that the Lacedaemonians are law-breakers, and that too in the most important affairs—they who are regarded as the most law-abiding of men. But then, for Heaven's sake, Hippias, what sort of discourses are those for which they applaud you and which they enjoy hearing? Or are they evidently those which you understand most admirably, those about the stars and the phenomena of the heavens?

HIPP. Not in the least; they won't even endure those.

SOC. But they enjoy hearing about geometry?

HIPP. Not at all, since one might say that many of them do not even know how to count.

SOC. Then they are far from enduring a lecture by you on the processes of thought.

HIPP. Far from it indeed, by Zeus.

SOC. Well, then, those matters which you of all men know best how to discuss, concerning the value of letters and syllables and rhythms and harmonies?

HIPP. Harmonies indeed, my good fellow, and letters!

SOC. But then what are the things about which they like to listen to you and which they applaud? Tell me yourself, for I cannot discover them.

HIPP. They are very fond of hearing about the genealogies of heroes and men, Socrates, and the foundations of cities in ancient times and, in short, about antiquity in general, so that for their sake I have been obliged to learn all that sort of thing by heart and practise it thoroughly.

SOC. By Zeus, Hippias, it is lucky for you that the Lacedaemonians do not enjoy hearing one recite the list of our archons from Solon's time; if they did, you would have trouble in learning it by heart.

HIPP. How so, Socrates? After hearing them once, I can remember fifty names.

SOC. True, but I did not understand that you possess the science of memory; and so I understand that the Lacedaemonians naturally enjoy you as one who knows many things, and they make use of you as children make use of old women, to tell stories agreeably.

HIPP. And by Zeus, Socrates, I have just lately gained reputation there by telling about noble or beautiful pursuits, recounting what those of a young man should be. For I have a very beautiful discourse composed about them, well arranged in its words and also in other respects. And the plan of the discourse, and its beginning, is something like this: After the fall of Troy, the story goes that Neoptolemus asked Nestor what the noble and beautiful pursuits were, by following which a young man would become most famous; so after that we have Nestor speaking and suggesting to him very many lawful and most beautiful pursuits. That discourse, then, I delivered there and intend to deliver here the day after to-morrow in Pheidostratus's schoolroom, with many other things worth hearing; for Eudicus, the son of Apemantus, asked me to do so. Now be sure to be there yourself and to bring others who are able to judge of discourses that they hear.

SOC. Well, that shall be done, God willing, Hippias. Now, however, give me a brief answer to a question about your discourse, for you reminded me of the beautiful just at the right moment. For recently, my most excellent friend, as I was finding fault with some things in certain speeches as ugly and praising other things as beautiful, a man threw me into confusion by questioning me very insolently somewhat after this fashion: "How, if you please, do you know, Socrates," said he, "what sort of things are beautiful and ugly? For, come now, could you tell me what the beautiful is?" And I, being of no account, was at a loss and could not answer him properly; and so, as I was going away from the company, I was angry with myself and reproached myself, and threatened that the first time I met one of you wise men, I would hear and learn and practise and then go back to the man who questioned me to renew the wordy strife. So now, as I say, you have come at the right moment; just teach me satisfactorily what the absolute beautiful is, and try in replying to speak as accurately as possible, that I may not be confuted a second time and be made ridiculous again. for you doubtless know clearly, and this would doubtless be but a small example of your learning.

HIPP. Yes, surely, by Zeus, a small one, Socrates, and, I may say, of no value.

SOC. Then I shall learn it easily, and nobody will confute me any more.

HIPP. Nobody, surely; for in that case my profession would be worthless and ordinary.

SOC. That is good, by Hera, Hippias, if we are to worst the fellow. But may I without hindering you imitate him, and when you answer, take exception to what you say, in order that you may give me as much practice as possible? For I am more or less experienced in taking exceptions. So, if it is all the same to you, I wish to take exceptions, that I may learn more vigorously.

HIPP. Oh yes, take exceptions. For, as I said just now, the question is no great matter, but I could teach you to answer much harder ones than this, so that nobody in the world could confute you.

SOC. Oh how good that is! But come, since you tell me to do so, now let me try to play that man's part, so far as possible, and ask you questions. For if you were to deliver for him this discourse that you mention, the one about beautiful pursuits, when he had heard it, after you had stopped speaking, the very first thing he would ask about would be the beautiful; for he has that sort of habit, and he would say, "Stranger from Elis, is it not by justice that the just are just?" So answer, Hippias, as though he were asking the question.

HIPP. I shall answer that it is by justice.

SOC. "Then this—I mean justice—is something?"

HIPP. Certainly.

SOC. "Then, too, by wisdom the wise are wise and by the good all things are good, are they not?"

HIPP. Of course.

SOC. "And justice, wisdom, and so forth are something; for the just, wise, and so forth would not be such by them, if they were not something."

HIPP. To be sure, they are something.

SOC. "Then are not all beautiful things beautiful by the beautiful?"

HIPP. Yes by the beautiful.

SOC. "By the beautiful, which is something?"

HIPP. Yes, for what alternative is there?

SOC. "Tell me, then stranger," he will say, "what is this, the beautiful?"

HIPP. Well, Socrates, does he who asks this question want to find out anything else than what is beautiful?

SOC. I do not think that is what he wants to find out, but what the beautiful is.

HIPP. And what difference is there between the two?

SOC. Do you think there is none?

HIPP. Yes, for there is no difference.

SOC. Well, surely it is plain that you know best; but still, my good friend, consider; for he asked you, not what is beautiful, but what the beautiful is.

HIPP. I understand, my good friend, and I

will answer and tell him what the beautiful is, and I shall never be confuted. For be assured, Socrates, if I must speak the truth, a beautiful maiden is beautiful.

SOC. Beautifully answered, Hippias, by the dog, and notably! Then if I give this answer, I shall have answered the question that was asked, and shall have answered it correctly, and shall never be confuted?

HIPP. Yes, for how could you, Socrates, be confuted, when you say what everybody thinks, and when all who hear it will bear witness that what you say is correct?

SOC. Very well; certainly. Come, then, Hippias, let me rehearse to myself what you say. The man will question me in some such fashion as this: "Come Socrates, answer me. All these things which you say are beautiful, if the absolute beautiful is anything, would be beautiful?" And I shall say that if a beautiful maiden is beautiful, there is something by reason of which these things would be beautiful.

HIPP. Do you think, then, that he will still attempt to refute you and to show that what you say is not beautiful, or, if he does attempt it, that he will not be ridiculous?

SOC. That he will attempt it, my admirable friend, I am sure; but whether the attempt will make him ridiculous, the event will show. However, I should like to tell you what he will ask.

HIPP. Do so.

SOC. "How charming you are, Socrates!" he will say. "But is not a beautiful mare beautiful, which even the god praised in his oracle?"[61] What shall we say, Hippias? Shall we not say that the mare is beautiful, I mean the beautiful mare? For how could we dare to deny that the beautiful thing is beautiful?

HIPP. Quite true, Socrates; for what the god said is quite correct, too; for very beautiful mares are bred in our country.

SOC. "Very well," he will say, "and how about a beautiful lyre? Is it not beautiful?" Shall we agree, Hippias?

HIPP. Yes.

SOC. After this, then, the man will ask, I am sure, judging by his character: "You most excellent man, how about a beautiful pot? Is it, then, not beautiful?"

HIPP. Socrates, who is the fellow? What an uncultivated person, who has the face to mention such worthless things in a dignified discussion!

SOC. That's the kind of person he is, Hippias, not elegant, but vulgar, thinking of nothing but the truth. But nevertheless the man must be answered, and I will declare my opinion beforehand: if the pot were made by a good potter, were smooth and round and well fired, as are some of the two-handled pots, those that hold six choes,[62] very beautiful ones —if that were the kind of pot he asked about, we must agree that it is beautiful; for how could we say that being beautiful it is not beautiful?

HIPP. We could not at all, Socrates.

SOC. "Then," he will say, "a beautiful pot also is beautiful, is it not? Answer."

HIPP. Well, Socrates, it is like this, I think. This utensil, when well wrought, is beautiful, but absolutely considered it does not deserve to be regarded as beautiful in comparison with a mare and a maiden and all the beautiful things.

SOC. Very well; I understand, Hippias, that the proper reply to him who asks these questions is this: "Sir, you are not aware that the saying of Heracleitus is good, that 'the most beautiful of monkeys is ugly compared with the race of man,' and the most beautiful of pots is ugly compared with the race of maidens, as Hippias the wise man says." Is it not so, Hippias?

[61] "Better than all other land is the land of Pelasgian Argos, Thracian mares are the best, and the Lacedaemonian women."
To be sure, nothing is said about the beauty of the mares, and the reference to Elis contained in *παρ' ἡμῖν* just below is hard to reconcile with the Thracian mares of the oracle.

[62] The *χοῦς* was 5.76 pints.

HIPP. Certainly, Socrates; you replied rightly.

SOC. Listen then. For I am sure that after this he will say: "Yes, but, Socrates, if we compare maidens with gods, will not the same thing happen to them that happened to pots when compared with maidens? Will not the most beautiful maiden appear ugly? Or does not Heracleitus, whom you cite, mean just this, that the wisest of men, if compared with a god, will appear a monkey, both in wisdom and in beauty and in everything else? Shall we agree, Hippias, that the most beautiful maiden is ugly if compared with the gods?

HIPP. Yes, for who would deny that, Socrates?

SOC. If, then, we agree to that, he will laugh and say: "Socrates, do you remember the question you were asked?" "I do," I shall say, "the question was what the absolute beautiful is." "Then," he will say, "when you were asked for the beautiful, do you give as your reply what is, as you yourself say, no more beautiful than ugly?" "So it seems," I shall say; or what do you, my friend, advise me to say?

HIPP. That is what I advise; for, of course, in saying that the human race is not beautiful in comparison with gods, you will be speaking the truth.

SOC. "But if I had asked you," he will say, "in the beginning what is beautiful and ugly, if you had replied as you now do, would you not have replied correctly? But do you still think that the absolute beautiful, by the addition of which all other things are adorned and made to appear beautiful, when its form is added to any of them—do you think that is a maiden or a mare or a lyre?"

HIPP. Well, certainly, Socrates, if that is what he is looking for, nothing is easier than to answer and tell him what the beautiful is, by which all other things are adorned and by the addition of which they are made to appear beautiful. So the fellow is very simple-minded and knows nothing about beautiful possessions. For if you reply to him: "This that you ask about, the beautiful, is nothing else but gold," he will be thrown into confusion and will not attempt to confute you. For we all know, I fancy, that wherever this is added, even what before appears ugly will appear beautiful when adorned with gold.

SOC. You don't know the man, Hippias, what a wretch he is, and how certain not to accept anything easily.

HIPP. What of that, then, Socrates? For he must perforce accept what is correct, or if he does not accept it, be ridiculous.

SOC. This reply, my most excellent friend, he not only will certainly not accept, but he will even jeer at me grossly and will say: "You lunatic, do you think Pheidias is a bad craftsman?" And I shall say, "Not in the least,"

HIPP. And you will be right, Socrates.

SOC. Yes, to be sure. Consequently when I agree that Pheidias is a good craftsman, "Well, then," he will say, "do you imagine that Pheidias did not know this beautiful that you speak of?" "Why do you ask that?" I shall say. "Because," he will say, "he did not make the eyes of his Athena of gold, nor the rest of her face, nor her hands and feet, if, that is, they were sure to appear most beautiful provided only they were made of gold, but he made them of ivory; evidently he made this mistake through ignorance, not knowing that it is gold which makes everything beautiful to which it is added." When he says that, what reply shall we make to him, Hippias?

HIPP. That is easy; for we shall say that Pheidias did right; for ivory, I think, is beautiful.

SOC. "Why, then," he will say, "did he not make the middle parts of the eyes also of ivory, but of stone, procuring stone as similar as possible to the ivory? Or is beautiful stone also beautiful?" Shall we say that it is, Hippias?

HIPP. Surely we shall say so, that is, where it is appropriate.

SOC. "But ugly when not appropriate?" Shall I agree or not?

HIPP. Agree, that is, when it is not appropriate.

SOC. "What then? Do not gold and ivory," he will say, "when they are appropriate, make things beautiful, and when they are not appropriate, ugly?" Shall we deny that, or agree that what he says is correct?

HIPP. We shall agree to this, at any rate, that whatever is appropriate to any particular thing makes that thing beautiful.

SOC. "Well then," he will say, "when some one has boiled the pot of which we were speaking just now, the beautiful one, full of beautiful soup, is a golden ladle appropriate to it, or one made of fig wood?"

HIPP. Heracles! What a fellow this is that you speak of! Won't you tell me who he is?

SOC. You would not know him if I should tell you his name.

HIPP. But even now I know that he is an ignoramus.

SOC. He is a great nuisance, Hippias; but yet, what shall we say? Which of the two ladles shall we say is appropriate to the soup and the pot? Is it not evidently the one of fig wood? For it is likely to make the soup smell better, and besides, my friend, it would not break the pot, thereby spilling the soup, putting out the fire, and making those who are to be entertained go without their splendid soup; whereas the golden ladle would do all those things, so that it seems to me that we must say that the wooden ladle is more appropriate than the golden one, unless you disagree.

HIPP. No, for it is more appropriate, Socrates; however, I, for my part, would not talk with the fellow when he asks such questions.

SOC. Quite right, my friend; for it would not be appropriate for you to be filled up with such words, you who are so beautifully clad, so beautifully shod, and so famous for your wisdom among all the Greeks; but for me it doesn't matter if I do associate with the fellow; so instruct me and for my sake answer him. "For if the wooden one is more appropriate than the golden one," the fellow will say, "would it not be more beautiful, since you agreed, Socrates, that the appropriate is more beautiful than that which is not appropriate?" Shall we not agree, Hippias, that the wooden one is more beautiful than the golden?

HIPP. Do you wish me to tell you, Socrates, what definition of the beautiful will enable you to free yourself from long discussion?

SOC. Certainly; but not until after you have told me which of the two ladles I just spoke of I shall reply is appropriate and more beautiful.

HIPP. Well, if you like, reply to him that it is the one made of fig wood.

SOC. Now, then, say what you were just now going to say. For by this reply, if I say that the beautiful is gold, it seems to me that gold will be shown to be no more beautiful than fig wood; but what do you now, once more, say that the beautiful is?

HIPP. I will tell you; for you seem to me to be seeking to reply that the beautiful is something of such sort that it will never appear ugly anywhere to anybody.

SOC. Certainly, Hippias; now you understand beautifully.

HIPP. Listen, then; for, mind you, if anyone has anything to say against this, you may say I know nothing at all.

SOC. Then for Heaven's sake, speak as quickly as you can.

HIPP. I say, then, that for every man and everywhere it is most beautiful to be rich and healthy and honoured by the Greeks, to reach old age, and, after providing a beautiful funeral for his deceased parents, to be beautifully and splendidly buried by his own offspring.

SOC. Bravo, bravo, Hippias! You have spoken in a way that is wonderful and great and worthy of you; and now, by Hera, I thank you, because you are kindly coming to my assistance to the best of your ability. But our shots are not hitting the man; no, he will laugh at us now more than ever, be sure of that.

HIPP. A wretched laugh, Socrates; for when he has nothing to say to this, but laughs, he will be laughing at himself and will himself be laughed at by those present.

SOC. Perhaps, that is so; perhaps, however, after this reply, he will, I foresee, be likely to do more than laugh at me.

HIPP. Why do you say that, pray?

SOC. Because, if he happens to have a stick, unless I get away in a hurry, he will try to fetch me a good one.

HIPP. What? Is the fellow some sort of master of yours, and if he does that, will he not be arrested and have to pay for it? Or does your city disregard justice and allow the citizens to beat one another unjustly?

SOC. Oh no; that is not allowed at all.

HIPP. Then he will have to pay a penalty for beating you unjustly.

SOC. I do not think so, Hippias. No, if I were to make that reply, the beating would be just, I think.

HIPP. Then I think so, too, Socrates, since that is your own belief.

SOC. Shall I, then, not tell you why it is my own belief that the beating would be just, if I made that reply? Or will you also beat me without trial? Or will you listen to what I have to say?

HIPP. It would be shocking if I would not listen; but what have you to say?

SOC. I will tell you, imitating him in the same way as a while ago, that I may not use to you such harsh and uncouth words as he uses to me. For you may be sure, "Tell me, Socrates," he will say, "do you think it would be unjust if you got a beating for singing such a long dithyramb so unmusically and so far from the question?" "How so?" I shall say. "How so?" he will say; "are you not able to remember that I asked for the absolute beautiful, by which everything to which it is added has the property of being beautiful, both stone and stick and man and god and every act and every acquisition of knowledge? For what I am asking is this, man: what is absolute beauty? and I cannot make you hear what I say any more than if you were a stone sitting beside me, and a millstone at that, having neither ears nor brain." Would you, then, not be angry, Hippias, if I should be frightened and should reply in this way? "Well, but Hippias said that this was the beautiful; and yet I asked him, just as you asked me, what is beautiful to all and always." What do you say? Will you not be angry if I say that?

HIPP. I know very well, Socrates, that this which I said was beautiful is beautiful to all and will seem so.

SOC. "And will it be so, too?" he will say; "for the beautiful is always beautiful, is it not?"

HIPP. Certainly.

SOC. "Then was it so, too?" he will say.

HIPP. It was so, too.

SOC. "And," he will say, "did the stranger from Elis say also that for Achilles it was beautiful to be buried later than his parents, and for his grandfather Aeacus, and all the others who were born of gods, and for the gods themselves?"

HIPP. What's that? Confound it! These questions of the fellow's are not even respectful to religion.

SOC. Well, then, when another asks the question, perhaps it is not quite disrespectful to religion to say that these things are so?

HIPP. Perhaps.

SOC. "Perhaps, then, you are the man," he will say, "who says that it is beautiful for every one and always to be buried by one's offspring, and to bury one's parents; or was not Heracles included in 'every one,' he and all those whom we just now mentioned?"

HIPP. But I did not say it was so for the gods.

SOC. "Nor for the heroes either, apparently."

HIPP. Not those who were children of gods.

SOC. "But those who were not?"

HIPP. Certainly.

SOC. "Then again, according to your statement, among the heroes it is terrible and impious and disgraceful for Tantalus and Dardanus and Zethus, but beautiful for Pelops[63] and the others who were born as he was?"

HIPP. I think so.

SOC. "You think, then, what you did not say just now, that to bury one's parents and be buried by one's offspring is sometimes and for some persons disgraceful; and it is still more impossible, as it seems, for this to become and to be beautiful for all, so that the same thing has happened to this as to the things we mentioned before, the maiden and the pot, in a still more ridiculous way than to them; it is beautiful for some and not beautiful for others. And you are not able yet, even to-day, Socrates," he will say, "to answer what is asked about the beautiful, namely what it is." With these words and the like he will rebuke me, if I reply to him in this way. For the most part, Hippias, he talks with me in some such way as that; but sometimes, as if in pity for my inexperience and lack of training, he himself volunteers a question, and asks whether I think the beautiful is so and so—or whatever else it is which happens to be the subject of our questions and our discussion.

HIPP. What do you mean by that, Socrates?

SOC. I will tell you. "Oh, my dear Socrates," he says, "stop making replies of this sort and in this way—for they are too silly and easy to refute; but see if something like this does not seem to you to be beautiful, which we got hold of just now in our reply, when we said that gold was beautiful for those things for which it was appropriate, but not for those for which it was not, and that all the other things were beautiful to which this quality pertains; so examine this very thing, the appropriate, and see if it is perchance the beautiful." Now I am accustomed to agree to such things every time; for I don't know what to say; but now does it seem to you that the appropriate is the beautiful?

HIPP. Yes, certainly, Socrates.

SOC. Let us consider, lest we make a mistake somehow.

HIPP. Yes, we must consider.

SOC. See, then; do we say that the appropriate is that which, when it is added, makes each of those things to which it is added appear beautiful, or which makes them be beautiful, or neither of these?

HIPP. I think so.

SOC. Which?

HIPP. That which makes them appear beautiful; as when a man takes clothes or shoes that fit, even if he be ridiculous, he appears more beautiful.

SOC. Then if the appropriate makes him appear more beautiful than he is, the appropriate would be a sort of deceit in respect to the beautiful, and would not be that which we are looking for, would it, Hippias? For we were rather looking for that by which all beautiful things are beautiful—like that by which all great things are great, that is, excess; for it is by this that all great things are great; for even if they do not appear great, but exceed, they are of necessity great; so, then, we say, what would the beautiful be, by which all things are beautiful, whether they appear so or not? For it could not be the appropriate, since that, by your statement, makes things appear more beautiful than they are, but does not let them appear such as they are. But we must try to say what that is which makes things be beautiful, as I said just now, whether they appear so or not; for that is what we are looking for, since we are looking for the beautiful.

HIPP. But the appropriate, Socrates, makes things both be and appear beautiful by its presence.

SOC. Is it impossible, then, for things which

63 Pelops as the son of a mortal (Tantalus); the others mentioned were sons of gods.

are really beautiful not to appear to be beautiful, at any rate when that is present which makes them appear so?

HIPP. It is impossible.

SOC. Shall we, then, agree to this, Hippias, that all things which are really beautiful, both uses and pursuits, are always believed to be beautiful by all, and appear so to them, or, quite the contrary, that people are ignorant about them, and that there is more strife and contention about them than about anything else, both in private between individuals and in public between states?

HIPP. The latter rather, Socrates; that people are ignorant about them.

SOC. They would not be so, if the appearance of beauty were added to them; and it would be added, if the appropriate were beautiful and made things not only to be beautiful, but also to appear so. So that the appropriate, if it is that which makes things be beautiful, would be the beautiful which we are looking for, but would not be that which makes things appear beautiful; but if, on the other hand, the appropriate is that which makes things appear beautiful, it would not be the beautiful for which we are looking. For that makes things be beautiful, but the same element could not make things both appear and be beautiful, nor could it make them both appear and be anything else whatsoever. Let us choose, then, whether we think that the appropriate is that which makes things appear or be beautiful.

HIPP. That which makes them appear so, in my opinion, Socrates.

SOC. Whew! Our perception of what the beautiful is has fled away and gone, Hippias, since the appropriate has been found to be something other than the beautiful.

HIPP. Yes, by Zeus, Socrates, and to me that is very queer.

SOC. However, my friend, let us not yet give it up, for I still have hopes that what the beautiful is will be made clear.

HIPP. Certainly, to be sure, Socrates, for it is not hard to find. Now I know that if I should go away into solitude and meditate alone by myself, I could tell it to you with the most perfect accuracy.

SOC. Ah, don't boast, Hippias. You see how much trouble it has caused us already; I'm afraid it may get angry and run away more than ever. And yet that is nonsense; for you, I think, will easily find it when you go away by yourself. But for Heaven's sake, find it in my presence, or, if you please, join me, as you are now doing, in looking for it. And if we find it, that will be splendid, but if we do not, I shall, I suppose, accept my lot, and you will go away and find it easily. And if we find it now, I shall certainly not be a nuisance to you by asking what that was which you found by yourself; but now once more see if this is in your opinion beautiful: I say, then, that it is—but consider, paying close attention to me, that I may not talk nonsense—for I say, then, whatever is useful shall be for us beautiful. But I said it with this reason for my thought; beautiful eyes, we say, are not such as seem to be so, which are unable to see, but those which are able and useful for seeing. Is that right?

HIPP. Yes.

SOC. Then, too, in the same way we say that the whole body is beautiful, part of it for running, part for wrestling; and again all the animals, a beautiful horse or cock or quail; and all utensils and land vehicles, and on the sea freight-ships and ships of war; and all instruments in music and in the other arts, and, if you like, customs and laws also—pretty well all these we call beautiful in the same way; looking at each of them—how it is formed by nature, how it is wrought, how it has been enacted—the useful we call beautiful, and beautiful in the way in which it is useful, and for the purpose for which it is useful, and at the time when it is useful; and that which is in all these aspects useless we say is ugly. Now is not this your opinion also, Hippias?

HIPP. It is.

SOC. Then are we right in saying that the useful rather than everything else is beautiful?

HIPP. We are right, surely, Socrates.

SOC. Now that which has power to accomplish anything is useful for that for which it has power, but that which is powerless is useless, is it not?

HIPP. Certainly.

SOC. Power, then, is beautiful, and want of power is disgraceful or ugly.

HIPP. Decidedly. Now other things, Socrates, testify for us that this is so, but especially political affairs; for in political affairs and in one's own state to be powerful is the most beautiful of all things, but to be powerless is the most disgraceful of all.

SOC. Good! Then, for Heaven's sake, Hippias, is wisdom also for this reason the most beautiful of all things and ignorance the most disgraceful of all things?

HIPP. Well, what do you suppose, Socrates?

SOC. Just keep quiet, my dear friend; I am so afraid and wondering what in the world we are saying again.

HIPP. What are you afraid of again, Socrates, since now your discussion has gone ahead most beautifully?

SOC. I wish that might be the case; but consider this point with me: could a person do what he did not know how and was utterly powerless to do?

HIPP. By no means; for how could he do what he was powerless to do?

SOC. Then those who commit errors and accomplish and do bad things involuntarily, if they were powerless to do those things, would not do them?

HIPP. Evidently not.

SOC. But yet it is by power that those are powerful who are powerful; for surely it is not by powerlessness.

HIPP. Certainly not.

SOC. And all who do, have power to do what they do?

HIPP. Yes.

SOC. Men do many more bad things than good, from childhood up, and commit many errors involuntarily.

HIPP. That is true.

SOC. Well, then, this power and these useful things, which are useful for accomplishing something bad—shall we say that they are beautiful, or far from it?

HIPP. Far from it, in my opinion, Socrates.

SOC. Then, Hippias, the powerful and the useful are not, as it seems, our beautiful.

HIPP. They are, Socrates, if they are powerful and useful for good.

SOC. Then that assertion, that the powerful and useful are beautiful without qualification, is gone; but was this, Hippias, what our soul wished to say, that the useful and the powerful for doing something good is the beautiful?

HIPP. Yes, in my opinion.

SOC. But surely this is beneficial; or is it not?

HIPP. Certainly.

SOC. So by this argument the beautiful persons and beautiful customs and all that we mentioned just now are beautiful because they are beneficial.

HIPP. Evidently.

SOC. Then the beneficial seems to us to be the beautiful, Hippias.

HIPP. Yes, certainly, Socrates.

SOC. But the beneficial is that which creates good.

HIPP. Yes, it is.

SOC. But that which creates is nothing else than the cause; am I right?

HIPP. It is so.

SOC. Then the beautiful is the cause of the good.

HIPP. Yes, it is.

SOC. But surely, Hippias, the cause and that of which the cause is the cause are different; for the cause could not well be the cause of the cause. But look at it in this way: was not the cause seen to be creating?

HIPP. Yes, certainly.

SOC. By that which creates, then, only that is created which comes into being, but not that which creates. Is not that true?

HIPP. That is true.

SOC. The cause, then, is not the cause of the cause, but of that which comes into being through it.

HIPP. Certainly.

SOC. If, then, the beautiful is the cause of good, the good would come into being through the beautiful; and this is why we are eager for wisdom and all the other beautiful things, because their offspring, the good, is worthy of eagerness, and, from what we are finding, it looks as if the beautiful were a sort of father of the good.

HIPP. Certainly; for what you say is well said, Socrates.

SOC. Then is this well said, too, that the father is not the son, and the son not father?

HIPP. To be sure it is well said.

SOC. And neither is the cause that which comes into being, nor is that which comes into being the cause.

HIPP. True.

SOC. By Zeus, my good friend, then neither is the beautiful good, nor the good beautiful; or does it seem to you possible, after what has been said?

HIPP. No, by Zeus, it does not appear so to me.

SOC. Does it please us, and should we be willing to say that the beautiful is not good, and the good not beautiful?

HIPP. No, by Zeus, it does not please me at all.

SOC. Right, by Zeus, Hippias! And it pleases me least of all the things we have said.

HIPP. Yes, that is likely.

SOC. Then there is a good chance that the statement that the beneficial and the useful and the powerful to create something good are beautiful, is not, as it appeared to be, the most beautiful of our statements, but, if that be possible, is even more ridiculous than those first ones in which we thought the maiden was the beautiful, and each of the various other things we spoke of before.

HIPP. That is likely.

SOC. And Hippias, I no longer know where to turn; I am at a loss; but have you anything to say?

HIPP. Not at the moment, but, as I said just now, I am sure I shall find it after meditation.

SOC. But it seems to me that I am so eager to know that I cannot wait for you while you delay; for I believe I have just now found a way out. Just see; how would it help us towards our goal if we were to say that that is beautiful which makes us feel joy; I do not mean all pleasures, but that which makes us feel joy through hearing and sight? For surely beautiful human beings, Hippias, and all decorations, and paintings and works of sculpture which are beautiful, delight us when we see them; and beautiful sounds and music in general and speeches and stories do the same thing, so that if we were to reply to that impudent fellow, "My excellent man, the beautiful is that which is pleasing through hearing and sight," don't you think that we should put a stop to his impudence?

HIPP. To me, at any rate, Socrates, it seems that the nature of the beautiful is now well stated.

SOC. But what then? Shall we say, Hippias, that beautiful customs and laws are beautiful because they are pleasing through hearing and sight, or that they have some other form of beauty?

HIPP. Perhaps, Socrates, these things might slip past the man unnoticed.

SOC. No, by dog, Hippias—not past the man before whom I should be most ashamed of talking nonsense and pretending that I was talking sense when I was not.

HIPP. What man is that?

SOC. Socrates, the son of Sophroniscus, who

would no more permit me to say these things carelessly without investigation than to say that I know what I do not know.

HIPP. But certainly I also, now that you have mentioned it, think that this about the laws is something different.

SOC. Not too fast, Hippias; for very likely we have fallen into the same perplexity about the beautiful in which we were a while ago, although we think we have found another way out.

HIPP. What do you mean by that, Socrates?

SOC. I will tell you what presents itself to me, if perhaps there may be some sense in it. For perhaps these matters of laws and customs might be shown to be not outside of the perception which we have through hearing and sight; but let us stick to the statement that that which is pleasing through the senses is beautiful, without interjecting the matter of the laws. But if this man of whom I speak, or anyone else whosoever, should ask us: "Hippias and Socrates, did you make the distinction that in the category of 'the pleasing' that which is pleasing in the way you mention is beautiful, whereas you say that that which is pleasing according to the other senses—those concerned with food and drink and sexual love and all such things—is not beautiful? Or do you say that such things are not even pleasing and that there is no pleasure at all in them, nor in anything else except sight and hearing?" What shall we say, Hippias?

HIPP. Certainly, by all means, Socrates, we shall say that there are very great pleasures in the other things also.

SOC. "Why, then," he will say, "if they are pleasures no less than the others, do you take from them this designation and deprive them of being beautiful?" "Because," we shall say, "everybody would laugh at us if we should say that eating is not pleasant but is beautiful, and that a pleasant odour is not pleasant but is beautiful; and as to the act of sexual love, we should all, no doubt, contend that it is most pleasant, but that one must, if he perform it, do it so that no one else shall see, because it is most repulsive to see." If we say this, Hippias, "I too understand," he will perhaps say, "that you have all along been ashamed to say that these pleasures are beautiful, because they do not seem so to people; but that is not what I asked, what seems to most people to be beautiful, but what is so." We shall, then, I fancy, say, as we suggested, "We say that that part of the pleasant which comes by sight and hearing is beautiful." Do you think the statement is of any use, Hippias, or shall we say something else?

HIPP. Inevitably, in view of what has been said, Socrates, we must say just that.

SOC. "Excellent!" he will say. "Then if that which is pleasant through sight and hearing is beautiful, that among pleasant things which does not happen to be of that sort would evidently not be beautiful?" Shall we agree?

HIPP. Yes.

SOC. "Is, then, that which is pleasant through sight," he will say, "pleasant through sight and hearing, or is that which is pleasant through hearing pleasant through hearing and sight?" "No," we shall say, "that which is pleasant through each of these would not in the least be pleasant through both—for that is what you appear to us to mean—but we said that either of these pleasant things would be beautiful alone by itself, and both together." Is not that the reply we shall make?

HIPP. Certainly.

SOC. "Does, then," he will say, "any pleasant thing whatsoever differ from any pleasant thing whatsoever by this, by being pleasant? I ask not whether any pleasure is greater or smaller or more or less, but whether it differs by just this very thing, by the fact that one of the pleasures is a pleasure and the other is not a pleasure." "We do not think so." Do we?

HIPP. No, we do not.

SOC. "Is it not, then," he will say, "for

some other reason than because they are pleasures that you chose these pleasures out from the other pleasures—it was because you saw some quality in both, since they have something different from the others, in view of which you say that they are beautiful? For the reason why that which is pleasant through sight is beautiful, is not, I imagine, because it is through sight; for if that were the cause of its being beautiful, the other pleasure, that through hearing, would not be beautiful; it certainly is not pleasure through sight." Shall we say "What you say is true?"

HIPP. Yes, we shall.

SOC. "Nor, again, is the pleasure through hearing beautiful for the reason that it is through hearing; for in that case, again, the pleasure through sight would not be beautiful; it certainly is not pleasure through hearing." Shall we say, Hippias, that the man who says that speaks the truth?

HIPP. Yes, he speaks the truth.

SOC. "But yet both are beautiful, as you say." We do say that, do we not?

HIPP. We do.

SOC. "They have, then, something identical which makes them to be beautiful, this common quality which pertains to both of them in common and to each individually; for otherwise they would not both collectively and each individually be beautiful." Answer me, as if you were answering him.

HIPP. I answer, and I think it is as you say.

SOC. If, then, these pleasures are both affected in any way collectively, but each individually is not so affected, it is not by this affection that they would be beautiful.

HIPP. And how could that be, Socrates, when neither of them individually is affected by some affection or other, that then both are affected by that affection by which neither is affected?

SOC. You think it cannot be?

HIPP. I should have to be very inexperienced both in the nature of these things and in the language of our present discussion.

SOC. Very pretty, Hippias. But there is a chance that I think I see a case of that kind which you say is impossible, but do not really see it.

HIPP. There's no chance about it, Socrates, but you quite purposely see wrongly.

SOC. And certainly many such cases appear before my mind, but I mistrust them because they do not appear to you, a man has made more money by wisdom than anyone now living, but to me who never made any money at all; and the thought disturbs me that you are playing with me and purposely deceiving me, they appear to me in such numbers and with such force.

HIPP. Nobody, Socrates, will know better than you whether I am playing with you or not, if you proceed to tell these things that appear to you; for it will be apparent to you that you are talking nonsense. For you will never find that you and I are both affected by an affection by which neither of us is affected.

SOC. What are you saying, Hippias? Perhaps you are talking sense, and I fail to understand; but let me tell more clearly what I wish to say. For it appears to me that it is possible for us both to be so affected as to be something which I am not so affected as to be, and which I am not and you are not either; and again for neither of us to be so affected as to be other things which we both are.

HIPP. Your reply, Socrates seems to involve miracles again even greater than those of your previous reply. For consider: if we are both just, would not each of us be just also, and if each is unjust, would not both again also be unjust, or if both are healthy, each of us also? Or if each of us were to be tired or wounded or struck or affected in any other way whatsoever, should we not both of us be affected in the same way? Then, too, if we were to be golden or of silver or of ivory, or, if you please, noble or wise or honoured or old or young or whatever else you like of all that flesh is heir to, is it not quite inevitable that each of us be that also?

SOC. Absolutely.

HIPP. But you see, Socrates, you do not consider the entirety of things, nor do they with whom you are in the habit of conversing, but you all test the beautiful and each individual entity by taking them separately and cutting them to pieces. For this reason you fail to observe that embodiments of reality are by nature so great and undivided. And now you have failed to observe to such a degree that you think there is some affection or reality which pertains to both of these together, but not to each individually, or again to each, but not to both; so unreasoning and undiscerning and foolish and unreflecting is your state of mind.

SOC. Human affairs, Hippias, are not what a man wishes, but what he can, as the proverb goes which people are constantly citing; but you are always aiding us with admonitions. For now too, until we were admonished by you of our foolish state of mind—shall I continue to speak and make you a still further exhibition of our thoughts on the subject, or shall I not speak?

HIPP. You will speak to one who knows, Socrates, for I know the state of mind of all who are concerned with discussions; but nevertheless, if you prefer, speak.

SOC. Well, I do prefer. For we, my friend, were so stupid, before you spoke, as to have an opinion concerning you and me, that each of us was one, but that we were not both that which each of us was—for we are not one, but two—so foolish were we. But now we have been taught by you that if we are both two, then each of us is inevitably two, and if each is one, then both are inevitably one; for it is impossible, by the continuous doctrine of reality according to Hippias, that it be otherwise, but what we both are, that each is, and what each is, both are. So now I have been convinced by you, and I hold this position. But first, Hippias, refresh my memory: Are you and I one, or are you two and I two?

HIPP. What do you mean, Socrates?

SOC. Just what I say; for I am afraid to speak plainly to you, because you are vexed with me, when you think you are talking sensibly; however, tell me further: Is not each of us one and affected in such a way as to be one?

HIPP. Certainly.

SOC. Then each of us, if one, would be an odd number; or do you not consider one an odd number?

HIPP. I do.

SOC. Then are we both an odd number, being two?

HIPP. That could not be, Socrates,

SOC. But we are both an even number, are we not?

HIPP. Certainly.

SOC. Then because we are both even, is each of us on that account even?

HIPP. No, surely not.

SOC. Then it is not absolutely inevitable, as you said just now, that what both are, each is, and what each is, both are.

HIPP. Not things of this sort, but such as I mentioned before.

SOC. That suffices, Hippias; for even this is welcome, since it appears that some things are so and some are not so. For I said, if you remember the beginning of this discussion, that pleasure through sight and through hearing were beautiful, not by that by which each of them was so affected as to be beautiful, but not both, nor both but not each, but by that by which both and each were so affected, because you conceded that both and each were beautiful. For this reason I thought that if both are beautiful they must be beautiful by that essence which belongs to both, but not by that which is lacking in each; and I still think so. But tell me, as in the beginning: If pleasure through sight and pleasure through hearing are both and each beautiful, does not that which makes them beautiful belong to both and to each?

HIPP. Certainly.

SOC. Is it, then, for this reason, because each is a pleasure and both are pleasures, that they would be beautiful? Or would all other pleasures be for this reason no less beautiful than they? For we saw, if you remember, that they were no less pleasures.

HIPP. Yes, I remember.

SOC. But for this reason, because these pleasures were through sight and hearing, it was said that they are beautiful.

HIPP. Yes, that is what was said.

SOC. See if what I say is true. For it was said, if my memory serves me, that *this* "pleasant" was beautiful, not *all* "pleasant," but that which is through sight and hearing.

HIPP. True.

SOC. Now this quality belongs to both, but not to each, does it not? For surely each of them, as was said before, is not through both senses, but both are through both, and each is not. Is that true?

HIPP. It is.

SOC. Then it is not by that which does not belong to each that each of them is beautiful; for "both" does not belong to each; so that it is possible, according to our hypothesis, to say that they both are beautiful, but not to say that each is so; or what shall we say? Is that not inevitable?

HIPP. It appears so.

SOC. Shall we say, then, that both are beautiful, but that each is not?

HIPP. What is to prevent?

SOC. This seems to me, my friend, to prevent, that there were some attributes thus belonging to individual things, which belonged, we thought, to each, if they belonged to both, and to both, if they belonged to each—I mean all those attributes which you specified. Am I right?

HIPP. Yes.

SOC. But those again which I specified did not; and among those were precisely "each" and "both." Is that so?

HIPP. It is.

SOC. To which group, then, Hippias, does the beautiful seem to you to belong? To the group of those that you mentioned? If I am strong and you also, are we both collectively strong, and if I am just and you also, are we both collectively just, and if both collectively, then each individually; so, too, if I am beautiful and you also, are we both collectively beautiful, and if both collectively, then each individually? Or is there nothing to prevent this, as in the case that when given things are both collectively even, they may perhaps individually be odd, or perhaps even, and again, when things are individually irrational quantities they may perhaps both collectively be rational, or perhaps irrational, and countless other cases which, you know, I said appeared before my mind? To which group do you assign the beautiful? Or have you the same view about it as I? For to me it seems great foolishness that we collectively are beautiful, but each of us is not so, or that each of us is so, but both are not, or anything else of that sort. Do you choose in this way, as I do, or in some other way?

HIPP. In this way, Socrates.

SOC. You choose well, Hippias, that we may be free from the need of further search; for if the beautiful is in this group, that which is pleasing through sight and hearing would no longer be the beautiful. For the expression "through sight and hearing" makes both collectively beautiful, but not each individually; and this was impossible, as you and I agree.

HIPP. Yes, we agree.

SOC. It is, then, impossible that the pleasant through sight and hearing be the beautiful, since in becoming beautiful it offers an impossibility.

HIPP. That is true.

SOC. "Then tell us again," he will say, "from the beginning, since you failed this time; what do you say that this 'beautiful,' belonging to both the pleasures, is, on account of which you honoured them before the rest and called them beautiful?" It seems to me, Hippias, inevitable that we say that these are the most harmless and the best of pleasures, both of them collectively and each of them individually; or have you anything else to suggest, by which they excel the rest?

HIPP. Not at all; for really they are the best.

SOC. "This, then," he will say, "you say is the beautiful, beneficial pleasure?" "It seems that we do," I shall say; and you?

HIPP. I also.

SOC. "Well, then," he will say, "beneficial is that which creates the good, but that which creates and that which is created were just now seen to be different, and our argument has come round to the earlier argument, has it not? For neither could the good be beautiful nor the beautiful good, if each of them is different from the other." "Absolutely true," we shall say, if we are reasonable; for it is inadmissable to disagree with him who says what is right.

HIPP. But now, Socrates, what do you think all this amounts to? It is mere scrapings and shavings of discourse, as I said a while ago, divided into bits; but that other ability is beautiful and of great worth, the ability to produce a discourse well and beautifully in a court of law or a council-house or before any other public body before which the discourse may be delivered, to convince the audience and to carry off, not the smallest, but the greatest of prizes, the salvation of oneself, one's property, and one's friends. For these things, therefore, one must strive, renouncing these petty arguments, that one may not, by busying oneself, as at present, with mere talk and nonsense, appear to be a fool.

SOC. My dear Hippias, you are blessed because you know the things a man ought to practise, and have, as you say, practised them satisfactorily. But I, as it seems, am possessed by some accursed fortune, so that I am always wandering and perplexed, and, exhibiting my perplexity to you wise men, am in turn reviled by you in speech whenever I exhibit it. For you say of me, what you are now saying, that I busy myself with silly little matters of no account; but when in turn I am convinced by you and say what you say, that it is by far the best thing to be able to produce a discourse well and beautifully and gain one's end in a court of law or in any other assemblage, I am called everything that is bad by some other men here and especially by that man who is continually refuting me; for he is a very near relative of mine and lives in the same house. So whenever I go home to my own house, and he hears me saying these things, he asks me if I am not ashamed that I have the face to talk about beautiful practices, when it is so plainly shown, to my confusion, that I do not even know what the beautiful itself is. "And yet how are you to know," he will say, "either who produced a discourse, or anything else whatsoever, beautifully, or not, when you are ignorant of the beautiful? And when you are in such a condition, do you think it is better for you to be alive than dead?" So it has come about, as I say, that I am abused and reviled by you and by him. But perhaps it is necessary to endure all this, for it is quite reasonable that I might be benefited by it. So I think, Hippias, that I have been benefited by conversation with both of you; for I think I know the meaning of the proverb: "beautiful things are difficult."

Eros; poetry as creation; creative men; absolute beauty and its experience

Symposium 201D–205C

SOCRATES. . . . She was[64] my instructress in the art of love, and I shall try to repeat to you what she said to me, beginning with the propositions on which Agathon and I are agreed; I will do the best I can do without any help. As you, Agathon, suggested, it is proper to speak first of the being and nature of Love,

[64] Following selections taken from *The Dialogues of Plato*, translated by Benjamin Jowett, 4th ed., 1953. By permission of the Clarendon Press, Oxford.

and then of his works. (I think it will be easiest for me if in recounting my conversation with the wise woman I follow its actual course of question and answer.) First I said to her in nearly the same words which he used to me, that Love was a mighty god, and likewise fair; and she proved to me, as I proved to him, that by my own showing Love was neither fair nor good. 'What do you mean, Diotima,' I said, 'is Love then evil and foul?' 'Hush,' she cried; 'must that be foul which is not fair?' 'Certainly,' I said. 'And is that which is not wise, ignorant? do you not see that there is a mean between wisdom and ignorance?' 'And what may that be?' I said. 'Right opinion,' she replied; 'which, as you know, being incapable of giving a reason, is not knowledge (for how can knowledge be devoid of reason?) nor again ignorance (for neither can ignorance attain the truth), but is clearly something which is a mean between ignorance and wisdom.' 'Quite true,' I replied. 'Do not then insist,' she said, 'that what is not fair is of necessity foul, or what is not good evil; or infer that because Love is not fair and good he is therefore foul and evil; for he is in a mean between them.' 'Well,' I said, 'Love is surely admitted by all to be a great god.' 'By those who know or by those who do not know?' 'By all.' 'And how, Socrates,' she said with a smile, 'can Love be acknowledged to be a great god by those who say that he is not a god at all?' 'And who are they?' I said. 'You and I are two of them,' she replied. 'How can that be?' I said. 'It is quite intelligible,' she replied; 'for you yourself would acknowledge that the gods are happy and fair—of course you would—would you dare to say that any god was not?' 'Certainly not,' I replied. 'And you mean by the happy, those who are the possessors of things good and things fair?' 'Yes.' 'And you admitted that Love, because he was in want, desires those good and fair things of which he is in want?' 'Yes, I did.' 'But how can he be a god who has no portion in what is good and fair?' 'Impossible.' 'Then you see that you also deny the divinity of Love.'

'What then is Love?' I asked; 'Is he mortal?' 'No.' 'What then?' 'As in the former instance, he is neither mortal nor immortal, but in a mean between the two.' 'What is he, Diotima?' 'He is a great spirit (δαίμων), and like all spirits he is intermediate between the divine and the mortal.' 'And what,' I said, 'is his power?' 'He interprets between gods and men, conveying and taking across to the gods the prayers and sacrifices of men, and to men the commands of the gods and the benefits they return; he is the mediator who spans the chasm which divides them, and therefore by him the universe is bound together, and through him the arts of the prophet and the priest, their sacrifices and mysteries and charms, and all prophecy and incantation, find their way. For God mingles not with man; but through Love all the intercourse and converse of gods with men, whether they be awake or asleep, is carried on. The wisdom which understands this is spiritual; all other wisdom, such as that of arts and handicrafts, is mean and vulgar. Now these spirits or intermediate powers are many and diverse, and one of them is Love.' 'And who,' I said, 'was his father, and who his mother?' 'The tale,' she said, 'will take time; nevertheless I will tell you. On the day when Aphrodite was born there was a feast of all the gods, among them the god Poros or Plenty, who is the son of Metis or Sagacity. When the feast was over, Penia or Poverty, as the manner is on such occasions, came about the doors to beg. Now Plenty, who was the worse for nectar (there was no wine in those days), went into the garden of Zeus and fell into a heavy sleep; and Poverty considering that for her there was no plenty, plotted to have a child by him, and accordingly she lay down at his side and conceived Love, who partly because he is naturally a lover of the beautiful, and because Aphrodite is herself beautiful, and also because he was begotten during her birthday feast, is her follower and attendant. And as his parentage is, so also are his fortunes. In the first place he is always poor, and anything but tender and fair, as the many imagine him; and he is rough and squalid, and has no shoes, nor a house to dwell in; on the bare earth exposed he lies under the open heaven, in the streets, or at the doors of houses, taking his rest; and like his mother he is always in distress. Like his father too, whom he also partly resembles, he is always plotting against the fair and good; he is bold, enterprising, strong, a mighty hunter, always weaving some intrigue or other, keen in the pursuit of wisdom, fertile in resources; a philosopher at all times, terrible as an enchanter, sorcerer, sophist. He is by nature neither mortal nor immortal, but alive and flourishing at one moment when he is in plenty, and dead at another moment in the same day, and again alive by reason of his father's nature. But that which is always flowing in is always flowing out, and so he is never in want and never in wealth; and, further, he is in a mean between ignorance and knowledge. The truth of the matter is this: No god is a philosopher or seeker after wisdom, for he is wise already; nor does any man who is wise seek after wisdom. Neither do the ignorant seek after wisdom; for herein is the evil of ignorance, that he who is neither a man of honour nor wise is nevertheless satisfied with himself: there is no desire when there is no feeling of want.' 'But who then, Diotima,' I said, 'are the lovers of wisdom, if they are neither the wise nor the foolish?' 'A child may answer that question,' she replied; 'they are those who are in a mean between the two; Love is one of them. For wisdom is a most beautiful thing, and Love is of the beautiful; and therefore Love is also a philosopher or lover of wisdom, and being a lover of wisdom is in a mean between the wise and the ignorant. And of this, too, his birth is the cause; for his father is wealthy and wise, and his mother poor and foolish. Such, my dear Socrates, is the nature of the spirit Love. The error in your conception of him was very natural; from what you say yourself, I infer that it arose because you thought that Love is that which is loved, not that which loves; and for that reason, I think, Love appeared to you supremely beautiful. For the beloved is the truly beautiful, and delicate, and perfect, and blessed; but the active principle of love is of another nature, and is such as I have described.'

I said: 'O thou stranger woman, thou sayest well; but, assuming Love to be such as you say, what is the use of him to men?' 'That, Socrates,' she replied, 'I will attempt to unfold: of his nature and birth I have already spoken; and you acknowledge that love is of the beautiful. But someone will say: What does it consist in, Socrates and Diotima?—or rather let me put the question more clearly, and ask: When a man loves the beautiful, what does his love desire?' I answered her 'That the beautiful may be his.' 'Still,' she said, 'the answer suggests a further question: What is given by the possession of beauty?' 'To what you have asked,' I replied, 'I have no answer ready.' 'Then,' she said, 'let me put the word "good" in the place of the beautiful, and repeat the question once more: If he who loves loves the good, what is it then that he loves?' 'The possession of the good.' 'And what does he gain who possesses the good?' 'Happiness,' I replied; 'there is less difficulty in answering that question.' 'Yes,' she said, 'the happy are made happy by the acquisition of good things. Nor is there any need to ask why a man desires happiness; the answer is already final.' 'You are right,' I said. 'And is this wish and this desire common to all? and do all men always desire their own good, or only some men?—what say you?' 'All men,' I replied; 'the desire is common to all.' 'Why, then,' she rejoined, 'are not all men, Socrates, said to love, but only some of them? whereas you say that all men are always loving the same things.' 'I myself wonder,' I said, 'why this is.' 'There is nothing to wonder at,' she replied; 'the reason is that one part of love is separated off and receives the name of the whole, but the other parts have other names.' 'Give an illustration,' I said. She answered me as follows: There is creative activity which, as you know, is complex and manifold. All that causes the passage of non-being into being is a "poesy" or creation, and the processes of all art are creative; and the masters of arts are all poets or creators.' 'Very true.' 'Still,' she said, 'you know that they are not called poets, but have other names; only that one portion of creative activity which is separated off from the rest, and is concerned with music and metre, is called by the name of the whole and is termed poetry, and they who possess poetry in this sense of the word are called poets.' . . . .

——208E–212A . . . 'Those who are pregnant in the body only, betake themselves to women and beget children—this is the character of their love; their offspring, as they hope, will preserve their memory and give them the blessedness and immortality which they desire for all future time. But souls which are pregnant—for there certainly are men who are more creative in their souls than in their bodies, creative of that which is proper for the soul to conceive and bring forth: and if you ask me what are these conceptions, I answer, wisdom, and virtue in general—among such souls are all creative poets and all artists who are deserving of the name inventor. But the greatest and fairest sort of wisdom by far is that which is concerned with the ordering of states and families, and which is called temperance and justice. And he who in youth has the seed of these implanted in his soul, when he grows up and comes to maturity desires to beget and generate. He wanders about seeking beauty that he may get offspring—for from deformity he will beget nothing—and naturally embraces the beautiful rather than the deformed body; above all, when he finds a fair and noble and well-nurtured soul, he embraces the two in one person, and to such a one he is full of speech about virtue and the nature and pursuits of a good man, and he tries to educate him. At the touch and in the society of the beautiful which is ever present to his memory, even when absent, he brings forth that which he had conceived long before, and in company with him tends that which he brings forth; and they are married by a far nearer tie and have a closer friendship than those who beget mortal children, for the children who are their common offspring are fairer and more immortal. Who, when he thinks of Homer and Hesiod and other great poets, would not rather have their children than ordinary human ones? Who would not emulate them in the creation of children such as theirs, which have preserved their memory and given them everlasting glory? Or who would not have such children as Lycurgus left behind him to be the saviours, not only of Lacedaemon, but of Hellas, as one may say? There is Solon, too, who is the revered father of Athenian laws; and many others there are in many other places, both among Hellenes and barbarians, who have given to the world many noble works, and have been the parents of virtue of every kind; and many temples have been raised in their honour for the sake of children such as theirs; which were never raised in honour of anyone, for the sake of his mortal children.

'These are the lesser mysteries of love, into which even you, Socrates, may enter; to the greater and more hidden ones which are the crown of these, and to which, if you pursue them in a right spirit, they will lead, I know not whether you will be able to attain. But I will do my utmost to inform you, and do you follow if you can. For he who would proceed aright in this matter should begin in youth to seek the company of corporeal beauty; and first, if he be guided by his instructor aright, to love one beautiful body only—out of that he should create fair thoughts; and soon he will of himself perceive that the beauty of one body is akin to the beauty of another and then if beauty of form in general is his pursuit, how foolish would he be not to recognize that the beauty in every body is one and the same! And when he perceives this he will abate his violent love of the one, which he will despise and deem a small thing, and will become a steadfast lover of all beautiful bodies. In the next stage he will consider that the beauty of the soul is more precious than the beauty of the outward form; so that if a virtuous soul have but a little comeliness, he will be content to love and tend him, and will search out and bring to the birth thoughts which may improve the young, until he is compelled next to contemplate and see the beauty in institutions and laws, and to understand that the beauty of them all is of one family, and that personal beauty is a trifle; and after institutions his guide will lead him on to the sciences, in order that, beholding the wide region already occupied by beauty, he may cease to be like a servant in love with one beauty only, that of a particular youth or man or institution, himself a slave mean and narrow-minded; but drawing towards and contemplating the vast sea of beauty, he will create many fair and noble thoughts and discourses in boundless love of wisdom, until on that shore he grows and waxes strong, and at last the vision is revealed to him of a single science, which is the science of beauty everywhere. To this I will proceed; please to give me your very best attention:

'He who has been instructed thus far in the things of love, and who has learned to see the beautiful in due order and succession, when he comes toward the end will suddenly perceive a nature of wondrous beauty (and this, Socrates, is the final cause of all our former toils)—a nature which in the first place is everlasting, knowing not birth or death, growth or decay; secondly, not fair in one point of view and foul in another, or at one time or in one relation or at one place fair, at another time or in another relation or at another place foul, as if fair to some and foul to others, or in the likeness of a face or hands or any other part of the bodily frame, or in any form of speech or knowledge, or existing in any individual being, as for example, in a living creature, whether in heaven, or in earth, or anywhere else; but beauty absolute, separate, simple, and everlasting, which is imparted to the ever growing and perishing beauties of all other beautiful things, without itself suffering diminution, or increase, or any change. He who, ascending from these earthly things under the influence of true love, begins to perceive that beauty, is not far from the end. And the true order of going, or being led by another, to the things of love, is to begin from the beauties of earth and mount upwards for the sake of that other beauty, using these as steps only, and from one going on to two, and from two to all fair bodily forms, and from fair bodily forms to fair practices, and from fair practices to fair sciences, until from fair sciences he arrives at the science of which I have spoken, the science which has no other object than absolute beauty, and at last knows that which is beautiful by itself alone. This, my dear Socrates,' said the stranger of Mantinea, 'is that life above all others which man should live, in the contemplation of beauty absolute; a beauty which if you once beheld, you would see not to be after the measure of gold, and garments, and fair boys and youths, whose presence now entrances you; and you and many a one would be content to live seeing them only and conversing with them without meat or drink, if that were possible—you only want to look at them and to be with them. But what if a man had eyes to see the true beauty—the divine beauty, I mean, pure and clear and unalloyed, not infected with the pollutions of the flesh and all the colours and vanities of mortal life—thither looking, and holding converse with the true beauty simple and divine? Remember how in that communion only, beholding beauty with that by which it can be beheld, he will be enabled to bring forth, not images of beauty, but realities (for he has hold not of an image but of a reality), and bringing forth and nourishing true virtue will properly become the friend of God and be immortal, if mortal man may. Would that be an ignoble life?' . . . .

The madness that inspires frenzy; the world of ideas; the experience of true beauty Phaedrus 243E–251A

SOCRATES. Know then, fair youth, that the former discourse was the word of Phaedrus, the son of Pythocles, of the deme Myrrhina. And this which I am about to utter is the recantation of Stesichorus the son of Euphemus, who comes from the town of Himera, and is to the following effect: 'False was that word of mine' that the beloved ought to accept the non-lover when he might have the lover, because the one is sane, and the other mad. It might be so if madness were simply an evil; but there is also a madness which is a divine gift, and the source of the chiefest blessings granted to men. For prophecy is a madness, and the prophetess at Delphi and the priestesses at Dodona when out of their senses have conferred great benefits on Hellas, both in public and private life, but when in their senses few or none. And I might also tell you how the Sibyl and other inspired persons have given to many an one many an intimation of the future which has saved them from falling. But it would be tedious to speak of what every one knows.

There will be more reason in appealing to the ancient inventors of names,[65] who would never have connected prophecy (μαντική), which foretells the future and is the noblest of arts, with madness (μανική), or called them both by the same name, if they had deemed madness to be a disgrace or dishonour;—they must have thought that there was an inspired madness which was a noble thing; for the two words, μαντική and μανική, are really the same, and the letter τ is only a modern and tasteless insertion. And this is confirmed by the name which was given by them to the rational investigation of futurity, whether made by the help of birds or other signs—this, for as much as it is an art which supplies from the reasoning faculty mind (νοῦς) and information (ἱστορία) to human thought (οἴησις), they originally termed οἰονοιστική , but the word has been lately altered and made sonorous by the modern introduction of the letter Omega (οἰονοιστική and οἰωνιστική), and in proportion as prophecy (μαντική) is more perfect and august than augury, both in name and fact, in the same proportion, as the ancients testify, is madness superior to a sane mind (σωφροσύνη), for the one is only of human, but the other of divine, origin. Again, where plagues and mightiest woes have bred in certain families, owing to some ancient blood-guiltiness, there madness, inspiring and taking possession of those whom destiny has appointed, has found deliverance, having recourse to prayers and religious rites. And learning thence the use of purifications and mysteries, it has sheltered from evil, future as well as present, the man who has some part in this gift, and has afforded a release from his present calamity to one who is truly possessed, and duly out of his mind. The third kind is the madness of those who are possessed by the Muses; which taking hold of a delicate and virgin soul, and there inspiring frenzy, awakens lyrical and all other numbers; with these adorning the myriad actions of ancient heroes for the instruction of posterity. But he who, having no touch of the Muses' madness in his soul, comes to the door and thinks that he will get into the temple by the help of art—he, I say, and his poetry are not admitted; the sane man disappears and is nowhere when he enters into rivalry with the madman.

I might tell of many other noble deeds which have sprung from inspired madness. And therefore, let not the mere thought of this frighten

[65] Cf. *Crat.* 388 foll.

us, and let us not be scared and confused by an argument which says that the temperate friend is to be chosen rather than the inspired, but let him further show that love is not sent by the gods for any good to lover or beloved; if he can do so we will allow him to carry off the palm. And we, on our part, must prove in answer to him that the madness of love is the greatest of heaven's blessings, and the proof shall be one which the wise will receive, and the witling disbelieve. But first of all, let us view the affections and actions of the soul divine and human, and try to ascertain the truth about them. The beginning of our proof is as follows:—

The soul through all her being is immortal, for that which is ever in motion is immortal; but that which moves another and is moved by another, in ceasing to move ceases also to live. Only the self-moving, since it cannot depart from itself, never ceases to move, and is the fountain and beginning of motion to all that moves besides. Now, the beginning is unbegotten, for that which is begotten must have a beginning; but this itself cannot be begotten of anything, for if it were dependent upon something, then the begotten would not come from a *beginning*. But since it is unbegotten, it must also be indestructible. For surely if a beginning were destroyed, then it could neither come into being itself from any source, nor serve as the beginning of other things, if it be true that all things must have a beginning. Thus it is proved that the self-moving is the beginning of motion; and this can neither be destroyed nor begotten, else the whole heavens and all creation would collapse and stand still, and, lacking all power of motion, never again have birth. But whereas the self-moving is proved to be immortal, he who affirms that this is the very meaning and essence of the soul will not be put to confusion. For every body which is moved from without is soul-less, but that which is self-moved from within is animate, and our usage makes it plain what is the nature of the soul. But if this be true, that the soul is identical with the self-moving, it must follow of necessity that the soul is unbegotten and immortal. Enough of her immortality: let us pass to the description of her form.

To show her true nature would be a theme of large and more than mortal discourse, but an image of it may be given in a briefer discourse within the scope of man; in this way, then, let us speak. Let the soul be compared to a pair of winged horses and charioteer joined in natural union. Now the horses and the charioteers of the gods are all of them noble and of noble descent, but those of other races are mixed. First, you must know that the human charioteeer drives a pair; and next, that one of his horses is noble and of noble breed, and the other is ignoble and of ignoble breed; so that the management of the human chariot cannot but be a difficult and anxious task. I will endeavour to explain to you in what way the mortal differs from the immortal creature. The soul in her totality has the care of inanimate being everywhere, and traverses the whole heaven in divers forms appearing;—when perfect and fully winged she soars upward, and orders the whole world; whereas the imperfect soul, losing her wings and drooping in her flight at last settles on the solid ground—there, finding a home, she receives an earthly frame which appears to be self-moved, but is really moved by her power; and this composition of soul and body is called a living and mortal creature. For immortal no such union can be reasonably believed to be; although fancy, not having seen nor surely known the nature of God, may imagine an immortal creature having both a body and also a soul which are united throughout all time. Let that, however, be as God wills, and be spoken of acceptably to him. And now let us ask the reason why the soul loses her wings!

The wing is the corporeal element which is most akin to the divine, and which by nature tends to soar aloft and carry that which gravitates downwards into the upper region, which is the habitation of the gods. The divine is beauty, wisdom, goodness, and the like; and by these the wing of the soul is nourished, and grows apace; but when fed upon evil and foulness and the opposite of good, wastes and falls away. Zeus, the mighty lord, holding the reins of a winged chariot, leads the way in heaven, ordering all and taking care of all; and there follows him the array of gods and demigods, marshalled in eleven bands; Hestia alone abides at home in the house of heaven; of the rest they who are reckoned among the princely twelve march in their appointed order. They see many blessed sights in the inner heaven, and there are many ways to and fro, along which the blessed gods are passing, every one doing his own work; he may follow who will and can, for jealousy has no place in the celestial choir. But when they go to banquet and festival, then they move up the steep to the top of the vault of heaven. The chariots of the gods in even poise, obeying the rein, glide rapidly; but the others labour, for the vicious steed goes heavily, weighing down the charioteer to the earth when his steed has not been thoroughly trained:—and this is the hour of agony and extremest conflict for the soul. For the immortals, when they are at the end of their course, go forth and stand upon the outside of heaven; its revolution carries them round, and they behold the things beyond. But of the heaven which is above the heavens, what earthly poet ever did or ever will sing worthily? It is such as I will describe; for I must dare to speak the truth, when truth is my theme. There abides the very being with which true knowledge is concerned; the colourless, formless, intangible essence, visible only to mind, the pilot of the soul. The divine intelligence, being nurtured upon mind and pure knowledge, and the intelligence of every soul which is capable of receiving the food proper to it, rejoices at beholding reality once more, after so long a time, and gazing upon truth, is replenished and made glad, until the revolution of the world brings her round again to the same place. In the revolution she beholds justice, and temperance, and knowledge absolute, not that to which becoming belongs, nor that which is found, in varying forms, in one or other of those regions which we men call *real*, but real knowledge really present where true being is. And beholding the other true existences in like manner, and feasting upon them, she passes down into the interior of the heavens and returns home; and there the charioteer putting up his horses at the stall, gives them ambrosia to eat and nectar to drink.

Such is the life of the gods; but of other souls, that which follows God best and is likest to him lifts the head of the charioteer into the outer world, and is carried round in the revolution, troubled indeed by the steeds, and with difficulty beholding true being; while another only rises and falls, and sees, and again fails to see by reason of the unruliness of the steeds. The rest of the souls are also longing after the upper world and they all follow, but not being strong enough they are carried round below the surface, plunging, treading on one another, each striving to be first; and there is confusion and perspiration and the extremity of effort; and many of them are lamed or have their wings broken through the ill driving of the charioteers; and all of them after a fruitless toil, not having attained to the mysteries of true being, go away, and feed upon opinion [or appearance]. The reason why the souls exhibit this exceeding eagerness to behold the Plain of Truth is that pasturage is found there, which is suited to the highest part of the soul; and the wing on which the soul soars is nourished with this. And there is a law of Destiny, that the soul which attains any vision of truth in company with a god is preserved from harm until the next period, and if attaining always is always unharmed. But when she is unable to follow, and fails to behold the truth, and through some ill-hap sinks beneath the double load of forgetfulness and vice, and her wings fall from her and she drops to the ground, then the law ordains that this soul shall at her first birth pass, not into any other animal, but only into man; and the soul which has seen most of truth shall be placed in the seed from which a philosopher, or artist, or some musical and loving nature will spring; that which has seen truth in the second degree shall be some righteous king or warrior chief; the soul which is of the third class shall be a politician, or economist, or trader; the fourth shall be a lover of gymnastic toils, or a physician; the fifth shall lead the life of a prophet or hierophant; to the sixth the character of a poet or some other imitative artist will be assigned; to the seventh the life of an artisan or husbandman; to the eigth that of a sophist or demagogue; to the ninth that of a tyrant;—all these are states of probation, in which he who does righteously improves, and he who does unrighteously deteriorates, his lot.

Ten thousand years must elapse before the soul of each one can return to the place from whence she came, for she cannot grow her wings less, save only the soul of a philosopher, guileless and true, or of a lover, who has been guided by philosophy. And these when the third period comes round, if they have chosen this life three times in succession, have wings given them, and go away at the end of three thousand years. But the others[66] receive judgment when they have completed their first life, and after the judgment they go, some of them to the houses of correction which are under the earth, and are punished; others to some place in heaven whither they are lightly borne by justice, and there they live in a manner worthy of the life which they led here when in the form of men. And in the thousandth year, both arrive at a place where they must draw lots and choose their second life, and they may take any which they please. And now the soul of a man may pass into the life of a beast, or that which has once been a man return again from the beast into human form. But the soul which has never seen the truth will not pass into the human form. For a man must have intelligence by what is called the Idea, a unity gathered[67] together by reason from the many particulars of sense. This is the recollection of those things which our soul once saw while following God—when regardless of that which we now call being she raised her head up towards the true being. And therefore the mind of the philosopher alone has wings; and this is just, for he is always, according to the measure of his abilities, clinging in recollection to those things in which God abides, and in beholding which He is what He is. And he who employs aright these memories is ever being initiated into perfect mysteries and alone becomes truly perfect. But, as he forgets earthly interests and is rapt in the divine, the vulgar deem him mad, and rebuke him; they do not see that he is inspired.

Thus far I have been speaking of the fourth and the last kind of madness, which is imputed to him who, when he sees the beauty of earth, is transported with the recollection of the true beauty; he would like to fly away, but he cannot; he is like a bird fluttering and looking upward and careless of the world below; and he is therefore thought to be mad. And I have shown this of all inspirations to be the noblest and highest and the offspring of the highest to him who has or shares in it, and that he who loves the beautiful is called a lover because he partakes of it. For, as has been already said, every soul of man has in the way of nature beheld true being; this was the condition of her passing into the form of man. But all souls do not easily recall the things of the other world; they may have seen them for a short

[66] The philosopher alone is not subject to judgment (κρίσιϛ), for he has never lost the vision of truth.

[67] [Plato proposes here an etymology of the word ξυνιέναι, understand.]

time only, or they may have been unfortunate in their earthly lot, and, having had their hearts turned to unrighteousness through some corrupting influence, they may have lost the memory of the holy things which once they saw. Few only retain an adequate remembrance of them; and they, when they behold here any image of that other world, are rapt in amazement; but they are ignorant of what this rapture means, because they do not clearly perceive. For there is no radiance in our earthly copies of justice or temperance or those other things which are precious to souls: they are seen through a glass dimly; and there are few who, going to the images, behold in them the realities, and these only with difficulty. But beauty could be seen, brightly shining, by all who were with that happy band,—we philosophers following in the train of Zeus, others in company with other gods; at which time we beheld the beatific vision and were initiated into a mystery which may be truly called most blessed, celebrated by us in our state of innocence, before we had any experience of evils to come, when we were admitted to the sight of apparitions innocent and simple and calm and happy, which we beheld shining in pure light, pure ourselves and not yet enshrined in that living tomb which we carry about, now that we are imprisoned in the body, like an oyster in his shell. Let me linger over the memory of scenes which have passed away.

But of beauty, I repeat that we saw her there shining in company with the celestial forms; and coming to earth we find her here too, shining in clearness through the clearest aperture of sense. For sight is the most piercing of our bodily senses; though not by that is wisdom seen; her loveliness would have been transporting if there had been a visible image of her, and the other ideas, if they had visible counterparts, would be equally lovely. But this is the privilege of beauty, that being the loveliest she is also the most palpable to sight. Now he who is not newly initiated or who has become corrupted, does not easily rise out of this world to the sight of true beauty in the other, when he contemplates her earthly namesake, and instead of being awed at the sight of her, he is given over to pleasure, and like a brutish beast he rushes on to enjoy and beget; he consorts with wantonness, and is not afraid or ashamed of pursuing pleasure in violation of nature. But he whose initiation is recent, and who has been the spectator of many glories in the other world, is amazed when he sees anyone having a godlike face or form, which is the expression of divine beauty . . . .

The man inspired is out of his wits and cannot judge of the vision he sees or the words he utters

Timaeus 71E

. . . No man, when in his wits, attains prophetic truth and inspiration; but when he receives the inspired word, either his intelligence is enthralled in sleep, or he is demented by some distemper or possession. And he who would understand what he remembers to have been said, whether in a dream or when he was awake, by the prophetic and inspired nature, or would determine by reason the meaning of the apparitions which he has seen, and what indications they afford to this man or that, of past, present or future good and evil, must first recover his wits. But, while he continues demented, he cannot judge of the visions which he sees or the words which he utters. . . . And for this reason it is customary to appoint interpreters to be judges of the true inspiration . . . .

The Demiurge makes the cosmos; the pattern and the material; the making of man

Timaeus 27A–31B

CRITIAS. Let me proceed to explain to you, Socrates, the order in which we have arranged our entertainment. Our intention is, that Timaeus, who is the most of an astronomer amongst us, and has made the nature of the universe his special study, should speak first, beginning with the generation of the world and going down to the creation of man; next, I am to receive the men whom he has created, and of whom some will have profited by the excellent education which you have given them; and then, in accordance with the tale of Solon, and equally with his law, we will bring them into court and make them citizens, as if they were those very Athenians whom the sacred Egyptian record has recovered from oblivion, and thenceforward we will speak of them as Athenians and fellow citizens.

SOCRATES. I see that I shall receive in my turn a perfect and splendid feast of reason. And now, Timaeus, you, I suppose, should speak next, after duly calling upon the Gods.

TIMAEUS. All men, Socrates, who have any degree of right feeling, at the beginning of every enterprise, whether small or great, always call upon God. And we, too, who are going to discourse of the nature of the universe, how created or how existing without creation, if we be not altogether out of our wits, must invoke the aid of Gods and Goddesses and pray that our words may be above all acceptable to them and in consequence to ourselves. Let this, then, be our invocation of the Gods, to which I add an exhortation of myself to speak in such manner as will be most intelligible to you, and will most accord with my own intent.

First then, in my judgment, we must make a distinction and ask, What is that which always is and has no becoming; and what is that which is always becoming and never is? That which is apprehended by intelligence and reason is always in the same state; but that which is conceived by opinion with the help of sensation and without reason, is always in a process of becoming and perishing and never really is. Now everything that becomes or is created must of necessity be created by some cause, for without a cause nothing can be created. The work of the creator, whenever he looks to the unchangeable and fashions the form and nature of his work after an unchangeable pattern, must necessarily be made fair and perfect; but when he looks to the created only, and uses a created pattern, it is not fair or perfect. Was the heaven then or the world, whether called by this or by any other more appropriate name—assuming the name, I am asking a question which has to be asked at the beginning of an inquiry about anything—was the world, I say, always in existence and without beginning? or created, and had it a beginning? Created, I reply, being visible and tangible and having a body, and therefore sensible; and all sensible things are apprehended by opinion and sense and are in a process of creation and created. Now that which is created must, as we affirm, of necessity be created by a cause. But the father and maker af all this universe is past finding out; and even if we found him, to tell of him to all men would be impossible. This question, however, we must ask about the world: Which of the patterns had the artificer in view when he made it,—the pattern of the unchangeable, or of that which is created? If the world be indeed fair and the artificer good, it is manifest that he must have looked to that which is eternal; but if what cannot be said without blasphemy is true, then to the created pattern. Everyone will see that he must have looked to the eternal; for the world is the fairest of creations and he is the best of causes. And having been created in this way, the world has been framed in the likeness of that which is apprehended by reason and mind and is unchangeable, and must therefore of necessity, if this is admitted, be a copy of something. Now it is all-important that the beginning of everything should be according to nature. And in speaking of the copy and the original we may assume that the words are akin to the matter which they describe; when they relate to the lasting and permanent and intelligible, they ought to be lasting and unalterable, and, as far as their nature allows, irrefutable and invincible—nothing less. But when they express only the copy or likeness and not the eternal things themselves, they need only be likely and analogous to the former words: as being is to becoming, so is truth to belief. If then, Socrates, amid the many opinions about the gods and the generation of the universe, we are not able to give notions which are altogether and in every respect exact and consistent with one another, do not be surprised. Enough, if we adduce probabilities as likely as any others; for we must remember that I who am the speaker, and you who are the judges, are only mortal men, and we ought to accept the tale which is probable and inquire no further.

SOC. Excellent, Timaeus; and we will do precisely as you bid us. The prelude is charming, and is already accepted by us—may we beg of you to proceed to the strain?

TIM. Let me tell you then why the creator made this world of generation. He was good, and the good can never have any jealousy of anything. And being free from jealousy, he desired that all things should be as like himself as they could be. This is in the truest sense the origin of creation and of the world, as we shall do well in believing on the testimony of wise men: God desired that all things should be good and nothing bad, so far as this was attainable. Wherefore also finding the whole visible sphere not at rest, but moving in an irregular and disorderly fashion, out of disorder he brought order, considering that this was in every way better than the other. Now the deeds of the best could never be or have been other than the fairest; and the creator, reflecting on the things which are by nature visible, found that no unintelligent creature taken as a whole could ever be fairer than the intelligent taken as a whole; and again that intelligence could not be present in anything which was devoid of soul. For which reason, when he was framing the universe, he put intelligence in soul, and soul in body, that he might be the creator of a work which was by nature fairest and best. On this wise, using the language of probability, we may say that the world came into being—a living creature truly endowed with soul and intelligence by the providence of God.

This being supposed, let us proceed to the next stage: In the likeness of what animal did the Creator make the world? It would be an unworthy thing to liken it to any nature which exists as a part only; for nothing can be beautiful which is like any imperfect thing; but let us suppose the world to be the very image of that whole of which all other animals both individually and in their tribes are portions. For the original of the universe contains in itself all intelligible beings, just as this world comprehends us and all other visible creatures. For the Deity, intending to make this world like the fairest and most perfect of intelligible beings, framed one visible animal comprehending within itself all other animals of a kindred nature. Are we right in saying that there is one world, or that they are many and infinite? There must be one only, if the created copy is to accord with the original. For that which includes all other intelligible creatures cannot have a second or companion; in that case there would be need of another living being which would include both, and of which they would be parts, and the likeness would be truly said to resemble not them, but that other which included them. In order then that the world might be solitary, like the perfect animal, the creator made not two worlds or an infinite number of them; but there is and ever will be one only-begotten and created heaven . . . .

——32C. Now the creation took up the whole of each of the four elements; for the Creator compounded the world out of all the fire and all the water and all the air and all the earth, leaving no part of any of them nor any power of them outside. His intention was, in the first place, that the animal should be as far as possible a perfect whole and of perfect parts: secondly, that it should be one, leaving no remnants out of which another such world might be created: and also that it should be free from old age and unaffected by disease. Considering that if heat and cold and other powerful forces surround composite bodies and attack them from without, they decompose them before their time, and by bringing diseases and old age upon them, make them waste away —for this cause and on these grounds he made the world one whole, having every part entire, and being therefore perfect and not liable to old age and disease. And he gave to the world the figure which was suitable and also natural. Now to the animal which was to comprehend all animals, that figure would be suitable which comprehends within itself all other figures. Wherefore he made the world in the form of a globe, round as from a lathe, having its extremes in every direction equidistant from the centre, the most perfect and the most like itself of all figures; for he considered that the like is infinitely fairer than the unlike . . . .

——44D. First, then, the gods, imitating the spherical shape of the universe, enclosed the two divine courses in a spherical body, that, namely, which we now term the head, being the most divine part of us and the lord of all that is in us: to this the gods, when they put together the body, gave all the other members to be servants, considering that it must partake of every sort of motion. In order then that it might not tumble about among the high and deep places of the earth, but might be able to get over the one and out of the other, they provided the body to be its vehicle and means of locomotion; which consequently had length and was furnished with four limbs extended and flexible; these God contrived to be instruments of locomotion with which it might take hold and find support, and so be able to pass through all places, carrying on high the dwelling-place of the most sacred and divine part of us . . . .

——51E. Wherefore also we must acknowledge that one kind of being is the form which is always the same, uncreated and indestructable, never receiving anything into itself from without, nor itself going out to any other, but invisible and imperceptible by any sense, and of which the contemplation is granted to intelligence only. And there is another nature of the same name with it, and like to it, perceived by sense, created, always in motion, becoming in place and again vanishing out of place, which is apprehended by opinion jointly with sense. And there is a third nature, which is space, and is eternal, and admits not of destruction and provides a home for all created things . . . .

Pure pleasure and the mathematical arts

The claims of pleasure and wisdom to be the good; the true pleasures got in the experience of non-imitative, mathematical forms

Philebus 11

SOCRATES. Observe, Protarchus, the nature of the position which you are now going to take from Philebus, and what the other position is which I maintain, and which, if you do not approve of it, is to be controverted by you. Shall you and I sum up the two sides?

PROTARCHUS. By all means.

SOC. Philebus was saying that enjoyment and pleasure and delight, and the class of feelings akin to them, are a good to every living being, whereas I contend, that not these, but wisdom and intelligence and memory, and their kindred, right opinion and true reasoning, are better and more desirable than pleasure for all who are able to partake of them, and that to all such who are or ever will be, the possession of them is the most advantageous thing in the world. Have I not given, Philebus, a fair statement of the two sides of the argument?

PHILEBUS. Nothing could be fairer, Socrates.

SOC. And do you, Protarchus, accept the position which is assigned to you?

PRO. I cannot do otherwise, since our fair Philebus has left the field.

SOC. Surely the truth about these matters ought, by all means, to be ascertained.

PRO. Certainly.

SOC. Shall we further agree—

PRO. To what?

SOC. That you and I must now try to indicate some state and disposition of the soul which has the property of making all men happy.

PRO. Yes, by all means.

SOC. And you say that pleasure, and I say that wisdom, is such a state?

PRO. True.

SOC. And what if there be a third state, which is better than either? Then both of us are vanquished—are we not? But if this life, which can be relied upon to make men happy, turns out to be more akin to pleasure than to wisdom, the life of pleasure may still have the advantage over the life of wisdom.

PRO. True. . . .

——51B. PRO. Then what pleasures, Socrates, should we be right in conceiving to be true?

SOC. True pleasures are those which are given by beauty of colour and form, and most of those which arise from smells; those of sound, again, and in general those of which the want is painless and unconscious, and of which the fruition is palpable to sense and pleasant and unalloyed with pain.

PRO. Once more, Socrates, I must ask what you mean.

SOC. My meaning is certainly not obvious, and I will endeavour to be plainer. I do not mean by beauty of form such beauty as that of animals or pictures, which the many would suppose to be my meaning; but, says the argument, understand me to mean straight lines and circles, and the plane or solid figures which are formed out of them by turning-lathes and rulers and measurers of angles; for these I affirm to be not only relatively beautiful, like other things, but they are eternally and absolutely beautiful, and they have peculiar pleasures, quite unlike the pleasures of scratching. And there are colours which are of the same character, and have similar pleasures; now do you understand my meaning?

PRO. I am trying to understand, Socrates, and I hope that you will try to make your meaning clearer.

SOC. When sounds are smooth and clear, and have a single pure tone, then I mean to say that they are not relatively but absolutely beautiful, and have natural pleasures of the same character.

PRO. Yes, there are such pleasures.

SOC. The pleasures of smell are of a less ethereal sort, but in having no necessary admixture of pain, in the manner in which the enjoyment is felt, and the subject which feels it, in all this I deem them analogous to the others. Here then are two kinds of our unmixed pleasures. . . .

The most beautiful of the four most beautiful bodies which are unlike one another

Timaeus 53E–54B

SOCRATES. And next we have to determine what are the four most beautiful bodies which could be formed, unlike one another, yet in some instances capable of resolution into one another; for having discovered thus much, we shall know the true origin of earth and fire and of the proportionate and intermediate elements. For we shall not be willing to allow that there are any distinct kinds of visible bodies fairer than these. Wherefore we must endeavour to construct the four forms of bodies which excel in beauty, and secure the right to say that we have sufficiently apprehended their nature. Now of the two triangles, the isosceles has one form only; the scalene or unequal-sided has an infinite number. Of the infinite forms we must again select the most beautiful, if we are to proceed in due order, and anyone who can point out a more beautiful form than ours for the construction of these bodies shall carry off the palm, not as an enemy, but as a friend. Now, the one which we maintain to be the most beautiful of all the many triangles (and we need not speak of the others) is that of which the double forms a third triangle which is equilateral; the reason of this would be long to tell; he who disproves what we are saying, and shows that we are mistaken, may claim a friendly victory. . . .

Art and education
The exile of the poet: The modes of music

Republic III 398A–399C

. . . And therefore when any one of these pantomimic gentlemen, who are so clever that they can imitate anything, comes to us and makes a proposal to exhibit himself and his poetry, we will fall down and worship him as a sacred, marvellous and delightful being; but we must also inform him that in our State such as he are not permitted to exist; the law will not allow them. And so when we have anointed him with myrrh, and set a garland of wool upon his head, we shall send him away to another city. For we mean to employ for our souls' health the rougher and severer poet or story-teller, who will imitate the style of the virtuous only, and will follow those models which we prescribed at first when we began the education of our soldiers.

We certainly will, he said, if we have the power.

Then now, my friend, I said, that part of music or literary education which relates to the story or myth may be considered to be finished; for the matter and manner have both been discussed.

I think so too, he said.

Next in order will follow melody and song.

That is obvious.

Everyone now would be able to discover what we ought to say about them, if we are to be consistent with ourselves.

I fear, said Glaucon, laughing, that the word 'everyone' hardly includes me, for I cannot at the moment say what they should be, though I have a suspicion.

At any rate you are aware that a song or ode has three parts—the words, the melody, and the rhythm.

Yes, he said; so much as that I know.

And as for the words, there will surely be no difference which are and which are not set to music; both will conform to the same laws, and these have been already determined by us?

Yes.

And the melody and rhythm will be in conformity with the words?

Certainly.

We were saying, when we spoke of the

subject-matter, that we had no need of lamentation and strains of sorrow?

True.

And which are the harmonies expressive of sorrow? You are musical, and can tell me.

The harmonies which you mean are the mixed or tenor Lydian, and the full-toned or bass Lydian, and such-like.

These then, I said, must be banished; even to women who have a character to maintain they are of no use, and much less to men.

Certainly.

In the next place, drunkenness and softness and indolence are utterly unbecoming the character of our guardians.

Utterly unbecoming.

And which are the soft and convivial harmonies?

The Ionian, he replied, and some of the Lydian which are termed 'relaxed'.

Well, and are these of any use for warlike men?

Quite the reverse, he replied; and if so the Dorian and the Phrygian are the only ones which you have left.

I answered: Of the harmonies I know nothing, but would have you leave me one which can render the note or accent which a brave man utters in warlike action and in stern resolve; and when his cause is failing, and he is going to wounds or death or is overtaken by disaster in some other form, at every such crisis he meets the blows of fortune with firm step and a determination to endure; and an opposite kind for times of peace and freedom of action, when there is no pressure of necessity, and he is seeking to persuade God by prayer, or man by instruction and admonition, or when on the other hand he is expressing his willingness to yield to the persuasion or entreaty or admonition of others. And when in this manner he has attained his end, I would have the music show him not carried away by his success, but acting moderately and wisely in all circumstances, and acquiescing in the event. These two harmonies I ask you to leave; the strain of necessity and the strain of freedom, the strain of the unfortunate and the strain of the fortunate, the strain of courage, and the strain of temperance; these, I say, leave.

And these, he replied, are the Dorian and Phrygian harmonies of which I was just now speaking.

Then, I said, if these and these only are to be used in our songs and melodies, we shall not want multiplicity of strings or a panharmonic scale?

I suppose not.

Then we shall not maintain the artificers of lyres with three corners and complex scales, or the makers of any other many-stringed, curiously harmonized instruments?

Certainly not.

But what do you say to flute-makers and flute-players? Would you admit them into our State when you reflect that in this composite use of harmony the flute is worse than any stringed instrument; even the panharmonic music is only an imitation of the flute?

Clearly not.

There remain then only the lyre and the harp for use in the city, and the shepherds in the country may have some kind of pipe.

That is surely the conclusion to be drawn from the argument.

The preferring of Apollo and his instruments to Marsyas and his instruments is not at all strange, I said.

Not at all, he replied.

And so, by the dog of Egypt, we have been unconsciously purging the State, which not long ago we termed luxurious.

And we have done wisely, he replied. . . .

The harmony of a beautiful soul and a beautiful form

Republic III 402B–D

SOCRATES. . . . Even so, as I maintain, neither we nor the guardians, whom we say that we have to educate, can ever become musical until we and they know the essential forms of temperance, courage, liberality, magnanimity, and their kindred, as well as the contrary forms, in all their combinations, and can recognize them and their images wherever they are found, not slighting them either in small things or great, but believing them all to be within the sphere of one art and study.

ADEIMANTUS. Most assuredly.

And when nobility of soul is observed in harmonious union with beauty of form, and both are cast from the same mould, that will be the fairest of sights to him who has an eye to see it?

The fairest indeed.

And the fairest is also the loveliest?

That may be assumed.

And it is with human beings who most display such harmony that a musical man will be most in love; but he will not love any who do not possess it. . . .

Tragedy and comedy

Philebus 48A–50B

SOCRATES. And you remember also how at the sight of tragedies the spectators smile through their tears?

PROTARCHUS. Certainly I do.

SOC. And are you aware that even at a comedy the soul experiences a mixed feeling of pain and pleasure?

PRO. I do not quite understand you.

SOC. I admit, Protarchus, that there is some difficulty in recognizing this mixture of feelings at a comedy.

PRO. There is, I think.

SOC. And the greater the obscurity of the case the more desirable is the examination of it, because the difficulty in detecting other cases of mixed pleasures and pains will be less.

PRO. Proceed.

SOC. I have just mentioned envy; would you not call that a pain of the soul?

PRO. Yes.

SOC. And yet the envious man evidently finds something in the misfortunes of his neighbours at which he is pleased?

PRO. Certainly.

SOC. And ignorance, and what is termed clownishness, are surely an evil?

PRO. To be sure.

SOC. From these considerations learn to know the nature of the ridiculous.

PRO. Explain.

SOC. The ridiculous is in short the specific name which is used to describe the vicious form of a certain habit; and of vice in general it is that kind which is most at variance with the inscription at Delphi.

PRO. You mean, Socrates, 'Know thyself.'

SOC. I do; and the opposite would be, 'Know not thyself.'

PRO. Certainly.

SOC. And now, O Protarchus, try to divide this into three.

PRO. Indeed I am afraid that I cannot.

SOC. Do you mean to say that I must make the division for you?

PRO. Yes, and what is more, I beg that you will.

SOC. Are there not three ways in which ignorance of self may be shown?

PRO. What are they?

SOC. In the first place, about money, the ignorant may fancy himself richer than he is.

PRO. Yes, that is a very common error.

SOC. And still more often he will fancy that

he is taller or fairer than he is, or that he has some other advantage of person which he really has not.

PRO. Of course.

SOC. And yet surely by far the greatest number err about the third class of goods, those of the soul; they imagine themselves to be much better men than they are.

PRO. Yes, that is by far the commonest delusion.

SOC. And of all the virtues, is not wisdom the one which the mass of mankind are always claiming, and which most arouses in them a spirit of contention and lying conceit of wisdom?

PRO. Certainly.

SOC. And may not all this be truly called an evil condition?

PRO. Very evil.

SOC. But we must make a further twofold division, Protarchus, if we would see in envy of the childish sort a singular mixture of pleasure and pain. What, then, is our next step? All who are silly enough to entertain this lying conceit of themselves may of course be divided, like the rest of mankind, into two classes—one having power and might; and the other the reverse.

PRO. Certainly.

SOC. Let this, then, be the principle of division; those of them who are weak and unable to revenge themselves, when they are laughed at, may be truly called ridiculous, but those who are powerful and can defend themselves may be more truly described as formidable and hateful; for ignorance in the powerful is hateful and horrible, because hurtful to others both in reality and in fiction, but powerless ignorance may be reckoned, and in truth is, ridiculous.

PRO. That is very true, but I do not as yet see where is the admixture of pleasures and pains.

SOC. Well, then, let us examine the nature of envy.

PRO. Proceed.

SOC. Is not envy an unrighteous pleasure, and also an unrighteous pain?

PRO. Most true.

SOC. There is nothing envious or wrong in rejoicing at the misfortunes of enemies?

PRO. Certainly not.

SOC. But to feel joy instead of sorrow at the sight of our friends' misfortunes—is not that wrong?

PRO. Undoubtedly.

SOC. Did we not say that ignorance was always an evil?

PRO. True.

SOC. And the three kinds of vain conceit in our friends which we enumerated—the vain conceit of beauty, of wisdom, and of wealth, are ridiculous if they are weak, and detestable when they are powerful: may we not say, as I was saying before, that our friends who are in this state of mind, when harmless to others, are simply ridiculous?

PRO. They are ridiculous.

SOC. And do we not acknowledge this state of mind, like all ignorance, to be a misfortune?

PRO. Certainly.

SOC. And do we feel pain or pleasure in laughing at it?

PRO. Clearly we feel pleasure.

SOC. And we agreed that the source of this pleasure which we feel at the misfortunes of friends was envy?

PRO. Certainly.

SOC. Then the argument shows that when we laugh at the folly of our friends, pleasure, in mingling with envy, mingles with pain, for envy has been acknowledged by us to be mental pain, and laughter is pleasant; and on such occasions we envy and laugh at the same instant.

PRO. True.

SOC. And the argument implies that there are combinations of pleasure and pain in lamentations, and in tragedy and comedy, not only on the stage, but on the greater stage of human life; and so in endless other cases.

PRO. I do not see how any one can deny what you say, Socrates, however eager he may be to assert the opposite opinion.

SOC. I mentioned anger, desire, sorrow, fear, love, emulation, envy, and similar emotions, as examples in which we should find a mixture of the two elements so often named. . . .

Art in terms of function

Republic I. 345D–346E

SOCRATES. Yet surely the art of the shepherd is concerned only with the good of his subjects; he has only to provide the best for them, since the perfection of the art itself is already ensured whenever the shepherd's work is perfectly performed. And that was what I was saying just now about the ruler. I conceived that the art of the ruler, considered as ruler, whether in a state or in private life, could only have regard to the maximum good of his flock or subjects; whereas you seem to think that the rulers in states, that is to say, the true rulers, like being in authority.

THRASYMACHUS. Think! Nay, I am sure of it.

Then why in the case of lesser offices do men never take them willingly without payment, unless because they assume that their rule is to be advantageous not to themselves but to the governed? Let me ask you a question: Are not the several arts different, by reason of their each having a separate function? And, my dear illustrious friend, do say what you think, that we may make a little progress.

Yes, that is the difference, he replied.

And each art gives us a particular good and not merely a general one—medicine, for example, gives us health; navigation, safety at sea, and so on?

Yes, he said.

And the art of earning has the special function of giving pay: but we do not confuse this with other arts, any more than the art of the pilot is to be confused with the art of medicine, because the health of the pilot may be improved by a sea voyage. You would not be inclined to say, would you, that navigation is the art of medicine, at least if we are to adopt your exact use of language?

Certainly not.

Or because a man is in good health when he receives pay, you would not say that the art of earning is medicine?

I should not.

Nor would you say that medicine is the art of receiving pay, because a man takes fees when he is engaged in healing?

No.

And we have admitted, I said, that the good of each art is specially confined to the art?

Let us take it for granted.

Then, if there be any good which all craftsmen have in common, that is to be attributed to something of which they all make common use?

True, he replied.

Moreover, we say that if the craftsman is benefited by receiving pay, that comes from his use of the art of earning in addition to his own?

He gave a reluctant assent to this.

Then the benefit, or receipt of pay, is not derived by the several craftsmen from their respective crafts. But it is more accurate to say that while the art of medicine gives health, and the art of the builder builds a house, another art attends them which is the art of earning. The various arts may be doing their own business and benefiting that over which they preside, but would the craftsman receive any benefit from his art unless he were paid as well?

I suppose not.

But does he therefore confer no benefit when he works for nothing?

Certainly, he confers a benefit.

Then now, Thrasymachus, there is no longer any doubt that neither arts nor governments provide for their own interests; but, as we were before saying, they rule and provide for the interests of their subjects who are the weaker and not the stronger—to their good they attend and not to the good of the superior. . . .

On Organic Wholes and the Analogy of the State to the Sculptured Figure

IV. 419–420D

Here Adeimantus interposed a question: How would you answer, Socrates, said he, if a person were to say that you are not making these men very happy, and that they are themselves to blame; the city in fact belongs to them, but they reap no advantage from it; whereas other men acquire lands, and build large and handsome houses, and have everything handsome about them, offering sacrifices to the gods on their own account, and practising hospitality; moreover, they have the gold and silver which you have just mentioned, and all that is usual among the favourites of fortune; but our poor citizens are no better than mercenaries who are quartered in the city and are always mounting guard?

Yes, I said; and you may add that they are only fed, and not paid in addition to their food like other men; and therefore they cannot, if they would, take a private journey abroad; they have no money to spend on a mistress or any other luxurious fancy, which, as the world goes, is thought to be happiness; and many other accusations of the same nature might be added.

But, said he, let us suppose all this to be included in the charge.

You mean to ask, I said, what will be our answer?

Yes.

If we proceed along the old path, my belief, I said, is that we shall find the answer. And our answer will be that, even as they are, our guardians may very likely be the happiest of men; but that our aim in founding the State was not the disproportionate happiness of any one class, but the greatest happiness of the whole; we thought that in a State which is ordered with a view to the good of the whole we should be most likely to find justice, and in the worst-ordered State injustice: and, having found them, we might then decide upon the answer to our first question. At present, I take it, we are fashioning the happy State, not piecemeal, or with a view of making a few happy citizens, but as a whole; and by-and-by we will proceed to view the opposite kind of State. Suppose that we were painting a statue, and someone came up to us and said, Why do you not put the most beautiful colours on the most beautiful parts of the body—the eyes ought to be purple, but you have made them black—to him we might fairly answer, 'Sir, you would not surely have us beautify the eyes to such a degree that they are no longer eyes; consider rather whether, by giving this and the other features their due proportion, we make the whole beautiful. . . .

The arts and the systematization of parts into a whole

Gorgias 501D–504C

SOCRATES. Can you tell me the pursuits which delight mankind—or rather, if you would prefer, let me ask, and do you answer, which of them belong to the pleasurable class, and which of them not? In the first place, what say you of flute-playing? Does not that appear to be an art which seeks only pleasure, Callicles, and thinks of nothing else?

CALLICLES. I assent.

SOC. And is not the same true of all similar arts, as, for example, the art of playing the lyre at festivals?

CAL. Yes.

SOC. And what do you say of the choral art and of dithyrambic poetry?—are not they of the same nature? Do you imagine that Cinesias the son of Meles cares about what will tend to the moral improvement of his hearers, or about what will give pleasure to the multitude?

CAL. There can be no mistake about Cinesias, Socrates.

SOC. And what do you say of his father, Meles the harp-player? When he sang to the harp, did you suppose that he had his eye on the highest good? Perhaps he indeed could scarcely be said to regard even the greatest pleasure, since his singing was an infliction to his audience? In fact, would you not say that all music of the harp and dithyrambic poetry in general have been invented for the sake of pleasure?

CAL. I should.

SOC. And as for the Muse of Tragedy, that solemn and august personage—what are her aspirations? Is all her aim and desire only to give pleasure to the spectators, or does she strive to refrain her tongue from all that pleases and charms them but is vicious? to proclaim, in speech and song, truth that is salutary but unpleasant, whether they welcome it or not?—which in your judgement is of the nature of tragic poetry?

CAL. There can be no doubt, Socrates, that Tragedy has her face turned towards pleasure and the gratification of the audience.

SOC. And is not that the sort of thing, Callicles, which we were just now describing as flattery?

CAL. Quite true.

SOC. Well now, suppose that we strip all poetry of melody and rhythm and metre, there will remain speech?[68]

CAL. To be sure.

SOC. And this speech is addressed to a crowd of people?

CAL. Yes.

SOC. Then poetry is a sort of public speaking?

CAL. True.

SOC. And it is a rhetorical sort of public speaking; do not the poets in the theatres seem to you to be rhetoricians?

CAL. Yes.

SOC. Then now we have discovered a sort of rhetoric which is addressed to a crowd of men, women, and children, freemen and slaves. And it is not much to our taste, for we have described it as having the nature of flattery.

CAL. Quite true.

SOC. Very good. And what do you say of that other rhetoric which addresses the Athenian Assembly and the assemblies of freemen in other states? Do the rhetoricians appear to you always to aim at what is best, and do they seek to improve the citizens by their speeches, or are they too, like the rest of mankind, bent upon giving them pleasure, forgetting the public good in the thought of their own interest, playing with the people as with children, and trying only to gratify them, but never considering whether they will be better or worse for this?

CAL. The question does not admit of a simple answer. There are some who have a real care of the public in what they say, while others are such as you describe.

SOC. That is enough for me: If rhetoric also is twofold, one part of it will be mere flattery and disgraceful declamation; the other noble, aiming at the improvement of the souls of the citizens, and striving to say what is best, whether welcome or unwelcome to the audience. But you have never known such a rhetoric; or

[68] Cf. *Rep.* iii. 392 foll.

if you have, and can point out any rhetorician who is of this stamp, who is he?

CAL. But, indeed, I am afraid that I cannot tell you of any such among the orators who are at present living.

SOC. Well, then, can you mention anyone of a former generation, of whom the Athenians have cause to say that as soon as he began to make speeches he advanced them in virtue? for indeed, I do not know of such a man.

CAL. What! did you never hear that Themistocles was a good man, and Cimon and Miltiades and Pericles, who is just lately dead. and whom you heard yourself?

SOC. Yes, Callicles, they were good men, if, as you said at first, true virtue consists only in the satisfaction of our own desires and those of others; but if not, and if, as we were afterwards compelled to acknowledge, the satisfaction of some desires makes us better, and of others, worse, and we ought to gratify the one and not the other, and there is an art in distinguishing them, then I cannot name one of these statesmen to whom I can attribute such a character.

CAL. You will find one, if you search properly.

SOC. Suppose that we just calmly consider whether any of these was such as I have described. Will not the good man, who says whatever he says with a view to the best, speak with a reference to some standard and not at random; just as all other artists strive to give a definite form to their work, instead of choosing at random what they apply to it. Look at the painter, the builder, the shipwright, any craftsman you like; see how he disposes all things in order, and compels the one part to harmonize and accord with the other part, until he has constructed a regular and systematic whole; and this is true of all artists, and in the same way the trainers and physicians, of whom we spoke before, give order and regularity to the body: do you deny this?

CAL. No; I am ready to admit it.

SOC. Then the house in which order and regularity prevail is good; that in which there is disorder, evil?

CAL. Yes.

SOC. And the same is true of a ship?

CAL. Yes.

SOC. And the same may be said of the human body?

CAL. Yes.

SOC. And what would you say of the soul? Will the good soul be that in which disorder is prevalent, or that in which there is harmony and order?

CAL. The latter follows from our previous admissions.

SOC. What is the name which is given to the effect of harmony and order in the body?

CAL. I suppose that you mean health and strength?

SOC. Yes, I do; and what is the name which you would give to the effect of harmony and order in the soul? Try and discover a name for this as well as for the other . . . .

Monumental sculpture and the Egyptian canon

Fantastic and True Images in Sculpture

Sophist 235B–236C

STRANGER. Then, clearly, we ought as soon as possible to divide the image-making art, and go down to the net, and, if the Sophist does not run away from us, to seize him according to the royal command of Reason, to whom he should be delivered over with a report of the capture; and if he creeps into the recesses of the imitative art, and secretes himself in one of them, to divide again and follow him up until in some subsection of imitation he is caught. For our method of tackling each and all is one which neither he nor any other creature will ever escape in triumph.

THEAETETUS. Well said; and let us do as you propose.

STR. Well, then, pursuing the same analytic method as before, I think that I can discern two divisions of the imitative art, but I am not as yet able to see in which of them the desired form is to be found.

THEAET. Will you tell me first what are the two divisions of which you are speaking?

STR. One is the art of likeness-making;—generally a likeness of anything is made by producing a copy which is executed according to the proportions of the original, similar in length and breadth and depth, each thing receiving also its appropriate colour.

THEAET. Is not this always the aim of imitation?

STR. Not always; in works either of sculpture or of painting, which are of any magnitude, there is a certain degree of deception; for if artists were to give the true proportions of their fair models, the upper part, which is farther off, would appear to be out of proportion in comparison with the lower, which is nearer; and so they give up the truth in their images and make only the proportions which appear to be beautiful, disregarding the real ones.

THEAET. Quite true.

STR. And that which being other is also like, may we not fairly call a likeness or image?

THEAET. Yes.

STR. And may we not, as I did just now, call that part of the imitative art which is concerned with making such images the art of likeness-making?

THEAET. Let that be the name.

STR. And what shall we call those resemblances of the beautiful, which appear such owing to the unfavourable position of the spectator, whereas if a person had the power of getting a correct view of works of such magnitude, they would appear not even like that to which they profess to be like? May we not call these 'appearances', since they appear only and are not really like?

THEAET. Certainly.

STR. There is a great deal of this kind of thing in painting, and in all imitation.

THEAET. Of course.

STR. And may we not fairly call the sort of art, which produces an appearance and not an image, phantastic art?

THEAET. Most fairly.

STR. These then are the two kinds of image-making—the art of making likenesses, and phantastic or the art of making appearances?

THEAET. True . . . .

Laws II. 654E. *Let us follow the scent like hounds, and go in pursuit of beauty of figure, and melody, and song, and dance, if these escape us, there will be no use in talking about true education, whether Hellenic or barbarian . . .*

——*656C–657B.* [*The praise of the Egyptian canon.*]

ATHENIAN STRANGER. Then in a city which has good laws, or in future ages is to have them, bearing in mind the instruction and amusement which are given by music, can we suppose that the poets are to be allowed to teach in the dance anything which they themselves like, in the way of rhythm, or melody, or words, to the young children of any well-conditioned parents? Is the poet to train his choruses as he pleases, without reference to virtue or vice?

CLEINIAS. That is surely quite unreasonable, and is not to be thought of.

ATH. And yet he may do this in almost any state with the exception of Egypt.

CLE. And what are the laws about music and dancing in Egypt?

ATH. You will wonder when I tell you: Long ago they appear to have recognized the very principle of which we are now speaking—that their young citizens must be habituated to forms and strains of virtue. These they fixed, and exhibited the patterns of them in their temples; and no painter, no other representative artist is allowed to innovate upon them, or to leave the traditional forms and invent new ones. To this day, no alteration is allowed either in these arts, or in music at all. And you find that their works of art are painted or moulded in the same forms which they had ten thousand years ago;—this is literally true and no exaggeration,—their ancient paintings and sculptures are not a whit better or worse than the work of today, but are made with just the same skill.

CLE. How extraordinary!

ATH. I should rather say, How statesmanlike, how worthy of a legislator! I know that other things in Egypt are not so well. But what I am telling you about music is true and deserving of consideration, because showing that a lawgiver may institute melodies which have a natural truth and correctness without any fear of failure. To do this, however, must be the work of God, or of a divine person; in Egypt they have a tradition that their ancient chants which have been preserved for so many ages are the composition of the Goddess Isis. And therefore, as I was saying, if a person can only find in any way the natural melodies, he may confidently embody them in a fixed and legal form. For the love of novelty which arises out of pleasure in the new and weariness of the old, has not strength enough to corrupt the consecrated song and dance, under the plea that they have become antiquated. At any rate, they are far from being corrupted in Egypt.

Painting, architecture, music

On the painter of an ideal of a perfectly beautiful man

Republic IV. 472C–D

SOCRATES. It was in order to have an ideal that we were inquiring into the nature of absolute justice and into the character of the supposed perfectly just man, and into injustice and the perfectly unjust man. We were to look at these two extremes in order that we might judge of our own happiness and unhappiness according to the standard of happiness and misery which they exhibited and the degree in which we resembled them, but not with any view of showing that they could exist in fact.

ADEIMANTUS. True, he said.

Would a painter, in your view, be less expert because, after having delineated with consummate art an ideal of a perfectly beautiful man, he was unable to show that any such man could ever have existed?

No, indeed . . . .

The architect rules the workmen; painting and poetry can imitate violent actions

Statesman 259E–260B: The Eleatic Stranger

You may remember that we made an art of calculation? . . . Which was, unmistakeably, one of the cognitive sciences? . . . And to this art of calculation which discerns the differences of numbers shall we assign any other function except to pass judgment on their differences? . . . You know that the master-builder does not work himself, but is the ruler of workmen? . . . He contributes science, not manual labour? . . . And may therefore be justly said to share in theoretical science? . . . But he ought not, like the calculator, to regard his functions as at an end when he has formed a judgment;—he must assign to the individual workmen their appropriate task until they have completed the work . . . Are not all such sciences cognitive, no less than arithmetic and the like; and is not the difference between the two classes, that the one sort has the power of judging only, and the other of command as well? . . . May we not very properly say, that of all cognitive science, there are two divisions—one which commands, and the other which judges? . . . .

Strains of music are our laws

Laws VII. 799E–803A

ATHENIAN STRANGER. Let us then affirm the paradox that strains of music are our laws (νόμοι), and this latter being the name which the ancients gave to lyric songs, they probably would not have very much objected to our proposed application of the word. Some one, either asleep or awake, must have had a dreamy suspicion of their nature. And let our decree be as follows:—No one in singing or dancing shall offend against public and consecrated models, and the general fashion among the youth, any more then he would offend against any other law. And he who observes this law shall be blameless; but he who is disobedient, as I was saying, shall be punished by the guardians of the laws, and by the priests and priestesses. Suppose that we imagine this to be our law.

CLEINIAS. Very good.

ATH. Can anyone who makes such laws escape ridicule? Let us see. I think that our only safety will be in first framing certain models for composers. One of these models shall be as follows:—If a sacrifice has been offered, and the victims burnt according to law,—if, I say, anyone who may be a son or brother, standing by another at the altar and over the victims, horribly blasphemes, will not his words inspire despondency and evil omens and forebodings in the mind of his father and of his other kinsmen?

CLE. Of course.

ATH. And this is just what takes place in almost all our cities. A magistrate offers a public sacrifice, and there come in not one but many choruses, who take up a position a little way from the altar, and from time to time pour forth all sorts of horrible blasphemies on the sacred rites, exciting the souls of the audience with words and rhythms and melodies most sorrowful to hear; and he who at the moment when the city has offered sacrifice makes the citizens weep most, carries away the palm of victory. Now, ought we not to forbid such strains as these? And if ever our citizens must hear such lamentations, then on some unblest and inauspicious day let there be choruses of foreign and hired minstrels, like those hirelings who accompany the departed at funerals with barbarous Carian chants. That is the sort of thing which will be appropriate if we have such strains at all; and let the apparel of the singers of the funeral dirge be, not circles and ornaments of gold, but the reverse. Enough of all this. I will simply ask once more whether we shall lay down as one of our principles of song——

CLE. What?

ATH. That we should avoid every word of evil omen; let that kind of song which is of good omen be heard everywhere and always in our state. I need hardly ask again, but shall assume that you agree with me.

CLE. By all means; that law is approved by the suffrages of us all.

ATH. But what shall be our next musical law or type? Ought not prayers to be offered up to the Gods when we sacrifice?

CLE. Certainly.

ATH. And our third law, if I am not mistaken, will be to the effect that our poets, understanding prayers to be requests which we make to the Gods, will take especial heed that they do not by mistake ask for evil instead of good. To make such a prayer would surely be too ridiculous.

CLE. Very true.

ATH. Were we not a little while ago quite convinced that no silver or golden Plutus should dwell in our state?

CLE. To be sure.

ATH. And what has it been the object of our argument to show? Did we not imply that the poets are not always quite capable of knowing what is good or evil? And if one of them utters a mistaken prayer in song or words, he will make our citizens pray for the opposite of what we ordain in matters of the highest import; than which, as I was saying, there can be few greater mistakes. Shall we then propose as one of our laws and models relating to the Muses——

CLE. What?—will you explain the law more precisely?

ATH. Shall we make a law that the poet shall compose nothing contrary to the ideas of the lawful, or just, or beautiful, or good, which are allowed in the state? nor shall he be permitted to communicate his compositions to any private individuals, until he shall have shown them to the appointed judges and the guardians of the law, and they are satisfied with them. As to the persons whom we appoint to be our legislators about music and as the director of education, these have been already indicated. Once more then, as I have asked more than once, shall this be our third law, and type, and model—What do you say?

CLE. Let it be so, by all means.

ATH. Then it will be proper to have hymns and praises of the Gods, intermingled with prayers; and after the Gods prayers and praises should be offered in like manner to demigods and heroes, suitable to their several characters.

CLE. Certainly.

ATH. In the next place there will be no objection to a law, that citizens who are departed and have done good and energetic deeds, either with their souls or with their bodies, and have been obedient to the laws, should receive eulogies; this will be very fitting.

CLE. Quite true.

ATH. But to honour with hymns and panegyrics those who are still alive is not safe; a man should run his course, and make a fair ending, and then we will praise him; and let praise be given equally to women as well as men who have been distinguished in virtue. The order of songs and dances shall be as follows:—There are many ancient musical compositions and dances which are excellent, and from these it is fair to select what is proper and suitable to the newly-founded city; and they shall choose judges of not less than fifty years of age, who shall make the selection, and any of the old poems which they deem sufficient they shall include; any that are deficient or altogether unsuitable, they shall either utterly throw aside, or examine and amend, taking into their counsel poets and musicians, and making use of their poetical genius; but explaining to them the wishes of the legislator in order that they may regulate dancing, music, and all choral strains, according to the mind of the judges; and not allowing them to indulge, except in some few matters, their individual pleasures and fancies. Now the irregular strain of music is always made ten thousand times better by attaining to law and order, and rejecting the honeyed Muse—not however that we mean wholly to exclude pleasure, which is the characteristic of all music. And if a man be brought up from childhood to the age of discretion and maturity in the use of the orderly and severe music, when he hears the opposite he detests it, and calls it illiberal; but if trained in the sweet and vulgar music, he deems the severer kind cold and displeasing. So that, as I was saying before, while he who hears them gains no more pleasure from the one than from the other, the one has the advantage of making those who are trained in it better men, whereas the other makes them worse.

CLE. Very true.

ATH. Again, we must distinguish and determine on some general principle what songs are suitable to women, and what to men, and must assign to them their proper melodies and rhythms. It is shocking for a whole harmony to be inharmonical, or for a rhythm to be unrhythmical, and this will happen when the melody is inappropriate to them. And therefore the legislator must assign to these also their forms. Now both sexes have melodies and rhythms which of necessity belong to them; and those of women are clearly enough indicated by their natural difference. The grand, and that which tends to courage, may be fairly called manly; but that which inclines to moderation and temperance, may be declared both in law and in ordinary speech to be the more womanly quality. This, then, will be the general order of them . . . .

The attack on imitative art and on tragedy

Tragedy and its experience. Imitative art thrice removed from truth

Republic X. 595A–608C

SOCRATES. Of the many excellences which I perceive in the order of our State, there is none which upon reflection pleases me better than the rule about poetry.

To what do you refer?

To our refusal to admit the imitative kind of poetry, for it certainly ought not to be received; as I see far more clearly now that the parts of the soul have been distinguished.

What do you mean?

Speaking in confidence, for you will not denounce me to the tragedians and the rest of the imitative tribe, all poetical imitations are ruinous to the understanding of the hearers, unless as an antidote they possess the knowledge of the true nature of the originals.

Explain the purport of your remark.

Well, I will tell you, although I have always from my earliest youth had an awe and love of Homer which even now makes the words falter on my lips, for he seems to be the great captain and teacher of the whole of that noble tragic company; but a man is not to be reverenced more than the truth, and therefore I will speak out.

Very good, he said.

Listen to me then, or rather, answer me.

Put your question.

Can you give me a general definition of imitation? for I really do not myself understand what it professes to be.

A likely thing, then, that I should know.

There would be nothing strange in that, for the duller eye may often see a thing sooner than the keener.

Very true, he said; but in your presence, even if I had any faint notion, I could not muster courage to utter it. Will you inquire yourself?

Well then, shall we begin the inquiry at this point, following our usual method: Whenever a number of individuals have a common name, we assume that there is one corresponding idea or form:—do you understand me?

I do.

Let us take, for our present purpose, any instance of such a group; there are beds and tables in the world—many of each, are there not?

Yes.

But there are only two ideas or forms of such furniture—one the idea of a bed, the other of a table.

True.

And the maker of either of them makes a bed or he makes a table for our use, in accordance with the idea—that is our way of speaking in this and similar instances—but no artificer makes the idea itself: how could he?

Impossible.

And there is another artificer,—I should like to know what you would say of him.

Who is he?

One who is the maker of all the works of all other workmen.

What an extraordinary man!

Wait a little, and there will be more reason for your saying so. For this is the craftsman who is able to make not only furniture of every kind, but all that grows out of the earth, and all living creatures, himself included; and besides these he can make earth and sky and the gods, and all the things which are in heaven or in the realm of Hades under the earth.

He must be a wizard and no mistake.

Oh! you are incredulous, are you? Do you mean that there is no such maker or creator, or that in one sense there might be a maker of all these things but in another not? Do you see that there is a way in which you could make them all yourself?

And what way is this? he asked.

An easy way enough; or rather, there are many ways in which the feat might be quickly and easily accomplished, none quicker than that of turning a mirror round and round—you would soon enough make the sun and the heavens, and the earth and yourself, and other animals and plants, and furniture and all the other things of which we were just now speaking, in the mirror.

Yes, he said; but they would be appearances only.

Very good, I said, you are coming to the point now. And the painter too is, as I conceive, just such another—a creator of appearances, is he not?

Of course.

But then I suppose you will say that what he creates is untrue. And yet there is a sense in which the painter also creates a bed? Is there not?

Yes, he said, but here again, an appearance only.

And what of the maker of the bed? were you not saying that he too makes, not the idea which according to our view is the real object denoted by the word bed, but only a particular bed?

Yes, I did.

Then if he does not make a real object he cannot make what *is*, but only some semblance of existence; and if any one were to say that the work of the maker of the bed, or of any other workman, has real existence, he could hardly be supposed to be speaking the truth.

Not, at least, he replied, in the view of those who make a business of these discussions.

No wonder, then, that his work too is an indistinct expression of truth.

No wonder.

Suppose now that by the light of the examples just offered we inquire who this imitator is?

If you please.

Well then, here we find three beds: one existing in nature, which is made by God, as I think that we may say—for no one else can be the maker?

No one, I think.

There is another which is the work of the carpenter?

Yes.

And the work of the painter is a third?

Yes.

Beds, then, are of three kinds, and there are three artists who superintend them: God, the maker of the bed, and the painter?

Yes, there are three of them.

God, whether from choice or from necessity, made one bed in nature and one only; two or more such beds neither ever have been nor ever will be made by God.

Why is that?

Because even if He had made but two, a third would still appear behind them of which they again both possessed the form, and that would be the real bed and not the two others.

Very true, he said.

God knew this, I suppose, and He desired to be the real maker of a real bed, not a kind of maker of a kind of bed, and therefore He created a bed which is essentially and by nature one only.

So it seems.

Shall we, then, speak of Him as the natural author or maker of the bed?

Yes, he replied; inasmuch as by the natural process of creation He is the author of this and of all other things.

And what shall we say of the carpenter—is not he also the maker of a bed?

Yes.

But would you call the painter an artificer and maker?

Certainly not.

Yet if he is not the maker, what is he in relation to the bed?

I think, he said, that we may fairly designate him as the imitator of that which the others make.

Good, I said; then you call him whose product is third in the descent from nature, an imitator?

Certainly, he said.

And so if the tragic poet is an imitator, he too is thrice removed from the king and from the truth; and so are all other imitators.

That appears to be so.

Then about the imitator we are agreed. And what about the painter?—Do you think he tries to imitate in each case that which originally exists in nature, or only the creations of artificers?

The latter.

As they are or as they appear? you have still to determine this.

What do you mean?

I mean to ask whether a bed really becomes different when it is seen from different points of view, obliquely or directly or from any other point of view? Or does it simply appear different, without being really so? And the same of all things.

Yes, he said, the difference is only apparent.

Now let me ask you another question: Which is the art of painting designed to be—an imitation of things as they are, or as they appear—of appearance or of reality?

Of appearance, he said.

Then the imitator is a long way off the truth, and can reproduce all things because he lightly touches on a small part of them, and that part an image. For example: A painter will paint a cobbler, carpenter, or any other artisan, though he knows nothing of their arts; and, if he is a good painter, he may deceive children or simple persons when he shows them his picture of a carpenter from a distance, and they will fancy that they are looking at a real carpenter.

Certainly.

And surely, my friend, this is how we should regard all such claims: whenever any one informs us that he has found a man who knows all the arts, and all things else that anybody knows, and every single thing with a higher degree of accuracy than any other man—whoever tells us this, I think that we can only retort that he is a simple creature who seems to have been deceived by some wizard or imitator whom he met, and whom he thought all-knowing, because he himself was unable to analyse the nature of knowledge and ignorance and imitation.

Most true.

And next, I said, we have to consider tragedy and its leader, Homer; for we hear some persons saying that these poets know all the arts; and all things human; where virtue and vice are concerned, and indeed all divine things too; because the good poet cannot compose well unless he knows his subject, and he who has not this knowledge can never be a poet. We ought to consider whether here also there may not be a similar illusion. Perhaps they may have come across imitators and been deceived by them; they may not have remembered when they saw their works that these were thrice removed from the truth, and could easily be made without any knowledge of the truth, because they are appearances only and not realities? Or, after all, they may be in the right, and good poets do really know the things about which they seem to the many to speak so well?

The question, he said, should by all means be considered.

Now do you suppose that if a person were able to make the original as well as the image, he would seriously devote himself to the image-making branch? Would he allow imitation to be the ruling principle of his life, as if he had nothing higher in him?

I should say not.

But the real artist, who had real knowledge of those things which he chose also to imitate, would be interested in realities and not in imitations; and would desire to leave as memorials of himself works many and fair; and, instead of being the author of encomiums, he would prefer to be the theme of them.

Yes, he said, that would be to him a source of much greater honour and profit.

Now let us refrain, I said, from calling Homer or any other poet to account regarding those arts to which his poems incidentally refer: we will not ask them, in case any poet has been a doctor and not a mere imitator of medical parlance, to show what patients have been restored to health by a poet, ancient or modern, as they were by Asclepius; or what disciples in medicine a poet has left behind him, like the Asclepiads. Nor shall we press the same question upon them about the other arts. But we have a right to know respecting warfare, strategy, the administration of States and the education of man, which are the chiefest and noblest subjects of his poems, and we may fairly ask him about them. 'Friend Homer,' then we say to him, 'if you are only in the second remove from truth in what you say of virtue, and not in the third—not an image maker, that is, by our definition, an imitator—and if you are able to discern what pursuits make men better or worse in private or public life, tell us what State was ever better governed by your help? The good order of Lacedaemon is due to Lycurgus, and many other cities great and small have been similarly benefited by others; but who says that you have been a good legislator to them and have done them any good? Italy and Sicily boast of Charondas, and there is Solon who is renowned among us; but what city has anything to say about you? Is there any city which he might name?

I think not, said Glaucon; not even the Homerids themselves pretend that he was a legislator.

Well, but is there any war on record which was carried on successfully owing to his leadership or counsel?

There is not.

Or is there anything comparable to those clever improvements in the arts, or in other operations, which are said to have been due to men of practical genius such as Thales the Milesian or Anacharsis the Scythian?

There is absolutely nothing of the kind.

But, if Homer never did any public service, was he privately a guide or teacher of any? Had he in his lifetime friends who loved to associate with him, and who handed down to posterity an Homeric way of life, such as was established by Pythagoras who was especially beloved for this reason and whose followers are to this day conspicuous among others by what they term as the Pythagorean way of life?

Nothing of the kind is recorded of him. For surely, Socrates, Creophylus, the companion of Homer, that child of flesh, whose name always makes us laugh, might be more justly ridiculed for his want of breeding, if what is said is true, that Homer was greatly neglected by him in his own day when he was alive?

Yes, I replied, that is the tradition. But can you imagine, Glaucon, that if Homer had really been able to educate and improve mankind—if he had been capable of knowledge and not been a mere imitator—can you imagine, I say, that he would not have attracted many followers, and been honoured and loved by them? Protagoras of Abdera, Prodicus of Ceos, and a host of others, have only to whisper to their contemporaries: 'You will never be able to manage either your own house or your own State until you appoint us to be your ministers of education'—and this ingenious device of theirs has such an effect in making men love them that their companions all but carry them about on their shoulders. And is it conceivable that the contemporaries of Homer, or again of Hesiod, would have allowed either of them to go about as rhapsodists, if they had really been able to help mankind forward in virtue? Would they not have been as unwilling to part with them as with gold, and have compelled them to stay at home with them? Or, if the master would not stay, then the disciples would have followed him about everywhere, until they had got education enough?

Yes, Socrates, that, I think, is quite true.

Then must we not infer that all these poetical individuals, beginning with Homer, are only imitators, who copy images of virtue and the other themes of their poetry, but have no contact with the truth? The poet is like a painter who, as we have already observed, will make a likeness of a cobbler though he understands nothing of cobbling; and his picture is good enough for those who know no more than he does, and judge only by colours and figures.

Quite so.

In like manner the poet with his words and phrases[69] may be said to lay on the colours of the several arts, himself understanding their nature only enough to imitate them; and other people, who are as ignorant as he is, and judge only from his words, imagine that if he speaks of cobbling, or of military tactics, or of anything else, in metre and harmony and rhythm, he speaks very well—such is the sweet influence which melody and rhythm by nature have. For I am sure that you know what a poor appearance the works of poets make when stripped of the colours which art puts upon them, and recited in simple prose. You have seen some examples?

Yes, he said.

They are like faces which were never really beautiful, but only blooming, seen when the bloom of youth has passed away from them?

Exactly.

Come now, and observe this point: The imitator or maker of the image knows nothing, we have said, of true existence; he knows appearances only. Am I not right?

Yes.

Then let us have a clear understanding, and not be satisfied with half an explanation.

Proceed.

Of the painter we say that he will paint reins, and he will paint a bit?

Yes.

And the worker in leather and brass will make them?

Certainly.

But does the painter know the right form of the bit and reins? Nay, hardly even the workers in brass and leather who make them; only the horseman who knows how to use them —he knows the right form.

Most true.

And may we not say the same of all things?

What?

That there are three arts which are concerned with all things: one which uses, another which makes, a third which imitates them?

Yes.

[69] Or, 'with his nouns and verbs'.

And the excellence and beauty and rightness of every structure, animate or inanimate, and of every action of man, is relative solely to the use for which nature or the artist has intended them.

True.

Then beyond doubt it is the user who has the greatest experience of them, and he must report to the maker the good or bad qualities which develop themselves in use; for example, the flute-player will tell the flute-maker which of his flutes is satisfactory to the performer;[70] he will tell him how he ought to make them, and the other will attend to his instructions?

Of course.

So the one pronounces with knowledge about the goodness and badness of flutes, while the other, confiding in him, will make them accordingly?

True.

The instrument is the same, but about the excellence or badness of it the maker will possess a correct belief, since he associates with one who knows, and is compelled to hear what he has to say; whereas the user will have knowledge?

True.

But will the imitator have either? Will he know from use whether or no that which he paints is correct or beautiful? or will he have right opinion from being compelled to associate with another who knows and gives him instructions about what he should paint?

Neither.

Then an imitator will no more have true opinion than he will have knowledge about the goodness or badness of his models?

I suppose not.

The imitative poet will be in a brilliant state of intelligence about the theme of his poetry?

Nay, very much the reverse.

And still he will go on imitating without knowing what makes a thing good or bad, and may be expected therefore to imitate only that which appears to be good to the ignorant multitude?

Just so.

Thus far then we are pretty well agreed that the imitator has no knowledge worth mentioning of what he imitates. Imitation is only a kind of play or sport, and the tragic poets, whether they write in iambic or in heroic verse, are imitators in the highest degree?

Very true.

And now tell me, I conjure you, — this imitation is concerned with an object which is thrice removed from the truth?

Certainly.

And what kind of faculty in man is that to which imitation makes its special appeal?

What do you mean?

I will explain: The same body does not appear equal to our sight when seen near and when seen at a distance?

True.

And the same objects appear straight when looked at out of the water, and crooked when in the water; and the concave becomes convex, owing to the illusion about colours to which the sight is liable. Thus every sort of confusion is revealed within us; and this is that weakness of the human mind on which the art of painting in light and shadow, the art of conjuring, and many other ingenious devices impose, having an effect upon us like magic.

True.

And the arts of measuring and numbering and weighing come to the rescue of the human understanding—there is the beauty of them—with the result that the apparent greater or less, or more or heavier, no longer have the mastery over us, but give way before the power of calculation and measuring and weighing?

Most true.

And this, surely, must be the work of the

[70] [Or, to avoid the repetition of ὑπηρετεῖν in a different sense: 'will make a report to the flute-maker, *who assists him in his playing,* about the flutes'.]

calculating and rational principle in the soul?

To be sure.

And often when this principle measures and certifies that some things are equal, or that some are greater or less than others, it is, at the same time, contradicted by the appearance which the objects present?

True.

But did we not say that such a contradiction is impossible—the same faculty cannot have contrary opinions at the same time about the same thing?

We did; and rightly.

Then that part of the soul which has an opinion contrary to measure can hardly be the same with that which has an opinion in accordance with measure?

True.

And the part of the soul which trusts to measure and calculation is likely to be the better one?

Certainly.

And therefore that which is opposed to this is probably an inferior principle in our nature?

No doubt.

This was the conclusion at which I was seeking to arrive when I said that painting or drawing, and imitation in general, are engaged upon productions which are far removed from truth, and are also the companions and friends and associates of a principle within us which is equally removed from reason, and that they have no true or healthy aim.

Exactly.

The imitative art is an inferior who from intercourse with an inferior has inferior offspring.

Very true.

And is this confined to the sight only, or does it extend to the hearing also, relating in fact to what we term poetry?

Probably the same would be true of poetry.

Do not rely, I said, on a probability derived from the analogy of painting; but let us once more go directly to that faculty of the mind with which imitative poetry has converse, and see whether it is good or bad.

By all means.

We may state the question thus:—Imitation imitates the actions of men, whether voluntary or involuntary, on which, as they imagine, a good or bad result has ensued, and they rejoice or sorrow accordingly. Is there anything more?

No, there is nothing else.

But in all this variety of circumstances is the man at unity with himself—or rather, as in the instance of sight there was confusion and opposition in his opinions about the same things, so here also is there not strife and inconsistency in his life? Though I need hardly raise the question again, for I remember that all this has been already admitted; and the soul has been acknowledged by us to be full of these and ten thousand similar oppositions occurring at the same moment?

And we were right, he said.

Yes, I said, thus far we were right; but there was an omission which must now be supplied.

What was the omission?

Were we not saying that a good man, who has the misfortune to lose his son or anything else which is most dear to him, will bear the loss with more equanimity than another?

Yes, indeed.

But will he have no sorrow, or shall we say that although he cannot help sorrowing, he will moderate his sorrow?

The latter, he said, is the truer statement.

Tell me: will he be more likely to struggle and hold out against his sorrow when he is seen by his equals, or when he is alone in a deserted place?

The fact of being seen will make a great difference, he said.

When he is by himself he will not mind saying many things which he would be ashamed of any one hearing, and also doing many things which he would not care to be seen doing?

True.

And doubtless it is the law and reason in him which bids him resist; while it is the affliction itself which is urging him to indulge his sorrow?

True.

But when a man is drawn in two opposite directions, to and from the same object, this, as we affirm, necessarily implies two distinct principles in him?

Certainly.

One of them is ready to follow the guidance of the law?

How do you mean?

The law would say that to be patient under calamity is best, and that we should not give way to impatience, as the good and evil in such things are not clear, and nothing is gained by impatience; also, because no human thing is of serious importance, and grief stands in the way of that which at the moment is most required.

What is most required? he asked.

That we should take counsel about what happened, and when the dice have been thrown, according to their fall, order our affairs in the way which reason deems best; not, like children who have had a fall, keeping hold of the part struck and wasting time in setting up a howl, but always accustoming the soul forthwith to apply a remedy, raising up that which is sickly and fallen, banishing the cry of sorrow by the healing art.

Yes, he said, that is the true way of meeting the attacks of fortune.

Well then, I said, the higher principle is ready to follow this suggestion of reason?

Clearly.

But the other principle, which inclines us to recollection of our troubles and to lamentation, and can never have enough of them, we may call irrational, useless, and cowardly?

Indeed, we may.

Now does not the principle which is thus inclined to complaint, furnish a great variety of materials for imitation? Whereas the wise and calm temperament, being always nearly equable, is not easy to imitate or to appreciate when imitated, especially at a public festival when a promiscuous crowd is assembled in a theatre. For the feeling represented is one to which they are strangers.

Certainly.

Then the imitative poet who aims at being popular is not by nature made, nor is his art intended, to please or to affect the rational principle in the soul; but he will appeal rather to the lachrymose and fitful temper, which is easily imitated?

Clearly.

And now we may fairly take him and place him by the side of the painter, for he is like him in two ways: first, inasmuch as his creations have an inferior degree of truth—in this, I say, he is like him; and he is also like him in being the associate of an inferior part of the soul; and this is enough to show that we shall be right in refusing to admit him into a State which is to be well ordered, because he awakens and nourishes this part of the soul, and by strengthening it impairs the reason. As in a city when the evil are permitted to wield power and the finer men are put out of the way, so in the soul of each man, as we shall maintain, the imitative poet implants an evil constitution, for he indulges the irrational nature which has no discernment of greater and less, but thinks the same thing at one time great and at another small—he is an imitator of images and is very far removed from the truth.

Exactly.

But we have not yet brought forward the heaviest count in our accusation:—the power which poetry has of harming even the good (and there are very few who are not harmed), is surely an awful thing?

Yes, certainly, if the effect is what you say.

Hear and judge: The best of us, as I conceive, when we listen to a passage of Homer or one of the tragedians, in which he represents some hero who is drawling out his sorrows in a long oration, or singing, and smiting his breast—the best of us, you know, delight in giving way to sympathy, and are in raptures at the excellence of the poet who stirs our feelings most.

Yes, of course I know.

But when any sorrow of our own happens to us, then you may observe that we pride ourselves on the opposite quality—we would fain be quiet and patient; this is considered the manly part, and the other which delighted us in the recitation is now deemed to be the part of a woman.

Very true, he said.

Now can we be right in praising and admiring another who is doing that which any one of us would abominate and be ashamed of in his own person?

No, he said, that is certainly not reasonable.

Nay, I said, quite reasonable from one point of view.

What point of view?

If you consider, I said, that when in misfortune we feel a natural hunger and desire to relieve our sorrow by weeping and lamentation, and that this very feeling which is starved and suppressed in our own calamities is satisfied and delighted by the poets;—the better nature in each of us, not having been sufficiently trained by reason or habit, allows the sympathetic element to break loose because the sorrow is another's; and the spectator fancies that there can be no disgrace to himself in praising and pitying any one who while professing to be a brave man, gives way to untimely lamentation; he thinks that the pleasure is a gain, and is far from wishing to lose it by rejection of the whole poem. Few persons ever reflect, as I should imagine, that the contagion must pass from others to themselves. For the pity which has been nourished and strengthened in the misfortunes of others is with difficulty repressed in our own.

How very true!

And does not the same hold also the ridiculous? There are jests which you would be ashamed to make yourself, and yet on the comic stage, or indeed in private, when you hear them, you are greatly amused by them, and are not at all disgusted at their unseemliness;—the case of pity is repeated;—there is a principle in human nature which is disposed to raise a laugh, and this, which you once restrained by reason because you were afraid of being thought a buffoon, is now let out again; and having stimulated the risible faculty at the theatre, you are betrayed unconsciously to yourself into playing the comic poet at home.

Quite true, he said.

And the same may be said of lust and anger and all the other affections, of desire and pain and pleasure, which are held to be inseparable from every action—in all of them poetry has a like effect; it feeds and waters the passions instead of drying them up; she lets them rule, although they ought to be controlled if mankind are ever to increase in happiness and virtue.

I cannot deny it.

Therefore, Glaucon, I said, whenever you meet with any of the eulogists of Homer declaring that he has been the educator of Hellas, and that he is profitable for education and for the ordering of human things, and that you should take him up again and again and get to know him and regulate your whole life according to him, we may love and honour those who say these things—they are excellent people, as far as their lights extend; and we are ready to acknowledge that Homer is the greatest of poets and first of tragedy writers; but we must remain firm in our conviction that hymns to the gods and praises of famous men are the only poetry which ought to be admitted into our State. For if you go beyond this and allow the honeyed Muse to enter, either in epic or lyric verse, not law and the reason of mankind, which by common consent have ever been deemed best,[71] but pleasure and pain will be the rulers in our State.

That is most true, he said.

And now since we have reverted to the subject of poetry, let this our defence serve to show the reasonableness of our former judgment in sending away out of our State an art having the tendencies which we have described; for reason constrained us. But that she may not impute to us any harshness or want of politeness, let us tell her that there is an ancient quarrel between philosophy and poetry; of which there are many proofs, such as the saying of 'the yelping hound howling at her lord', or of one 'mighty in the vain talk of fools', and 'the mob of sages circumventing Zeus', and the 'subtle thinkers who are beggars after all';[72] and there are innumerable other signs of ancient enmity between them. Notwithstanding this, let us assure the poetry which aims at pleasure, and the art of imitation, that if she will only prove her title to exist in a well-ordered State we shall be delighted to receive her—we are very conscious of her charms; but it would not be right on that account to betray the truth. I dare say, Glaucon, that you are as much charmed by her as I am, especially when she appears in Homer?

Yes, indeed, I am greatly charmed.

Shall I propose, then, that she be allowed to return from exile, but upon this condition only—that she make a defence of herself in some lyrical or other metre?

Certainly.

And we may further grant to those of her defenders who are lovers of poetry and yet not poets the permission to speak in prose on her behalf: let them show not only that she is pleasant but also useful to States and to human life, and we will listen in a kindly spirit; for we shall surely be the gainers if this can be proved, that there is a use in poetry as well as a delight?

Certainly, he said, we shall be the gainers.

If her defence fails, then, my dear friend, like other persons who are enamoured of something, but put a restraint upon themselves when they think their desires are opposed to their interests, so too must we after the manner of lovers give her up, though not without a struggle. We too are inspired by that love of such poetry which the education of noble States has implanted in us, and therefore we shall be glad if she appears at her best and truest; but so long as she is unable to make good her defence, this argument of ours shall be a charm to us, which we will repeat to ourselves while we listen to her strains; that we may not fall away into the childish love of her which captivates the many. At all events we are well aware[73] that poetry,[74] such as we have described, is not to be regarded seriously as attaining to the truth; and he who listens to her, fearing for the safety of the city which is within him, should be on his guard against her seductions and make our words his law.

Yes, he said, I quite agree with you.

Yes, I said, my dear Glaucon, for great is the issue at stake, greater than appears, whether a man is to be good or bad. And what will any one be profited if under the influence of honour or money or power, aye, or under the excitement of poetry, he neglect justice and virtue?

Yes, he said; I have been convinced by the argument, as I believe that anyone else would have been. . . .

[71] [Or: 'law, and the principle which the community in every case has pronounced to be the best'.]

[72] [Reading and sense uncertain. The origin of all these quotations is unknown.]

[73] Or, if we accept Madvig's ingenious but unnecessary emendation ᾀσόμεθα, 'At all events we will sing, that', &c.

[74] [i.e. *imitative* poetry. The word imitation, in the recent argument, had not the same sense as in Book III; but it has always been implied that there might be poetry which is not imitative.]

Dance and Song; Art as Play

Art in the state; on dance and song; a play-theory of art; on judgments of music and poetry; on excellence of art

Laws II. 654C–661D

ATHENIAN STRANGER. We will supose that he knows the good to be good, and the bad to be bad, and makes use of them accordingly: which now is the better trained in dancing and music—he who is able to move his body and use his voice in what he understands to be the right manner, but has no delight in good or hatred of evil; or he who is scarcely correct in gesture and voice and in understanding, but is right in his sense of pleasure and pain, and welcomes what is good, and is offended at what is evil?

CLEINIAS. There is a great difference, stranger, in the two kinds of education.

ATH. If we three know what is good in song and dance, then we truly know also who is educated and who is uneducated; but if not, then we certainly shall not know wherein lies the safeguard of education, and whether there is any or not.

CLE. True.

ATH. Let us follow the scent like hounds, and go in pursuit of beauty of figure, and melody, and song, and dance; if these escape us, there will be no use in talking about true education, whether Hellenic or barbarian.

CLE. Yes.

ATH. Now what is meant by beauty of figure, or beautiful melody? When a manly soul is in trouble, and when a cowardly soul is in similar case, are they likely to use the same figures and gestures, or to give utterance to the same sounds?

CLE. How can they, when the very colours of their faces differ?

ATH. Good my friend; I may observe, however, in passing, that in music there certainly are figures and there are melodies: and music is concerned with harmony and rhythm, so that you may speak of a melody or figure having a good rhythm or good harmony—the term is correct enough; but to speak metaphorically of a melody or figure having a 'good colour', as the masters of choruses do, is not allowable, although you can speak of the melodies or figures of the brave and the coward, praising the one and censuring the other. And not to be tedious, let us say that the figures and melodies which are expressive of virtue of soul of body, or of images of virtue, are without exception good, and those which are expressive of vice are the reverse of good.

CLE. Your suggestion is excellent; and let us answer that these things are so.

ATH. Once more, are all of us equally delighted with every sort of dance?

CLE. Far otherwise.

ATH. What, then, leads us astray? Are beautiful things not the same to us all, or are they the same in themselves, but not in our opinion of them? For no one will admit that forms of vice in the dance are more beautiful than forms of virtue, or that he himself delights in the forms of vice, and others in a muse of another character. And yet most persons say, that the excellence of music is to give pleasure to our souls. But this is intolerable and blasphemous; there is, however, a much more plausible account of the delusion.

CLE. What?

ATH. The adaptation of art to the characters of men. Choric movements are imitations of manners and the performers range over all the various actions and chances of life with characterization and mimicry; and those to whom the words, or songs, or dances are suited, either by nature or habit or both, cannot help feeling pleasure in them and applauding them, and calling them beautiful. But those whose natures, or ways, or habits are unsuited to them, cannot delight in them or applaud them, and they call them base. There are others, again, whose natures are right and their habits wrong, or whose habits are right and their natures wrong, and they praise one thing, but are pleased at another. For they say that all these imitations are pleasant, but not good. And in the presence of those whom they think wise, they are ashamed of dancing and singing in the baser manner, in a way which would indicate deliberate approval; and yet they have a secret pleasure in them.

CLE. Very true.

ATH. And is any harm done to the lover of vicious dances or songs, or any good done to the approver of the opposite sort of pleasure?

CLE. I think that there is.

ATH. 'I think' is not the word, but I would say, rather, 'I am certain'. For must they not have the same effect as when a man associates with bad characters, whom he likes and approves rather than dislikes, and only censures playfully because he has but a suspicion of their badness? In that case, he who takes pleasure in them will surely become like those in whom he takes pleasure, even though he be ashamed to praise them. This result is quite certain; and what greater good or evil can a human being undergo?

CLE. I know of none.

ATH. Then in a city which has good laws, or in future ages is to have them, bearing in mind the instruction and amusement which are given by music, can we suppose that the poets are to be allowed to teach in the dance anything which they themselves like, in the way of rhythm, or melody, or words, to the young children of any well-conditioned parents? Is the poet to train his choruses as he pleases, without reference to virtue or vice?

CLE. That is surely quite unreasonable, and is not to be thought of.

ATH. And yet he may do this in almost any state with the exception of Egypt.

CLE. And what are the laws about music and dancing in Egypt?

ATH. You will wonder when I tell you: Long ago they appear to have recognized the very principle of which we are now speaking—that their young citizens must be habituated to forms and strains of virtue. These they fixed, and exhibited the patterns of them in their temples; and no painter, no other representative artist is allowed to innovate upon them, or to leave the traditional forms and invent new ones. To this day, no alteration is allowed either in these arts, or in music at all. And you find that their works of art are painted or moulded in the same forms which they had ten thousand years ago;—this is literally true and no exaggeration,—their ancient paintings and sculptures are not a whit better or worse than the work of today, but are made with just the same skill.

CLE. How extraordinary!

ATH. I should rather say, How statesmanlike, how worthy of a legislator! I know that other things in Egypt are not so well. But what I am telling you about music is true and deserving of consideration, because showing that a lawgiver may institute melodies which have a natural truth and correctness without any fear of failure. To do this, however, must be the work of God, or of a divine person; in Egypt they have a tradition that their ancient chants which have been preserved for so many ages are the composition of the Goddess Isis. And therefore, as I was saying, if a person can only find in any way the natural melodies, he may confidently embody them in a fixed and legal form. For the love of novelty which arises out of pleasure in the new and weariness of the old, has not strength enough to corrupt the consecrated song and dance, under the plea that they have become antiquated. At any rate, they are far from being corrupted in Egypt.

CLE. Your arguments seem to prove your point.

ATH. May we not confidently say that the true use of music and of choral festivities is as follows: We rejoice when we think that we prosper, and again we think that we prosper when we rejoice?

CLE. Exactly.

ATH. And when rejoicing in our good fortune, we are unable to be still?

CLE. True.

ATH. Our young men break forth into dancing and singing, and we who are their elders deem that we are fulfilling our part in life when we look on at them. Having lost our agility, we delight in their sports and merry-making, because we love to think of our former selves; and gladly institute contests for those who are able to awaken in us the memory of our youth.

CLE. Very true.

ATH. Is it altogether unmeaning to say, as the common people do about festivals, that he should be adjudged the wisest of men and the winner of the palm, who gives us the greatest amount of pleasure and mirth? For on such occasions, and when mirth is the order of the day, ought not he to be honoured most, and, as I was saying, bear the palm, who gives most mirth to the greatest number? Now is this a true way of speaking or of acting?

CLE. Possibly.

ATH. But, my dear friend, let us distinguish between different cases, and not be hasty in forming a judgment: One way of considering the question will be to imagine a festival at which there are entertainments of all sorts, including gymnastic, musical, and equestrian contests: the citizens are assembled; prizes are offered, and proclamation is made that anyone who likes may enter the lists, and that he is to bear the palm who gives the most pleasure to the spectators—there is to be no regulation about the manner how; but he who is most successful in giving pleasure is to be crowned victor, and deemed to be the pleasantest of the candidates. What is likely to be the result of such a proclamation?

CLE. In what respect?

ATH. There would be various exhibitions: one man, like Homer, will exhibit a rhapsody, another a performance on the lute; one will have a tragedy, and another a comedy. Nor would there be anything astonishing in someone imagining that he could gain the prize by exhibiting a puppet-show. Suppose these competitors to meet, and not these only, but innumerable others as well—can you tell me who ought to be the victor?

CLE. I do not see how anyone can answer you, or pretend to know, unless he has heard with his own ears the several competitors; the question is absurd.

ATH. Well, then, if neither of you can answer, shall I answer this question which you deem so absurd?

CLE. By all means.

ATH. If very small children are to determine the question, they will decide for the puppet-show.

CLE. Of course.

ATH. The older children will be advocates of comedy; educated women, and young men, and people in general, will favour tragedy.

CLE. Very likely.

ATH. And I believe that we old men would have the greatest pleasure in hearing a rhapsodist recite well the Iliad and Odyssey, or one of the Hesiodic poems, and would award an overwhelming victory to him. But, who would really be the victor?—that is the question.

CLE. Yes.

ATH. Clearly you and I will have to declare that those whom we old men adjudge victors ought to win; for our ways are far and away better than any which at present exist anywhere in the world.

CLE. Certainly.

ATH. Thus far I too should agree with the many, that the excellence of music is to be measured by pleasure. But the pleasure must not be that of chance persons; the fairest music is that which delights the best and best educated, and especially that which delights the one man who is pre-eminent in virtue and education. And therefore the judges must be men of character, for they will require wisdom and have still greater need of courage; the true judge must not draw his inspiration from the theatre, nor ought he to be unnerved by the clamour of the many and his own incapacity; nor again, knowing the truth, ought he through cowardice and unmanliness carelessly to deliver a lying judgment, with the very same lips which have just appealed to the Gods before he judged. He is sitting not as the disciple of the theatre, but, in his proper place, as their instructor, and he ought to be the enemy of all pandering to the pleasure of the spectators.[75] The ancient and common custom of Hellas was the reverse of that which now prevails in Italy and Sicily, where the judgment is left to the body of spectators, who determine the victor by show of hands. But this custom has been the destruction of the poets themselves; for they are now in the habit of composing with a view to please the bad taste of their judges, and the result is that the spectators instruct themselves;—and also it has been the ruin of the theatre; they ought to be having characters put before them better than their own, and so receiving a higher pleasure, but now by their own act the opposite result follows. What inference is to be drawn from all this? Shall I tell you?

CLE. What?

ATH. The inference at which we arrive for the third or fourth time is, that education is the constraining and directing of youth towards that right reason, which the law affirms, and which the experience of the eldest and best has agreed to be truly right. In order, then, that the soul of the child may not be habituated to feel joy and sorrow in a manner at variance with the law, and those who obey the law, but may rather follow the law and rejoice and sorrow at the same things as the aged—in order, I say, to produce this effect, chants appear to have been invented, which really enchant, and are designed to implant that harmony of which we speak. And, because the mind of the child is incapable of enduring serious training, they are called plays and songs, and are performed in play; just as when men are sick and ailing in their bodies, their attendants give them wholesome diet in pleasant meats and drinks, but unwholesome diet in disagreeable things, in order that they may learn, as they ought, to like the one, and to dislike the other. And similarly the true legislator will persuade, and, if he cannot persuade, will compel the poet to express, as he ought, by fair and noble words, in his rhythms, the figures, and in his melodies, the music of temperate and brave and in every way good men.

CLE. But do you really imagine, stranger, that this is the way in which poets generally compose in states at the present day? As far as I can observe, except among us and among the Lacedaemonians, there are no regulations like those of which you speak; in other places novelties are always being introduced in dancing and music, generally not under the authority of any law, but at the instigation of lawless pleasures; and these pleasures are so far from being stable and governed by principles, as are those of the Egyptians by your account, that they have no consistency at all.

ATH. Most true, Cleinias; and I dare say that I may have expressed myself obscurely, and so led you to imagine that I was speaking of some really existing state of things, whereas I was only saying what regulations I would like to have about music; and hence there occurred a misapprehension on your part. For when evils are far gone and irremediable, the task of censuring them is never pleasant, although at times necessary. But as we do not really differ, will you let me ask you whether you consider such institutions to be more prevalent among

[75] [Or, taking τοῖς with θεαταῖς, 'the enemy of all spectators who respond with pleasure in a mistaken and unsuitable way'.]

the Cretans and Lacedaemonians than among the other Hellenes?

CLE. Certainly they are.

ATH. And if they were extended to the other Hellenes, would it be an improvement on the present state of things?

CLE. A very great improvement, if the customs which prevail among them were such as prevail among us and the Lacedaemonians, and such as you were just now saying ought to prevail.

ATH. Let us see whether we understand one another:—Are not the principles of education and music which prevail among you as follows: you compel your poets to say that the good man, if he be temperate and just, is fortunate and happy; and this whether he be great and strong or small and weak, and whether he be rich or poor; and, on the other hand, if he have a wealth passing that of Cinyras or Midas, and be unjust, he is wretched and lives in misery? As the poet says, and with truth: 'I sing not, I care not about him' who accomplishes all things reputed noble, not having justice; let him who 'draws near and stretches out his hand against his enemies' be a just man. But if he be unjust, I would not have him 'look calmly upon bloody death,' nor surpass in swiftness 'Thracian Boreas'; and let no other thing that is called good ever be his. For the goods of which the many speak are not really good: first in the catalogue is placed health, beauty next, wealth third; and then innumerable others, as for example to have a keen eye or a quick ear, and in general to have all the senses perfect; or, again, to be a tyrant and do as you like; and the final consummation of happiness is to have acquired all these things, and when you have acquired them to become at once immortal. But you and I say, that while to the just and holy all these things are the best of possessions, to the unjust they are all, including even health, the greatest of evils. For in truth, to have sight, and hearing, and the use of the senses, or to live at all without justice and virtue, even though a man be rich in all the so-called goods of fortune, is the greatest of evils, if life be immortal; but not so great, if the bad man lives only a very short time. These are the truths which, if I am not mistaken, you will persuade or compel your poets to utter with suitable accompaniments of harmony and rhythm, and in these they must train up your youth. Am I not right? For I plainly declare that evils as they are termed are goods to the unjust, and only evils to the just, and that goods are truly good to the good, but evil to the evil. Let me ask again, Are you and I agreed about this?

CLE. I think that we partly agree, and partly are opposed . . . .

Art as play and preparatory to serious activities

Laws I. 643B–C

ATHENIAN STRANGER. According to my view, anyone who would be good at anything must practise that thing from his youth upwards, both in sport and earnest, in its several branches: for example, he who is to be a good builder, should play at building children's houses; he who is to be a good husbandman, at tilling the ground; and those who have the care of their education should provide them when young with mimic tools. They should learn beforehand the knowledge which they will afterwards require for their art. For example, the future carpenter should learn to measure or apply the line in play; and the future warrior should learn riding, or some other exercise, for amusement, and the teacher should endeavour to direct the children's inclinations and pleasures, by the help of amusements, to their final aim in life. The most important part of education is right training in the nursery . . . .

Criteria of excellence in art

The criteria for sound judgments of imitative art

Laws II. 668D–671A

ATHENIAN STRANGER. There are ten thousand likenesses which we apprehend by sight? . . . Even in their case, can he who does not know what the exact object is which is imitated, ever know whether the resemblance is truthfully executed? I mean, for example, whether a statue has the proportions of a body, and the true situation of the parts; what those proportions are, and how the parts fit into one another in due order; also their colours and conformations, or whether this is all confused in the execution: do you think that anyone can know about this, who does not know what the animal is which has been imitated?

CLEINIAS. Impossible.

ATH. But even if we know that the thing pictured or sculptured is man, who has received at the hand of the artist all his proper parts and colours and shapes, shall we therefore know at once, and of necessity, whether the work is beautiful or in any respect deficient in beauty?

CLE. If this were true, stranger, we should almost all of us be judges of beauty.

ATH. Very true; and may we not say that in everything imitated, whether in drawing, music, or any other art, he who is to be a competent judge must possess three things;—he must know, in the first place, of what the imitation is; secondly, he must know that it is true; and thirdly, that it has been well executed in words and melodies and rhythms?

CLE. Certainly.

ATH. Then let us not faint in discussing the peculiar difficulty of music. Music is more celebrated than any other kind of imitation, and therefore requires the greatest care of them all. For if a man makes a mistake here, he may do himself the greatest injury by welcoming evil dispositions, and the mistake may be very difficult to discern, because the poets are artists very inferior in character to the Muses themselves, who would never fall into the monstrous error of assigning to the words of men the intonation and song of women; nor after combining the melodies with the gestures of freemen would they add on the rhythms of slaves and men of the baser sort; nor, beginning with the rhythms and gestures of freemen, would they assign to them a melody or words which are of an opposite character; nor would they mix up the voices and sounds of animals and of men and instruments, and every other sort of noise, as if they were all one. But human poets are fond of introducing this sort of inconsistent mixture, and so make themselves ridiculous in the eyes of those who, as Orpheus says, 'are ripe for true pleasure'. The experienced see all this confusion, and yet the poets go on and make still further havoc by separating the rhythm and the figure of the dance from the melody, setting bare words to metre, and also separating the melody and the rhythm from the words, using the lyre or the flute alone. For when there are no words, it is very difficult to recognize the meaning of the harmony and rhythm, or to see that any worthy object is imitated by them. And we must acknowledge that all this sort of thing, which aims at only swiftness and smoothness and a brutish noise, and uses the flute and the lyre not as the mere accompaniments of the dance and song, is exceedingly coarse and tasteless. The use of either instrument, when unaccompanied, leads to every sort of irregularity and trickery. This is all rational enough. But we are considering not how our choristers, who are from thirty to fifty years of age, and may be over fifty, are not to use the Muses, but how they are to use them. And the considerations which we have urged seem to show that these fifty-years-old choristers who are to sing, will require something better than a mere choral training. For they need have a quick perception and knowledge of harmonies and rhythms; otherwise, how can they ever know whether a melody would be rightly sung to the Dorian mode, or to the rhythm which the poet has assigned to it?

CLE. Clearly they cannot.

ATH. The many are ridiculous in imagining that they know what is in proper harmony and rhythm, and what is not, when they can only be made by force to sing to the flute and step in rhythm; it never occurs to them that they are ignorant of what they are doing. Now every melody is right when it has suitable harmony and rhythm, and wrong when unsuitable.

CLE. That is most certain.

ATH. But can a man who does not know a thing, as we were saying, know that the thing is right?

CLE. Impossible.

ATH. Then now, as would appear, we are making the discovery that our newly appointed choristers, whom we hereby invite and, although they are their own masters, compel to sing, must be educated to such an extent as to be able to follow the steps of the rhythm and the notes of the song, that they may review the harmonies and rhythms, and be able to select what are suitable for men of their age and character to sing; and may sing them, and have innocent pleasure from their own performance, and also lead younger men to receive the virtues of character with the welcome which they deserve. Having such training, they will attain a more accurate knowledge than falls to the lot of the common people, or even of the poets themselves. For the poet need not know the third point, viz. whether the imitation is good or not, though he can hardly help knowing the laws of melody and rhythm. But our critics must know all the three, that they may choose the best, and that which is nearest to the best; for otherwise they will never be able to charm the souls of young men in the way of virtue. And now the original design of the argument which was intended to show that we were wise to lend support to the chorus of Dionysus, has been accomplished to the best of our ability . . . .

The Artists and Problems of the Specific Arts. The painter

Philebus 39B

SOCRATES. I must bespeak your favour also for another artist, who is busy at the same time in the chambers of the soul.

PROTARCHUS. Who is he?

SOC. The painter, who, after the scribe has done his work, draws images in the soul of the things which he has described.

PRO. But when and how does he do this?

SOC. When a man, besides receiving from sight or some other sense certain opinions or statements, sees in his mind the images of the subjects of them;—is not this a very common mental phenomenon?

The writers of comedy and tragedy

Republic III. 395A

SOCRATES. Then the same person will hardly be able to play a serious part in life, and at the same time to be an imitator and imitate many other parts as well; for even when two species of imitation are nearly allied, the same persons cannot succeed in both, as, for example, the writers of tragedy and comedy—did you not just now call them imitations?

ADEIMANTUS. Yes, I did; and you are right in thinking that the same persons cannot succeed in both.

SOC. Any more than they can be rhapsodists and actors at once? . . . Neither do comic and tragic writers employ the same actors; yet all these things are imitations . . . .

Symposium 223B

APOLLODORUS. Aristodemus said that Eryximachus, Phaedrus, and others went away—he himself fell asleep, and as the nights were long took a good rest: he was awakened towards daybreak by a crowing of cocks, and when he awoke, the others were either asleep, or had gone away; there remained only Socrates, Aristophanes, and Agathon, who were drinking out of a large goblet which they passed round, and Socrates was discoursing to them. Aristodemus was only half awake, and he did not hear the beginning of the discourse; the chief thing which he remembered was Socrates compelling the other two to acknowledge that the genius of comedy was the same with that of tragedy, and that the true artist in tragedy was an artist in comedy also. To this they were constrained to assent, being drowsy, and not quite following the argument . . . .

Painters can represent violent events

Statesman 306C–307B

STRANGER. Then let us carefully investigate whether this is universally true, or whether there are not parts of virtue which are at war with their kindred in some respect . . . We must extend our inquiry to all those things which we consider beautiful and at the same time place in two opposite classes . . . Acuteness and quickness, whether in body or soul or in the movement of sound, and the imitations of them which painting and music supply, you must have praised yourself before now, or been present when others praised them . . . And do you remember the terms in which, in such instances, they are praised?

YOUNG SOCRATES. I do not.

STRANGER. I wonder whether I can explain to you in words the thought which is passing in my mind.

YOUNG SOCRATES. Why not?

STRANGER. You fancy that this is all so easy: well, let us consider these notions with reference to the opposite classes under which they fall. When we admire quickness and energy and acuteness, whether of thought or body or sound, as we do in numerous instances of action, we express our praise of the quality which we admire by one word, and that one word is manliness or courage . . . And on the contrary, do we often praise the quiet strain of action also? . . . And do we not then say the opposite of what we said of the other? . . . We exclaim, How calm! How temperate! in admiration of the slow and quiet working of the intellect, and of steadiness and gentleness in action, of smoothness and depth of voice, and of all rhythmical movement and of music in general, when these have a proper solemnity. Of all such actions we predicate not courage, but a name indicative of order . . . .

We are more easily satisfied with the imitation by the painter if he presents unfamiliar subject matter than a copy of the human form with which we are more familiar and so can ascertain more easily the defects

Critias 107A–108A

CRITIAS. . . . I shall argue that to seem to speak well of the gods to men is far easier than to speak well of men to men: for the inexperience and utter ignorance of his hearers about any subject is a great assistance to him who has to speak of it, and we know how ignorant we are concerning the gods. But I should like to make my meaning clearer, if you will follow me. All that is said by any of us can only be imitation and representation. And if we consider the likenesses of bodies divine and human, and the different degrees of resemblance which the spectator requires from the painter according to the difficulty of his task, we shall see that we are satisfied with the artist who is able in any degree to imitate the earth and its mountains, and the rivers, and the woods, and the universe, and the things that are and move therein, and further, that knowing nothing precise about such matters, we do not examine or analyse the painting; all that is required is a sort of indistinct and deceptive mode of shadowing them forth. But when a person endeavours to paint the human form we are quick at finding out defects, and our familiar knowledge makes us severe judges of any one who does not render every point of similarity. And we may observe the same thing to happen in discourse; we are satisfied with a picture of divine and heavenly things which has very little likeness to them; but we are more precise in our criticism of mortal and human things. Wherefore if at the moment of speaking I cannot suitably express my meaning, you must excuse me, considering that to form approved likenesses of human things is the reverse of easy. This is what I want to suggest to you, and at the same time to beg, Socrates, that I may have not less, but more indulgence conceded to me in what I am about to say. Which favour, if I am right in asking, I hope that you will be ready to grant . . . .

On Sculpture

Republic III. 401B–402A

But shall our superintendence go no further, and are the poets only to be required by us to express the image of the good in their works, on pain, if they do anything else, of expulsion from our State? Or is the same control to be extended to other artists, and are they also to be prohibited from exhibiting the opposite forms of vice and intemperance and meanness and deformity in sculpture and building and the other creative arts; and is he who cannot conform to this rule of ours to be prevented from practising his art in our State, lest the taste of our citizens be corrupted by him? We would not have our guardians grow up amid images of mortal deformity, as in some noxious pasture, and there browse and feed upon many a baneful herb and flower day by day, little by little, until they silently gather a festering mass of corruption in their own soul. Let us rather search for artists who are gifted to discern the true nature of the beautiful and graceful; then will our youth dwell in a land of health, amid fair sights and sounds, and receive the good in everything; and beauty, the effluence of fair works, shall flow into the eye and ear, like a health-giving breeze from a purer region, and insensibly draw the soul from earliest years into the likeness and sympathy with the beauty of reason . . . .

And therefore, I said, Glaucon, musical training is a more potent instrument than any other, because rhythm and harmony find their way into the inward places of the soul, on which they mightily fasten, imparting grace, and making the soul of him who is rightly educated graceful, or of him who is ill-educated ungraceful; and also because he who has received this true education of the inner being will most shrewdly perceive omissions or faults in art and nature, and with a true taste, while he praises and rejoices over and receives into his soul the good, and becomes noble and good, he will justly blame and hate the bad, now in the days of his youth, even before he is able to know the reason why; and when reason comes he will recognize and salute the friend with whom his education has made him long familiar . . . .

The Poet is unable to distinguish truth from falsehood

Laws IV. 719B–C Athenian Stranger

Did we not hear you just now saying, that the legislator ought not to allow the poets to do what they liked? For that they would not know in which of their words they went against the laws, to the hurt of the state. . . . May we not fairly make answer to him on behalf of the poets, . . . That the poet, according to the tradition which has ever prevailed among us, and is accepted of all men, when he sits down on the tripod of the muse, is not in his right mind; like a fountain, he allows to flow out freely whatever comes in, and his art being imitative, he is often compelled to represent men of opposite dispositions, and thus to contradict himself; neither can he tell whether there is more truth in one thing that he has said than in another . . . .

A Classification of the Arts

Philebus 55E–56C (arranged)

SOCRATES. Then now let us divide the arts of which we were speaking into two kinds,—the arts which, like music, are less exact in their results, and those which, like carpentering, are more exact . . . Of the latter class, the most exact of all are those which we just now spoke of as primary . . . arithmetic, and the kindred arts of weighing and measuring . . . I mean to say, that if arithmetic, mensuration, and weighing be taken away from any art, that which remains will not be much . . . The rest will be only conjecture, and the better use of the senses which is given by experience and practice, with the help of a certain power of guessing, which is commonly called art, and is perfected by attention and pains . . . Music, for instance, is full of this empiricism; for sounds are harmonized, not by measure, but by skilful conjecture; the music of the flute is always trying to guess the pitch of each vibrating note, and is therefore mixed up with much that is doubtful and has little which is certain . . . The art of the builder, on the other hand, which uses a number of measures and instruments, attains by their help to a greater degree of accuracy than the other arts . . . In ship-building and house-building, and in other branches of the art of carpentering, the builder has his rule, lathe, compass, line, and a most ingenious machine for straightening wood. . . .

Chapter 4

Aristotle

384–322 B.C.

A. Life

Aristotle's *Poetics* is beyond doubt the single volume on an art and the arts that has exerted both the most extensive and profound influence on Philosophy of Art and Aesthetics. For Dante, Aristotle was "the master of them that know"—and with good reason, for he took in its entirety the scope of man's knowledge as his province.

Aristotle was born in Stagira, on the peninsula of Chalcidice in Macedonia and, in accord with the name of his birthplace, he is sometimes referred to as "the Stagarite." His father was Nicomachus—the name Aristotle gave his own son—a court physician to Amyntas II, King of Macedonia and father of Philip the Great. Aristotle was descended through his father from a line of men trained in medicine and belonging to the caste, Asclepius. Aristotle was left an orphan and had as a guardian Proxenus of Atarneus. At the age of 17 or 18 years, in 368–367 B.C., Aristotle entered Plato's Academy in Athens, bringing about the extraordinary relation of teachers and pupils of Socrates, Plato, and Aristotle. Aristotle remained in the Academy for 19 or 20 years, where he was known as "the brain of the Academy" and "the Mind of the School."

Aristotle was in Atarneus when Plato died. Speusippus, Plato's nephew, succeeded to the headship of the Academy and at the age of 37 Aristotle left Athens for Atarneus. He was accompanied by Xenocrates, another of Plato's pupils, and the two men went to Assos, where Plato's former pupils, Erastus and Coriscus, were teaching Platonic philosophy. Aristotle had come to know Hermias, Tyrant of Atarneus. Aristotle and Xenocrates joined the Platonic circle in Scepsis, on the slope of Mount Ida, and there Aristotle remained for three years, to be joined by Theophrastus, the man who became his own most distinguished pupil.

Aristotle married Hermias' niece and in 344 B.C. moved to the island of Lesbos, where he remained for two years. In 343–342 B.C. he was invited by King Philip to Pella, the Macedonian court, to serve as tutor to Philip's son, the Alexander who was to conquer the world. Alexander was much influenced by Aristotle, more particularly in the realms of politics and morals. He is said to have remarked that "To my father I owe my life, to Aristotle the knowledge how to live worthily."

Aristotle, however, was not only a superb moral and political philosopher, but he was also a shrewd man. "When he thought he had stayed long enough with Alexander," he left Pella, warning his kinsmen and successor, Callisthenes, not to talk with too much freedom to the king. Callisthenes disregarded the advice. Alexander had Callisthenes imprisoned in an iron cage, covered with vermin, and, finally, thrown to a lion.

Aristotle went to Athens and founded the Lyceum, which soon outshone the Academy in renown. For the next ten or twelve years, from 335–322 B.C., Aristotle directed the research in the Lyceum. He worked in a small wooden building on the grounds of the institution.

Since, while in Atarneus, Aristotle had married the adopted daughter of Hermias, the Tyrant of Atarneus, in Athens he was not only a foreigner—a Macedonian—but one who had married a barbarian. When the Athenians began their rebellion against Macedonian domination, feeling arose against Aristotle, as he was thought to be master of Alexander's spy-system. He left Athens for Chalcis in 323 B.C., remarking that he did so lest Athens sin twice against philosophy. Aristotle died in Chalcis in 322 B.C. He left a daughter by Hermias' step-daughter and a son by a second marriage. Aristotle is said to have been slender, elegant in his dress, and to have spoken with a lisp.

The selections given below include the *Poetics,* as well as excerpts concerning art and the arts drawn from Aristotle's many and diverse writings. There is general agreement that Aristotle's principal work on art, the *Poetics,* belongs to the second of his sojourns in Athens.

B. Philosophy of Art

It will be recalled that Aristotle replied to the question, "Why do we spend so much time with the beautiful?" with "That is a blind man's question." This ancient anecdote might well suffice to lead one to wonder that this greatest product of the Platonic Academy—itself clearly a center for speculation on art and beauty—has not infrequently been held to be insensitive both to art and beauty. Still, if sound evidence and not hearsay be required to refute the charge, Aristotle's *Poetics* provides it in abundance. The *Poetics* is in all likelihood the most powerful—and certainly it is the most influential—single writing on art. It lacks both the superb prose of Plato's myth of Diotima in the *Symposium* [1] and the tremendous thrust of imagination in Plato's *Ion* and *Phaedrus* [2] which make of Plato's Philosophy of Art a system which transcends its age despite its outmoded theory of imitation. But "the Reader," the "Mind of the school," the tutor of the young man who became Alexander the Great, the founder of the Lyceum, and the author of more writings pre-eminent in more fields of philosophy than any other single man, was in fact so sensitive to the power of Euripides' plays that he judged their author to be the most tragic of the poets and did so in spite of his own harsh opinion of the plays' technical deficiencies. Moreover, Aristotle clearly was so interested in the metaphysics of beauty that he devotes much of two books of the *Meta-*

[1] See above, pp. 83 et seq.

[2] See above, pp. 54 et seq. and 89 et seq.

physics[3] to Pythagorean doctrines that emerge from Pythagoras' own theory of harmony.

There is little doubt that what remains of the corpus of Aristotle's writings bears no comparison to Plato's dialogues in style, but then it may be said that there are few if any sustained writings in prose that do rival the works of "the Son of Apollo." It is likely, however, that a contrast between Aristotle's writings and Plato's is not in fact the ground for the occasional adverse criticism of the Peripatetic philosopher's attitude towards art. Rather, it would seem to result from Aristotle's consistently dim view of Plato's theory of Ideas or forms. The difficulty arises in Plato's philosophy in relating the universals to objects and events in the world of change. Aristotle incorporated into his own philosophy the theory of universals, but he denied the transcendence of the forms, and was consistently critical of the separation of universals from things.[4] For Aristotle, universals are in things. The differences between Plato and Aristotle on this point are profound and significant. Plato could say in jest that "Aristotle spurns me, as colts kick out at the mother who bore them," but despite both the differences and the jest, it is likely that the basic relation between the two philosophers is accurately described by Diogenes Laertius: "Aristotle was Plato's most genuine disciple." Aristotle himself, writing critically in the *Metaphysics*, uses the word "we" as readily as other members of Plato's Academy must have done. Even in attacking the theory of forms in the *Nicomachean Ethics*, Aristotle writes that "we had perhaps better consider the universal good and discuss thoroughly what is meant by it, although such an inquiry is made an uphill one by the fact that the Forms have been introduced by friends of our own. . . ."

Even if it be granted that the field of philosophy of art is a limited one, it is essential to indicate the difference between Plato's theory of beauty and Aristotle's theory of art, and to do this requires a brief discussion of philosophical principles in general. The systematic change introduced by Aristotle with his own speculation no longer makes of beauty a universal conterminous with good, as it was for Plato. Therefore, for Aristotle there can be no single principle that will account for the whole of philosophy as a single science related to such an explanatory principle.[5] For Aristotle, there is scientific knowledge, the object of which is certainty. The object of such knowledge is "of necessity."[6] There is also the realm of the variable,[7] in which are included "both things made and things done." Art and making are the preconditions for Aristotle's analyses of works of art. Making differs from acting, for art is identical with a "reasoned state of capacity to make." This involves "a true course of reasoning" and is "concerned with coming into being, i.e., with contriving and considering how something may come into being which is capable of either being or not being, and whose origin is in the maker and not in the thing made." Art is not concerned with necessity, i.e., not with things that are or come into being by necessity, "nor with things which do so in accordance with nature (since these have their origin in themselves)." Because making is concerned with the variable, our judgments in this realm are probable. There is excellence in art, i.e., "we ascribe in the arts *wisdom* to their most finished exponents," such as to Pheidias as a sculptor and to Polycleitus as a maker of portrait-statues.

Aristotle's confidence in art as an intelligible and demonstrable technique is strikingly

[3] See above, pp. 26 et seq., 69 et seq.

[4] See below, p. 137 for his definition of beauty and also the *Poetics* 7. 1451 a 1 sq.

[5] Aristotle, *Nicomachean Ethics* VI. Cf. Plato, *Republic* V-VII.

[6] Aristotle, *Nicomachean Ethics* VI. 1139 b 22. See below, pp. 136 et seq.

[7] *Ibid.* 1140 a 5. *Posterior Analytics* II. 100 b 5, quoted below, p. 135.

illustrated in the passage in *De Sophisticis Elenchis*.[8] It is notable that Aristotle tells us here that the program in the art of logic has been completed. He believes, however, that it is important not to "omit to notice what has happened in regard to this inquiry." What happened, in a field in which nothing systematic had existed before the work in the Lyceum, was that for which Aristotle and his students worked out the "art". Aristotle obviously favored the "art", not its "products".

For Aristotle, art imitates nature.[9] It involves, however, the intervention of the agent as an external efficient cause of the work of art, a cause not present to such natural processes as that by which the acorn is actualized in the oak. ". . . Art partly completes what nature cannot bring to a finish." As we turn to the product of Art, two points should be made. First, the object produced is an object or event separated from the maker in space and in time. Secondly, making involves the imposition of a form upon a matter.

Presumably this form is identical with that in the mind of the maker before it is embodied in the material. Consequently, once the object is made and is in the medium of the work of art, what was before only an object made is now a sign signified,[10] since it is an external symbol of the form in the artist's mind. In the *Rhetoric* (1413 b 20), Aristotle goes so far as to suggest that "it was naturally the poets who first set the movement (i.e. the predominance of diction over thought in set speeches) going; for words represent things. . . ." Precisely how far Aristotle had left behind the Platonic comparison of the artist to a mirror is evident in the *Politics* (1340 a 30): ". . . Figures and colours are not imitations, but signs, of moral habits, indications which the body gives of states of feeling. . . ."

If we ask, How do the signs get to the object from the artist? the answer lies in the Aristotelian conception of art, tools, and maker and ends of art. Of the main tool needed for making, we have the extraordinary suggestion that Nature has given man the hand, "whose range of uses is extensive," and which in fact appears "to be not one single instrument but many, as if it were an instrument which represents many instruments." It is of use as a maker of instruments principally because we can retract our thumbs.[11]

Aristotle evidently believes that the language we can construct for art, in terms of the genus, imitation, and the arts as species of imitation correspond to the means and ends used by the craftsman to produce the work of art. "The habit of feeling pleasure or pain at mere representations," he writes in the *Politics* (1340 a 24) "is not far removed from the same feeling about realities." Moreover, we learn from the *Poetics*[12] that it is from the identical instinct for imitation that the maker imitates and that we take pleasure in the imitation.

I have expressly stated the matter in these terms because Aristotle means that imitation, being natural to man from childhood—he is "the most imitative creature in the world, and learns at first by imitation,"—also means that man rationalizes the instincts in transferring a form to a matter in the process of making. Change means the imposition of a form by means of an activity. Unlike change in nature, making is a rationally directed procedure. In poetry and other arts, making is directed to the end of an increase in knowledge by means of recognition, as well as to the rational pleasure that is concomitant to this activity.

So it is that tragedy,[13] which originates in

[8] Aristotle, *De Sophisticis Elenchis* XXXIV. 183 b 16. Quoted below, pp. 135 et seq.

[9] See *Poetics* I. 1447 a. See below, pp. 149 et seq.

[10] See Aristotle, *Politics* 1340 a 19 and *Generation of Animals* 729 a 22. Quoted below, pp. 142 et seq. and 138 et seq.

[11] *Parts of Animals* IV.1. 687 a 8 et seq. See below, pp. 139 et seq.

[12] *Poetics* 4. 1448 b 4 sq. See below, p. 149.

[13] Aristotle, *Poetics* IV. 1449 a 10. Quoted below, pp. 150.

the dithyramb is brought to its "natural" state, as tragedy, by a maker. The dithyramb is prior to the tragedy in time; but the tragedy, the actuality of the dithyramb, is prior to the dithyramb conceptually.

This means that Aristotle is writing a Philosophy of Art on "natural" grounds. The word "natural" occurs many times in the *Poetics.* Here, we need merely make explicit its principal implications. The artist proposes to describe not what has happened, but what may happen and is free in the natural sense to choose to do this rather than that. The end of art is pleasure of a rational kind, and this constitutes a rational end for making. Even more specifically, in terms of a "natural" theory, Aristotle makes no mention of such images as Plato's Eros, does not accept the Platonic conception of inspiration, and abandons the conception of the inspired man suspended from the magnetic rings. For Aristotle, Homer is beyond compare. Nevertheless Plato's genius, bereft of his senses, undergoes a radical change in Aristotle's philosophy—Aristotle's genius is not the man possessed but one affected by black bile.[14]

In contrast to Plato, Aristotle holds that the artist may err. He also believes that there are differences in the kinds of error that affect the art.[15] It is important to see that for Aristotle a man may choose either to make or not to produce an imitation. The imitative artist is no mere reflecting mirror. He chooses to do what is better than, worse than, or the same as what is imitated.[16]

It is fascinating to observe Aristotle introduce the great problems of philosophy into the ostensibly simple *Poetics*: that a probable impossibility is to be preferred to a possible improbability;[17] that poetry is more universal than history;[18] and that the unity of a work of art is not mathematical but has a unity analogous to that of an organism.[19]

There is no more important part of the *Poetics,* however, than that in which Aristotle asserts that we delight to look upon ugly and painful things, provided that they are imitated.[20] The argument for the transforming and transmuting capacity of Art has never been so forcefully expressed—and Aristotle's is the first of many a rational theory of ugliness.[21]

Who exercises this great power? To say that it is the man who possesses "a rational state of capacity to make" obviously will not suffice to differentiate the maker from the nonmaker. Aristotle answers this question in the *Nicomachean Ethics* (1124 a 34.). There he draws the analogy between the magnificent man and the artist.[22] He, like the artist, "can see what is fitting," although it is doubtful that the artist, like the magnificent man, can "spend large sums tastefully." The criterion for both the magnificent man and the artist is appropriateness, and by it we judge the artist to be a skilled artisan. Again, the magnificent man will "consider how the result can be made most beautiful and most becoming rather than for how much it can be produced and how it can be produced most cheaply." And in the same passage, Aristotle sagely observes that art's product possesses a value beyond that of a mere possession—for the most valuable possession is that which is worth most, whereas the most valuable work of art is that which is "great and beautiful (for the contemplation of such a work inspires admiration)" as does magnificence.

[14] Aristotle, *Problems* XXX. 935 a 1. 1Q. See below, pp. 140 et seq. (The passage has been attributed to Theophrastus.)

[15] *Poetics* XXV. 1461 b 6. See below, p. 165 et seq.

[16] See Aristotle, *Poetics* XXV. See below, p. 165 et seq.

[17] *Ibid.,* XXV.

[18] *Ibid.,* IX. 1451 b 2. See below, p. 153.

[19] *Ibid.,* VII. 1450 b 2. See below, p. 152.

[20] *Ibid.,* IV. 1448 b 3. See below, p. 149.

[21] The *Poetics* is quoted below, p. 147. See Kant, *Critique of Judgement,* Sec. 48 below, p. 414; Plotinus, *Enneads* 1. 6. 6 below, p. 223; St. Augustine, *The City of God* XI. 23 below, p. 238.

[22] See below, pp. 140 et seq.

What, then, of the experience of art? In this "natural" system, it is clearly neither being possessed nor being taken out of oneself. Nor is it, as Plato expresses it in *Ion*,[23] the imitation of what the artist has produced. Aristotle writes specifically of our experience of tragedy and music and in doing so has produced the most vexing and controversial statement in the history of the Philosophy of Art. To various commentaries on the Aristotelian theory of the *catharsis* of pity and terror, we shall turn to the next chapter.[24] In concluding the present chapter, it is enough to draw the reader's attention to the fact that whatever interpretation he may place upon the theory of *catharsis*, there can be no doubt that it describes a specific form of response to stimuli.

[23] See above, p. 55.

[24] See below, p. 169 et seq.

Aristotle

The Systematic Distinctions of Art from Science and Acting

Posterior Analytics II, Ch. 19, 100 *b* 5.

Now of the [25] thinking states by which we grasp truth, some are unfailingly true, others admit of error—opinion, for instance, and calculation, whereas scientific knowledge and intuition are always true. . . .

On the Superiority of Art

De Sophisticis Elenchis 183 *b* 16

. . . That our [26] programme, then, has been adequately completed is clear. But we must not omit to notice what has happened in regard to this inquiry. For in the case of all discoveries the results of previous labours that have been handed down from others have been advanced bit by bit by those who have taken them on, whereas the original discoveries generally make an advance that is small at first though much more useful than the development which later springs out of them. For it may be that in everything, as the saying is, 'the first start is the main part': and for this reason also it is the most difficult; for in proportion as it is most potent in its influence, so it is smallest in its compass and therefore most difficult to see: whereas when this is once discovered, it is easier to add and develop the remainder in connexion with it. This is in fact what has happened in regard to rhetorical speeches and to practically all the other arts: for those who discovered the beginnings of them advanced them in all only a little way, whereas the celebrities of to-day are the heirs (so to speak) of a long succession of men who have advanced them bit by bit, and so have developed them to their present form, Tisias coming next after the first founders, then Thrasymachus after Tisias, and Theodorus next to him, while several people have made their several contributions to it: and therefore it is not to be wondered at that the art has attained considerable dimensions. Of this inquiry, on the other hand, it was not the case that part of the work had been thoroughly done before, while part had not. Nothing existed at all. For the training given by the paid professors of contentious arguments was like the treatment of the matter by Gorgias. For they used to hand out speeches to be learned by heart, some rhetorical, others in the form of question and answer, each side supposing that their arguments on either side generally fall among them. And therefore the

[25] Aristotle, *Analytica Posteriora* 100 b 5; Translated by G. R. G. Mure from *The Oxford Translation of Aristotle,* W. D. Ross ed., Vol. 1, 1928. By permission of the Clarendon Press, Oxford.

[26] Aristotle, *De Sophisticis Elenchis* 183 b 16 translated by W. A. Pickard-Cambridge from *The Oxford Translation of Aristotle,* W. D. Ross ed., Vol. 1, 1928. By permission of the Clarendon Press, Oxford.

teaching they gave their pupils was ready but rough. For they used to suppose that they trained people by imparting to them not the art but its products, as though any one professing that he would impart a form of knowledge to obviate any pain in the feet, were then not to teach a man the art of shoe-making or the sources whence he can acquire anything of the kind, but were to present him with several kinds of shoes of all sorts: for he has helped him to meet his need, but has not imparted an art to him. Moreover, on the subject of Rhetoric there exists much that has been said long ago, whereas on the subject of reasoning we had nothing else of an earlier date to speak of at all, but were kept at work for a long time in experimental researches. If, then, it seems to you after inspection that, such being the situation as it existed at the start, our investigation is in a satisfactory condition compared with the other inquiries that have been developed by tradition, there must remain for all of you, or for our students, the task of extending us your pardon for the shortcomings of the inquiry, and for the discoveries thereof your warm thanks.

Science, Art and Practical Wisdom: Things made and things done

Aristotle, Nicomachean Ethics VI.3. 1139 *b* 14

3. Let us begin,[27] then, from the beginning, and discuss these states once more. Let it be assumed that the states by virtue of which the soul possesses truth by way of affirmation or denial are five in number, i.e. art, scientific knowledge, practical wisdom, philosophic wisdom, intuitive reason; we do not include judgment and opinion because in these we may be mistaken.

Now what *scientific knowledge* is, if we are to speak exactly and not follow mere similarities, is plain from what follows. We all suppose that what we know is not even capable of being otherwise; of things capable of being otherwise we do not know, when they have passed outside our observation, whether they exist or not. Therefore the object of scientific knowledge is of necessity. Therefore it is eternal; for things that are of necessity in the unqualified sense are all eternal; and things that are eternal are ungenerated and imperishable. Again, every science is thought to be capable of being taught, and its object of being learned. And all teaching starts from what is already known, as we maintain in the *Analytics* also; for it proceeds sometimes through induction and sometimes by syllogism. Now induction is the starting-point which knowledge even of the universal presupposes, while syllogism proceeds *from* universals. There are therefore starting-points from which syllogism proceeds, which are not reached by syllogism; it is therefore by induction that they are acquired. Scientific knowledge is, then, a state of capacity to demonstrate, and has the other limiting characteristics which we specify in the *Analytics*; for it is when a man believes in a certain way and the starting-points are known to him that he has scientific knowledge, since if they are not better known to him than the conclusion, he will have his knowledge only incidentally.

Let this, then, be taken as our account of scientific knowledge.

In the variable are included both things made and things done; making and acting are different (for their nature we treat even the discussions outside our school as reliable); so that the reasoned state of capacity to act is different from the reasoned state of capacity to make. Hence too they are not included one in the other; for neither is acting making nor is

[27] Aristotle, *Nicomachean Ethics*, translated by W. D. Ross from *The Oxford Translation* of *Aristotle*, W. D. Ross ed., Vol IX, 1925. By permission of Clarendon Press, Oxford.

making acting. Now since architecture is an art and is essentially a reasoned state of capacity to make, and there is neither any art that is not such a state nor any such state that is not an art, *art* is identical with a state of capacity to make, involving a true course of reasoning. All art is concerned with coming into being, i.e. with contriving and considering how something may come into being which is capable of either being or not being, and whose origin is in the maker and not in the thing made; for art is concerned neither with things that are, or come into being, by necessity, nor with things that do so in accordance with nature (since these have their origin in themselves). Making and acting being different, art must be a matter of making, not of acting. And in a sense chance and art are concerned with the same objects; as Agathon says, "art loves chance and chance loves art". Art, then, as has been said, is a state concerned with making, involving a true course of reasoning, and lack of art on the contrary is a state concerned with making, involving a false course of reasoning; both are concerned with the variable.

Wisdom (1) in the arts we ascribe to their most finished exponents, e.g. to Phidias as a sculptor and to Polyclitus as a maker of portrait-statues, and here we mean nothing by wisdom except excellence in art; but (2) we think that some people are wise in general, not in some particular field or in any other limited respect, as Homer says in the *Margites*.

Him did the gods make neither a digger nor yet
  a ploughman
Nor wise in anything else . . .

The Definition of Beauty

Metaphysics XIII. 1078 *b* 1

The chief forms [28] of beauty are order and symmetry and definiteness, which the mathematical sciences demonstrate in a special degree. And since these (e.g., order and definiteness) are obviously causes of many things, evidently these sciences must treat this sort of causative principle (i.e., the beautiful) as in some sense a cause . . .

The Relation of Form and Matter: the Process of Making and Art

——— 1069 *b* 35

Note, next, that neither the matter nor the form comes to be—and I mean the last matter and form. For everything that changes is something and is changed by something and into something. That by which it is changed is the immediate mover; that which is changed, the matter; that into which it is changed, the form. The process, then, will go on to infinity, if not only the bronze comes to be round but also the round or the bronze comes to be; therefore there must be a stop.

Note, next, that each substance comes into being out of something that shares its name. (Natural objects and other things both rank as substances.) For things come into being either by art or by nature or by luck or by spontaneity. Now art is a principle of movement in something other than the thing moved, nature is a principle in the thing itself (for man begets man), and the other causes are privations of these two.

[28] Aristotle, *Metaphysics,* translated by W. D. Ross from the *Oxford Translation of Aristotle,* Vol. 8, 2nd ed. 1928. By permission of the Clarendon Press, Oxford.

The Physics 194 *a* 20

In reading[29] the ancients one might well suppose that the physicist's only concern was with the material; for Empedocles and Democritus have remarkably little to say about kinds of things and what is the constituent essence of them. But if art imitates Nature, and if in the arts and crafts it pertains to the same branch of knowledge both to study its own distinctive aspect of things and likewise (up to a point) the material in which the same is manifested (as the physicians, for instance, must study health and also bile and phlegm, the state of which constitutes health; and the builder must know what the house is to be like and also that it is built of bricks and timber; and so in all other cases), it seems to follow that physics must take cognisance both of the formal and of the material aspect of Nature.

And further the same inquiry must embrace both the purpose or end and the means to that end . . . For in the arts, too, it is in view of the end that the materials are either made or suitably prepared, and we make use of all the things that we have at our command as though they existed for our sake; for we too are, in some part, a goal ourselves. For the expression "that for the sake of which" a thing exists or is done has two senses . . . Accordingly, the arts which control the material and possess the necessary knowledge are two: the art which uses the product and the art of the master-craftsman who directs the manufacture. (Cf. Plato, *Cratylus* 390 and *Politics* 259 E). Hence the art of the user also may in a sense be called the master-art; the difference is that this art is concerned with knowing the form, the other, which is supreme as controlling the manufacture, with knowing the material. Thus, the helmsman knows which are the distinctive characteristics of the helm as such—that is to say, its form—and gives his orders accordingly; while what the other knows is out of what wood and by what manipulations the helm is produced. In the crafts, then, it is we that prepare the material for the sake of the function it is to fulfil, but in natural products Nature herself has provided the material. In both cases, however, the preparation of the material is commanded by the end to which it is directed.

And again, the conception of "material" is relative, for it is different material that is suited to receive the several forms.

How far then, is the physicist concerned with the form and identifying essence of things and how far with the material? With the form primarily and essentially, as the physician is with health; with the material up to a certain point, as the physician is with sinew and the smith with bronze . . .

[29] Reprinted by permission of the publishers and The Loeb Classical Library from P. H. Wicksteed and F. N. Cornford's translation of Aristotle, *The Physics*, pp. 121 et seq. Cambridge, Mass.: Harvard University Press; London: Heinemann, 1929–34.

Form, Matter and the Intelligibility of What is Formed

Generation of Animals 729 *a* 22

Thus,[30] there must be that which generates, and that of out which it generates; and even if these two be united in one, at any rate they must differ in kind, and in that the *logos* of each of them is distinct . . . If we consider the matter on general grounds, we see that when some one thing is formed from the conjunction of an active partner with a passive one, the active partner is not situated within the thing which is being formed; and we may generalise this still further by substituting "moving" and

[30] Reprinted by permission of the publishers and The Loeb Classical Library from A. L. Peck's translation of Aristotle, *Generation of Animals*. Cambridge, Mass.: Harvard University Press, 1943.

"moved" for "active" and "passive". Taking, then, the widest formulation of each of these two opposites, viz., regarding the male *qua* active and causing movement, and the female *qua* passive and being set in movement, we see that the one thing which is formed is formed *from them* only in the sense in which a bedstead is formed from the carpenter and the wood, or a ball from the wax and the form. It is plain, then, that there is no necessity for any substance to pass from the male; and if any does pass, this does not mean that the offspring is formed from it as from something situated within itself during the process, but as from that which has imparted movement to it, or that which is its "form" . . . XXII 730 b 8. After all, the carpenter is close by his timber, and the potter close by his clay; and to put it in general terms, the working or treatment of any material, and the ultimate movement which acts upon it, is in all cases close by the material, *e.g.*, the location of the activity of house-building is in the houses which are being built . . . In the same way, nothing passes from the carpenter into the pieces of timber, which are *his* material, and there is no part of the art of carpentry present in the object which is being fashioned: it is the shape and the form which pass from the carpenter, and they come into being by means of the movement in the material. It is his soul, wherein is the "form", and his knowledge, which cause his hands (or some other part of his body) to move in a particular way (different ways for different products, and always the same way for any one product); his hands move his tools and his tools move the materials . . . just as when objects are being produced by any art the tools are in movement, because the movement which belongs to the art is, in a way, situated in them . . . The result is that here Nature resembles a modeller in clay rather than a carpenter; she does not rely upon contact exerted at second hand when fashioning the object which is being given shape, but uses the parts of her own very self to handle it . . . In all her workmanship herein Nature acts in every particular as reason would expect . . .

The Hand: An Instrument that Represents Many Instruments

Parts of Animals 687 *a* 2

We have [31] now stated why it is that some animals have two feet, some many, some none at all; why some creatures are plants and some animals; and why man is the only one of the animals that stands upright. And since man stands upright, he has no need of legs in front; instead of them Nature has given him arms and hands. Anaxagoras indeed asserts that it is his possession of hands that makes man the most intelligent of the animals; but surely the reasonable point of view is that it is because he is the most intelligent animal that he has got hands. Hands are an instrument; and Nature, like a sensible human being, always assigns an organ to the animal that can use it (as it is more in keeping to give flutes to a man who is already a flute-player than to provide a man who possesses flutes with the skill to play them); thus Nature has provided that which is less an addition to that which is greater and superior; not *vice versa.* We may conclude, then, that, if this is the *better way,* and if Nature always does the *best* she can in the circumstances, it is not true to say that man is the most intelligent animal because he possesses hands, but he has hands because he is the most intelligent animal. We should expect the most intelligent to be able to employ the greatest number of organs or instruments to good purpose; now the hand would appear to be not

[31] Reprinted by permission of the publishers and The Loeb Classical Library from A. L. Peck's translation of Aristotle, *Parts of Animals.* Cambridge, Mass.: Harvard University Press; London: Heinemann, 1937.

one single instrument but many, as it were an instrument that represents many instruments. . . . For man [in contrast to other creatures], on the other hand, many means of defence are available, and he can change them at any time, and above all he can choose what weapon he will have and where. Take the hand: this is as good as a talon, or a claw, or a horn, or again, a spear or a sword, or any other weapon or tool: it can be all of these, because it can seize and hold them all. And Nature has admirably contrived the actual shape of the hand so as to fit in with this arrangement. It is not all of one piece, but it branches into several pieces; which gives the possibility of its coming together into one piece, whereas the reverse order of events would be impossible . . ."

Poetic Genius Attributed to Black Bile

Problems XXX. 953 *a* 1. 10

Why is it[32] that all men who are outstanding in philosophy, poetry or the arts are melancholic, and some to the extent that they are infected by the diseases arising from black bile, as the story of Heracles among the heroes tells? . . . In later times also there have been Empedocles, Plato, Socrates and many other well-known men. The same is true of most of those who have handled poetry. For such men have suffered from diseases which arise from this mixture in the body, and in others their nature evidently inclines to troubles of this sort. In any case they are all, as has been said, naturally of this character. First of all, we must consider the cause of this, using wine as a natural example. For wine in large quantities seems to make men of the type we have described melancholic, and where it is drunk produces a variety of qualities, making men ill-tempered, kindly, merciful or hasty but neither honey nor milk nor water nor any such thing produces these effects. . . . Those for instance in whom the bile is considerable and cold become sluggish and stupid, while those with whom it is excessive and hot become mad, good-natured or amorous and easily moved by passion and desire, and some become more talkative. But many, because this heat is near to the seat of the mind, are affected by the diseases of madness or frenzy, which accounts for the Sibyls, Bacis and all inspired persons, when their condition is due not to disease but to a natural mixture. Maracus, the Syracusan, was an even better poet when he was mad. . . .

[32] Reprinted by permission of the publishers and The Loeb Classical Library from W. S. Hett's translation of Aristotle, *Problems XXX*. Cambridge, Mass.: Harvard University Press, 1936–37. The passage has been attributed to Theophrastus.

The Magnificent Man Compared to the Artist

Nicomachean Ethics 1122 *a* 34

The magnificent man[33] is like an artist; for he can see what is fitting and spend large sums tastefully. For, as we said at the beginning, a state of character is determined by its activities and by its objects. Now the expenses of the magnificent man are large and fitting. Such, therefore, are also his results; for thus there will be a great expenditure and one that is fitting to its result. Therefore the result should be worthy of the expense, and the expense should be worthy of the result, or should even exceed it. And the magnificent man will spend such sums for honour's sake; for this is common to the virtues. And further he will do so gladly and lavishly; for nice calculation

[33] Aristotle, *Nicomachean Ethics,* translated by W. D. Ross from *The Oxford Translation of Aristotle,* W. D. Ross ed., Vol. ix, 1925.

is a niggardly thing. And he will consider how the result can be made most beautiful and most becoming rather than for how much it can be produced and how it can be produced most cheaply. It is necessary, then, that the magnificent man be also liberal. For the liberal man also will spend what he ought and as he ought; and it is in these matters that the greatness implied in the name of the magnificent man—his bigness, as it were—is manifested, since liberality is concerned with these matters; and at an equal expense he will produce a more magnificent work of art. For a possession and a work of art have not the same excellence. The most valuable possession is that which is worth most, e.g. gold, but the most valuable work of art is that which is great and beautiful (for the contemplation of such a work inspires admiration, and so does magnificence); and a work has an excellence—viz. magnificence—which involves magnitude. Magnificence is an attribute of expenditures of the kind which we call honourable, e.g. those connected with the gods—votive offerings, buildings, and sacrifices—and similarly with any form of religious worship, and all those that are proper objects of public-spirited ambition, as when people think they ought to equip a chorus or a trireme, or entertain the city, in a brilliant way. But in all cases, as has been said, we have regard to the agent as well and ask who he is and what means he has; for the expenditure should be worthy of his means, and suit not only the result but also the producer. Hence a poor man cannot be magnificent, since he has not the means with which to spend large sums fittingly; and he who tries is a fool, since he spends beyond what can be expected of him and what is proper, but it is *right* expenditure that is virtuous. But great expenditure is becoming to those who have suitable means to start with, acquired by their own efforts or from ancestors or connexions, and to people of high birth or reputation, and so on; for all these things bring with them greatness and prestige. Primarily, then, the magnificent man is of this sort, and magnificence is shown in expenditures of this sort, as has been said; for these are the greatest and most honourable. Of *private* occasions of expenditure the most suitable are those that take place once for all, e.g. a wedding or anything of the kind, or anything that interests the whole city or the people of position in it, and also the receiving of foreign guests and the sending of them on their way, and gifts and counter-gifts; for the magnificent man spends not on himself but on public objects, and gifts bear some resemblance to votive offerings. A magnificent man will also furnish his house suitably to his wealth (for even a house is a sort of public ornament), and will spend by preference on those works that are lasting (for these are the most beautiful), and on every class of things he will spend what is becoming; for the same things are not suitable for gods and for men, nor in a temple and in a tomb. And since each expenditure may be great of its kind, and what is most magnificent absolutely is great expenditure on a great object, but what is magnificent *here* is what is great in *these* circumstances, and greatness in the work differs from greatness in the expense (for the most beautiful ball or bottle is magnificent as a gift to a child, but the price of it is small and mean),—therefore it is characteristic of the magnificent man, whatever kind of result he is producing, to produce it magnificently (for such a result is not easily surpassed) and to make it worthy of the expenditure.

Such, then, is the magnificent man; the man who goes to excess and is vulgar exceeds, as has been said, by spending beyond what is right. For on small objects of expenditure he spends much and displays a tasteless showiness; e.g. he gives a club dinner on the scale of a wedding banquet, and when he provides the chorus for a comedy he brings them on to the stage in purple, as they do at Megara. And all such things he will do not for honour's sake but to show off his wealth, and because he thinks he is admired for these things, and where he ought to spend much he spends little and where little, much. The niggardly man on the other hand will fall short in everything, and after spending the greatest sums will spoil the beauty of the result for a trifle, and whatever he is doing he will hesitate and consider how he may spend least, and lament even that, and think he is doing everything on a bigger scale than he ought.

Various Statements by Aristotle Concerning Art and the Arts

On Rhythm and Melody

Politics 1340 *a* 19

Rhythm and melody[34] supply imitations of anger and gentleness, and also of courage and temperance, and of all the qualities contrary to these, and of the other qualities of character, which hardly fall short of the actual affections, as we know from our own experience, for in listening to such strains our souls undergo a change. The habit of feeling pleasure or pain at mere representations is not far removed from the same feeling about realities; (cf. *Rep.* III. 395) for example, if any one delights in the sight of a statue for its beauty only, it necessarily follows that the sight of the original will be pleasant for him. . . . Again, figures and colours are not imitations, but signs, of moral habits, indications which the body gives of states of feeling. The connexion of them with morals is slight, but in so far as there is any, young men should be taught to look, not at the works of Pauson, but at those of Polygnotus, (cf. *Poetics* 1448 a 5, 1450 a 26) or any other painter or sculptor who expresses moral ideas. On the other hand, even in mere melodies there is an imitation of character, for the musical modes differ essentially from one another and those who hear them are differently affected by each. Some of them make men sad and grave, like the so-called Mixolydian, others enfeeble the mind, like the relaxed modes, another, again, produces a moderate and settled temper, which appears to be the peculiar effect of the Dorian; the Phrygian inspires enthusiasm. . . .

There is a meaning also in the myth of the ancients, which tells how Athene invented the flute and then threw it away. It was not a bad idea of theirs, that the Goddess disliked the instrument because it made the face ugly; but with still more reason may we say that she rejected it because the acquirement of flute-playing contributes nothing to the mind, since to Athene we ascribe both knowledge and art.

Thus then we reject the professional instruments and also the professional mode of education in music (and by professional we mean that which is adopted in contests), for in this the performer practises the art, not for the sake of his own improvement, but in order to give pleasure, and that of a vulgar sort, to his hearers. For this reason the execution of such music is not the part of a freeman but of a paid performer, and the result is that the performers are vulgarized, for the end at which they aim is bad. The vulgarity of the spectator tends to lower the character of the music and therefore of the performers; they look to him—he makes them what they are, and fashions even their bodies by the movements which he expects them to exhibit.

We have also to consider rhythms and modes, and their use in education. Shall we use them all or make a distinction? and shall the same distinction be made for those who practise music with a view to education, or shall it be

[34] Aristotle's *Politica,* translated by Benjamin Jowett from *The Oxford Translation of Aristotle,* W. D. Ross ed., Vol. 10, 1921. By permission of The Clarendon Press, Oxford.

some other? Now we see that music is produced by melody and rhythm, and we ought to know what influence these have respectively on education, and whether we should prefer excellence in melody or excellence in rhythm. But as the subject has been very well treated by many musicians of the present day, and also by philosophers who have had considerable experience of musical education, to those we would refer the more exact student of the subject; we shall only speak of it now after the manner of the legislator, stating the general principles.

We accept the division of melodies proposed by certain philosophers into ethical melodies, melodies of action, and passionate or inspiring melodies, each having as they say, a mode corresponding to it. But we maintain further that music should be studied, not for the sake of one, but of many benefits, that is to say, with a view to (1) education, (2) purgation (the word 'purgation' we use at present without explanation, but when hereafter we speak of poetry,[35] we will treat the subject with more precision); music may also serve (3) for intellectual enjoyment, for relaxation and for recreation after exertion. It is clear, therefore, that all the modes must be employed by us, but not all of them in the same manner. In education the most ethical modes are to be preferred, but in listening to the performances of others we may admit the modes of action and passion also. For feelings such as pity and fear, or, again, enthusiasm, exist very strongly in some souls, and have more or less influence over all. Some persons fall into a religious frenzy, whom we see as a result of the sacred melodies—when they have used the melodies that excite the soul to mystic frenzy—restored as though they had found healing and purgation. Those who are influenced by pity or fear, and every emotional nature, must have a like experience, and others in so far as each is susceptible to such emotions, and all are in a manner purged and their souls lightened and delighted. The purgative melodies likewise give an innocent pleasure to mankind. Such are the modes and the melodies in which those who perform music at the theatre should be invited to compete. But since the spectators are of two kinds—the one free and educated, and the other a vulgar crowd composed of mechanics, labourers, and the like—there ought to be contests and exhibitions instituted for the relaxation of the second class also. And the music will correspond to their minds; for as their minds are perverted from the natural state, so there are perverted modes and highly strung and unnaturally coloured melodies. A man receives pleasure from what is natural to him, and therefore professional musicians may be allowed to practise this lower sort of music before an audience of a lower type. But, for the purposes of education, as I have already said, those modes and melodies should be employed which are ethical, such as the Dorian, as we said before; though we may include any others which are approved by philosophers who have had a musical education. The Socrates of the *Republic* is wrong in retaining only the Phrygian mode along with the Dorian, and the more so because he rejects the flute; for the Phrygian is to the modes what the flute is to musical instruments—both of them are exciting and emotional. Poetry proves this, for Bacchic frenzy and all similar emotions are most suitably expressed by the flute, and are better set to the Phrygian than to any other mode. The dithyramb, for example, is acknowledged to be Phrygian, a fact of which the connoisseurs of music offer many proofs, saying, among other things, that Philoxenus, having attempted to compose his *Mysians* as a dithyramb in the Dorian mode, found it impossible, and fell back by the very nature of things into the more appropriate Phrygian. All men agree that the Dorian music is the gravest and manliest. And

[35] Cp. *Poet.* 1449b 27, though the promise is really unfulfilled. The reference is probably to a lost part of the *Poetics.*

whereas we say that the extremes should be avoided and the mean followed, and whereas the Dorian is a mean between the other modes, it is evident that our youth should be taught the Dorian music.

Two principles have to be kept in view, what is possible, what is becoming: at these every man ought to aim. But even these are relative to age; the old, who have lost their powers, cannot very well sing the high-strung modes, and nature herself seems to suggest that their songs should be of the more relaxed kind. Wherefore the musicians likewise blame Socrates, and with justice, for rejecting the relaxed modes in education under the idea that they are intoxicating, not in the ordinary sense of intoxication (for wine rather tends to excite men), but because they have no strength in them. And so, with a view also to the time of life when men begin to grow old, they ought to practise the gentler modes and melodies as well as the others, and, further, any modes, such as the Lydian above all others appears to be, which is suited to children of tender age, and possesses the elements both of order and of education. Thus it is clear that education should be based upon three principles—the mean, the possible, the becoming, these three.

On Old Paintings

Topica 140 *a* 15

Moreover,[36] see if from the expression used the definition of the contrary be not clear; for definitions that have been correctly rendered also indicate their contraries as well. Or, again, see if, when it is merely stated by itself, it is not evident what it defines; just as in the works of the old painters, unless there were an inscription, the figures used to be unrecognizable.

The Bronze

Metaphysics 1029 *a* 4

By the matter[37] I mean, for instance, the bronze, by the shape the pattern of its form, and by the compound of these the statue, the concrete whole. Therefore if the form is prior to the matter and more real, it will be prior also to the compound of both, for the same reason.

The Color of the Statue

———— 1033 *a* 5

As for that out of which as matter they are produced, some things are said, when they have been produced, to be not that but 'thaten'; e.g. the statue is not gold but golden.

The Product of Art

———— 1035 *a* 24

And it is clear from what has been said that in a sense every product of art is produced

[36] Aristotle, *Topica and Sophisticis Elenchis*, translated by W. A. Pickard-Cambridge from *The Oxford Translation of Aristotle*, W. D. Ross ed., Vol. I, 1928. By permission of the Clarendon Press, Oxford.

[37] Aristotle, *Metaphysics* translated by W. D. Ross from *The Oxford Translation of Aristotle*, W. D. Ross ed., Vol. 8, 2nd ed., 1928. By permission of The Clarendon Press, Oxford.

from a thing which shares its name (as natural products are produced), or from a part of itself which shares its name (e.g. the house is produced from a house, *qua* produced by reason; for the art of building is the form of the house), or from something which contains a part of it—if we exclude things produced by accident; for the cause of the thing's producing the product directly *per se* is a part of the product.

On Statues

Politics 1254 *b* 34

And doubtless [38] if men differed from one another in the mere forms of their bodies as much as the statues of the Gods do from men, all would acknowledge that the inferior class should be slaves of the superior. . . .

On Proportions in Painting

——— 1284 *b* 8

The same thing may be observed in the arts and sciences, for the painter will not allow the figure to have a foot which, however beautiful, is not in proportion, nor will the shipbuilder allow the stern or any other part of the vessel be unduly large, any more than the chorus-master will allow any one who sings louder or better than all the rest to sing in the choir. . . .

On Symmetry

——— 1302 *b* 36

For as a body is made up of many members, and every member ought to grow in proportion, that symmetry may be preserved; but loses its nature if the foot be four cubits long and the rest of the body two spans . . . even so a state has many parts, of which someone may often grow imperceptibly. . . .

On Censorship

——— 1336 *b* 12

And since we do not allow improper language, clearly we should also banish pictures or speeches from the stage which are indecent. Let the rulers take care that there be no image or picture representing unseemly actions, except in the temples of those Gods at whose festivals the law permits even ribaldry, and whom the law also permits to be worshipped by persons of mature age on behalf of themselves, their children, and their wives. But the legislator should not allow youth to be spectators of iambi or of comedy until they are of an age to sit at the public tables and to drink strong wine; by that time education will have armed them against the evil influence of such representations.

[38] Aristotle, *Politica,* translated by Benjamin Jowett from *The Oxford Translation of Aristotle,* W. D. Ross ed., Vol. 10, 1921. By permission of The Clarendon Press, Oxford.

Aristotle's Poetics [39]

ANALYSIS OF CONTENTS

I. 'Imitation' (μίμησις) the common principle of the Arts of Poetry, Music, Dancing, Painting, and Sculpture. These Arts distinguished according to the Medium or material Vehicle, the Objects, and the Manner of Imitation. The Medium of Imitation is Rhythm, Language, and 'Harmony' (or Melody), taken singly or combined.

II. The Objects of Imitation.

Higher or lower types are represented in all the Imitative Arts. In Poetry this is the basis of the distinction between Tragedy and Comedy.

III. The Manner of Imitation.

Poetry may be in form either dramatic narrative, pure narrative (including lyric poetry), or pure drama. A digression follows on the name and original home of the Drama.

IV. The Origin and Development of Poetry.

Psychologically, Poetry may be traced to two causes, the instinct of Imitation, and the instinct of Harmony and Rhythm.

Historically viewed, Poetry diverged early in two directions: traces of this twofold tendency are found in the Homeric poems: Tragedy and Comedy exhibit the distinction in a developed form.

The successive steps in the history of Tragedy are enumerated.

V. Definition of the Ludicrous (τὸ γελοῖον), and a brief sketch of the rise of Comedy. Points of comparison between Epic Poetry and Tragedy. (The chapter is fragmentary.)

VI. Definition of Tragedy. Six elements in Tragedy: three external — namely, Scenic Presentment (ὁ τῆς ὄψεως κόσμος or ὄψις), Lyrical Song (μελοποιία), Diction (λέξις); three internal—namely, Plot (μῦθος), Character (ἦθος), and Thought (διάνοια). Plot, or the representation of the action, is of primary importance; Character and Thought come next in order.

VII. The Plot must be a Whole, complete in itself, and of adequate magnitude.

VIII. The Plot must be a Unity. Unity of Plot consists not in Unity of Hero, but in Unity of Action.

The parts must be organically connected.

IX. (Plot continued.) Dramatic Unity can be attained only by the observance of Poetic as distinct from Historic Truth; for Poetry is an expression of the Universal, History of the Particular. The rule of probable or necessary sequence as applied to the incidents. Certain plots condemned for want of Unity.

The best Tragic effects depend on the combination of the Inevitable and the Unexpected.

X. (Plot continued.) Definitions of Simple (ἁπλοῖ) and Complex (πεπλεγμένοι) Plots.

XI. (Plot continued.) Sudden Reversal or Recoil of the Action (περιπέτεια), Recognition (ἀναγνώρισις), and Tragic or disastrous Incident (πάθος) defined and explained.

XII. The 'quantitative parts' (μέρη κατὰ τὸ ποσόν) of Tragedy defined:—Prologue, Episode, etc. (Probably an interpolation.)

XIII. (Plot continued.) What constitutes Tragic Action. The change of fortune and the character of the hero as requisite to an ideal Tragedy. The unhappy ending more truly tragic than the 'poetic justice' which is in favour with a popular audience, and belongs rather to Comedy.

XIV. (Plot continued.) The tragic emotions of pity and fear should spring out of the Plot itself. To produce them by

[39] Translated by S. H. Butcher. *Aristotle's Theory of Poetry and Fine Art.* . . . London, Macmillan and Co., Ltd., 1898.

Scenery or Spectacular effect is entirely against the spirit of Tragedy. Examples of Tragic Incidents designed to heighten the emotional effect.

XV. The element of Character (as the manifestation of moral purpose) in Tragedy. Requisites of ethical portraiture. The rule of necessity or probability applicable to Character as to Plot. The 'Deus ex Machina' (a passage out of place here). How Character is idealised.

XVI. (Plot continued.) Recognition: its various kinds, with examples.

XVII. Practical rules for the Tragic Poet:

(1) To place the scene before his eyes, and to act the parts himself in order to enter into vivid sympathy with the *dramatis personae.*

(2) To sketch the bare outline of the action before proceeding to fill in the episodes.

The Episodes of Tragedy are here incidentally contrasted with those of Epic Poetry.

XVIII. Further rules for the Tragic Poet:

(1) To be careful about the Complication (δέσις) and *Dénouement* (λύσις) of the Plot; especially the *Dénouement.*

(2) To unite, if possible, varied forms of poetic excellence.

(3) Not to overcharge a Tragedy with details appropriate to Epic Poetry.

(4) To make the Choral Odes—like the Dialogue—an organic part of the whole.

XIX. Thought (διάνοια), or the Intellectual element, and Diction in Tragedy.

Thought may be expressed either by the dramatic speeches—composed according to the rules of Rhetoric—or through the dramatic incidents, which speak for themselves.

Diction falls largely within the domain of the Art of Declamation, rather than of Poetry.

XX. Diction, or Language in general. An analysis of the parts of speech, and other grammatical details. (Probably interpolated.)

XXI. Poetic Diction. The words and modes of speech admissible in Poetry: including Metaphor, in particular.

A passage—probably interpolated—on the Gender of Nouns.

XXII. (Poetic Diction continued.) How Poetry combines elevation of language with perspicuity.

XXIII. Epic Poetry. It agrees with Tragedy in Unity of Action: herein contrasted with History.

XXIV. (Epic Poetry continued.) Further points of agreement with Tragedy. The points of difference are enumerated and illustrated,—namely, (1) the length of the poem; (2) the metre; (3) the art of imparting a plausible air to incredible fiction.

XXV. Critical Objections brought against Poetry, and the principles on which they are to be answered. In particular, an elucidation of the meaning of Poetic Truth, and its difference from common reality.

XXVI. A general estimate of the comparative worth of Epic Poetry and Tragedy. The alleged defects of Tragedy are not essential to it. Its positive merits entitle it to the higher rank of the two.

ARISTOTLE'S POETICS

I

I propose to treat of Poetry in itself and of its various kinds, noting the essential quality of each; to inquire into the structure of the plot as requisite to a good poem; into the number and nature of the parts of which a poem is composed; and similarly into whatever else falls within the same inquiry. Following, then, the order of nature, let us begin with the principles which come first.

Epic poetry and Tragedy, Comedy also

and dithyrambic poetry, and the music of the flute and of the lyre in most of their forms, are all in their general conception modes of imitation. They differ, however, from one another in three respects,—the medium, the objects, the manner or modes of imitation, being in each case distinct.

For as there are persons who, by conscious art or mere habit, imitate and represent various objects through the medium of colour and form, or again by the voice; so in the arts above mentioned, taken as a whole, the imitation is produced by rhythm, language, or "harmony", either singly or combined.

Thus in the music of the flute and the lyre, "harmony" and rhythm alone are employed; also in other arts, such as that of the shepherd's pipe, which are essentially similar to these. In dancing, rhythm alone is used without "harmony"; for even dancing imitates character, emotion, and action, by rhythmical movement. There is another art which imitates by means of language alone, and that either in prose or verse—which verse, again, may either combine different metres or consist of but one kind—but this has hitherto been without a name.

For there is no common term we could apply to the mimes of Sophron and Xenarchus and the Socratic dialogues on the one hand; and, on the other, to poetic imitations in iambic, elegiac, or any similar metre. People do, indeed, add the word "maker" or "poet" to the name of the metre, and speak of elegiac poets, or epic (that is, hexameter) poets, as if it were not the imitation that makes the poet, but the verse that entitles them all indiscriminately to the name. Even when a treatise on medicine or natural science is brought out in verse, the name of poet is by custom given to the author; and yet Homer and Empedocles have nothing in common but the metre, so that it would be right to call the one poet, the other physicist rather than poet. On the same principle, even if a writer in his poetic imitation were to combine all metres, as Chaeremon did in his Centaur, which is a medley composed of metres of all kinds, we should bring him too under the general term poet. So much then for these distinctions.

There are, again, some arts which employ all the means above mentioned,—namely, rhythm, tune and metre. Such are dithyrambic and nomic poetry, and also Tragedy and Comedy; but between them the difference is, that in the first two cases these means are all employed in combination, in the latter, now one means is employed, now another.

Such, then, are the differences of the arts with respect to the medium of imitation.

II

Since the objects of imitation are men in action, and these men must be either of a higher or a lower type (for moral character mainly answers to these divisions, goodness and badness being the distinguishing marks of moral differences), it follows that we must represent men either as better than in real life, or as worse, or as they are. It is the same in painting. Polygnotus depicted men as nobler than they are, Pauson as less noble, Dionysius drew them true to life.

Now it is evident that each of the modes of imitation above mentioned will exhibit these differences, and become a distinct kind in imitating objects that are thus distinct. Such diversities may be found even in dancing, flute-playing, and lyre-playing. So again in language, whether prose or verse unaccompanied by music. Homer, for example, makes men better than they are; Cleophon as they are; Hegemon the Thasian, the inventor of parodies, and Nicochares, the author of the Deliad, worse than they are. The same thing holds good of dithyrambs and nomes; here too one may portray different types, as Timotheus and Philoxenus differed in representing the Cyclopes. The same distinction marks off Tragedy from Comedy; for Comedy aims at representing men as worse, Tragedy better than in actual life.

III

There is still a third difference—the manner in which each of these objects may be imitated. For the medium being the same, and the objects the same, the poet may imitate by narration—in which case he can either take another personality as Homer does, or speak in his own person, unchanged—or he may present all his characters as living and moving before us.

These, then, as we said at the beginning, are the three differences which distinguish artistic imitation,—the medium, the objects, and the manner. So that from one point of view, Sophocles is an imitator of the same kind as Homer—for both imitate higher types of character; from another point of view, of the same kind as Aristophanes—for both imitate persons acting and doing. Hence, some say, the name of "drama" is given to such poems, as representing action. For the same reason the Dorians claim the invention both of Tragedy and Comedy. The claim to Comedy is put forward by the Megarians,—not only by those of Greece proper, who allege that it originated under their democracy, but also by the Megarians of Sicily, for the poet Epicharmus, who is much earlier than Chionides and Magnes, belonged to that country. Tragedy too is claimed by certain Dorians of the Peloponnese. In each case they appeal to the evidence of language. Villages, they say, are by them called *κῶμαι*, by the Athenians *δῆμοι*: and they assume that Comedians were so named not from *κωάζειν*, "to revel", but because they wandered from village to village (*κατὰ κώμας*), being excluded contemptuously from the city. They add also that the Dorian word for "doing" is *δρᾶν*, and the Athenian, *πράττειν*.

This may suffice as to the number and nature of the various modes of imitation.

IV

Poetry in general seems to have sprung from two causes, each of them lying deep in our nature. First, the instinct of imitation is implanted in man from childhood, one difference between him and other animals being that he is the most imitative of living creatures; and through imitation he learns his earliest lessons; and no less universal is the pleasure felt in things imitated. We have evidence of this in the facts of experience. Objects which in themselves we view with pain, we delight to contemplate when reproduced with minute fidelity: such as the forms of the most ignoble animals and of dead bodies. The cause of this again is, that to learn gives the liveliest pleasure, not only to philosophers but to men in general; whose capacity, however, of learning is more limited. Thus the reason why men enjoy seeing a likeness is, that in contemplating it they find themselves learning or inferring, and saying perhaps, "Ah, that is he". For if you happen not to have seen the original, the pleasure will be due not to the imitation as such, but to the execution, the colouring, or some such other cause.

Imitation, then, is one instinct of our nature. Next, there is the instinct for "harmony" and rhythm, metres being manifestly sections of rhythm. Persons, therefore, starting with this natural gift developed by degrees their special aptitudes, till their rude improvisations gave birth to Poetry.

Poetry now diverged in two directions, according to the individual character of the writers. The graver spirits imitated noble actions, and the actions of good men. The more trivial sort imitated the actions of meaner persons, at first composing satires, as the former did hymns to the gods and the praises of famous men. A poem of the satirical kind cannot indeed be put down to any author earlier than Homer; though many such writers probably there were. But from Homer onward, instances can be cited,—his own Margites, for example, and other similar compositions. The appropriate metre was also here introduced; hence the measure is still called the iambic or lampooning measure, being that in which people lampooned one another. Thus the older poets were distinguished as writers of heroic or of lampooning verse.

As, in the serious style, Homer is pre-eminent among poets, standing alone not only in the excellence, but also in the dramatic form of his imitations, so he too first laid down the main lines of Comedy, by dramatising the ludicrous instead of writing personal satire. His Margites bears the same relation to Comedy that the Iliad and Odyssey do to Tragedy. But when Tragedy and Comedy came to light, the two classes of poets still followed their natural bent: the lampooners became writers of Comedy, and the Epic poets were succeeded by Tragedians, since the drama was a larger and higher form of art.

Whether Tragedy has as yet perfected its proper types or not; and whether it is to be judged in itself, or in relation also to the audience,—this raises another question. Be that as it may, Tragedy—as also Comedy—was at first mere improvisation. The one originated with the leaders of the dithyramb, the other with those of the phallic songs, which are still in use in many of our cities. Tragedy advanced by slow degrees; each new element that showed itself was in turn developed. Having passed through many changes, it found its natural form, and there it stopped.

Aeschylus first introduced a second actor; he diminished the importance of the Chorus, and assigned the leading part to the dialogue. Sophocles raised the number of actors to three, and added scene-painting. It was not till late that the short plot was discarded for one of greater compass, and the grotesque diction of the earlier satyric form for the stately manner of Tragedy. The iambic measure then replaced the trochaic tetrameter, which was originally employed when the poetry was of the satyric order, and had greater affinities with dancing. Once dialogue had come in, Nature herself discovered the appropriate measure. For the iambic is, of all measures, the most colloquial: we see it in the fact that conversational speech runs into iambic form more frequently than into any other kind of verse; rarely into hexameters, and only when we drop the colloquial intonation. The number of "episodes" or acts was also increased, and the other embellishments added, of which tradition tells. These we need not here discuss; to enter into them in detail would, doubtless, be a large undertaking.

V

Comedy is, as we have said, an imitation of characters of a lower type,—not, however, in the full sense of the word bad, the Ludicrous being merely a subdivision of the ugly. It consists in some defect or ugliness which is not painful or destructive. To take an obvious example, the comic mask is ugly and distorted, but does not imply pain.

The successive changes through which Tragedy passed, and the authors of these changes, are well known, whereas Comedy has had no history, because it was not at first treated seriously. It was late before the Archon granted a comic chorus to a poet; the performers were till then voluntary. Comedy had already taken definite shape when comic poets, distinctively so called are heard of. Who introduced masks, or prologues, or increased the number of actors,—these and other similar details remain unknown. As for the plot, it came originally from Sicily; but of Athenian writers Crates was the first who, abandoning the "iambic" or lampooning form, generalised his themes and plots.

Epic poetry agrees with Tragedy in so far as it is an imitation in verse of characters of a higher type. They differ, in that Epic poetry admits but one kind of metre, and is narrative in form. They differ, again, in the length of the action: for Tragedy endeavours, as far as possible, to confine itself to a single revolution of the sun, or but slightly to exceed this limit; whereas the Epic action has no limits of time. This, then, is a second point of difference; though at first the same freedom was admitted in Tragedy as in Epic poetry.

Of their constituent parts some are common to both, some peculiar to Tragedy. Whoever, therefore, knows what is good or bad Tragedy, knows also about Epic poetry: for all the elements of an Epic poem are found in Tragedy, but the elements of a Tragedy are not all found in the Epic poem.

VI

Of the poetry which imitates in hexameter verse, and of Comedy, we will speak hereafter. Let us now discuss Tragedy, resuming its formal definition, as resulting from what has been already said.

Tragedy, then, is an imitation of an action that is serious, complete, and of a certain magnitude; in language embellished with each kind of artistic ornament, the several kinds being found in separate parts of the play; in the form of action, not of narrative; through pity and fear effecting the proper purgation of these emotions. By "language embellished", I mean language into which rhythm, "harmony", and song enter. By "the several kinds in separate parts", I mean, that some parts are rendered through the medium of verse alone, others again with the aid of song.

Now as tragic imitation implies persons acting, it necessarily follows, in the first place, that Scenic equipment will be a part of Tragedy. Next, Song and Diction, for these are the medium of imitation. By "Diction" I mean the mere metrical arrangement of the words: as for "Song", it is a term whose sense every one understands.

Again, Tragedy is the imitation of an action; and an action implies personal agents, who necessarily possess certain distinctive qualities both of character and thought. It is these that determine the qualities of actions themselves; these—thought and character—are the two natural causes from which actions spring: on these causes, again, all success or failure depends. Hence, the Plot is the imitation of the action:—for by plot I here mean the arrangement of the incidents. By Character I mean that in virtue of which we ascribe certain qualities to the agents. Thought is required wherever a statement is proved, or, it may be, a general truth enunciated. Every Tragedy, therefore, must have six parts, which parts determine its quality—namely, Plot, Character, Diction, Thought, Scenery, Song. Two of the parts constitute the medium of imitation, one the manner, and three the objects of imitation. And these complete the list. These elements have been employed, we may say, by the poets to a man; in fact, every play contains Scenic accessories as well as Character, Plot, Diction, Song, and Thought.

But most important of all is the structure of the incidents. For Tragedy is an imitation, not of men, but of an action and of life, and consists of action, and its end is a mode of action, not a quality. Now character determines men's qualities, but it is by their actions that they are happy or the reverse. Dramatic action, therefore, is not with a view to the representation of character: character comes in as subsidiary to the action. Hence the incidents and the plot are the end of a tragedy; and the end is the chief thing of all. Again, without action there cannot be a tragedy; there may be without character. The tragedies of most of our modern poets fail in the rendering of character; and of poets in general this is often true. It is the same in painting; and here lies the difference between Zeuxis and Polygnotus. Polygnotus delineates character well: the style of Zeuxis is devoid of ethical quality. Again, if you string together a set of speeches expressive of character, and well finished in point of diction and thought, you will not produce the essential tragic effect nearly so well as with a play which, however deficient in these respects, yet has a plot and artistically constructed incidents. Besides which, the most powerful elements of emotional interest in Tragedy—Reversal or Recoil of the Action, and Recognition scenes—are parts of the plot. A further proof is, that novices in the art attain to finish of diction and precision of portraiture before they can construct the plot. It is the same with almost all the early poets.

The Plot, then, is the first principle, and, as it were, the soul of a tragedy: Character holds the second place. A similar fact is seen in painting. The most beautiful colours, laid on confusedly, will not give as much pleasure as the chalk outline of a portrait. Thus Tragedy is the imitation of an action, and of the agents, mainly with a view to the action.

Third in order is Thought,—that is, the faculty of saying what is possible and pertinent in given circumstances. In the case of oratory, this is the function of the political art and of the art of rhetoric: and so indeed the older poets make their characters speak the language of civic life; the poets of our time, the language of the rhetoricians. Character is that which reveals moral purpose, showing what kind of things a man chooses or avoids. Speeches, therefore, which do not make this manifest, or in which the speaker does not choose or avoid anything whatever, are not expressive of character. Thought, on the other hand, is found where something is proved to be or not to be, or a general maxim is enunciated.

Fourth among the elements enumerated comes Diction; by which I mean, as has been already said, the expression of our meaning in words; and its essence is the same both in verse and prose.

Of the remaining elements Song holds the chief place among the embellishments.

Scenery has, indeed, an emotional attraction of its own, but, of all the parts, it is the least artistic, and connected least with the art of poetry. For the power of Tragedy, we may be sure, is felt even apart from representation and actors. Besides, the production of spectacular effects depends more on the art of the stage machinist than on that of the poet.

VII

These principles being established, let us now discuss the proper structure of the Plot, since this is the first and most important part of Tragedy.

Now, according to our definition, Tragedy is an imitation of an action that is complete, and whole, and of a certain magnitude; for there may be a whole that is wanting in magnitude. A whole is that which has a beginning, a middle, and an end. A beginning is that which does not itself follow anything by causal necessity, but after which something naturally is or comes to be. An end, on the contrary, is that which itself naturally follows some other thing, either by necessity, or as a rule, but has nothing following it. A middle is that which follows something as some other thing follows it. A well constructed plot, therefore, must neither begin nor end at haphazard, but conform to these principles.

Again, a beautiful object, whether it be a picture of a living organism or any whole composed of parts, must not only have an orderly arrangement of parts, but must also be of a certain magnitude; for beauty depends on magnitude and order. Hence an exceedingly small picture cannot be beautiful; for the view of it is confused, the object being seen in an almost imperceptible moment of time. Nor, again, can one of vast size be beautiful; for as the eye cannot take it all in at once, the unity and sense of the whole is lost for the spectator; as for instance if there were a picture a thousand miles long. As, therefore, in the case of animate bodies and pictures a certain magnitude is necessary, and a magnitude which may be easily embraced in one view; so in the plot, a certain length is necessary, and a length which can be easily embraced by the memory. The limit of length in relation to dramatic competition and sensuous presentment, is no part of artistic theory. For had it been the rule for a hundred tragedies to compete together, the performance would have been regulated by the water-clock,—as indeed is the practice in certain other contests. But the limit as fixed by the nature of the drama itself is this:—the greater the length, the more beautiful will the piece be, so far as beauty depends on size, provided that the whole be perspicuous. And to define the matter roughly, we may say that the proper magnitude is comprised within such limits, that the sequence of events, according to the law of probability or necessity, will admit of a change from bad fortune to good, or from good fortune to bad.

VIII

Unity of plot does not, as some persons think, consist in the unity of the hero. For infinitely various are the incidents in one man's life, which cannot be reduced to unity; and so, too, there are many actions of one man out of which we cannot make one action. Hence the error, as it appears, of all poets who have composed a Heracleid, a Theseid, or other poems of the kind. They imagine that as Heracles was one man, the story of Heracles must also be unity. But Homer, as in all else he is of surpassing merit, here too—whether from art or natural genius—seems to have happily discerned the truth. In composing the Odyssey he did not include all the adventures of Odysseus—such as his wound on Parnassus, or his feigned madness at the mustering of the host—incidents between which there was no necessary or probable connexion: but he made the Odyssey, and likewise the Iliad, to centre round an action, that in our sense of the word is one. As therefore, in the other imitative arts, the imitation is one, when the object imitated is one, so the plot, being an imitation of an action, must imitate one action and that a whole, the structural union of the parts being such that, if any one of them is displayed or removed, the whole will be disjointed and disturbed. For a thing whose presence or absence makes no visible difference, is not an organic part of the whole.

IX

It is, moreover, evident from what has been said, that it is not the function of the poet to relate what has happened, but what may happen,—what is possible according to the law of probability or necessity. The poet and the historian differ not by writing in verse or in prose. The work of Herodotus might be put into verse, and it would still be a species of history, with metre no less than without it. The true difference is that one relates what has happened, the other what may happen. Poetry, therefore, is a more philosophical and a higher thing than history: for poetry tends to express the universal, history the particular. By the universal I mean how a person of given character will on occasion speak or act, according to the law of probability or necessity; and it is this universality at which poetry aims in the names she attaches to the personages. The particular is—for example—what Alcibiades did or suffered. In Comedy this is already apparent: for here the poet first constructs the plot on the lines of probability, and then inserts characteristic names;—unlike the lampooners who write about particular individuals. But tragedians still keep to real names, the reason being that what is possible is credible: what has not happened we do not at once feel sure to be possible: but what has happened is manifestly possible; otherwise it would not have happened. Still there are some tragedies in which there are only one or two well known names, the rest being fictitious. In others, none are well known,—as in Agathon's Flower, where incidents and names alike are fictitious, and yet they give none the less pleasure. We must not, therefore, at all costs keep to the received legends, which are the usual subjects of Tragedy. Indeed, it would be absurd to attempt it; for even familiar subjects are familiar only to a few, and yet give pleasure to all. It clearly follows that the poet or "maker" should be the maker of plots rather than of verses; since he is a poet because he imitates, and what he imitates are actions. And even if he chances to take an historical subject, he is none the less a poet; for there is no reason why some events that have actually happened should not conform to the law of the probable and possible, and in virtue of that quality in them he is their poet or maker.

Of all plots and actions the epeisodic are the worst. I call a plot "epeisodic" in which the episodes or acts succeed one another without probable or necessary sequence. Bad poets compose such pieces by their own fault, good poets, to please the players; for, as they write show pieces for competition, they stretch the plot beyond its capacity, and are often forced to break the natural continuity.

But again, Tragedy is an imitation not only of a complete action, but of events terrible and pitiful. Such an effect is best produced when the events come on us by surprise; and the effect is heightened when, at the same time, they follow from one another. The tragic wonder will then be greater than if they happened of themselves or by accident; for even coincidences are most striking when they have an air of design. We may instance the statue of Mitys at Argos, which fell upon his murderer while he was a spectator at a festival, and killed him. Such events seem not to be due to mere chance. Plots, therefore, constructed on these principles are necessarily the best.

X

Plots are either Simple or Complex, for the actions in real life, of which the plots are an imitation, obviously show a similar distinction. An action which is one and continuous in the sense above defined, I call Simple, when the change of fortune takes place without Reversal (or Recoil) of the Action and without Recognition.

A Complex action is one in which the change is accompanied by such Reversal, or by Recognition, or by both. These last should arise from the internal structure of the plot, so that what follows should be the necessary or probable result of the preceding action. It makes all the difference whether any given event is a case of *propter hoc* or *post hoc*.

XI

Reversal (or Recoil) is a change by which a train of action produces the opposite of the effect intended, subject always to our rule of probability or necessity. Thus in the Oedipus, the messenger comes to cheer Oedipus and free him from his alarms about his mother, but by revealing who he is, he produces the opposite effect. Again in the Lynceus, Lynceus is being led away to his death, and Danaus goes with him, meaning to slay him; but the outcome of the action is, that Danaus is killed and Lynceus saved.

Recognition, as the name indicates, is a change from ignorance to knowledge, producing love or hate between the persons destined by the poet for good or bad fortune. The best form of recognition is coincident with a Reversal (or Recoil), as in the Oedipus. There are indeed other forms. Even inanimate things of the most trivial kind may sometimes be objects of recognition. Again, we may recognise or discover whether a person has done a thing or not. But the recognition which is most intimately connected with the plot and action is, as we have said, the recognition of persons. This recognition, combined with Reversal, will produce either pity or fear; and actions producing these effects are those which, by our definition, Tragedy represents. Moreover, it is upon such issues that fortune or misfortune will turn. Recognition, then, being between persons, it may happen that one person only is recognised by the other—when the latter is already known—or it may be necessary that the recognition should be on both sides. Thus Iphigenia is revealed to Orestes by the sending of the letter; but another act of recognition is required to make Orestes known to Iphigenia.

Two parts, then, of the Plot—Reversal and Recognition—turn upon surprises. A third part is the Tragic Incident. The Tragic Incident is a destructive or painful action, such as death on the stage, bodily agony, wounds and the like.

XII

[The parts of Tragedy, which must be treated as elements of the whole, have been already mentioned. We now come to the quantitative parts—the separate parts into which Tragedy is divided—namely, Prologue, Episode, Exodos, Choric song; this last being divided into Parados and Stasimon. These are common to all plays: peculiar to some are the songs of actors from the stage and the Commoi.

The Prologos is that entire part of a tragedy which precedes the Parodos of the Chorus. The Episode is that entire part of a tragedy which is between complete choric songs. The Exodos is that entire part of a tragedy which has no choric song after it. Of the Choric part the Parados is the first undivided utterance of the Chorus: the Stasimon is a Choric ode without anapaests or trochees: the Commos is a joint lamentation of Chorus and actors. The parts of Tragedy which must be treated as elements of the whole have been already mentioned. The quantitative parts—the separate parts into which it is divided—are here enumerated.]

XIII

As the sequel to what has already been said, we must proceed to consider what the poet should aim at, and what he should avoid, in constructing his plots; and by what means the specific effect of Tragedy will be produced.

A perfect tragedy should, as we have seen, be arranged not on the simple but on the complex plan. It should, moreover, imitate actions which excite pity and fear, this being the distinctive mark of tragic imitation. It follows plainly, in the first place, that the change of fortune presented must not be the spectacle of a virtuous man brought from prosperity to adversity: for this moves neither pity nor fear; it merely shocks us. Nor again, that of a bad man passing from adversity to prosperity: for nothing can be more alien to the spirit of Tragedy; it possesses no single tragic quality; it neither satisfies the moral sense, nor calls forth pity or fear. Nor, again, should the downfall of the utter villain be exhibited. A plot of this kind would, doubtless, satisfy the moral sense, but it would inspire neither pity nor fear; for pity is aroused by unmerited misfortune, fear by the misfortune of a man like ourselves. Such an event, therefore, will be neither pitiful nor terrible. There remains, then, the character between these two extremes—that of a man who is not eminently good and just, yet whose misfortune is brought about not by vice or depravity, but by some error or frailty. He must be one who is highly renowned and prosperous—a personage like Oedipus, Thyestes, or other illustrious men of such families.

A well constructed plot should, therefore, be single in its issue, rather than double as some maintain. The change of fortune should be not from bad to good, but, reversely, from good to bad. It should come about as the result not of vice, but of some great error or frailty, in a character either such as we have described, or better rather than worse. The practice of the stage bears out our view. At first the poets recounted any legend that came in their way. Now, tragedies are founded on the story of a few houses — on the fortunes of Alcmaeon, Oedipus, Orestes, Meleager, Thyestes, Telephus, and those others who have done or suffered something terrible. A tragedy, then, to be perfect according to the rules of art should be of this construction. Hence they are in error who censure Euripides just because he follows this principle in his plays, many of which end unhappily. It is, as we have said, the right ending. The best proof is that on the stage and in dramatic competition, such plays, if they are well represented, are the most tragic in effect; and Euripides, faulty as he is in the general management of his subject, yet is felt to be the most tragic of the poets.

In the second rank comes the kind of tragedy which some place first. Like the Odyssey, it has a double thread of plot, and also an opposite catastrophe for the good and for the bad. It is accounted the best because of the weakness of the spectators; for the poet is guided in what he writes by the wishes of his audience. The pleasure, however, thence derived is not the true tragic pleasure. It is proper rather to Comedy, where those who, in the piece, are the deadliest enemies—like Orestes and Aegisthus—quit the stage as friends at the close, and no one slays or is slain.

XIV

Fear and pity may be aroused by spectacular means; but they may also result from the inner structure of the piece, which is the better way, and indicates a superior poet. For the plot ought to be so constructed that, even without the aid of the eye, he who hears the tale told will thrill with horror and melt to pity at what takes place. This is the impression we should receive from hearing the story of the Oedipus. But to produce this effect by the mere spectacle is a less artistic method, and dependent on extraneous aids. Those who employ spectacular means to create a sense not of the terrible but of the monstrous, are strangers to the purpose of Tragedy; for we must not demand of Tragedy any and every kind of pleasure, but only that which is proper to it. And since the pleasure which the poet should afford is that which comes from pity and fear through imitation, it is evident that this quality must be impressed upon the incidents.

Let us then determine what are the circumstances which strike us as terrible or pitiful.

Actions capable of this effect must happen between persons who are either friends or enemies or indifferent to one another. If an enemy kills an enemy, there is nothing to excite pity either in the act or the intention—except so far as the suffering in itself is pitiful. So again with indifferent persons. But when the tragic incident occurs between those who are near or dear to one another—if, for example, a brother kills, or intends to kill, a brother, a son his father, a mother her son, a son his mother, or any other deed of the kind is done—these are the situations to be looked for by the poet. He may not indeed destroy the framework of the received legends—the fact, for instance, that Clytemnestra was slain by Orestes and Eriphyle by Alcmaeon—but he ought to show invention of his own, and skilfully handle the traditional material. Let us explain more clearly what is meant by skilful handling.

The action may be done consciously and with knowledge of the persons, in the manner of the older poets. It is thus indeed that Euripides makes Medea slay her children. Or, again, the deed of horror may be done, but done in ignorance, and the tie of kinship or friendship be discovered afterwards. The Oedipus of Sophocles is an example. Here, indeed, the incident is outside the drama proper; but cases occur where it falls within the action of the play: one may cite the Alcmaeon of Astydamas, or Telegonus in the Wounded Odysseus. Again, there is a third case, where some one is just about to do some irreparable deed through ignorance, and makes the discovery before it is done. These are the only possible ways. For the deed must either be done or not done,—and that wittingly or unwittingly. But of all these ways, to be about to act knowing the persons, and then not to act, is the worst. It is shocking without being tragic, for no disaster follows. It is, therefore, never, or very rarely, found in poetry. One instance, however, is in the Antigone, where Haemon threatens to kill Creon. The next and better way is that the deed should be perpetuated. Still better, that it should be perpetuated in ignorance, and the discovery made afterwards. There is then nothing to shock us, while the discovery produces a startling effect. The last case is the best, as when in the Cresphontes Merope is about to slay her son, but, recognising who he is, spares his life. So in the Iphigenia, the sister recognises the brother just in time. Again in the Helle, the son recognises the mother when on the point of giving her up. This, then, is why a few families only, as has been already observed, furnish the subjects of tragedy. It was not art, but happy chance, that led poets to look for such situations and so impress the tragic quality upon their plots. They are compelled, therefore, to have recourse to those houses whose history contains moving incidents like these.

Enough has now been said concerning the structure of the incidents, and the proper constitutions of the plot.

XV

In respect of Character there are four things to be aimed at. First, and most important, it must be good. Now any speech or action that manifests moral purpose of any kind will be expressive of character: the character will be good if the purpose is good. This rule is relative to each class. Even a woman may be good, and also a slave; though the woman may be said to be an inferior being, and the slave quite worthless. The second thing to aim at is propriety. There is a type of manly valour; but for a woman to be valiant, or terrible, would be inappropriate. Thirdly, character must be true to life: for this is a distinct thing from goodness and propriety, as here described. The fourth point is consistency: for though the subject of the imitation, who suggested the type, be inconsistent, still he must be consistently inconsistent. As an example of character gratuitously bad, we have Menelaus in the Orestes: of character indecorous and inappropriate, the lament of Odysseus in the Scylla, and the speech of Melanippe: of inconsistency, the Iphigenia at Aulis,—for Iphigenia the suppliant in no way resembles her later self.

As in the structure of the plot, so too in the portraiture of character, the poet should always aim either at the necessary or the probable. Thus a person of a given character should speak or act in a given way, by the rule either of necessity or of probability; just as this event should follow that by necessary or probable sequence. It is therefore evident that the unravelling of the plot, no less than the complication, must arise out of the plot itself, it must not be brought about by the *Deus ex Machina*,—as in the Medea, or in the Return of the Greeks in the Iliad. The *Deus ex Machina* should be employed only for events external to the drama,—for antecedent or subsequent events, which lie beyond the range of human knowledge, and which require to be reported or foretold; for to the gods we ascribe the power of seeing all things. Within the action there must be nothing irrational. If the irrational cannot be excluded, it should be outside the scope of the tragedy. Such is the irrational element in the Oedipus of Sophocles.

Again, since Tragedy is an imitation of persons who are above the common level, the example of good portrait-painters should be followed. They, while reproducing the distinctive form of the original, make a likeness which is true to life and yet more beautiful. So too the poet, in representing men who are irascible or indolent, or have other defects of character, should preserve the type and yet ennoble it. In this way Achilles is portrayed by Agathon and Homer.

These are rules the poet should observe. Nor should he neglect those appeals to the senses, which, though not among the essentials, are the concomitants of poetry; for here too there is much room for error. But of this enough has been said in the published treatises.

XVI

What Recognition is has been already explained. We will now enumerate its kinds.

First, the least artistic form, which from poverty of wit, is most commonly employed—recognition by signs. Of these some are congenital,—such as "the spear which the earth-born race bear on their bodies", or the stars introduced by Carcinus in his Thyestes. Others are acquired after birth; and of these some are bodily marks, as scars; some external tokens, as necklaces, or the little ark in the Tyro by which the discovery is effected. Even these admit of more or less skilful treatment. Thus in the recognition of Odysseus by his scar, the discovery is made in one way by the nurse, in another by the herdsmen. The use of tokens for the express purpose of proof—and, indeed, any formal proof with or without tokens—is a less artistic mode of recognition. A better kind is that which comes about by a turn of incident, as in the Bath Scene in the Odyssey.

Next come the recognitions invented at will by the poet, and on that account wanting in art. For example, Orestes in the Iphigenia reveals the fact that he is Orestes. She, indeed, makes herself known by the letter; but he, by speaking himself, and saying what the poet, not what the plot requires. This, therefore, is nearly allied to the fault above mentioned:—for Orestes might as well have brought tokens with him. Another similar instance is the "voice of the shuttle" in the Tereus of Sophocles.

The third kind depends on memory when the sight of some object awakens a feeling: as in the Cyprians of Dicaeogenes, where the hero breaks into tears on seeing the picture; or again in the "Lay of Alcinous", where Odysseus, hearing the minstrel play the lyre, recalls the past and weeps; and hence the recognition.

The fourth kind is by process of reasoning. Thus in the Choephori:—"Some one resembling me has come: no one resembles me but Orestes: therefore Orestes has come". Such too is the discovery made by Iphigenia in the play of Polyeidus the Sophist. It was a natural reflection for Orestes to make, "So I too must die at the altar like my sister". So, again, in the Tydeus of Theodectes, the father says, "I came to find my son, and I lose my own life". So too in the Phineidae: the women, on seeing the place, inferred their fate:—"Here we are doomed to die, for here we were cast forth". Again, there is a recognition combined with a false inference on the part of one of the characters, as in the Odysseus Disguised as a Messenger. A man said he would know the bow,—which, however, he had not seen. This remark led Odysseus to imagine that the other would recognise him through the bow, thus suggesting a false inference.

But, of all recognitions, the best is that which arises from the incidents themselves, where the startling discovery is made by natural means. Such is that in the Oedipus of Sophocles, and in the Iphigenia; for it was natural that Iphigenia should wish to despatch a letter. These recognitions alone dispense with the artificial aid of tokens or necklaces. Next come the recognitions by process of reasoning.

XVII

In constructing the plot and working it out with the proper diction, the poet should place the scene, as far as possible, before his eyes. In this way, seeing everything with the utmost vividness, as if he were a spectator of the action, he will discover what is in keeping with it, and be most unlikely to overlook inconsistencies. The need of such a rule is shown by the fault found in Carcinus. Amphiaraus was on his way from the temple. This fact escaped the observation of one who did not see the situation. On the stage, however, the piece failed, the audience being offended at the oversight.

Again, the poet should work out his play, to the best of his power, with appropriate gestures; for those who feel emotion are most convincing by force of sympathy. One who is agitated storms, one who is angry rages, with the most life-like reality. Hence poetry implies either a happy gift of nature or a strain of madness. In the one case a man can take the mould of any character; in the other, he is lifted out of his proper self.

As for the story, whether the poet takes it ready made or constructs it for himself, he should first sketch its general outline, and then fill in the episodes and amplify in detail. The general plan may be illustrated by the Iphigenia. A young girl is sacrificed; she disappears mysteriously from the eyes of those who sacrificed her; she is transported to another country, where the custom is to offer up all strangers to the goddess. To this ministry she is appointed. Some time later her brother chances to arrive. The fact that the oracle for some reason ordered him to go there, is outside the general plan of the play. The purpose, again, of his coming is outside the action proper. However, he comes, he is seized, and when on the point of being sacrificed, reveals who he is. The mode of recognition may be either that of Euripides or of Polyeidus, in whose play he exclaims very naturally:—"So it was not my sister only, but I too, who was doomed to be sacrificed"; and by that remark he is saved.

After this, the names being once given, it remains to fill in the episodes. We must see that they are relevant to the action. In the case of Orestes, for example, there is the madness which led to his capture, and his deliverance by means of the purificatory rite. In the drama, the episodes are short, but it is these that give extension to Epic poetry. Thus the story of the Odyssey can be stated briefly. A certain man is absent from home for many years; he is jealously watched by Poseidon, and left desolate. Meanwhile his home is in a wretched plight—suitors are wasting his substance and plotting against his son. At length, tempest-tost, he arrives and reveals his true self; he attacks his enemies, destroys them and is himself preserved. This is the essence of the plot; the rest is episode.

XVIII

Every tragedy falls into two parts,—Complication and Unravelling (or *Dénouement*). Incidents extraneous to the action are frequently combined with a portion of the action proper, to form the Complication; the rest is the Unravelling. By the Complication I mean all that comes between the beginning of the action and the part which marks the turning-point to good or bad fortune. The Unravelling is that which comes between the beginning of the change and the end. Thus, in the Lynceus of Theodectes, the Complication consists of the incidents presupposed in the drama, the seizure of the child, and then again * * <The Unravelling> extends from the accusation of murder to the end.

There are four kinds of Tragedy,—first, the <Simple, then> the Complex, depending entirely on Reversal and Recognition; next, the Pathetic (where the motive is passion),—such as the tragedies on Ajax and Ixion; next, the Ethical (where the motives are ethical),—such as the Phthiotides and the Peleus. <We here exclude the supernatural kind>, such as the Phorcides, the Prometheus, and tragedies whose scene is the lower world. The poet should endeavour, if possible, to combine all poetic merits; or failing that, the greatest number and those the most important; the more so, in face of the cavilling criticism of the day. For whereas there have hitherto been good poets, each in his own branch, the critics now expect one man to surpass all others in their several lines of excellence.

In speaking of a tragedy as the same or different, the best test to take is the plot. Identity exists where the Complication and Unravelling are the same. Many poets tie the knot well, but unravel it ill. Both arts, however, should always be mastered.

Again, the poet should remember what has been often said, and not make a Tragedy into an Epic structure. By an Epic structure I mean one with a multiplicity of plots: as if, for instance, you were to make a tragedy out of the entire story of the Iliad. In the Epic poem, owing to its length, each part assumes its proper magnitude. In the drama the result is far from answering to the poet's expectation. The proof is that the poets who have dramatised the whole story of the Fall of Troy, instead of selecting portions, like Euripides; or who have taken the whole tale of Niobe, and not a part of her story, like Aeschylus, either fail utterly or meet with poor success on the stage. Even Agathon has been known to fail from this one defect. In his Reversals of the Action, however, he shows a marvellous skill in the effort to hit the popular taste,—to produce a tragic effect that satisfies the moral sense. This effect is produced when the clever rogue, like Sisyphus, is outwitted, or the brave villain defeated. Such an event is, moreover, probable in Agathon's sense of the word: "it is probable", he says, "that many things should happen contrary to probability."

The Chorus too should be regarded as one of the actors; it should be an integral part of the whole, and share in the action, in the manner not of Euripides but of Sophocles. As for the later poets, their choral songs pertain as little to the subject of the piece as to that of any other tragedy. They are, therefore, sung as mere interludes,—a practice first begun by Agathon. Yet what difference is there between introducing such choral interludes, and transferring a speech, or even a whole act, from one play to another?

XIX

It remains to speak of Diction and Thought, the other parts of Tragedy having been already discussed. Concerning Thought, we may assume what is said in the Rhetoric, to which inquiry the subject more strictly belongs. Under Thought is included every effect which has to be produced by speech; in particular,—proof and refutation; the excitation of the feelings, such as pity, fear, anger, and the like; the suggestion of importance or its opposite. Further, it is evident that the dramatic incidents must be treated from the same points of view as the dramatic speeches, when the object is to evoke the sense of pity, fear, importance, or probability. The only difference is, that the incidents should speak for themselves without verbal exposition; while the effects aimed at in a speech should be produced by the speaker, and as a result of the speech. For what were the need of a speaker, if the proper impression were at once conveyed, quite apart from what he says?

Next, as regards Diction. One branch of the inquiry treats of the Modes of Expression. But this province of knowledge belongs to the art of Declamation, and to the masters of that science. It includes, for instance,—what is a command, a prayer, a narrative, a threat, a question, an answer, and so forth. To know or not to know these things involves no serious censure upon the poet's art. For who can admit the fault imputed to Homer by Protagoras,—that in the words, "Sing, goddess, of the wrath," he gives a command under the idea that he utters a prayer? For to tell some one to do a thing or not to do it is, he says, a command. We may, therefore, pass this over as an inquiry that belongs to another art, not to poetry.

XX

[Language in general includes the following parts:—the Letter, the Syllable, the Connecting word, the Noun, the Verb, the Inflexion or Case, the Proposition or Phrase.

A Letter is an indivisible sound, yet not every such sound, but only one which can form part of a group of sounds. For even brutes utter indivisible sounds, none of which I call a letter. The sound I mean may be either a vowel, a semi-vowel, or a mute. A vowel is that which without impact of tongue or lip has an audible sound. A semi-vowel, that which with such impact has an audible sound, as S and R. A mute, that which with such impact has by itself no sound, but joined to a vowel sound becomes audible, as G and D. These are distinguished according to the form assumed by the mouth, and the place where they are produced; according as they are aspirated or smooth, long or short; as they are acute, grave, or of an intermediate tone; which inquiry belongs in detail to a treatise on metre.

A Syllable is a non-significant sound, composed of a mute and a vowel <or of a mute, a semi-vowel> and a vowel: for GR without A is not a syllable, but with A it is,—GRA. But the investigation of these differences belongs also to metrical science.

A Connecting word is a non-significant sound, which neither causes nor hinders the union of many sounds into one significant sound; it may be placed at either end or in the middle of a sentence. Or a non-significant sound, which out of several sounds, each of them significant, is capable of forming one significant sound,—as ἀμφι', περί, and the like. Or, a non-significant sound, which marks the beginning, end, or division of a sentence; such, however, that it cannot correctly stand by itself at the beginning of a sentence,— as μέν, ἤτοι, δέ.

A Noun is a composite significant sound, not marking time, of which no part is in itself significant; for in double or compound words we do not employ the separate parts as if each were in itself significant. Thus in Theodorus, "god-given", the δῶρον or "gift" is not in itself significant.

A Verb is a composite significant sound, marking time, in which, as in the noun, no part is in itself significant. For "man", or "white" does not express the idea of "when"; but "he walks", or "he has walked" does connote time, present or past.

Inflexion belongs both to the noun and verb, and expresses either the relation "of", "to", or the like; or that of number, whether one or many, as "man" or "men"; or the modes or tones in actual delivery, e.g. a question or a command. "Did he go?" and "go" are verbal inflexions of this kind.

A Proposition or Phrase is a composite significant sound, some at least of whose parts are in themselves significant; for not every such group of words consists of verbs and nouns—"the definition of man", for example—but it may dispense even with the verb. Still it will always have some significant part, as "in walking", or "Cleon son of Cleon". A proposition or phrase may form a unity in two ways,—either as signifying one thing, or as consisting of several parts linked together. Thus the Iliad is one by the linking together of parts, the definition of man by the unity of the thing signified.]

XXI

Words are of two kinds, simple and double. By simple I mean those composed of non-significant elements, such as γῆ. By double or compound, those composed either of a significant and non-significant element (though within the whole word no element is significant), or of elements that are both significant. A word may likewise be triple, quadruple, or multiple in form, like so many Massilian expressions, e.g. "Hermo-caico-xanthus <who prayed to Father Zeus".>

Every word is either current, or strange, or metaphorical, or ornamental, or newly-coined, or lengthened, or contracted, or altered.

By a current or proper word I mean one which is in general use among a people; by a strange word, one which is in use in another country. Plainly, therefore, the same word may be at once strange and current, but not in relation to the same people. The word σίγυνον, "lance", is to the Cyprians a current term but to us a strange one.

Metaphor is the application of an alien name by transference either from genus to species, or from species to genus, or from species to species, or by analogy, that is, proportion. Thus from genus to species, as: "There lies my ship"; for lying at anchor is a species of lying. From species to genus, as: "Verily ten thousand noble deeds hath Odysseus wrought"; for ten thousand is a species of large number, and is here used for a large number generally. From species to species, as: "With blade of bronze drew away the life", and "Cleft the water with the vessel of unyielding bronze". Here ἀρύσαι, "to draw away", is used for ταμεῖν, "to cleave", and ταμεῖν again for ἀρύσαι,—each being a species of taking away. Analogy or proportion is when the second term is to the first as the fourth to the third. We may then use the fourth for the second, or the second for the fourth. Sometimes too we qualify the metaphor by adding the term to which the proper word is relative. Thus the cup is to Dionysus as the shield to Ares. The cup may, therefore, be called "the shield of Dionysus", and the shield "the cup of Ares". Or, again, as old age is to life, so is evening to day. Evening may therefore be called "the old age of the day", and old age, "the evening of life" or, in the phrase of Empedocles, "life's setting sun." In some cases one of the terms of the proportion has no specific name; still, the metaphor may be used. For instance, to scatter seed is called sowing: but the action of the sun in scattering his rays is nameless. Still this process bears to the sun the same relation as sowing to the seed. Hence the expression of the poet, "sowing the god-created light." There is another way in which this kind of metaphor may be employed. We may apply an alien term, and then deny of that term one of its proper attributes; as if we were to call the shield, not "the cup of Ares", but "the wineless cup."

A newly-coined word is one which has never been even in local use, but is invented by the poet himself. Some such words there appear to be: as *ἐρνύγες*, "sprouters", for *κέρατα*, "horns", and *ἀρητήρ*, "supplicator", for *ἱερεύς*, "priest".

A word is lengthened when its own vowel is exchanged for a longer one, or when a syllable is inserted. A word is contracted when some part of it is removed. Instances of lengthening are.— *πόληος* for *πόλεως*, Πηληος for Πηλέος, and Πηληιάδεω for Πηλείδου : of contraction,— *κρῖ*, *δῶ*, and *ὄψ*, as in *μία γίνεται ἀμφοτέρων ὄψ*.

An altered word is one in which part of the ordinary form is left unchanged, and part is re-cast; as in *δεξιτερὸν κατὰ μαζόν*, *δεξιτερόν* is for *δεξιόν*.

[Nouns in themselves are either masculine, feminine, or neuter. Masculine are such as end in *ν*, *ρ*, *ς*, or in some letter compounded with *ς*,—these being two, *ψ* and *ξ*. Feminine, such as end in vowels that are always long, as *η* and *ω*, and—of vowels that admit of lengthening—those in *α*. Thus the number of letters in which nouns masculine and feminine end is the same; for *ψ* and *ξ* are equivalent to endings in *ς*. No noun ends in a mute or a vowel short by nature. Three only end in *ι*,— *μέλι*, *κόμμι*, *πέπερι*: five end in *υ*. Neuter nouns end in these two latter vowels; also in *ν* and *ς*.]

XXII

The perfection of style is to be clear without being mean. The clearest style is that which uses only current or proper words; at the same time it is mean:—witness the poetry of Cleophon and of Sthenelus. That diction, on the other hand, is lofty and raised above the commonplace which employs unusual words. By unusual, I mean strange (or rare) words, metaphorical, lengthened,—anything, in short, that differs from the normal idiom. Yet a style wholly composed of such words is either a riddle or a jargon; a riddle, if it consists of metaphors; a jargon, if it consists of strange (or rare) words. For the essence of a riddle is to express true facts under impossible combinations. Now this cannot be done by any arrangement of ordinary words, but by the use of metaphor it can. Such is the riddle:—"A man I saw who on another man had glued the bronze by aid of fire", and others of the same kind. A diction that is made up of strange (or rare) terms is a jargon. A certain infusion, therefore, of these elements is necessary to style; for the strange (or rare) word, the metaphorical, the ornamental, and the other kinds above mentioned, will raise it above the commonplace and mean, while the use of proper words will make it perspicuous. But nothing contributes more to produce a clearness of diction that is remote from commonness than the lengthening, contraction, and alteration of words. For by deviating in exceptional cases from the normal idiom, the language will gain distinction; while, at the same time, the partial conformity with usage will give perspicuity. The critics, therefore, are in error who censure these licenses of speech, and hold the author up to ridicule. Thus Eucleides, the elder, declared that it would be an easy matter to be a poet if you might lengthen syllables at will. He caricatured the practice in the very form of his diction, as in the verse:

Ἐπιχάρην εἶδον Μαραθῶνάδε βαδίζνοτα,

or,

οὐκ ἄνγ' ἐράμενος τόν ἐκείνου ἐλλέβορον.

To employ such license at all obtrusively is, no doubt, grotesque; but in any mode of poetic diction there must be moderation. Even metaphors, strange (or rare) words, or any similar forms of speech, would produce the like effect if used without propriety, and with the express purpose of being ludicrous. How great a difference is made by the appropriate use of lengthening, may be seen in Epic poetry by the insertion of ordinary forms in the verse. So, again, if we take a strange (or rare) word, a metaphor, or any similar mode of expression, and replace it by the current or proper term, the truth of our observation will be manifest. For example Aeschylus and Euripides each composed the same iambic line. But the alteration of a single word by Euripides, who employed the rarer term instead of the ordinary one, makes one verse appear beautiful and the other trivial. Aeschylus in his Philoctetes says:

φαγέδαινα <δ'> ἥ μου σάρκας ἐσθίει ποδός.

Euripides substitutes θοινᾶται "feasts on" for ἐσθίει "feeds on". Again, in the line,

νῦν δέ μ' ἐὼν ὀλίγος τε καὶ οὐτιδανὸς καὶ ἀεικής.

the difference will be felt if we substitute the common words,

νῦν δέ μ' ἐὼν μικρός τε καὶ ἀσθενικὸς καὶ ἀειδής.

Or, if for the line,

δίφρον [τ'] ἀεικέλιον καταθεὶς ὀλίγην τε τράπεζαν,

we read,

δίφρον μοχθηρὸν καταθεὶς μικράν τε τράπεζαν.

Or, for ἠιόνες βοόωσιν, ἠιόνες κράζουσιν.

Again, Ariphrades ridiculed the tragedians for using phrases which no one would employ in ordinary speech: for example, δωμάτων ἄπο instead of ἀπό δωμάτων, σέθεν, ἐγὼ δέ νιν, Ἀχιλλέως πέρι instead of περὶ Ἀχιλλέως, and the like. It is precisely because such phrases are not part of the current idiom that they give distinction to the style. This, however, he failed to see.

It is a great matter to observe propriety in these several modes of expression—compound words, strange (or rare) words, and so forth. But the greatest thing by far is to have a command of metaphor. This alone cannot be imparted by another; it is the mark of genius,—for to make good metaphors implies an eye for resemblances.

Of the various kinds of words, the compound are best adapted to dithyrambs, rare words to heroic poetry, metaphors to iambic. In heroic poetry, indeed, all these varieties are serviceable. But in iambic verse, which reproduces, as far as may be, familiar speech, the most appropriate words are those which are found even in prose. These are,—the current or proper, the metaphorical, the ornamental.

Concerning Tragedy and imitation by means of action, this may suffice.

XXIII

As to that poetic imitation which is narrative in form and employs a single metre, the plot manifestly ought, as in a tragedy, to be constructed on dramatic principles. It should have for its subject a single action, whole and complete, with a beginning, a middle, and an end. It will thus resemble a single and coherent picture of a living being, and produce the pleasure proper to it. It will differ in structure from historical compositions, which of necessity present not a single action, but a single period, and all that happened within that period to one person or to many, little connected together as the events may be. For as the sea-fight at Salamis and the battle with the Carthaginians in Sicily took place at the same time, but did not tend to one result, so in the sequence of events, one thing sometimes follows another, and yet the two may not work up to any common end. Such is the practice, we may say, of most poets. Here again, then, as has been already observed, the transcendent excellence of Homer is manifest. He never attempts to make the whole war of Troy the subject of his poem, though that war had a beginning and an end. It would have been too vast a theme, and not easily embraced in a single view. If, again, he had kept it within moderate limits, it must have been over-complicated by the variety of the incidents. As it is, he detaches a single portion, and admits as episodes many events from the general story of the war—such as the Catalogue of the ships and others—thus diversifying the poem. All other poets take a single hero, a single period, or an action single indeed, but with a multiplicity of parts. Thus did the author of the Cypria and of the Little Iliad. For this reason the Iliad and the Odyssey each furnish the subject of one tragedy, or, at most, of two; while the Cypria supplies materials for many, and the Little Iliad eight—the Award of the Arms, the Philoctetes, the Neoptolemus, Eurypylus, the Mendicant Odysseus, the Laconian Women, the Fall of Ilium, the Departure of the Fleet.

XXIV

Again, Epic poetry must have as many kinds as Tragedy: it must be simple, or complex, or "ethical", or "pathetic". The parts also, with the exception of song and scenery, are the same; for it requires Reversals, Recognitions, and Tragic Incidents. Moreover, the thoughts and the diction must be artistic. In all these respects Homer is our earliest and sufficient model. Indeed each of his poems has a twofold character. The Iliad is at once simple and "pathetic", and the Odyssey complex (for Recognition scenes run through it), and at the same time "ethical". Moreover, in diction and thought he is supreme.

Epic poetry differs from Tragedy in the scale on which it is constructed, and in its metre. As regards scale or length, we have already laid down an adequate limit:—the beginning and the end must be capable of being brought within a single view. This condition will be satisfied by poems on a smaller scale than the old epics, and answering in length to the group of tragedies presented at a single sitting.

Epic poetry has, however, a great—a special—capacity for enlarging its dimensions, and we can see the reason. In Tragedy we cannot imitate several actions carried on at one and the same time; we must confine ourselves to the action on the stage and the part taken by the players. But in Epic poetry, owing to the narrative form, many events simultaneously transacted can be presented; and these, if relevant to the subject, add mass and dignity to the poem. The Epic has here an advantage, and one that conduces to grandeur of effect, also diverting the mind of the hearer and relieving the story with varying episodes. For sameness of incident soon produces satiety, and makes tragedies fail on the stage.

As for the metre, the heroic measure has proved its fitness by the test of experience. If a narrative poem in any other metre or in many metres were now composed, it would be found incongruous. For of all measures the heroic is the stateliest and the most massive; and hence it most readily admits rare words and metaphors, which is another point in which the narrative form of imitation stands alone. On the other hand, the iambic and the trochaic tetrameter are stirring measures, the latter being akin to dancing, the former expressive of action. Still more absurd would it be to mix together different metres, as was done by Chaeremon. Hence no one has ever composed a poem on a great scale in any other than heroic verse. Nature herself, as we have said, teaches the choice of the proper measure.

Homer, admirable in all respects, has the special merit of being the only poet who rightly appreciates the part he should take himself. The poet should speak as little as possible in his own person, for it is not this that makes him an imitator. Other poets appear themselves upon the scene throughout, and imitate but little and rarely. Homer, after a few prefatory words, at once brings in a man, or woman, or other personage; none of them wanting in characteristic qualities, but each with a character of his own.

The element of the wonderful is admitted in Tragedy. The irrational, on which the wonderful depends for its chief effects, has wider scope in Epic poetry, because there the person acting is not seen. Thus, the pursuit of Hector would be ludicrous if placed upon the stage—the Greeks standing still and not joining in the pursuit, and Achilles waving them back. But in the Epic poem the absurdity passes unnoticed. Now the wonderful is pleasing: as may be inferred from the fact that, in telling a story, every one adds something startling of his own, knowing that his hearers like it. It is Homer who has chiefly taught other poets the art of telling lies skilfully. The secret of it lies in a fallacy. For, assuming that if one thing is or becomes, a second is or becomes, men imagine that, if the second is, the first likewise is or becomes. But this is a false inference. Hence, where the first thing is untrue, it is quite unnecessary, provided the second be true, to add that the first is or has become. For the mind, knowing the second to be true, falsely infers the truth of the first. There is an example of this in the Bath Scene of the Odyssey.

Accordingly, the poet should prefer probable impossibilities to improbable possibilities. The tragic plot must now be composed of irrational parts. Everything irrational should, if possible, be excluded; or, at all events, it should lie outside the action of the day (as, in the Oedipus, the hero's ignorance as to the manner of Laius' death); not within the drama,—as in the Electra, the messenger's account of the Pythian games; or, as in the Mysians, the man who comes from Tegea to Mysia without speaking. The plea that otherwise the plot would have been ruined, is ridiculous. Such a plot should not in the first instance be constructed. But once it has been framed and an air of likelihood imparted to it, the absurdity itself should be tolerated. Take the irrational incidents in the Odyssey, where Odysseus is left upon the shore of Ithaca. How intolerable even these might have been would be apparent if an inferior poet were to treat the subject. As it is, the absurdity is veiled by the poetic charm with which the poet invests it.

The diction should be elaborated in the pauses of the action, where there is no expression of character or thought. For, conversely, character and thought are merely obscured by a diction that is over brilliant.

XXV

With respect to critical difficulties and their solutions, the number and nature of the sources from which they may be drawn may be thus exhibited.

The poet being an imitator, like a painter or any other artist, must of necessity imitate one of three objects,—things as they were or are, things as they are said or thought to be, or things as they ought to be. The vehicle of expression is language,—either current terms or, it may be, rare words or metaphors. There are also many modifications of language, which we concede to the poets. Add to this, that the standard of correctness is not the same in poetry and politics, any more than in poetry and any other art. Within the art of poetry itself there are two kinds of faults,—those which touch its essence, and those which are accidental. If a poet has proposed to himself to imitate something, <but has imitated it incorrectly> through want of capacity, the error is inherent in the poetry. But if the failure is due to the thing he has proposed to do—if he has represented a horse as throwing out both his off legs at once, or introduced technical inaccuracies in medicine, for example, or in any other art—the error is not essential to the poetry. These are the points of view from which we should consider and answer the objections raised by the critics.

First we will suppose the poet has represented things impossible according to the laws of his own art. It is an error; but the error may be justified, if the end of the art be thereby attained (the end being that already mentioned),—if, that is, the effect of this or any other part of the poem is thus rendered more striking. A case in point is the pursuit of Hector. If, however, the end might have been as well, or better, attained without violating the special rules of the poetic art, the error is not justified: for every kind of error should, if possible, be avoided.

Again, does the error touch the essentials of the poetic art, or some accident of it? For example,—not to know that a hind has no horns is a less serious matter than to paint it inartistically.

Further, if it be objected that the description is not true to fact, the poet may perhaps reply,—"But the objects are as they ought to be": just as Sophocles said that he drew men as they ought to be; Euripides, as they are. In this way the objection may be met. If, however, the representation be of neither kind, the poet may answer,—"This is how men say the thing is." This applies to tales about the gods. It may well be that these stories are not higher than fact nor yet true to fact: they are, very possibly, what Xenophanes says of them. But anyhow, "this is what is said." Again, a description may be no better than the fact: "still, it was the fact"; as in the passage about the arms: "Upright upon their butt-ends stood the spears." This was the custom then, as it now is among the Illyrians.

Again, in examining whether what has been said or done by some one is poetically right or not, we must now look merely to the particular act or saying, and ask whether it is poetically good or bad. We must also consider by whom it is said or done, to whom, when, in whose interest, or for what end; whether, for instance, it be to secure a greater good, or avert a greater evil.

Other difficulties may be resolved by due regard to the diction. We may note a rare word, as in *οὐρῆας μὲν πρῶτον*, where the poet perhaps employs *οὐρῆας* not in the sense of mules, but of sentinels. So, again, of Dolon: "ill-favoured indeed he was to look upon." It is not meant that his body was ill-shaped, but that his face was ugly; for the Cretans use the word *εὐειδές*, "well-favoured", to denote a fair face. Again *ζωρότερον δὲ κέραιε*, "mix the drink livelier", does not mean "mix it stronger" as for hard drinkers, but "mix it quicker."

Sometimes an expression is metaphorical, as "Now all gods and men were sleeping through the night,"—while at the same time the poet says: "Often indeed as he turned his gaze to the Trojan plain, he marvelled at the sound of flutes and pipes." "All" is here used metaphorically for "many," all being a species of many. So in the verse,—"alone she hath no part . . .," *οἴη*, "alone," is metaphorical; for the best known may be called the only one.

Again, the solution may depend upon accent or breathing. Thus Hippias of Thasos solved the difficulties in the lines,— *δίδομεν* (*διδόμεν*) *δέ οἱ*, and *τὸ μὲν οὗ* (*οὐ*) *καταπύθεται ὄμβρῳ*.

Or again, the question may be solved by punctuation, as in Empedocles,—"Of a sudden things became mortal that before had learnt to be immortal, and things unmixed before mixed."

Or again, by ambiguity of construction,—as in *παρῴχηκεν δὲ πλέω νύξ*, where the word *πλέω* is ambiguous.

Or by the usage of language. Thus any mixed drink is called *οἶνος*, "wine". Hence Ganymede is said "to pour the wine to Zeus," though the gods do not drink wine. So too workers in iron are called *χαλκέας*, or workers in bronze. This, however, may also be taken as a metaphor.

Again, when a word seems to involve some

inconsistency of meaning, we should consider how many senses it may bear in the particular passage. For example: "there was stayed the spear of bronze"—we should ask in how many ways we may take "being checked there." The true mode of interpretation is the precise opposite of what Glaucus mentions. Critics, he says, jump at certain groundless conclusions; they pass adverse judgment and then proceed to reason on it; and, assuming that the poet has said whatever they happen to think, find fault if a thing is inconsistent with their own fancy. The question about Icarius has been treated in this fashion. The critics imagine he was a Lacedaemonian. They think it strange, therefore, that Telemachus should not have met him when he went to Lacedaemon. But the Cephallenian story may perhaps be the true one. They allege that Odysseus took a wife from among themselves, and that her father was Icadius not Icarius. It is merely a mistake, then, that gives plausibility to the objection.

In general, the impossible must be justified by reference to artistic requirements, or to the higher reality, or to received opinion. With respect to the requirements of art, a probable impossibility is to be preferred to a thing improbable and yet possible. Again, it may be impossible that there should be men such as Zeuxis painted. "Yes", we say, "but the impossible is the higher thing; for the ideal type must surpass the reality". To justify the irrational, we appeal to what is commonly said to be. In addition to which, we urge that the irrational sometimes does not violate reason; just as "it is probable that a thing may happen contrary to probability."

Things that sound contradictory should be examined by the same rules as in dialectical refutation—whether the same thing is meant, in the same relation, and in the same sense. We should therefore solve the question by reference to what the poet says himself, or to what is tacitly assumed by a person of intelligence.

The element of the irrational, and, similarly, depravity of character, are justly censured when there is no inner necessity for introducing them. Such is the irrational element in the Aegeus of Euripides, and the badness of Menelaus in the Orestes.

Thus, there are five sources from which critical objections are drawn. Things are censured either as impossible, or irrational, or morally hurtful, or contradictory, or contrary to artistic correctness. The answers should be sought under the twelve heads above mentioned.

XXVI

The question may be raised whether the Epic or Tragic mode of imitation is the higher. If the more refined art is the higher, and the more refined in every case is that which appeals to the better sort of audience, the art which imitates anything and everything is manifestly most unrefined. The audience is supposed to be too dull to comprehend unless something of their own is thrown in by the performers, who therefore indulge in restless movements. Bad flute-players twist and twirl, if they have to represent "the quoit-throw", or hustle the coryphaeus when they perform the "Scylla." Tragedy, it is said, has this same defect. We may compare the opinion that the older actors entertained of their successors. Mynniscus used to call Callippides "ape" on account of the extravagance of his action, and the same view was held of Pindarus. Tragic art, then, as a whole, stands to Epic in the same relation as the younger to the elder actors. So we are told that Epic poetry is addressed to a cultivated audience, who do not need gesture; Tragedy, to an inferior public. Being then unrefined, it is evidently the lower of the two.

Now, in the first place, this censure attaches not to the poetic but to the histrionic art; for gesticulation may be equally overdone in epic recitation, as by Sosistratus, or in lyrical competition, as by Mnasitheus the Opuntian. Next, all action is not to be condemned—any more than all dancing—but only that of bad performers. Such was the fault found in Callippides, as also in others of our own day, who are censured for representing degraded women.

Again, Tragedy like Epic poetry produces its effect even without action; it reveals its power by mere reading. If, then, in all other respects it is superior, this fault, we say, is not inherent in it.

And superior it is, because it has all the epic elements—it may even use the epic metre—with the music and scenic effects as important accessories; and these produce the most vivid of pleasures. Further, it has vividness of impression in reading as well as in representation. Moreover, the art attains its end within narrower limits; for the concentrated effect is more pleasurable than one which is spread over a long time and so diluted. What, for example, would be the effect of the Oedipus of Sophocles, if it were cast into a form as long as the Iliad? Once more, the Epic imitation has less unity; as is shown by this,—that any Epic poem will furnish subjects for several tragedies. Now if the story be worked into a unity, it will, if concisely told, appear truncated; or, if it conform to the Epic canon of length, it will seem weak and watery. * * * What I mean by a story composed of several actions may be illustrated from the Iliad and Odyssey, which have many parts, each with a certain magnitude of its own. Yet these poems are as perfect as possible in structure; each is, in the highest degree attainable, an imitation of a single action.

If, then, Tragedy is superior to Epic poetry in all these respects, and, moreover, fulfils its specific function better as an art—for each art ought to produce, not any chance pleasure, but the pleasure proper to it, as already stated—it plainly follows that Tragedy is the higher art, as attaining its end more perfectly.

Thus much may suffice concerning Tragic and Epic poetry in general; their several kinds and parts, with the number of each and their differences; the causes that make a poem good or bad; the objections of the critics and the answers to these objections.

Chapter 5

Aristotle's Theory of Catharsis. The Work of Art as Stimulus to Response

There is little doubt that Aristotle's theory that tragedy and some music inspire fear, pity, and "such-like emotions" is at once the most widely known and controversial contention ever put forward in the history of Philosophy of Art. To various of the interpretations of what Aristotle said in the *Poetics*[1] and the *Politics*,[2] we shall come shortly. It is of value, however, to suggest various points that may help us to understand the background of the theory and its general nature.

Within the context of Aristotle's philosophy, a catharsis of feeling such as is mentioned in the *Poetics* and in the *Politics* belongs properly to a Philosophy of Art in which the work of art is regarded as a stimulus to a response or, more specifically, as a stimulus of a specific response of an appropriate kind. But the theory has had such a powerful influence upon philosophers, poets, critics, and dramatists that it has served not only the classical philosophers who wrote of art in terms of imitation and took works of art and events in nature to serve as models and as external stimuli but also modern theorists whose philosophies of art and aesthetic theories are grounded on expression and imagination. What once served to describe a response has thus at times become a statement concerning the initiation of feelings and images by the aesthetic perceiver.

As regards Aristotle's indebtedness to Plato in this matter of the theory of catharsis, any conclusion must necessarily be ambivalent. Plato denies[3] the precise theory that Aristotle adopts for his philosophy of art and adapts to it: "If you consider . . . that there is in us a natural feeling which is just hungering after sorrow and weeping, and desiring to be indulged, and that this feeling, which is kept under control in our own calamities," writes Plato, "is the same which is satisfied and delighted by the poets:—the better nature in each of us . . . is taken unawares because the sorrow is another's; and the spectator fancies that there can be no disgrace to himself in praising or pitying any one who comes telling him what a good man he is, and making unseasonable lamentations—he thinks that the pleasure is a gain which he must not lose by the rejection of the poem. For the reflection is not often made that . . . the feeling of pity which has been nursed, and has acquired

[1] See Aristotle, *Poetics*, chapter XIV, 1453 b 4 et seq., quoted above, p. 156.

[2] See Aristotle, *Politics*, 1342 a 8, quoted above, p. 173.

[3] Plato, *Republic* 605–606. Compare *Philebus* 48A. For Plato on music, see *Republic* 398A, above, pp. 97 et seq., *Laws* 799, above, pp. 107 et seq.

strength at the sight of the misfortunes of others, will come out in our own misfortunes, and cannot be easily controlled."

This is an anticipation of Aristotle's theory that the poet may induce in some way a harmless response to the drama. Plato obviously believes that excitation is not likely to reduce feeling in intensity. Despite this disagreement concerning the value of the exercise of feeling and its results, Plato provides the structure for a theory of purgation that is among the best known of all formulations—that written by John Milton. The poet's interpretation of Aristotle's theory of the purgation of pity and fear appears in the preface to *Samson Agonistes*[4] and in lines in the tragedy itself.[5] Milton's is an interpretation accurately described as "homeopathic". For tragedy, according to the poet, is "of power, by raising pity and fear, or terror, to purge the mind of those and such like passions. . . ." The sound imitation of these passions acts as do analogous things in Nature, i.e. in Physic "things of melancholic hue and quality are us'd against melancholy, sowr against sowr, salt to remove salt humours. . . ." In the *Laws,* Plato[6] had argued that we may learn a lesson from experience, in this instance from the practice of nurses and the rites of the Corybantes, namely that "when mothers want their restless children to go to sleep they do not employ rest, but, on the contrary, motion—rocking them in their arms; nor do they give them silence, but they sing to them and lap them in sweet strains; and the Bacchic women are cured of their frenzy in the same manner by the use of dance and of music."

Upon being asked why this is the case, the Athenian Stranger in the *Laws* replies that "the affection both of the Corybantes and of the children is an emotion of fear," a feeling springing from an evil habit of the soul and one best exorcized by the application of an external agitation that gets the better of the violent internal one and "produces a peace and calm in the soul. . . ." How little removed this passage in the *Laws* is from what Aristotle believes is evident from the argument in the *Politics.*[7] Aristotle tells us that feelings such as "pity and fear, or, again, enthusiasm, exist very strongly in some souls, and have more or less influence over all." This fact he relates to the religious frenzy into which some people fall. Some are healed and purged as a result of the sacred melodies. "Those who are influenced by pity and fear, and every emotional nature, must have a like experience, and all are in a manner purged and their souls lightened and delighted."

This is, of course, not the only interpretation of catharsis that scholars have brought from the context of Greek religious life and from its medical theory. In their *"Notes on Katharsis",* F. Susemihl and R. D. Hicks[8] enumerate some usages of the term. They cite the following:

Briefly, *katharsis* means "simple cleansing" (*Sophist* 226 D-231 E); "lustration", (Euripides' *Ion,* 101 ff.) i.e. external, ceremonial in a liturgical or religious sense and "lustration" as a cure for madness (*Phaedrus* 244 D-E.); as purification or purging of impurity (*Republic* 364 E, *Phaedo* 82 D); as a medical term for purgation and discharge (*Timaeus* 39, 40, 82 ff.). In the readings that follow, the authors' views of the relations between the man who experiences tragedy or music and the object or event he is experiencing present sufficiently divergent interpretations of Aristotle's theory of the catharsis of feelings to suggest a pattern for a more general theory of aesthetic response. As for the nature and experience of tragedy itself, various theories are offered in later pages of this book.[9]

[4] See below, p. 174.

[5] See below, p. 174.

[6] Plato, *Laws,* 790 et seq. Cf. Ibid. 653–4.

[7] *Politics* 1342 a 5. Quoted below, p. 143.

[8] F. Susemihl and R. D. Hicks, *The Politics of Aristotle* (London, 1894), pp. 648 sq.

[9] See below: Dante Alighieri's "Letter to Can Grande," pp. 250 et seq.; Hegel's writing on *Antigone,* pp. 429 et seq.; Schopenhauer on the relation of tragedy and the Will, pp. 517 et seq.; Nietzsche, pp. 527 et seq.

The readings include Bywater's interpretation [10] in *Aristotle on the Art of Poetry,* in which emphasis is placed upon objective factors external to the tragedy; John Milton's *Preface to Samson Agonistes,*[11] in which the poet offers a homeopathic theory of Aristotle's remarks; Goethe's *Supplement to Aristotle's Poetics,*[12] in which it is argued that the catharsis is a purgation of the tragedy itself; S. H. Butcher's interpretation of catharsis in *Aristotle's Theory of Poetry and Fine Art,*[13] in which it is maintained that the feelings themselves are altered; E. Zeller's analysis in *Aristotle and the Later Peripatetics,*[14] which concentrates on the interrelation of subjective and objective factors in the work of art; Gerald Frank Else's [15] view that the tragedy itself is purged; and M. C. Nahm's [16] comment on the principal deficiency in many interpretations of Aristotle's theory.

[10] See below, pp. 172 et seq. for Bywater's commentary.

[11] See below, pp. 174 et seq. for Milton's writing.

[12] See below, pp. 175 et seq. for Goethe's *Supplement.*

[13] See below, pp. 180 et seq. for Butcher's commentary.

[14] See below, pp. 178 et seq. for Zeller's argument.

[15] See below, pp. 183 for Else's interpretation.

[16] See below, pp. 186 et seq. for Nahm's argument.

Ingram Bywater

1840–1914

A. Life

Ingram Bywater was Regius Professor of Greek at Oxford from 1893 until 1908. He was born in London in 1840, attended Queen's College, Oxford, was a Fellow of Exeter College. He is best known for his text of the fragments of Heraclitus' philosophy and for the *Aristotle on the Art of Poetry* (1909), from which the selection that follows is abstracted.

B. Commentary

Cartharsis is explained by the infrequency of dramatic performances

This tolerance [17] of the enthusiastic harmonies in a well-ordered state Aristotle justifies by showing that they stand in much the same position as Tragedy. There are certain emotions, he tells us, which arise in some degree in every man's soul, and in a disquieting degree . . . in certain of us, e.g., pity and fear. Enthusiasm is one of these disturbing emotions. Experience, however, shows that the enthusiastic music (that of the hymns of Olympus, for instance) has a salutary effect on those subject to accesses . . . of enthusiasm, restoring them to a normal condition of calm and peace, . . . just as though they had undergone a cure or *catharsis* at the hands of a physician. . . . The same sort of treatment . . . is required of other emotional natures also, e.g., by those liable to accesses of pity and fear, and by the rest of mankind likewise, in so far as they share in these feelings; all want a certain *catharsis,* a pleasurable relief . . . from emotion. . . . In Greek physiology and pathology κάθαρςις is a very general term for a physical clearance or discharge, the removal by art or an effort of nature of some bodily product . . . which, if allowed to remain, would cause discomfort or harm. The κάθαρςις of the soul as described in the Politics is a similar process . . . the tacit assumption being apparently that the emotions

[17] *Aristotle on the Art of Poetry,* translated by Ingram Bywater, Oxford, The Clarendon Press, 1909, pp. 154–56. By permission of the Clarendon Press, Oxford.

in question are analogous to these peccant humours in the body which, according to the ancient humoral theory of medicine, have to be expelled from the system by the appropriate κάθαρςις . . . Pity and fear are elements in human nature, and in some men . . . are present in a disquieting degree. . . . With these latter the tragic excitement is a necessity . . . ; but it is also in a certain sense good for all. It serves as a sort of medicine, producing a *catharsis* to lighten and relieve the soul . . . of the accumulated emotion within it; and as the relief is wanted, there is always a harmless pleasure attending the process of relief. This, then, may be taken as Aristotle's answer to the Platonic argument in the Republic. . . . A *catharsis* in the medical sense of the word is . . . only for occasional use; and its analogue . . . may very well be presumed to resemble it in this respect. In assuming Tragedy, therefore, to have a cathartic rather than a permanent moral effect, Aristotle would seem to have been mindful of the position of the Drama in Greek life, and to have seen that the dramatic performances in the theatre were not sufficiently frequent or continuous to generate a moral habit, or make a lasting impression for good or evil on character. . . .

John Milton

1608–1674

A. Life

The great English poet was born in Cheapside, London, Dec. 9, 1608, and died in Bunhill at the age of 65 years. He attended St. Paul's School and Cambridge University, where he wrote *L'Allegro* and *Il Penseroso.* He travelled in Italy, where he met Galileo. In 1644, Milton published *Areopagitica, A Speech of Mr. John Milton for the Liberty of Unlicensed Printing, to the Parliament of England.* He accepted the Secretaryship for Foreign Tongues to the Council of State of the Commonwealth in 1648 and, at the Restoration of Charles II, escaped execution, probably through the intervention of Davenant or Marvell or both. In 1667, Milton printed *Paradise Lost,* in 1671, *Paradise Regained. Samson Agonistes,* for which the selection printed below is the Preface, was printed in 1671.

B. Commentary

A homeopathic theory

Nothing is here for tears, nothing to wail
Or knock the breast, no weakness, no contempt,
And what may quiet us in a death so noble. . . .

–John Milton, *Samson Agonistes*

Preface to Samson Agonistes

Of that sort of dramatic poem which is called tragedy

Tragedy, as it[18] was antiently compos'd, hath been ever held the gravest, moralest, and most profitable of all other Poems: therefore said by *Aristotle* to be of power, by raising pity and fear, or terror, to purge the mind of those and such like passions, that is, to temper and reduce them to just measure with a kind of delight, stirr'd up by reading or seeing those passions well imitated. Nor is Nature wanting in her own effects to make good his assertion; for so, in Physic, things of melancholic hue and quality are us'd against melancholy, sowr against sowr, salt to remove salt humours. . . .

[18] John Milton, *Samson Agonistes* (London, 1671).

Johann Wolfgang Von Goethe

1749–1832

A. Life

The great poet and dramatist was born in Frankfurt am Main on August 28, 1749. In 1765, he entered the University of Leipzig and in 1770 saw for the first time the Gothic Cathedral in Strassburg, an experience concerning which he wrote a notable essay. Goethe was trained as a lawyer, but his interests went far beyond the law into literature and philosophy. His journey to Italy in 1786–88 proved a notable experience for him and for succeeding generations of lovers of that country. Goethe's best known work is *Faust,* which he wrote at the Court at Weimar. Among his many writings are *Dichtung und Wahrheit, Die Lieder des jungen Werther* and *Wilhelm Meister*. Goethe died in Weimar, March 22, 1832.

B. Commentary

Tragedy does not purify the spectator's emotions . . . The drama must close on the stage with a reconciliation of pity and fear

Supplement to Aristotle's Poetics [19] (1827)

Every one [20] who has concerned himself at all about the theory of poetic art—and of tragedy in particular—will remember a passage in Aristotle which has caused the commentators much difficulty, without their ever having been able to convince themselves wholly of its meaning. In his definition of tragedy this great writer seems to demand of it that, through the representation of stirring deeds and events,

[19] "I have just re-read the *Poetics* of Aristotle with the greatest pleasure; intelligence in its highest manifestation is a fine thing. It is really remarkable how Aristotle limits himself entirely to experience, and so appears, if perhaps somewhat material, for the most part all the more solid. It was also stimulating to me to see with what liberality he always shields the poet against the fault-finders and the hypercritical, how he always insists on essentials, and in everything else is so lax that in more than one place I was simply amazed. It is this that makes his whole view of poetry, and especially of his favorite forms, so vivifying that I shall soon take up the book again, especially in regard to some important passages which are not quite clear and the meaning of which I wish to investigate further."—Goethe to Schiller, April 28, 1797.

[20] *Goethe's Literary Essays,* arranged by J. E. Spingarn. Frederick Ungar Publishing Co., New York, 1964, pp. 104–108.

which should arouse pity and fear, the soul of the spectator should be purified of these passions.

My thoughts and convictions in regard to this passage I can best impart by a translation of it:—

"Tragedy is the imitation of a significant and complete action, which has a certain extension in time and is portrayed in beautiful language by separate individuals, each of whom plays a rôle, instead of having all represented by one person as the narration of a story or epic. After a course of events arousing pity and fear, the action closes with the equilibration of these passions."

In the foregoing translation, I believe I have made this hitherto dubious passage clear; it will only be necessary to add the following remarks: Could Aristotle, notwithstanding his always objective manner,—as, for instance, here, where he seems to be speaking exclusively of the technique of tragedy,—be really thinking of the effect, indeed the distant effect, upon the *spectator?* By no means! He speaks clearly and definitely: When the course of action is one arousing pity and fear, the tragedy must close *on the stage* with an equilibration, a reconciliation, of these emotions.

By "catharsis", he understands this reconciling culmination, which is demanded of all drama, indeed of all poetical works.

This occurs in the tragedy through a kind of human sacrifice, whether it be rigidly worked out with the death of the victim, or, under the influence of a favoring divinity, be satisfied by a substitute, as in the case of Abraham and Agamemnon. But this reconciliation, this release, is necessary at the end if the tragedy is to be a perfect work of art. This release, on the other hand, when effected through a favorable or desirable outcome, rather makes the work resemble an intermediate species of art, as in the return of Alcestis. In comedy, on the contrary, for the clearing up of all complications, which in themselves are of little significance from the point of view of arousing fear and hope, a marriage is usually introduced; and this, even if it does not end life completely, does make in it an important and serious break. Nobody wants to die, everybody to marry; and in this lies the half-jocose, half-serious difference between tragedy and comedy in practical aesthetics.

We shall perceive further that the Greeks did make use of their "trilogy" for such a purpose; for there is no loftier "catharsis" than the *Oedipus of Kolonus,* where a half-guilty delinquent,—a man who, through a demonic strain in his nature, through the sombre vehemence as well as greatness of his character, and through a headstrong course of action, puts himself at the mercy of the ever-inscrutable, unalterable powers,—plunges himself and his family into the deepest, irreparable misery, and yet finally, after having made atonement and reparation, is raised to the company of the gods, as the auspicious protecting spirit of a region, revered with special sacrifices and services.

Here we find the principle of the great master, that the hero of a tragedy must be regarded and represented neither as wholly guilty nor as wholly innocent. In the first case the catharsis would merely result from the nature of the story, and the murdered wretch would appear only to have escaped the common justice which would have fallen upon him anyway by law. In the second case, it is not feasible either; for then there would seem to fall on human power or fate the weight of an all too heavy burden of injustice.

But on this subject I do not wish to wax polemical, any more than on any other; I have only to point out here how up to the present time people have been inclined to put up with a dubious interpretation of this passage. Aristotle had said in the *Politics* that music could be made use of in education for ethical purposes, since by means of the sacred melodies the minds of those raised to frenzy by the orgies were quieted and soothed again; thus he thought other emotions and passions could be calmed and equilibrated. That the argument here is from analogous cases we cannot deny; yet we think they are not identical. The effect of music depends on its particular character, as Handel has worked out in his "Alexander's Feast," and as we can see evidenced at every ball, where perhaps after a chaste and dignified polonaise, a waltz is played and whirls the whole company of young people away in a bacchic frenzy.

For music, like all the arts, has little power directly to influence morality, and it is always wrong to demand such results from them. Philosophy and Religion alone can accomplish this. If piety and duty must be stimulated, the arts can only casually effect this stimulation. What they can accomplish, however, is a softening of crude manners and morals; yet even this may, on the other hand, soon degenerate into effeminacy.

Whoever is on the path of a truly moral and spiritual self-cultivation, will feel and acknowledge that tragedy and tragic romance do not quiet and satisfy the mind, but rather tend to unsettle the emotions and what we call the heart, and induce a vague, unquiet mood. Youth is apt to love this mood and is for that reason passionately devoted to such productions.

We now return to our original point, and repeat: Aristotle speaks of the *technique* of tragedy, in the sense that the poet, making it the object of his attention, contrives to create something pleasing to eye and ear in a course of a completed action.

If the poet has fulfilled this purpose and his duty on his side, tying together his knots of meaning and unraveling them again, the same process will pass before the mind of the spectator; the complications will perplex him, the solution enlighten him, but he will not go home any the better for it all. He will be inclined perhaps, if he is given to reflection, to be amazed at the state of mind in which he finds himself at home again—just as frivolous, as obstinate, as zealous, as weak, as tender or as cynical as he was when he went out. On this point we believe we have said all we can until a further working out of the whole subject makes it possible to understand it more clearly.

Eduard Zeller

1814–1908

A. Life

Eduard Zeller was born in Kleinbottwer (Würtemburg) in 1814. He served as *Privatdocent* in the University of Tübingen and became Professor of Theology at Berne in 1847. He held chairs at the Universities of Marburg and Heidelberg before going to Berlin, where he remained from 1872 until 1894. Zeller was an enormously learned scholar and his *Die Philosophie der Griechen* (1844, 1846, 1852) is a landmark in classical and philosophical scholarship. In 1883, Zeller published *Grundriss der Geschichte der Griechischen Philosophie.* The passage quoted below, but not in its entirety, is from the *History of Greek Philosophy,* the second volume of *Aristotle and the Earlier Peripatetics.*

B. Commentary

The importance of the universal and the law manifest in the work of art

". . . The purification [21] of the emotions is the chief end . . . of serious poetry . . . and . . . Aristotle regards this purifying effect of art as standing in the closest relation to intellectual culture. . . . To this day, after all the endless discussions to which Aristotle's definition of Tragedy has given rise, no agreement has been arrived at upon the question wherein, according to his view, it [the purifying effect of art] consists and what are the conditions of its production. . . .

He describes purification . . . as a species of healing and as a mental alleviation accompanied by pleasure, and accordingly looks for it not in any improvement of the will or in the production of virtuous inclinations, but in the equalization of disturbances produced by violent emotions and the restoration of equanimity. It is here of less importance, in point of actual fact, whether it is the religious or the

[21] E. Zeller, *Aristotle and the Earlier Peripatetics,* London, Longmans, Green and Co., 1897, II. 309 et seq.

medical meaning of "purification" that is prominent in Aristotle's mind; since in either case alike we are dealing with a figurative expression, in the sense that the term does not admit of being transferred literally from one sphere to another. . . . It seems probable that he took *κάθαρςις* as we might use "purgation" . . . to mean expulsion from the body of burdensome or injurious matter, but that inasmuch as he was here dealing with the application of this conception to states of the emotion, he came to connect with it, as he went on, the idea of deliverance from pollution and spiritual disease as well.

. . . When we ask How does Art affect this removal? (the answer is) the "catharsis" is indeed effected in his view by exciting the emotions and is a homeopathic cure of them but this effect is not to be expected from all excitements indifferently, but only from such as are artistic—and by artistic Aristotle here means, as we clearly gather from his account of tragedy, not that which produces the most violent emotion in us, but that which produces emotion in the right way. . . . Art . . . purifies and soothes the emotions in that it delivers us from such as are morbid or oppressive by exciting such as are subordinate to its law, directing them, not towards what is merely personal, but towards what is universal in man, controlling their course upon a fixed principle and setting a definite limit to their force. . . . (Real life) presents us only with the particular, (art) with the universal in the particular; in the latter chance largely rules, the former must reveal to us in its creations the fixity of law. . . . Tragedy in the fate of its heroes gives us a glimpse into the universal lot of man, and at the same time into an eternal law of justice; music calms mental excitement and holds it spellbound by its rhythm and harmony. . . . The tragic poet sets before us in his heroes and in their fate universal types of human nature and life, our sympathies do not confine themselves to these particular characters, but extend to the common elements of human nature; . . . our personal woes are silenced at the spectacle of universal destiny, we are delivered from the oppressions that weigh on us, and our emotions find peace in the recognition of those eternal laws which the course of the piece reveals to us. . . .

S. H. Butcher

1850–1910

A. Life

Samuel Henry Butcher was born in Dublin, April 16, 1850. He attended St. Paul's School and Trinity College, Cambridge, and became a Fellow of Exeter College, Oxford. He was appointed Professor of Greek at Edinburgh, 1882–83. He was a member of the Royal Academy of Letters. Butcher and Andrew Lang produced in 1879 their famous translation of the *Odyssey.* His *Aristotle's Theory of Poetry and Fine Art* is at once an excellent translation and perhaps the best commentary on Aristotle's text in English. It was first published in 1895.

B. Commentary

The feelings undergo qualitative changes in the experience of tragedy

The original [22] metaphor [catharsis] is in itself a guide to the full aesthetic significance of the term. In the medical language of the school of Hippocrates it strictly denotes the removal of a painful or disturbing element from the organism, and hence the purifying of what remains, by the elimination of alien matter. Applying this to tragedy we observe that the feelings of pity and fear in real life contain a morbid and disturbing element. In the process of tragic excitation they find relief, and the morbid element is thrown off. As the tragic action progresses, when the tumult of the mind, first roused has afterwards subsided, the lower forms of emotion are found to have been transmuted into higher and more refined forms. The painful element in the pity and fear of reality is purged away; the emotions themselves are purged. The curative and tranquillising influence that tragedy exercises follows as an immediate accompaniment of the transformation of feeling. Tragedy, then, does more than effect the homeopathic cure of certain passions. Its function on this view is not merely to provide an outlet for pity or fear, but to provide for them a distinctively

[22] S. H. Butcher, "The Function of Tragedy," *Aristotle's Theory of Poetry and Fine Art,* London, Macmillan and Co., 1932, pp. 248 et seq.

aesthetic satisfaction, to purify and clarify them through the medium of art. . . . Pity and fear in Aristotle are strictly correlated feelings. . . . (253) The conditions of dramatic representation, and above all the combined appeal which tragedy makes to both feelings will considerably modify the emotions as they are known in actual reality. Pity in itself undergoes no essential change. . . . The emotion of fear is profoundly altered when it is transferred from the real to the imaginative world. It is no longer the direct apprehension of misfortune impending over our own life. It is not caused by the actual approach of danger. (256) The pressure of immediate reality is removed. . . . We have here part of the refining process which the tragic emotions undergo within the region of art. They are discharged from the petty interests of self, and are on the way to being universalized. The tragic fear, though modified in passing under the conditions of art, is not, in Aristotle, a languid sympathy. Being refracted through pity, it differs from the crushing apprehension of personal disaster . . . Yet a thrill runs through us, a shudder of horror or of vague foreboding. . . .

We are here brought back to Aristotle's theory of poetry as a representation of the universal. Tragedy exemplifies with concentrated power this highest function of the poetic art. The characters it depicts; the actions and fortunes of the persons with whom it acquaints us, possess a typical and universal value. The artistic unity of plot, binding together the several parts of the play in close inward coherence, reveals the law of human destiny, the causes and effects of suffering. The incidents which thrill us are intensified in their effect, when to the shock of surprise is added the discovery that each thing as it has happened could not be otherwise; it stands in organic relation to what has gone before. Pity and fear awakened in connexion with these larger aspects of human suffering, and kept in close alliance with one another, become universalized emotions. What is purely personal and self-regarding drops away. The spectator who is brought face to face with grander sufferings than his own experiences a sympathetic ecstasy, or lifting out of himself. It is precisely in this transport of feeling, which carries a man outside his individual self, that the distinctive tragic pleasure resides. Pity and fear are purged of the impure element which clings to them in life. In the glow of tragic excitement these feelings are so transformed that the net result is a noble emotional satisfaction.

The *katharsis*, viewed as a refining process, may have primarily implied no more to Aristotle than the expulsion of the disturbing element, namely, the pain, which enters into pity and fear when aroused by real objects. The mere fact of such an expulsion would have supplied him with a point of argument against Plato, in addition to the main line of reply above indicated. In the *Philebus* Plato had described the mixed (μιχθεῖσαι) or impure (ἀκάθαρτοι) pleasures as those which have in them an alloy of pain; and the pleasure of tragedy was stated to be of the mixed order. The Aristotelian theory asserts that the emotions on which tragedy works do indeed in real life contain a large admixture of pain, but that by artistic treatment the painful element is expelled or overpowered. . . .

Let us assume, then, that the tragic *katharsis* involves not only the idea of an emotional relief, but the further idea of the purifying of the emotions so relieved. In accepting this interpretation we do not ascribe to tragedy a direct moral purpose and influence. Tragedy, according to the definition, acts on the feelings, not on the will. It does not make men better, but removes certain hindrances to virtue. The refinement of feeling under temporary and artificial excitement is still far removed from moral improvement. Aristotle would probably admit that indirectly the drama has a moral influence, in enabling the emotional system to throw off some perilous stuff, certain elements of feeling, which, if left to themselves, might develop dangerous energy, and impede the free play of those vital functions on which the exercise of virtue depends. The excitation of noble emotions will probably in time exert an influence on the will. But whatever may be the indirect effect of the repeated operation of the *katharsis,* we may confidently say that Aristotle in his definition of tragedy is thinking, not of any such remote result, but of the immediate end of the art, of the aesthetic function it fulfils.

It is only under certain conditions of art that the homeopathic cure of pity and fear by similar emotions is possible. Fear cannot be combined with the proper measure of pity, unless the subject matter admits of being universalized. . . .

Tragedy, as it has been here explained, satisfies a universal human need. The fear and pity on and through which it operates are not, as some have maintained, rare and abnormal emotions. All men, as Aristotle says, are susceptible to them, some persons in an overpowering measure. For the modern, as for the ancient world, they are still among the primary instincts; always present, if below the surface, and ready to be called into activity. The Greeks, from temperament, circumstances, and religious beliefs, may have been more sensitive to their influence than we are, and more likely to suffer from them in a morbid form. Greek tragedy, indeed, in its beginnings was but a wild religious excitement, a bacchic ecstasy. This aimless ecstasy was brought under artistic law. It was ennobled by objects worthy of an ideal emotion. The poets found out how the transport of human pity and human fear might, under the excitation of art, be dissolved in joy, and the pain escape in the purified tide of human sympathy.

Gerald Frank Else

1908–

A. Life

Gerald Frank Else was born in Redfield, South Dakota, July 1, 1908. He was educated at the University of Nebraska and Harvard University. He is Professor of Classics at the University of Michigan and Director of the Center for Co-ordination of Ancient and Modern Studies there. He is the author of *Aristotle's Poetics: The Argument.*

B. Commentary

. . . To return to our question,[23] then: what will be the judgments and the feelings of a normal spectator or hearer or reader when confronted with a tragic story? First of all, so far as the plot as a whole is concerned, if it is to gain his sympathy and ultimately his fear and/or pity, he must make two judgments (one or the other, and, for the best effect, both): (1) that the hero is "like himself", and (2) that he does not deserve his misfortune. These judgments are not after-effects of the spectator's feeling, they are the prerequisites to it, the conditions which must be satisfied *before his psyche* (that is, the rational element in his soul) *will allow the emotions to be felt.*

The analogy between these judgments and those which an Athenian was called upon to make in a murder trial becomes much closer when we bring the question down to the specific issues that are before us in chapter 14: those, namely, that cluster around the tragic act. Before us is a person—Oedipus, Alcmeon, Medea, Heracles—who has killed or is about to kill a "dear one": father, mother, children. In itself the act, or even the intention, is impure and abhorrent in the highest degree. We have seen in what solemn and special tones Plato dealt with such crimes against one's own blood, and with what horror they were still regarded, what taboos and perils still surrounded them,

[23] Reprinted by permission of the publishers from ARISTOTLE'S POETICS: THE ARGUMENT by Gerald F. Else, Cambridge, Mass.: Harvard University Press, 1957, pp. 436–39.

even in the relatively enlightened Athens of the fourth century. Such outrages against god and nature are fearful, there can be no mistake about that. But under what circumstances can I bring myself to pity the murderer or would-be murderer? I can pity him if I judge that *he did not intend the parricide, matricide, or whatever, as such:* in other words, if it is established to my satisfaction that he performed or intended the fearful act δι' ἁμαρτιάν τινά, because of some error.

Let us be precise. The category "slaying of a close blood-relation because of ignorance of his identity" did not appear as such in Plato's code. Book 5 of the *Ethics* showed us Aristotle striving for a closer definition than Plato's of those cases of wrong-doing (including homicide) which lie between full intent and mere unforeseeable accident. Similarly in book 3 he defined the deed which rates pity and forgiveness, instead of reprobation, as the one performed out of ignorance of details. Beyond these specific parallels lies the general fact of the development of the sense of equity (ἐπιείχ εια) in the fourth century—a concept to which Aristotle explicitly attached his discussion in book 5. This is the sphere in which we are moving in tragedy. The deeds or intended deeds before us are such as comported the full horror of blood-pollution and stirred even Plato to a severity which was inconsistent with his own ideas. But they are also deeds caused (not merely accompanied) by ignorance, and therefore having a claim upon our sense of equity and pity. The claim might not lie in a court of law, but it will suffice here because we are sitting in judgment as a court of fellow human-beings, fallible and exposed to misfortune as the hero is. We must and do judge, but as men, not ministers of the law.

I would argue, then, that the spectator or reader of the play is the judge in whose sight the tragic act must be "purified", so that he may pity instead of execrating the doer. But again let us be precise. The spectator or reader does not *perform* the purification, any more than the judges at the Delphinion or in Plato's state did so. The purification, that is, the proof of the purity of the hero's motive in performing an otherwise "unclean" act, is *presented* to him, and his conscience accepts and certifies it to his emotions, issues a license, so to speak, which says: "You may pity this man, for he is like us, a good man rather than a bad, and he is χαθαρός, free of pollution".

But this is not enough either. The hero, who come before us with hands dripping with his father's or mother's blood, is not merely presented to us by the dramatist on a platter bearing the label "pure". The question is how the catharsis is operated, and the answer is that it is operated ("carried forward, brought to completion": περαινόυσα) by the *plot* (the μίμησις). To some extent this is achieved by all that we see and hear about the hero in the play. All that we see of Oedipus assures us that he is a strong-willed, excitable, hot-tempered man, but also a kind, loving, and public-spirited one. Such a person cannot, we feel, have killed his father and married his mother in cold blood. But these reassurances are not enough. Aristotle himself tells us in book 3 of the *Ethics* (3. 2. 1110b19, 1111a20) what it is that guarantees the innocence of motive of the person who has done wrong δι' ἄγνοιαν: it is his remorse when the truth is discovered. And the complex plot offers precisely this kind of certification, in the recognition and the hero's subsequent behaviour. It is Oedipus' self-blinding, his transport of grief and remorse when he learns the truth, that finally assures us of his "purity" and releases our tears. Thus recognition is the structural device which makes it possible for the hero to prove that he did indeed act δι' ἀμαρτίαν τινά and so deserves our pity. For the *Oedipus* the sequence would be: (*pathos,* i.e., deed of horror, inherently μιαρόν but performed in ignorance→) steady augmentation of the horror as the climax approaches→recognition, undoing (reversing) the ignorance→grief and remorse of the doer, certifying the ignorance as cause of the deed and the deed therefore as *οὐ μιαρόν* → pity (→tragic pleasure).

Thus the catharsis is not a change or end-product in the spectator's soul, or in the fear and pity (i.e., the dispositions to them) in his soul, but a process carried forward in the emotional material of the play by its structural elements, above all by the recognition. For the recognition is the pay-off, to use a vulgar but expressive modernism; or in more conventional figure, it is the hinge on which the emotional structure of the play turns. The catharsis, that is, the purification of the tragic act by the demonstration that its motive was not *μιαρόν*, is accomplished by the whole structure of the drama, but above all by the recognition.

This interpretation makes catharsis a transitive or operational factor within the tragic structure itself, precedent to the release of pity, and ultimately of the tragic pleasure, rather than the be-all and end-all of tragedy itself. By so much, it robs our aesthetic vocabulary of one of those "Prachtausdrücke", as Bernays put it, "die jedem Gebildeten geläufig und keinem Denkenden deutlich sind". The great virtue, but also the great vice, of "catharsis" in modern interpretation has been its incurable vagueness. Every variety of moral, aesthetic, and therapeutic effect that is or could be experienced from tragedy has been subsumed under the venerable word at one time or another. Thus, to cite one obvious example out of many, in Butcher's essays on *Aristotle's Theory of Poetry and Fine Art*—which for all their shortcomings are still the best whole treatment of the subject—catharsis rises to the universal plane and ultimately means or implies a notion of "universalising the emotions and ridding them of an intrusive element that belongs to the sphere of the accidental and individual. . . ."

Milton Charles Nahm

1903–

A. Life

Milton C. Nahm was born in Las Vegas, New Mexico, Dec. 12, 1903. He attended the University of Pennsylvania and the University of Oxford. He is author and editor of *Selections from Early Greek Philosophy, Aesthetic Experience and Its Presuppositions, Aristotle on Poetry and Music, The Artist as Creator, Genius and Creativity,* and *The Relation of Criticism and Aesthetics.* He is Professor Emeritus of Philosophy at Bryn Mawr College.

B. Commentary

The theory of catharsis provides only negative criteria for judging art

Tragedy and Value

The more general views of the present editor have been expressed fairly fully in *Aesthetic Experience and Its Presuppositions* and in *Aristotle on Poetry and Music.* Concerning the specific problems raised by the readings chosen for this book, it is of some importance to offer a succinct evaluation, if only because the theory of catharsis appears so frequently as a description of aesthetic experience and because perhaps the most radical change in speculation on art that has occurred between classical and modern times is the emphasis upon imagination rather than upon imitation. That change precludes, in my opinion, the adoption of Aristotle's theory as a wholly satisfactory answer to the questions raised by the experience of moving art.

As for the interpretations of Aristotle's theory of the purgation of feelings, I doubt that a play such as *Medea* would permit Aristotle to argue that the tragedy had been purged by the time the last lines were spoken. As for the explanations offered to explain the purgation of the spectators' feelings, I am inclined to agree with Plato and to doubt that the exercise of feeling tends to purge them. There is a stronger objection, however, to Aristotle's theory as a solution to conflicts in the drama. In my opinion, Aristotle's theory of catharsis provides only a negative criterion for judging tragedy. It is of negative value in the explanation of the tragic experience. Butcher remarked long ago that an inferior tragedy may excite only one of the two emotions generally called tragic. It is here that the difficulty emerges. Aristotle's famous theory provides an instrument which serves to help us determine not what is of value but what is not of value. Schiller wrote that we have the greatest pity for those tragic figures who are whirled into situations over which they have no control. Some characters, however, in "flawed tragedies" arouse only our fear and not our pity. They are beyond human reaction to the forces which arouse our deepest pity. Some characters arouse only our pity, but they may be of such insignificant worth as to achieve no tragic stature.

There is an additional and basic defect in Aristotle's theory of the purgation of the feelings by tragedy. No wholly satisfactory theory of tragedy may ignore the basic fact that tragedy is endurable only if in its construction by the artist or in its experience by the perceiver, values are created. Nothing in Aristotle's theory suggests that such creativity is accounted for.

PART TWO

HELLENIST AND MEDIAEVAL PHILOSOPHIES OF ART

Chapter 6

Hellenist and Mediaeval Philosophers of Art and Beauty

Aristotle's Philosophy of Art is an integral part of speculation upon the artist, the work of art, the techniques employed to produce the object of art, and the end of art. It may accurately be called a "natural" theory, in contrast, for example, to Plato's, in which there are "supranatural", i.e., transcendant elements. For Aristotle, the universal is in the thing; for Plato, it is separate from and prior to the thing. Plato's Philosophy of Art requires for its completeness a doctrine of divine inspiration. This implies that the beautiful work of art is ultimately as far beyond definition as is the Idea of Beauty. Plato's theory places the product of inspired genius beyond the universe in which correctness or error in judgment apply and therefore beyond the scope of complete intelligibility. Aristotle clearly believes that genus and species suffice both to explain imitation and to account for the experience of mimetic objects. As we have observed, however, various difficulties arise in this "natural" philosophy of art, more particularly from the fact that the making of "metaphor" is not teachable and in the implication that it is not technique that makes of Euripides "the most tragic" of the dramatists. For Plato, art is condemned both because it is a copy of a copy and because it affects the feelings. In contrast, Aristotle holds that art begins in the instinct for imitation and is the rationalization of that instinct to imitate and to take pleasure in imitation. Similarly, tragedy is rationalized from its potentiality, the dithyramb, into its actualization as drama.

In the period of Hellenism with which we are concerned in this chapter, both Platonic and Aristotelian elements are present in significant degree. In the later period, the Mediaeval, Aristotelian influences come to be predominant. For the historian of philosophy, both the earlier and the later periods are characterized by epistemological dualism. Theorists of knowledge try to account for truth in terms both of Revelation and Reason. For the philosopher of art, the earlier period is marked by the development of a theory of artistic creativity derived from Plato, whereas the later and Aristotelian period tends to emphasize art as making and right procedure, as well as by close attention to definition and distinction in theories of art and of criticism.

We begin with a direct, powerful, but unsophisticated—in the sense that it is not systematic—denial by Philostratus of the theory that the artist is of necessity one who imitates. We shall then indicate some of the background for Plotinus' philosophy of art and beauty. We shall proceed thereafter to an examination of Longinus *de Sublimitate,* to St. Augustine's philosophy of art, and to Dionysius the Areopagite's assertion of the transcendence of Beauty in the *Divine Names.* We shall conclude with a brief consideration of St. Thomas Aquinas' writings on art and Dante's remarks in a Thomist vein on various aspects of art and more particularly on tragedy.

Philostratus, Longinus, Plotinus

Plotinus is the most powerful thinker and the preeminent philosopher among the Neo-Platonists. Nonetheless, Philostratus, Longinus, and St. Augustine cope with one of the subject's central problems in their endeavour to make evident the meaning of creativity.

There are passages in the writings of various Stoics that anticipate what Philostratus believed concerning imitation and imagination. Such suggestions as are made by Cicero and Seneca,[1] among others, fit into a context of an ordered philosophy, whereas the passage in the Sixth book of *Philostratus* [2] *Life of Apollodorus* is at once powerful and original, evidently expressing a deep conviction rather than a deeply rooted philosophical argument.

Philostratus [3] recounts an argument between an Egyptian, Thespesion, and a Greek, Apollonius, in which the latter asserts that there is no need for Pheidias and Praxiteles actually to have seen the gods: "Imagination wrought these works, a wiser and subtler artist by far than imitation." The entire dialogue is of extraordinary interest but what should be noted particularly is that we are introduced here to creative imagination as a form of human freedom. Imagination in contrast to imitation, is autonomous. It "marches undismayed to the goal which it has itself laid down," whereas imitation proceeds to "conceive of its goal with reference to reality" and is often baffled by the problem.

The identical issue is presented in different terms, that is, in terms of inspiration rather than imagination, by one of the greatest of critics. This Hellenist, Longinus, author of *de Sublimitate,*[4] stoutly denies value to the very criterion Plato used to justify the exile of the imitative artist. Whereas Plato insisted that imitative art is inferior because the mimetic artist is twice removed from truth, Longinus maintains that great art is not to be judged in terms of the criterion of "minute correctness." [5] The poet himself need not be trained or taught.[6]

The inspired genius, who needs neither teaching nor training and, indeed, whose work may be flawed, approaches the divine: " . . . Other qualities prove their possessors

[1] See, for example, Cicero, *Orator* II.9 and Seneca the Elder, *Rhet. Controv.* X. 34.

[2] See below, pp. 205 et seq. for the translation of this passage.

[3] See below, p. 205, for Philostratus' life and writing.

[4] See below, pp. 207 et seq. for the selections from Longinus' *de Sublimitate.*

[5] Longinus maintained that great art was not intended to "persuade" but rather to "transport". His contention that the inspired artist thought little of "minute correctness" and that geniuses were men who were "far removed from flawlessness" exerted an enormous influence upon writers of the 18th century who were in revolt against the rules laid down by Aristotelians. See Longinus' *de Sublimitate* XXXVI, pp. 217–18 below.

[6] Ibid. II.1. See below, p. 208. Cf. Plato, *Ion* above, pp. 51 et seq. on the general theory of inspiration implied. See below, Edward Young, pp. 385 et seq. I. Kant, pp. 411–12 and B. Croce, pp. 533, 559 et seq.

men, sublimity lifts them near the mighty mind of God." It is not the least significant part of this perhaps second greatest critical writing in the West that the author of *de Sublimitate* moves radically away not only from the Platonic circumscription of art within mastery of a whole art[7] but from the conviction that works of art are stimuli intended to produce specific reactions.[8] Not only is great art not to be judged in terms of "minute correctness" but Longinus maintains that it is profoundly moving, a view which radically affects the evaluation of creative powers both in the artist and in the perceiver. The inspired artist is carried out of himself. The genius is "born"[9] and endowed with powers not attainable by means of instruction, Longinus grants, however, that some effects of natural genius alone can only be attained by art. But " . . . Inspired wonder casts a spell upon us . . ." and it can do so because the sublimity which lifts the genius near "the mighty mind of God," has also the power to create. It is important to observe that what is created are ideas in the perceiver which "often pass beyond the limits that enring us."[10] Longinus' most important question is, "What then was in the mind of those demigods who aimed only at what is greatest in writing?" His answer, reminiscent of Plato's in the *Symposium*,[11] makes the end of art the creating of creativity in his auditors:

> Among other things this, that Nature . . . therefore from the first breathed into our hearts an unconquerable passion for whatever is great and more divine than ourselves. Thus within the scope of human enterprise there lie such powers of contemplation and thought that even the whole universe cannot satisfy them, but our ideas often pass beyond the limits that enring us.

[7] See Plato *Ion* 532, above p. 53.

[8] See above, Aristotle, Chap. IV, p. 134 and Chap. V.

[9] *Ibid.* II. 1-3. See below, p. 208.

[10] *Ibid.* XXXV. See below, pp. 216–17.

[11] See above, pp. 87 et seq.

Plotinus, to whose Philosophy of Art we now turn,[12] is said to have remarked of Cassius Longinus—who may have been the author of *de Sublimitate*—that the writer of *On First Principles* might be a scholar but that he was no philosopher. However much this may suggest that Plotinus is not affected by the brilliance of the connection between great art and creativity in its experience, there can be no doubt that Plotinus, the author of the *Enneads*, is a speculative philosopher of first rank. Nor can it be doubted that with him Hellenist philosophy receives its most powerful statement. Not only is this Neo-Platonism profound in itself, but it exerted one of the most pervasive influences ever brought to bear by a highly complex and difficult system of thought upon artists and philosophers alike. It exerted its spell not only on Platonic Academies in the Renaissance but the philosophy affected men as diverse in temperament and thinking as St. Augustine, St. Thomas Aquinas, Marsilio Ficino, Leone Ebreo, Michelangelo Buonarotti, John Milton, Percy Bysshe Shelley, Robert Bridges, as well as a host of others.[13]

We shall here attend largely to Philosophy of Art and to the problem of creativity which, as we have already observed, pervades the writings of Philostratus and Longinus. In Plotinus' philosophy, there are elements that can be properly understood only in the light of Alexandrian speculation as it influenced scholarly interpretations of Plato's and Aristotle's Philosophies of Art. The Jews of Alexandria were orthodox believers in the truths revealed in the Old Testament. Still, theologians and philosophers, of whom the most eminent was Philo Judaeus, were profoundly influenced by Greek philosophy. They felt the need to reconcile Hebraic revelation and Greek philosophy. The method used was the well-

[12] See below, pp. 218 et seq., for Plotinus' life and for selections from his writings.

[13] See below for Augustine, Aquinas, Leone Ebreo, Michelangelo and Milton.

known "allegorical interpretation", which permitted the reading of the Old Testament both literally and allegorically. The principal point of interest for the philosopher of art concerns Philo's interpretation of God and man in terms of the freedom each possesses as creators. We shall examine some of the implications of these problems in the selections which concern the "Great Analogy" of the artist to God.[14] Here it is sufficient to indicate the thinking from which the conception of artistic creativity grew. For Plato, God is an artisan and a maker of the cosmos and man is a microcosm of the macrocosm.[15] For Aristotle, the universe is everlasting and the "analogy" between the artist and God is of little importance, whereas that between Art and Nature is a recurrent theme. Aristotle's theory of "genesis" concerns the making actual of what is potential in the matter upon which the artist works.[16] Philo's God, however, is the God of *Genesis*. He creates the universe not out of preexisting materials but out of nothing. There are traces of Platonic cosmology as well, for Philo's God is the architect of the universe and the creator of man.[17]

Man is created in God's image and is endowed with freedom of will. Yet, Philo's creative God is not only the architect of the cosmos; he is transcendent and "has shown his nature to none." For Philo, therefore, God as absolutely transcendent is beyond rational experience and beyond prediction. Yet, he is ultimate reality.

We have observed that for Plato the *Demiurge* makes the cosmos after the pattern of Ideas he does not create. For Philo, God creates the Ideas, which are immanent in God's mind and have their *locus* in the *Logos*, the first emanation in the system. Philo asserts (*De Opificio Mundi IV*) that God created the Ideas because without beautiful prototypes nothing beautiful could be created.[18]

Thus, for Philo, whereas God is beyond thought, the Platonic Ideas, with their locus in the *Logos*, which constitutes the world of intellect, are created on the first day. The *Logos* flows from God's essence and is the complete aspect of God as He reveals himself to the world. Philo holds that the *Logos* is at once a personification and God in process of thinking. In contrast to Plato's *Demiurgos*, who is conditioned externally by Ideas and by "matter", neither of which he creates, Philo's [19] God is externally conditioned neither by Ideas, which are in the *Logos*, nor by matter, which is nonexistent.

We are introduced in the Philonic philosophy to epistemological dualism, of which mention was made earlier. The sources of knowledge are two-fold: Revelation and Reason. For the philosopher of art, it is difficult to overestimate the importance of this speculation. It influenced the systematic philosophies of Plotinus and St. Augustine, two of the most influential thinkers on art and beauty in the history of philosophy.

As we turn to Plotinus,[20] it is well to observe that whereas Plato argues that the artist makes an imitation of an imitation which, in turn, is an imitation of an Idea, Plotinus' Platonism endows the work of art with value—not, it is true, of the highest but nevertheless to an immeasurably greater degree than does

[14] See above, pp. 10 et seq.

[15] See above, Ibid. and above, *Timaeus*, pp. 93 et seq.

[16] See above, pp. 137 et seq.

[17] See below, pp. 203 et seq. for Philo's life and writings.

[18] See below, p. 203. Compare St. Thomas Aquinas, *Summa Theolog.* 1.15:1. "Now because the world has not come about by accident but was created by God by an act of his intellect, there necessarily must be present in the divine mind a divine form (*divina sit forma*) according to whose model the world was made. And herein consists the rational nature of the idea."

[19] See below, p. 203.

[20] See below, pp. 218 et seq. for Plotinus' life and writings.

Plato. For Plotinus, the ultimately real is the One, the original Being, and it is beyond predication. The One creates the world out of itself and the process by which plurality derives from its source is emanation: ". . . The One . . . has overflowed, and its exuberance has produced the new." (*Enneads* 5. 2. 1.) From the One flow *Nous* or mind, *Psyche* or Soul and, finally, matter. Plotinus holds that in the process of emanation, mind turns towards its source and in knowing the One establishes the dualism of knowing and object known. Since the One is nameless and not the object of rational knowledge, it can be known only in a communion or ecstatic state, as the soul returns to its source.

Immanence and transcendence provide the grounds for a philosophy in which the One is not separated, as are Plato's Ideas, from the world. Plotinus' artists do not merely imitate. Rather, they return to the principles of things and add to what is missing. They possess beauty. The arts go back to "the Ideas from which Nature itself derives," and have their power to improve on Nature.[21] In one of the most famous passages in Philosophy of Art, Plotinus tells us [22] that Pheidias produces his Zeus according to nothing visible but made him such as Zeus himself would appear, should he wish to reveal himself to our eyes. Plotinus writes that the arts "are holders of beauty and add where Nature is lacking."

This is an important step away from the restrictive interpretation Plato laid upon art. Moreover, it is an improvement upon the Aristotelian theory that the form is in the material and is to be made explicit by art. Nonetheless, Neo-Platonism has its problems—as does every speculative Philosophy of Art; serious ones which become imbedded in the history of both art and philosophy. One problem arises from the assumption that Plotinus makes, that Art is superior to what Art produces. The artist's freedom consists in rationality in technique, but the block of stone made into a statue is not beautiful because of the stone but because of the form or shape lent to it by Art, precisely as the beauty of Nature is in the radiance of the Idea but is inferior to its source.[23] This form or shape was in the artist's mind before it came into the stone. The beauty resides in the mind of the artist and does not enter into the stone. What enters the stone is only a lesser beauty derived from the greater and is revealed only insofar as the stone is obedient to art.[24]

For Plotinus, the arts give more than a bare representation of the thing seen.[25] The block of marble becomes beauty, although the form or idea introduced by art "is in the designer before ever it enters the stone." [26]

Despite this high evaluation of art, however, there is a denigration of the function played by the media of art. This, in turn, derives precisely from the presumed superiority of the form over the formed material, which in turn derives from an ambiguity in Plotinus' thought concerning the status of matter in his system of philosophy. On one interpretation, Neo-Platonism asserts that matter exists and grants some value to it. In this way, Plotinus accounts for ugliness in terms of contrast. The suggestion is that a whole may be beautiful, although its parts, or some of them, may be ugly.[27] "An artist would not make an animal all eyes," writes Plotinus [28] and proceeds to the well-known suggestion [29] that should we ask that the world be otherwise than it is,

[21] Plotinus, *Enneads* 5.8.1. See below, pp.226 et seq.

[22] *Ibid.* 5.8.1. See below, p. 226 et seq.

[23] *Ibid.* 1.6.2 and 1.6.3. See below, pp. 221 et seq.

[24] *Ibid.* 1.6.9 and 1.6.1. See below, pp. 225 and 219.

[25] *Ibid.* 5.8.1. See below, p. 226.

[26] *Ibid.*

[27] *Ibid.* 3.2.3 and 3.2.5.

[28] *Ibid.* 3.2.11. See below, pp. 231.

[29] *Ibid.*

We are like people ignorant of painting, who complain that the colours are not beautiful everywhere in the picture: but the Artist has laid on the appropriate tint to every spot. Or we are censuring a drama because the persons are not all heroes but include a servant and rustic and some scurrilous clown; yet take away the low characters and the power of the drama is gone; these are part and parcel of it.

The second interpretation of matter asserts its non-existence,[30] This theory has little aesthetic value. It is primarily intended to account for the evil for which the One cannot be made responsible.[31]

In the combination of Neo-Platonism, Christian theology, and the genius of a great father of the Church, St. Augustine's Philosophy of Art [32] moves outside the area of freedom in terms of external conditions to the complete creativity in art which is the aesthetic correlative to freedom of will.

For Philo, as we have observed, God is a creator, but the making of the cosmos is the function of the Logos. For St. Augustine, there are no entities intervening between God and the world. In accordance with *Genesis,* Augustine holds that God created the cosmos. There are no external conditions. For Plato, the *Demiurge* makes the world after the pattern of Ideas and out of matter, neither of which he creates. For St. Augustine, God needs no pattern."[33] He creates the world out of nothing.[34] The Aristotelian theory of freedom of choice [35] is supplanted by the Augustinean theory of freedom of will.

For Plato, man is a microcosm of the macrocosm.[36] He possesses freedom to choose. For Augustine, man is created in God's image [37] and possesses freedom of will, although his freedom is not comparable to God's.[38] For Plato, the order of nature is one of fixed laws. For Augustine, God may intervene with miracles.

Within the scope of the enormous speculative changes summarized above, we may set about providing a brief statement concerning St. Augustine's Philosophy of Art.

St. Augustine is more Platonic than is Plotinus in his interpretation of art, at least in the sense that for him mathematics is a sound tool for the understanding of what the artist produces. For Plotinus,[39] despite the fact that almost everyone "declares that the symmetry of parts towards each other and towards a whole . . . constitutes the beauty appealing to the eye," the fact is for him that to urge that "to be beautiful is to be symmetrical and fashioned after a certain measure," means that ". . . by this teaching, of necessity, only a compound can be beautiful, never anything simple."

St. Augustine, on the contrary, emphasises the significance of mathematics for art. In *De Ordine,* we are reminded of Plato's *Phaedrus,*[40] for "reason turns to the domain of sight," to a domain in which "it is beauty that pleases the sight, in beauty, figures; in measures, numbers. . . ." On this hypothesis, St. Augustine examines harmony in architecture and comments upon the pervasiveness of *design* to "all the arts and creations of man." [41] It may be

[30] *Ibid.* 3.6.7.

[31] Cf. *Ibid.* 3.2.3, 3.2.5.

[32] An Account of St. Augustine's life and the selections begin below, pp. 232 et seq.

[33] *De Diversis Quaestionibus* LXXXIII. See below, pp. 233. Compare George Puttenham, *The Arte of English Poetry,* below pp. 384 et seq.

[34] *Confessions* XI, ch. See below, p. 233.

[35] See above, Aristotle, *Nicomachean Ethics* Bk. VI. See above pp. 136 et seq.

[36] See above, p. 93. Plato, *Timaeus* 28 C–D.

[37] St. Augustine, *De Trinitate* XIV. xii. 16. See below, pp. 233.

[38] *Confessions* XII, 23. See below, p. 236 et seq.

[39] Plotinus, *Enneads* 1. 6. See below, pp. 219 et seq.

[40] See below, pp. 241–42.

[41] See below, pp. 239 et seq. for *De Ordine* and compare *The City of God* XII, 4 and *De Vera Rel.,* 21, "in quantum est, quidquid est, bonum est." See below, Ibid.

pointed out in this connection that in *De Vera Religione,* Augustine holds that the balance of equal arches "pleases because it is beautiful, and it is beautiful because the parts are alike and are brought by a certain bond to a single harmony." The search for the most beautiful geometrical figure leads Augustine along the same path that it led Plato. The Patristic philosopher tends to favor, however, the circle rather than the dodecahedron as the solution to the problem of what is the most beautiful figure.[42]

In the final analysis, however, although Augustine considers the circle's indivisibility to be a factor to be considered, it is the point rather than the circle that is chosen, on the ground that the former is indivisible, unified and conceptual.

Thus far, St. Augustine's mathematical philosophy of art is but a distant and not particularly interesting echo of the Platonic thesis that mathematical objects are the most beautiful forms. St. Augustine's *De Musica*[43] is mathematical, but as a study of the art it is at once less abstract and more inclusive than Plato's theory. It makes an inference from sounds to numbers and it stresses creativity. The study is dominated by the conception of God as Creator of the world in space and time. For Augustine, simple sights and sounds are not aesthetic,[44] because they are in space and time. Moreover, sensuous perception is inferior to reason, the object of which is God. Personal taste does enter into our preference for numbers, although the form of numbers is universal. Numbers provide the variety necessary in the form, but unity is provided by God, who is not in space and time.

The procedure and Neo-Platonic tone of *De Musica* merits close attention, as a few quotations will indicate. In Book Six, Chapter 17, we are told that "all this is done by God's Providence." For God has created and He rules all things and "even the sinful and miserable soul may be moved by numbers and set numbers moving even in the lowest corruption of the flesh." Although these numbers may be less beautiful, "they cannot lack beauty entire." In this sense, numbers participate in ideal numbers and, too, the artisan "can operate the sensible numbers of his habit by the reasonable numbers of his art." It should be noted that in the 9th Chapter of *De Musica* St. Augustine remarks that the "sense of delight" is favorable to equal numbers rather than to "perturbed ones" because it, that is, the "sense of delight," is imbued with numbers.

The theological presuppositions of the writings on arts manifest themselves significantly at two points. In the first place, St. Augustine—as did Plotinus—examines the ugly, and in the second, he is led to compare the beauty of works of art with the beauty of God. Let us take these in order. As we have observed, God created the world by an act of will. He created matter. The world is made of "a formless matter, which matter, out of nothing." The corruption of beauty is ugliness, for God is not responsible for evil or ugliness. "God made all things from nothing." [45] In his argument concerning matter, St. Augustine is not wholly consistent. Matter is the receptacle of forms. As he holds in *De Genesis contra Manicheos,* it is also the principle of change. Likewise, it is nonexistent, Augustine writes of those "who affirm that there is a nature which God Almighty did not create, but of which at the same time He fashioned the world," and we begin to learn how the issue arises: There are those who deny that God is almighty reason. They do so "from their carnal familiarity with

[42] *De Quantitate Animae,* Chs. VIII, IX and XI.

[43] See below, pp. 240–41 et seq. for selection from *De Musica.*

[44] For a startling contrast to St. Augustine on music, see above, pp. 35 et seq. for the Pythagorean theory and below, pp. 304 et seq., for Descartes' letters on the subject.

[45] *De Fide et Symbolo* II.2. See below, p. 233.

the sight of craftsmen and housebuilders, and artisans of all descriptions, who have no power to make good the effect of their art unless they get the help of materials already prepared."[46]

We are told in *De Vera Religione* that "Measure, form, and order are said to be bad when they are inferior to that which they should be, or when they are applied to objects where they do not agree, or when applied inharmoniously." The issue is more basic, however, than the application of these criteria. All beautiful mundane things derive their beauty from God. (*Nulla essent pulchra, nisi abs te.*) The beautiful is "temporal, carnal, and a lower kind of good." Beauty is above "the souls" and beautiful things made by the artist derive from *pulchritudo* which is single and which transcends all beautiful things. The forms or ideas in the mind of God are eternal. St. Augustine draws the inference:[47]

> What numberless things, made by divers arts and manufactures, both in our apparel, shoes, vessels, and every kind of work, in pictures, too, and sundry images, and these going far beyond necessary and moderate use and holy signification, have men added for the enthrallment of the eyes . . . following outwardly Him by whom they were made, forsaking inwardly Him by whom they were made . . . But I . . . do hence also sing a hymn unto Thee, because those beautiful patterns, which through the medium of men's souls are conveyed into their artistic hands, emanate from that Beauty which is above our souls, which my soul sigheth after day and night . . . And I, . . . impede my course with such beauties . . .

It is clear that Augustine is convinced that art is but "wind and smoke." Although the beauty of things is acknowledged to be the product of man's creative acts or will, his attention is primarily directed to the supreme beauty which is beyond those things, however admirable may be the beauty of the most beautiful mathematical figures. Plato's Ideas are now integral to God's creativity; they are not external to Him. All other "beauties" take their meaning from these *rationes* which are external to them.

Many of the implications of St. Augustine's Philosophy of Art—which in its turn transformed Plato's metaphysics into a theology—are made explicit for beauty by the *Pseudo-Areopagite.*[48] For *Dionysius the Areopagite,* ". . . The One above conception is inconceivable to all conceptions; and the Good above word is unutterable by word." For St. Augustine, God is transcendent, beyond the Aristotelian categories, and not describable as substance but as *essentia.* Nevertheless, for St. Augustine, God is Creator of the world in time and space. For the Areopagite, God is absolutely transcendent. God is beauty and God transcends reason. No predication can be made concerning Him. The supreme aesthetic value is apprehended in mystical union. In the Mystical Theology, the theory of beauty has got "beyond science and beyond reason to the truth of faith and revelation." The names of God are not descriptive of His own nature, but describe corresponding qualities in us. God is, in fact, Nameless and the Many-named. As the Areopagite writes, "As pain does not grieve and joy does not rejoice, so the primitive life does not live and the original light is not illumined."

Plato had concluded that the Idea of Beauty is both substantival and adjectival. For Dionysius, what can be said is that causes are not similar to effects, although "effects assume as much as they can of cause and try to become similar to it." Philonic as well as Platonic influences enter to produce one passage of special interest for the philosopher of art. There is a sharply drawn dualism between beauty and beautiful, following upon the interpretation of

[46] *Ibid.*

[47] *Confessions* X.xxxiv. See below, pp. 234 et seq. Cf. Ibid XXXIV, below, p. 240.

[48] See below pp. 243 et seq. for a brief life and a selection from the writings of the Pseudo-Areopagite.

God as both Nameless and Many-named. Beauty becomes absolute and transcendent. To ascribe beauty to God or to predicate it of Him is to ascribe a term to the Nameless. Beauty is the source of all beautiful objects.[49] And because God is transcendent, both sense and intellect must be abandoned if we are to apprehend Him. Only in an absolute ecstasy, by standing outside the self in all purity, "wilt thou be carried on high to the superessential ray of all darkness."

The sentence just quoted is from *de Pulchro et de Bono*,[50] variously attributed to Albertus Magnus and to St. Thomas Aquinas. That in terms of Platonism it enormously influenced Scholastic philosophy is evident from the sentence in the "Expositio" in which the author maintains that the essence of the thing pertains to brilliance, whereas its ordering in terms of the end pertains to harmony.

St. Thomas Aquinas[51] maintains that "It is impossible for the natural reason to arrive at the knowledge of the divine persons. By natural reason, we may know those things which pertain to the unity of the divine essence, but not those which pertain to the distinction of the divine persons, and he who attempts to prove by the natural reason the trinity of persons, detracts from the rights of faith."[52] The issue here is of importance for the Thomist Philosophy of Art and for followers of St. Thomas' doctrine. In Thomas' view, there is much on which Reason is silent and Scripture teaches much that Reason has neither the capacity to understand nor to demonstrate. In Scholasticism, however, it is held that there is a segment of knowledge common to Reason and Revelation. Reason can prove God's existence but Reason cannot remain in opposition to Revelation. If there appears to be disagreement, there is something wrong with the arguments in question. Reason may be employed to refute the arguments of the rationalists. Faith transcends reason.

A dichotomy results in Philosophy of Art, one ultimately traceable to the Hebraic-Christian belief that God created the cosmos out of nothing, from the Philonic-Augustinean hypothesis that the form or idea exists in God, and from the Aristotelian theory of art as making. We have observed in Philo's philosophy the Philonic[53] and Plotinean reinterpretation of the Platonic–Aristotelian conception of God as an architect. In the *Summa Theologiae*,[54] Aquinas writes that it is necessary for a likeness of the form to be in the producer. This occurs in two ways: ". . . in some effective agents there pre-exists the form of the thing to be produced by way of *natural* existence. . . ." One illustration of this is man begetting man. The second way is by *intelligible* existence, "as in those beings which operate by the mind." An illustration of thesis is provided by the house that preexists in the mind of the architect, which "can be designated as the Idea of the house." This is explained in terms of the intention of the artist to assimilate the made house to the identical form he has conceived in his mind. The world was not brought into existence by accident but was created by God "by an act of Intellect" and for this the requirement is that a form be present to the divine mind according to the pattern according to which the world was made. Aquinas argues that in this consists "the conceptual nature of God."[55]

[49] See below, pp. 244, *Concerning Divine Names,* III.7.

[50] The full title is Opusculum LXVIII, *De Pulchro et De Bono Ex Commentario S. Thomae Aquinatis, in Librum S. Dionysii De Divinis Nominibus,* Cap. IV. Lect. V. The book has been listed among the writings of St. Thomas which are not genuine. M. De Wulf has argued that it was written by Albertus Magnus.

[51] See below, pp. 246 et seq., for life and writings of St. Thomas Aquinas.

[52] St. Thomas Aquinas, *Summa Theol.* I.Qu.32, Art. 1.

[53] See above, pp. 203–04, *de Opif. Mundi.*

[54] *Summa Theol.* 1.15.1.

[55] *De Div. Nom.* cap. iv., lesson 5 and 6 and *Commentary of St. Thomas.*

God is beautiful and imparts beauty to all things. Art makes a work of art. The artist is a craftsman. His technique does not necessarily produce beauty.[56] Beauty produces beauty and from God all beauty is imparted. Beauty is the "splendor of form shining on the proportioned parts of matter." [57]

Some arts tend to produce works of beauty. These, however, are inferior, belonging as they do to the world of created things. So far as the beautiful is concerned, "three things are requisite: ". . . For beauty includes three conditions, *integrity,* or *perfection,* since those things which are impaired are by the very fact ugly; due *proportion* or *harmony;* and lastly, *brightness,* or *clarity,* whence things are called beautiful which have a bright color."[58] Although they are fundamentally identical in a thing, they being based on the form and goodness praised as beauty, they differ logically. Goodness belongs to the appetite, whereas beauty relates to the cognitive faculty. Beautiful things "are those which please when seen." Beauty, therefore, consists in "due proportion." The senses delight in things duly proportioned, "as in what is after their own kind—because even sense is a sort of reason, just as is every cognitive faculty." Aquinas concludes that "since knowledge is by assimilation, and similarity relates to form, beauty properly belongs to the nature of a formal cause."

In the *Exposition of Dionysius on the Divine Names,* Chapter IV, Lecture 4-5, there appears an examination of the problem, "Beautiful Things Participate in Divine Beauty." The writing is not listed among St. Thomas' writings and de Bryne and de Wulf hold that it was written by Albertus Magnus. However that may be, *de Pulchro* shows clearly one problem which the Schoolmen encountered in Philosophy of Art. Dionysius is quoted to the effect that "God, Who is the supersubstantially beautiful, is called Beauty," because ". . . He gives beauty to all created beings in accord with the limitations of each." In the *Summa Theol.,*[59] however, it is said of Art that it is "nothing but right reasoning concerning works that are to be made." Art is "an operative habit." Maritain points out [60] in *Art and Scholasticism,* however, that "the production of beauty belongs to God alone as His true property." According to the same author, should the artist attempt to produce beauty, the effort is a denial of the conditions of making and, in certain circumstances, an arrogation of the aseity of God. Here is the argument in the context of Maritain's essay on "The Frontiers of Poetry." Maritain,[61] writes that

> Here is a gleam of metaphysics thrown on the movement which impels—or only the other day impelled—our generation to search for *abstract music, abstract painting, abstract drama, abstract poetry* . . . To order contemporary art *to exist* as abstract art, discarding every condition determining its existence in the human subject, is to have it arrogate to itself the aseity of God. To require it *to tend* to abstract art like a curve to its asymptote, without rejecting the servitude of its human estate, but ceaselessly overcoming them, by straining its created bonds to the extreme limit of elasticity, is to require it to realise more fully its radical spirituality. Here is pride, there magnanimity, both aiming at the impossible, either of folly or heroism . . . To particularise: the whole discussion resolves itself into this, that art is faced by an antinomy (it is not alone in such a situation) between the supreme postulates of *its essential being* considered in itself and transcendentally, and the *conditions of existence* demanded by the same being as it is realised on this earth . . .

[56] *Commentary on Ethics.*

[57] Compare below, p. 246.

[58] *Pers. in Refer. to Essence,* Q. 39, Art. 8. See below, p. 246. This is amplified in *Ibid.* Q. 5. Art 5, see below, p. 246, where the distinction is drawn between beauty and goodness.

[59] St. Thomas Aquinas, *Summa Theol.* I–II, 57, 3, c, replies to Obj. 1-3.

[60] *Ibid.,* p. 60. See below, p. 247.

[61] J. Maritain, *Art and Scholasticism,* pp. 90-91, 109.

Where would the notion of abstract art, driven to its furthest logical extremes lead, to an art completely isolated from everything which was not its own peculiar rules of operation and the object to be created as such—in other words, separate and exempt from, and perfectly disinterested in regard to man and things . . . By showing us where moral truth and the genuine supernatural are situate, religion saves poetry from the absurdity of believing itself destined to transform ethics and life: saves it from overweening arrogance.

There is another side to the influence of Thomism on theories of art and it concerns art rather than beauty as transcendental. Such a theory asks the question, as does Eric Gill in his *Art*,[62] "How are things made? What is necessary to the making of anything?" The answer he finds in Aristotelian and Thomist thought: "First or all there is an idea in the mind. Second there is the material of which the thing is to be made." To this Gill adds tools and the the will to act. What he is writing comes quite clear: he explains art in terms of Aristotle's four causes: Final, Efficient, Material, and Formal.

If we now return to the Middle Ages, after examining the contemporary interpretation of Scholasticism in Jacques Maritain's writings, our most fortunate encounter is with Dante Alighieri.[63] In his writing abstract philosophy is transformed within the body of great poetry. Dante is of importance and influence within the confines of Philosophy of Art. He reiterates, it is true, the ancient theory of the relation of parts to wholes.[64] He expresses succinctly and clearly the analogy between the artist and God.[65] But it is unlikely that anything Dante ever wrote on art has exceeded in influence the definitions of tragedy and comedy contained in the poet's letter to Lord Can Grande.[66] For these reasons alone, it is evident that Dante was not merely the versifier of Thomas Aquinas,[67] although it is no less evident that he was enormously influenced by Thomist philosophy. In some instances in *The Divine Comedy*,[68] Dante translates abstract Thomist theology into the language of the artist. For example, he writes in the following passage of the creative power of the "idea":

. . . That which dies not,
And that which can die, are each but the beam
Of that idea, which our Sovereign Sire
Engendered loving; for that lively light,
Which passeth from his brightness, not disjoin'd
From him, nor from his love triune with them,
Doth, through his bounty, congregate itself,
Mirror'd, as 't were in new existences,
Itself unalterable and ever one . . .
Descending hence unto the lower powers,
Its energy so sinks, at last it makes
But brief contingencies: for so I name
Things generated, which the heav'nly orbs
Moving, with seed or without seed, produce.
Their wax, and that which molds it, differ much:
And thence with lustre, more or less, it shows
Th' ideal stamp imprest: so that one tree
According to his kind, hath better fruit,
Or worse: and, at your birth, ye, mortal men,
Are in your talents various. Were the wax
Molded with nice exactness, and the heav'n
In its disposing influence supreme,
The lustre of the seal should be complete:
But nature renders it imperfect ever,
Resembling thus the artist in her work,
Whose faltering hand is faithless to his skill . . .

The emanation of the idea into nature and the stigma of inferiority as the artist impresses the idea on the medium with "faltering hand," "faithless to his skill," is thoroughly Neo-

[62] Eric Gill, *Art* (London, 1934), p. 1.

[63] For Dante's life and selections from his writings, see below, pp. 249 et seq.

[64] See below, p. 250.

[65] See below, p. 249–50.

[66] See below, p. 250.

[67] The opinion is widely expressed. See below, p. 202 et seq.

[68] *Paradiso* XIII. 48 (Translation, H. F. Cary), p. 202.

Platonic and Thomist to the degree that St. Thomas follows Dionysius and St. Augustine. In this connection, it should be noted that Dorothy L. Sayers, who translated Dante's *Inferno*,[69] remarks in "The Divine Poet and the Angelic Doctor," that "It was formerly the critical fashion to imply that the *Comedy*, theologically considered, was little more than a versified paraphrase of the *Summa*." Miss Sayers herself holds that

> For Dante and Aquinas . . . the universe meant something; it made sense; it had order. And the order was a Christian order . . . Such, then, is the image which Dante found for the Thomist synthesis. So far as they go, human wisdom is valid, art is valid, science and philosophy and natural ethics, and even natural religion are valid; they can avail to preserve the soul from the lowest deeps—they can by proof and reason establish an overwhelming case for theism, and, under the authority of religion and in the power of Grace, they can sustain and fortify the soul for a long way on its journey. But of themselves they do not form a substitute for the redeemed life of grace— . . . The Heavenly Paradise belongs to another universe of discourse altogether . . .

In fact, Dante did "versify" some of St. Thomas. But the important point—and it is one that, strangely enough, Miss Sayers does not mention—is that Dante wrote superb poetry. This is evident in Miss Sayers' own translation of the lines:

> The little brooks the ripple from the hills
> Of the green Casentin to Arno river,
> Softening their channels with their cooling rills,
> Are in my eyes and in my ears for ever . . .[70]

[69] Dorothy L. Sayers, *Further Papers on Dante* (London: Harper & Company; New York: Harper & Row), pp. 38, 43, 50. Reprinted by permission of Harold Ober Associates Incorporated. Copyright © 1957 by Dorothy L. Sayers.

[70] *The Comedy of Dante Alighieri the Florentine*. Cantica I. Hell (L'Inferno). Translated by Dorothy L. Sayers. Canto XXX, 64–67, pp. 259–60. London, Penguin Books, Ltd., 1957.

Philo

ca. 25 B.C.–50 A.D.

A. Life

Philo Judaeus' name is most notably associated with the allegorical interpretation of the Old Testament and with the city of Alexandria in Egypt where that method of interpretation was the principal instrument employed in efforts to relate Hebraic and Greek thought. In the year 40 A.D., Philo was a member of a group of Jews sent from Alexandria on a mission to the Roman Emperor Gaius to ask that the Jews not be required to offer him divine honor. Philo's writings include *De Mundi Opificio, Vita Mosis,* and *A Treatise on the Cherubim.*

B. Philosophy of Art

God, the Architect and the Pattern

For God,[71] as being God, anticipating that there could never be a beautiful imitation without a beautiful pattern, or any perceptible thing faultless which was not modelled in conformity with an archetypal and intelligible idea, when he wished to fabricate this visible cosmos, first shaped forth the intelligible, in order that, using an immaterial and most God-like pattern, he might work out the material cosmos, a more recent copy of an older one, destined to contain as many perceptible genera as there were intelligible in the other. But it is not to be said or supposed that the cosmos which consists of the ideas is in any place; but in what way it subsists we shall know by following up an example of what takes place among ourselves. Whenever a city is founded to gratify the high ambition of some king or emperor, claiming autocratic authority, and at the same time brilliant in thought, adding splendour to his good fortune, sometimes a trained architect having offered his services, and inspected the suitability of the place, describes first within himself almost all

[71] Translated by James Drummond, *Philo Judaeus; or, The Jewish-Alexandrian Philosophy,* II. 75. Williams and Norgate, London, 1888.

the parts of the city that is to be erected, temples, gymnasia, town-halls, market-places, harbours, docks, lanes, equipment of walls, foundations of houses and other public edifices. Then, having received the forms of each in his own soul, as in wax, he bears the figure of an intelligible city, and having stirred up the images of this in his memory, and, still more, having sealed there its characters, looking, like a good workman, to the pattern, he begins to prepare the well proportioned mixture made of stones and timber, making the material substances like each of the immaterial ideas. Similarly, then, we must think about God, who, when he purposed founding the great city, first devised its forms, out of which, having composed an intelligible cosmos, he completes the perceptible, using the former as a pattern. As, then, the city which was first formed within the architect had no exterior place, but had been sealed in the artist's soul, in the same way not even the cosmos that consists of the ideas could have any other place than the divine Logos which disposed these things into a cosmos. For what other place could there be for his powers which would be adequate to receive and contain, I do not say all, but any one unmixed?

Philostratus

ca. 170–240 A.D.

A. Life

Flavius Philostratus, the Athenian, was the author of the *Life of Apollonius of Tyana.* The book was dedicated to Julia Domna, mother of Caracalla. Philostratus also wrote the *Lives of the Sophists.* Little is known of Philostratus' life, but it is usually assumed that he was born in Lemnos, that he taught in Athens, and that he lived in Rome. Considerable doubt has been brought to bear on the *Life of Apollonius.* It has frequently been dismissed as a series of highly subjective impressions having little to do with the actual lives of the subjects of whom the author writes.

B. Philosophy of Art

Imagination and its superiority over imitation

[Apollonius engages Thespesion, an Egyptian, in conversation concerning Egypt's gods and the talk turns to imitation and imagination:]

APOLLONIUS.[72] My first question shall be about the gods. On what principle have you given the people of this country such absurd and ludicrous shapes of gods, all but a few—a few? Why, they are few indeed who are scientifically represented by their images and in a godlike form. The rest of your temples seem more like honours rendered to irrational and unworthy animals than to gods.

THESPESION. (*angrily*). And your images? Pray, how do they represent them in your country?

APOLL. With such craftsmanship as ideal beauty and devotion prescribe for divine effigies.

THESP. I suppose you mean the Zeus at Olympia, and the image of Athena, and those of the Cnidian and the Argive goddesses, and others equally beautiful and instinct with grace?

[72] *Philostratus in Honour of Apollonius of Tyana,* translated by J. S. Phillimore. Vol. II, 1912. By permission of the Clarendon Press, Oxford. Book VI, pp. 122–23.

APOLL. Not those only; I assert that, in general, the statuary of other nations has a feeling for decency, whereas yours is rather a mockery than a worship of the godhead.

THESP. Did your Pheidias and your Praxiteles go up into heaven, and model the gods from the life, before they made their artistic representations of them, or had they something else that guided their plastic skill?

APOLL. Something else, and something full of ingenuity.

THESP. What can that have been? You will not find any other principle besides mimicry.

APOLL. Imagination produced these effects, and imagination is a more cunning craftsman than mimicry. Imitation can portray in art what it has seen; imagination, even what it has not seen, for it will suppose the unseen by the analogy of the real. Mimicry is often disconcerted by wonder and awe, but nothing disconcerts imagination, which moves with imperturbable advance towards its ideal goal. The man who meditates a design for Zeus must see him with heavens and seasons and stars, as Pheidias did in that eager sally of ambition; the man who will carve an Athena must think of camps, and wisdom, and the arts, and how she sprang to birth from Zeus himself. But when you make a hawk, or an owl, or a wolf, or a dog, and take that to a temple in lieu of Hermes, Athena, and Apollo, the beasts and birds are no doubt to be congratulated on their effigies, but it must be a grave derogation from the divine honour.

THESP. I do not think that your criticism of our usages shows much discernment. If there is one point in which the Egyptians show Science, it is in not presuming to take a free hand with divine effigies, but making them symbolical and implicitly significant: for thus they gain in reverence. . . .

Longinus

Third Century A.D.

A. Life

The author of *On the Sublime,* one of the most remarkable works of criticism in the West, probably lived in the third century A.D. He has been identified as Cassius Longinus, ca. 213–273 A.D., and if the identification is correct, he would be the Cassius Longinus who was born in Syria, studied at Alexandria, and taught in Athens. This Longinus engaged in dispute with Plotinus and had a reputation for great learning. Eunapius called him "a living library and a walking museum". He was executed in Rome, by order of Emperor Aurelian.

There are grave doubts, however, that the author of *Problemata Homeri* is the author of *de Sublimitate.* In any case, the book on the sublime was written in the third century or earlier. The oldest manuscript dates from the tenth century and is only two-thirds complete. The first modern edition was issued in Basel in 1554 and the first English translation was published in 1652.

B. Philosophy of Art

Dionysius or Longinus on the Sublime

1. You know,[73] my dear Postumius Terentianus, that when we were studying together Cecilius's [74] little treatise on the Sublime we found it was too trivial to satisfy the full demands of the subject and omitted altogether to touch upon the main points, and that consequently it does not render to its readers very much of that assistance which should be an author's chief aim. Moreover, in every systematic treatise there are two requisites: the author must first define his subject, and secondly, though this is really more important, he must show us how and by what

[73] Reprinted by permission of the publishers and the Loeb Classical Library from W. Hamilton Fyfe's translation of Longinus, *Dionysius or Longinus on the Sublime* (Cambridge, Mass.. Harvard University Press; London: Heinemann, 1939).

[74] A Sicilian rhetorician, in religion a Jew, who taught at Rome in the time of Augustus.

means of study we may reach the goal ourselves. Cecilius, however, while assuming our ignorance and endeavouring by a thousand instances to demonstrate the nature of the sublime, apparently thought it unnecessary to deal with the means by which we may be enabled to educate our natures to the proper pitch of elevation. Still, so far as Cecilius is concerned, we ought perhaps rather to praise him for the mere conception of such a treatise and the trouble spent upon it than to blame him for his omissions. But since you have now required me in my turn to prepare some notes on the sublime purely for your own sake, let us then see whether our views have any real value for public speakers; and in the details of our inquiry you yourself, my friend, will, I am sure, do what duty and your heart alike dictate and give me the benefit of your unbiased judgement. For he spoke well who, in answer to the question, "What have we in common with the gods?" said "Kindness and Truth." Further, writing for a man of such learning and culture as yourself, dear friend, I almost feel freed from the need of a lengthy preface showing how the Sublime consists in a consummate excellence and distinction of language, and that this alone gave to the greatest poets and historians their pre-eminence and clothed them with immortal fame. For the effect of genius is not to persuade the audience but rather to transport them out of themselves. Invariably what inspires wonder casts a spell upon us and is always superior to what is merely convincing and pleasing. For our convictions are usually under our own control, while such passages exercise an irresistible power of mastery and get the upper hand with every member of the audience.

Again inventive skill and the due disposal and marshalling of facts do not show themselves in one or two touches: they gradually emerge from the whole tissue of the composition, while, on the other hand, a well-timed flash of sublimity scatters everything before it like a bolt of lighting and reveals the full power of the speaker at a single stroke. But, as I say, my dear Terentianus, these and other such hints you with your experience could supply yourself.

2. We must begin now by raising the question whether there is an art of sublimity or profundity, for some think those are wholly at fault who try to bring such matters under systematic rules. Genius, it is said, is born and does not come of teaching, and the only art for producing it is nature. Works of natural genius, so people think, are spoiled and utterly demeaned by being reduced to the dry bones of rule and precept. For my part I hold that the opposite may be proved, if we consider that while in lofty emotion Nature for the most part knows no law, yet it is not the way of Nature to work at random and wholly without system. In all production Nature is the prime cause, the great exemplar; but as to all questions of degree, of the happy moment in each case, and again of the safest rules of practice and use, such prescriptions are the proper contribution of an art or system. We must remember also that mere grandeur runs the greater risk, if left to itself without the stay and ballast of scientific method, and abandoned to the impetus of uninstructed enterprise. For genius needs the curb as often as the spur. Speaking of the common life of men Demosthenes declares that the greatest of all blessings is good fortune, and that next comes good judgement, which is indeed quite as important, since the lack of it often completely cancels the advantage of the former. We may apply this to literature and say that Nature fills the place of good fortune, Art that of good judgement. And above all we must remember this: the very fact that in literature some effects come of natural genius alone can only be learnt from art. If then, I say, those who censure the students of this art would lay these considerations to heart, they would not, I fancy, be any longer inclined to consider the

study of these subjects superfluous and useless.

[*Two pages of the MS. are missing here.*]

3 . . .

Yea, though they check the chimney's towering flame.
For, if I spy one hearthholder alone,
I'll weave one torrent coronal of flame
And fire the steading to a heap of ash.
But not yet have I blown the noble strain.

All this has lost the tone of tragedy: it is pseudo-tragic,—the "coronals" and "spewing to heaven" and making Boreas a flute-player and all the rest of it. The phrasing is turbid, while the images make for confusion rather than intensity. Examine each in the light of day and it gradually declines from the terrible to the ridiculous. Now seeing that in tragedy, which is essentially a majestic matter and admits of bombast, misplaced tumidity is none the less unpardonable, surely it is not likely to suit real speeches. Thus it is that people laugh at Gorgias of Leontini for calling Xerxes "the Persian Zeus," and vultures "living sepulchres"; also at certain phrases of Callisthenes which are not sublime but high-falutin, and still more at some of Cleitarchus's efforts, an affected creature, blowing, as Sophocles says, "on scrannel pipes, yet wasting all his wind." You find the same sort of thing in Amphicrates too, and in Hegesias and Matris. For often when they think themselves inspired, their supposed ecstasy is merely childish folly. Speaking generally, tumidity seems one of the hardest faults to guard against. For all who aim at grandeur, in trying to avoid the charge of being feeble and arid, fall somehow into this fault, pinning their faith to the maxim that "to miss a high aim is to fail without shame." Tumours are bad things whether in books or bodies, those empty inflations, void of sincerity, as likely as not producing the opposite to the effect intended. For, as they say, "there's naught so dry as dropsy."

Tumidity then comes of trying to outdo the sublime. Puerility, on the other hand, is the exact opposite of grandeur; utterly abject, mean-spirited, and in fact the most ignoble of faults. What then is puerility? Is it not obviously the academic attitude, where over-elaboration ends in frigid failure? Writers fall into this fault through trying to be uncommon and exquisite, and above all to please, and founder instead upon the tinsel reefs of affectation. Closely allied to this is a third kind of fault peculiar to emotional passages, what Theodorus used to call "Parenthyrson." This is emotion misplaced and pointless where none is needed, or unrestrained where restraint is required. For writers often behave as if they were drunk and give way to outbursts of emotion which the subject no longer warrants. Such emotion is purely subjective and consequently tedious, so that to an audience which feels none of it their behaviour looks unseemly. And naturally so, for while they are in ecstasy, the audience are not. However we have reserved another place in which to treat of emotional passages.

4. The second fault of which we spoke above is Frigidity, or which there are many examples in Timaeus, in other respects a capable writer and sometimes far from barren in greatness of style, learned, and full of ideas. Yet while keenly critical of others' faults, he is blind and deaf to his own, and his insatiable passion for starting strange conceits often lands him in the most puerile bathos. I will only quote one or two examples from Timaeus, as Cecilius has forestalled me with most of them. In his eulogy of Alexander the Great he speaks of "one who subdued the whole of Asia in fewer years than Isocrates took to write his *Panegyric* urging war on Persia." Surely this is an odd comparison on the Macedonian to the sophist, for it is obvious, friend Timaeus, that on this showing Isocrates was a far better man

than the Spartans, since they spent thirty years in subduing Messene, while he composed his *Panegyric* in no more than ten! Again, take his denunciation of the Athenian prisoners in Sicily: "Having committed sacrilege against Hermes and mutilated his statues they were therefore punished, mainly owing to the action of a single man, who was kin on his father's side to the injured deity, Hermocrates the son of Hermon." This makes me wonder, my dear Terentianus, why he does not write of the tyrant Dionysius that "Having shown impiety towards Zeus and Heracles, he was therefore deprived of his tyranny by Dion and Heracleides." But why speak of Timaeus when those very demi-gods, Xenophon and Plato, for all their training in the school of Socrates, yet sometimes forget themselves in their fondness for such cheap effects. In his *Constitution of Sparta* Xenophon says, "Certainly you would hear as little speech from these Spartans as from marble statues, and could as easily catch the eye of a bronze figure; indeed you might well think them as modest as the maidens in their eyes." It would have better suited Amphicrates than Xenophon to speak of the pupils in our eyes as modest maidens. And fancy believing that every single man of them had modest pupils, when they say that people show their immodesty in nothing so much as their eyes! Why, an impudent fellow is called "Heavy with wine, with the eyes of a dog." However, Timaeus, laying hands as it were on stolen goods, could not leave even this frigid conceit to Xenophon. For example, speaking of Agathocles when he carried off his cousin from the unveiling ceremony although she had been given in marriage to another, he says, "Who could have done such a thing, had he not harlots instead of maidens in his eyes?" And what of the otherwise divine Plato? "They will inscribe and store in the temples," he says, "cypress memorials," meaning wooden tablets: and again, "As for walls, Megillus, I would consent with Sparta to let the walls lie slumbering on the ground and never rise again." Herodotus's phrase for fair women is not much better: "eye torture" he calls them. Yet he has some excuse, for in Herodotus this is said by the barbarians, who are, moreover, in their cups. Yet even in the mouths of such characters as these it is not right to display an unseemly triviality before an audience of all the ages. . . .

7. We must realize, dear friend, that as in our everyday life nothing is really great which it is a mark of greatness to despise, I mean, for instance, wealth, position, reputation, sovereignty, and all the other things which possess a deal of theatrical attraction, and yet to a wise man would not seem supremely good, since contempt for them is itself eminently good—certainly men feel less admiration for those who have these things than for those who could have them but are big enough to slight them—well, so it is with the grand style in poetry and prose. We must consider whether some of these passages have merely some such outward show of grandeur with a rich moulding of casual accretions, and whether, if all this is peeled off, they may not turn out to be empty bombast which it is more noble to despise than to admire? For the true sublime, by some virtue of its nature, elevates us: uplifted with a sense of proud possession, we are filled with joyful pride, as if we had ourselves produced the very thing we heard. If, then, a man of sense, well-versed in literature, after hearing a passage several times finds that it does not affect him with a sense of sublimity, and does not leave behind in his mind more food for thought than the mere words at first suggest, but rather that on careful consideration it sinks in his esteem, then it cannot really be the true sublime, if its effect does not outlast the moment of utterance. For what is truly great gives abundant food for thought: it is irksome, nay, impossible, to resist its effect: the memory of it is stubborn and indelible. To speak, generally, you should consider that to

be truly beautiful and sublime which pleases all people at all times. For when men who differ in their habits, their lives, their tastes, their ages, their dates, all agree together in holding one and the same view about the same writings, then the unanimous verdict, as it were, of such discordant judges makes our faith in the admired passage strong and indisputable.

8. There are, one may say, some five genuine sources of the sublime in literature, the common groundwork, as it were, of all five being a natural faculty of expression, without which nothing can be done. The first and most powerful is the command of full-blooded ideas —I have defined this in my book on Xenophon —and the second is the inspiration of vehement emotion. These two constituents of the sublime are for the most part congenital. But the other three come partly of art, namely the proper construction of figures—these being probably of two kinds, figures of thought and figures of speech—and, over and above these, nobility of phrase, which again may be resolved into choice of words and the use of metaphor and elaborated diction. The fifth cause of grandeur, which embraces all those already mentioned, is the general effect of dignity and elevation.[75] Let us then consider all that is involved under each of these heads, merely prefacing this, that Cecilius has omitted some of these five classes, one obvious omission being that of emotion. Now if he thought that sublimity and emotion were the same thing, and that one always essentially involved the other, he is wrong. For one can find emotion that is mean and devoid of sublimity, for instance feelings of commiseration, annoyance, and fear. On the other hand, many sublime passages are quite apart from emotion. There are thousands of examples, for instance, the poet's daring lines about the Aloadae:

> Ossa then up on Olympus they strove to set, then upon Ossa Pelion, ashiver with leaves, to build them a ladder to Heaven;

and the still greater conception that follows,

> Yea and indeed they had done it.

Then again in the orators their eulogies and ceremonial speeches and show pieces throughout include touches of dignity and sublimity, yet are usually void of emotion. The result is that emotional orators excel least in eulogy, while panegyrists equally lack emotion. If, on the other hand, it never entered Cecilius's head that emotion sometimes contributes towards sublimity, and he therefore omitted it as undeserving of mention, then great indeed is his mistake. I would confidently lay it down that nothing makes so much for grandeur as genuine emotion in the right place. It inspires the words as it were with a fine frenzy and fills them with divine afflatus.

9. Now, since the first, I meant natural genius, plays a greater part than all the others, here too, although it is rather a gift than an acquired quality, we should still do our utmost to train our minds into sympathy with what is noble and, as it were, impregnate them again and again with lofty inspiration. "How?" you will ask. Well, elsewhere I have written something like this, "Sublimity is the true ring of a noble mind." And so even without being spoken the bare idea often of itself wins admiration for its inherent genius. How grand, for instance, is the silence of Ajax in the Summoning of the Ghosts, more sublime than any speech. In the first place, then, it is absolutely necessary to suggest its source and to show that the mind of the genuine orator must be neither small nor ignoble. For it is impossible that those whose thoughts and habits all their lives long

[75] The five "sources" are (1) the command of full-blooded ideas; (2) emotion; (3) the proper use of "figures"; (4) nobility of phrase; (5) general effect. In chapter xxxix, σύνθεσις means the arrangement of words. Here the phrase seems to mean the putting together of the words and clauses into a total effect of grandeur, making a whole of them.

are petty and servile should flash out anything wonderful, worthy of immortal life. No, a great style is the natural outcome of weighty thoughts, and sublime sayings naturally fall to men of spirit. . . .

10. Well, then, let us see further whether we could find anything else that can make style sublime. Since with all things there are associated certain elements, essentially inherent in their substance, it follows that we shall find one factor of sublimity in a consistently happy choice of these constituent elements, and in the power of combining them together as it were into an organic whole. One writer for instance attracts the reader by the selection of ideas, another by the soldering of these selected. Sappho, for instance, never fails to take the emotions incident to the passion of love from the symptoms which accompany it in real life. And wherein does she show her excellence? In the skill with which she selects and combines the most striking and intense of those symptoms.

I think him God's peer that sits near thee face to face and listens to thy sweet speech and lovely laughter.
'Tis this that makes my heart flutter in my breast. If I see thee but for a little, my voice comes no more and my tongue is broken.
At once a delicate flame runs through my limbs; my eyes are blinded and my ears thunder.
The sweat pours down: shivers hunt me all over. I am grown paler than grass, and very near to death I feel.

Is it not wonderful how she summons at the same time, soul, body, hearing, tongue, sight, colour, all as though they had wandered off apart from herself? She feels contradictory sensations, freezes, burns, raves, reasons—for one that is at the point of death is clearly beside herself. She wants to display not a single emotion, but a whole congress of emotions. Lovers all show such symptoms as these, but what gives supreme merit to her art is, as I said, the skill with which she chooses the most striking and combines them into a single whole. It is, I fancy, much in the same way that the poet in describing storms picks out the most alarming circumstances. The author of the *Arimaspeia*, to be sure, thinks these lines awe-inspiring:

Here is another thing also that fills us with feelings of wonder,
Men that dwell in the water, away from the earth, on the ocean.
Sorrowful wretches they are, and theirs is a grievous employment:
Ever they rivet their eyes on the stars, their thoughts on the waters.
Often, I ween, to the gods they lift up their hands and they pray;
Ever their innermost parts are terribly tossed to and fro.

Anyone can see, I fancy, that this is more flowery than fearful. But how does Homer do it? Let us take one example of many:

He fell on the host as a wave of the sea on a hurrying vessel,
Rising up under the clouds, a boisterous son of the stormwind.
The good ship is lost in the shroud of the foam, and the breath of the tempest
Terribly roars in the sails; and the sailors for fear are atremble,
By the breadth of a hand swept out from under the jaws of destruction.

Aratus, too, tried to adapt this same idea:

'Tis but the tiniest plank that bars them from bitter destruction.

But he has demeaned the idea and made it elegant instead of awe-inspiring. Moreover, he defines the danger when he says, "A plank keeps off destruction." Why then, it *does* keep it off. Homer, on the other hand, instead of defining the danger once and for all, depicts the sailors as being all the time, again and again, with every wave on the very brink of death. Moreover, in the phrase "out from under the jaws of destruction," by forcing into an abnormal union prepositions not usually compounded he has tortured his language into conformity with the impending disaster, magnificently figured the disaster by the compression of his language and almost stamped on the diction the form and feature of the danger—"swept out from under the jaws of destruction." Comparable to this is the passage of Archilochus about the shipwreck and the description of the arrival of the news in Demosthenes. "Now it was evening," etc. What they have done is to make a clean sweep, as it were, of all the main points by order of merit, and to bring them together, allowing nothing affected or undignified or pedantic to intervene. For all such irrelevancies are like the introduction of gaps or open tracery in architecture: they utterly spoil the effect of sublime ideas, well ordered and built into one coherent structure.

15. Weight, grandeur, and energy in writing are very largely produced, dear pupil, by the use of "images." (That at least is what some people call the actual mental pictures.) For the term Imagination is applied in general to an idea which enters the mind from any source and engenders speech, but the word has now come to be used predominantly of passages where, inspired by strong emotion, you seem to see what you describe and bring it vividly before the eyes of your audience. That imagination means one thing in oratory and another in poetry you will yourself detect, and also that the object of poetry is to enthral, of prose writing to present things vividly, though both indeed aim at this latter and at excited feeling.

Mother, I beg thee tarre not on against me
These snake-like hags with silent bloody feet.
See there! See there! They leap upon me close.

And

Ah, she will slay me, whither shall I flee?

In these passages the poet himself had Furies before his eyes and almost compelled the audience to see what he imaged. Now Euripides spends his fondest efforts in presenting these two emotions, madness and love, in tragic guise, and succeeds more brilliantly with these emotions than, I think, with any others; not that he lacks enterprise to attack other forms of imagination as well. While his natural genius is certainly not sublime, yet in many places he forces it into the tragic mould and invariably in his grand passages, as the poet says,

His tail at his ribs and his flanks now lashes on this, now on that side,
Ever he spurs himself on to share in the joys of the battle.

For instance, when Helios hands over the reins to Phaëthon:—

" And see thou drive not to the Libyan clime.
Its torrid air with no damp humour tempered
Will fire thy wheel and melt it."

And he goes on,

" But for the seven Pleiads shape thy course."
This heard, young Phaëthon caught up the reins,
Slashed at the flanks of his wing-wafted team,
And launched them flying to the cloudy coombs.
Behind, his sire, astride the Dog-star's back,
Rode, schooling thus his son. "Now, drive thou there,
Now this way wheel thy car, this way."

Would you not say that the writer's feelings are aboard the car, sharing the perilous flight of those winged horses? Never could he have shown such imagination, had he not run neck and neck with those celestial doings. You find the same in his Cassandra's speech beginning

Nay, Trojans, lovers of horse flesh.

Aeschylus ventures upon imaginative passages of the true heroic mould. For instance he says of his *Seven against Thebes*:

Seven resistless captains o'er a shield
Black-bound with hide have slit a bullock's throat,
And dipped their fingers in the bullock's blood,
Swearing a mighty oath by War and Havoc
And Panic, bloodshed's lover—

where they all pledge themselves to each other to die "apart from pity." Sometimes, however, he introduces rough ideas, all woolly, as it were, and ragged, and yet Euripides' emulation leads him to embark on the same perilous path. Aeschylus uses a startling phrase of Lycurgus's palace, magically possessed at the appearance of Dionysus,

The house breathes ecstasy, the roof-tree revels.

Euripides expressed the same idea differently, softening it down,

And all the mountain felt
And worshipped with them.

Sophocles describes with superb imagination the dying Oedipus, conducting his own burial amid strange portents in the sky; and Achilles at the departure of the Greeks, when he appears above his tomb to those embarking, a scene which nobody perhaps has depicted so vividly as Simonides. But to give all the instances would be endless. However, as I said, these examples from poetry show a romantic exaggeration, far exceeding the limits of credibility, whereas the most perfect effect of imagination in oratory is always one of reality and truth. The exceptions to this rule have a strange, outlandish air, when the texture of the speech is poetical and romantic and deviates into all sorts of impossibilities. For instance, our wonderful modern orators—save the mark!—are like so many tragedians in seeing Furies, and the fine fellows cannot even understand that when Orestes says,

Avaunt! Of mine own Furies art thou one
That clip my waist to cast me down to Hell,

he only imagines that, because he is mad. What then is the use of imagination in rhetoric? It may be said generally to introduce a great deal of vigour and emotion into one's speeches, but when combined with argumentative treatment it not only convinces the audience, it positively masters them. Take Demosthenes: "And yet, suppose that at this very moment we were to hear an uproar in front of the law courts and someone were to tell us, 'The prison has been broken open and the prisoners are escaping,' there is no man, old or young, so careless that he would not run to give all the assistance in his power. But suppose someone were to come and actually tell us that this was the man who set them free, he would be killed on the moment without a hearing." And then, to be sure, there is Hypereides on his trial, when he had moved the enfranchisement of the slaves after the Athenian reverse. "It was not the speaker that framed this measure, but the battle of Chaeroneia." There, besides developing his technical argument the orator uses his imagination and consequently his conception far exceeds the limits of mere persuasion. In all such cases the stronger accents seem naturally to catch our ears, so that our attention is drawn from the reasoning to the enthralling effect of the imagination, and the technique is concealed in a halo of brilliance. And this effect on us is natural enough; set two forces side by side and the stronger always borrows the virtues of the other.

This must suffice for our treatment of sublimity in ideas, as produced by nobility of mind or imitation or imagination. . . .

32. As to the proper number of metaphors, Cecilius seems on the side of those who

lay down a law that two or at the most three should be used together. Demosthenes assurdly is the canon in these matters too. And what decides the occasion for their use? Why, the right moment, when emotion sweeps on like a flood and inevitably carries the multitude of metaphors along it. "Men," he says, "of evil life, flatterers, who have each foully mutilated their own country and pledged their liberty in a cup of wine first to Philip and now to Alexander, men who measure happiness by their bellies and their basest appetites, and have strewn in ruins that liberty and freedom from despotism which to Greeks of older days was the canon and standard of all that was good." Here it is the orator's indignation against the traitors which screens the multitude of metaphors. Accordingly, Aristotle and Theophrastus say that bold metaphors are softened by inserting "as if" or "as it were" or "if one may say so" or "if one may risk the expression." The apology, they tell us, mitigates the audacity of the language. I accept this, but at the same time, as I said in speaking of "figures," the proper antidote for a multitude of daring metaphors is strong and timely emotion and genuine sublimity. These by their nature sweep everything along in the forward surge of their current, or rather they positively demand bold imagery as essential to their effect, and do not give the hearer time to examine how many metaphors there are, because he shares the excitement of the speaker.

Moreover in the treatment of a commonplace and in descriptions there is nothing so expressive as a sustained series of metaphors. It is thus that in Xenophon the anatomy of the human tabernacle is magnificently depicted, and still more divinely in Plato. The head he calls the citadel of the body, the neck is an isthmus built between the head and chest, and the vertebrae, he says, are planted beneath like hinges; pleasure is evil's bait for man, and the tongue is the touchstone of taste. The heart is a knot of veins and the source whence the blood runs vigorously round, and it has its station in the guard-house of the body. The passage-ways of the body he calls alleys, and "for the leaping of the heart in the expectation of danger or the arising of wrath, since this was due to fiery heat, the gods devised a support by implanting the lungs, making them a sort of buffer, soft and bloodless and full of pores inside, so that when anger boiled up in the heart it might throb against a yielding surface and get no damage." The seat of the desires he compares to the women's apartments and the seat of anger to the men's. The spleen again is the napkin of the entrails, "whence it is filled with the offscourings and becomes swollen and fetid." "After this," he goes on, "they shrouded the whole in a covering of flesh, like a felt mat, to shield it from the outer world." Blood he calls the fodder of the flesh, and adds, "For purposes of nutriment they irrigated the body, cutting channels as one does in a garden, and thus, the body being a conduit full of passages, the streams in the veins were able to flow as it were from a running stream." And when the end comes, the soul, he says, is loosed like a ship from its moorings and set free. These and thousands of similar metaphors occur throughout. Those we have pointed out suffice to show that figurative writing has a natural grandeur and that metaphors make for sublimity: also that emotional and descriptive passages are most glad of them. However, that the use of metaphor, like all the other beauties of style, always tempts writers to excess is obvious without my stating it. Indeed it is for these passages in particular that critics pull Plato to pieces, on the ground that he is often carried away by the intoxication of his language into harsh and intemperate metaphor and allegorical bombast. "It is by no means easy to see," he says, "that a city needs mixing like a wine-bowl, where the mad wine seethes as it is poured in, but is chastened by another and a sober god and finding good company makes a excellent and temperate drink." To call water "a sober god" and mixing "chastisement," say the critics, is the language of a poet who is far from sober.

Cecilius, too, laying his finger on such defects as this, has actually had the face to declare in his writings in praise of Lysias that Lysias is altogether superior to Plato. Here he has given way to two uncritical impulses: for though he loves Lysias even better than himself, yet his hatred for Plato altogether outweighs his love for Lysias. However he is the victim of prejudice and even his premisses are not, as he supposed, admitted. For he prefers his orator on the ground that he is immaculate and never makes a mistake, whereas Plato is full of mistakes. But the truth, we find, is different, very different indeed.

33. Suppose we illustrate this by taking some altogether immaculate and unimpeachable writer, must we not in this very connexion raise the general question: Which is the better in poetry and in prose, grandeur with a few flaws or correct composition of mediocre quality, yet entirely sound and impeccable? Yes, and we must surely ask the further question whether in literature the first place is rightly due to the largest number of merits or to the merits that are greatest in themselves. These inquiries are proper to a treatise on the sublime and on every ground demand decision. Now I am well aware that the greatest natures are least immaculate. Perfect precision runs the risk of triviality, whereas in great writing as in great wealth there must needs be something overlooked. Perhaps it is inevitable that the humble, mediocre natures, because they never run any risks, never aim at the heights, should remain to a large extent safe from error, while in great natures their very greatness spells danger. Not indeed that I am ignorant of this second point, that whatever men do is always inevitably regarded from the worst side: faults make an ineradicable impression, but beauties soon slip from our memory·. I have myself noted a good many faults in Homer and the other greatest authors, and though these slips certainly offend my taste, yet I prefer to call them not wilful mistakes but careless oversights, let in casually almost and at random by the heedlessness of genius. In spite, then, of these faults I still think that great excellence, even if it is not sustained throughout at the same level, should always be voted the first place, if for nothing else, for its inherent nobility. Apollonius, for instance in his *Argonautica* is an impeccable poet and Theocritus—except in a few extraneous matters—is supremely successful in his pastorals. Yet would you not rather be Homer than Apollonius? And what of Eratosthenes in his *Erigone*? Wholly blameless as the little poem is, do you therefore think him a greater poet than Archilochus with all the manifold irrelevance he carries on his flood; greater than those outbursts of divine inspiration, which are so troublesome to bring under any rule? In lyrics, again, would you choose to be Bacchylides rather than Pindar, or in tragedy Ion of Chios rather than (save the mark!) Sophocles? In both cases the former is impeccable and a master of elegance in the smooth style. On the other hand Pindar and Sophocles sometimes seem to fire the whole landscape as they sweep across it, while often their fire is unaccountably quenched and they fall miserably flat. Yet would anyone in his senses give the single tragedy of *Oedipus* for all the works of Ion in a row?. . . .

35. There is, as I said, a further point of difference in the case of Plato. Lysias is far inferior both in the greatness and the number of his merits; and the excess of his faults is still greater than the defect of his merits. What then was in the mind of those demigods who aimed only at what is greatest in writing and scorned detailed accuracy? Among many other things this, that Nature has distinguished man, as a creature of no mean or ignoble quality.

As if she were inviting us rather to some great gathering, she has called us into life, into the whole universe, there to be spectators of all that she has made and eager competitors for honour; and she therefore from the first breathed into our hearts an unconquerable passion for whatever is great and more divine than ourselves. Thus within the scope of human enterprise there lie such powers of contemplation and thought that even the whole universe cannot satisfy them, but our ideas often pass beyond the limits that enring us. Look at life from all sides and see how in all things the extraordinary, the great, the beautiful stand supreme, and you will soon realize the object of our creation. So it is by some natural instinct that we admire, surely not the small streams, clear and useful as they are, but the Nile, the Danube, the Rhine, and far above all, the sea. The little fire we kindle for ourselves keeps clear and steady, yet we do not therefore regard it with more amazement than the fires of Heaven, which are often darkened, or think it more wonderful than the craters of Etna in eruption, hurling up rocks and whole hills from their depths and sometimes shooting forth rivers of that pure Titanic fire. But on all such matters I would only say this, that what is useful and indeed necessary is cheap enough; it is always the unusual which wins our wonder.

36. In dealing, then, with writers of genius, whose grandeur is of a kind that comes within the limits of use and profit, we must at the outset form the conclusion that, while they are far from unerring, yet they are all more than human. Other qualities prove their possessors men, sublimity lifts them near the mighty mind of God. Correctness escapes censure: greatness earns admiration as well. We need hardly add that each of these great men again and again redeems all his mistakes by a single touch of sublimity and true excellence; and, what is finally decisive, if we were to pick out all the faults in Homer, Demosthenes, Plato and all the other greatest authors and put them together, we should find them a tiny fraction, not the ten-thousandth part, of the true excellence to be found on every page of these demi-gods. That is why the judgement of all ages, which no jealousy can prove to be amiss, has awarded them the crown of victory, guarding it as their inalienable right, and is likely so to preserve it,

So long as the rivers run and the tall trees flourish
in green.

As to the statement that the faulty Colossus is no better than Polycleitus's spearman, there are many obvious answers to that. In art we admire accuracy, in nature grandeur; and it is nature that has given man the power of using words. Also we expect a statue to resemble a man, but in literature, as I said before, we look for something greater than human. However, to come back again to the doctrine with which we began our treatise, since the merit of impeccable correctness is, generally speaking, due to art, and the height of excellence, though not sustained, to genius, it is proper that art should always assist Nature. Their co-operation may thus result in perfection. This much had to be said to decide the questions before us. But everyone is welcome to his own tastes. . . .

Plotinus

204–269 A.D.

A. Life

Porphyry, Plotinus' disciple, wrote of his master that the great philosopher never wanted any feast or sacrifice on his own birthday but "he himself sacrificed on the traditional birthdays of Plato and Socrates, afterwards giving a banquet at which every member of the circle who was able was expected to deliver an address. . . ."

Plotinus was born in Lycopolis in Egypt and educated in Alexandria, where he studied under Ammonias Saccas. He served under the Emperor Gordian in military campaigns against the Persians. He came to Rome in 242 A.D. to become a teacher. His students included an emperor and empress, poets, doctors, and rhetoricians. In the process of his teaching in Rome, Plotinus radically altered Plato's philosophy. It was Plotinus who almost succeeded in convincing the Roman Emperor that he should build Platonopolis, a city for philosophers modeled after Plato's Republic.

His writings occupied fifty-four *Corpuscles.* Porphyry brought them together in six *Enneads.*

B. Philosophy of Art

The Enneads

Third Tractate

ON DIALECTIC (THE UPWARD WAY)

I.3.1

What art [76] is there, what method, what discipline to bring us there where we must go?

[76] Reprinted from THE ENNEADS, 3rd Edition, by Plotinus, translated by Stephen MacKenna. (Pantheon Books, a Division of Random House, Inc.) All rights reserved. Also reprinted by permission of Faber and Faber Ltd. from *Plotinus: The Enneads.*

The Term at which we must arrive we may take as agreed: we have established elsewhere, by many considerations, that our journey is to the Good, to the Primal-Principle; and, indeed, the very reasoning which discovered the Term was itself something like an initiation.

But what order of beings will attain the Term?

Surely, as we read, those that have already seen all or most things, those who at their first birth have entered into the life-germ from which is to spring a metaphysician, a musician or a born lover, the metaphysician taking to the path by instinct, the musician and the nature peculiarly susceptible to love needing outside guidance.

But how lies the course? Is it alike for all, or is there a distinct method for each class of temperament?

For all there are two stages of the path, as they are making upwards or have already gained the upper sphere.

The first degree is the conversion from the lower life; the second—held by those that have already made their way to the sphere of the Intelligibles, have set as it were a footprint there but must still advance within the realm —lasts until they reach the extreme hold of the place, the Term attained when the topmost peak of the Intellectual realm is won.

But this highest degree must bide its time: let us first try to speak of the initial process of conversion.

We must begin by distinguishing the three types. Let us take the musician first and indicate his temperamental equipment for the task.

The musician we may think of as being exceedingly quick to beauty, drawn in a very rapture to it: somewhat slow to stir of his own impulse, he answers at once to the outer stimulus: as the timid are sensitive to noise so he to tones and the beauty they convey; all that offends against unison or harmony in melodies and rhythms repels him; he longs for measure and shapely pattern.

This natural tendency must be made the starting-point to such a man; he must be drawn by the tone, rhythm and design in things of sense: he must learn to distinguish the material forms from the Authentic-Existent which is the source of all these correspondences and of the entire reasoned scheme in the work of art: he must be led to the Beauty that manifests itself through these forms; he must be shown that what ravished him was no other than the Harmony of the Intellectual world and the Beauty in that sphere, not some one shape of beauty but the All-Beauty, the Absolute Beauty, and the truths of philosophy must be implanted in him to lead him to faith in that which, unknowing it, he possesses within himself. What these truths are we will show later.

The born lover, to whose degree the musician also may attain—and then either come to a stand or pass beyond—has a certain memory of beauty but, severed from it now, he no longer comprehends it: spell-bound by visible loveliness he clings amazed about that. His lesson must be to fall down no longer in bewildered delight before some, one embodied form; he must be led, under a system of mental discipline, to beauty everywhere and made to discern the One Principle underlying all, a Principle apart from the material forms, springing from another source, and elsewhere more truly present. The beauty, for example, in a noble course of life and in an admirably organised social system may be pointed out to him—a first training this in the loveliness of the immaterial—he must learn to recognise the beauty in the arts, sciences, virtues; then these severed and particular forms must be brought under the one principle by the explanation of their origin. From the virtues he is to be led to the Intellectual-Principle, to the Authentic-Existent; thence onward, he treads the upward way. . . .

Sixth Tractate

BEAUTY

I.6.1

Beauty addresses itself chiefly to sight; but there is a beauty for the hearing too, as in certain combinations of words and in all kinds of music, for melodies and cadences are beautiful; and minds that lift themselves above the realm of sense to a higher order are aware of beauty in the conduct of life, in actions, in character, in the pursuits of the intellect; and there is the beauty of the virtues. What loftier beauty there may be, yet, our argument will bring to light.

What, then, is it that gives comeliness to material forms and draws the ear to the sweetness perceived in sounds, and what is the secret of the beauty there is in all that derives from Soul?

Is there some One Principle from which all take their grace, or is there a beauty peculiar to the embodied and another for the bodiless? Finally, one or many, what would such a Principle be?

Consider that some things, material shapes for instance, are gracious not by anything inherent but by something communicated, while others are lovely of themselves, as, for example, Virtue.

The same bodies appear sometimes beautiful, sometimes not; so that there is a good deal between being body and being beautiful.

What, then, is this something that shows itself in certain material forms? This is the natural beginning of our enquiry.

What is it that attracts the eyes of those to whom a beautiful object is presented, and calls them, lures them, towards it, and fills them with joy at the sight? If we possess ourselves of this, we have at once a standpoint for the wider survey.

Almost everyone declares that the symmetry of parts towards each other and towards a whole, with, besides, a certain charm of colour, constitutes the beauty recognised by the eye, that in visible things, as indeed in all else, universally, the beautiful thing is essentially symmetrical, patterned.

But think what this means.

Only a compound can be beautiful, never anything devoid of parts; and only a whole; the several parts will have beauty, not in themselves, but only as working together to give a comely total. Yet beauty in an aggregate demands beauty in details; it cannot be constructed out of ugliness; its law must run throughout.

All the loveliness of colour and even the light of the sun, being devoid of parts and so not beautiful by symmetry, must be ruled out of the realm of beauty. And how comes gold to be a beautiful thing? And lightning by night, and the stars, why are these so fair?

In sounds also the simple must be proscribed, though often in a whole noble composition each several tone is delicious in itself.

Again since the one face, constant in symmetry, appears sometimes fair and sometimes not, can we doubt that beauty is something more than symmetry, that symmetry itself owes its beauty to a remoter principle?

Turn to what is attractive in methods of life or in the expression of thought; are we to call in symmetry here? What symmetry is to be found in noble conduct, or excellent laws, in any form of mental pursuit?

What symmetry can there be in points of abstract thought?

The symmetry of being accordant with each other? But there may be accordance or entire identity where there is nothing but ugliness: the proposition that honesty is merely a generous artlessness chimes in the most perfect harmony with the proposition that morality means weakness of will; the accordance is complete.

Then again, all the virtues are a beauty of the soul, a beauty authentic beyond any of these others; but how does symmetry enter here? The soul, it is true, is not a simple unity, but still its virtue cannot have the symmetry of size or of number: what standard of measurement could preside over the compromise or the coalescence of the soul's faculties or purposes?

Finally, how by this theory would there be beauty in the Intellectual-Principle, essentially the solitary?

2.

Let us, then, go back to the source, and indicate at once the Principle that bestows beauty on material things.

Undoubtedly this Principle exists; it is something that is perceived at the first glance, something which the soul names as from an ancient knowledge and, recognising, welcomes it, enters into unison with it.

But let the soul fall in with the Ugly and at once it shrinks within itself, denies the thing, turns away from it, not accordant, resenting it.

Our interpretation is that the soul—by the very truth of its nature, by its affiliation to the noblest Existents in the hierarchy of Being—when it sees anything of that kin, or any trace of that kinship, thrills with an immediate delight, takes its own to itself, and thus stirs anew to the sense of its nature and of all its affinity.

But, is there any such likeness between the loveliness of this world and the splendours in the Supreme? Such a likeness in the particulars would make the two orders alike: but what is there in common between beauty here and beauty There?

We hold that all the loveliness of this world comes by communion in Ideal-Form.

All shapelessness whose kind admits of pattern and form, as long as it remains outside of Reason and Idea, is ugly by that very isolation from the Divine-Thought. And this is the Absolute Ugly: an ugly thing is something that has not been entirely mastered by pattern, that is by Reason, the Matter not yielding at all points and in all respects to Ideal-Form.

But where the Ideal-Form has entered, it has grouped and co-ordinated what from a diversity of parts was to become a unity: it has rallied confusion into co-operation: it has made the sum one harmonious coherence: for the Idea is a unity and what it moulds must come to unity as far as multiplicity may.

And on what has thus been compacted to unity, Beauty enthrones itself, giving itself to the parts as to the sum: when it lights on some natural unity, a thing of like parts, then it gives itself to that whole. Thus, for an illustration, there is the beauty, conferred by craftsmanship, of all a house with all its parts, and the beauty which some natural quality may give to a single stone.

This, then, is how the material thing becomes beautiful—by communicating in the thought that flows from the Divine.

3.

And the soul includes a faculty peculiarly addressed to Beauty—one incomparably sure in the appreciation of its own, never in doubt whenever any lovely thing presents itself for judgement.

Or perhaps the soul itself acts immediately, affirming the Beautiful where it finds something accordant with the Ideal-Form within itself, using this Idea as a canon of accuracy in its decision.

But what accordance is there between the material and that which antedates all Matter?

On what principle does the architect, when he finds the house standing before him correspondent with his inner ideal of a house, pronounce it beautiful? Is it not that the house before him, the stones apart, is the inner idea stamped upon the mass of exterior matter, the indivisible exhibited in diversity?

So with the perceptive faculty: discerning in certain objects the Ideal-Form which has bound and controlled shapeless matter, opposed in nature to Idea, seeing further stamped upon the common shapes some shape excellent above the common, it gathers into unity what still remains fragmentary, catches it up and carries it within, no longer a thing of parts, and presents it to the Ideal-Principle as something concordant and congenial, a natural friend: the joy here is like that of a good man who discerns in a youth the early signs of a virtue consonant with the achieved perfection within his own soul.

The beauty of colour is also the outcome of a unification: it derives from shape, from the conquest of the darkness inherent in Matter by the pouring-in of light, the unembodied, which is a Rational-Principle and an Ideal-Form.

Hence it is that Fire itself is splendid beyond all material bodies, holding the rank of Ideal-Principle to the other elements, making ever upwards, the subtlest and sprightliest of all bodies, as very near to the unembodied; itself alone admitting no other, all the others penetrated by it: for they take warmth but this is never cold; it has colour primally; they receive the Form of colour from it: hence the splendour of its light, the splendour that belongs to the Idea. And all that has resisted and is but uncertainly held by its light remains outside of beauty, as not having absorbed the plenitude of the Form of colour.

And harmonies unheard in sound create the harmonies we hear and wake the soul to the consciousness of beauty, showing it the one essence in another kind: for the measures of our sensible music are not arbitrary but are determined by the Principle whose labour is to dominate Matter and bring pattern into being.

Thus far of the beauties of the realm of sense, images and shadow-pictures, fugitives that have entered into Matter—to adorn, and to ravish, where they are seen.

4.

But there are earlier and loftier beauties than these. In the sense-bound life we are no longer granted to know them, but the soul, taking no help from the organs, sees and proclaims them. To the vision of these we must mount, leaving sense to its own low place.

As it is not for those to speak of the graceful forms of the material world who have never seen them or known their grace—men born blind, let us suppose—in the same way those must be silent upon the beauty of noble conduct and of learning and all that order who have never cared for such things, nor may those tell of the splendour of virtue who have never known the face of Justice and of Moral-Wisdom beautiful beyond the beauty of Evening and of Dawn.

Such vision is for those only who see with the Soul's sight—and at the vision, they will rejoice, and awe will fall upon them and a trouble deeper than all the rest could ever stir, for now they are moving in the realm of Truth.

This is the spirit that Beauty must ever induce, wonderment and a delicious trouble, longing and love and a trembling that is all delight. For the unseen all this may be felt as for the seen; and this the Souls feel for it, every soul in some degree, but those the more deeply that are the more truly apt to this higher love—just as all take delight in the beauty of the body but all are not stung as sharply, and those only that feel the keener wound are known as Lovers.

5.

These Lovers, then, lovers of the beauty outside of sense, must be made to declare themselves.

What do you feel in presence of the grace you discern in actions, in manners, in sound morality, in all the works and fruits of virtue, in the beauty of souls? When you see that you yourselves are beautiful within, what do you feel? What is this Dionysiac exultation that thrills through your being, this straining upwards of all your Soul, this longing to break away from the body and live sunken within the veritable self?

These are no other than the emotions of Souls under the spell of love.

But what is it that awakens all this passion? No shape, no colour, no grandeur of mass: all is for Soul, something whose beauty rests upon no colour, for the moral wisdom the Soul enshrines and all the other hueless splendour of the virtues. It is that you find in yourself, or admire in another, loftiness of spirit; righteousness of life; disciplined purity; courage of the majestic face; gravity; modesty that goes fearless and tranquil and passionless; and, shining down upon all, the light of god-like Intellection.

All these noble qualities are to be reverenced and loved, no doubt, but what entitles them to be called beautiful?

They exist: they manifest themselves to us: anyone that sees them must admit that they have reality of Being; and is not Real-Being, really beautiful?

But we have not yet shown by what property in them they have wrought the Soul to loveliness: what is this grace, this splendour as of Light, resting upon all the virtues?

Let us take the contrary, the ugliness of the Soul, and set that against its beauty: to understand, at once, what this ugliness is and how it comes to appear in the Soul will certainly open our way before us.

Let us then suppose an ugly Soul, dissolute, unrighteous: teeming with all the lusts; torn by internal discord; beset by the fears of its cowardice and the envies of its pettiness; thinking, in the little thought it has, only of the perishable and the base; perverse in all its impulses; the friend of unclean pleasures; living the life of abandonment to bodily sensation and delighting in its deformity.

What must we think but that all this shame is something that has gathered about the Soul, some foreign bane outraging it, soiling it, so that, encumbered with all manner of turpitude, it has no longer a clean activity or a clean sensation, but commands only a life smouldering dully under the crust of evil; that, sunk in manifold death, it no longer sees what a Soul should see, may no longer rest in its own being, dragged ever as it is towards the outer, the lower, the dark?

An unclean thing, I dare to say; flickering hither and thither at the call of objects of sense, deeply infected with the taint of body, occupied always in Matter, and absorbing Matter into itself; in its commerce with the Ignoble it has trafficked away for an alien nature its own essential Idea.

If a man has been immersed in filth or daubed with mud his native comeliness disappears and all that is seen is the foul stuff besmearing him: his ugly condition is due to alien matter that has encrusted him, and if he is to win back his grace it must be his business to scour and purify himself and make himself what he was.

So, we may justly say, a Soul becomes ugly—by something foisted upon it, by sinking itself into the alien, by a fall, a descent into body, into Matter. The dishonour of the Soul is in its ceasing to be clean and apart. Gold is degraded when it is mixed with earthly particles; if these be worked out, the gold is left and is beautiful, isolated from all that is foreign, gold with gold alone. And so the Soul; let it be but cleared of the desires that come by its too intimate converse with the body, emancipated from all the passions, purged of all the embodiment has thrust upon it, withdrawn, a solitary, to itself again—in that moment the ugliness that came only from the alien is stripped away.

6.

For, as the ancient teaching was, moral-discipline and courage and every virtue, not even excepting Wisdom itself, all is purification.

Hence the Mysteries with good reason adumbrate the immersion of the unpurified in filth, even in the Nether-World, since the unclean loves filth for its very filthiness, and swine foul of body find their joy in foulness.

What else is Sophrosyny, rightly so-called,

but to take no part in the pleasures of the body, to break away from them as unclean and unworthy of the clean? So too, Courage is but being fearless of the death which is but the parting of the Soul from the body, an event which no one can dread whose delight is to be his unmingled self. And Magnanimity is but disregard for the lure of things here. And Wisdom is but the Act of the Intellectual-Principle withdrawn from the lower places and leading the Soul to the Above.

The Soul thus cleansed is all Idea and Reason, wholly free of body, intellective, entirely of that divine order from which the wellspring of Beauty rises and all the race of Beauty.

Hence the Soul heightened to the Intellectual-Principle is beautiful to all its power. For Intellection and all that proceeds from Intellection are the Soul's beauty, a graciousness native to it and not foreign, for only with these is it truly Soul. And it is just to say that in the Soul's becoming a good and beautiful thing is its becoming like to God, for from the Divine comes all the Beauty and all the Good in beings.

We may even say that Beauty *is* the Authentic-Existents and Ugliness is the Principle contrary to Existence: and the Ugly is also the primal evil; therefore its contrary is at once good and beautiful, or is Good and Beauty: and hence the one method will discover to us the Beauty-Good and the Ugliness-Evil.

And Beauty, this Beauty which is also The Good, must be posed as The First: directly deriving from this First is the Intellectual-Principle which is pre-eminently the manifestation of Beauty; through the Intellectual-Principle Soul is beautiful. The beauty in things of a lower order—actions and pursuits for instance—comes by operation of the shaping Soul which is also the author of the beauty found in the world of sense. For the Soul, a divine thing, a fragment as it were of the Primal Beauty, makes beautiful to the fulness of their capacity all things whatsoever that it grasps and moulds.

7.

Therefore we must ascend again towards the Good, the desired of every Soul. Anyone that has seen This, knows what I intend when I say that it is beautiful. Even the desire of it is to be desired as a Good. To attain it is for those that will take the upward path, who will set all their forces towards it, who will divest themselves of all that we have put on in our descent:—so, to those that approach the Holy Celebrations of the Mysteries, there are appointed purifications and the laying aside of the garments worn before, and the entry in nakedness—until, passing, on the upward way, all that is other than the God, each in the solitude of himself shall behold that solitary-dwelling Existence, the Apart, the Unmingled, the Pure, that from Which all things depend, for Which all look and live and act and know, the Source of Life and of Intellection and of Being.

And one that shall know this vision—with what passion of love shall he not be seized, with what pang of desire, what longing to be molten into one with This, what wondering delight! If he that has never seen this Being must hunger for It as for all his welfare, he that has known must love and reverence It as the very Beauty; he will be flooded with awe and gladness, stricken by a salutary terror; he loves with a veritable love, with sharp desire; all other loves than this he must despise, and disdain all that once seemed fair.

This, indeed, is the mood even of those who, having witnessed the manifestation of Gods or Supernals, can never again feel the old delight in the comeliness of material forms: what then are we to think of one that contemplates Absolute Beauty in Its essential integrity, no accumulation of flesh and matter, no dweller on earth or in the heavens—so perfect Its purity—far above all such things in that they are non-essential, composite, not primal but descending from This?

Beholding this Being—the Choragos of all Existence, the Self-Intent that ever gives forth and never takes—resting, rapt, in the vision and possession of so lofty a loveliness, growing to Its likeness, what Beauty can the soul yet lack? For This, the Beauty supreme, the absolute and the primal, fashions Its lovers to Beauty and makes them also worthy of love.

And for This, the sternest and the uttermost combat is set before the Souls; all our labour is for This, lest we be left without part in this noblest vision, which to attain is to be blessed in the blissful sight, which to fail of is to fail utterly.

For not he that has failed of the joy that is in colour or in visible forms, not he that has failed of power or of honours or of kingdom has failed, but only he that has failed of only This, for Whose winning he should renounce kingdoms and command over earth and ocean and sky, if only, spurning the world of sense from beneath his feet, and straining to This, he may see.

8.

But what must we do? How lies the path? How come to vision of the inaccessible Beauty, dwelling as if in consecrated precincts, apart from the common ways where all may see, even the profane?

He that has the strength, let him arise and withdraw into himself, foregoing all that is known by the eyes, turning away for ever from the material beauty that once made his joy. When he perceives those shapes of grace that show in body, let him not pursue: he must know them for copies, vestiges, shadows, and hasten away towards That they tell of. For if anyone follow what is like a beautiful shape playing over water—is there not a myth telling in symbol of such a dupe, how he sank into the depths of the current and was swept away to nothingness? So too, one that is held by material beauty and will not break free shall be precipitated, not in body but in Soul, down to the dark depths loathed of the Intellective-Being, where, blind even in the Lower-World, he shall have commerce only with shadows, there as here.

"Let us flee then to the beloved Fatherland": this is the soundest counsel. But what is this flight? How are we to gain the open sea? For Odysseus is surely a parable to us when he commands the flight from the sorceries of Circe or Calypso—not content to linger for all the pleasure offered to his eyes and all the delight of sense filling his days.

The Fatherland to us is There whence we have come, and There is The Father.

What then is our course, what the manner of our flight? This is not a journey for the feet; the feet bring us only from land to land; nor need you think of coach or ship to carry you away; all this order of things you must set aside and refuse to see: you must close the eyes and call instead upon another vision which is to be waked within you, a vision, the birthright of all, which few turn to use.

9.

And this inner vision, what is its operation?

Newly awakened it is all too feeble to bear the ultimate splendour. Therefore the Soul must be trained—to the habit of remarking, first, all noble pursuits, then the works of beauty produced not by the labour of the arts but by the virtue of men known for their goodness: lastly, you must search the souls of those that have shaped these beautiful forms.

But how are you to see into a virtuous soul and know its loveliness?

Withdraw into yourself and look. And if you do not find yourself beautiful yet, act as does the creator of a statue that is to be made beautiful: he cuts away here, he smoothes there, he makes this line lighter, this other purer, until a lovely face has grown upon his work. So do you also: cut away all that is excessive, straighten all that is crooked, bring light to all that is overcast, labour to make all one glow of beauty and never cease chiselling your statue, until there shall shine out on you from it the godlike splendour of virtue, until you shall see the perfect goodness surely established in the stainless shrine.

When you know that you have become this perfect work, when you are self-gathered in the purity of your being, nothing now remaining that can shatter that inner unity, nothing from without clinging to the authentic man, when you find yourself wholly true to your essential nature, wholly that only veritable Light which is not measured by space, not narrowed to any circumscribed form nor again diffused as a thing void of term, but ever unmeasurable as something greater than all measure and more than all quantity—when you perceive that you have grown to this, you are now become very vision: now call up all your confidence, strike forward yet a step—you need a guide no longer—strain, and see.

This is the only eye that sees the mighty Beauty. If the eye that adventures the vision be dimmed by vice, impure, or weak, and unable in its cowardly blenching to see the uttermost brightness, then it sees nothing even though another point to what lies plain to sight before it. To any vision must be brought an eye adapted to what is to be seen, and having some likeness to it. Never did eye see the sun unless it had first become sunlike, and never can the soul have vision of the First Beauty unless itself be beautiful.

Therefore, first let each become godlike and each beautiful who cares to see God and Beauty. So, mounting, the Soul will come first to the Intellectual-Principle and survey all the beautiful Ideas in the Supreme and will avow that this is Beauty, that the Ideas are Beauty. For by their efficacy comes all Beauty else, by the offspring and essence of the Intellectual-Being. What is beyond the Intellectual-Principle we affirm to be the nature of Good radiating Beauty before it. So that, treating the Intellectual-Kosmos as one, the first is the Beautiful: if we make distinction there, the Realm of Ideas constitutes the Beauty of the Intellectual Sphere; and The Good, which lies beyond, is the Fountain at once and Principle of Beauty: the Primal Good and the Primal Beauty have the one dwelling-place and, thus, always, Beauty's seat is There.

Eighth Tractate

ON THE INTELLECTUAL BEAUTY

V.8.1.

It is a principle with us that one who has attained to the vision of the Intellectual Beauty and grasped the beauty of the Authentic Intellect will be able also to come to understand the Father and Transcendent of that Divine Being. It concerns us, then, to try to see and say, for ourselves and as far as such matters may be told, how the Beauty of the divine Intellect and of the Intellectual Kosmos may be revealed to contemplation.

Let us go to the realm of magnitudes:—Suppose two blocks of stone lying side by side: one is unpatterned, quite untouched by art; the other has been minutely wrought by the craftsman's hands into some statue of god or man, a Grace or a Muse, or if a human being, not a portrait but a creation in which the sculptor's art has concentrated all loveliness.

Now it must be seen that the stone thus brought under the artist's hand to the beauty of form is beautiful not as stone—for so the crude block would be as pleasant—but in virtue of the form or idea introduced by the art. This form is not in the material; it is in the designer before ever it enters the stone;

and the artificer holds it not by his equipment of eyes and hands but by his participation in his art. The beauty, therefore, exists in a far higher state in the art; for it does not come over integrally into the work; that original beauty is not transferred; what comes over is a derivative and a minor: and even that shows itself upon the statue not integrally and with entire realisation of intention but only in so far as it has subdued the resistance of the material.

Art, then, creating in the image of its own nature and content, and working by the Idea or Reason-Principle of the beautiful object it is to produce, must itself be beautiful in a far higher and purer degree since it is the seat and source of that beauty, indwelling in the art, which must naturally be more complete than any comeliness of the external. In the degree in which the beauty is diffused by entering into matter, it is so much the weaker than that concentrated in unity; everything that reaches outwards is the less for it, strength less strong, heat less hot, every power less potent, and so beauty less beautiful.

Then again every prime cause must be, within itself, more powerful than its effect can be: the musical does not derive from an unmusical source but from music; and so the art exhibited in the material work derives from an art yet higher.

Still the arts are not to be slighted on the ground that they create by imitation of natural objects; for, to begin with, these natural objects are themselves imitations; then, we must recognise that they give no bare reproduction of the thing seen but go back to the Ideas from which Nature itself derives, and, furthermore, that much of their work is all their own; they are holders of beauty and add where nature is lacking. Thus Pheidias wrought the Zeus upon no model among things of sense but by apprehending what form Zeus must take if he chose to become manifest to sight.

2.

But let us leave the arts and consider those works produced by Nature and admitted to be naturally beautiful which the creations of art are charged with imitating, all reasoning life and unreasoning things alike, but especially the consummate among them, where the moulder and maker has subdued the material and given the form he desired. Now what is the beauty here? It has nothing to do with the blood or the menstrual process: either there is also a colour and form apart from all this or there is nothing unless sheer ugliness or (at best) a bare recipient, as it were the mere Matter of beauty.

Whence shone forth the beauty of Helen, battle-sought; or of all those women like in loveliness to Aphrodite; or of Aphrodite herself; or of any human being that has been perfect in beauty; or of any of these gods manifest to sight, or unseen but carrying what would be beauty if we saw?

In all these is it not the Idea, something of that realm but communicated to the produced from within the producer just as in works of art, we held, it is communicated from the arts to their creations? Now we can surely not believe that, while the made thing and the Idea thus impressed upon Matter are beautiful, yet the Idea not so alloyed but resting still with the creator—the Idea primal, immaterial, firmly a unity—is not Beauty.

If material extension were in itself the ground of beauty, then the creating principle, being without extension, could not be beautiful: but beauty cannot be made to depend upon magnitude since, whether in a large object or a small, the one Idea equally moves and forms the mind by its inherent power. A further indication is that as long as the object remains outside us we know nothing of it; it affects us by entry; but only as an Idea can it enter through the eyes which are not of scope to take an extended mass: we are, no doubt, simultaneously possessed of the magnitude which, however, we take in not as mass but by an elaboration upon the presented form.

Then again the principle producing the beauty must be, itself, ugly, neutral or beautiful: ugly, it could not produce the opposite; neutral, why should its product be the one rather than the other? The Nature, then, which creates things so lovely must be itself of a far earlier beauty; we, undisciplined in discernment of the inward, knowing nothing of it, run after the outer, never understanding that it is the inner which stirs us; we are in the case of one who sees his own reflection but not realising whence it comes goes in pursuit of it.

But that the thing we are pursuing is something different and that the beauty is not in the concrete object is manifest from the beauty there is in matters of study, in conduct and custom; briefly in soul or mind. And it is precisely here that the greater beauty lies, perceived whenever you look to the wisdom in a man and delight in it, not wasting attention on the face, which may be hideous, but passing all appearance by and catching only at the inner comeliness, the truly personal; if you are still unmoved and cannot acknowledge beauty under such conditions, then looking to your own inner being you will find no beauty to delight you and it will be futile in that state to seek the greater vision, for you will be questing it through the ugly and impure.

This is why such matters are not spoken of to everyone; you, if you are conscious of beauty within, remember.

3.

Thus there is in the Nature-Principle itself an Ideal archetype of the beauty that is found in material forms and, of that archetype again, the still more beautiful archetype in Soul, source of that in Nature. In the proficient soul this is brighter and of more advanced loveliness: adorning the soul and bringing to it a light from that greater light which is beauty primally, its immediate presence sets the soul reflecting upon the quality of this prior, the archetype which has no such entries, and is present nowhere but remains in itself alone, and thus is not even to be called a Reason-Principle but is the creative source of the very first Reason-Principle which is the Beauty to which Soul serves as Matter.

This prior, then, is the Intellectual-Principle, the veritable, abiding and not fluctuant since not taking intellectual quality from outside itself. By what image thus, can we represent it? We have nowhere to go but to what is less. Only from itself can we take an image of it; that is, there can be no representation of it, except in the sense that we represent gold by some portion of gold—purified, either actually or mentally, if it be impure—insisting at the same time that this is not the total thing gold, but merely the particular gold of a particular parcel. In the same way we learn in this matter from the purified Intellect in ourselves or, if you like, from the Gods and the glory of the Intellect in them.

For assuredly all the gods are august and beautiful in a beauty beyond our speech. And what makes them so? Intellect; and especially Intellect operating within them (the divine sun and stars) to visibility. It is not through the loveliness of their corporeal forms: even those that have body are not gods by that beauty; it is in virtue of Intellect that they, too, are gods, and as gods beautiful. . . .

8.

This then is Beauty primally: it is entire and omnipresent as an entirety; and therefore in none of its parts or members lacking in beauty; beautiful thus beyond denial. Certainly it cannot be anything (be, for example, Beauty) without being wholly that thing; it can be nothing which it is to possess partially or in which it utterly fails (and therefore it must entirely be Beauty entire).

If this principle were not beautiful, what

other could be? Its prior does not deign to be beautiful; that which is the first to manifest itself—Form and object of vision to the intellect—cannot but be lovely to see. It is to indicate this that Plato, drawing on something well within our observation, represents the Creator as approving the work he has achieved: the intention is to make us feel the lovable beauty of the autotype and of the Divine Idea; for to admire a representation is to admire the original upon which it was made.

It is not surprising if we fail to recognise what is passing within us: lovers, and those in general that admire beauty here, do not stay to reflect that it is to be traced, as of course it must be, to the Beauty There. That the admiration of the Demiurge is to be referred to the Ideal Exemplar is deliberately made evident by the rest of the passage: "He admired; and determined to bring the work into still closer likeness with the Exemplar": he makes us feel the magnificent beauty of the Exemplar by telling us that the Beauty sprung from this world is, itself, a copy from That.

And indeed if the divine did not exist, the transcendently beautiful, in a beauty beyond all thought, what could be lovelier than the things we see? Certainly no reproach can rightly be brought against this world save only that it is not That.

9.

. . . The power in that other world has merely Being and Beauty of Being. Beauty without Being could not be, nor Being voided of Beauty: abandoned of Beauty, Being loses something of its essence. Being is desirable because it is identical with Beauty; and Beauty is loved because it is Being. How then can we debate which is the cause of the other, where the nature is one? The very figment of Being needs some imposed image of Beauty to make it passable, and even to ensure its existence; it exists to the degree in which it has taken some share in the beauty of Idea; and the more deeply it has drawn on this, the less imperfect it is, precisely because the nature which is essentially the beautiful has entered into it the more intimately.

11.

Similarly any one, unable to see himself, but possessed by that God, has but to bring that divine-within before his consciousness and at once he sees an image of himself, himself lifted to a better beauty: now let him ignore that image, lovely though it is, and sink into a perfect self-identity, no such separation remaining; at once he forms a multiple unity with the God silently present; in the degree of his power and will, the two become one, should he turn back to the former duality, still he is pure and remains very near to the God; he has but to look again and the same presence is there.

This conversion brings gain: at the first stage, that of separation, a man is aware of self; but retreating inwards, he becomes possessor of all; he puts sense away behind him in dread of the separated life and becomes one in the Divine; if he plans to see in separation, he sets himself outside.

The novice must hold himself constantly under some image of the Divine Being and seek in the light of a clear conception; knowing thus, in a deep conviction, whither he is going —into what a sublimity he penetrates—he must give himself forthwith to the inner and, radiant with the Divine Intellections (with which he is now one), be no longer the seer, but, as that place has made him, the seen.

Still, we will be told, one cannot be in beauty and yet fail to see it. The very contrary: to see the divine as something external is to be outside of it; to become it is to be most truly in beauty: since sight deals with the external, there can here be no vision unless in the sense of identification with the object.

And this identification amounts to a self-knowing, a self-consciousness, guarded by the fear of losing the self in the desire of a too wide awareness.

It must be remembered that sensations of the ugly and evil impress us more violently than those of what is agreeable and yet leave less knowledge as the residue of the shock: sickness makes the rougher mark, but health, tranquilly present, explains itself better; it takes the first place, it is the natural thing, it belongs to our being; illness is alien, unnatural and thus makes itself felt by its very incongruity, while the other conditions are native and we take no notice. Such being our nature, we are most completely aware of ourselves when we are most completely identified with the object of our knowledge.

This is why in that other sphere, when we are deepest in that knowledge by intellection, we are aware of none; we are expecting some impression on sense, which has nothing to report since it has seen nothing and never could in that order see anything. The unbelieving element is sense; it is the other, the Intellectual-Principle, that sees; and if this too doubted, it could not even credit its own existence, for it can never stand away and with bodily eyes apprehend itself as a visible object.

12.

We have told how this vision is to be procured, whether by the mode of separation or in identity: now, seen in either way, what does it give to report?

The vision has been of God in travail of a beautiful offspring, God engendering a universe within himself in a painless labour and—rejoiced in what he has brought into being, proud of his children—keeping all closely by Him, for the pleasure He has in his radiance and in theirs.

Of this offspring—all beautiful, but most beautiful those that have remained within—only one has become manifest without; from him (Zeus, sovran over the visible universe) the youngest born, we may gather, as from some image, the greatness of the Father and of the Brothers that remain within the Father's house.

Still the manifested God cannot think that he has come forth in vain from the father; for through him another universe has arisen, beautiful as the image of beauty, and it could not be lawful that Beauty and Being should fail of a beautiful image.

This second Kosmos at every point copies the archetype: it has life and being in copy, and has beauty as springing from that diviner world. In its character of image it holds, too, that divine perpetuity without which it would only at times be truly representative and sometimes fail like a construction of art; for every image whose existence lies in the nature of things must stand during the entire existence of the archetype.

Hence it is false to put an end to the visible sphere as long as the Intellectual endures, or to found it upon a decision taken by its maker at some given moment.

That teaching shirks the penetration of such a making as is here involved: it fails to see that as long as the Supreme is radiant there can be no failing of its sequel but, that existing, all exists. And—since the necessity of conveying our meaning compels such terms—the Supreme has existed for ever and for ever will exist.

13.

. . . Soul also has beauty, but is less beautiful than Intellect as being its image and therefore, though beautiful in nature, taking increase of beauty by looking to that original. Since then the All-Soul—to use the more familiar term—since Aphrodite herself is so beautiful, what name can we give to that other? If Soul is so lovely in its own right, of what quality must that prior be? And since its being is derived, what must that power be from which the Soul takes the double beauty, the borrowed and the inherent?

We ourselves possess beauty when we are true to our own being; our ugliness is in going over to another order; our self knowledge, that is to say, is our beauty; in self-ignorance we are ugly.

Thus beauty is of the Divine and comes Thence only.

Do these considerations suffice to a clear understanding of the Intellectual Sphere or must we make yet another attempt by another road?

III.2.11.

Are we, then, to conclude that particular things are determined by Necessities rooted in Nature and by the sequences of causes, and that everything is as good as anything can be?

No: the Reason-Principle is the sovereign, making all: it wills things as they are and, in its reasonable act, it produces even what we know as evil: it cannot desire all to be good: an artist would not make an animal all eyes; and in the same way, the Reason-Principle would not make all divine; it makes Gods but also celestial spirits, the intermediate order, then men, then the animals; all is graded succession, and this in no spirit of grudging but in the expression of a Reason teeming with intellectual variety.

We are like people ignorant of painting who complain that the colours are not beautiful everywhere in the picture: but the Artist has laid on the appropriate tint to every spot. Or we are censuring a drama because the persons are not all heroes but include a servant and a rustic and some scurrilous clown; yet take away the low characters and the power of the drama is gone; these are part and parcel of it.

St. Augustine

354–430

A. Life

In the writings of St. Augustine,[77] Bishop of Hippo Regius, the Platonism of the ecclesiastical doctrine of the Patristic period is elaborated. In his writings it is noteworthy also that the Platonism at the core of Neo-Platonic philosophy exerts the strongest influence upon Augustine's thinking. Augustine is sometimes referred to as "the Plato born of Christianity" and his writings on philosophy of art clearly warrant the appelation. Augustine Aurelius was born in Thagaste, Numidia, of a pagan father and a Christian mother. He was educated in Madaura and Carthage. He sought faith in the Manichaean doctrines, in the Platonic Academy, and in Neo-Platonism. At last he was converted in 387 to Christianity under the influence of Platonic thought, the sermons of St. Ambrose, and the moral force of his mother. St. Augustine spent the years 384–86 in Milan but returned to Hippo Regius in Africa. He was an enormously able and industrious administrator, as well as a voluminous author. His best known writings are *The Confessions* and *The City of God*. St. Augustine died in Africa in 430 A.D.

B. Philosophy of Art and Beauty

The Nature of Divine Creating: Ex Nihilo and Unconditioned by External Ideas

De Trinitate XIV. xii. 16

There is, then, a nature not made, which made all other natures . . . and is without doubt more excellent than those which it made . . . than the mind of man, made after the image of Him who made it.

[77] Selections from St. Augustine's writings are quoted below, pp. 232 et seq.

The Confessions XI. 5

For it[78] was not as a human worker fashioning body from body. . . . He (the human worker) assigns to it already existing, as it were having a being, a form, as clay, or stone, or wood, or gold, or such like.

De Fide et Symbolo II.2

God made all things from nothing.

God and the Relation of External Ideas

De Diversis Quaestionibus LXXXIII. Q. 46; de ideis (30)

What man[79] religiously disposed and imbued with pure religion would dare deny this vision, even though he were still incapable of it? On the contrary, would he not proclaim that all things in existence have been created by God, their Cause—all things, that is, whose capacity for existence is determined in kind by their own specific nature; and that it is by this Cause that all living things have their life, and that the entire conservation of things as well as the very order whereby changing realities accomplish their periodic courses in definite directions, are maintained and governed by the laws of the Most-High God?

Once this is established and granted, who can dare to declare that God has made everything in an irrational manner? If one can not really say or believe such a thing, then it follows that all things have been fashioned according to an intelligible principle (*ratione*). Neither has man been made by the same intelligible principle as the horse, since this is an absurd supposition. Each thing, therefore, has been created according to its own intellectual principle. But where are we to suppose that these intelligible principles exist, if not in the very Mind of the Creator? He was not fixing His gaze upon anything located outside Himself to serve as a model when He made the things He created, for such a view is blasphemous. But if the intelligible principles of things created, and of those to be created, are contained in the Divine Mind and if only the eternal and changeless can exist there—Plato called these Original Exemplars the Ideas—then not only are these realities Ideas but they are themselves true, seeing that they are external and, as such, remain unchangeable in their existence. It is by participating in these Ideas that a thing comes to exist, whatever its mode of being.

[78] *The Confessions*, translated by J. G. Pilkington, *A Select Library of the Nicene and Post-Nicene Fathers of the Christian Church*, 1886–1890. Vol. 1.

[79] *De Diversis Quaestionibus* LXXXIII, translated by Robert P. Russell, O.S.A., Ph.D. Translated for and published in M. C. Nahm, *Genius and Creativity*, pp. 70–71, Harper and Row, New York, 1965. Reprinted by permission of the author.

God's creating not necessitated

The City of God, Bk. XI, Ch. XXII

. . . And in the greatest[80] is God the great workman, yet no lesser in the less: which little things are not to be measured to their own greatness, being near to nothing, but by their Maker's wisdom: as in a man's shape, shave his eyebrow, a very nothing to the body, yet how must does it deform him, his beauty consisting more of proportion and parility of parts,

[80] St. Augustine, *The City of God, A Select Library, The Nicene and Post-Nicene Fathers of the Christian Church*, Vol. 2 (Buffalo, N.Y. The Christian Library Co., 1887). Translated by the Rev. M. Dods.

than magnitude. Nor is it a wonder that those that hold some nature bad, and produced from a bad beginning, do not receive God's goodness for the cause of the creation, but rather think that He was compelled by this rebellious evil of mere necessity to fall a-creating, and mixing of His own good nature with evil in the suppression and reforming thereof, by which it was so foiled, and so toiled, that He had much ado to recreate and mundify it: nor can yet cleanse it all, but that which He could cleanse, serves as the future prison of the captived enemy. This was not the Manichees' foolishness, but their madness: which they should abandon, would they like Christians believe that God's nature is unchangeable, incorruptible, impassible, and that the soul (which may be changed by the will, unto worse, and by the corruption of sin be deprived of that unchangeable light) is no part of God nor God's nature, but by Him created of a far inferior mould.

The status of beautiful things in relation to Beauty external to man's soul

The Confessions, Book X, Ch. XXXIV.[81]

What numberless things, made by divers arts and manufactures, both in our apparel, shoes, vessels, and every kind of work, in pictures, too, and sundry images, and these going far beyond necessary and moderate use and holy signification, have men added for the enthrallment of the eyes; . . . following outwardly Him by whom they were made. . . . But I . . . do hence also sing a hymn to Thee —because those beautiful patterns, which through the medium of men's souls are conveyed into their artistic hands emanate from that Beauty which is above our souls, which my soul sigheth after day and night. . . . And I . . . impede my course with such beauties. . . . "

[81] *The Confessions,* translated by J. G. Pilkington, *A Select Library of the Nicene and Post-Nicene Fathers of the Christian Church,* 1886–1890. Vol. 1.

The beauty of the world: the world not eternal

The City of God, Bk. XI, Ch. IV.

. . . But what made God[82] create heaven and earth, then, not sooner? They that say this to import an eternity of the world, being not by God created, are damnably, and impiously deceived and infected. For (to except all prophecy) the very order, disposition, beauty, and change of the world and all therein proclaims itself to have been made (and not possible to have been made but) by God, that ineffable, invisible Great One, ineffably and invisibly beauteous. But they that say God made the world, and yet allow it no temporal, but only a formal original, being made after a manner almost incomprehensible, they seem to say somewhat in God's defence from that chanceful rashness, to take a thing into His head that was not therein before, viz., to make the world, and to be subject to change of will, He being wholly unchangeable and for ever. But I see not how their reason can stand in other respects, chiefly in that of the soul, which if they do co-eternize with God, they can never show how that misery befalls it anew, that was never accident to it before. If they say that the happiness and misery have been co-eternal ever, then must they be so still, and then follows this absurdity, that the soul being called happy, shall not be happy in this, that it foresees the misery to come. If it do neither

[82] St. Augustine, *The City of God.*

foresee their bliss nor their bale, then is it happily a false understanding: and that were a most fond assertion. But if they hold that the misery and the bliss have succeeded each other from all eternity, but that afterwards the soul being once blessed, returns no more to misery, yet does not this save them from being convicted that the soul was never truly happy before; but then begins to enjoy a new and uncertain happiness: and so they confess that this so strange and unexpected a thing befalls the soul then, that never befell it before: which new changes cause if they deny that God eternally foreknew, they deny Him also to be the author of that happiness (which were wicked to do). And then if they should say that He had newly resolved that the soul should not become eternally blessed, how far are they from quitting Him from that mutability which they disallow? But if they acknowledge that it had a true temporal beginning, but shall never have temporal end, and having once tried misery, and gotten clear of it, shall never be miserable more, this they may boldly affirm with prejudice to God's immutability of will. And so they may believe that the world had a temporal original, and yet that God did not alter His eternal resolution in creating of it.

The City of God, Bk. XI, Ch. V.

. . . But as it is not consequent that God followed chance rather than reason in placing of the world's frame where it now stands, and in no other place, though this place had no merit to deserve it before the infinite others: (yet no man's reason can comprehend why the divine will placed it so): even so no more is it consequent that we should think that it was any chance made God create this world then, rather than at any other time, whereas all times before had their equal course, and none was more meritorious of the creation than another: but if they say, men are fond to think there is any place besides that wherein the word is: so are they (say we) to imagine any time for God to be idle in, since there was no time before the world's creation.

The City of God, Bk. XI, Ch. V.

. . . The Scripture indeed calls the Holy Ghost the manifold spirit of wisdom, because the powers of it are many: but all one with the essence, and all included in one, for the wisdom thereof is not manifold, but one, and therein are infinite and immeasurable treasuries of things intelligible, wherein are all the immutable and inscrutable causes of all things, both visible and mutable, which are thereby created: for God did nothing unwittingly, it were disgrace to say so of any human artificer. Buf if He made all knowing, then made He but what He knew. This now produces a wonder, but yet a truth in our minds: that the world could not be known unto us, but that it is now extant: but it could not have been at all but that God knew it.

The City of God, Bk. XI, Ch. XXI

Of God's eternal unchanging will and knowledge wherein He pleased to create all things in form as they were created.

What means that saying that goes through all, "And God saw that it was good," but the approbation of the work made according to the workman's art, God's wisdom? God does not see it is good, being made, as if He saw it not so ere it was made: but in seeing that it is good being made, which could not have been made so but that He foresaw it, He teaches, but learns not, that it is good. Plato durst go further, and say, "That God had great joy in the beauty of the universe." He was not so fond to think the newness of the work increased God's joy; but he showed that that pleased Him, being effected, which had pleased His wisdom to foreknow should be so effected, not that God's knowledge varies, or apprehends diversely of things past, present and future. He does not foresee things to come as we do, nor behold things present, nor remember things past as we do: but in a manner far different from our imagination. He sees them not by change in thought, but immutably, be they past or not past, to come or not to come, all these has He eternally present, nor thus in His eye and thus in His mind (He consists not of body and soul), nor thus now, and otherwise hereafter, or heretofore: His knowledge is not as ours is, admitting alteration by circumstance of time, but exempted from all change, and all variation of moments: for His intention runs not from thought to thought; all things he knows are in His unbodily presence. He has no temporal notions of the time, nor moved He the time by any temporal notions in Himself. Therefore He saw that which He had made was good, because He foresaw that He should make it good. Nor doubted His knowledge in seeing it made, or augmented it, as if it had been less ere He made it; He could not do His works in such absolute perfection, but out of His most perfect knowledge. Wherefore if one urges with, "Who made this light?" it suffices to answer, God: if we be asked by what means, suffices this, "God said, Let there be light, and there was light:" God making it by His very word. But because there are three necessary questions of every creature, who made it, how He made it, and wherefore He made it? God says, quoth Moses, "Let there be light, and there was light, and God saw the light that it was good." Who made it? God. How? God said but "Let it be, and it was:" wherefore? It was good. No better author can there be than God, no better art than His word, no better cause why, than that a good God should make a good creature. And this Plato praised as the justest cause of the world's creation: whether he had read it, or heard it, or got it by speculation of the creatures, or learned it of those that had this speculation.

Man in God's image, his creative powers conditioned

The City of God, Bk. XII, Ch. XXIII

Of the nature of the human soul created in the image of God.

God, then, made man in His own image. For he created for him a soul endowed with reason and intelligence, so that he might excel all the creatures of earth, air, and sea, which were not so gifted. And when He had formed the man out of the dust of the earth, and had willed that his soul should be such as I have said,—whether He had already made it, and now by breathing imparted it to man, or rather made it by breathing, so that that breath which God made by breathing (for what else is "to breathe" than to make breath?) is the soul,—He made also a wife for him, to aid him in the work of generating his kind, and her He formed of a bone taken out of the man's side, working in a divine manner. For we are not to conceive of this work in a carnal fashion, as if God wrought as we commonly see artisans, who use their hands, and material furnished to them, that by their artistic skill they may fashion some material object. God's hand is God's power; and He, working invisibly, effects visible results. But this seems fabulous rather than true to men, who measure by customary and everyday works the power and wisdom of God, whereby He understands and produces without seeds even seeds themselves . . . .

The City of God, Bk. XII, Ch. XXV

That God alone is the Creator of every kind of creature, whatever its nature or form.

For whereas there is one form which is given from without to every bodily substance,—such as the form which is constructed by potters and smiths, and that class of artists who paint and fashion forms like the body of animals,—but another and internal form which is not itself constructed, but, as the efficient cause, produces not only the natural bodily forms, but even the life itself of the living creatures and which proceeds from the secret and hidden choice of an intelligent and living nature,—let that first-mentioned form be attributed to every artificer, but this latter to one only, God, the Creator and Originator who made the world itself and the angels, without the help of world or angels. For the same divine and, so to speak, creative energy, which cannot be made, but makes, and which gave to the earth and sky their roundness,—this same divine, effective, and creative energy gave their roundness to the eye and to the apple; and the other natural objects which we anywhere see, received also their form, not from without, but from the secret and profound might of the Creator, who said, "Do not I fill heaven and earth?" and whose wisdom it is that "reacheth from one end to another mightily; and sweetly doth she order all things." Wherefore I know not what kind of aid the angels, themselves created first, afforded to the Creator in making other things. I cannot ascribe to them what perhaps they cannot do, neither ought I to deny them such faculty as they have. But by their leave, I attribute the creating and originating work which gave being to all natures to God, to whom they themselves thankfully ascribe their existence. We do not call gardeners the creators of their fruits, for we read, "Neither is he that planteth anything, neither he that watereth, but God that giveth the increase." Nay, not even the earth itself do we call a creator, though she seems to be the prolific mother of all things which she aids in germinating and bursting forth from the seed, and which she keeps rooted in her own breast; for we likewise read, "God giveth it a body, as it hath pleased Him, and to every seed his own body." . . . .

The City of God, Bk. XV, Ch. XXI

Freedom of will.

. . . For will, being a nature which was made good by the good God, but mutable by the immutable, because it was made out of nothing, can both decline from good to do evil, which takes place when it freely chooses, and can also escape the evil and do good, which takes place only by divine assistance.

The City of God, Bk. XV, Ch. XXII

Of the fall of the sons of God who were captivated by the daughters of men, whereby all, with the exception of eight persons, deservedly perished in the deluge.

When the human race, in the exercise of this freedom of will, increased and advanced, there arose a mixture and confusion of the two cities by their participation in a common iniquity. And this calamity, as well as the first, was occasioned by woman, though not in the same way; for these women were not themselves betrayed, neither did they persuade the men to sin, but having belonged to the earthly city and society of the earthly, they had been of corrupt manners from the first, and were loved for their bodily beauty by the sons of God, or the citizens of the other city which sojourns in this world. Beauty is indeed a good gift of God; but that the good may not think it a great good, God dispenses it even to the wicked. And thus, when the good that is great and proper to the good was abandoned by the sons of God, they fell to a paltry good which is not peculiar to the good, but common to the good and the evil; and when they were captivated by the daughters of men, they adopted the manners of the earthly to win them as brides, and forsook the godly ways they had followed in their own holy society. And thus beauty, which is indeed God's handiwork, but only a temporal, carnal, and lower kind of good, is not fitly loved in preference to God, the eternal, spiritual, and unchangeable good. When the miser prefers his gold to justice, it is through no fault of the gold, but of the man, and so with every created thing. For though it be good, it may be loved with an evil as well as with a good love: it is loved rightly when it is loved ordinately; evilly, when inordinately. It is this which some one has briefly said in these verses in praise of the Creator: "These are Thine, they are good, because Thou art good who didst create them. There is in them nothing of ours, unless the sin we commit when we forget the order of things, and instead of Thee love that which Thou hast made."

Earthly beauty composed of contrarieties

The City of God, Bk. XI, Ch. XVIII

For God would never have foreknown vice in any work of His, angel or man, but that He knew in like manner what good use to put it unto, so making the world's course, like a fair poem, more gracious by antithetic figures. *Antitheta,* called in Latin, opposites, are the most decent figures of all elocution: some, more expressly call them contra-posites. But we have no use of this word, though for the figure, the Latin, and all the tongues of the world, use it. St. Paul uses it rarely upon that place to the Corinthians where he says: "By the armour of righteousness on the right hand, and the left, by honour and dishonour, by evil report and good, as deceivers, and yet true, as unknown and yet known, as dying and behold we live, as chastened, and yet not killed, as sorrowing and yet ever glad, as poor and yet making many rich, as having nothing, yet possessing all things." Thus as these contraries opposed do give the saying an excellent grace, so is the world's beauty composed of contrarieties, not in figure but in nature. This is plain in Ecclesiasticus, in this verse: "Against evil is good, and against death is life, so is the godly against the sinner: so look for in all the works of the highest two and two, one against one."

We fail to perceive some beauties because we do not know the whole

The City of God, Bk. XII, Ch. IV

Of the nature of irrational and lifeless creatures, which in their own kind and order do not mar the beauty of the universe.

But it is ridiculous to condemn the faults of beasts and trees, and other such mortal and mutable things as are void of intelligence, sensation, or life, even though these faults should destroy their corruptible nature; for these creatures received, at their Creator's will, an existence fitting them, by passing away and giving place to others, to secure that lowest form of beauty, the beauty of seasons, which in its own place is a requisite part of this world. For things earthly were neither to be made equal to things heavenly, nor were they though inferior, to be quite omitted from the universe. Since, then, in those situations where such things are appropriate, some perish to make way for others that are born in their room, and the less succumb to the greater, and the things that are overcome are transformed into the quality of those that have the mastery, this is the appointed order of things transitory. Of this order the beauty does not strike us, because by our mortal frailty we are so involved in a part of it, that we cannot perceive the whole, in which these fragments that offend us are harmonized with the most accurate fitness and beauty. And therefore, where we are not so well able to perceive the wisdom of the Creator, we are very properly enjoined to believe it, lest in the vanity of human rashness we presume to find any fault with the work of so great an Artificer. At the same time, if we attentively consider even these faults of earthly things, which are neither voluntary nor penal, they seem to illustrate the excellence of the natures themselves, which are all originated and created by God; for it is that which pleases us in this nature which we are displeased to see removed by the fault, —unless even the natures themselves displease men, as often happens when they become hurtful to them, and then men estimate them not by their nature, but by their utility; as in the case of those animals whose swarms scourged the pride of the Egyptians. But in this way of estimating, they may find fault with the sun itself; for certain criminals or debtors are sentenced by the judges to be set in the sun. Therefore it is not with respect to our convenience or discomfort, but with respect to their own nature, that the creatures are glorifying to their Artificer. Thus even the nature of the eternal fire, penal though it be to the condemned sinners, is most assuredly worthy of praise. For what is more beautiful than fire flaming, blazing, and shining? What more useful than fire for warming, restoring, cooking, though nothing is more destructive than fire burning and consuming? The same thing, then, when applied in one way, is destructive, but when applied suitably, is most beneficial. For who can find words to tell its uses throughout the world? We must not listen, then, to those who praise the light of fire but find fault with its heat, judging it not by its nature, but by their convenience or discomfort. For they wish to see, but not to be burnt. But they forget that this very light which is so pleasant to them, disagrees with and hurts weak eyes; and in that heat which is disagreeable to them, some animals find the most suitable conditions of a healthy life.

The vision of beauty

De Ordine, Bk. II. XV. 51

But when the soul[83] has properly adjusted and disposed itself, and has rendered itself harmonious and beautiful, then will it venture to see God, the very source of all truth and the very Father of Truth. O great God, What kind of eyes shall those be! How pure! How beautiful! How powerful! How constant! How serene! How blessed! And what is that which they can see! What is it? I ask. What should we surmise? What should we believe? What should we say? Everyday expressions present themselves, but they have been rendered sordid by things of least worth. I shall say no more, except that to us is promised a vision of beauty —the beauty of whose imitation all other

[83] St. Augustine, *De Ordine*, translated by Robert Russell. Originally published by Cosmopolitan Science and Art Service, New York, 1942. Now included in Fathers of the Church, Vol. 5, Catholic University Press, Washington, D.C.

things are beautiful, and by comparison with which all other things are unsightly. Whosoever will have glimpsed this beauty—and he will see it, who lives well, prays well, studies well—how will it ever trouble him why one man, desiring to have children, has them not, while another man casts out his own offspring as being unduly numerous; why one man hates children before they are born, and another man loves them after birth; or how it is not absurd that nothing will come to pass which is not with God—and therefore it is inevitable that all things come into being in accordance with order — and nevertheless God is not petitioned in vain?

Finally, how will any burdens, dangers, scorns, or smiles of fortune disturb a just man? In this world of sense, it is indeed necessary to examine carefully what time and place are, so that what delights in a portion of place or time, may be understood to be far less beautiful than the whole of which it is a portion. . . . .

Beautiful things emanate from Beauty and are inferior

The Confessions, Ch. XXXIV. 53.

What numberless things,[84] made by divers arts and manufactures, both in our apparel, shoes, vessels, and every kind of work, in pictures, too, and sundry images, and these going far beyond necessary and moderate use and holy signfication, have men added for the enthralment of the eyes; following outwardly what they make, forsaking inwardly Him by whom they were made, yea, and destroying that which they themselves were made! But I, O my God and my Joy, do hence also sing a hymn unto Thee, and offer a sacrifice of praise unto my Sanctifier, because those beautiful patterns, which through the medium of men's souls are conveyed into their artistic hands, emanate from that Beauty which is above our souls, which my soul sigheth after day and night. But as for the makers and followers of those outward beauties, they from thence derive the way of approving them, but not of using them. And though they see Him not, yet is He there, that they might not go astray, but keep their strength for Thee, and not dissipate it upon delicious lassitudes. And I, though I both say and perceive this, impede my course with such beauties, but Thou dost rescue me, O Lord, Thou dost rescue me; "for Thy loving-kindness is before mine eyes." For I am taken miserably, and Thou rescuest me mercifully; sometimes not perceiving it, in that I had come upon them hesitatingly; at other times with pain, because I was held fast by them.

[84] *The Confessions,* translated by J. G. Pilkington, *A Select Library of the Nicene and Post-Nicene Fathers of the Christian Church,* 1886–1890. Vol. 1.

These numbers are pre-eminent by virtue of the beauty of ratio

On Music, Book VI. 31

And so,[85] to return to the subject all this was said for, these numbers are pre-eminent by virtue of the beauty of ratio. And if we were absolutely separated from them, then whenever we should be disposed to the body, the advancing numbers would not alter the sensuous numbers. But by moving bodies they produce the sensible beauties of times. And so reacting numbers are also made opposed to

[85] St. Augustine, *On Music,* translated by Robert Taliaferro. Originally published by Cima Publishing Co., New York, 1947. Now included in Fathers of the Church, Vol. 4, Catholic University Press, Washington, D.C.

sounding numbers. And the same soul receiving all its own motions multiplies, you might say, in itself, and makes them subject to recall. And this force it has is called memory, a great help in the everyday business of this life.

The love of lower beauty

On Music, Book VI. 46

It's not those numbers below reason and beautiful in their kind do soil the soul, then, but the love of lower beauty. And whenever the soul finds to love in it not only equality, concerning which we have said enough for this work, but also order, it has lost its own order. Nor yet does it depart from the order of things even at this point, and so it is whenever and however a thing is, it is highly ordered. For it is one thing to keep order and another to be kept by order. That soul keeps order that, with its whole self, loves Him above itself, that is, God and fellow souls as itself. In virtue of this love it orders lower things and suffers no disorder from them. And what degrades it is not evil, for the body also is a creature of God and is adorned in its own beauty, although of the lowest kind, but in view of the soul's dignity is lightly esteemed, just as the value of gold is degraded by a mixture with the finest silver. And so whatever numbers result from our criminal mortality, we shall not except them from the making of Divine Providence, since they are beautiful in their own kind, but let us not love them to become happy in their enjoyment. For we shall keep free of them since they are temporal, by using them well, as with a board in a flood by not throwing them aside as burdensome and not grasping them as stable. But the love of our neighbor commanded us is our most certain ascent to inhere in God and not so much to be kept by His ordering as to keep our own order firm and sure.

Reason turns to the domain of sight; on design and harmony in architecture

De Ordine, Bk. II. XV. 42

From this stage,[86] reason advanced to the province of the eyes. And scanning the earth and the heavens, it realized that nothing pleased it but beauty; and in beauty, design; and in design, dimensions; and in dimensions, number. And it asked itself whether any line or curve or any other form or shape in that realm was of such kind as intelligence comprehended. It found that they were far inferior; and that nothing which the eyes beheld, could in any way be compared with what the mind discerned. These distinct and separate realities, it also reduced to a branch of learning, and called it geometry.

De Ordine, Bk. II. XI. 34

Wherefore, considering carefully the parts of this very building, we cannot but be displeased because we see one doorway towards the side and another situated almost, but not exactly, in the middle. In things constructed, a proportion of parts that is faulty, without any compelling necessity, unquestionably seems to inflict, as it were, a kind of injury upon one's gaze. But the fact that three windows inside, one in the middle and two at the sides, pour light at equal intervals on the bathing place—how much that delights and enraptures us as

[86] St. Augustine, *De Ordine,* translated by Robert Russell. Originally published by Cosmopolitan Science and Art Service, New York, 1942. Now included in Fathers of the Church, Vol. 5, Catholic University Press, Washington D.C.

we gaze attentively, is a thing already manifest, and need not be shown to you in many words. In their own terminology, architects themselves call this *design*; and they say that parts unsymmetrically placed, are without *design*. This is very general; it pervades all the arts and creations of man. . . .

De Vera Religione, XXXVI. 66

[The balance of equal arches] pleases because it is beautiful, and it is beautiful because the parts are alike and are brought by a certain bond to a single harmony.

Pseudo-Dionysius

fl. 482–513 A.D.

A. Life

We need not enter in detail into the puzzles concerning the dates of the life of the Pseudo-Dionysius (Dionysius the Areopagite), or into the puzzles raised by the question of the authenticity of the writings attributed to him. It is sufficient to mention the fact that scholars are still not in agreement concerning either answers to the questions raised, or the date at which the writings attributed to him actually appeared. Pope Martin used the writings in 649, and they are first mentioned in Constantinople in 533. From 649, Dionysius' writings held sway in the East and their powerful influence continued until the fifteenth century. Laurentius Valla in his "Notes to the New Testament" cast doubt on the authenticity of the writings, a doubt shared by Erasmus. Out of this dispute concerning the authenticity of the writings attributed to Dionysius came the charge that a portion of them contained deliberate fraud. Various writers maintained, however, that there was no fraud but that the author had misinterpreted various sources. It is generally agreed that 482 A.D. is the date before which the writings could not have been produced. There is some agreement that the works were written between the years 482 and 513.

Whatever the answers to the questions concerning the date and the authenticity of the writings, there is a general tendency among scholars to assume that they represent the thought of a Christian expressing his faith in terms that Platonists could understand. In any case, Dionysius the Areopagite is as important for the history of mysticism as St. Augustine is for the scholasticism of the Middle Ages. His most important writings are *De Divinis Nominibus, De Caelesti Hierarchia,* and *De Mystica Theologia.*

It will be helpful to understand the passage quoted below from *De Divinis Nominibus* if we realize that in making his faith in Christianity comprehensible to the Platonists from whom his speculations arise, Dionysius is arguing throughout his writings for a faith which transcends his philosophical Platonism. Consequently, his contribution to Philosophy of Art may be traced to those of his writings which concern God, who transcends reason and is not comprehensible to the senses. As he writes [86] in *De Mystica Theologia,*

> . . . But thou, O dear Timothy, by thy persistent commerce with the mystic visions, leave behind both sensible perceptions and intellectual

[86] Dionysius the Areopagite, *De Mystica Theologia,* Ch. I, Sect. 1.

efforts, and all objects of sense and intelligence, and all things not being and being, and be raised aloft unknowingly to the union, as far as attainable, with Him Who is above every essence and knowledge. For by the resistless and absolute ecstasy in all purity, from thyself and all, thou wilt be carried on high, to the superessential ray of the Divine darkness, when thou hast cast away all, and become free of all . . .

The conception of divine transcendence embodied in this passage does not mean that God is not the cause, ground, and being of everything. Scripture has made these presumably contrary statements intelligible. God's unity, plurality, and being have been made clear in the Scriptures, where they are clothed in symbols. Thus the theologian praises God as the Nameless and the Many-named, for names are mere symbols. Dionysius gives many illustrations of his point. Pain does not grieve nor does joy rejoice. In the selections from *Concerning Divine Names,* one such illustration is given. It has been sought out and quoted again and again in mystical literature and in turn by mystics in art and its criticism.

B. Philosophy of Beauty and the Beautiful

God as Beautiful and Absolute Beauty

This God[87] is celebrated by the sacred theologians, both as beautiful and as Beauty—and all the other Divine Names which beseem the beautifying and highly-favored comeliness. But the beautiful and Beauty are not to be divided, as regards the Cause which has embraced the whole in one. For, with regard to all created things, by dividing them into participations and participants, we call beautiful that which participates in Beauty; but beauty, the participation of the beautifying Cause of all the beautiful things. But, the super-essential Beautiful is called Beauty, on account of the beauty communicated from Itself to all beautiful things, in a manner appropriate to each, and as Cause of the good harmony and brightness of all things which flashes like light to all the beautifying distributions of its fontal ray, and as calling . . . all things to Itself (whence it is called Beauty) . . . and as collecting all in all to Itself. (And it is called) Beautiful, as (being) at once beautiful and super-beautiful, and always being under the same conditions and in the same manner beautiful, and neither coming into being nor perishing, neither waxing nor waning; neither in this beautiful, nor in that ugly nor at one time beautiful, and at another, not; nor in relation to one thing beautiful, and in relation to another ugly, nor here, and not there, as being beautiful to some, and not beautiful to others; but as Itself, in Itself, with Itself, uniform, always being beautiful, and as having beforehand in Itself pre-eminently the fontal beauty of everything beautiful. For, by the simplex and supernatural nature of all beautiful things, all beauty, and everything beautiful, pre-existed uniquely as to Cause. From this Beautiful (comes) being to all existing things—that each is beautiful in its proper order; and by reason of the Beautiful are the adaptations of all things, and friendships, and

[87] Dionysius the Areopagite, *Concerning Divine Names,* III. 7, pp. 39–41. *The Works of Dionysius the Areopagite,* translated by The Reverend John Parker. London, J. Parker and Co., 1897.

inter-communions, and by the Beautiful all things are made one, and the Beautiful is origin of all things, as a creating Cause, both by moving and whole and holding it together by the love of its own peculiar Beauty; and end of all things and beloved, as final Cause (for all things exist for the sake of the Beautiful) and exemplary (Cause), because all things are determined according to It . . .

. . . Moreover, all things whatever, which are and come to being, are and come to being by reason of the Beautiful and Good; and to It all things look, and by It are moved and held together, and for the sake of It, and by reason of It, and in It, is every source exemplary, final, creative, formative, elemental, and in one word, every beginning, every bond, every term or to speak summarily, all things existing are from the Beautiful and Good; and all things non-existing are superessentially in the Beautiful and Good; and it is of all, beginning and term, above beginning and above term, because from It, and through It, and in It, and to It, are all things, as says the Sacred Word.

By all things, then, the Beautiful and Good is desired and beloved and cherished; and, by reason of It, and for the sake of It, the less love the greater suppliantly; and those of the same rank, their fellows brotherly; and the greater, the less considerately; and these severally love the things of themselves continuously; and all things by aspiring to the Beautiful and Good, do and wish all things whatever they do and wish. Further, it may be boldly said with truth, that even the very Author of all things, by reason of overflowing Goodness, loves all, makes all, perfects all, sustains all, attracts all; and even the Divine Love is Good of Good, by reason of the Good. For Love itself, the benefactor of things that be, pre-existing overflowingly in the Good, did not permit itself to remain unproductive in itself, but moved itself to creation, as befits the overflow which is generative of all . . .

St. Thomas Aquinas

1224–1274

A. Life

St. Thomas Aquinas was the founder of the Dominican tradition and the philosopher who in the Middle Ages exercised the greatest influence as a follower of Aristotle. He was born in Aquino, Italy, and studied at the University of Naples. He decided to enter the Dominican Order, studied in Cologne under Albertus Magnus, and received his degree in Paris in 1257, where he lectured until 1261. He was called to Italy by the Pope in 1261 and lectured in Pisa, Rome and Bologna. His principal works are the *Summa Theologia* and the *Summa Contra Gentiles.*

B. Philosophy of Art

Beauty includes three conditions

Persons in Reference to Essence. Q. 39. Art. 8

For beauty[88] includes three conditions, *integrity* or *perfection,* since those things which are impaired are by the very fact ugly; due *proportion* or *harmony;* and lastly, *brightness,* or *clarity,* whence things are called beautiful which have a bright colour . . . An image is said to be beautiful, if it perfectly represents even an ugly thing . . .

[88] *Basic Writings of Saint Thomas Aquinas,* translated by Father Lawrence Shapcote, O.P., Vol. II, pp. 433 et seq. (Based on the English Dominican Translation, begun in 1911.) New York: Random House, 1945. Copyright © 1945.

Goodness in General, Q. 5. Art. 5

REPLY OBJ. 1

Beauty and goodness[89] in a thing are identical fundamentally; for they are based

[89] Ibid.

upon the same thing, namely, the form; and consequently goodness is praised as beauty. But they differ logically, for goodness properly relates to appetite (goodness being what all things desire); and therefore it has the aspect of an end (the appetite being a kind of movement towards a thing). On the other hand, beauty relates to the cognitive faculty; for beautiful things are those which please when seen. Hence beauty consists in due proportion; for the senses delight in things duly proportioned, as in what is after their own kind—because even sense is a sort of reason, just as is every cognitive faculty. Now, since knowledge is by assimilation, and similarity relates to form, beauty properly belongs to the nature of a formal cause . . .

Whether the Intellectual Habit ART is a Virtue?[90]

We proceed thus to the Third Article:—

Objection 1. It would seem that art is not an intellectual virtue. For Augustine says that *no one makes bad use of virtue.* But one may make bad use of art, for a craftsman can work badly according to the science of his art. Therefore art is not a virtue.

Obj. 2. Further, there is no virtue of a virtue. But *there is a virtue of art,* according to the Philosopher. Therefore art is not a virtue.

Obj. 3. Further, the liberal arts excel the mechanical arts. But just as the mechanical arts are practical, so the liberal arts are speculative. Therefore, if art were an intellectual virtue, it would have to be reckoned among the speculative virtues.

On the contrary, The Philosopher says that art is a virtue. However, he does not reckon it among the speculative virtues, which, according to him, reside in the scientific part of the soul.

I answer that, Art is nothing else but *the right reason about certain works to be made.* And yet the good of these things depends, not on the disposition of man's appetite, but on the goodness of the work done. For a craftsman as such is commendable, not for the will with which he does a work, but for the quality of the work. Art, therefore, properly speaking is an operative habit. And yet it has something in common with the speculative habits, since the disposition of the things considered by them is a matter of concern to the speculative habits also, although they are not concerned with the disposition of the appetite towards their objects. For as long as the geometrician demonstrates the truth, it matters not how his appetite is disposed, whether he be joyful or angry; even as neither does this matter in a craftsman, as we have observed. And so art has the nature of a virtue in the same way as the speculative habits, in so far, namely, as neither art nor a speculative habit makes a good work as regards the use of the habit, which is distinctive of a virtue that perfects the appetite, but only as regards the ability to work well.

Reply Obj. 1. When anyone endowed with an art produces bad workmanship, this is not the work of that art; in fact, it is contrary to the art. In the same way, when a man lies, while knowing the truth, his words are not in accord with what he knows, but contrary thereto. Therefore, just as science has always a relation to good, as was stated above, so it is with art; and it is for this reason that it is called a virtue. And yet it falls short of being a perfect virtue, because it does not make its possessor to use it well; for which purpose something further is requisite, even though there cannot be a good use without the art.

Reply Obj. 2. In order that a man may

[90] *Summa Theologiae* Q. 57, Art. 3. See above, p. 200.

make good use of the art he has, he needs a good will, which is perfected by moral virtue; and for this reason the Philosopher says there is a virtue of art, namely, a moral virtue, in so far as the good use of art requires a moral virtue. For it is evident that a craftsman is inclined by justice, which rectifies his will, to do his work faithfully.

Reply Obj. 3. Even in speculative matters there is something by way of work: *e.g.,* the making of a syllogism or of a fitting speech, or the work of counting or measuring. Hence whatever habits are ordained to such works of the speculative reason are, by a kind of comparison, called arts indeed, but *liberal* arts, in order to distinguish them from those arts that are ordained to works done by the body; for these arts are, in a fashion, servile, inasmuch as the body is in servile subjection to the soul, and man, as regards his soul, is free [*liber*]. On the other hand, those sciences which are not ordained to any such work are called sciences absolute, and not arts. Nor, if the liberal arts be more excellent, does it follow that the notion of art is more applicable to them.

Dante Alighieri

1265–1321

A. Life

The greatest of Italian poets and one of the great poets of all times, Dante Alighieri, was born in Florence, was exiled from Venice where he had held the chief magistracy of the Republic, and died in Ravenna. He wrote the *Vita Nova* and the famous *De Monarchia,* the latter in anticipation of the visit to Italy of Emperor Henry VII. In Ravenna in 1317 Dante completed the *Divine Comedy,* the allegorical account of human life with its visions of Hell, Purgatory and Paradise.

B. Philosophy of Art

Dante [91] has been called Thomas Aquinas in verse. It is true that in the *Tractate* Dante all but paraphrases the great Scholastic's words concerning art and beauty. He makes an enormous contribution of his own, however, to Philosophy of Art in his letter to Lord Can Grande.[92] His definition of tragedy and comedy, couched in integral terms, has had great influence not only on the theory but also upon the practice of drama. "Tragedy in its beginning," he writes "is admirable and quiet, in its ending or catastrophe foul and horrible. . . . Comedy . . . beginneth with some adverse circumstances, but its theme hath a happy termination. . . ." [93]

De Monarchia II. 2.

Art exists in a three-fold degree.

It [94] must be understood, therefore, that as art exists in a threefold degree, in the mind of the artist, in the instrument, and in the matter informed by art, so may Nature be looked upon as threefold. For Nature exists in the mind of the Primal Motor, who is God,

[91] See above for a brief life of Dante and below for selections from his writings.

[92] Quoted below, p. 250.

[93] Chaucer's version of Dante's interpretation of tragedy is of interest. It appears in the *Monk's Tale*:

> Tragedie is to seyn a certeyn storie,
> As olde bokes maken in memorie,
> Of him that stood in greet prosperitee
> And is y-fallen out of heigh degree
> Into miserie, and endeth wretchedly.

[94] *The De Monarchia of Dante Alighieri,* translated by Aurelia Henry (New York, 1904), pp. 71–4.

and then in heaven, as in the instrument through whose mediation the likeness of eternal goodness is unfolded on fluid matter. When the artist is perfect, and his instrument without fault, any flaw that may appear in the form of the art can then be imputed to the matter only. Thus, since God is ultimate perfection, and since heaven, his instrument, suffers no defect in its required perfectness (as a philosophic study of heaven makes clear), it is evident that whatever flaw mars lesser things is a flaw in the subjected material, and outside the intention of God working through Nature, and of heaven; and that whatever good is in lesser things cannot come from the material itself, which exists only potentially, but must come first from the artist, God, and secondly from the instrument of divine art, heaven, which men generally call Nature.

Letter to Can Grande

The title of the book is: [95] "Here beginneth the Comedy of Dante Alighieri, a Florentine by birth, but not by character." And for the comprehension of this it must be understood that the word "comedy" is derived from *κώμη*, village, and ῳδή, which meaneth song; hence comedy is, as it were, a *village song*. Comedy is in truth a certain kind of poetical narrative that differeth from all others. It differeth from Tragedy in its subject matter,—in this way, that Tragedy in its beginning is admirable and quiet, in its ending or catastrophe foul and horrible; and because of this the word "tragedy" is derived from *τράγος*, which meaneth *goat*, and ῳδή. Tragedy is, then, as it were, a *goatish song;* that is, foul like a goat, as doth appear in the tragedies of Seneca. Comedy, indeed, beginneth with some adverse circumstances, but its theme hath a happy termination, as doth appear in the comedies of Terence. And hence certain writers were accustomed to say in their salutations in place of a greeting, "a tragic beginning and a comic ending." Likewise they differ in their style of language, for Tragedy is lofty and sublime, Comedy, mild and humble,—as Horace says in his "Poetica," where he concedeth that sometimes comedians speak like tragedians and conversely: —

> " Interdum tamen et vocem comoedia tollit,
> Iratusque Chremes tumido delitigat ore;
> Et tragicus plerumque dolet sermone pedestri."

From this it is evident why the present work is called a comedy. For if we consider the theme, in its beginning it is horrible and foul, because it is Hell; in its ending, fortunate, desirable, and joyful, because it is Paradise; and if we consider the style of language, the style is careless and humble, because it is the vulgar tongue, in which even housewives hold converse. There are also other kinds of poetic narration: namely, the bucolic song, the elegy, the satire, and the votive hymn, as likewise can be seen in the "Poetica" of Horace; but of these at present nothing need be said.

[95] *A Translation of Dante's Eleven Letters,* translated by Charles Sterrett (Boston, 1892).

PART THREE

TWO RENAISSANCE WRITERS ON PHILOSOPHY OF ART

Chapter 7

Leone Ebreo and Leonardo da Vinci

There are almost unlimited possibilities for choice among important writings on philosophy of art in the Renaissance. In selecting from those of Leone Ebreo and Leonardo da Vinci, the choice was made in terms of contrast as well as of importance. The views of both men in philosophy and art derive from speculation in classical times. Leone Ebreo is a Neo-Platonist, as well as a thinker deeply influenced by the theology of the Old Testament. Leonardo da Vinci's thinking returns to rationalist Pre-Socratic philosophy and his speculation reflects, as well, his interest in classical thinkers in mathematics. Both men anticipate in their writings the intense interest shown by philosophers and literary men in the meaning of artistic originality. They differ radically, however, in their search for the grounds for creativity in art. Da Vinci argues his theory in terms of time and of whole and part. His argument pays little heed to the analogy implicit in many writings of the Renaissance between God and man in the area of creativity. He does say that "The divinity which is the science of painting transmutes the painter's mind into a resemblance of the divine mind," but remarks of this kind perform a radically different function in da Vinci's thought than does the conception of deity integrated into the philosophies of the Neo-Platonists. Leone Ebreo provides an extraordinary illustration of a Platonist metaphysic in which the conceptions of God as Creator *ex nihilo* and God as a *Demiurgos* rest somewhat uncomfortably together. In this, he carries on the tradition of Plato in *Timaeus*[1] and of Philo Judaeus.[2] Finally, both Leone and Leonardo commit themselves to not dissimilar interpretations of art as technique and of the artist as craftsman, although in metaphysical terms Leone Ebreo's conception directs attention to Platonic Ideas and their locus, whereas Leonardo's conception of the free artist depends almost wholly upon interpretation of the work of art in mathematical terms and of the craftsman in terms of imagination and technique.

The two Renaissance writers differ in background and in interests almost as much as they do in their philosophies. Leone Ebreo,[3]

[1] See above, pp. 12, 93, 95, 104.

[2] See above, pp. 203 et seq.

[3] For Leone Ebreo's life and for selections from his book, see below, pp. 264 et seq. *The numbers in parentheses at the end of each passage refer to the pages of the English translation of his* Dialoghi.

born after 1460, was the distinguished son of Isaac Abrabanel, the most eminent Jew in the Portugal of the fifteenth century. Leonardo da Vinci,[4] born April 15, 1452, was the illegitimate offspring of a notary living in Vinci in Tuscany. Leone Ebreo shared with his father the expulsion of the Jews from Portugal. He studied in the great Academies in Italy with such scholars at Pico della Mirandola and Mariano Lenzi. The *Dialoghi d'Amore* was published in 1535, although Leone wrote it in 1501–2 These dialogues, from which selections are given here as part of *The Philosophy of Love,* provided the most popular study of Platonism of its time. The book was issued in five editions in the original Italian, was translated twice into French, three times into Spanish, and appeared both in Latin and Hebrew. Camoens, Montaigne, Castiglione, Burton, Vives, and Bruno knew Leone's work and Spinoza owned a copy of it.

Leonardo da Vinci is generally regarded as one of the supreme geniuses, not only of the Renaissance, but of all time. A painter of superb power, an extraordinarily inventive thinker, an engineer among whose projects was the draining of the Valley of the Po River, and a speculative mind with boundless interests, Leonardo is widely regarded as "the Renaissance Man." Leonardo's *Notebooks,* written from right to left, are adorned with sketches on the widest variety of subjects. He is a prodigious figure in Italian art and it may justly be said that when he left Italy for the French court in 1514, the Renaissance moved with him to France.

As is true of many Neo-Platonists, Leone Ebreo in his speculation upon art is interested in accounting for the manner in which the Ideas manifest themselves in the world of change (407).[5] Leonardo da Vinci's speculative roots are in Pre-Socratic philosophy, more particularly in the writings of Anaxagoras and Zeno, but the classical philosophies are radically altered by his experimentation, his interest in mathematics, and his superb powers of observation. Of perhaps as great interest, however, is that Leone's speculation, like Spinoza's is God-centered, whereas Leonardo, so far as his thinking concerning art is concerned, is rather little preoccupied with problems arising from historical conceptions of Deity. What Leonardo argues in terms of an intelligible theory of time, of the canon of proportions, and of imagination, Leone Ebreo puts forward against a background of a Platonic conception of a world-artisan (123, 423, 440)[6] and of a creative God. Creativity or generation, for Leone Ebreo, is interpreted in terms of Plato's argument in *Symposium* and of Plato's interest in that Dialogue in Eros.

We obtain a clearer understanding of the issues of creativity and originality with which both Leone Ebreo and Leonardo do Vinci are concerned if we return to one line of Scholastic speculation upon the subject. Jacques Maritain, discussing art and beauty in terms of Thomist philosophy,[7] argues that the artist is in the sphere of "making" and exists in "a strange and pathetic condition, the very image of man's condition in the world, where he is condemned to wear himself out among bodies and live with mind." Maritain believes that this is true because ". . . The production of beauty belongs to God alone," a position almost diametrically opposed to that adopted by the Platonists. Their speculative problems in this area are clearly delineated in the eleventh century by St. Anselm, in arguments to be echoed by Pico della Mirandola and Leone Ebreo. In the *Monologium,*[8] St. Anselm asks "in what sense those things which were created may be said to have been nothing before their creation."

[4] See below, pp. 281 et seq. for a brief life of Leonardo and for selections from his writings.

[5] *The Philosophy of Love.* See below, p. 264. The numbers refer to the pages of the English translation, which begins below.

[6] *Ibid.,* pp. 265, 275, 279.

[7] J. Maritain, *Art and Scholasticism,* p. 35. Compare above, p. 200.

[8] St. Anselm, *Monologium,* IX, pp. 55 et seq.

He answers that nothing can conceivably be created by anyone "unless there is, in the mind of the creative agent, some example, as it were, or (as is more fittingly supposed) some model, or likeness, or rule." Anselm concludes that "it is evident, then, that before the world was created, it was in the thought of the supreme Nature, what, and of what sort, and how, it should be." There is an analogy implicit between God's creation and man's. Before he is about to create a something by using his craft, man, too, "first expresses it to himself through a concept." The analogy, Anselm believes, is, however, "very incomplete": God's creation is *ex nihilo,* whereas the artisan must learn from external objects and he requires a material in which to work.[9]

For Pico della Mirandola,[10] God is not only the Father, but He is also the "supreme Architect," a phrase used by Philo.[11] God is the builder of the "cosmic home," the most sacred temple of His godhead." He builds the universe but, "when the work is finished, the Craftsman kept wishing that there were someone to ponder the plan of so great a work, to love its beauty, and to wonder at its vastness." It is significant that whereas Pico's universe is basically Platonic in conception, the account of man's creation is, for him, in contrast, Hebraic–Christian in derivation. When all else was done, writes Pico, "(as Moses and Timaeus bear witness), He finally took thought concerning the creation of man, But," adds Pico, "there was not among His archetypes that from which he could fashion a new offspring." Because of this, man is evidently unique; he belongs to no class which preexisted him, as the Ideas preexist other particulars. "At last," writes Pico, "the best of artisans ordained that the creature to whom He had been able to give nothing proper to himself should have joint possession of whatever had been peculiar to each of the different kinds of being. . . ."

In Pico della Mirandola's account, there is emphasis upon the uniqueness of man, a subject upon which essayists in the eighteenth century seized in order to explain the analogy of God to man. It should be noted, however, that it is not with Pico but with another of the eminent Florentine Neo-Platonists, Marsilio Ficino, that we more nearly approach that interest in visible earthly things which also marks off the *Dialoghi* of Ebreo. According to Ficino, we know and can know visible earthly beautiful things because we have an innate notion of the invisible Idea of Beauty. To the degree that the particular beautiful thing agrees with the Idea of beauty, to that degree the object is beautiful. The sensible object is referred to the formula in our minds by means of which the Idea is experienced by us.

The Neo-Platonic philosophies of art of Leone Ebreo and of Ficino tend to remain abstract, in terms of the problem of the relation of the Idea of Beauty to beautiful objects and in contrast to the speculation and findings of such a largely empirical mind as Leonardo's. It is nonetheless true, however, that an occasionally brilliant insight lights up more than the speculative metaphysics. One such passage (387)[12] in Leone's philosophy of love is an answer to the question concerning the origin of beautiful things. The author argues that "the beauty of natural things is derived from natural forms . . ." and this leads to the inference that "form is most beautiful without body, just as body is infinitely ugly without form." Thus far, we have Platonism pure and simple. What is not Platonist is the suggestion that "the greater the mastery of the form over the roughness and ugliness of matter, the greater the beauty of the artificial object. . . ." Another indication of the movement of Leone's speculation away from abstraction to concrete

[9] See above, St. Augustine, pp. 197, 231 et seq. Cf. above, p. 10.

[10] Pico della Mirandola, *Oration on the Dignity of Man, The Renaissance Philosophy of Man* (Chicago, 1948), p. 224 (tr. E. L. Forbes).

[11] See above, pp. 203.

[12] *The Philosophy of Love.* See below, p. 275.

problems is evident in his argument that there are many things which are neither beautiful nor ugly (429). Leone undertakes to explain how the "artificial forms" are derived from the mind of the "human artificer . . . in which they first exist with greater perfection and beauty than in the object . . . beautifully designed" (386).[13] The author is in fact arguing the superiority of form over formed matter. For "true and first artificial beauty is the knowledge and art pre-existing in the mind of the craftsman" (399).

This is to suggest the central analogy to God, who is, however, a creator who creates *ex nihilo,* who is not beautiful by participation, "like His creatures, but is the first creator of beauty" (423).[14] The universe was created by the supreme Creator through the medium of love (440).[15] Leone Ebreo here cites Plato: ". . . The end of love, as Plato says, is birth in the beautiful." The gap is bridged because "our soul is formed in the image of the highest beauty, and by its nature desires to return to its divine origin. . . ." (465;[16] cf. 251). It is bridged, also, by the fact that "true and first artificial beauty is the knowledge and art pre-existing in the mind of the craftsman. . . ." (399).[17] The master Craftsman is God, who perfects the beauty of every created thing (375).[18] God is thus not only a Creator but a Craftsman. The universe is a macrocosm, man is a microcosm (105).[19] Corporeal beauty is, however, the mere image of spiritual beauty (378)[20] and its love enslaves the beholder (379).[21] It is difficult to determine precisely how Leone Ebreo conjoins "making" in the sense of engendering by love and "making" as craft. But he clearly tries to bring the explanation of the beauty of natural and of artificial things. The natural forms of bodies are derived from the incorporeal and spiritual soul of the world and the artificial forms are derived from the mind of the human artificer, "in which they first exist in greater perfection" (386).[22] The beautiful in the mind of the artist as a single idea of a work of art is more beautiful than if it is diffused through the material object (387).[23] The beauty of design is more beautiful than the thing designed—which is precisely what Plotinus held.

Out of this extraordinary theory, largely Neo-Platonic, in which God creates a world as in *Genesis,* but one which is nonetheless Platonic in that God is also an Architect and a Master Craftsman in Whom exist the Ideas (336),[24] we come upon an analogy of the human craftsman to God. We come, also to an echo of Plotinus' philosophy of art, for Art is superior—because First or prior—to what Art makes. This superiority of the technique (399)[25] is believed to hold both for divine and human creating. As we have observed, God is both begetter and creator (375, 440)[26] of all things (123)[27] and the extent of His power is indicated by the assertion that "formless chaos" must have been created "from eternity" by God. This view is attributed to Plato, but the basic conception of creativity is derived from *Genesis.* Only when men make explicit the implications of imagination, does it become possible for philosophers of art to solve the problems presented by Leone Ebreo's *Dialoghi d'Amore*: the conjoining artistic originality and artistic intelligibility. As the argument stands in *The Philosophy of Love,* man emerges both as similar to the creator and to the *Demiurgos,* but the two conceptions are not reconciled. Man

[13] *Ibid.*, see below, p. 275.
[14] *Ibid.*, see below, pp. 275-76.
[15] *Ibid.*, see below, p. 277.
[16] *Ibid.*, see below,p. 280.
[17] *Ibid.*, see below, p. 275.
[18] *Ibid.*, see below, p. 271.
[19] *Ibid.*, see below, p. 265.
[20] *Ibid.*, see below, p. 271 et seq.
[21] *Ibid.*, see below, p. 273.
[22] *Ibid.*, see below, p. 274.
[23] *Ibid.*, see below, p. 274.
[24] *Ibid.*, see below, p. 269.
[25] *Ibid.*, see below, p. 275.
[26] *Ibid.*, see below, pp. 275, 277-78.
[27] *Ibid.*, see below, p. 266.

remains primarily a craftsman (399, 375).[28] And within this *schema,* Leone Ebreo offers sound statements concerning the reasons for differences in judgments of works of art and for the beauty of artificial things (385).[29] The analogy of the production of beauty by love and of beautiful things by craft is only justified on the grounds of the priority of ideas in the mind of the artist (372-3, 375-9 and 385, 399).[30]

No inconsiderable portion of Leone Ebreo's *The Philosophy of Love* is presented as a wholly intelligible theory of art and beauty. The author prefers the beauty provided through sight; there is a considered suggestion concerning the problem of judgment; there is an instructive concern for a rational display of the meaning of the technique by which artificial objects are made. It should be noted, however, that there are two aspects of the Philosophy of Art and beauty which are not open to analysis in rational terms. The first is the view, adopted from the domain of revealed religion, that God creates the cosmos *ex nihilo,* although Leone tries to relate this to Plato's description of the making of the world in *Timaeus.* The second is the view that "love in the created intellect is the advance from the first intellection of the beautiful object of mind to that of final and perfect union with it" (456).[31] The mind cannot perceive "how great is the beauty of the beautiful beloved" (466; see the entire passage, 454 seq.).[32]

The conception of inexplicable creativity is as alien to Leonardo da Vinci's thinking as is the echo of Plato's *Symposium* with its suggestion of "communion," "ecstasy," and inexplicable experience of beauty. Both Leone Ebreo and Leonardo da Vinci are part and parcel of the tradition that accepts the intelligibility of Art. Leone however, accepts as well that aspect of Platonism and Neo-Platonism which puts beauty beyond definition. Both men introduce the problem of creativity into their writings but Leonardo, in order to cope with it formulates a metaphysic in which time and the relation of parts to wholes play a fundamental role. Nor is it unimportant to note that imagination—even in a primitive form—begins to play a significant role in Leonardo's thoughts concerning art.

Giorgio Vasari wrote of Leonardo as this man of "regal boldness and magnanimous bearing who "had so rare a gift of talent and ability" that "to whatever subject he turned his attention, however difficult, he presently made himself absolute master of it." To him have been ascribed inventions and "creations" of the most extraordinary kind and in the most diverse fields: warfare, engineering, hydraulics, anatomy, mathematics. It has been said [33] that Leonardo "revolutionized the casually discursive style of the late fifteenth century . . . [and] . . . fertilized European art with profound spirituality." The word "genius" has been used in discussing Leonardo perhaps as frequently as it has been applied to any single individual. What has usually been meant is that he is the first man to accomplish or to discover or understand or produce something—for example, to account for fossils found on the tops of mountains. The question here is not whether Leonardo did in fact invent or discover "first"—in most instances he did not do this—but that to him has attached the accolade of "genius" and this has primarily meant that what he produced is wholly new as a creation, inexplicable or beyond duplication.

It is paradoxical to read what men have said and their estimates of Leonardo in this vein and then to turn to da Vinci's own writings. On the main point, Leonardo is explicit:

[28] *Ibid.,* see below, pp. 275, 271.

[29] *Ibid.,* see below, p. 273.

[30] *Ibid.,* see below, pp. 270-71, 271-73, 273 et seq. and 275.

[31] *Ibid.,* see below, p. 279.

[32] *Ibid.,* see below, pp. 280, 278-79.

[33] David M. Robb and J. J. Garrison, *Art in the Western World,* pp. 669-671.

Man, he asserts,[34] "has no power to create any natural thing except another like himself, that is his children." His theory of art does not rest on a Platonic philosophy of ideas. Neither is it derived from a theory of beauty engendered by love, nor is it based upon a "communion" with beauty. "There is no certainty," he believes, "where one can neither apply any of the mathematical sciences nor any of those which are based upon the mathematical sciences."

Leonardo's rationalism is such, however, that he believes that the original mind can produce "new discoveries" and be stimulated to "new inventions." The main problem is one of determining how Leonardo established this hypothesis within the framework of his conception of mathematics and science.

We may best begin with certain general statements concerning "art," "perception," "imitation," and "imagination," which appear in Leonardo's works and which the reader will come upon in those selections[35] in which Leonardo compares and contrasts painting, poetry, and sculpture, as well as in scattered passages throughout his *Notebooks*. Leonardo evidently prefers to account for art in terms of perception rather than imagination and, in fact, adheres to a rather strict interpretation of art as imitation. Painting, for him, is "the sole imitator of all the visible works of nature." The true and scientific principles of painting "are understood by the mind alone and entail no manual operation." Nevertheless, he echoes Neo-Platonism and also holds that "Whatever exists in the universe . . . the painter has first in his mind and then in his hands. . . ." It is important to note that the artist is freer than other men, not only because he has in his mind what needs no manual perfecting but also because he can present "a base, ugly, monstrous thing," as Leonardo himself does in the sketch of the hanged man, Bernardo di Bandino. This is true because painting is the presentation of the works of nature in an imitative science which externalizes what is imitated. It is also a "harmonious concord," one in which the hands "design what is in the imagination."

If we move from this—a statement in fact concerning the artist's freedom to choose and make—to the philosophy of originality, it is clear that for Leonardo painting is also philosophy, the subject that deals with the "increase and decrease of motion of bodies and of their coloring, because an object as it recedes from the eye loses in size and color in proportion to the increase in distance."

The problem clearly is that of the continuity of science and art. Leonardo's conception of philosophy or science or art—and it would be difficult to distinguish them—is primarily a renaissance of Pre-Socratic naturalism. This naturalism is fortified by an explicit search for a mathematical statement of science. Of perspective, for example, he argues that it is "the bridle and rudder of painting." Leonardo's philosophy differs from its Greek prototype in its emphasis upon time but not in its subscription to the law of necessity in nature. It is in the context of this demand for a description of nature explained in terms of rigorous law that the question must be asked: how can thinking of this kind permit even the assumption of originality?

A closer inspection of the problem leads us directly to the ancient Atomists and to their founder, Leucippus. "Nothing occurs at random," the early thinker tells us, "but everything for a reason and by necessity." The echo of this is Leonardo's "Necessity is the mistress and guide of nature. Necessity is the theme and inventress of nature, the curb and law and theme." The "first mover" is apostrophized in the same terms: "Thou has not permitted that any force should fail of the order or quality of its necessary results." To the rigor of ancient

[34] F. McCurdy, *The Notebooks of Leonardo da Vinci,* 1.180.

[35] See below, pp. 282 et seq. The selections are from Irma A. Richter's edition of Leonardo da Vinci's *Paragone.*

Atomism, Leonardo weds the ancient mathematical ideal of Pythagoreanism: "No human investigation can be called true science without passing through mathematical tests. . . ." [36] There is no certainty in science when one of the mathematical sciences cannot be applied.

The adoption of the principle[37] of necessity and of the ideal of mathematical rigor does not mean for Leonardo that man ever wholly comprehends nature. Nature is full of infinite causes "that have never occurred in experience." [38] Nonetheless, experience, "the interpreter between formative nature and the human race, teaches how that nature acts among mortals," at which point the identical law holds, i.e., how that nature "being constrained by necessity cannot act otherwise than as reason, which is its helm, requires it to act."[39]

Nature, for Leonardo is "a spiritual power," specified as force. Leonardo emphasizes the function of the element of water, which he describes as the "driver of nature" and the "vital humour" of the "terrestrial machine," moved by water's own "natural heat." This is the world of Heraclitean change, of flux and becoming. At this juncture, the full force of the theory of mechanism is conveyed to us. Every action is caused by motion and movement is the cause of life. Not only does Leonardo subscribe to this mechanistic doctrine, but he also describes man in terms of the ancient rationalist theory of microcosm and macrocosm. Man is regarded by the ancients as a world in miniature, and with this Leonardo agrees: ". . . Man is composed of earth, water, air, and fire, his body resembles that of the earth; and as man has in his bones, the support and framework of his flesh, the world has its rocks, the support of the earth. . . . [40]

[36] See below, p. 259.

[37] This portion of this chapter is drawn from my "Leonardo da Vinci's Philosophy of Originality," *Bucknell Review*, Vol. 8 (No. 1, December 1958), pp. 1-10. Reprinted by permission of the Bucknell University Press.

[38] J. P. Richter, *The Literary Works of Leonardo*

[39] *Ibid.*, II, 1149.

The Atomists marked out the field and willed the problem of freedom and originality to their heirs. These, in their turn, could only introduce a declination of the atom to account for such deviations of movement as would tell us how compounded and perceptible objects appear—in contrast to imperceptible atoms—and how men may exercise freedom of will by a deviation of atoms at the moment of willing. It is evident, however, that such a chance motion of atoms destroys the necessity that as the central doctrine of the Atomism served as the model of classical philosophies of nature. certainly, Leonardo could not subscribe to such an inconsistency in theory.

It is important to notice in this connection that Lucretius, who adopts the theory of the Greek Atomists, criticizes the philosophy of Anaxagoras, another great Pre-Socratic thinker. He does so on the ground that Anaxagoras's theory, that all things are latent in all things, does not account for the fact that "the begetting bodies of matter do beget different things." The point is crucial for an understanding of Leonardo, who agrees with Anaxagoras. "Anaxagoras: Everything proceeds from everything, and everything becomes everything, and everything can be turned into everything else, because that which exists in the elements is composed of those elements." [41] Now it should be recalled that for Lucretius and other Atomists "no atom has any color." Only compounds of atoms are qualified as colors, odors, tastes, and sounds. Anaxagoras held, on the contrary, that the qualities of compounds—hot, cold, wet, and dry—can be what they are because the original seeds or elements also have these qualities. It is clear that Leonardo agrees with Anaxagoras rather than with Lucretius. "Force," for him, "is the same throughout the whole and the whole is in every part of it." [42]

[40] *Ibid.*, II, 929.

[41] *Ibid.*, II, 1473.

[42] *Ibid.*, II, 1136.

If we begin with the basic fact that for Leonardo no fundamental distinction may be drawn between element and compound, we are led directly to his theory of originality. We must, first of all, distinguish between mathematical abstractions and temporal events. If we do so, the issue that arises for the Atomists because atoms and compounds are distinguished need not arise. The second point is that the problem of originality should be examined at the level of compounds, i.e., of parts and wholes.

The first point is of interest, because as we have seen, Leonardo believes that the principal instrument of science is mathematics. Yet, though, as we have observed, "there is no certainty where one can neither apply any of the mathematical sciences nor any of those which are based upon the mathematical sciences," he cautions himself to "write of the nature of time as distinct from its geometry." The distinction leads Leonardo to differentiate between what I should call mathematical "objects" and "events" in time. Leonardo appears to hold that while what we might call "actual events" are subject to mathematical expression, they properly belong to two fields, that of mechanics ("the Paradise of mathematical science, because here we come to the fruits of mathematics") and that of perception (in which "all our knowledge has its origin").[43]

If we accept this explanation of Leonardo's position in terms of an "event-philosophy," the supporting argument is one which in its turn requires an analysis of time. Leonardo discusses "force" as a form of dynamism. Consistent with this is the hypothesis that motion *is,* but is not initiated. Division must stop "at the indivisible substance . . . and not continue to infinity." This point is insisted upon with great firmness: ". . . That which is divisible in fact is in potentiality also; but not all quantities which are divisible in potentiality are divisible in fact." A particular application of this assertion involves the mathematical point, "than which there can be nothing smaller." Neither in nature nor in the human mind can there be anything which originates the point, and the point is the beginning of geometry. The point has no part and, therefore, is not "divisible in fact." By analogy, the point in time may be compared to the instant. "An instant has no time," Leonardo writes; and the important inference is that, although the instant has no time and therefore is not "divisible in fact," time itself is made "of movements of the instant and instants are the boundaries of time." The conclusion follows: "The stroke of indivisible time is movement" and "no movement can be so slow that a moment of stability is found in it. . . . Movement can acquire infinite degrees of slowness."

Time, for Leonardo, is not reducible to moments of stability. Like the point, time is not divisible *ad infinitum.* As elements contain elements and force contains force and as neither can be reduced to nothing, time contains time and movement. We are in a world in which every action is an event caused by motion. Motion is the cause of life. Water is the vital moisture of the earthly machine. The doctrine of Heraclitus, that everything flows, is the rule of necessity in a world in which there are no exceptions to the law of nature.

The additional substantiation for the argument concerning "events" and the ground for considering events (called in Leonardo's writings "part" and "whole") are found in Leonardo's remarks concerning "nothingness." "Nothingness," he believes, is found only in time and speech.[44] It is found in time "between the past and the future and retains nothing of the present." It is found in speech "when the things spoken of do not exist or are impossible." It "does not extend among the things of nature."

[43] *Ibid.,* II, 1147.

[44] E. MacCurdy, *The Notebooks of Leonardo da Vinci* (London, 1938), I, 79.

Distinctions fail if "nothingness" is employed as a principle of nature, simply because in such a state of nature "the part is equal to the whole and the whole to the part" and the distinction between the divisible and the indivisible disappears.

In this treatment of "nothingness" there is again the echo of Anaxagoras's philosophy. "Neither is there a least of what is small but there is always a less," wrote the Pre-Socratic. In Leonardo's interpretation, we may speculate about "element" and "instant"; but in dealing with "actual events," if we attempt to get by continuous and repeated division to the existing elements or instants, our science is involved in paradox. If we try to show how the gap between element and compound is bridged, the law of necessity breaks down—as it does when Epicurus introduces the notion of declination of atoms. Philosophical explanation then becomes unintelligible because the basic distinction between mathematical constructs and temporal events is ignored.

At the level of compounds or of events which we experience in time, two classes claim especial attention. These are the classes of events called part and of the whole. They present a contrast among compounds, not between element and compound. The distinction between part and whole in the world of events is crucial, and upon it Leonardo rests his own case for originality. It is a distinction as old in rationalist philosophy as the speculations of Plato and Aristotle. And, it is against this rationalist background that Leonardo himself is able to assert that "necessity is the inventress" of nature, not its creator, and that man is a microcosm of the rational microcosm, rather than a creator created in God's image.

A similar rationalism characterizes Leonardo's approach to the problem of knowledge. His is a natural theory of perception. "To me," he writes, "it seems that all sciences are vain and full of errors that are not born of experience, mother of all certainty, and that are not tested by experience, that is to say, that do not at their origin, middle, or end pass through any of the five senses." Imagination is subordinated to direct sense perception. Imagination is to reality as "the shadow to the body" and cannot visualize such beauty as is seen by the eye.[45] This is true, he believes, because the eye receives the actual semblance or image of the object and transmits it through the senses to the understanding, where it is judged. Imagination, on the contrary, operates only to bring the image to the memory, where what is imagined "stops and dies . . . if the imagined object is not of great beauty. . . ."

What should the painter do? He ought to be solitary and "consider what he sees, discussing it with himself in order to select the most excellent parts of whatever he sees." He should act as a mirror; he will thus "seem to be a second nature." He is primarily free to choose, and he is original in this sense because Leonardo's preference for perception rather than imagination delivers us from the domain of speculation in which philosophy is used principally in a prohibitory way. Leonardo suggests in fact certain percepts, a new means of study, which he believes will be extremely useful in arousing the mind to various inventions. In doing so, however, he makes evident also the degree to which his own solution to the problem of originality by means of relating parts to whole may be judged in positive terms. What he writes concerning the new means of study is well known:

> I cannot forbear to mention among these precepts a new device for study which, although it may seem but trivial and almost ludicrous, is nevertheless extremely useful in arousing the mind to various inventions. And this is, when you look at a wall spotted with stains, or with a mixture of stones, if you have to devise some scene, you may discover a resemblance to various landscapes, beautified with mountains, rivers, rocks, trees,

[45] See below, p. 286.

plains, wide valleys and hills in varied arrangement; or, again, you may see battles and figures in action; or strange faces and costumes, and an endless variety of objects, *which you could reduce to complete and well-drawn forms.* And these appear on such walls confusedly, like the sound of bells in whose jangle you may find any name or word you choose to imagine.[46]

The significant phrase is "reduce to complete and well-drawn forms." Some of the contrast between "nothingness" and the world of events in time turns upon two points. In the notion of "nothingness," part and whole are indiscriminable; in the notion of "events," part and whole are decisively distinguished. Natural and artistic orderings in the world of events make a difference; and they do so, evidently, because in Leonardo's conception of the world "the part always tends to reunite with its whole in order to escape from its imperfection."[47] Of the painter's powers in the matter of reducing what he perceives "to complete and well-drawn forms," it suffices to quote Leonardo: "In fact, whatever exists in the universe, in essence, in appearance, in the imagination, the painter has first in his mind and then in his hands; and these are of such excellence that they are able to present a proportioned and harmonious view of the whole that can be seen simultaneously, at one glance, just as things in nature."[48]

This is da Vinci's solution to the problem of originality. Nature and man differ in that nature "is concerned only with the production of elementary things," whereas man, "nature's chiefest instrument," is he who with nature's elementary things, "produces an infinite number of compounds, although he has no power to create any natural thing except another like himself, that is his children."[49] But differ though they may in this respect, nature and man are inventive, not creative,[50] Both invent when they produce wholes from parts. Their perfection is achieved in harmonious, i.e., mathematically demonstrable wholes.

What is produced in this way is new in one sense; that is, a harmonious whole differs from its ingredient parts.[51] It appears that for Leonardo uniqueness as complete novelty is not and could not be intelligible. Part and whole do differ; moreover, the laws under which they operate differ. Yet both part and whole are intelligible. Parts do not originate miraculously, *ex nihilo*; wholes are made up of parts. Whether product of nature or of art, part and whole are demonstrable in mathematical terms. There is no break in nature. There is no dispute "as to whether twice three is more or less than six or whether the angles of a triangle are less than two right angles." "Proportion," Leonardo writes, "is not only found in figures and measurements, but also in sound, weight, time and position, and in whatever power which exists." Of painting, he maintains, that it "extends to the surface, colours, and shape of all things created by nature." More than this, painting "presents its subject to thee in one instant through the sense sight, through the same organ that transmits the natural objects to the mind; and at the same time the har-

[46] J. P. Richter, op cit I. 508.

[47] Ibid., II. 1142.

[48] See p. 287. Leonardo argues that "a poem which aims at the representation of perfect beauty has to describe separately each particular part that makes up the harmony of a picture; and its charm is no greater than that which would arise if in music each voice were to be heard separately at different times without producing any concord, or if a face were to be revealed bit by bit with the part previously shown covered up, so that we are prevented by our forgetfulness from composing any harmony of proportions because the eye cannot embrace the whole simultaneously in its field of vision."

[49] Quoted from Leonardo's writings on "Anatomy" (MacCurdy, I.180). It should be noted that nature is "continually producing" and that she "does not change the ordinary kinds of things which she creates."

[50] Leonardo remarks of alchemists that they have "never either by chance or deliberate experiment succeeded in creating the smallest thing that can be created by nature . . ." (MacCurdy, *Ibid.*, I.150–151.)

[51] Quoted by Irma A. Richter, *Paragone*, pp. 60–61.

monious proportions of the parts composing the whole react and delight the eye."

This, then, is the intelligible theory of originality which Leonardo employed systematically. He is not everywhere clear and consistent. Still, what seems to be an inconsistency may not be one in fact. For example, Leonardo, in formulating a canon of human beauty appears to invalidate the argument by presupposing the solution he seeks. He remarks that for our measurements we should choose "a man of three braccia in height and measure him by the rule I will give you." But we are also told that "If you tell me that I may be mistaken and judge a man to be well proportioned who does not conform to this division, I answer that you must look at many men of 3 braccia, and out of the larger number who are alike in their limbs one of those who are most graceful and take your measurements." We should not be too certain that this is an instance of putting the cart before the horse. We should recall the difference between mathematical objects and temporal events and also recall that Leonardo remarks of the mathematical sciences that ". . . as the geometrician reduces every area circumscribed by lines to the square and every body to the cube; and arithmetic does likewise with its cubic and square roots, these two sciences do not extend beyond the study of continuous and discontinuous quantities." What he insists upon is clear: ". . . [the mathematical sciences] do not deal with the quality of things which constitutes the beauty of the works of nature and the ornament of the world." Such beauty belongs to the dynamic world of temporal events, not to constructs of mathematics divorced from time.

Leone Ebreo

Born after 1460. Died 1520

A. Life

Leone Ebreo, a member of the distinguished Abrabanel family, the son of Don Isaac ben Judah Abrabanel, statesman, financier and scholar, was born in Lisbon *ca.* 1460. The family fled to Toledo in 1483, when Isaac Abrabanel was accused of complicity in a conspiracy led by the Duke of Braganza against King Alfonso. Isaac Abrabanel served Ferdinand and Isabella and raised money for the siege of Granada and for Columbus' first voyage.

With the exile of the Jews in 1492, the Abrabanel family settled in Naples, where Don Isaac again served a royal house and where his son became a physician. From Naples, Leone Ebreo travelled to various cities in Italy, returning to Naples to serve the "Great Captain," Don Gonsalvo de Cordoba.

In Italy, Leone Ebreo came to know some of the most distinguished scholars of his day, among them Pico della Mirandola and Mariano Lanzi, and studied Neo-Platonic philosophy in the various Academies of the day. Marsilio Ficino had completed his commentary on Plato's *Symposium* in 1483–84 and Leone wrote, 1501–2, his *Dialoghi d'Amore Composti per Leone Medico, de Natione Hebreo, et di poi Fatto Christiano*. The book was published in 1535—"rescued from the shade in which it was buried." Five editions in Italian followed within the next twenty years.

Leone Ebreo died not long after 1520.

B. Philosophy of Beauty and Art

The Philosophy of Love [52]

THE FIVE FACULTIES OF MIND, INCLUDING ART

SOPHIA. What and how many are these faculties of the intellect?

PHILO. I distinguish five: [53] Art, Prudence, Understanding, Science and Wisdom.

SOPHIA. How do you define them?

PHILO. Art is the faculty of producing things according to reason which require the

[52] *The Philosophy of Love,* translated by F. Friedeberg-Seeley and Jean H. Barnes. By permission of The Soncino Press Ltd. (London 1937). The first dialogue is entitled "On the Universality of Love".

[53] Compare Aristotle, *Nicomachean Ethics,* VI. See above, pp. 136 et seq.

work of our hands or physical labour: this includes all mechanical crafts to which our bodies are instrumental. Prudence is the faculty of acting according to reason, and consists in the practice of human morality, which includes all virtues springing from the will or from the two chief affects of the will: love and desire. Understanding is the faculty and principle which apprehends those axioms, which everyone naturally admits, as soon as he has grasped their sense, as that: good is to be pursued, evil to be shunned, or that: opposites cannot be predicated of the same subject, and others of the same kind, in which our intellectual faculty manifests its earliest activities. Science is the faculty of knowledge and inference based on the just mentioned principles; and under it we range the seven liberal arts, in which our intellect displays its medial activity. Wisdom is a faculty concerned alike with the principles and the conclusions touching all that exists; it alone attains to the highest knowledge of spiritual things, which the Greeks call θεολογία, i.e. Science of the Divine, and which is also called First Philosophy, as being the crown of all the sciences. And therein it is that our intellect acts according to its ultimate and most perfect nature (37) . . . .

MICROCOSM AND MACROCOSM

P. The head of Man, which forms the upper part of his body, is an image of the spiritual world. And this, according to godlike Plato,[54] with whom Aristotle does not disagree, comprises three degrees: soul, intellect and godhead. The soul is the source of the motion of Heaven, and oversees and governs the nature of the lower world, even as in that lower world Nature governs first matter. This corresponds to the brain in Man with its two powers of perception and voluntary movement: which are included in the sensitive soul: analogous to the Soul of the Universe, which directs and moves all bodies. Next, Man possesses potential intellect, which is the highest human form and corresponds to the intellect of the Universe, which embraces all angelic creatures. Lastly Man possesses active intellect, which, when conjoined with potential intellect, becomes actual, fulfilled with perfection and the grace of God, in union with His sacred Godhead. This it is, which corresponds in Man to the Divine Fount, from which all things proceed, to which all tend, and in which all rest as their last end. So much must suffice you, O Sophia, in this familiar discourse of ours, concerning the likeness of Man to the whole Universe, and how the ancients were right in calling him a microcosm. There are many other similarities of detail which would be redundant and alien to our purpose. Of what we have already said we shall make use when we discuss the birth and origin of love, and then you will understand that it is not for nothing that the members of the Universe love one another,—the exalted, the base; and the base, the exalted—since they are all parts of one body and contribute to one whole and perfection. (105)

[54] See Plato, *Timaeus*, quoted above pp. 93-95 et seq.

GOD, CREATOR AND BEGETTER

S. Tell me the meaning of this fable of Demogorgon's procreation.

P. It denotes the begetting or production of all things by God the supreme Creator. Eternity is said to have been His companion because He alone is the true Eternal, as He is and was and ever will be origin and cause of all things, while there is in Him no temporal succession. And they name Chaos too as His eternal companion—Chaos, which is, as Ovid explains, the indeterminate matter of all things promiscuously commingled, which the ancients held co-eternal with God. And from this He generated at His pleasure all created things, being their true father, as matter is the common mother of all things born. Therefore they predicate eternity and ingenerability only of the two parents of all things: their father and mother. But they held the father to be the main cause and the mother the accessory and concomitant cause; and it appears that such was the opinion of Plato too in the 'Timaeus' about the new generation of things produced by the Supreme God out of eternal indeterminate matter. In this, however, they might be criticised: for God, being the Creator of all things must have created too the matter from which they are produced. But we should understand them to mean, when they make Chaos the eternal companion of God, that it was created by Him from all eternity and that God created all other things freshly out of that Chaos at the beginning of time (according to the Platonic belief); and they call it 'companion', despite the fact that it was created, because it was created from all eternity and for ever attends on God. And being the Creator's Companion in the creation and production of all things, and His consort in engendering them (for it was produced immediately by God, but all other things by God in conjunction with this same chaos or matter), this chaos may with reason be called God's companion. Nevertheless it was created of God from all eternity, even as Eve, created of Adam, because his companion and consort and from these two all men sprang.

S. It does indeed appear that this legend was intended to symbolise the procreation of the Universe by omnipotent God, as father, and Chaos, or matter, as mother. (123-4). . . .

ON PLATO: OF EROS AND BEAUTY [55]

S. Tell me why love and desire must necessarily be predicated of God because others are defective; for nothing is wanting in Him, and truly I find this but rough justice.

P. You must know that this was why Plato maintained that the gods do not love, and that love is neither a god nor an Idea of the Supreme Intellect; for love, according to his definition, is the desire of something beautiful that is wanting, and cannot be ascribed to the gods, who have all beauty and lack for nothing. He therefore makes love to be a great spirit, intermediate between the gods and men, who conveys to the gods the good deeds and pure spirits of men, and to men the gifts and blessings of the gods, for all is carried on through the medium of love. And Plato's meaning is that love is not actually beautiful, for if he were, he would neither love or desire beauty (since we do not desire what we already possess); but that love is potentially beautiful and loves and desires actual beauty. He is therefore a mean between the beautiful and the ugly, or compounded of both, as potentiality is composed of being and privation (251). . . .

THE PECULIAR PROPERTY OF THE BEAUTIFUL

P. You are deceived if you believe that the beautiful and the good are in everything the same.

S. Do you then make some distinction between the good and the beautiful?

P. Certainly I do.

S. And how?

P. In that a man may desire the good for himself, or for another whom he loves, but the beautiful he may only desire exclusively for himself.

S. What reason have you in support of this?

[55] "On the Origin of Love," of which the following excerpts are a part, belongs to Dialogue III of *The Philosophy of Love.*

P. The reason is that the beautiful is the peculiar [property] of him who loves it; for what seems beautiful to one does not to another, and therefore what is beautiful to one is not beautiful to another. The good, on the contrary, is universal in itself, and a good thing is more often esteemed as good by many people. Therefore, he who desires the beautiful always desires it for himself because it is lacking in him; but he who desires the good may desire it for himself or for a friend who has need of it.

S. I in no way understand this distinction which you make between the beautiful and the good; for as you say that a beautiful thing may seem beautiful to one person and not to another, so I say, and with truth, that a thing may seem good to one person and not to another. And you must have observed how the wicked man esteems evil to be good, and therefore follows it, and how he shuns good because he holds it to be evil, and his actions are accordingly the opposite of those of the virtuous man. What is true of the beautiful is, therefore, also true of the good.

P. All men of sane judgment and upright and well-balanced character recognise the true nature of good and evil, just as all who have the normal faculty of taste find sweet food sweet to their palate and bitter food bitter; but to those of diseased and corrupted character and distempered appetite, good appears as evil and evil as good, just as sweet tastes bitter to the sick man and bitter is sometimes sweet to his palate. And as sweetness, although it may seem bitter, to the sick is no less sweet in reality, so good, although esteemed as evil by the diseased intellect, does not therefore cease to be truly and universally good.

S. And is not the beautiful the same?

P. Certainly not, for the beautiful is not the same for all men of sane judgment and virtuous character. For although a beautiful object is universally recognised as good, it will appear of such beauty to one virtuous man that he will be moved to love it, whereas to another it will seem good but not beautiful, nor will he be inspired to love it. And just as good and evil in their relation to the mind resemble sweet and bitter with respect to taste, so the beautiful and the non-beautiful are to the mind as the savoury or delectable and the non-savoury to the taste, and likewise the ugly and deformed to what is abhorrent and nauseous to the palate. Therefore as a dish which is sweet to everyone with a normal power of taste may yet be relished by one and not by another, so a person or object may be recognised as good by every virtuous person, but to one will be so beautiful that its beauty incites him to love, and to another will have no beauty whatsoever (256-7). . . .

NOT EVERY BEAUTIFUL THING IS GOOD

S. . . . I am still in doubt as to why you make such a difference between the beautiful which figures in Plato's definition of love, and the good by means of which Aristotle defined it; in fact, the beautiful and the good seem to me to be one and the same.

P. Therein lies your error.

S. How can you deny that every beautiful thing is good?

P. I do not deny it, but it is commonly denied.

S. How?

P. It is said that not every beautiful thing is good; for some things which seem beautiful are bad in reality, and some things which seem ugly are good.

S. This cannot be: because if a thing seems beautiful, in so far as it is beautiful it also seems good, and if it is truly good, it is truly beautiful. Again, if a thing seems ugly, that which is ugly in it also seems bad, and if in reality it is good, it is not truly ugly.

P. Your refutation is good, although, as I have told you, the beautiful has more part than the good in appearance, and the good more part than the beautiful in reality. My reply, however, is that although, as you say, every beautiful thing is good, either in essence or in appearance, it does not follow that everything is beautiful.

S. What kind of good thing is not beautiful?

P. Sweet and invigorating food and drink, a rare fragrance, a temperate clime,—you will not deny that these are good things, but you would not call them beautiful.

S. Although I would not actually call them beautiful, yet I believe that they are so; for if good things are not beautiful they must needs be ugly, and goodness and ugliness seem to me to be incompatible.

P. I wish that your reasoning were more accurate, Sophia. It is true that goodness and ugliness cannot exist together in respect of the same [subject or mode of a subject] but it is not true that everything which is not beautiful is ugly.

S. What is it then?

P. Like many good things, it is neither beautiful nor ugly; for you may see that amongst humans who are subject to beauty and ugliness, there are some who are neither beautiful nor ugly. Which is true, *a fortiori*, of many species of good things, which possess neither beauty nor ugliness; and such as the examples I have given you, which truly are subject to neither of these qualities. There is this difference, however, between persons and things: of persons we say that they are neither beautiful nor ugly when they are beautiful in one part and ugly in another, so that they are neither wholly beautiful nor wholly ugly; but the good things which I named to you have neither beauty nor ugliness in their whole or in their parts (262-3). . . .

GOD AS CREATOR EX NIHILO

S. Explain this doubt which has troubled men's minds concerning the time of the creation of the world, and we shall straightway understand the difficulty which depends upon it as to when love was born; for once it has been clearly stated you will find the way to a solution more quickly.

P. Listen, and I will tell you. All men grant that the supreme God, the father and creator of the world, is eternal without any beginning in time; but they are divided in their opinion concerning the creation of the world, whether it exists from eternity or was produced at some later time. Many philosophers hold that it was produced from eternity by God, and is like God in that it never had a temporal beginning, and amongst them, the great philosopher, Aristotle, and all the Peripatetics.

S. And what difference, then, would there be between God and the world if both existed from eternity?

P. The difference between them would still be great, because God would have been the creator from eternity, and the world would have been created from eternity: the one the eternal cause, the other the eternal effect: but the faithful and all those who believe in the sacred law of Moses hold that the world was not created from eternity, but *ex nihilo* in the beginning of time, and certain philosophers also seem to believe this. Amongst them is Plato, godlike in his wisdom, who, in the Timaeus, says that the world was made and begotten of God, and created out of chaos, that confused material which went to the making of all things. And though Plotinus, his follower, tries to reconcile him with the theory of the eternity of the world, saying the Platonic generation and production of the world is understood to be from eternity, yet Plato's words seem to assign to it a beginning in time, and it was understood thus by other illustrious Platonists. It is certainly true that he makes chaos, out of which everything is made, to be eternal, that is eternally created by God. And this the faithful do not believe; for they hold that up to the time of the Creation God alone existed without the world and without chaos, and that the omnipotence of God created all things out of nothing in the beginning of time. And indeed Moses nowhere gives any clear indication that he held matter to be coeternal with God. (277-8)

ACTUALITY, POTENTIALITY AND ARTIFICIAL THINGS

P. A perfection may only be lacking in actuality, but not in potentiality, and this is properly called lack; or it may be lacking both actually and potentially, and this is called absolute privation.

S. Give me an example of both of these.

P. Amongst artificial things you may see a piece of rough wood which lacks the form and beauty of a statue of Apollo, nevertheless it has these qualities potentially; water, however, lacks the form of the statue both actually and potentially, because a statue cannot be made of water as it can of wood. The former lack, which does not exclude potentiality, is called lack, the second, which covers actuality and potentiality is called absolute privation. And in nature, the first matter which is in fire and water, though actually lacking the form and essence of air, is not, however, potentially lacking in it, because air can be obtained from fire and from water; but it lacks the form of the stars, sun and moon, or of a heavenly being, not only actually but potentially, for first matter has no power or possibility of becoming heavenly or stellar. (321)

IN THE MIND OF GOD IS LAID UP THE PATTERN OF THE WHOLE UNIVERSE

P. . . . The foremost seat of love, therefore, is that first and most perfect created intelligence, which by reason of its love enjoys in union the highest beauty of its Creator, upon Whom it depends. From it the other intelligences and heavenly creatures are successively derived, descending from one degree to another down to the lower world, where man alone can be likened to it in his love of the divine beauty through his immortal intellect which the Creator vouchsafed to bestow upon his mortal frame. And it is only through the love of man for the divine beauty that the lower world, which is his domain, is united to the Divinity, the first cause and final end of the universe and the highest beauty universally loved and desired; for otherwise the lower world would be wholly cut off from God. Love, therefore, was born in the created universe in its angelic part, and was thence imparted to its other parts.

S. My mind would be contented with this account, and I could certainly grant that love was first born in the angelic world, where it reaches the peak of its desire, did it not seem strange to me to associate the smallest lack of beauty with the greatest knowledge and desire of what is lacking, as you affirm to be true of the intellectual world. For, as I have already told you, these things should logically be proportional and the knowledge and desire of the beauty which is lacking should be proportionate to the lack. And although, Philo, you with your subtle reasoning allege the contrary to be true and your arguments cannot be refuted, none the less your conclusion seems contradictory in that it makes the lack disproportionate to the desire and knowledge of that which is lacking. (313)

THE MIND OF GOD COMPARED TO THAT OF THE CRAFTSMAN

. . . And in the mind of God is laid up the pattern of the whole universe as the form of his work in the mind of the craftsman. But the Forms in the mind of God do not imply multiplication of His essence, nay, in respect of Him they are one: though they are multiplied in His work because it lacks the perfection of its Maker. Thus the Ideas of the Divinity are many relative to the created essences, but inasmuch as they are in the divine mind they are one with it. Averroes, therefore, maintains that divine beauty is directly impressed on all the intelligences which move the heavens, and that they are all immediately derived from it, together with their respective spheres, and all the Forms, first matter, and the human intellect, which alone are eternal in the lower world. Altogether, however, they all receive this impression directly, none the less it is graded according to whether the impression is greater or less. For the divine beauty is impressed on the first intelligence with greater nobility, spirituality and perfection, and with a greater resemblance to its pattern, than on the second, and on the second with greater perfection than on the third, and thus in continual succession down to the human intellect, which is the least of the intelligences. In corporeal substances the manner of its impression is inferior, for there it can be measured and divided; nevertheless it is impressed more perfectly on the first sphere than on the second, and so in succession until, reaching the sphere of the moon, it comes to first matter, whereon all the Ideas of the divine beauty are impressed, as they are on each of the intelligences, the motors and souls of the heavens, and on the wise and active human intellect. The impression, however, is not so clear and luminous, but overcast and subject to corporeal potentiality; and the impression on first matter bears the same relation to that on heavenly bodies as the impression on the potential human intellect to that on all the other actual intellects. And there is no difference between these two impressions save that in first matter all the formal Ideas are impressed potentially and corporeally, since it is the least of all corporeal substances, and in the potential intellect they are impressed potentially, yet not corporeally but spiritually or intellectually. To these successive degrees of impression of the divine beauty corresponds the love and desire of it in the intellectual world, passing from one degree to another, from the highest intelligence to the potential or lowest form of human intellect. And in the corporeal world, where love depends on the intellectual, it passes in the same way from the highest heaven down to first matter, which thus resembles each one of the heavenly spheres: for as these in the insatiable love which they have for divine beauty, and to increase their participation in and enjoyment of it, move in perpetual circular motion and know no rest, so first matter, in its insatiable desire to partake of divine beauty by the reception of forms, moves continually from one form to another in the unceasing circular motion of generation and corruption (336-7). . . .

THE FORM OF THE BEAUTIFUL IN THE MIND OF THE LOVER

S. . . . You say that the mother of love is the knowledge of the beautiful which is lacking, and on the other hand that she is first made pregnant of the form of the beautiful, and therefore desires and loves it. The contradiction is this: if the mind of the knower is pregnant of the beautiful he does not lack it; nay, he even possesses it, just as the woman who is with child can in no wise be called barren.

P. If the form of the beautiful were not in the mind of the lover in its aspect of beautiful, good and pleasant, he would never be able to love the beautiful; because those who are entirely without beauty have no desire for it, but he who desires it is not entirely without it, since he has knowledge of it and his mind is impregnated with the form of its beauty. But because he lacks the essential, to wit, perfect union with the beautiful, the desire of this all-important effect which he lacks comes to him, namely the desire of the enjoyment in union of the beautiful. And its form impressed on his mind incites him to desire, just as the woman with child looks for the day of her delivery that she may bring forth to the world the secret contents of her womb. Thus the mother of love, that is the lover, though wanting in perfect union with the beloved, is not entirely without the form and copy of its beauty, which causes her love and desire to union with the beauty which is lacking.

S. I like well what you say, but one difficulty remains. It seems that the mother and lover made pregnant by the beautiful father brings forth and conceives as her son the father himself; for you say that generation and child-birth are none other than the active enjoyment of union with this same father.

P. Your argument is subtle, but if it were yet more penetrating you would see the solution: that the act of enjoying union with the beautiful is not absolutely and entirely the same as the beautiful itself, though resembling it as the child his own father. For to this paternal likeness is joined a maternal impression of the knowledge of the lover. And the act would not be one of enjoyment if it were not, on the part of the knower and lover with respect to the beautiful, the object of his knowledge and love. In this way it is the true son of lover and beloved, and takes its material part from maternal cognition and its formal part from paternal beauty. And as Plato shows, love is a desire of that which is made pregnant of beauty to give birth to it in the likeness of the father; and such is the love not only of the mind but also of the body (372-3). . . .

THE ART OF THE CRAFTSMAN

P. Do not marvel, Sophia, that beauty should be that which makes every beloved thing to be loved and every lover to love, and that it should be the beginning, middle and end of all love, to wit, the beginning in the beloved, the middle in its repercussion on the lover, and the end in the enjoyment and union of the lover with its beginning, the beloved. For since the supremely beautiful is the most high Maker of the universe, the beauty of every created thing is the perfection of the work of the master Craftsman in its construction, and it is in respect of this quality that the thing made bears the greatest resemblance and relationship to the maker, and the created to the creator. And since this Divinity is diffused throughout the whole universe, it is not strange, but only natural, that it should be prior to every other being and should be that which makes its recipients lovable and those who are acquainted with them, lovers, desirous of partaking of them, and through their medium, of the divine beauty of the craftsman. And this is not only prior to the love in created things, whether corporeal, corruptible and heavenly, or incorporeal, spiritual and angelic; but also to the love which comes from God for His creatures: for this is none other than the wish that the beauty of His creatures may grow to be like the supreme beauty of their Creator in Whose image they were created. Beauty, therefore, must precede love in God, just as something beautiful and lovable is a prior condition of the existence of a lover.

S. I am considering your reply to my question, and although it seems to give you satisfaction it brings none to me, because I do not well understand the greatness of the dignity and excellence of this beauty, nor do I see how it is of such importance that it can be the beginning of all excellent and perfect things, as you allege. I wish that you would set my mind at rest concerning the essence of beauty. I remember well that once you defined it to me as grace which delights the mind that has knowledge of it, moving it to love; but I have still the same thirst to learn of the essence of this grace and of its supreme importance for the

Creator and for the whole universe, even as I desire to learn of the essence of beauty, defined in this way.

P. I also remember that I showed you part of the spiritual essence of beauty. For I told you that of the five external senses beauty is not apprehended by the three material, to wit, touch, taste, and smell (for the temperate qualities and the pleasures of sexual intercourse are not called beautiful, nor yet a taste sweet to the palate or a soft fragrance); but only by the two spiritual senses: that is, partly through hearing—fine speeches, excellent reasoning, beautiful verses, sweet music, and beautiful and harmonious melodies—and for the most part through the eyes, in beautiful forms and colours, regular patterns, and light in all its varied splendour and so on. This will show you that beauty must be a spiritual thing, abstracted from the body. I have also proved for you that the greatest beauty inheres in those faculties of the soul which are most exalted above the body, namely: firstly, in the imagination the seat of beautiful images and thoughts inventions; in a higher degree, in the understanding separated from matter, which finds beauty in learning, art, science, and the practice of virtue; and even more perfectly in the pure intellect, seat of the highest human wisdom, which is the true image of the highest beauty. This, therefore, may serve as an introduction in showing you how beauty is in itself foreign to matter and to the body, and how it is imparted spiritually to matter.

S. Yet the vulgar commonly attribute beauty principally to bodies, as proper to their essence, and it certainly seems to pertain more truly to them [than to things of the spirit]. And if incorporeal things are called beautiful it seems as if it were only metaphorically, as, for example, when they are called great after the manner of bodies, such as great mind, great intellect, great memory, great art, although the incorporeal is in itself non-dimensional, and can in truth be neither great nor small except [metaphorically] by comparison with corporeal objects, which are measurable. Beauty, likewise, seems to be a property of bodies and alien to incorporeal objects, in which it is only spoken of by imagery.

P. Although this is true of greatness because it is proper to quantity and quantity to the body, what reason have you to suppose that beauty is the same?

S. Besides the uses of speech which apply the word beauty to bodies, corporeal beauty is reputed by the vulgar to be the true beauty, and there is another reason: for beauty seems to be the proportion of the parts to the whole and the symmetry of the whole with its parts, as, indeed, many philosophers have defined it. Therefore it is a property of measurable body and of a whole composed of parts, and properly presupposes a body characterised by quantity. And if it is attributed to incorporeal things, such as harmony and reasoned oratory, this is because they, like the body, have parts of which they are composed in due proportion, and therefore they are termed beautiful, like the composite and proportioned body. In this way in the thoughts of the imagination, understanding and intellect, the relation of the parts to the whole is copied from the body, which is truly composed of proportionate parts which are called beautiful. Therefore the true home of beauty, as of magnitude, appears to be body, which is the proper substance for quantity and composition of parts.

P. The use of this word beautiful by the vulgar is in like proportion to the knowledge they have of beauty. For because they can understand no beauty save that apprehended by corporeal sight or hearing, they believe there to be none else besides this, unless it be fictitious or dreamed or imagined. But those whose mental vision is clear and who see far beyond corporeal things have a greater knowledge of incorporeal beauty than those whose pleasure is in sensual delights. And they know that the beauty of the body is of little price and mere outward show compared with that of the spirit; for corporeal beauty is the shadow and image of spiritual beauty, from which it is derived, and is none other than the splendour which the spiritual world imparts to the corporeal. They see also that the beauty of corporeal objects does not proceed from their corporeal or material nature: for then every body and every material thing would have the same mode of beauty, since matter and corporeality is the same in every substance; or again, the greatest would be the most beautiful, which frequently does not hold in reality, for beauty abhors extremes and the largest body, like the smallest, is misshapen. And [the wiser spirits] know that the beauty in bodies is derived from participation in that of the incorporeal beings higher than they; and the incompleteness of their participation gives the measure of imperfection of their beauty: so that deformity is inherent in body and beauty comes to it from its spiritual benefactor. The eyes of your body, Sophia, are therefore not sufficient for the perception of beautiful things: you must behold them with the eyes of the spirit and you will recognise true beauty such as the vulgar can never know. For as the physically blind cannot apprehend beautiful forms and colours, so those who are mentally blind can neither apprehend nor rejoice in the brightest spiritual beauties. And there is no pleasure in beauty where there is no knowledge of it, and he who tastes not of its waters is deprived of the sweetest of delights. If, then, corporeal beauty, which is but the shadow of the spiritual, so delights the beholder that it seizes control of all his [actions and thoughts] and not only enslaves him, but kills in him all desire to shake off his yoke, how much greater will be the effect of unsullied intellectual beauty, of which the corporeal is only the shadow and image, in those who are worthy to behold it! May you, therefore, Sophia, be numbered amongst those who dedicate themselves not to the shadow of beauty but to that which is its master, the highest beauty and gladness (375-9). . . .

THE BEAUTY OF ARTIFICIAL THINGS

S. I understand how all natural beauty in the corporeal world derives from the form or forms impressed upon its material substance; but I do not yet understand the origin of the beauty of artificial things, since it does not come from the spiritual or heavenly source of the natural forms, nor is it of their number and nature.

P. As the beauty of natural things is derived from natural forms, whether essential or accidental, so the beauty of artificial things derives from artificial forms. Therefore the definition of both kinds of beauty is the same.

S. And what is this definition?

P. Formal grace, which delights and moves him who apprehends it to love; and as this formal grace belongs to natural form in natural beauty so it belongs to artificial form in artificial beauty. If you would understand how the beauty of artificial objects comes from the form of the art [with which they are fashioned], imagine two pieces of wood of the same size, one carved in the form of a most beautiful Venus, the other untouched, and you will recognise that it is not the wood which makes the Venus beautiful, because the other similar piece of wood has no beauty, and therefore its form or artificial design must be its beauty and that which makes it beautiful. And as the natural forms of bodies are derived from an incorporeal and spiritual origin which is the soul of the world, and ultimately from the first divine intellect, in which two spiritual beings all forms first, exist with more exalted essence, perfection and beauty than in lower bodies subject to division; so the artificial forms are derived from the mind of the human artificer in which they first exist with greater perfection and beauty than in the object, [though it be] beautifully designed. And as when we ignore the material of an object the better to consider the beauty of its design we are left only with the Idea in the mind of the craftsman, so, subtracting matter from beautiful natural objects, only their ideal forms remain, pre-existing in the first intellect and thence imparted to the soul of the world. You will easily recognise, Sophia, how much more beautiful must be the single idea of a work of art in the mind of the artist than when it is dismembered and diffused throughout the material object: because union enhances all beauty and perfection, and division detracts from it, and the elements of the beauty of the wooden statue of Venus are separated, each standing on its own merit, so that the beauty of the created statue will be less vivid and weaker than that which is in the mind of the craftsman. For he conceives the form of his work with all its parts, the one setting off the other and increasing its beauty, and the beauty of the whole is contained in each part and that of each in the whole without discord or division. If, therefore, a man were to see the one and the other, he would know that the beauty of the design is beyond comparison with that of the beauty of the design is beyond comparison with that of the thing designed as being the cause of its beauty; and in the company of corporeal substance it decreases in perfection as the substance increases. For the greater the mastery of form over the roughness and ugliness of matter, the greater the beauty of the artificial object, and the greater the opposition of matter to form the less will be this beauty. It follows, therefore, that form is most beautiful without body, just as body is infinitely ugly without form. And natural things are of the manner of artificial things: because it is clear that those forms which make natural bodies beautiful exist with a far higher degree of beauty in the mind of the Creator and true architect of the world, that is in the divine intellect; for there they are all abstracted from matter, mutation or alteration, and from all manner of division and multiplication; and the beauty of the whole makes each one of them beautiful, and the beauty of each is found in the whole. These forms are also all contained in the soul of the world, which is its second artificer, though not with that measure of beauty which is in the first creative intellect, because in the soul they do not exist in pure union, but with some multiplication or ordered diversity, the soul being the mean between the creator and the created. In the world soul, however, they enjoy a far greater measure of beauty than in corporeal things, for there they exist spiritually in ordered unity, abstracted from matter, mutation and motion. And from the world soul emanate all the souls and natural forms in the lower world, distributed amongst the various bodies, and all subject to change and motion with successive generation and corruption, save only the rational human soul, which is free from corruption, mutation and corporeal motion (though with some intellectual motion and spiritual reception of the forms). For it is not combined with body like the other souls and natural forms, of which (as we said of the artificial) those which predominate in their association with matter are more beautiful in themselves and make the body which they inform more beautiful, and those which are submerged in matter are less beautiful in themselves and make the body which they inform defective. And the opposite is true of natural bodies, for the most beautiful is that which is elevated by its form and is the most subjected to it, and the ugly is that which resists its form and draws it down to itself. You, Sophia, will recognise from this discourse how beauty of lower natural and artificial bodies is none other than the grace which each has from its own form, whether essential or accidental, or from its artificial form. And you will understand that the forms in themselves, of one kind or the other, are more beautiful than that which they inform, and are far more excellent in beauty in their spiritual than in their corporeal being, even though their corporeal beauty is apprehended partly by corporeal vision and partly by corporeal hearing, unlike the spiritual which is apprehended by the eyes of the soul or of the intellect which are capable and worthy of such perception (385-8). . . .

. . . P. In beautiful artificial things, as you have heard, beauty is nothing more than the art of the craftsman diffused throughout the objects which he makes and throughout their several parts. Hence true and first artificial beauty is the knowledge and art pre-existing in the mind of the craftsman, upon which the beauty of artificial objects depends, as on their original Idea communicated to them all. In the same way, the beauty of all natural bodies is none other than the splendour of their Ideas, and therefore these are the true beauty by which all things are made beautiful (399). . . .

THE PRIORITY OF BEAUTY

P. Even did I grant you that the Idea of the universe contained many different Ideas of the parts in it, it is undoubtedly true that as the beauty of the universe is prior to the beauty of its parts, because the beauty of each is derived from that of the whole, so the beauty of the Idea of the whole universe is prior to the beauty of the Ideas of its parts. And, being the first, it is the true beauty, and by giving of itself to the other Ideas of the parts, it makes them beautiful in varying degrees. Moreover, the separate multiplication of the Ideas cannot be allowed, because although the first Idea of the universe, which is in the mind of its highest Creator, reflects the ordered multiplicity of its essential parts, this multiplicity does not therefore induce any essential or separable diversity in the Idea nor a dimensional or numerical division, as it does in the parts of the universe, but the first Idea is multifarious in such a way that it remains indivisible, pure and absolutely simple in itself, and in perfect unity, containing the plurality of all the parts of the created universe, together with the order of all their degrees, so that where one is there are they all, and the whole does not take away from the unity of the one (407). . . .

S. You have entirely satisfied me with this example of the reflection of the sun's rays by the two kinds of recipients, to wit, the gross and opaque and the subtle and diaphanous, which may be compared with the representation of the divine intellectual Idea in the created universe in the two recipient natures, the corporeal and the spiritual and intellectual. For the sun with its light, as you have already told me, is not only an example of the divine Idea and intellect, but a true copy made by it in its own image. Therefore as the sun imparts its shining beauty as a whole or separately to the various gross and opaque bodies, so the divine intellect imparts its ideal beauty as a whole and separately to all the essences of the different corporeal parts of the universe; and just as the sun imparts the light of its beauty with multiform unity to subtle and diaphanous bodies, so the divine intellect imparts its ideal beauty with multiform unity to the created intellects, whether human, heavenly, or angelic (410). . . .

BEAUTY AND LOVE

. . . Thus the all simple unity of highest beauty is hidden by reason of its lofty station above all created beings. Again, he invokes beauty that she may impart of herself to the bodies of the universe, not only by her visible presence, but by her voice and speech that she may be apprehended of the created intellect. And Solomon, in his love of the highest beauty, relates many other things in his Song of Songs pertaining to her which I must omit lest our discussion should never find its end. Only this will I tell you: that as he signified as ideal wisdom the highest beauty, so God, from Whom beauty emanates, he called the supremely beautiful, saying 'Behold, thou art fair, my beloved, yea, pleasant: also our bed is green', which means that He is not beautiful by participation like His creatures, but the first [of all being and the] creator of beauty. And he denotes the bond and union of the highest beauty with the supremely beautiful from which it emanates, saying that their bed is green, which means that God in conjunction with the highest beauty makes the whole universe beautiful, bringing forth fruits and flowers. Again, in Ecclesiastes, he declares beauty to be imparted to the universe in the words: 'He hath made everything beautiful in his time', which saying is taken from that of Moses: 'and God saw everything that He had made, and, behold, it was very good'. And God is said to have seen every part of the universe, that it was good, and the whole that it was very good, because good means beautiful; and therefore it is associated with vision, for goodness which is seen is always beauty. And He who sees it to be good is God, because it was the vision and supreme wisdom of God which made beautiful or imparted beauty to every part of the world and made the whole very beautiful and good through the joint impression of all divine wisdom and beauty (423). . . .

. . . . Those things which are exceedingly beautiful bestow beauty in like proportion upon their lovers. It is therefore right, Sophia, that we should set aside trivial beauty mingled with deformity and ugliness, such as that of matter and of the body, and only love it in so far as it leads to a knowledge and love of perfect spiritual beauty, and hate it and flee from it in so far as it prevents the enjoyment of pure spiritual beauty. And we ought principally to love the higher forms of beauty separated from formless matter and gross corporeality, such as the virtues and sciences, which are ever beautiful and devoid of all ugliness and defect; and here again we may ascend through a hierarchy of beauty, from the lesser to the greater and from the pure to the purest, [as if a ladder were set up] leading to the knowledge and love, not only of the most beautiful intelligences, souls and motors of the heavenly bodies, but also of the highest beauty and of the supremely beautiful, the giver of all beauty, life, intelligence and being. We may scale this ladder only when we put away earthly garments and material affection, not only despising their meaner beauty in comparison with the highest, upon which they and others more exalted depend, but also hating them and fleeing from them, since they prevent us from attaining to true beauty in which our good consists. To behold this beauty we must put on the spiritual garments of inviolacy and purity, after the manner of the high priest who, on the Day of Atonement when he enters into the Holy of Holies, puts off his vestments of gold, studded with precious gems, and clothed in white raiment and spotless apparel, implores divine mercy and pardon. For when we have attained to a knowledge of the highest beauty and of the supremely beautiful, our love of it will be of such strength that we shall forsake all else for the love of these two, with all the powers of our intellect united in His pure mind. Thus we shall become exceeding beautiful, as lovers of the supremely beautiful and participants of its beauty, and we shall enjoy sweet union with it, which is the ultimate happiness and desired beatitude of the enlightened soul and pure intellect. For the supremely beautiful being our father, first beauty our mother, and the highest wisdom our native land whence we are sprung, our good and our happiness consist in returning to that bourn and in being gathered to our parents, rejoicing in sweet sight of and joyous union with them.

S. God grant that we fall not by the way

and are not cut off from such divine joy, but that we may be amongst the elect who attain to ultimate happiness and final beatitude. You have no less contented me with your answer to my fourth question concerning the parents of love than with your solution of the other three, to wit, if, when and where love was born. Now only my fifth question remains why love was born in the universe ,and to what end it was produced.

P. Since you have already received the answer to your four previous questions concerning the birth of love, a lengthy reply is not needed to this last one. We shall readily understand the end for which love was born in the universe if we consider the end of individual love between humans and other creatures. The end of all love is the pleasure of the lover in the beloved, just as the end of hatred is to avoid the pain which the hated object would produce. Because the end which is obtained by love is contrary to that avoided by hatred, and so the means to attain these ends are contrary. And the means of love are hope and pursuit of pleasure, and those of hatred, fear and flight from pain. Therefore if the end of hatred is to separate oneself from grief as bad and ugly, the end of love is approach to pleasure as good and beautiful (426-7). . . .

GOD AS CREATOR THROUGH THE MEDIUM OF LOVE

S. I now understand that your opinion is indeed the true one, and that the end of all individual love is the pleasure of the lover in union with the beloved. Will you not increase my knowledge still further, and tell me what is the universal end for which love was born in the universe? For it will not be so simple to prove that pleasure is its end as it is of the love of men and animals one for another.

P. It is fully time to answer your question. You know at any rate that the world was produced by the supreme Creator through the medium of love. For He, as the supremely good, beholding His immense beauty and loving it, and she likewise Him as the supremely beautiful, He created and engendered in her likeness the beautiful universe; for the end of love, as Plato says, is birth in the beautiful. The universe, therefore, having been produced by its supreme Creator in the likeness or image of His immense wisdom, His love was born towards this universe, not as of the imperfect for the perfect, but as of the supremely perfect for the lower and less perfect and as of the father for the son and the cause for its single effect. So the end of this love is not that the lover may acquire the beauty which he lacks, nor even find pleasure in union with the beloved, but that the latter may acquire that perfection which it would lack were it not imparted to it through the love of the lover, and that the divine Lover may take pleasure in the increased beauty of His beloved, the universe, which increase is the result of the divine love. And the same is true of the four cases of the love of the cause for its effect, to wit: of the superior for the inferior, the father for the son, the master for the disciple, and all benefactors for those whom they benefit; for their love is the desire that those inferior to them may attain to the highest degree of perfection and beauty. And it is in the attainment thereof by the beloved that the lovers delight, and it is this pleasure in the perfection and beauty of the latter which is the end of their love.

S. I remember you told me of this distinction between the love of the superior for the inferior and the inferior for the superior, and your account was almost identical in matter if not in form. And I know that although the end of each of these loves is the pleasure of the lover in the acquired beauty of the beloved, yet the love of the inferior for the superior is for the sake of the beauty of the superior and beloved which he lacks, and the end of this love is the pleasure of the lover in union with the beauty of the superior and beloved which is lacking in him; whereas the love of the superior for the inferior is for the sake of the beauty which is lacking in the inferior and beloved, and the lover rejoices in the acquisition of this beauty by the beloved as in the end of his love, just as the beloved rejoices in his possession of that beauty and union with it, which before was lacking in him and therefore the object of his love and desire. I know, moreover, that the love of the highest Creator for the created universe is of this kind (440-41). . . .

DIVINE AND MORTAL LOVE

P. . . . Even as this activity is highest in being the union of the universe with the highest beauty, so the pleasure to which it gives rise, which is the true end of love, is immeasurably great and the peak of all pleasure of created beings. And I have already told you that the pleasure of the lover is none other than union with the beauty which he loves. When that beauty is finite the pleasure is finite, and greater or less according to the measure of beauty. And because it is [in]finite in the love of the created universe, that is its intellectual part, for the highest good, the end of that love is boundless and infinite pleasure; and this is the end of the love of the whole created world, and the reason why love was born in the universe. For without the love and desire to return to the highest beauty nothing could have been created or gone forth from the Divinity; and without paternal love and procreative desire similar to that of God one degree of being could not have sprung from or been produced by its superior in an ever descending hierarchy from the Divinity to first matter. For it is paternal or creative love which governs the whole of the first half circle from the highest being down to the lowest chaos. In the same way created beings could never return to union with the Divinity, from which the most distant point is first matter, nor could they acquire the highest pleasure in which the perfection and happiness of the whole world consists, were it not for the love and desire for this very return as for their ultimate perfection, leading to the final and actual happiness of the universe. Therefore, as the end of the productive love of the first half circle was the love for 'return' of the second, and the end of the latter the ultimate perfection and beatitude of the universe, it follows that love was born in the universe to lead it to its final happiness.

S. I have now true knowledge that love was born in the universe, firstly that it might be created in ordered succession, and secondly that it might be blessed with the highest pleasure, by procuring its union with the supreme good, its first beginning. With this I am satisfied in respect of my fifth question of the end for which love was born in the universe. Three things only relating to this matter I would still know. Firstly, although pleasure must be the end of natural or sensuous love, to wit, of that love which proceeds from the soul and faculties of the body, yet it does not seem meet that it should also be the end of intellectual love. For pleasure is an affection, and the intellect separated from matter is not passive, nor is it right that it, and still less the angelic and divine intellects, should be subject to any affection. Pleasure, therefore, should not be the true end of their love, so that it cannot be the common end of all love, as you have said. Secondly, although the end of all the love for 'return' is pleasure, as you have told me, this would not seem to be the end of creative love: for no one finds pleasure in joining himself to something less beautiful than himself, and therefore the end of productive love would seem rather to consist in giving and imparting beauty where it does not exist than in taking its own pleasure, as you have asserted, since there can be no pleasure where there is no beauty. Thirdly, you told me that the love which the Creator bears the created universe is that which leads it back to its perfection, just as the love which He has for His own beauty is the cause of its creation; and now you tell me that the love which leads it back to its true perfection is that which the universe has, through its intellectual part, for the highest divine beauty. The love of God for the universe, therefore, is not that which brings it to its perfection, but that of the universe for God. Solve these three difficulties for me, and I will acknowledge that you have fulfilled the promise you made to tell me of the birth of love.

P. I would not remain in debt for so small a sum. Sensuous pleasure, like sensuous love, is an affection of the sensitive soul, save that love is the first of its affections and pleasure the last and the end of that love. Intellectual pleasure, however, is not an affection in the intellect which loves. And if you allow that there can be love in the intellectual beings which is not an affection, you must also allow that they can have pleasure without affection; and this is the end of their love, and more perfect and abstracted than the activity of love itself.

S. If the love and pleasure of intellectual beings are not affections, then what are they?

P. They are intellectual activities (as I have told you), free from all natural affection, although we have no other name to give them, because similar activities are called affections in sensible bodies. And I have already told you that love in the created intellect is the advance from first intellection of the beautiful object of mind to that of final and perfect union with it; and the pleasure of the intellect is none other than this same unitive intellection of the highest intelligible beauty.

S. And what are love and pleasure in the divine intellect?

P. Divine love is the inclination of the most beautiful wisdom of the Divinity towards the likeness of its own beauty, to wit, the universe created by it, together with its return to union with that supreme wisdom; and divine pleasure is the perfect union of the image of God with Himself as Creator: wherefore David says, 'The Lord shall rejoice in His works' (454-6). . . .

THE PROCREATIVE LOVE OF GOD

. . . For the procreative love of the father for the son is not love of the son, who does not yet exist, but the love of himself which causes the birth of the son; for he desires to become a father to increase his own perfection, begetting a child in his own image. There is another and second love, that of the son when he is born, and this it is which makes the father to nurture and raise him up and educate him in every possible accomplishment. In the same way the procreative love of God for the universe is not the only love which He bears the universe, but another prior to it, to wit, the love of Himself, desirous of imparting this supreme beauty to the universe created by Him in His image and likeness. For there is no perfection or beauty which does not grow when it is communicated: thus the tree which bears fruit is always more beautiful than that which is barren, and running waters leaping from their fountains are worthy of greater admiration than those which remain enclosed and imprisoned within banks. When the universe was created God's love for it also came into being, as that of the father for the newborn son. The end of this love was not only to preserve the universe in its first created state, but also, and more truly, to guide it to its ultimate perfection in blissful union with divine beauty.

S. Although by reason of the paternal likeness divine love for the universe seems to be that which leads it to its end and final perfection, none the less this seems to be the true function of the love which the universe bears for the divine beauty, since it is thereby inclined to union with that beauty in which its happiness lies (459). . . .

P. . . . Since our soul is formed in the image of the highest beauty, and by its nature desires to return to its divine origin, it is ever impregnated with this natural desire. When, therefore, it perceives a beautiful person whose beauty is in harmony with itself, it recognises in and through this beauty, divine beauty, in the image of which this person also is made. And the image of this beloved in the mind of the lover quickens with its beauty the latent divine beauty which is the very soul, and gives it actuality, as if it were to receive it from the beauty of the divine original itself. Therefore the [image] is made divine and its beauty is increased, even as divine beauty is greater than human. And the love of it becomes so intense, ardent and active that it steals away sense, imagination and the whole mind, as if it were divine beauty withdrawing the human soul to itself in contemplation. And the image of the beloved person is revered in the mind of the lover as divine in so far as the beauty of the soul and body of the beloved is more excellent and more similar to divine beauty and as it reflects the highest wisdom more clearly. This is conditioned by the nature of the mind of the lover which receives the image: for if the divine beauty is so latent and sunk so deep that it is wholly overwhelmed by matter and corporeality, although the beloved be of surpassing beauty it can hardly be made divine, because so little of this divinity shines forth in the receiving mind. Nor can that mind perceive how great is the beauty of the beautiful beloved. Therefore it rarely happens that souls of low estate, immersed in matter, bear love for great and true beauty, and that their love is of high price; but when a person of the highest beauty is loved by a soul full of light and raised above matter, in which the highest divine beauty shines forth with exceeding brightness, then does this person truly assume the cloak of divinity in the mind of the lover who for ever adores her as divine and is filled with most intense, mighty and ardent love for her. Now my love for you, Sophia, confers a large measure of the divine upon that corporeal and spiritual beauty which you bear within you. And although the clarity of my intellect is not proportionate to such an end, nor capable of bestowing that divinity upon your image which is its due, yet the excellence of your beauty supplies this deficiency in my darkened mind (465-6). . . .

Leonardo da Vinci

1452–1519

A. Life

Possessed of one of the most extraordinary and inventive minds in the Renaissance, Leonardo da Vinci wrote on as wide a variety of subjects as his activities as painter, engineer, geologist, anatomist, astronomer, and mathematician extended.[56] He was born on April 15, 1452, in Vinci, near Empoli, the illegitimate son of Piero, a notary, and a servant-maid. He was trained as a painter in the studio of Andrea Verrocchio and became a member of the Florentine Guild in 1472. After 1477, Leonardo probably worked for his patron, Lorenzo de Medici. In 1479, Leonardo made a drawing of Bernardo Bandini, who had been hanged for the murder of Giuliano de Medici and in 1481 he painted an Adoration for the Monastery of San Donato.

Leonardo spent the years 1482–1499 in Milan, where his work is principally associated with the name of Lodovico Sforza, Il Moro, Duke of Milan. There he served as engineer in the Valley of the Po River, and there he produced the *Last Supper*. Upon the French invasion of Milan, Leonardo returned to Florence, acting as a military engineer for Cesare Borgia. Between 1500 and 1504, he painted the *Mona Lisa,* the portrait of the wife of a Florentine official. Da Vinci returned to Milan in 1506 and served under Francis I of France as painter and engineer. He died May 2, 1519, at Cloux, near Amboise, in France.

Leonardo's *Notebooks* are in his own words, "a collection without order, taken from many papers, which I have copied here, hoping afterwards to arrange them according to the subjects of which they treat. . . ." They were never arranged nor ordered by Leonardo. Jean Paul Richter's *Literary Works of Leonardo da Vinci* attests at once to the enormous skill and intelligence of the great Renaissance figure and the extraordinary skill of the editor.

[56] Selections from da Vinci's writings are quoted below, pp. 282 et seq.

B. Philosophy of Art

Book on Painting of Leonardo da Vinci

First part[57]

1. IS PAINTING A SCIENCE OR NOT?

Science is an investigation by the mind which begins with the ultimate origin of a subject beyond which nothing in nature can be found to form part of that subject. Take, for example, the continuous quantity in the science of geometry: if we begin with the surface of a body we find that it is derived from lines, the boundaries of this surface. But we do not let the matter rest there, for we know that the line (in its turn) is terminated by points, and that the point is that (ultimate unit) than which there can be nothing smaller. Therefore the point is the first beginning of geometry, and neither in nature nor in the human mind can there be anything which can originate the point. . . .

No human investigation can be called true science without passing through mathematical tests, and if you say that the sciences which begin and end in the mind contain truth, this cannot be conceded, and must be denied for many reasons. First and foremost because in such mental discourses experience does not come in, without which nothing reveals itself with certainty.

[57] *Paragone: A Comparison of the Arts by Leonardo da Vinci,* Irma A. Richter, editor and translator. London-New York, Oxford University Press, 1949. By kind permission of Gisela M. A. Richter.

2. THE FIRST BEGINNING OF THE SCIENCE OF PAINTING

The science of painting begins with the point, then comes the line, the plane comes third, and the fourth the body in its vesture of planes. This is as far as the representation of objects goes. For painting does not, as a matter of fact, extend beyond the surface and it is by these surfaces that it represents the shapes of all visible things.

5. WHERETO THE SCIENCE OF PAINTING EXTENDS

The science of painting deals with all the colours of the surfaces of bodies and with the shapes of the bodies thus enclosed; with their relative nearness and distance; with the degrees of diminutions required as distances gradually increase; moreover, this science is the mother of perspective, that is, of the science of visual rays.

Perspective is divided into three parts, of which the first deals with the line-drawing of bodies; the second with the toning down of colours as they recede into the distance; the third with the loss of distinctness of bodies at various distances.

Now the first part which deals only with lines and contours of bodies is called drawing, that is to say, the figuration of any body. From it springs another science that deals with shade and light, also called chiaroscuro, which requires much explanation. But the science of the visual rays has given birth to the science of astronomy, which is simply a form of perspective since it entirely depends on visual rays and sections of pyramids.

6. WHICH SCIENCE IS MECHANICAL AND WHICH IS NOT?

They say that knowledge born of experience is mechanical, but that knowledge born and consummated in the mind is scientific, while knowledge born of science and culminating in manual work is semi-mechanical. But to me it seems that all sciences are vain and full of errors that are not born of experience, mother of all certainty, and that are not tested by experience, that is to say, that do not at their origin, middle, or end pass through any of the five senses. (For if we are doubtful about the certainty of things that pass through the senses how much more should we question the many things against which these senses rebel, such as the nature of God and the soul and the like, about which there are endless disputes and controversies. And truly it so happens that where reason is not, its place is taken by clamour. This never occurs when things are certain. Therefore, where there are quarrels, there true science is not; because truth can only end one way—wherever it is known, controversy is silenced for all time, and should controversy nevertheless again arise, then our conclusions must have been uncertain and confused and not truth which is reborn.) All true sciences are the result of experience which has passed through our senses, thus silencing the tongues of litigants. Experience does not feed investigators on dreams, but always proceeds from accurately determined first principles, step by step in true sequences, to the end; as can be seen in the elements of mathematics founded on numbers and measures called arithmetic and geometry, which deal with discontinuous and continuous quantities with absolute truth. Here no one argues as to whether twice three is more or less than six or whether the angles of a triangle are less than two right angles. Here all argument is destroyed by eternal silence and these sciences can be enjoyed by their devotees in peace. This the deceptive purely speculative sciences cannot achieve. If you say that these true sciences that are founded on observation must be classed as mechanical because they do not accomplish their end, without manual work, I reply that all arts that pass through the hands of scribes are in the same position, for they are a kind of drawing which is a branch of painting.

Astronomy and the other sciences also entail manual operations although they have their beginning in the mind, like painting, which arises in the mind of the contemplator but cannot be accomplished without manual operation. The scientific and true principles of painting first determine what is a shaded object, what is direct shadow, what is cast shadow, and what is light, that is to say, darkness, light, colour, body, figure, position, distance, nearness, motion, and rest. These are understood by the mind alone and entail no manual operation; and they constitute the science of painting which remains in the mind of its contemplators; and from it is then born the actual creation, which is far superior in dignity to the contemplation or science which precedes it.

7. WHICH SCIENCE IS THE MORE USEFUL AND IN WHAT DOES ITS USEFULNESS CONSIST?

That science is the most useful whose fruit is most communicable, and conversely, that is less useful which is less communicable. The result of painting is communicable to all generations of the universe, because it depends on the visual faculty; the way through the ear to our understanding is not the same as the way through the eye; because the latter way has no need of interpreters for the various languages as letters have, and thus painting gives satisfaction at once to mankind, in the same way as things, created by nature, and not only to mankind but also to animals, as was shown by a painting representing the father of a family which was caressed by infants who were still in their swaddling clothes, and also by the dog and the cat in the same house—a spectacle marvellous to behold.

Painting presents the works of nature to our understanding with more truth and accuracy than do words or letters; but letters represent words with more truth than does painting. But we affirm that a science representing the works of nature is more wonderful than one representing the works of a worker, that is to say, the works of man, such as words in poetry and the like, which are expressed by the human tongue.

7a. All sciences which end in words are dead the moment they come to life, except for their manual part, that is to say, the writing, which is the mechanical part.

8. OF IMITABLE SCIENCES

In imitable sciences the student can attain equality with the master and can produce similar fruit. These sciences are useful to the imitator, but they are not of such excellence as those which cannot be passed on in heritage like other goods. Among inimitable sciences painting comes first. It cannot be taught to those not endowed by nature like mathematics, where the pupil takes in as much as the master gives. It cannot be copied like letters where the copy has the same value as the original. It cannot be moulded as in sculpture where the cast is equal in merit to the original; it cannot be reproduced indefinitely as is done in the printing of books. It remains peerless in its nobility; alone it does honour to its author, remaining unique and precious; it never engenders offspring equal to it; and this singleness makes it finer than the sciences which are published everywhere. Do we not see great kings of the East go about veiled and covered because they think they might diminish their fame by showing themselves in public and divulging their presence. Do we not see that pictures representing deity are kept constantly concealed under costly draperies and that before they are uncovered great ecclesiastical rites are performed with singing to the strains of instruments; and at the moment of unveiling the great multitude of peoples who have flocked there throw themselves to the ground, worshipping and praying to Him whose image is represented for the recovery of their health and for their eternal salvation as if the Deity were present in person.

The like does not happen with any other science or any other work of man; and if you assert that it is not due to the merit of the painter but to the subject represented we answer that if that were so men might remain peacefully in their beds provided their imagination were satisfied instead of going to wearisome and perilous places as we see them doing constantly on pilgrimages. And what necessity impels these men to go on pilgrimages? You certainly will agree that the image of the Deity is the cause and that no amount of writing could produce the equal of such an image either in form or in power. It would seem, therefore, that the Deity loves such a painting and loves those who adore and revere it and prefers to be worshipped in this rather than in another form of imitation, and bestows grace and deliverance through it according to the belief of those who assemble in such a spot.

9. HOW PAINTING EMBRACES ALL THE SURFACES OF BODIES AND EXTENDS TO THESE

Painting extends only to the surface of bodies; perspective deals with the increase and decrease of bodies and of their colouring, because an object as it recedes from the eye loses in size and colour in proportion to the increase of distance.

Therefore painting is philosophy, because philosophy deals with the increase and decrease through motion as set forth in the above proposition; or we may reverse the statement and say that the object seen by the eye gains in size, importance, and colour as the space interposed between it and the eye which sees it diminishes.

Painting can be shown to be philosophy because it deals with the motion of bodies in the promptitude of their actions, and philosophy too deals with motion.

10. PAINTING EMBRACES THE SURFACES, SHAPES, AND COLOURS OF NATURAL BODIES, AND PHILOSOPHY ONLY EXTENDS TO THEIR NATURAL PROPERTIES

Painting extends to the surfaces, colours, and shapes of all things created by nature; while philosophy penetrates below the surface in order to arrive at the inherent properties, but it does not carry the same conviction, and in this is unlike the work of the painter who apprehends the foremost truth of these bodies, as the eye errs less.

12. WHY PAINTING IS NOT NUMBERED AMONG THE SCIENCES

As the scribes have had no knowledge of the science of painting they could not assign to it its rightful place or share; and painting does not display her accomplishment in words; therefore she was classed below the sciences, through ignorance—but she does not thereby lose any of her divine quality.

And truly, it was not without reason that they did not confer honours upon her, since she proclaims her own glory without the help of tongues in the same way as do the excellent works of nature. And it is not the fault of painting if painters have not described their art and reduced it to a science, she is not the less noble for that, since few painters profess to be writers because life is too short for the understanding of art. . . .

13. HE WHO DEPRECATES PAINTING LOVES NEITHER PHILOSOPHY NOR NATURE

If you despise painting, which is the sole imitator of all visible works of nature, you certainly will be despising subtle invention which brings philosophy and subtle speculation to bear on the nature of all forms—sea and land, plants and animals, grasses and flowers—which are enveloped in shade and light. Truly painting is a science, the true-born child of nature. For painting is born of nature; to be more correct we should call it the grandchild of nature, since all visible things were brought forth by nature and these, her children, have given birth to painting. Therefore we may justly speak of it as the grandchild of nature and as related to God.

13a. Whoso speaks ill of painting speaks ill of nature, because the works of the painter represent the works of nature, and therefore such a detractor lacks feeling.

16. OF THE EYE

The eye whereby the beauty of the world is reflected by beholders is of such excellence that whoso consents to its loss deprives himself of the representation of all the works of nature. Because we can see these things owing to our eyes the soul is content to stay imprisoned in the human body; for through the eyes all the various things of nature are represented to the soul. Who loses his eyes leaves his soul in a dark prison without hope of ever again seeing the sun, light of all the world; and how many there are to whom the darkness of night is hateful though it is of but short duration; what would they do if such darkness were to be their companion for life?

Certainly there is nobody who would not prefer to lose his hearing and his sense of smell rather than the sight of his eyes. Although in consenting to the loss of hearing he relinquishes all knowledge that depends on words; he only consents to it in order not to lose the beauty of the world, which consists of the surfaces of the bodies with both their accidental and their natural qualities as reflected in the human eye.

17. SIMILARITY AND DIFFERENCE BETWEEN PAINTING AND POETRY

The imagination is to reality as the shadow to the body that casts it and as poetry is to painting, because poetry puts down her subjects in imaginary written characters, while painting puts down the identical reflections that the eye receives, as if they were real, and poetry does not give the actual likeness of things, and does not, like painting, impress the consciousness through the organ of sight.

18. A COMPARISON BETWEEN POETRY AND PAINTING

The imagination cannot visualize such beauty as is seen by the eye, because the eye receives the actual semblances or images of objects and transmits them through the sense organ to the understanding where they are judged. But the imagination never gets outside the understanding (sensus communis); it reaches the memory and stops and dies there if the imagined object is not of great beauty; thus poetry is born in the mind or rather in the imagination of the poet who, because he describes the same things as the painter, claims to be the painter's equal! But in truth he is far removed, as has been shown above. Therefore, in regard to imitation, it is true to say that the science of painting stands to poetry in the same relation as a body to its cast shadow; but the difference is even greater; because a shadow penetrates through the eye to the understanding while the object of the imagination does not come from without but is born in the darkness of the mind's eye. What a difference between forming a mental image of such light in the darkness of the mind's eye and actually perceiving it outside the darkness!

If you, poet, had to represent a murderous battle you would have to describe the air obscured and darkened by fumes from frightful and deadly engines mixed with thick clouds of dust polluting the atmosphere, and the panicky flight of wretches fearful of horrible death. In that case the painter will be your superior, because your pen will be worn out before you can fully describe what the painter can demonstrate forthwith by the aid of his science, and your tongue will be parched with thirst and your body overcome by sleep and hunger before you can describe with words what a painter is able to show you in an instant. In his picture only the soul is wanting; each figure is represented so as to show completely that part which faces the given direction. What long and tedious work it would be for poetry to describe all the movements of the fighters in such a battle and the actions of their limbs and their ornaments. This is accomplished with great directness and truth in painting and placed before you, and in such a picture only the sound of the engines, the shouts of the terrifying victors, and the cries and wailing of the terrified victims are wanting, and neither can the poet convey these to the sense of hearing.

It may be said, therefore, that poetry is the science for the blind and painting for the deaf. But painting is nobler than poetry inasmuch as it serves the nobler sense.

The only true office of the poet is to invent the words of people who are conversing together—only then can he transmit to the sense of hearing an equivalent of nature, for the words created by the human voice are natural phenomena in themselves.

But in everything else he is outstripped by the painter. The many-sidedness which painting commands is incomparably greater than can be attained by words because the painter can express an infinite variety of things which words cannot describe for want of appropriate terms. Now do you not see to what an abundance of inventions the painter may resort if he wishes to portray animals or devils in hell?

19. THE PAINTER IS LORD OF ALL TYPES OF PEOPLE AND OF ALL THINGS

If the painter wishes to see beauties that charm him it lies in his power to create them, and if he wishes to see monstrosities that are frightful, buffoonish, or ridiculous, or pitiable, he can be lord and God (creator) thereof; and if he wishes to produce inhabited regions or deserts, or dark and shady (cool) retreats from the heat, or warm places for cold weather, he can do so. If he wants valleys (likewise) if he wants from high mountain tops to unfold a great plain extending down to the sea's horizon, he is lord to do so; and likewise if from low plains he wishes to see high mountains, or from high mountains low plains and the sea shore. In fact, whatever exists in the universe, in essence, in appearance, in the imagination, the painter has first in his mind and then in his hands; and these are of such excellence that they are able to present a proportioned and harmonious view of the whole that can be seen simultaneously, at one glance, just as things in nature.

20. ON PAINTING AND POETRY

Poetry is superior to painting in the presentation of words, and painting is superior to poetry in the presentation of facts. And painting is to poetry in the same relation as facts are to words. Since facts are subject to the eye and words are subject to the ear, the relation which these senses have to one another also exists between their respective objects. For this reason I judge painting to be superior to poetry. But as painters did not know how to plead for their own art she was left without advocates for a long time. For painting does not talk; but reveals herself as she is, ending in reality; and Poetry ends in words in which she eloquently sings her own praises.

21. THE PAINTER'S DISPUTE WITH THE POET

What poet can represent to you in words, oh lover, the true image of your ideal as faithfully as the painter will do? Who can show you the courses of rivers, the forests, valleys, and fields, and call up memories of past pleasures therein with more truth than the painter?

And if you say: painting is poetry, which in itself is mute unless there is some one to expound it and explain what it represents, do you not see that your book is worse off because even if there is a man to expound it, one cannot see anything of what he is saying, while he who speaks of pictures will speak of things that can be seen, and these pictures will be understood as if they could speak, if the actions of the figures are well attuned to their states of mind.

22. THE POET AND THE PAINTER

Painting serves a nobler sense than poetry and represents the works of nature with more truth than the poet. The works of nature are much nobler than speech which was invented by man; for the works of man are to the works of nature as man is to God. Therefore, it is a nobler profession to imitate the things of nature which are the true and actual likenesses than to imitate in words the actions and speeches of men. And if you, poet, wish to confine yourself exclusively to your own profession in describing the works of nature, representing diverse places and forms of various objects, you will be out-distanced by the painter's infinitely greater power. . . .

24. THE DIFFERENCE BETWEEN PAINTING AND POETRY

Painting is poetry which is seen and not heard, and poetry is a painting which is heard but not seen. These two arts, you may call them both either poetry or painting, have here interchanged the senses by which they penetrate to the intellect. Whatever is painted must pass by the eye, which is the nobler sense, and whatever is poetry must pass through a less noble sense, namely the ear, to the understanding. Therefore, let the painting be judged by a man born deaf, and the poetry by one born blind. If in the painting the actions of the figures are in every case expressive of the purpose in their minds, the beholder, though born deaf, is sure to understand what is intended, but the listener born blind will never understand the things the poet describes which reflect honour on the poem, including such important parts as the indication of gestures, the compositions of the stories, the description of beautiful and delightful places with limpid waters through which the green bed of the stream can be seen, and the play of the waves rolling through meadows and over pebbles, mingling with blades of grass and with playful fishes, and similar subtle detail which may as well be addressed to a stone as to a man born blind who never in his life has seen what makes the beauty of the world, namely, light, shade, colour, body, figure, position, distance, nearness, motion, and rest—these ten ornaments of nature. But the deaf man who has lost a sense less noble, even though he may thereby be deprived of speech (for never having heard anybody talk he could not learn any language), will understand all the actions of the human body better than one who can speak and hear, and he will therefore be able to understand the works of painters and recognize the actions of their figures.

25. THE DIFFERENCE BETWEEN PAINTING AND POETRY

Painting is mute poetry, and poetry is blind painting. Both aim at imitating nature as closely as lies in their power, and both can be used for expounding divers customs and morals, as Apelles did in his "Calumny".

And from painting which serves the eye, the noblest sense, arises harmony of proportions; just as many different voices joined together and singing simultaneously produce a harmonious proportion which gives such satisfaction to the sense of hearing that listeners remain spellbound with admiration as if half alive. But the effect of the beautiful proportion of an angelic face in a painting is much greater, for these proportions produce a harmonious concord which reaches the eye simultaneously, just as (a chord in) music affects the ear; and if this beautiful harmony be shown to the lover of her whose beauties are portrayed, he will without doubt remain spellbound in admiration and in a joy without parallel and superior to all other sensations. . . .

26. THE DIFFERENCE BETWEEN POETRY AND PAINTING

Painting presents the impression which the artist wished to convey all at once and gives as much pleasure to the noblest sense as any work created by nature. But a poet, wishing to convey the same things to the "sensus communis" through the inferior sense of hearing, gives no more pleasure to the eye than if one were listening to something.

Now look what difference there is between listening for a long time to a tale about something which gives pleasure to the eye and actually seeing it all at once as works of nature are seen. Moreover, the works of poets are read at long intervals; they are often not understood and require many explanations, and commentators very rarely know what was in the poet's mind; often only a small part of the poet's works is read for want of time. But the work of the painter is immediately understood by its beholders.

27. OF THE DIFFERENCE AND ALSO THE SIMILARITY WHICH PAINTING HAS WITH POETRY

Painting presents its subject to thee in one instant through the sense sight, through the same organ that transmits the natural objects to the mind: and at the same time the harmonious proportions of the parts composing the whole react and delight the eye. Poetry transmits the same subject through a sense which is less noble and which impresses on the mind the shapes of the objects it describes more slowly and confusedly than the eye, which is the true and direct intermediary between the object and the mind, and which transmits with the greatest accuracy the surfaces and shapes of whatever presents itself. And from these shapes is born the proportionality called harmony, which delights the sense of sight with sweet concord just as the proportions of diverse voices delight the sense of hearing. But the harmony of music is less noble than the harmony which appeals to the eye, because sound dies as soon as it is born, and its death is as swift as its birth, and this cannot happen with the sense of sight. For if you present to the eye the beauty of a human figure composed of fine proportions, these beauties will not be as transient nor will they be destroyed as swiftly as in music. On the contrary, beauty has a long life; it can be enjoyed and examined at leisure without having to be continually reborn like music which has to be played again and again, and it will not weary you; on the contrary, it will inspire you with love and not only the eye but all your senses with a longing for possession; and all the senses will seem to compete with the eye; as if the mouth would like to swallow it bodily, as if the ear took pleasure in listening to the descriptions of its beauty, as if the sense of touch liked to draw it in through all its pores and as if the nose would like to inhale the air which continually breathes from it.

In nature time destroys the beauty of such harmony in a few years; this does not happen to the same beauty imitated by the painter; time will preserve it for a long while. And the eye, exercising its function, will take as much pleasure in the painted beauty as it did in the living beauty which it has lost; the sense of touch at the same time is made senior brother, and as it will have been satisfied will leave reason unimpeded to the contemplation of the divine beauty.

And in this case the painting can take the place of the original which is destroyed, while the description of the poet is not able to do so. The poet who tries to emulate in this the painter does not take into account that the words which he uses to describe the various elements of beauty are separated from one another by lapses of time which introduce oblivion and sever the proportions. These he cannot describe without using long phrases, and he cannot therefore with words convey the harmonious relation of the divine proportions. Beauty cannot be described in words in the same time which it takes to view beauty in a painting. It is a sin against nature to want to give to the ear what is meant for the eye. Let music enter there and do not try to put in her place the science of painting, the true imitator of all the shapes of nature.

What induces you, oh man, to depart from your home in town, to leave parents and friends, and go to the country-side over mountains and valleys, if it is not the beauty of the world of nature which, on considering, you can only enjoy through the sense of sight; and as the poet in this also wants to compete with the painter, why do you not take the poet's descriptions of such landscapes and stay at home without exposing yourself to the excessive heat of the sun? Would that not be more expedient and less fatiguing, since you could stay in a cool place without moving about and exposing yourself to illness? But your soul could not enjoy the pleasures that come to it through the eyes, the windows of its habitation, it could not receive the reflections of bright places, it could not see the shady valleys watered by the play of meandering rivers, it could not see the many flowers which with their various colours compose harmonies for the eye, nor all the other things which may present themselves to the eye.

But if a painter on a cold and severe winter's day shows you his paintings of these or other country-sides where you once enjoyed yourself, beside some fountain, and where you can see yourself again in flowery meadows as a lover by the side of your beloved under the cool, soft shadows of green trees, will it not give you much greater pleasure than listening to the poet's description of such a scene?

Here the poet replies and concedes the above reasons, but says he is superior to the painter because he can make men talk and argue as he pleases, inventing things that do not exist; and that he will rouse men to take up arms, that he will describe the sky, the stars, and nature and the arts and all things. To which we reply that none of the things which he enumerates pertain to his own profession and that he must admit that in the making of speeches and orations he will be beaten by the orator; that in speaking of the stars he is stealing his subject from the astronomer, in speaking of philosophy, from the philosopher; and that as a matter of fact poetry has no domain of its own and does not deserve to have one any more than a monger who collects all sorts of goods from different makers.

But the deity of the science of painting extends over works human as well as divine in so far as they are bound by surfaces, namely, the outlines of figures. With these she prescribes to the sculptor the perfection of his statues. By drawing, which is her beginning, she teaches the architect to make his edifices agreeable to the eye, she guides the potters in the making of various vases, the goldsmiths, the weavers and embroiderers. She has invented the characters in which the different languages are written, she has given the ciphers to the mathematician, and has described the figures of geometry, she teaches opticians, astronomers, mechanics, and engineers.

28. DISCUSSION BETWEEN THE POET AND THE PAINTER, AND WHAT IS THE DIFFERENCE BETWEEN POETRY AND PAINTING

The poet says that his science consists of invention and measure; invention as regards subject and measure as regards verse. This is the essence of poetry, its body, so to speak, which she then dresses up with all the sciences. The painter answers that similar principles govern the science of painting—invention and measure; invention as regards the subject-matter which he has to represent, and measure in the objects which he paints so that they should not be disproportioned; but that painting does not don the garments of the other three sciences, on the contrary, these partly clothe themselves in the garments of painting, as astrology cannot do anything without perspective which is a principal part of painting. I am speaking of mathematical astrology and not of that fallacious divination by the stars. May those who make their living thereby from fools forgive me for saying so. The poet says that he can describe in beautiful verse a thing which really stands for something else by way of simile. The painter replies that he can do the same and that in this respect he too is a poet. And if the poet says that he can kindle love in men which is the main motive of the species in the whole animal world, the painter has the power to do the same, the more so as he can place the true image of the beloved before the lover, who often kisses it and speaks to it, a thing he would not do to the description of the same beauties by the writer. The painter's power over men's minds is even greater, for he can induce them to love and fall in love with a picture which does not portray any living woman. It once happened to me that I made a picture representing a sacred subject which was bought by one who loved it and who then wished to remove the symbols of divinity in order that he might kiss her without misgivings. Finally his conscience prevailed over his sighs and lust and he felt constrained to remove the picture from his house.· Now let the poet go and try to rouse such desires in men by the description of a beauty which does not portray any living being. And if you say: I shall describe hell for you, and paradise or any other delights or terrors, there too the painter is your superior because he will place things before you which though silent will express such delights or terrors that will turn your courage into flight.

Painting will move the senses more readily than poetry. And if you say that with words you will move a people to tears or to laughter, my reply is that it is not the poet who moves, but the orator, by another science than poetry. But the painter will move you to laughter and not to tears, because weeping implies a more violent agitation than laughter. An artist painted a picture that whoever saw it at once yawned, and went on doing so as long as he kept his eyes on the picture, which represented a person who also was yawning. Other artists have represented acts of wantonness and lust which kindled these passions in the beholders. Poetry could not do as much. And if you write a description of Gods, such writing will never be worshipped in the same way as a painting of the deity. For to the picture many offerings and prayers will incessantly flow, many generations will flock to it from distant lands and from over the eastern Seas, and they will ask for help from such a painting, but not from writing.

29. THE POET'S ARGUMENT AGAINST THE PAINTER

You say, oh painter, that your art is the object of worship. Do not ascribe a power to yourself which is due to the subject of your painting. The painter then replies: "Oh poet, you who likewise try to imitate us, why don't you choose a subject for your poem that will move people to worship the written letters of your words in the same way?"

But nature has favoured the painter more than the poet; and more honour is due to the works of one favoured than to the works of one not so favoured.

Let us therefore give praise both to him who delights our ears with words and to him who with painting delights our sight; but less praise is due to him who uses words, as they are but accidental designations created by man, who is inferior to the creator of the works of nature which the painter imitates.

And nature is enclosed within the surfaces of shapes.

34b. If you say that the Sciences are not "mechanical" but purely of the mind, I reply that Painting is of the mind and that just as Music and Geometry deal with the proportions of continuous quantities and Arithmetic with non-continuous quantities, Painting deals with all continuous quantities, and it deals besides with the qualities of proportions, shadows and light and distances in perspective.

46. THE DIFFERENCE BETWEEN PAINTING AND SCULPTURE

. . . Perspective, a mathematical science entailing very subtle calculation and invention, which by means of lines makes what is near appear distant, and what is small, large. Here, in this case, sculpture is helped by nature, and does without the sculptor's invention.

PART FOUR

CONTINENTAL RATIONALISTS AS PHILOSOPHERS OF ART

Chapter 8

Continental Rationalists as Philosophers of Art

It is always difficult to generalize about the writings of great philosophers, the more so because the terms that indicate their places in history are likely to obscure divergences in their speculation and emphasise their common philosophical presuppositions. The point is well illustrated by the rather few ventures Descartes, Leibniz, and Spinoza made into the realm of philosophy of art. These men are the greatest of the "Continental Rationalists," and their philosophies have a common model, in mathematics. Yet, of the three, Descartes is the philosopher who, in writing upon music, uses the mathematical model most completely, whereas Spinoza, for systematic reasons, avails himself little of mathematics and stresses the subjective and nominalist character of art and beauty. Leibniz, inventor of the calculus, writes of the differences between collections and parts and ventures to explain music, not as Descartes did in terms of vibrating strings, but in terms of "hidden mathematics."

The differences among the Rationalists are perhaps best illustrated, however, if we refer, without overemphasising the importance of the point, to the theological background of the theory of the artist as creator. Here it functions as a denial rather than an affirmation. There is no place in Spinoza's speculations for a cosmic originator analogous to God the Creator, and the reason is not far to seek. In the Appendix to the first book of the *Ethic,* Spinoza writes that "it was looked upon as indisputable that the judgments of the gods far surpass our comprehension; and this opinion alone would have been sufficient to keep the human race in darkness to all eternity, if mathematics, which does not deal with ends, but with the essences and properties of forms, had not placed before us another rule of truth." On Spinoza's view, "universal prejudices" have kept men in bondage and among such are the commonly received notions concerning deity. Leibniz, on the other hand, echoes the ancient analogy: ". . . The soul imitates what God performs in the world." He echoes, as well, the ancient theory of inspiration.

It is nonetheless true that the Rationalists as a whole tend to emphasise art as a form of knowledge, confused though it may be, with precise relations to mathematics and with a norm of regularity. Theirs is not a rich

Philosophy of Art, a fact that underlines the point that history plays curious favorites. It was Alexander Gottlieb Baumgarten (1714–1762),[1] an exponent of Leibnizian rationalism, who gave Aesthetics its name. Baumgarten was not comparable in philosophical stature to the greatest of the Continental Rationalists, René Descartes, Gottfried Wilhelm Leibniz, and Benedict Spinoza, yet he succeeded in presenting in a clear and simplified fashion enough of the basic speculation of his intellectual ancestors to warrant quotation from his own writings and so provide an introduction to the Philosophies of Art that did not occupy the center of speculation for any one of the trio of preeminent rationalist philosophers of the seventeenth century.

In 1735, Baumgarten published his *Reflections on Poetry.* In it, he searches for the ground for "a science which might direct the lower cognitive faculty in knowing things sensately." He finds this in the distinction made by the Greek philosophers and the Church fathers, "between *things perceived* (αἰδητά) and *things known* (νοητά)" and remarks that neither philosophers nor theologians equated the latter with things of sense. Things of sense are "images" and as things perceived are known by the inferior faculty, as objects of the science of perception, or aesthetic. In contrast, *things known* are known by the superior faculty as objects of logic. Baumgarten notes that "that part of aesthetics which treats of such presentations as belong to things perceived" is more extensive than the corresponding part of logic.

In 1739, Baumgarten added to his treatment of Aesthetics. In *Metaphysics,* he notes [2] that an indistinct idea is called a sensuous idea and repeats his suggestion that sensuous perceptions are given by an inferior faculty. The appearance of perfection, or perfection obvious to taste, is, however, beauty, whereas "the corresponding imperfection" is ugliness.[3] In 1750, Baumgarten, writing in *Aesthetica,* is prepared to sum up his speculation. Aesthetics is the science of sensuous knowledge. It includes the theory of the fine arts, the theory of the lower kind of knowledge, the art of thinking beautifully, and the art of analogical reasoning. Beauty now becomes the perfection of sensuous perception and the end of Aesthetics. The defect of sensuous knowledge is to be avoided. Aesthetic truth, we are informed, contains no obvious falsehood but is not certain and can only attain to a degree of probability.[4] All that is not easily rejected by our senses is probable; it should not be rejected.[5]

Baumgarten held [6] that images are sensate representations and are less clear than sense impressions. It is also interesting in the light of the development of Aesthetics in the eighteenth century, and with the elaboration of the theory of representations and, more particularly, of imagination that Baumgarten's use of the word Aesthetics was only reluctantly accepted by Kant, who was to write the most powerful single work on the judgment of taste.[7] Kant wrote to Hertz in 1772 that the use of the word to signify the critique of taste was limited to the Germans, and he referred to the origin of the usage in Baumgarten's "abortive attempt . . . to bring the critical treatment of the beautiful under rational principles, and so to raise its rules to the rank of a science." Kant refers to Baumgarten as "that admirable analytic thinker" but he asserts that what the rationalist believed to be susceptible to scientific treatment could never yield a priori rules. The greater part of its chief sources was empirical. Kant

[1] See below pp. 296 et seq. for Baumgarten's Philosophy of Art. See above, pp. 5 et seq for an evaluation of Baumgarten's accomplishment.

[2] A. G. Baumgarten, *Metaphysics* 521.

[3] *Ibid.* 662.

[4] *Ibid.* 483.

[5] *Ibid.* 484.

[6] Baumgarten, *Reflections on Poetry,* 28 and 29.

[7] See below, pp. 334 et seq. See above, pp. 6, 8-9.

suggests that the word "aesthetic" be abandoned with reference to any critique of taste and reserved "for that doctrine of sensibility which is true science. . . ."

By 1787, however, Kant had altered his opinion. He writes on December 28 of that year and informs Reinhold that he is presently at work on a *Critique of Taste* and that he has been "in this way led to the discovery of another kind of *a priori* principles than I had formerly recognized. . . ." In 1790, Kant published the *Critique of Judgment*, the first part of which is called "The Critique of the Aesthetical Judgment."

If we turn now from one of the distinguished writers in the subject to which Baumgarten gave the name to the thinkers from whom he himself drew sustenance, we discover that the contributions of Descartes, Leibniz, and Spinoza to speculation on art and its experience, however important they may be historically, are sparse and arid. The great contributions of the three great Continental Rationalists were made in metaphysics, ethics, mathematics, psychology, theology, and cosmology. Modern Philosophy is ordinarily held to begin with Descartes, a thinker who is also in the first rank in mathematics as the inventor of the analytical geometry and in psychology with his study of the passions and his anticipation of the theory of conditioned reflexes. Leibniz is a philosopher of the widest range of interests, a writer on monadology, inventor of the calculus, jurist, diplomat, and theologian. Spinoza's life was brief but his is one of the great names in ethics and theology, in metaphysics, and in freedom of the press and of religion.

As is to be expected, the contributions of the three great Continental Rationalists to Philosophy of Art are integral parts of their systematic speculation. Descartes' principal interest in art is in music, and he writes of that art in the *Compendium Musicae* (1618) and in his *Correspondence* with his friend, Mersenne (1631). Before we come to these writings,[8] mention should be made of the justification Descartes offers for his reluctance to rely upon various of the other arts as possible foundations for the philosophy he proposes to construct in the *Discourse on Method*. As is well known, he plans "to accept nothing as true which I did not recognise to be so," and the criteria for his methods were those of clarity and distinctness. Descartes, in the course of proceeding to doubt of everything, examined what he had previously taken to be true. Eloquence and poetry he dismissed as "gifts of the mind rather than fruits of study," despite his high esteem of the former subject and the fact that he was "enamoured" of poetry. "Those who have the most delightful original ideas and who know how to express them with the maximum of style and suavity, would not fail to be the best poets even if the art of Poetry were unknown to them." This tacit acceptance of a theory of poetic inspiration and the denial of the value of technique for those whose gifts are poetic lead Descartes to turn elsewhere for certainty. Architecture provides him with one hint for the method he adopts. In Germany, during the wars, he remained one whole day "shut up alone in a stove-heated room." Occupied with his thoughts, the first consideration that came to him was "that there is very often less perfection in works composed of several portions, and carried out by the hands of various masters, than in those on which one individual alone has worked." He concludes that "buildings planned and carried out by one architect alone are usually more beautiful and better proportioned than those which many have tried to put in order and improve, making use of old walls which were built with other ends in view."

Descartes infers[9] that it is difficult to

[8] See below for a selection from Descartes' letters to Mersenne, pp. 306 et seq.

[9] R. Descartes, *Discourse on Method,* I. See below, p. 304.

bring about much that is satisfactory in operating only on the works of others and he cites in support of the inference the fact that in great towns which were originally villages the result is badly constructed in comparison to those regularly laid out by a surveyor free to follow his own ideas.

The emphasis is upon "regularity" and upon the superiority of reason guiding the will of men rather than in a dependence upon chance. Descartes decides that it is best in speculation to sweep away all opinions he has hitherto held and to replace them by a uniform and rational scheme. Architecture is a model, therefore, for the method he employs.

Benedetto Croce writes [10] of Descartes that "the French philosopher abhorred imagination, the outcome, according to him, of the agitation of the animal spirits: and though not utterly condemning poetry, he allowed it to exist only insofar as it was guided by intellect, that being the sole faculty able to save men from the caprices of the *folle du logis.* He tolerated it, but that was all. . . ." The result, Croce holds, is that "the mathematical spirit fostered on France by Descartes forbade all possibility of a serious consideration of poetry and art."

Whatever judgments we may make concerning the accuracy or inaccuracy of Croce's statement, his words do point up the fact that it is precisely the mathematical spirit in Descartes himself which directed his interest to the art of music, although he believes that beauty is primarily related to sight. As regards music, Descartes treated it "as a science of mathematical proportions, which proportions, when adhered to, give pleasurable sensations." It was Descartes who discovered that the frequency of the vibration of a string of a given tension and density varies inversely with its length. It will be recalled [11] that the Pythagorean discovery of the octave was based upon the measurement of the length of a tautened cord.

Descartes' *Compendium* contains much technical material, primarily of interest to the musicologist. Here it is sufficient to point out, before remarking on the *Letters to Mersenne*,[12] that the French philosopher maintains that the basis of music is sound and that its aim is to please and to arouse various emotions in us. He suggests, for example, that melodies can be at the same time sad and enjoyable. For Descartes, all senses are capable of experiencing pleasure, but for this pleasure there must be a proportional relation of some kind between the object and the sense itself. The noise of guns or thunder is not fit for music. Moreover, the object must be such that it does not fall on the sense in too complicated or confused a fashion. Objects are easier to perceive by the senses the smaller the difference of their parts. Descartes offers an interesting answer to the question, Which of the sense-objects is most agreeable? It is neither the object most difficult nor that easiest to perceive. Rather, it is that which does not quite gratify the natural desire by which the senses are carried to the objects, yet at the same time is not so complicated that it tires the senses.

Descartes suggests in the *Compendium* (1618), that there should be a discussion of the various powers that the consonances possess of evoking the emotions, but he dismisses the problem as one the discussion of which would exceed the limitations of the book, as well as one so varied and grounded on such imponderables as to require an entire volume for its investigation. The *Compendium* ends with more than a hint that Descartes had considered writing in detail concerning the emotions that music can arouse. It is no less clear that he believed such a study would require the correlation of such steps, consonances, meters, etc. as are instrumental in evoking correspond-

[10] B. Croce, *Aesthetic,* p. 204 (Ainslie's translation).

[11] See above, pp. 26, 37.

[12] See below, pp. 306 et seq.

ing emotions and this task, again, he remarks, is beyond the scope of the book.

In his letters to Mersenne (1631), Descartes dismisses the possibility that there is a correlation of the kind suggested in the *Compendium*: "I do not know," he writes, "any qualities in consonances which correspond to the passions." The letters to his friend express other views surprising in a philosopher who adheres so closely to rationalist principles. An illustration is provided by the judgment that the music of the ancients [13] may have been more powerful than is that of Descartes' contemporaries, "not because they were more learned, but because they were less so. . . ." The point, Descartes supposed, is that their freedom from constraint of rules would stimulate the imagination. Such would not be the case were the music based on knowledge of theory. Moreover, Descartes writes to Mersenne, "when you ask me by how much one consonance is more agreeable than another, you disturb me as much as if you were asking me by how much fruit is more agreeable for me to eat than fish."

The issue for Descartes is precisely that raised by later aestheticians and philosophers of art, namely, the difference between judgments of fact and judgments of taste or of aesthetic value. As Descartes phrases it in touching on the sweetness of consonances, two points must be distinguished. One is simplicity and harmony, the other is "what renders them more agreeable to the ear." He concludes that it is possible to say absolutely what is simplest and most harmonious, whereas what is agreeable is relative to the places in which the consonances are used. Neither beauty nor agreeableness signifies anything more than "a rapport between our judgment and the object" and since the judgment of men vary, beauty or agreeableness will have no determined measure. What will be called beautiful will be that which will please most people. Such agreement will ordinarily be found if the object is simple, but even in this instance one may not call one object absolutely more beautiful than another. Thus, the principal problem that was to preoccupy Kant in the *Critique of Judgment*—whether a judgment of taste may be shown to be both universal and subjective—is disposed of by Descartes on the grounds of subjectivity and fancy.

In the light of this important inference by Descartes, it is of singular interest for the historian as he turns to Leibniz [14] comparatively meager but nonetheless influential writings on Philosophy of Art, that the author of the *Monadology* anticipates one basic aspect of Kant's philosophy of art and runs completely counter to another. Like Kant, Leibniz believes that the man who is pleased by "the contemplation of a beautiful picture" loves it so to speak with a disinterested love.[15] Kant believes that the judgment of taste is disinterested, but this proposition he grounds on the fact that interest implies satisfaction in the existence of the object.[16] Leibniz' best known statement relating to an art concerns, as does Descartes', music. We come at this point upon a radical difference in Leibnizian Philosophy of Art from the Kantian Aesthetic. Briefly, Leibniz argues the implications of the statement that "Music charms us although its beauty only consists in the harmony of numbers, and in the account which we do not notice, but which the soul none the less takes, of the beating or vibration of sounding bodies, which meet one another at certain intervals." [17] Kant, on the other hand, argues [18] against all rationalist reduction of the judgments of taste to mathematical inferences, and, indeed, against the supposition that the

[13] See below, p. 306.

[14] See below, p. 315 et seq. for Leibniz's life and readings from his writings on art.

[15] Leibniz, *Juras et aequi elementa,* Cf. below, p. 317.

[16] See below, pp. 360-61 et seq. in Kant's *The Critique of Judgement.*

[17] Cf. below pp. 317-18.

[18] See *The Critique of Judgement,* Sect. 22.

judgment of taste is conceptual.[19] Kant, more specifically, denies validity to such Platonist philosophies of beauty as adduce "geometrically regular figures, such as a circle, a square, a cube, etc." as the "simplest and most indisputable examples of beauty . . .," precisely as he argues against the validity of the canon of beauty. But he is even more specific concerning the view of the seventeenth century rationalist that perfection may be predicated of beauty. It has in fact been regarded by celebrated philosophers, he writes,[20] "as the same as beauty, with the proviso, *if it is thought in a confused way.*" The object of his argument is not only Baumgarten, with his view that beauty is "perfection apprehended through the senses"—but Leibniz himself. For Kant, the judgment of taste is not conceptual. For Leibniz, knowledge that is clear is either confused or distinct; if it is confused, one cannot enumerate the marks that distinguish it from other objects. Such confused knowledge is got by sensation and is direct. Art, like sensation, is directly known: ". . . We sometimes see painters and other artists correctly judge what has been done well or badly; yet they are often unable to give a reason for their judgment but tell the inquirer that the work which displeases them lacks 'something, I know not what.' "[21] "Taste," he writes, "as distinguished from understanding consists of confused perceptions for which one cannot give an adequate reason."[22]

Leibniz defines a beautiful thing as that the contemplation of which is pleasant. Pleasure is a feeling of a perfection or an excellence; and, Leibniz adds, defects in parts of a painting or a musical composition may merely be necessary conditions for the achievement of a pleasing whole.[23]

"Look at the most lovely picture, and then cover it up, leaving uncovered only a tiny scrap of it. What else will you see there, even if you look as closely as possible, and the more so as you look from nearer and nearer at hand, but a kind of confused medley of colours, without selection, without art! And yet when you remove the covering, and looking upon the whole picture from the proper place, you will see that what previously seemed to you to have been aimlessly smeared on the canvas was in fact accomplished with the highest art by the author of the work . . ." The inference is that a part may be disturbed without upsetting the harmony of the whole.

For Leibniz, too, there is a reflection of the "great analogy" between the artist and God. ". . . The soul imitates what God performs in the world." God's superiority arises, however, not only because He makes the whole, but also because "the artisan has to seek for his material."[24] Of God's creative powers, Leibniz holds that "it is needful that God's invention should not be inferior to that of a workman; it must even go infinitely beyond it." God's superiority is not alone a matter of power; it derives from wisdom. God's machine "lasts longer and goes more correctly than that of any other mechanician whatever."

Not only is "the great analogy" of the artist to God the maker and God the creator embedded in his philosophy of art, but we encounter in Leibniz' writings as well the ancient theory of inspiration. Leibniz' remark that "Music is subordinate to Arithmetic" may well recall the Pythagoreans,[25] but his additional remark that "what a man needs in order to compose successfully are practice as well as the genius and vivid imagination in things of the ear," also reminds us that even Democritus needed inspiration in a rational philosophy to account for the beauty of a

[19] *Ibid.*

[20] See *Ibid,* Sect. 15.

[21] See below, pp. 316-17. See below, pp. 337 et seq. for Feijoo's essay, "I Know Not What."

[22] See below, p. 316.

[23] See above, Plato, p. 102; Plotinus, p. 220 and St. Augustine, p. 239. See below, Leibniz, p. 318 et seq.

[24] See above, St. Augustine, pp. 233 et seq.

[25] See above, pp. 26 et seq.

poem.[26] For Leibniz, ". . . imagining a beautiful melody . . ." requires that "our imagination itself acquires a habit after which it can be given the freedom to go its own way without consulting reason. . . ."

Spinoza, the third of the great Continental Rationalists, wrote little of primary interest to the philosopher of art or to the historian of Aesthetics. The contrast to Descartes' writing on music and Leibniz' interest in a variety of problems in art in terms of quantity should not obscure the fact, however, that what Spinoza did write displays, as does almost every area of speculation into which he ventured, a significant insight into a difficult but extraordinarily illuminating system of philosophy. Of the difficulty of philosophical speculation, Spinoza himself had no doubt. "If the way which, as I have shown," he writes at the end of the *Ethic*, "leads higher seem very difficult, it can nevertheless be found. It must indeed be difficult since it is so seldom discovered; for if salvation lay ready to hand and could be discovered without great labour, how could it be possible that it should be neglected almost by everybody? But all noble things are as difficult as they are rare." But Spinoza was no less certain of the tool to which philosophy was to be submitted than he was of the difficulty to be encountered in its application. The tool was mathematics. What Spinoza writes concerning beauty is intelligible in these terms, but it is not so much because Spinoza—like Plato, Descartes, Leibniz or Leonardo—believed that regularity is the criterion for beautiful figures, but rather because mathematics frees the human race from the tyranny of the judgment "that the gods far surpass our comprehension. . . ."

Teleology is a falsification of what is properly to be understood as objects and events in a mechanically defined universe.[27] Spinoza, in a letter written to Boxel in September, 1674,[28] concedes what, as an advocate of the geometrical method, he must concede: "As to beauty, there are things whose parts are proportionate in relation to others, and are better put together than others," because God has granted to man's understanding and judgment agreement and harmony with what is proportionate, but not with that which has no proportion. This echoes the ancient rationalist conviction that what is beautiful does not lack parts. It is of interest, however, that Spinoza does not pursue this line of reasoning in the letter but immediately proceeds to discuss "Whole" or "Universe" as the names given to the world. This in turn leads him to mention terms with which the reader of Spinoza's metaphysics is familiar: "eternal" and "temporal," "cause" and "effect," "finite" and "infinite," etc.

The systematic problem for Spinoza derives from his own belief that things regarded in themselves, or in relation to God, may be neither beautiful nor ugly. At the point at which this issue emerges in his letter to Boxel, Spinoza discusses the question of the relativism of the beauty of any object in terms of perceivers and the additional question, Whether or not God created the world to be beautiful? [29]

Spinoza concludes that the term Beauty, among others, is an idea highly confused; that objects we call beautiful should properly be described in terms of the motion of nerves; and that beauty is a word that is in fact, as some mediaevalists held, universal only "per voce." It is a universal "not formed by all persons in the same way." The meaning varies with the individual because in each instance the notion is formed in terms of the way the body is more frequently affected and in which the mind more easily imagines or recollects. In the Appendix to *Ethic I*,[30] Spinoza goes into detail concerning the forming of universal terms. Beauty,

[26] See above, pp. 45 et seq.

[27] See below, pp. 313 et seq. *Ethic,* I, Appendix. See below, pp. 310 et seq. for Spinoza's Life and Philosophy of Art.

[28] See below, pp. 312 et seq.

[29] See below, p. 312.

[30] See below, pp. 311 et seq.

among other general terms, is not an attribute of things; rather, it is one of the "modes in which the imagination is affected in different ways. . . ." Men consider all things as made for themselves, and in the instance of the so-called beautiful objects, "if the motion by which the nerves are affected by means of objects represented to the eye conduces to well-being," the objects are called beautiful. Such use of language, according to Spinoza, has led men to use the word "harmony" in such a way that "they have believed that God even is delighted with it." They call harmonious what is in fact a motion acting upon the ears. The use of such language is erroneous because the effects of motion vary with the individual. In each instance, the notion is formed in terms of the way the body is more frequently affected and in which the mind more easily imagines or recollects.

As Spinoza himself sums up his thinking on this subject in a letter to Oldenburg on November 20, 1665,[31] ". . . I do not attribute to Nature beauty or ugliness, order or confusion. For things cannot, except with respect to our imagination, be called beautiful, or ugly, ordered or confused." The closest Spinoza comes to granting that beauty is in objects is in the letter to Boxel referred to above. Here he expresses a basic tenet of Rationalist philosophy of art, one almost identical to that stated by Leibniz: "The perfection of a thing is also beautiful in so far as there is nothing lacking to it."

As we shall see in the next two chapters, the contrast between Rationalist writings of the seventeenth century and speculation on Philosophy of Art in the eighteenth century is indicative of the growing awareness of the need to make of Aesthetics a subject unique in fact as well as in name.

[31] See below, pp. 313 et seq.

René Descartes

1596–1650

A. Life

Modern philosophy, it has been maintained on sound grounds, begins with the speculation of the rationalist thinker, René Descartes. The inventor of analytic geometry, the formulator of a theory of universal doubt, and the author of a rationalist philosophy that served as a model for the great systematic philosophies of Leibniz and Spinoza, Descartes speaks primarily to the architect and musician in the arts, to the admirer of the mathematical arts as they serve to explain composition and town-planning.

Descartes was born in La Haye, in Touraine. He studied at the Jesuit school at La Flêche, where he was a fellow pupil of Marin Mersenne. It was with Mersenne that Descartes later carried on the extended correspondence that included Descartes' views on music, some of which follow below. It was his former schoolmate who defended Descartes when his philosophy was severely attacked on the grounds that it was unorthodox.

Descartes served as a soldier in the service of Prince Maurice of Orange. In 1619 he volunteered for military service in Bavaria, and in Neuberg on the Danube, in a warm room he began the speculation which brought forth the *Discourse of Method*. In the *Discourse,* architecture serves to illustrate the need for rational planning and the occasional need for the destruction of ancient foundations. Descartes settled in the Netherlands and there wrote *Meditations on First Philosophy* (1641). The *Principles of Philosophy* was published in Amsterdam in 1644. Descartes was invited to the Swedish court by Queen Christina, with whom he had corresponded on philosophical subjects and died in 1650 in Stockholm.

B. Philosophy of Art

The principal rules regarding the method: Illustration drawn from architecture

On Method II [32]

I was then in Germany, to which country I had been attracted by the wars which are not yet at an end. And as I was returning from the coronation of the Emperor to join the army, the setting in of winter detained me in a quarter where, since I found no society to divert me, while fortunately I had also no cares or passions to trouble me, I remained the whole day shut up alone in a stove-heated room, where I had complete leisure to occupy myself with my own thoughts. One of the first of the considerations that occurred to me was that there is very often less perfection in works composed of several portions, and carried out by the hands of various masters, than in those on which one individual alone has worked. Thus we see that buildings planned and carried out by one architect alone are usually more beautiful and better proportioned than those which many have tried to put in order and improve, making use of old walls which were built with other ends in view. In the same way also, those ancient cities which, originally mere villages, have become in the process of time great towns, are usually badly constructed in comparison with those which are regularly laid out on a plain by a surveyor who is free to follow his own ideas. Even though, considering their buildings each one apart, there is often as much or more display of skill in the one case than in the other, the former have large buildings indiscriminately placed together, thus rendering the streets crooked and irregular, so that it might be said that it was chance rather than the will of men guided by reason that led to such an arrangement. And if we consider that this happens despite the fact that from all time there have been certain officials who have had the special duty of looking after the buildings of private individuals in order that they may be public ornaments, we shall understand how difficult it is to bring about much that is satisfactory in operating only upon the works of others.. . . .

[32] *Descartes Selections,* ed. Ralph M. Eaton. New York: Charles Scribner's Sons, 1927, pp. 10–11 (by permission of Cambridge University Press, Publishers).

Compendium of Music

The basis of music is sound; its aim is to please and to arouse various emotions in us.[33] Melodies can be at the same time sad and enjoyable; nor is this so unique, for in the same way writers of elegies and tragedies please us most the more sorrow they awaken in us.

The means to this end, i.e., the attributes of sound, are principally two: namely, its differences of duration or time, and its differences of tension from high to low. The quality of tone itself (from what body and by what means it emanates in the most pleasing manner) is in the domain of the physicist.

The human voice seems most pleasing to us because it is most directly attuned to our souls. By the same token, the voice of a close friend is more agreeable than the voice of an

[33] René Descartes, *Compendium of Music,* pp. 11 et seq. Translated by Walter Robert, American Institute of Musicology, Rome, 1961. By permission of Dr. Armen Carapetyan, Director, American Institute of Musicology.

enemy because of sympathy or antipathy of feelings—just as it is said that a sheep-skin stretched over a drum will not give forth any sound when struck if a wolf's hide on another drum is sounding at the same time.

PRELIMINARIES

1. All senses are capable of experiencing pleasure.

2. For this pleasure a proportional relation of some kind between the object and the sense itself must be present. For example, the noise of guns or thunder is not fit for music, because it injures the ears, just as the excessive glare of the sun, if looked at directly, hurts the eyes.

3. The object must be such that it does not fall on the sense in too complicated or confused a fashion; therefore, a very complex design, even though it is regular, like the "matrix" on an astrolabe, is not as pleasing to the sight as another consisting of more equal lines, such as the "net" on the same astrolabe. The reason for this is that the sense finds more satisfaction in the latter than in the former, where there is much that it cannot distinctly perceive.

4. An object is perceived more easily by the senses when the difference of the parts is smaller.

5. We may say that the parts of a whole object are less different when there is greater proportion between them.

6. This proportion must be arithmetic, not geometric, the reason being that in the former there is less to perceive, as all differences are the same throughout. Therefore, in its attempt to perceive everything distinctly the sense will not be so strained. . . .

7. Among the sense-objects the most agreeable to the soul is neither that which is perceived most easily nor that which is perceived with the greatest difficulty; it is that which does not quite gratify the natural desire by which the senses are carried to the objects, yet is not so complicated that it tires the senses.

8. Finally, it must be observed that variety is in all things most pleasing. . . .

. . . As regards the various emotions which music can arouse by employing various meters, I will say that in general a slower pace arouses in us quieter feelings such as languor, sadness, fear, pride, etc. A faster pace arouses faster emotions, such as joy, etc. On the same basis one can state that duple meter, 4/4 and all meters divisible by two, are of slower types than triple meters, or those which consist of three parts. The reason for this is that the latter occupy the senses more, since there are more things to be noticed in them. For the latter contain three units, the former only two. But a more thorough investigation of this question depends on a detailed study of the movements of the soul, of which no more.

I cannot, however, pass over the fact that time in music has such power that it alone can be pleasurable by itself; such is the case with the military drum, where we have nothing [to perceive] but the beat; in this case I am of the opinion that here the meter can be composed not only of two or three units but perhaps even of five, seven, or more. For with such an instrument the ear has nothing to occupy its attention except the time; therefore, there can be more variety in time in order to hold the attention. . . .

. . . We should now discuss the various powers which the consonances possess of evoking emotions, but a more thorough investigation of this subject can be based on what we have already said, and it would exceed the limitations of this compendium. For these powers are so varied and based on such imponderable circumstances that a whole book would not suffice for the task. I shall therefore remark in regard to this only that the greatest variety arises from the use of these last four [consonances]. Of these the major third and the major sixth are more pleasing and more gay than the minor third and minor sixth; this is well known to composers and can easily be deduced from the aforesaid, where we have shown how the minor third is indirectly derived from the major third, whereas the major sixth is directly derived, since it is nothing but a composite major third. . . .

Descartes à Mersenne

December 18, 1629 [34]

. . . As to the Music of the ancients, I believe that it contained something of greater power than ours, not because they were more learned, but because they were less so: from which follows that those who had a great natural bent for music, not being constrained within the rules of our diatonic scale, did more through the sole force of the imagination than can be done by those who have corrupted this force through the knowledge of theory. Moreover, the ears of the listeners not being accustomed, as ours are, to a music so ordered, would be much more easily taken by surprise. If you care to take the trouble to make a little collection of everything that you have noticed touching upon today's practice, which passages are approved or disapproved, I should be very glad to employ three or four chapters of my treatise to state what I know about it and would acknowledge what I shall derive from you. But I would not want you to take the trouble to send it to me for eight or ten months, for I shall not have reached that point so soon and still I could not prevent myself from looking at it and I have too many other diversions: I wish to begin the study of anatomy. . . .

March 4, 1630

. . . 3. I had already written you that it is one thing to say that a consonance is sweeter than another and another thing to say that it is more agreeable. For everyone knows that honey is sweeter than olives and nevertheless many people will prefer to eat olives rather than honey. Thus everyone knows that the fifth is sweeter than the fourth, the latter than the major third and the major third than the minor; and nevertheless there are places where the minor third will please more than the fifth, even where a dissonance will be found more agreeable than a consonance.

4. I do not know any qualities in consonances which correspond to the passions.

5. When you ask me by how much one consonance is more agreeable than another, you disturb me as much as if you were asking me by how much fruit is more agreeable for me to eat than fish.

6. As to the composition of ratios, name them as you please, but you see clearly on your monochord [35] how a major tenth can be divided into an octave and a major third. . . .

March 18, 1630

. . . As to your question, to know whether one can establish the rule of the *beautiful,* it is just the same as what you were asking previously, why one sound is more agreeable than the other, except that the word *beautiful* seems more particularly to relate to the sense of sight. But, generally, neither beauty nor agreeableness signify anything but a rapport between our judgment and the object; and because the judgments of men are so different, one cannot say that beauty or agreeableness has any deter-

[34] *Oeuvres de Descartes. Correspondance I.* Publiées par Charles Adam et Paul Tannery sous les auspices du Ministère de l'Instruction Publique. Paris, 1897. Professor Pauline Jones, of the Department of French, and Professor Isabelle Cazeaux, of the Department of Music, Bryn Mawr College, have contributed valuable suggestions for this translation.

[35] Monochord. An acoustical instrument consisting of a long resonant box over which a single string of gut or wire is stretched.

mined measure. And I would not know how to explain it better than I have done elsewhere in my Music;[36] I shall set down here the same words because I have the Book in my hands:

> Among the sense-objects the most agreeable to the soul is neither that which is perceived most easily nor that which is perceived with the greatest difficulty; it is that which does not quite gratify the natural desire by which the senses are carried to the objects, yet is not so complicated that it tires the senses.[37]

I explain "that which is perceived easily or with difficulty", as for example, the divisions of a flower garden, which consist of only one or two kinds of patterns, arranged always in the same way, will be understood much more easily than if there were ten or twelve and arranged diversely; but that is not to say that one can call one absolutely more beautiful than the other, but according to the fancy of some, that of three sorts of figures will be the more beautiful, according to that of others one of four or of five, etc. But what will please most people can be called simply the most *beautiful*, something which cannot be determined.

Secondly, the same thing that makes some want to dance can make others want to weep. For this comes only from the fact that ideas, which are in our memory, are stimulated: thus, those who have at some other time taken pleasure in dancing when a certain air was being played, as soon as they hear the same, the desire to dance returns; on the contrary, if someone has never heard gaillards being played without at the same time experiencing some affliction, he would infallibly be saddened when he heard it another time. Which is so certain, that I judge that if one has beaten a dog hard five or six times, to the sound of a violin, as soon as he would hear this music another time, he would begin to cry and run away.

[36] Descartes *Compendium of Music.*
[37] *Ibid,* p. 13.

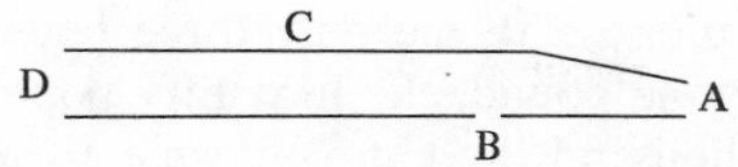

The sound of flutes is generated and modified in the following way. Let the flute be A B C D; the breath which has passed through A, having arrived at B, divides and one part goes out through hole B, the other passes the length of the flute to D. Now it must be noted that the wind which goes out through B is easily dissipated in the free air but that which wishes to pass the length of the tube, when it is still at B, would be unable to go further if it did not drive before it the air which is closest and if this latter did not at the same time push the air ahead of it and thus to D; and it is that which causes the sound to form at the same time in the entire concavity of the flute; as I shall endeavor to explain more distinctly in my Treatise. It is also the same thing which modifies it; for the longer the flute, the more the air, which is compressed in the aforesaid, resists the wind which comes from the mouth and in consequence is driven more slowly, from this it follows that the sound is lower. Now this is produced by minute impacts which correspond to the motions of strings to and fro. . . .

April 15, 1630

. . . To explain why the ear is not pleased by all sorts of intervals, I must make use of a comparison. I believe that you will certainly admit that there is a little more difficulty in recognizing the ratio which makes the fifth than in recognising the one which makes unison and a little more in recognizing that which makes the third than the fifth, just as there is a little more difficulty in lifting a weight of two pounds than in lifting one of one pound and more for one of three, etc. Now if you were to ask me how many pounds weight a single man can lift from the ground, I would say that this cannot be determined and that it varies according as men are more or less strong. But if you were to propose to me only three bodies, one weighing one pound, the next fifty pounds, the next a thousand, and if you were to ask me how many of these three bodies a man can lift, I would tell you absolutely that he could lift only the two which weigh fifty-one pounds. If you ask me whether this is because nature has limited the strength of man to fifty-one pounds, I would tell you no, but that it is because he could not lift more than fifty-one pounds if he had not yet lifted the whole weight of a thousand pounds, which exceeds the ordinary strength of men. Likewise, if you simply asked how many intervals there are in music which the ear can judge, I should say that that varies according as one has hearing more subtle than another; just as in fact I would be unable to distinguish the fifth from the octave and there are those who distinguish the major and minor half-tone; and there could be those who would be capable of recognizing the intervals of 6 to 7 and 10 to 11, etc. But when you ask me how many intervals there are which can be judged by ear, when they are put in a consort [38] of music, you are proposing to me that I consider in that case all the intervals which arise from the first, second and third bisection, linked in only three bodies, like the weights of 1 lb., 50 lb., and 1,000 lb. And I reply absolutely that there are only those which arise from the first and second bisection, which can be admitted in a concert; because if you admitted one more, it would be necessary to admit all those which arise from the third bisection, which all together exceed the capacity of the best ears.

A —————— B

The string A B at rest is equally stretched throughout; but in motion, because extension does not occur immediately, if the ends of the string are pulled, as usually happens, then the force is felt in the ends themselves before [it is felt] in the middle, and therefore it is broken there. If the extension were made without local movement of one of the extremities, as when the strings of a lute are swelled by the moisture of the air and snap of themselves, I am certain that they would break in the middle rather than elsewhere; you can experiment with this and inform me, for I have never done it. . . .

October, 1631

. . . Touching on the sweetness of consonance, there are two things to distinguish: namely, what renders them simpler and more harmonious and what renders them more agreeable to the ear. Now, as to what renders them more agreeable, that depends on the places in which they are used, and there are found places where even false fifths and other dissonances are more agreeable than consonances, the consequence being that one could not determine absolutely that one consonance is more agreeable than another. One can certainly say, however, that ordinarily thirds and sixths are more agreeable than the fourth; that in gay songs thirds and major sixths are more agreeable than the minor and the contrary in sad, etc., because there are found more occasions in which they can be employed agreeably. But one can say absolutely which consonances are the simplest and most harmonious; for that depends only upon the fact that their sounds unite more one with the other and that they approach more the nature of unison; consequently one can say absolutely that the fourth is more harmonious than the major third, although ordinarily it is not so agreeable, just as cassia is much sweeter than olives but not so agreeable to our taste. And to understand this really clearly, it is necessary to assume that the sound is nothing but a certain trembling of air which titilates our ears and that the motions to and fro of this trembling are proportionately faster as the

[38] "Consort" (archaic). "Union or symphony of various instruments playing in concert to one tune" (Grove's *Dictionary of Music and Musicians*).

sound is sharper; in consequence two sounds being an octave apart, the lower causes the air to tremble only once while the higher will make it tremble exactly twice and the same with other consonances. Thus it is necessary to assume that when two sounds strike the air at the same time, they are proportionately more harmonious as their tremblings begin again more often simultaneously and as they cause less inequality in the whole body of air. . . .

Benedict (Baruch) Spinoza

1637–1677

A. Life

Benedict Spinoza was born in Amsterdam and died at the Hague. His family were Spanish or Portuguese Jews, and Spinoza studied Hebrew until he was fifteen years of age. Doubtful of the cogency of Hebraic theology and fascinated by the physical and mathematical theories of the early seventeenth century, Spinoza expressed heretical views and was forced to leave the Synagogue in 1656. He earned a livelihood as a maker of lenses. He was offered but did not accept the chair of Philosophy at the University of Heidelberg; in 1661, he moved to Rhynsberg, near Leyden, where he began his writing of the *Ethic*. In 1670, he wrote the *Theological-Political Tractate,* in which he defended religious freedom as a right of man. He died in 1677. His house still stands in Amsterdam.

Spinoza knew the young Leibniz and carried on an extensive correspondence with, among others, Oldenburg and Boxel. Selections from the letters which discuss problems relating to beauty are given below.

Spinoza's brief writings on beauty and beautiful things are all of a piece. What men take to be objectively beautiful are called so as a result of our capacity to formulate universal terms. What men take to be beautiful as the products of God or Nature show in fact the predilection men have for reading into deity and nature their own feelings, images and purposes. Teleology is a falsification of what is properly understood as a mechanical universe, to be submitted to mathematics "which does not deal with ends."

B. Philosophy of Beauty

Beauty and deformity as modes of imagination: universals and highly confused ideas

. . . After men persuaded themselves [39] that everything which is created is created for their sake, they were bound to consider as the chief quality in everything that which is most useful to themselves, and to account those things the best of all which have the most beneficial effect on making. Further, they were bound to form abstract notions for the explanation of the nature of things, such as *goodness, badness, order, confusion, warmth, cold, beauty, deformity,* and so on; and from the belief that they are free agents arose the further notions *praise* and *blame, sin* and *merit*. . . .

. . . But all these prejudices which I have undertaken to point out depend upon this solely: that it is commonly supposed that all things in nature, like men, work to some end; and indeed it is thought to be certain that God Himself directs all things to some sure end, for it is said that God has made all things for man, and man that he may worship God. This, therefore, I will first investigate by inquiring, firstly, why so many rest in this prejudice, and why all are so naturally inclined to embrace it? I shall then show its falsity, and, finally, the manner in which there have arisen from it prejudices concerning *good* and *evil, merit* and *sin, praise* and *blame, order* and *disorder, beauty* and *deformity*, and so forth. . . . The other notions which I have mentioned are nothing but modes in which the imagination is affected in different ways, and nevertheless, they are regarded by the ignorant as being specially attributes of things, because, as we have remarked, men consider all things as made for themselves, and call the nature of a thing good, evil, sound, putrid, or corrupt, just as they are affected by it. For example, if the motion by which the nerves are affected by means of objects represented to the eye conduces to well-being, the objects by which it is caused are called *beautiful;* while those exciting a contrary motion are called *deformed*. Those things, too, . . . which act through the ears are said to make a noise, sound, or harmony, the last having caused men to lose their senses to such a degree that they have believed that God even is delighted with it. Indeed, philosophers may be found who have persuaded themselves that the celestial motions beget a harmony. All these things sufficiently show that every one judges things by the constitution of the brain, or rather accepts the affections of his imagination in the place of things. . . . So many heads, so many ways of thinking; Every one is satisfied with his own way of thinking; Differences of brains are not less common than differences of taste;—all which maxims show that men decided upon matters according to the constitution of their brains, and imagine rather than understand things. . . .

. . . For[40] it all comes to this, that these terms signify ideas in the highest degree confused. It is in this way that those notions have arisen which are called *Universal,* such as, *Man, Horse, Dog, &c.;* that is to say, so many images of men, for instance, are formed in the human body at once, that they exceed the power of the imagination, not entirely, but to such a degree that the mind has no power to imagine the determinate number of men and the small

[39] Benedict Spinoza, *Ethic I,* Appendix. *Spinoza's Ethics,* translated by W. H. White, Duckworth, London, 1899.

[40] *Ibid.* Pt. 2, prop. XL.

differences of each, such as colour and size, &c. It will therefore distinctly imagine that only in which all of them agree in so far as the body is affected by them, for by that the body was chiefly affected, that is to say, by each individual, and this it will express by the name *man,* covering thereby an infinite number of individuals; to imagine a determinate number of individuals being out of its power. But we must observe that these notions are not formed by all persons in the same way, but that they vary in each case according to the thing by which the body is more frequently affected, and which the mind more easily imagines or recollects. For example, those who have more frequently looked with admiration upon the stature of men, by the name *man* will understand an animal of erect stature, while those who have been in the habit of fixing their thoughts on something else, will form another common image of men, describing man, for instance, as an animal capable of laughter, a biped without features, a rational animal, and so on; each person forming universal images of things according to the temperament of his own body. . . ."

Beauty is not a quality of the object

. . . I too,[41] in order not to confuse the Divine with human nature, do not assign to God human attributes, such as Will, Understanding, attention, hearing, etc. Therefore, I say, as I have said just now, that the world is a necessary effect of the Divine Nature, and was not made by chance.

This, I think, will be sufficient to persuade you that the opinion of those (if indeed there are such persons) who say that the world was made by chance, is entirely opposed to my opinion. Relying on this foundation, I proceed to inquire into those reasons from which you conclude that all kinds of Spectres exist. What I can say of them in general is that they seem to be conjectures rather than reasons, and that I can find it difficult to believe that you hold them to be conclusive reasons. Let us see, however, whether they are conjectures or reasons, and whether we can accept them as established.

Your first reason is that the existence of Spectres is required for the beauty and perfection of the Universe. Beauty, most honoured Sir, is not so much a quality of the object which is perceived as an effect in him who perceives it. If our eyes were more long-sighted or more short-sighted, or if our temperament were other than it is, things which now appear to us beautiful would appear to be ugly and things which now appear to be ugly would appear to us beautiful. The most beautiful hand when seen through a microscope will appear horrible. Some things seen at a distance are beautiful, but seen at closer range are ugly. Therefore things regarded in themselves, or in relation to God, may be neither beautiful nor ugly. He, then, who says that God created the world to be beautiful must necessarily assert one of two alternatives, namely, either that God has made the world to suit the desire and the eyes of men, or the desire and the eyes of men to suit the world. Now, whether we assert the former or the latter, I do not see why God had to create Spectres and Spirits in order that one of these alternatives should result. Perfection and imperfection are designations which are not very different from those of beauty and ugliness. Therefore, not to be too diffuse, I only ask what will contribute more to the beauty and perfection of the world, is it the existence of Spectres, or that of numerous monsters, such as Centaurs, Hydras, Harpies, Satyrs, Griffins, Arguses, and more absurdities of this kind?

[41] Benedict Spinoza, *The Correspondence of Spinoza.* Letter LIV to Hugo Boxel, September, 1674. Translated by A. Wolf. George Allen and Unwin, Ltd., London, 1928. Boxel's reply, dated September, 1674, is No. LV in Wolf's edition. By permission of George Allen and Unwin.

The world would indeed have been well adorned had God for the pleasure of our Phantasy adorned and equipped it with these things which each man can easily imagine and dream for himself, but no one can ever understand. . . .

Beauty or ugliness not attributable to nature but are so called with respect to our imagination

. . . When you ask me [42] what I think about the question which turns on *the Knowledge how each part of Nature accords with the whole of it, and in what way it is connected with the other parts,* I think you mean to ask for the reasons on the strength of which we believe that each part of Nature accords with the whole of it, and is connected with the other parts. For I said in my preceding letter that I do not know how the parts are really interconnected, and how each part accords with the whole; for to know this it would be necessary to know the whole of Nature and all its Parts.

I shall therefore try to show the reason which compels me to make this assertion; but I should like first to warn you that I do not attribute to Nature beauty or ugliness, order or confusion. For things cannot, except with respect to our imagination, be called beautiful, or ugly, ordered or confused.

By connection of the parts, then, I mean nothing else than that the laws, or nature, of one part adapt themselves to the laws, or nature, of another part in such a way as to produce the least possible opposition. With regard to whole and parts, I consider things as parts of some whole, in so far as their natures are mutually adapted so that they are in accord among themselves, as far as possible; but in so far as things differ among themselves, each produces an idea in our mind, which is distinct from the others, and is therefore considered to be a whole, not a part. For instance, since the motions of the particles of lymph, chyle, etc., are so mutually adapted in respect of magnitude and figure that they clearly agree among themselves, and all together constitute one fluid, to that extent only, chyle, lymph, etc., are considered to be parts of the blood: but in so far as we conceive the lymph particles as differing in respect of figure and motion from the particles of chyle, to that extent we consider them to be a whole, not a part.

Let us now, if you please, imagine that a small worm lives in the blood, whose sight is keen enough to distinguish the particles of blood, lymph, etc., and his reason to observe how each part on collision with another either rebounds, or communicates a part of its own motion, etc. That worm would live in this blood as we live in this part of the universe, and he would consider each particle of blood to be a whole, and not a part. And he could not know how all the parts are controlled by the universal nature of blood, and are forced, as the universal nature of blood demands, to adapt themselves to one another, so as to harmonize with one another in a certain way. For if we imagine that there are no causes outside the blood to communicate new motions to the blood, and that outside the blood there is no space, and no other bodies, to which the particles of blood could transfer their motion, it is certain that the blood would remain always in its state, and its particles would suffer no changes other than those which can be conceived from the given relation of the motion of the blood to the lymph and chyle, etc., and so blood would have to be considered always to be a whole and not a part. But, since there are very many other causes which in a certain way control the laws of the nature of blood, and are in turn controlled by the blood, hence it comes about that other motions and other changes take place in the blood, which result not only from the mere relation of the motion of its parts to one

[42] *Ibid.,* Letter XXXII, to Oldenburg.

another, but from the relation of the motion of the blood and also of the external causes to one another: in this way the blood has the character of a part and not of a whole. I have only spoken of whole and part.

Now, all the bodies of nature can and should be conceived in the same way as we have here conceived the blood: for all bodies are surrounded by others, and are mutually determined to exist and to act in a definite and determined manner, while there is preserved in all together, that is, in the whole universe, the same proportion of motion and rest. Hence it follows that every body, in so far as it exists modified in a certain way, must be considered to be a part of the whole universe, to be in accord with the whole of it, and to be connected with the other parts. And since the nature of the universe is not limited, like the nature of the blood, but absolutely infinite, its parts are controlled by the nature of this infinite power in infinite ways, and are compelled to suffer infinite changes. But I conceive that with regard to substance each part has a closer union with its whole. For as I endeavoured to show in my first letter, which I wrote to you when I was still living at Rhynsburg, since it is of the nature of substance to be infinite, it follows that each part belongs to the nature of corporeal substance, and can neither exist nor be conceived without it. . . .

Gottfried Wilhelm Leibniz

1645–1716

A. Life

The great seventeenth century Rationalist philosopher, Gottfried Wilhelm Leibniz, was born in 1646 in Leipzig and died in Hanover in 1716. He was precocious, entering the University of Leipzig at the age of fifteen, and he was offered a professorship before he reached the age of twenty-one. Leibniz entered the service of the Elector of Mainz and in 1671 completed *A New Physical Hypothesis.* He spent three years in London and Paris, meeting Arnauld, the follower of Descartes, Tschirnhausen, a Spinozist, and Huygens, the distinguished Dutch mathematician. He knew the scientist Boyle, corresponded with Newton, and read the manuscript of the *Ethic,* which Spinoza showed him. He served as court counselor and librarian to the Duke of Hanover and published in 1684 his version of the differential calculus. Leibniz founded the Academy of Sciences in Berlin in 1700. His principal writings were *The Monadology, The Theodicy,* and *The Principles of Nature and Grace, New Essays on Human Understanding,* and the *Letters to Clarke.*

Leibniz did not write systematically on art or beauty. The following selections are drawn from a variety of sources in his writings and these sources are indicated in the text.[43]

B. Philosophy of Art

The 'I know not what' and 'sympathy'

Joy[44] is a pleasure which the soul feels in itself. *Pleasure* is the feeling of a perfection or an excellence, whether in ourselves or in something else. For the perfection of other beings also is agreeable, such as understanding, courage, and especially beauty in another human being, or in an animal or even in a

[43] I am deeply indebted to Clifford Brown for graciously providing me with some of the selections below. I should like to call special attention to Professor Brown's "Leibniz and Aesthetic," *Philosophy and Phenomenological Research,* XXVIII, 1.

[44] *On Wisdom* (in Gottfried Wilhelm Leibniz, *Philosophical Papers and Letters,* translated and edited by LeRoy E. Loemker; 2 Vols, (Chicago, 1956) II, 697-99). By permission of D. Reidel Publishing Co., Dordrecht, Holland.

lifeless creation, a painting or a work of craftsmanship, as well. For the image of such perfection in others, impressed upon us, causes some of this perfection to be implanted and aroused within ourselves. . . .

We do not always observe wherein the perfection of pleasing things consists, or what kind of perfection within ourselves they serve, yet our feelings (*Gemüth*) perceive it, even though our understanding does not. We commonly say, "There is something, I know not what, that pleases me in the matter." This we call "sympathy." But those who seek the causes of things will usually find a ground for this and understand that there is something at the bottom of the matter which, though unnoticed, really appeals to us. . . .

Music is a beautiful example of this. Everything that emits a sound contains a vibration or a transverse motion such as we see in strings, thus everything that emits sounds gives off invisible impulses. When these are not confused, but proceed together in order but with a certain variation, they are pleasing; in the same way, we also notice certain changes from long to short syllables, and a coincidence of rhymes in poetry, which contain a silent music, as it were, and when correctly constructed are pleasant even without being sung. Drum beats, the beat and cadence of the dance, and other motions of this kind in measure and rule derive their pleasureableness from their order, for all order is an aid to the emotions. And a regular though invisible order is found also in the artfully created beats and motions of vibrating strings, pipes, bells, and, indeed, even of the air itself, which these bring into uniform motion. Through our hearing, this creates a sympathetic echo in us, to which our animal spirits respond. This is why music is so well adapted to move our minds. . . .

There can be no doubt that, even in touch, taste, and smell, sweetness consists in a definite though insensible order and perfection or a fitness, which nature has put there to stimulate us and the animals to that which is otherwise needed. . . .

I call any elevation of being a perfection . . . perfection shows itself in great freedom and power of action, since all being consists in a kind of power. . . .

The greater any power is, moreover, the more there is found in it the many revealed through the one and in the one. . . . Now unity in plurality is nothing but harmony [Uebereinstimmung], and, since any particular being agrees with one rather than another being, there flows from this harmony the order from which beauty arises, and beauty awakens love.

Taste consists of confused perceptions

Taste[45] as distinguished from understanding consists of confused perceptions for which one cannot give an adequate reason. It is something like an instinct. Tastes are formed by nature and by habits. To have good taste, one must practice enjoying the good things which reason and experience have already authorized.

Confused knowledge and the "something, I know not what"

Knowledge[46] is *clear*, therefore, when it makes it possible for me to recognize the thing

[45] *Remarks on the Three Volumes Entitled "Characteristics of Men, Manners, Opinions, Times . . . "* (in Gottfried Wilhelm Leibniz, *Philosophical Papers and Letters,* translated and edited by LeRoy E. Loemker; 2 Vols. (Chicago, 1956) II, 1031). By permission of D. Reidel Publishing Co., Dordrecht, Holland.

[46] *Meditations on Knowledge, Truth, and Ideas* (in Gottfried Wilhelm Leibniz, *Philosophical Papers and Letters,* translated and edited by LeRoy E. Loemker; 2 Vols. (Chicago, 1956) I, 449). By permission of D. Reidel Publishing Co., Dordrecht, Holland.

represented. Clear knowledge, in turn, is either confused or distinct. It is *confused* when I cannot enumerate one by one the marks which are sufficient to distinguish the thing from others, even though the thing may in truth have such marks and constituents into which its concept can be resolved. Thus we know colors, odors, flavors, and other particular objects of the senses clearly enough and discern them from each other but only by the simple evidence of the senses and not by marks that can be expressed. So we cannot explain to a blind man what red is, nor can we explain such a quality to others except by bringing them into the presence of the thing and making them see, smell, or taste it, or at least by reminding them of some similar perception they have had in the past. Yet it is certain that the concepts of these qualities are composite and can be resolved, for they certainly have their causes. Likewise we sometimes see painters and other artists correctly judge what has been done well or badly; yet they are often unable to give a reason for their judgment but tell the inquirer that the work which displeases them lacks "something, I know not what."

Contemplation of beautiful things is pleasant in itself

Thus the contemplation of beautiful things [47] is itself pleasant, and a painting of Raphael affects him who understands it, even if it offers no material gains, so that he keeps it in his sight and takes delight in it, in a kind of image of love. But when the beautiful object is at the same time itself capable of happiness, this affection passes over into true love.

[47] *From the Preface of the CODEX JURIS GENTIUM DIPLOMATICUS* (in Gottfried Wilhelm Leibniz, *Philosophical Papers and Letters,* translated and edited by LeRoy E. Loemker; 2 Vols. (Chicago, 1956) II, 690-91). By permission of D. Reidel Publishing Co., Dordrecht, Holland.

Reason, imagination and the precepts of art

Music [48] is subordinate to Arithmetic and when we know a few fundamental experiments with harmonies and dissonances, all the remaining general precepts depend on numbers; I recall once drawing a harmonic line divided in such a fashion that one could determine with the compass the different compositions and properties of all musical intervals. Besides, we can show a man who does not know anything about music, the way to compose without mistakes. But as it is not enough to know Grammar and Prosody to compose a beautiful epigram, and since a schoolboy who is taught to avoid mistakes in his writing does not for that purpose have to compose a speech having the power of Cicero's eloquence, so in music what a man needs to compose successfully are practice as well as genius and vivid imagination in things of the ear. And as the making of beautiful verses requires a prior reading of good poets, noticing turns and expressions which gradually tinge one's own style, "as they who walk in the sun take on another tint," in the same way a Musician, after noticing in the compositions of talented men a thousand and one beautiful cadences and, so to speak, phrases of Music, will be able to give flight to his own imagination furnished with these fine materials. There are even those who are naturally musicians and who compose beautiful melodies just as there are natural poets who with a little aid and reading perform wonders, for there are things, especially those dependent

[48] *Precepts for Advancing the Sciences and Arts* (in *Leibniz Selections,* edited by Philip D. Wiener, Charles Scribners' Sons, New York, 1951, pp. 42-43). By permission of Charles Scribners' Sons.

on the senses, in which we do better by letting ourselves go automatically by imitation and practice than by sticking to dry precepts. And as playing the clavichord requires a habit which the fingers themselves have to acquire, so imagining a beautiful melody, making a good poem, promptly sketching architectural ornaments or the plan of a creative painting require that our imagination itself acquire a habit after which it can be given the freedom to go its own way without consulting reason, in the manner of an inspired Enthusiasm. The imagination will not fail to succeed in proportion to the genius and experience of the person, and we ourselves sometimes have the experience in dreams of shaping images which we should have great difficulty in creating while awake. But reason must afterwards examine and correct and polish the work of the imagination; that is where the precepts of art are needed to produce something finished and excellent . . . . we have said all these things only in order to forestall incidentally the false notions of those who might abuse what we have just said about the easy means of learning the sciences by some few precepts or principles of discovery.

Whole and part

. . . Look[49] at the most lovely picture, and then cover it up, leaving uncovered only a tiny scrap of it. What else will you see there, even if you look as closely as possible, and the more so as you look from nearer and nearer at hand, but a kind of confused medley of colours, without selection, without art! And yet when you remove the covering, and look upon the whole picture from the proper place, you will see that what previously seemed to you to have been aimlessly smeared on the canvas was in fact accomplished with the highest art by the author of the work. What happens to the eyes in painting is equally experienced by the ears in music. The great composers frequently mingle discords with harmonious chords so that the listener may be stimulated and pricked as it were, and may become eager to know what is going to happen; presently when all is restored to order he feels so much the more content. In the same way we may take pleasure in small dangers, or in the experience of ills, from the very sense or proof they give us of our own power or felicity. Or again at the spectacle of rope-walking or sword-dancing we are delighted by the very element of fear that is involved, and we ourselves in play with children hold them as if we were going to throw them out of the window, and half let them go—in very much the same way as the ape carried Christian, King of Denmark, when he was still an infant wrapped in long clothes, to the edge of the roof, and then, when everybody was in terror, turned it into jest and put him back into his cradle safe and sound. On the same principle it has an insipid effect if we always eat sweet things; sharp, acid, and even bitter things should be mixed in to stimulate the taste. He who has not tasted what is bitter has not earned what is sweet, nor will he appreciate it. This is the very law of enjoyment, that positive pleasure does not come from an even course; such things produce weariness, and make men dull, not joyful.

What I have said, however, about the possibility of a part being disturbed without upsetting the harmony of the whole must not be interpreted to mean that no account is taken of the parts; or that it is sufficient for the whole world to be completed at all points, even though it should turn out that the human race was wretched, and that there was in the universe no care for justice and no account was

[49] *On the Ultimate Origination of Things* (1697) From the book *The Philosophical Writings of Leibniz* by G. W. Leibniz. Selected and translated by Mary Morris. Introduction by C. R. Morris. Everyman's Library edition. Published by E. P. Dutton & Co. and reprinted with their permission. Also by permission of J. M. Dent and Sons Ltd. pp. 39 et seq.

taken of us—as is maintained by some people whose judgment about the sum of things is ill-grounded. For the truth is that, just as in a well regulated commonwealth care is taken that as far as possible things shall be to the interest of the individual, in the same way the universe would not be sufficiently perfect unless, as far as can be done without upsetting the universal harmony, the good of individual people is considered. Of this there could be established no better measure than the very law of justice itself, which dictates that each should have a part in the perfection of the universe and in his own happiness in proportion to his own virtue and to the extent to which his will is directed towards the common good; by which is fulfilled what we call the charity and love of God, in which alone, according to the judgment of wise theologians also, stands the whole force and power of the Christian religion. Nor ought it to seem remarkable that all this deference should be paid to minds in the universe, since they bear the closest resemblance to the image of the supreme Author, and their relation to Him is not that of machines to their artificer (like the rest of the world) but rather that of citizens to their prince; moreover they will endure as long as the universe itself, and they, in some manner, express and concentrate the whole in themselves; so that it might be said that minds are whole parts. . . .

God and the artisan contrasted

. . . The reason[50] why God is to be preferred above another mechanician is not only because He makes the whole, whereas the artisan has to seek for his material. This superiority would arise from power only. But there is another reason for the excellence of God, which arises from wisdom. This reason is that His machine also lasts longer and goes more correctly than that of any other mechanician whatever. The buyer of the watch does not trouble himself whether the workman made the whole of it, or whether he had the pieces of it made by other workmen and merely adjusted them himself, provided that it goes properly. And if the workman had received from God the gift of creating as well the material for the wheels, the buyer would not be satisfied if he had not also received the gift of adjusting them properly. And in the same way the man who wants to be satisfied with God's handiwork will not become so merely for the reason alleged here.

Thus it is needful that God's invention should not be inferior to that of a workman; it must even go infinitely beyond it. The mere production of everything would indeed exemplify the power of God, but it would not sufficiently show His wisdom. Those who maintain the opposite fall exactly into the error of the Materialists and of Spinoza, from whom they protest they differ. They recognize power, but not sufficient wisdom in the principle of things. . . .

[50] *New Essays on the Human Understanding.*

PART FIVE

THE EIGHTEENTH CENTURY: TASTE AND GENIUS

Chapter 9

Taste, a Central Problem for Philosophers of Art and Aestheticians in the Eighteenth Century

Speculation on art, on principles of Philosophy of Art, and on the basis of aesthetic judgments and judgments of taste in the eighteenth century is immensely rich and influential. For an aesthetician, the main issues raised and problems examined arise from the debates concerning the primacy of criticism or taste, the repeated efforts to supplant imitation and replace the mimetic interpretation of art by imagination, the conjoining of inspiration with a natural ground and the exclusion from speculation of reliance on divine intervention as an explanation for the artistic process, and the emergence of the ancient theory of the genius in new guises. Each effort has its roots in classical speculation. Of the more important problems, those concerning taste and genius have the deeper roots.

In the material that follows, the reader will find mention of the writings by the French genius, Voltaire; selections from the writings of the Spanish monk and reformer, Feijoo; one of the greatest of eighteenth century philosophers, David Hume; the essayist, Alexander Gerard; and the pre-eminent thinker, Immanuel Kant. The names of lesser men, but men who nonetheless made extraordinary contributions in their own right or in their influence upon others, are those of William Duff, and Edmund Burke. Their contributions are principally, as are those of Edward Young, Henry Home and Joseph Addison, to the theories of taste, of genius, and of imagination. Much of the current of this speculation flows into Kant's *The Critique of Judgement,* in which are systematized the problems of taste, genius, creativity, and imagination. Kant in his turn influenced Coleridge, Hegel, Schopenhauer, Nietzsche, Schiller, and Croce, as we shall observe in the next chapter.

The essays that follow have in common the subject of taste and the fact that all were written in the eighteenth century. The essayists differ, however, as radically in their methods and inferences as do the countries in which they lived and the professions they followed. As a literary figure, F. M. A. de Voltaire (1694–1778) is the most notable of the essayists included in this chapter. A man of universal genius, Voltaire's writings ranged from a study of the elements of Newton's philosophy to *Philosophical Letters,* in which he contrasts John Locke and René Descartes, as well as the French and the English governments. He set his face against superstition and dogma. Like Hume, he was a skeptic, but unlike the Scotsman he wrote the most cutting attacks against dogmatists and the clergy.

The two skeptics, Voltaire and Hume, are balanced in the following essays by a friar and a clergyman, the first a Spaniard, the second a Scotsman. The Spaniard, Friar Feijoo has had considerable influence as a critic on Spanish men of letters. Alexander Gerard, the Scotsman, was regarded by Kant as the greatest of the British writers on genius.

The Eighteenth Century: Critical Judgments and Judgments of Taste

For a student of Aesthetics, the issue drawn in the eighteenth century between the proponents of criticism and the advocates of taste is of primary importance. That there is an art of criticism, that it is autonomous, and that its results are valid is implicit in both the theory and practice of an age noted for the eminence of its critics and the quality of their work. That stout-hearted author of *The Lives of the Poets*, Dr. Samuel Johnson, was clearly not inclined to diminish by one iota his high regard for the critic. This is evident in his reply to the Boswell who appeared before him bemoaning the fact that he and Dempster had written a criticism of the tragedy, *Elvira.* Neither man, said Boswell, could have written a play "near so good." To this, Johnson justly replied, "You *may* abuse a tragedy, though you cannot write one. You may scold a carpenter who has made you a bad table. It is not your trade to make tables."

For most critics, inheritors as they were of a tradition that goes back to Aristotle's *Poetics,* sound criticism was authoritative, accurate, and analytical. It was an art to be practised with skill, but critics and criticism were to run into stormy seas. Two of the most distinguished philosophers of the century subjected the "art" to critical examination and judged it from the point of view of advocates of the man of taste. One, David Hume, approached criticism from the viewpoint of skeptic and empiricist, the other, Immanuel Kant, as the critical philosopher in search of an *a priori* ground for judgment. The result of their efforts and of those of many lesser men was a growing tendency to exile the critic from Aesthetics and elevate the man of taste to a place of eminence in aesthetic speculation.

Both Hume and Kant attack the assumption that criticism is an art. Kant quotes Hume with approval, selecting precisely the remark concerning criticism that the Scottish philosopher adopted from Aristotle, who had said in the *Nicomachean Ethics* (VII) that "the fact that no pleasure is the product of any art arises naturally enough; there is no art of any other activity either, but only the corresponding faculty. . . ." Aristotle added that "though for that matter the arts of the perfumer and the cook *are* thought to be arts of pleasure." Hume, interested in criticism and critics, transforms what Aristotle said into a snide remark concerning the art of criticism. In *The Skeptic,*[1] he writes that "Critics can reason and dispute more plausibly than cooks or perfumers" but adds that "this uniformity among human kind, hinders not, but that there is a considerable diversity in the sentiments of beauty and worth. . . ." Hume's main argument is that beauty and worth are "merely of

[1] David Hume, "The Skeptic", *Essays,* Part 1, XVIII. See below, pp. 347 et seq., particularly p. 349.

a relative nature. . . ." but Kant quotes with approval Hume's remark concerning critics: "Although as *Hume* says," he writes, "all critics can reason more plausibly than cooks, yet the same fate awaits them.[2] They cannot expect the determining ground of this judgment (to be derived) from the force of the proofs. . . ."

It is a matter of considerable importance to imply that criticism is unsound and that it should give way to taste. The writers upon taste in the eighteenth century did not underestimate their task. What was involved was not only the displacement of the critic from the central position he had occupied since Aristotle's time, but there was need to consider precisely the role taste was to play in its own turn. One answer was Kant's in the third Critique. It was a systematic approach to Aesthetics, and Kant sought to provide the ground for a universally valid judgment of taste, a ground resting on the reflection of the subject upon his own state of pleasure and pain. In this assertion, "all precepts and rules" are rejected. Kant argues that universal agreement may be imputed to all men, a point not too different from that made by most critics. But Kant, in addition, sought to establish the judgment of taste not only as a priori and necessary, but also subjective, and this did in fact run counter to what most critics sought. "A judgment of others," Kant writes, "which is unfavorable to ours may indeed rightly make us scrutinize our own with care, but it can never convince us of its incorrectness."

It is not in Kant's interest to argue that judgments of art and natural beauty are objective, convinced as he is that the judgment of taste is not conceptual. He holds that a man of taste can "impute" with confidence the judgment he makes to all other men, not on such empirical grounds as Edmund Burke[3] believed would lead a hundred men to agree that a given object is beautiful but, rather, on the ground that the judgment of taste is an harmonious interplay of the faculties of Understanding and Imagination. These faculties are integral to all cognition; all men cognise, therefore, Kant argues, the judgment of taste is universally valid.

Hume's skepticism is pronounced. He had argued that there are in every language certain terms that "import blame, and others praise . . . ," but he believes that "when critics come to particulars" the seeming unanimity in criticism vanishes. So far as the critic is concerned, Kant does not differ much in his opinion from Hume, who maintained that in fact ". . . Variety of taste is obvious to the most careless inquirer," and it will "be still greater in reality than in appearance." Kant urges the importance of *my* experience, arguing that "If any one reads me his poem, or brings me to a play, which, all said and done, fails to commend itself to my taste, then let him adduce *Batteux* or *Lessing,* or still older and more famous critics of taste, with all the host of rules laid down by them, as a proof of the beauty of his poem; let certain passages particularly displeasing to me accord completely with the rules of beauty, (as set out by these critics and universally recognized): I stop my ears: I do not want to hear any reasons for any arguing about the matter. I would prefer to suppose that those rules of the critics were at fault, or at least have no application, than to allow my judgement to be determined by a priori proofs. . . ."

It is illuminating that Kant draws the direct analogy between the experience of tasting food or wine and that of judging

[2] Immanuel Kant, *The Critique of Judgement,* Sect. 33. See below, pp. 360 et seq., for selections from Kant's writings. See also below, pp. 408 et seq.

[3] *A Philosophical Inquiry into the Origin of Our Ideas on the Sublime and the Beautiful.* London, J. Dodsley, 1770.

beauty. In doing so, he suggests the central problem of the period: "I try the dish with *my own* tongue and palate, and I pass judgement according to their verdict (not according to universal principles)." Kant knows full well that the analogy between the taste or food or wine and that of the judgment of taste is only an analogy.[4] Still, he uses the analogy to argue that in judgments of taste the representation of the tulip or the rose must be maintained in the imagination, as it does not do if we argue that "All tulips are beautiful." Kant believes that I feel pleasure in the aesthetic experience and that it is *my* pleasure.

We are, in part, back with Heraclitus[5] and with the author of the *Argument from Two Sides.*[6] There is this vast difference, however, that for Kant, if personal experience is a requisite, universal validity of judgment is no less so. In another sense, disputes concerning taste in the eighteenth century show an almost infinite diversity of attitudes towards the theme, *de gustibus non est disputandum.* To move from the skeptical Hume to the philosopher of universality, Kant, is to move from one extreme to another. Between these extremes, however, are among many others Voltaire, Feijoo and Gerard.

We shall come shortly to a more detailed account of Hume and Kant, as well as to some account of Voltaire, Feijoo, and Gerard. We shall understand them better and the eighteenth century attitudes toward taste and criticism more fully if we know something of the history of the change from the latter to the former and if we know, as well, something of the philosophical concepts that underlay the change.

The historical forces affecting the change from interest in criticism to speculation on taste are presented in a singularly valuable and informative essay,[7] written by Joel Spingarn at the turn of the century. Spingarn examines the historical developments in terms of the end-product, Benedetto Croce's theory of art as expression.[8] Here we shall be content to select such portions of Spingarn's writing as cast some light on the origins of the conception of taste in the eighteenth century and then turn briefly to the writers who make their contribution to the subject. But we may fairly do so only if we know the outcome of Spingarn's own speculations. In his later work, *Creative Criticism* (1912), Spingarn argues that if we ask the question, "What has the poet tried to express and how has he expressed it?" the only satisfactory answer is obtained if the critic, "if only for a moment of supreme power" becomes "at one with the creator."

In the earlier article, published in 1904, Spingarn tells us that the diffusion of Aristotle's *Poetics* came to furnish a standard of judgment in criticism, that the ideal of classical imitation was merged into the ideal of neoclassical rules, and that "imitation had been followed by theory and theory by law." According to Spingarn, the question, "What is poetry?" began to be replaced in the sixteenth century by the question, "What is criticism?" and in the seventeenth and eighteenth centuries "a new terminology" was being created, one that indicated a change in interest from the materials of literature "to the moods and faculties of the creative mind." What in fact emerges is the problem of taste.

Spingarn writes that in the sixteenth century, "the diffusion of Aristotle's *Poetics* was central in developing poetic theory and in furnishing a standard of judgment in criticism."

[4] He takes pains to differentiate the experience of gratification from the free judgment of taste. See below, pp. 361, 363, *The Critique of Judgement,* Sects. 3, 5.

[5] See below, Ibid., 8, 12, 16. For Heraclitus, see above, p. 40.

[6] See above, pp. 31 et seq.

[7] J. S. Spingarn, "The Origins of Modern Criticism," *Modern Philology,* Vol. 1, No. 4, April, 1904. Cf. Spingarn's *Creative Criticism* and below, pp. 559 et seq. and 536 et seq. for Croce's Aesthetic.

[8] See below, pp. 559 et seq.

The result was "that unified body of doctrine" called "Renaissance poetics," in which "the outworn criteria of *dottrina* and *eloquentia*, by which the humanists had tested all literary endeavor, were superseded by a thousand new ones—probability, verisimilitude, unity, the fixed norm for each literary *genre*, and the like." The ideal of classical imitation was merged into the ideal of neoclassical rules and "Imitation had been followed by theory, and theory by law." The immediate problem of criticism was the application of this body of poetic theory to the body of creative literature, past and present . . . " a task performed principally in terms of "*Bontà, dottrina, eloquenza* and *arte*."

To put briefly Spingarn's conclusion concerning the change, the new terminology created to take care of the new ideal indicated a change in interest from the materials of literature "to the moods and faculties of the creative mind." For, as quoted previously, if we try to answer the question, "What has the poet tried to express and how has he expressed it?", the answer can only be got if the critic, however briefly, is "at one with the creator." Taste must reproduce the work of art within itself in order to understand and judge it "and at the moment aesthetic judgment becomes nothing more nor less than creative art itself." The heart of criticism thus becomes not classification, but creativity.

Spingarn believes that this means an identification of genius and taste and this he calls the "final achievement of modern thought on the subject of art." We shall come to the problem of genius in Philosophy of Art in the next chapter, but here we may anticipate: "By genius is not merely meant the creative faculty," Spingarn writes, "but the power of self-expression, which we all share in varying degrees. By taste is meant the power to see and understand and enjoy the self-expression of others, a power which all of us must in some measure share or no art would be intelligible . . . We are all geniuses; we are all possessed of taste . . ."

It is clear that many eighteenth-century critics would regard this as the natural—and unwelcome—result of the abandonment of the rules and might well wish to apply the words, "too libertine," with which Sir William Temple describes not only poetry but the conception of taste. Not all earlier critics abandon Aristotle and the rules of criticism. Ben Jonson earlier advocates a temperate course. The dramatist believes that Aristotle was the first accurate critic and truest judge—"Nay, the greatest Philosopher the world ever had." Still, Honest Ben stoutly maintains that "Nothing is more ridiculous than to make an Author a *Dictator*" and, he adds, "Let *Aristotle* and others have their dues," but "no man, so soone as he knowest this or reades it, shall be able to write the better; but as he is adapted to it by Nature, he shall grow the perfecter writer."

The attack on Aristotle is mounted, nonetheless, and is more severe than the great Peripatetic merited. It is interesting that Charles Gildon, in *The Complete Art of Poetry* (1718) writes that Aristotle " is one of the greatest *Philosophers*, that ever was in the World," but "as regards the *Manner* in which he presents the Rules of art," Aristotle "gives not his *Rules* as Legislators do their Laws, without any other Reason than his Will; all that he advances is confirm'd by Reasons drawn from the common Sentiments of Mankind, . . . " Gildon adds that "They are the Laws of Nature, which always acts with Uniformity, renews them incessantly, and gives them a perpetuate existence." It was Aristotelian theory of criticism that had multiplied the rules. As for Aristotle, it has been observed [9] that in the *Nicomachean Ethics* he admonishes the magnificent man to use the artist as a model in the matter of taste.

[9] See below, pp. 140.

Aristotle had said that lack of liberality in the magnificent man is "lack of taste" or vulgarity and that expenditures on small objects show "a tasteless showiness." But while Aristotle in the *Ethics* is comparing the artist and the man of great wealth, he is doing so primarily in the area of expenditures. It is not this Aristotelian tradition that writers of the eighteen century follow but, rather, that of Plato and Longinus. They do so, as we have observed, to permit the artist and the judge of art to escape the rules of art. But they go farther and ally the notion of freedom of rules with inspiration and with the inspired genius.[10] It is of value to indicate that the ground for the theory of taste was laid, by Plato, primarily in *Ion* and *Symposium*, and by Longinus in *de Sublimitate.* Two points should be briefly noted: the first is the impact of the Platonic and Longinean theory; the second is the effort on the part of eighteenth-century theorists to provide some substitute in taste for the order and rules that they had sacrified when they abandoned criticism as the core of philosophy of art.

A statement by Daniel Webb in his *Remarks on the Beauties of Poetry* suggests what the eighteenth century made of a passage in Plato's *Laws,* once its writers had worked out the implications of the Platonic theory of the inspired poet and applied it to criticism. Webb wrote that the critic is ". . . a dependent, a sort of planet to his original," one who may do no more than "receive and reflect that light of which the poet is a fountain." Plato had written (*Laws* 719C) that "The poet . . . when he sits down on the tripod of the muse, is not in his right mind; like a fountain, he allows to flow out freely whatever comes in, and . . . he is often compelled . . . to contradict himself; neither can he tell whether there is more truth in one thing that he has said than in another. . . . " It is Plato's view (*Timaeus* 71E–72A) that "No man when in his wits . . . attains . . . inspiration," and adds that it is customary to appoint interpreters to be judges of the true inspiration." The implication, as will be evident once we come to the notion of the inspired genius, is that the inspired man is creative and original, but the judge or critic is not only lacking in originality but is doubtful that the products of originality are available for his judgment or criticism. It is clear that if the poet does not know whether he is in fact telling the truth or a falsehood and often contradicts himself, whereas the critic proceeds in terms of major and minor premise and conclusion, there are two separate and separated realms in the burgeoning Aesthetic of the eighteen century as it turns from Aristotle to Plato.

There is, in addition, the enormous impact of Longinus[11] to be considered in an evaluation of the problems of taste and criticism in the eighteenth century. It will suffice for the moment to illustrate the point by quoting Gibbon as he writes on his own experience in *Memoirs of My Life.* Gibbon tells us that until he had read Longinus' writing, he had believed criticism to be "an exact anatomy of the distinct beauties of a passage" and "whence they had sprung." But, he adds, Longinus taught him another form of criticism: "He tells me his own feelings upon reading and he tells them with such energy that he communicates them."

It is perhaps this substitution of the expression of his own feelings for the rules of art that presents the most formidable obstacle to the theorists of taste. How they surmount it is the subject of this and the succeeding chapters. If we now turn to the writers who seem characteristic of the century, we discover that feeling is but a part of the problem. For,

[10] See next Chapter, pp. 389 et seq.

[11] See above, pp. 192. et seq.

as Hume wrote, ". . . Variety of taste is obvious to the most careless inquirer" and it will "be still greater in reality than in appearance." The issue is the validity of the ancient saw, *de gustibus non est disputandum*.

Some eighteenth-century writers found the ground for their problem in Longinus' *de Sublimitate*. Thus, Thomas Warton, in *An Essay on the Genius and Writings of Pope,* judged that Longinus was a man of "exquisite taste" and "sensibility." Yet, among other criticisms, Warton argued that the author of the famous book on great poetry used a "method too loose" and that "Instead of discovering the secret power by which the sentiments and images affect the reader with pleasure, he is ever intent on producing something SUBLIME himself, and strokes of his own eloquence."

This is one price exacted for substituting taste for criticism—or so it would appear to be the price many believed must be paid for the acceptance of the argument, *de gustibus*. . . ." Part of the issue for philosophers of art and aestheticians turns on whether or not some portion of the objectivity of criticism may not be introduced into the conception of taste. The approaches to this issue vary with the writers. Hume remains skeptical but experimental, Voltaire writes a brilliant analysis of the external sense, *goût*. Feijoo, in revolt against the Scholastics in particular and the rationalists in general, adopts an empirical method. Alexander Gerard advocates the acceptance, as condition for the solution to the problem, of a reconciliation of Longinus and Aristotle. Kant undertakes the prodigious task of arguing the universality of the judgment of taste, along with its subjectivity. We shall turn to each in succession.

David Hume, as we have seen in *The Skeptic*, compares critics to cooks and perfumers and denies both to criticism and taste the unanimity and agreement some have maintained is possible. In the essay "Of the Standard of Taste,"[12] Hume gives his opinion that ". . . the same address and dexterity, which practice gives to the execution of any work, is also acquired by the same means, in judging of it." This, Hume maintains, is possible even though the rules of composition are not fixed by a priori reasonings nor are they "abstract conclusions of the understanding." What he calls the "nobler productions of genius" are explicable in terms of a mutual relation and correspondence of parts, as well as "a certain end or purpose for which it is calculated." It follows in his argument that it is possible for the critic to get at the truth; but it is also possible for him to err. Our errors arise because our thought may not be "capacious enough" to comprehend all these parts, and compare them with others, in order "to perceive the consistence and uniformity of the whole." We may err, also, because we may fail to retain in our view the end or purpose for which the work is fitted. We must be able to judge "how far the means employed are adapted to their respective purposes."

Hume's argument is empirical, based on "fact, not sentiment." Empirically, he holds that difference in the "degree of our approbation or blame" are due to different humors of particular men and to particular manners and opinions of our age and country. Hume argues that prejudices may prevail for a time but never "unite in celebrating any rival to the true genius. . . ." He goes so far as to argue that the principles of tastes are "universal, and nearly, if not entirely, the same for all men," but that individuals have imperfect organs of internal sensation and they may also criticize without sufficient practice."

The reader is made well aware of the acuteness of Hume's reasoning in these and in other instances of the principles of an empirical

[12] David Hume, "Of a Standard of Taste", *Essays, Literary Moral and Political by David Hume* (Essay XXII). See below, pp. 345 et seq. for a life of Hume and a selection from his writings.

criticism. It should be noted, in fact, how pervasive this empiricism is. Beauty is not a quality belonging to objects. Men may agree on the principles implicit in criticism but disagree that the specific instances in question embody the principles. Critical judgments are not matters of fact but of sentiment, and sentiments belong to the person entertaining them. Beauty marks a relation between the object and the subject. Critical judgment is dependent upon time and place and state of mind.

If we turn now from Hume to the Spanish monk, Benito Jerónimo Feijoo y Montenegro, we come to the writings of a man intent upon reducing the ignorance and superstitutions of his times and one bitterly attacked for his pains in doing so. He received general recognition for his *Teatro Critico* and the *Cartas Eruditas*. According to José M. Ferrater Mora, writing in his *Diccionario de Filosofía*, Feijoo's ideas were among the most advanced in the Europe of his time, the writer scorning the commonly held errors of his period in all fields. The limitations of Aristotelianism must be admitted, he argued, but the total surrender to "excessive Cartesian doubt" must not be permitted. Feijoo's search is for clarity and for the concrete, with emphasis upon experimentation and the use of logic as an instrumental technique. Philosophy lies midway between too great abstraction and what is too purely concrete and its method requires the recognition of a constant oscillation between these extremes in the subject.

For the philosopher of art and the aesthetician, Feijoo's most significant writing [13] is the essay "The 'I Know Not What.' " In it are found the view that "The investigation of principles is beyond access to the 'ingenio humano' " and that "without experience it is neither possible to study nature nor to have exact knowledge of it." More specifically, men, discouraged by their failure to explain a kind of "mysterious beauty" they find in the productions of nature and art, resort to the "formless" assertion "that a certain thing has an 'I know not what' which "pleases, which enchants, which bewitches." If one who resorts to this phrase finds pleasure and wonder in a building and finds, among other problems, that in it there is no exceptional observance of rules, they find neither words nor concepts "that satisfy their idea of it," and the beauty may torment their intelligence "in proportion as it pleases their taste."

Feijoo multiplies the instances in which the phrase, "I know not what" is used to describe the recognition of taste without the capacity to define. Indeed, he holds, there is no limit to the objects to which the sentence is applicable. It is applied to works of art—and Feijoo finds it in Pliny's account of Apelles—and to what is ugly. Discontented with this state of affairs, Feijoo sets himself the task of discovering "what this thing is that everyone says is unknowable." He proceeds to distinguish between simple and compound objects; draws the ancient conclusion that compound objects may please even though no part pleases the taste.[14] He infers that in these instances it is the mutual adaptation of the parts that provides the beauty of the compound object. The distinction between the beauty of the part and of the whole is stringently drawn. And although Feijoo admits that "there is nothing in the world which is to everyone's taste," he argues nonetheless, that the proportions between the compound object and the faculty of perception may provide a clue to the beauty, in spite of the fact that men's faculties, and therefore taste, differ.

[13] For a brief life of Feijoo and a translation of this essay, see below, pp. 336 et seq. Compare Leibniz, above, pp. 316 et seq.

[14] See Plato, *Republic* IV, above, p. 102, St. Augustine, above, pp. 238 et seq.; and Plotinus, above, pp. 220 et seq.

In an interesting passage, Feijoo further examines the problem in terms of dividing the possible answer to 'I know not what' into "what" and "why." ". . . He does not know what it is that pleases him . . ." or "why." As to the "what" in a voice that pleases him, Feijoo suggests that it is either the sound or the manner of handling it. It comes down eventually to the individual character, let us say, of the sound, which pleases. And the individual is never definable. Names do not explain the individual essence. Still, even though a single explanation will not fit all the cases of the word, some of the beauties in question can be explained and the 'I know not what' may be referred to one type of beauty or another. Feijoo then explains the three types to which he reduces all beauty.[15]

The author adds that imperfections of technique may escape the intelligence but nevertheless affect taste. This is indicated by an example contrasting a defect of pitch, which is not definable but diminishes the pleasure of the auditor.

Turning to the "Why" of 'I know not what,' Feijoo reverts to the factor of proportion, "the due and congruent proportion between the object and the perceptive faculty. . . ." Some men may like the type but the 'I know not what' is the individual quality of the given color. Feijoo argues that the 'I know not what' occurs most frequently in compound objects, principally because there are innumerable proportions different from the limited one we perceive. The efforts made by men to resolve the problem by reducing all beauties to one beauty is also a source for 'I know not what.'

The rules commonly used let us say in the construction of a building, will not curb the artist's soaring vision. He may and does know the rules and may have done everything according to rule. He may be obedient, however, to a higher rule in his mind.

At this juncture, Feijoo embarks on an examination of the problem of creativity. The professors of an art condemn the man who breaks the rules—but Feijoo echoes the ancient notion of inspiration. ". . . There are," he writes, "a number of compositions which break one rule or another and which please us enormously even in those passages where the rule is broken." He explains this on the ground that the common assumption that the rules are complete is erroneous. A soaring inspiration permits some men to perceive that the precepts and rules may in some circumstances be dispensed with. Excellent music does not go against the rules but only against a few limited and misunderstood ones.

The inference is drawn—and an important one it is—that "'I know not what' implies nothing other than being made according to art, but according to an art higher than that of the common rule." The distinction between art and fine art is implicit in this remark. Feijoo abandons this course of speculation at this point, indicating his belief in spiritual beauty—the complex, he writes, seems to be beautiful because it "shows forth the beauty of the soul." The beauty of a face is a strange grace that may be present even though the suitable proportions of the features are lacking. For Feijoo, the source of this aspect of "I know not what" is owing to the "good qualities of the soul."

A move such as Feijoo's from the establishment of "The I know not what" as the object of an empirically definable search to "beauty of the soul" as "I know not what" and as "a strange grace which may be present even though the suitable proportions of the features are lacking" is in fact an abandonment of the empirical and experimental method. It sets a problem, commented upon in ancient times by

[15] See below, Chapt. X, for Croce's criticism of types and his insistence on the individual. Referring to Feijoo, it is interesting to note that Croce refers as well to the fact that Spain from Vives to Feijoo was the land of freedom in criticism.

Socrates and Plato and resolved by them in terms of inspiration. It is implicit in the theory of genius, as we shall see in the next chapter, and there the problem emerges in efforts to define works of fine art and to examine the nature of the experience of objects and events that possess or display aesthetic value. As Feijoo expresses the problem, however, it runs counter to Hume's contention that "... the same address and dexterity, which practice gives to the execution of any work, is also acquired by the same means, in judging of it." Hume argues that even though rules of composition are not fixed by a priori reasonings, neither are they "abstract" givings of the understanding. Rules of composition are in fact "general observations, concerning what has been usually found to please in all countries and in all ages." And "if some negligent or irregular writers have pleased, they have not pleased by their transgressions of rule or order, but in spite of these transgressions they have possessed other beauties, which are conformable to just criticism. . . . The products of genius are dealt with on an empirical level. Like Feijoo, Hume argues that "unexpected or unaccountable" pleasures may be aroused by what is explicable in terms of "a mutual relation and correspondence of parts . . . as well as a certain end or purpose for which it is calculated." We may err but it is not necessary to abandon the empirical approach, even for a just criticism of "the nobler productions of genius."

Another but no less empirical tack is Voltaire's.[16] In his view, taste itself is the name for the external sense, a name that has been given a metaphorical meaning on occasion in all languages. This metaphorical interpretation of *taste* is the word we use to express "our perception of beauty, deformity, or defect in the several arts." But Voltaire is not content with the notion that *taste* is used metaphorically. Nor is he content to believe that it is a simple sensation. True, it is like the sensation of the palate, which anticipates reflexion. It is a quick discernment and a sudden perception. It is like the palate that is able to "relish what is good with an exquisite and voluptuous sensibility, and reject the contrary with loathing and disgust."

We begin to be aware of the complexity of Voltaire's conception of taste once we discover that the argument asserts that *goût* is often doubtful and bewildered. It does not know "whether it should relish or reject certain objects, and frequently requires the influence of habit to give it fixed and uniform determination."

We are prepared in this way for the brilliant inference Voltaire makes: "To have a *sense,* supposes something more than merely to perceive, and to discern with accuracy the beauty of any work or object. This beauty must be *felt*, as well as *perceived*; the mind must be touched and affected by it in a lively and sensible manner." Moreover, he adds, "This feeling . . . in order to constitute true *taste* must not be a vague and confused sensation but must be attended with a distinct view, a quick and comprehensive discernment of the various qualities, in their several relations and connexions, which entered into the composition of the object we contemplate. . . ."

The target of the attack is both taste as simple sensation and the confused feelings that

[16] Francois Marie Arouet de Voltaire (1694–1778) was one of the geniuses of the age. He was born in Paris, November 21, 1694, and died in that city in 1778. He was educated in the Jesuit College of Louis-le-Grand. He wrote the famous plays *OEdipe, Henriade, Artemire, Zaïre,* and *Merope.* Among his other writings of interest to the philosopher of art are *Lettres philosophiques sur les Anglais.* Voltaire was a superb satirist, Rousseau, the Church, and France itself being among his targets. The *Lettres* were condemned and burned. Voltaire suffered exile. The quotation given here is published in the *Encyclopédie* (Vol. VII, 1757). The eighteenth century translation used is the first of the three parts of the essay, "Goût". The remaining portions of the article are printed in *Questions sur l'Encyclopédie,* seixième partie, 1771.

rationalist philosophy had made central to speculation on art.

It is significant that Voltaire's essay on taste was translated into English and published in 1759 along with essays of related subjects by Montesquieu and D'Alembert, in Alexander Gerard's *An Essay on Taste.* Gerard, more explicitly but in the same spirit as Voltaire, is clearly in search of an analysis of the experience of art in which criticism and taste are dealt with so that the best aspects of each will make their contribution. In one superb sentence in *An Essay on Taste,* Gerard voices an opinion which, had Kant accepted and developed it instead of accepting Hume's opinion of critics, might well have altered the history of criticism and with it radically important portions of Philosophy of Art and Aesthetics. Instead, with Kant, as we have observed, comes the exile of critics from Aesthetics. Gerard had asserted that "As taste gives the last finishing to genius in the *author* or performer, so it is the fundamental ingredient in the *character* of the *critic.*" Refinement and justness of taste is necessary, but it is not sufficient. "A critic must not only *feel,* but possess that accuracy of discernment, which enables a person to *reflect* upon his feelings with distinctness, and to explain it to others."[17]

Kant fails to seize upon and develop the possibility that criticism might best be thought to reconcile feeling and reason, to combine Longinus' "fire" and Aristotle's rationality. Gerard himself had put forward a cogent and tempered theory of taste. A fine taste, he believes, is "neither wholly the gift of *Nature,* nor wholly the effect of art." [18] It originates in the powers of the mind to associate ideas, but it is the "interior senses" that, by their union, tend to form and perfect taste. Taste is not uniform among men of different nations and, indeed, taste and judgment may be united in very different proportions. "One *feels* what pleases," writes Gerard, whereas "the other knows what ought to gratify or disgust." He believes that sense has a kind of "instinctive infallibility" whereas judgment "often makes amends for dullness of imagination." He observes acutely that "one's chief entertainment from Works of genius lies in what he feels," whereas judgment leads one to enjoy principally the intellectual pleasure which results from "discovering the causes of his feelings."

Such argumentation leads Gerard to a comparison and contrast of Longinus and Aristotle.[19] In the former, the internal senses were "exquisitely delicate," but the judgment, "though good, was not in proportion." Longinus infuses his readers with his own rapture but does not always explain the reasons for that experience. Aristotle, on the other hand, "perfectly cool and unaffected" as he is, discovers no warmth of imagination and therefore does not transport his readers. Nevertheless, Aristotle's decisions are derived from "depth of penetration" and are both convincing and just.

We may leave Gerard's *An Essay on Taste* with his remarks on "the chief utility of criticism," turning to his theory of genius in the next chapter.[20] Gerard discovers the principal usefulness of criticism to lie in "promoting correctness of taste," a view that Kant adopts as well. The authority of the critic excites our attention and provokes inquiry; but "every one who really merits the name conveys much more momentous instruction and effectually teaches justness of thinking, by explaining the kind and degree of every excellence and blemish, by teaching us what are the qualities in things, to which we owe our pleasure or disgust, and what the principles of human nature, by which they are produced." Gerard lays down criteria for critics. The principles of taste include both judgment and all of the reflex senses. No critic combines all—culture, sensibility, refinement,

[17] For Gerard's life and writing, see below, pp. 352 et seq. and 404 et seq.

[18] See below, p. 352.

[19] See below, p. 357.

[20] See particularly pp. 404 et seq.

correctness, and the due proportion of all its parts in the qualities of his taste. Longinus, Dionysius of Halicarnasus, and Aristotle all possessed fine taste but "the first excelled in *sensibility,* the second in *refinement,* and the last in *correctness* and *enlargement.*"

Gerard's conception of taste as a combination of sensibility and its refinement on the one hand, and of correctness and its refinement on the other is a far cry from Burke's naive assumption that a considerable number of people congregated in a single room will agree that an object is beautiful. Still, Gerard's solution to the problem of making the "I know not what" into what is intelligible and demonstrable is an empirical one, based primarily upon the theory of the association of ideas. As Kant [21] undertakes to examine the problem of the nature of judgment and, more particularly, the judgment of taste, he abandons a posteriori for a priori principles. Kant's complex examination of the problem still has as its core the issue of providing an intelligible ground for taste while yet acknowledging that it is the taste and feeling of the individual perceiver that must be preserved in the process.

Whatever else "judgment of taste" means for Kant, it is not conceptual. The consequence is that the authority of the critic is abandoned, as are universal propositions such as "All tulips are beautiful." Still, Kant holds that the truth of the proposition, "This tulip is beautiful" may be established. The judgment of taste is an experience of a natural form such as the tulip, and we are made aware of it by the pleasure we enjoy. The pleasure is, however, not what we seek. Moreover, the pleasure is posterior to the harmonious interplay of the faculties of Imagination and Understanding.[22] The activity of the faculties is harmonious; it is a relation grounded on no concept; and the faculties in mutual agreement are brought into play more lively than in ordinary cognition. The faculties are in free play with reference to cognition in general. Imagination gathers the manifold of intuition, Understanding provides the unity of the concept uniting the representations. The judgment of taste is a state of mind in which we are aware that the harmonious interplay of the faculties is universally communicable, although not necessarily communicated.

As Kant develops his theory—and here only a brief statement of it can be presented—it is clear that he intends to establish the judgment of taste in an unique status. For his purposes, he abandons determinant judgment, in which the universal is given to find the particulars. In aesthetic experience, the particulars are given—delineations *à la grecque,* ripplemarks on the sand by the sea, tattoo marks, this rose, this tulip—and the universal is to be found. This is aesthetic as he sees it, and Kant classifies the judgment of taste as reflective, in contrast to determinant. The universal to be found is the universal judgment of taste based upon a cognitive state different from that in which we make moral, hedonic, ontological, or mathematical judgments. A judgment of taste is singular—it does not extend the judgment to objects but to the subject. Here the judgment is, because the interrelation of the faculties of Imagination and Understanding is integral to all cognition, imputable to all men. It is not commanded or demanded. We assume that once we have had the experience, it will be the same for all men since all men cognise.

Early in the *Critique,* Kant distinguishes the judgment of taste from the judgments, "that it is *good*" and "that it *gratifies.*" [23] Without going into the details of this differentiation, it is sufficient to point out that for Kant the judgment of taste is the only free and disinterested judgment. It is disinterested because we

[21] See below, pp. 359, 408 for a life of Kant and for selections from *The Critique of Judgement.*

[22] Kant, Ibid. Sect. 9. See below, pp. 368 et seq.

[23] *Ibid.,* Sects. 3–5. See below, pp. 361 et seq. See above, p. 317, for Leibniz similar inference.

are concerned with images or representations and are wholly unconcerned with the object's existence.

Kant's assertion that the judgment of taste is disinterested because we take interest in what is existent is a firm denial of any relevance of imitation to Aesthetics. Kant is wholly unconcerned with the issue of the accuracy or inaccuracy with which the image represents any possible source. In fact, neither the internal nor the external relations of the beautiful object are of concern to him. He has a more profound reason, however, for arguing the freedom of the judgment of taste than the mere denial of the validity of imitation. As we shall observe in the next chapter, the new Platonism and the revived Longinean philosophy of art grew to be more and more integral to imagination in the realm of art. Kant makes imagination integral to his Aesthetic, but it is not an imagination that is capricious and uncontrolled. Imagination permits the artist to convert the actual material that nature provides into another nature—one of imagination. It is a law-abiding nature to which the conversion is made. "The imagination, as a productive faculty of cognition, is a powerful agent for creating . . . a second nature . . . out of the material supplied to it by actual nature." [24] We are freed from the law of the association of ideas but freedom for Kant in its most meaningful sense does not mean freedom *from* rules but freedom under rules. Consequently, for him the principle of taste, for which no concept of the Object lies at the basis of the judgment, "can consist only in the subsumption of the imagination itself . . . under the conditions enabling the understanding in general to advance from the intuition to concepts." [25] Taste, for Kant, thus becomes the judgment subsuming the imagination under the understanding—the Imagination in its *freedom*, and of the understanding with *its conformity to law*.

At the hands of Kant and at the end of the eighteenth century, taste had been given a firm basis in freedom; but it had also been given a sound basis in intelligibility, in contrast to the "I know not what" which had hitherto pervaded philosophy of art and Aesthetics. Kant was not prepared to endow [26] taste with originality. He reserves originality for *genius* [27] and it remains for Croce to identify genius and taste.[28] To imagination in its creative role, we turn in the next chapter.

[24] Ibid., Sect. 49. See below, p. 415.

[25] Compare Sect. 49.

[26] Ibid., Sect. 48. See below, p. 414.

[27] *Ibid.*, Sect. 46. Kant remarks that originality is the first property of genius. See below, p. 411.

[28] See below, pp. 544 et seq. and above pp. 326. et seq.

Fr. Benito Jerónimo Feijoo

1676–1764

A. Life

Fray Benito Jeronimo Feijoo, one of the most important and influential figures in Spanish critical literature, was born in the province of Orense to a branch of a noble Galician family. In 1690, he entered the Monastery of Samos de la Orden de San Benito. After studying in Salamanca, he went in 1709 to Oviedo, to spend the remainder of his life at the University in writing and research in Theology and Literature. He had in fact an encyclopaedic mind and sought universal knowledge, writing in such diverse fields as medicine, philosophy, philosophy of art, criticism, witchcraft, religion, economics, and education. He fought against superstition and the rigor of scholastic dogma. He held to an empiricism expressed in the words "Without experience it is neither possible to study nature nor to have exact knowledge of it. She, and she alone, must determine the *fallos* of the judge, the judgments of the historian, the conclusions of the philosopher. . . . The investigation of principles is beyond access of the *ingenio humano."*

In the essay that follows, these principles are evident. Feijoo sought to deny the often assumed view that there is no disputing tastes by seeking the grounds for differences in men's judgments. For him, art is neither imitation nor subject to rules. The best art is creation.

B. Philosophy of Art

The "I Know Not What"

[SECTION I] [29]

In many productions of Nature and even of Art men find, beyond those perfections subject to their comprehension, another kind of mysterious beauty which torments their intelligence in proportion as it pleases their taste, which their senses can touch and reason cannot decipher; so it is that when they wish to explain it, not finding words or concepts that satisfy their idea of it, they let themselves fall, discouraged, into the formless assertion that a

[29] "the *No sé qué,"* by Friar Feijoo. Translated by Professor Willard F. King, Bryn Mawr College.

certain thing has an "I know not what" which pleases, which enchants, which bewitches; and there is no profit in asking them for a clearer revelation of this natural mystery.

They enter a building which at the very first sight fills them with pleasure and wonder. Examining it later more attentively, they find that neither by its grandeur or its abundance of light or the elegance of its basic materials or by its exact observance of the rules of architecture does it surpass, or perhaps even equal, others they have seen without finding pleasure or wonder in them. If they are asked what they find exquisite or beautiful in this building, they answer that it has an "I know not what" which entrances.

They come to a delightful spot whose pleasant aspect is due to Nature alone. They find nothing exquisite about its plants; nor in their situation, shape, or size that studied proportion which art employs in those plantings designed for the diversion of princes or peoples. The situation does not lack the crystalline beauty of running water, the necessary complement of all pleasant spots, but far from following in its course the measured direction, falls and rebounds with which the waves are made to play in royal gardens, it wanders aimlessly wherever the accidental opening of the terrain gives access to the stream. Nevertheless, the spot enchants the eye; a man cannot leave it, and his eyes are held more steadily by that natural carelessness than by all the artful beauties which provide a sumptuous and pleasing background for the country estates of great lords. What, then, does that natural spot have which does not appear in these? It has an "I know not what" which the latter do not have. And there is no point in pressing the spectator further, for he will not go beyond this statement.

They see a lady—or to give a clearer idea of the matter, let us express it in another way—they see a charming village maiden who has just come to the Court, and no sooner have they fixed their eyes on her than the image transmitted by them to the imagination prefigures for them an utterly pleasing object. The same people who looked with indifference or with tepid interest on the beautiful ladies most celebrated by the people can scarcely tear their eyes away from this rustic beauty. What singular quality do they find in her? Her skin is not so white as that of many others that they see every day, nor are her features more regular, nor her eyes wider, nor her lips redder, nor her forehead so broad, nor her figure so slender. It matters not. The village girl has an "I know not what" which is of more value than all the perfections of the others. There is no point in asking for further explanations, for they will say no more. This "I know not what" is the enchantment of their will and the stumbling block of their intelligence.

[SECTION II]

If one considers the matter insistently, there is no kind of object in which this "I know not what" may not be found. On occasion we are uplifted by the song of a voice which is neither clearer nor of so wide a range nor of such free play as others we have heard. Nevertheless this voice holds us more firmly than the others. How can that be if it is inferior to them in clarity, range, and elegance? It matters not. This voice has an "I know not what" which the others do not possess. We are enchanted by the style of an author which does not equal that of others we have read in its polish or brilliance, and does not exceed them in naturalness or propriety. Yet we interrupt the reading of those other authors without effort and we can scarcely let this author's book drop from our hands. What does this attraction consist in? In the fact that this author possesses in his method of expression an "I know not what" that makes us read with pleasure whatever he says. There is this same "I know not what" in the creations of all the arts. Painters have recognized it in their art under the name of "manner," a word which as interpreted by them means the same thing and with the same degree of confusion as the "I know not what," because they say that the manner of painting is a hidden and indefinable grace which is subject to no rule and depends only on the particular genius of the artist. Demontiotus (in *Praeamb. ad tract. de Pict.*) says that up to now no one has been able to explain what this mysterious grace is or in what it consists: *Quam nemo unquam scribendo potuit explicare,* which is the same thing as surrendering totally to the explanation of "I know not what."

This hidden grace, this "I know not what," was the quality which elevated the paintings of Apelles above all others of Antiquity: Apelles himself, who furthermore was very modest and a man who honoured greatly all the good practitioners of his art, bore witness to this fact when he said that in all the other perfections of painting there were others who equalled him or perhaps surpassed him in one or another aspect, but that he excelled them in that hidden grace which was lacking in all the rest. *Cum eadem aetate maximi Pictores essent: quorum opera cum admirarertur, collaudatis omnibus, deesse ijs unam illam Venerem dicebat, quam Graeci Charita vocant, caetera omnia contigisse, sed hac sola sibi neminem parem (Plin. Lib. 35, cap, 10).*[30] Here we should notice that even though Pliny, who relates the story, makes use of the Greek word *charita,* or *charis,* because he does not find in Latin a word capable of expressing the idea, neither does the Greek word explain it; because *charis* means *gracia* generically (so it is that the three pagan Graces are called in Greek *Charites*), from which we may infer that special beauty of Apelles is as indefinable a thing for the Greek as for the Roman and the Castilian.

[30] The entire passage from Pliny's *Historia Naturalis* XXXV is "Apelles of Kos, however, in the hundred and twelfth Olympiad (332–329 B.C.) excelled all painters who came before or after him. He of himself perhaps contributed more to painting than all the others together; he also wrote treatises on his theory of art. The grace of his genius remained quite unrivalled, although the very greatest painters were living at the time. He would admire their works, praising every beauty and yet observing that they failed in the grace, called χάρις in Greek, which was distinctively his own; everything else they had attained, but in this alone none equalled him . . ." (Translated by K. Jex-Blake, *The Elder Pliny's Chapters on the History of Art,* p. 121.)

[SECTION III]

The "I know not what" is extended not only to pleasing objects, but also to unpleasant ones; just as in some of the former there is a beauty which is inexplicable, in some of the latter there is an ugliness which cannot be explained. It is very commonly said that "So-and-so irritates me but I don't know why." There is no sense which does not register one or another displeasing object in which there is a certain irritating quality that resists all attempts by the intelligence to explain it; finally intelligence terms it an "I know not what" that displeases; and "I know not what" which annoys; an "I know not what" that forces itself on the attention; an "I know not what" that horrifies.

We shall try, then, in the present essay, to explain what no one has explained, to decipher this natural enigma, to draw this riddle out of the mysterious shadows where it has lurked until now; in fine, to say what this thing is that everyone says is unknowable.

[SECTION IV]

For this purpose I suppose first that objects which please us (let it be understood that what we say of them is equally applicable in their class to those which displease us) are divided into simple and compound. Two or three examples will explain this division. A sonorous voice pleases us, even though it is fixed on one note, which is to say that it does not vary or alter its tone and form any kind of melody. This voice is a simple object of the pleasure of the ear. We are also and even more pleased by the same voice when it proceeds along several notes so disposed as to form a musical combination agreeable to the ear. This is a compound object, which consists in that combination of various notes, disposed in such a proportion that the ear is captivated by it. Likewise our sight is pleased by an emerald green or a clear white. These are simple objects. But it is also pleased by the play of varied colours (for example, in a cloth, or in a garden) which are effectively placed in such a way as to make a harmony agreeable to the eyes, just as the disposition of different musical notes pleases the ears. This is a compound object.

Second, I suppose that many compound objects please or charm even though no single part of them considered by itself pleases the taste, which is to say that there are many objects whose beauty consists precisely in the reciprocal proportion, or the mutual adaptation, of the parts among themselves. Musical tones, when considered separately, hold no attraction for the ear, but when they are artfully disposed by a good composer, they can enchant the spirit. The same thing happens with regard to the component materials of a building, the various parts of a scene, the phrases of an oration, the different movements of a dance. Generally speaking, whether or not the separate parts considered individually are beautiful or attractive, it is certain that there is another beauty distinct from that of the single part, a compound beauty which consists in the pleasing disposition, order, and proportion, be it natural or artful, which obtains among the parts.

Third, I suppose that when an object pleases, there exists a kind of proportion or congruence between it and the faculty which perceives it (or the organ of the faculty, which comes to the same thing), without entering now on the attempt to explain what that proportion consists in. In the case of simple objects, there is only one proportion, that which obtains between them and the faculty; but in compound objects we must consider two proportions, the one which exists among the various parts, and the one obtaining between this collection of parts and the perceiving faculty, which rests upon the first proportion. The truth of this supposition appears clearly confirmed by the fact that the same object may please some people and displease others; indeed, it may be stated that there is nothing in the world which is to everyone's taste. Thus it can only be that a given object possesses a proportion of congruence with respect to the temper, texture, and disposition of the organs of one man, and disproportion with respect to those of another.

[SECTION V]

If these suppositions are granted, I would say that the doubt or lack of knowledge expressed in the "I know not what" can be understood if we limit it to two distinct things, to the "what" and to the "why." I shall explain my meaning by referring to the example of the curiously pleasing voice. When a person says: "This voice has an 'I know not what' which delights me more than do other voices," he may mean either that he does not know what it is that pleases him in that voice or that he does not know why that voice pleases him. Most often, even when the speaker's words seem to refer to the "what," in his own mind he is referring to the "why." But whether he is referring to one or to the other, we shall see that there is no mystery. The "what" of the voice may be reduced to one of two things, either to its sound (or what is commonly called the timbre of a voice) or to the manner of handling the voice; no more than a moment's reflexion will allow you to decide which has especially captivated you. If it is the sound, then you already know all there is to know about the "what." But you may reply. "My doubts are not resolved, because this sound has an 'I know not what' which is not to be found in the sounds of other voices." And I reply (heed well what I say to you) that the thing you call the "I know not what" is nothing other than the individual character of the sound itself which your ears perceive clearly and translate clearly in its essence to the understanding. You may despair because you cannot define or give a name to that sound according to its individual characteristics. But aren't you aware of the fact that the same thing happens with the sounds of all other voices that you hear? The individual is never definable. Even when they are freely imposed, names do not explain or definitely outline the individual essence. If a man is called Peter or Francis, does that name give me any idea of the particularity of the man's being, by which he is distinguished from all other men? Furthermore, don't you see that you never succeed in giving a particular name to any of the sounds of all other voices? Believe me, then, that you also understand whatever special quality there is in that sound, just as you understand the special quality of any of the others; you only need to understand that you understand.

If it is the handling of the voice in which you find the "I know not what" (although this, I think, seldom happens), I cannot give you a single explanation which will fit all cases of this sort, because all the beauties that may be found in the handling of the voice are not of the same kind. If I should hear that same voice, I would tell you with certainty what that grace that you call hidden consists in. But I can explain some of those beauties (perhaps all of them) which you have not succeeded in explaining, so that when the need arises you may decipher the "I know not what" by reference to one type of beauty or the other. I think that all the types of beauty may be reduced to three. The first is the ease with which the voice is employed. The second is the accuracy of intonation. The third is the complex of those soaring musical notes of which trills are composed.

The ease with which the voice is managed, by which all movements are produced without labor or anxiety, is a most gratifying thing for the auditor. Some people manage their voices with great celerity, but it is an affected celerity, or achieved by dint of the laborious efforts of the singer; and whatever is affected or violent, displeases. But few people understand this point, and so few would trace the "I know not what" to this origin.

The perfection of intonation is a beauty which is hidden even to musicians. Remember that I have said "the perfection of intonation." We should not misunderstand each other. Musicians distinguish very well deviations from the exact pitch up to a certain degree, even up to, for example, the fourth part of a tone, so that those with very fine ears may perceive, even when the inaccuracy is very slight, that the voice has not hit the note with complete accuracy, even though they may not be able to indicate the precise measure of the deviation. But when the deviation is much less, for example, the eighth part of a tone, no one thinks that the voice has even slightly missed the exact pitch. Nevertheless, this defect, which because of its delicacy escapes the intelligence, makes a sensible effect on the ear so that the piece no longer pleases so much as if it were sung by another voice that might hit the note more accurately; and if there is a voice which achieves perfection much more nearly, it pleases a great deal; and this is one of the cases in which we find in the handling of the voice an "I know not what" which enchants; and this "I know not what" deciphered is extreme accuracy in intonation. But it should be noticed that straying from the just pitch is very frequent, if not by a whole note, then in some minute part of it, so that, even though it seems that the voice is sure on, for example, *re,* it wavers upward or downward briefly from that indivisible spot on the scale of the diapason which *re* should occupy. This wavering spoils the song in greater or less degree, just as the absence of such a fault gives it a special grace.

Trills are a secondary or accidental music which serve to adorn the substance of the composition. This secondary music requires the same qualities as the primary in order to sound well. When the trill is a rapid passage of the voice from one note to another, when the disposition of the notes is proper and fitting, the trill will sound beautifully with respect to both the primary music and the words of the song; if these requisites are lacking, it will sound unpleasantly or will have no grace at all. This is what happens frequently even to singers whose throats are flexible and agile, who, lacking taste and talent, spoil their music more than they adorn it with tasteless and vain flutterings of the voice.

We have explained the "what" of the "I know not what" by the above example. There remains only the explanation of the "why." Herein enters the factor of proportion which we have already discussed. Once we know the "what" that pleases us in any object, the "why" should not elude us, for it consists in the due and congruent proportion between the object and the perceptive faculty, or the temper of the organ of perception. In order to prove that this matter requires no more elucidation, let the reader choose an object to his taste, an object in which he does not find that mysterious "I know not what," and let him tell me what it is to his taste and why it pleases him. He will not be able to find other reasons than the one I have indicated.

[SECTION VI]

The examples cited shed ample light on the problem of deciphering the "I know not what" in all objects, regardless of the sense to which they appeal. They explain suitably the what of simple objects and the why of simple and compound objects. The why is the same for all objects. The what of simple objects is that individual difference peculiar to each one, as we explained with reference to the voice. So it is that the only difference there is between agreeable objects which do not possess the mysterious "I know not what" and those that do, consists in fact that the former group please because they belong to a certain class, or by their generic character, while the latter please on account of their individual character. Some men like the color white because it is white; others like the color green because it is green. Here there is no mystery to solve. The type pleases them. But they may find a white or a green which, without being more intense than others, still pleases them much more than any other. Then they say that that white or that green has an "I know not what" that charms them. And I say that this "I know not what" is the individual quality of the given color, even though perhaps it may consist in the imperceptible admixture of another color, which would make the color belong to the class of compound objects, as we shall demonstrate later.

We should notice, however, that individual differences should not be understood here with such precise philosophical rigor that the same type of attraction is denied to all the other individuals of the same species. In all groups of individuals of one species there are some who are so alike that the senses barely distinguish among them. Consequently, if one of them pleases by its individual difference, the others will also please for the same reason.

I have said that the example of the voice explains appropriately the "what" of simple objects. Because some will perhaps complain that the explanation of the handling of the voice is not adaptable to other objects and therefore is useless as an explanation of the what of other objects, I answer that everything that has been said about the handling of the voice really applies to compound objects. Trills are compounds of several notes. Ease of handling and intonation do not constitute a perfection distinct from that inherent in music which is sung, which is also compound; that is to say, they are nothing but conditions necessary for music to sound well, since it is considerably spoiled when the proper intonation is lacking or when the song is produced with effort. But because I do not wish to leave the explanation of the "I know not what" of the voice incomplete, I extended myself to a discussion of the handling of it. Further, what has been said in this part may aid many readers to analyze other quite different objects.

[SECTION VII]

We shall now proceed to the explanation of the "I know not what" of compound objects. The "I know not what" occurs more frequently in them; indeed, the "I know not what" is rarely found in an object which is in no degree compound. And in what does the "I know not what" of compound objects consist? In their composition itself. I mean, in the proportion and congruence of the parts which compose them.

It will be objected that scarcely anyone is unaware that the symmetry and right disposition of their parts forms the principal, at times, the only, beauty of objects. Therefore this is not that mysterious grace to which is applied the term "I know not what" through ignorance or lack of penetration.

I answer that even though men understand this matter in some degree, they comprehend it with notable limitations, because they only succeed in perceiving a given proportion contained within extremely narrow limits or rules, while there are innumerable proportions different from that limited one which they perceive. An example will suffice to explain my meaning. It is certain that the beauty of a face consists in the proportion of its parts, or in a well-disposed combination of the color, size, and form of them. Since this matter interests people so much, they have, after much reflection, determined or specified this proportion, saying that the forehead must be formed in such a manner, the eyes in this way, the cheeks in another way, etc. But what frequently happens? People see this face or that face in which that studied proportion is not observed, and nevertheless they are much pleased by it. Then they say that, despite its fault or faults, that face has an "I know not what" that enchants. And I say that this "I know not what" is a certain proportion of the parts about which they have not thought any different from that proportion which they consider necessary to make a face pleasing to the eye.

God can make most beautiful faces in a thousand different ways and with innumerable and most diverse combinations of the parts. But men, carelessly measuring the immense amplitude of divine ideas by the limitation of their own, have thought they might reduce all beauty to one single combination, or at the most to a limited number of combinations. When beauty escapes from those limits, it is for them a mysterious "I know not what."

The same thing happens in the disposition of a building, in the proportion among the parts of a pleasant scene. That graceful "I know not what" which their eyes chance to find in the building or the scene is nothing else than a given symmetrical combination outside of the common rules. On occasion we find a building which in one part or another flouts the rules established by the architects but which nevertheless presents an admirable aspect to the eyes, pleasing us a great deal more than other buildings which conform more closely to the precepts of art. How does this happen? Because the artist who conceived it was unaware of those precepts? Decidedly not. Rather because he knew more and had a more soaring vision than ordinary artists. He did everything according to a rule, but according to a higher rule that exists in his mind, different from those common rules taught by the schools. Proportion there is, and imposing; symmetry there is, and highly appropriate, in all parts of the work; but it is not the symmetry which is usually studied but another higher symmetry to which the sublime concept of the architect climbed by virtue of his daring. If this happens in works of art, it is still more common in works of nature, since these are the creations of an artist of infinite wisdom whose concept infinitely exceeds, in both intention and execution, all human, or even angelic, ideas.

This maxim is nowhere more sensible than in musical compositions. Music has a system formed of various rules which its professors look upon as complete; therefore, when some one of them is violated, the professors damn the composition as defective. Nevertheless, there are a number of compositions which break one rule or another and which please us enormously even in those passages where the rule is broken. How does that happen? Because the system of rules that musicians have held to be complete is not so, but highly incomplete and reduced in scope. But this imperfection in the system is understood only by composers of soaring inspiration; these men perceive that the precepts can be dispensed with in certain circumstances, or they find a way to arrange their music so that, even when it breaks with the precepts, it may be harmonious and pleasing. Meanwhile composers of inferior competence cry out that this is heresy. But let them protest as they wish, for the sole and supreme judge of music is the ear. If music pleases the ear and pleases it a great deal, it is good and very good; and being very good, it cannot go absolutely against the rules but only against a few limited and ill understood rules. It will be said that this music goes against art but that nevertheless it has an "I know not what" which makes it seem good. And I say that "I know not what" implies nothing else than being made according to art, but according to an art higher than that of the common rule. When people began to introduce dissonances into music, I know that, even when they were opportunely disguised, the majority of composers cried out that they went against art; today everyone considers dissonances to be licit and according to art, because art, which before was extremely limited in range, was broadened by this discovery.

[SECTION VIII]

Although the explanation we have given up to now of the "I know not what" is adaptable to everything that may be hidden beneath this confused expression, we must confess that there is a certain "I know not what" characteristic of our species which by virtue of its special character demands a more precise explanation. We said earlier that grace or beauty of face to which, because it is not understood, the term "I know not what" is applied consists in a certain proportion of its parts, a proportion which is distinct from that which is commonly admitted as the unfailing model of beauty. But even though this may be true, there is in some faces another more particular grace which makes them very agreeable even though the grace of the suitable proportion of the features is lacking. This strange grace is due to that representation which the face makes of the good qualities of the soul (as we have explained in another connection in Vol. 5, Discourse 3, paragraphs 10 through 16; the reader may refer to that passage so that we can avoid repeating the argument here). In the complex of those various subtle movements of the parts of the face, especially of the eyes, by which this representation of the soul is expressed, we have to do not so much with corporeal as with spiritual beauty; or, in other words, that complex seems beautiful because it shows forth the beauty of the soul, which without doubt is much more attractive than that of the body. There are people who, just by those movements and disposition of the eyes which are required to produce a broad and gentle smile, reveal an exalted, noble, perspicacious, kind, sweet, loving, and active soul, which constrains all who see them to love them.

This is the supreme grace of the human countenance. This is the grace which, when found in the opposite sex, has kindled more violent and lasting passions than the snowy whiteness and perfect symmetry of features. And this is the grace which those very people whose passions have been inflamed by it never succeed in deciphering, even though they contemplate it constantly; so it is that, when they are forced by those who are attempting to correct them to point out the reason why such an object (an object which lacks the common perfections) has ensnared them, they find nothing else to say but that it possessed an "I know not what" which has wholly robbed them of their liberty. Let it be remembered (so as to forestall objections) that this grace, like all the rest which hide under the mantle of the "I know not what," is relative to the character, imagination, and knowledge of the one who perceives it. I had yet other things to say about this matter, but for various reasons I find it necessary to bring this essay to a close.

David Hume

1711–1776

A. Life

David Hume was born in Edinburgh in 1711 and died in the same city in 1776. He attended the University of Edinburgh, studied law there, and engaged in business in Bristol in 1734. Hume lived at La Flèche in France from 1734 until 1737 and it was there that he wrote *A Treatise on Human Nature.* This enormously important contribution to empirical philosophy was published in Edinburgh in 1739–1740. Its failure to find readers led Hume to rewrite Book III, which he published in 1751 as the *Enquiry concerning Human Understanding.* The *Essays, Moral and Political,* were brought out in 1757. In the same year, Hume published an *Essay on the Passions in Four Dissertations,* which was Book II of the *Enquiry concerning Principles of Morals.* He served as secretary in the English embassy in Vienna in 1751. His *Dialogues concerning Natural Religion* was written in 1751, his *Political Discourses* was published in 1752, and his *History of England* appeared from the year 1754 to 1761. He served as secretary of the English embassy in Paris from 1763 to 1765. Hume died in Edinburgh in 1776. He had attained great renown. But he was treated shabbily by at least two famous literary men: Hume was anathema to Dr. Samuel Johnson because of his skepticism, and, as Hume himself recounts in his letters, he was treated so badly by Rousseau that one can only understand the episodes in terms of Rousseau's mania. The full measure of Hume's stature as a philosopher has not yet been made but Humeian philosophy is in the ascendancy today. Still, the greatest philosopher of the eighteenth century, Immanuel Kant, wrote that Hume had awakened him from his "dogmatic slumber." More immediately relevant and significant for Philosophy of Art and Aesthetics is the fact that Kant exiles criticism from Aesthetics and that he does so quoting Hume's words, with consequences of enormous importance for later Aesthetics and criticism.

B. Philosophy of Art

Essay XVII—The Platonist

O philosopher! [31] thy wisdom is vain, and thy virtue unprofitable. Thou seekest the ignorant applauses of men, not the solid reflections of thy own conscience, or the more solid approbation of that being, who, with one regard of his all-seeing eye, penetrates the universe. Thou surely art conscious of the hollowness of thy pretended probity, whilst calling thyself a citizen, a son, a friend, thou forgettest thy higher sovereign, thy true father, thy greatest benefactor. Where is the adoration due to infinite perfection, whence every thing good and valuable is derived? Where is the gratitude, owing to thy creator, who called thee forth from nothing, who placed thee in all these relations to thy fellow-creatures, and requiring thee to fulfil the duty of each relation, forbids thee to neglect what thou owest to himself, the most perfect being, to whom thou art connected by the closest tye?

But thou art thyself thy own idol: Thou worshippest thy *imaginary* perfections: Or rather, sensible of thy *real* imperfections, thou seekest only to deceive the world, and to please thy fancy, by multiplying thy ignorant admirers. Thus, not content with neglecting what is most excellent in the universe, thou desirest to substitute in his place what is most vile and contemptible.

Consider all the works of men's hands; all the inventions of human wit, in which thou affectest so nice a discernment: Thou wilt find, that the most perfect production still proceeds from the most perfect thought, and that it is MIND alone, which we admire, while we bestow our applause on the graces of a well-proportioned statue, or the symmetry of a noble pile. The statuary, the architect comes still in view, and makes us reflect on the beauty of his art and contrivance, which, from a heap of unformed matter, could extract such expressions and proportions. This superior beauty of thought and intelligence thou thyself acknowledgest, while thou invitest us to contemplate, in thy conduct, the harmony of affections, the dignity of sentiments, and all those graces of a mind, which chiefly merit our attention. But why stoppest thou short? Seest thou nothing farther that is valuable? Amid thy rapturous applauses of beauty and order, art thou still ignorant where is to be found the most consummate beauty? the most perfect order? Compare the works of art with those of nature. The one are but imitations of the other. The nearer art approaches to nature, the more perfect is it esteemed. But still, how wide are its nearest approaches, and what an immense interval may be observed between them? Art copies only the outside of nature, leaving the inward and more admirable springs and principles; as exceeding her imitation; as beyond her comprehension. Art copies only the minute productions of nature, despairing to reach that grandeur and magnificence, which are so astonishing in the masterly works of her original. Can we then be so blind as not to discover an intelligence and a design in the exquisite and most stupendous contrivance of the universe? Can we be so stupid as not to feel the warmest raptures of worship and adoration, upon the contemplation of that intelligent being, so infinitely good and wise?

The most perfect happiness, surely, must

[31] *Essays Moral, Political, and Literary by David Hume.* Edited by T. H. Green and T. H. Grose. London. Longmans, Green, and Co., 1889. Vol. 1, pp. 212 et seq.

arise from the contemplation of the most perfect object. But what more perfect than beauty and virtue? And where is beauty to be found equal to that of the universe? Or virtue, which can be compared to the benevolence and justice of the Deity? If aught can diminish the pleasure of this contemplation, it must be either the narrowness of our faculties, which conceals from us the greatest part of these beauties and perfections; or the shortness of our lives, which allows not time sufficient to instruct us in them. But it is our comfort, that, if we employ worthily the faculties here assigned us, they will be enlarged in another state of existence, so as to render us more suitable worshippers of our maker: And that the task, which can never be finished in time, will be the business of an eternity.

Essay XVIII—The Sceptic

I have long entertained a suspicion, with regard to the decisions of philosophers upon all subjects, and found in myself a greater inclination to dispute, than assent to their conclusions. There is one mistake, to which they seem liable, almost without exception; they confine too much their principles, and make no account of that vast variety, which nature has so much affected in all her operations. When a philosopher has once laid hold of a favourite principle, which perhaps accounts for many natural effects, he extends the same principle over the whole creation, and reduces to it every phænomenon, though by the most violent and absurd reasoning. Our own mind being narrow and contracted, we cannot extend our conception to the variety and extent of nature; but imagine, that she is as much bounded in her operations, as we are in our speculation.

But if ever this infirmity of philosophers is to be suspected on any occasion, it is in their reasonings concerning human life, and the methods of attaining happiness. In that case, they are led astray, not only by the narrowness of their understandings, but by that also of their passions. Almost every one has a predominant inclination, to which his other desires and affections submit, and which governs him, though, perhaps, with some intervals, through the whole course of his life. It is difficult for him to apprehend, that anything, which appears totally indifferent to him, can ever give enjoyment to any person, or can possess charms, which altogether escape his observation. His own pursuits are always, in his account, the most engaging: The objects of his passion, the most valuable: And the road, which he pursues, the only one that leads to happiness.

But would these prejudiced reasoners reflect a moment, there are many obvious instances and arguments, sufficient to undeceive them, and make them enlarge their maxims and principles. Do they not see the vast variety of inclinations and pursuits among our species; where each man seems fully satisfied with his own course of life, and would esteem it the greatest unhappiness to be confined to that of his neighbour? Do they not feel in themselves, that what pleases at one time, displeases at another, by the change of inclination; and that it is not in their power, by their utmost efforts, to recall that taste or appetite, which formerly bestowed charms on what now appears indifferent or disagreeable? What is the meaning therefore of those general preferences of the town or country life, of a life of action or one of pleasure, of retirement or society; when besides the different inclinations of different men, every one's experience may convince him, that each of these kinds of life is agreeable in its turn, and that their variety or their judicious mixture chiefly contributes to the rendering all of them agreeable.

But shall this business be allowed to go altogether at adventures? And must a man consult only his humour and inclination, in order to determine his course of life, without employing his reason to inform him what road is preferable, and leads most surely to happiness! Is there no difference then between one man's conduct and another?

I answer, there is a great difference. One man, following his inclination, in chusing his course of life, may employ much surer means for succeeding than another, who is led by his inclination into the same course of life, and pursues the same object. *Are riches the chief object of your desires?* Acquire skill in your profession; be diligent in the exercise of it; enlarge the circle of your friends and acquaintance; avoid pleasure and expense; and never be generous, but with a view of gaining more than you could save by frugality. *Would you acquire the public esteem?* Guard equally against the extremes of arrogance and fawning. Let it appear that you set a value upon yourself, but without despising others. If you fall into either of the extremes, you either provoke men's pride by your insolence, or teach them to despise you by your timorous submission, and by the mean opinion which you seem to entertain of yourself.

These, you say, are the maxims of common prudence, and discretion; what every parent inculcates on his child, and what every man of sense pursues in the course of life, which he has chosen.—What is it then you desire more? Do you come to a philosopher as to a *cunning man*, to learn something by magic or witchcraft, beyond what can be known to common prudence and discretion? ———Yes; we come to a philosopher to be instructed, how we shall chuse our ends, more than the means for attaining these ends: We want to know what desire we shall gratify, what passion we shall comply with, what appetite we shall indulge. As to the rest, we trust to common sense, and the general maxims of the world for our instruction.

I am sorry then, I have pretended to be a philosopher: For I find your questions very perplexing; and am in danger, if my answer be too rigid and severe, of passing for a pedant and scholastic: if it be too easy and free, of being taken for a preacher of vice and immorality. However, to satisfy you, I shall deliver my opinion upon the matter, and shall only desire you to esteem it of as little consequence as I do myself. By that means you will neither think it worthy of your ridicule nor your anger.

If we can depend upon any principle, which we learn from philosophy, this, I think, may be considered as certain and undoubted, that there is nothing, in itself, valuable or despicable, desirable or hateful, beautiful or deformed; but that these attributes arise from the particular constitution and fabric of human sentiment and affection. What seems the most delicious food to one animal, appears loathsome to another: What affects the feeling of one with delight, produces uneasiness in another. This is confessedly the case with regard to all the bodily senses: But if we examine the matter more accurately, we shall find, that the same observation holds even where the mind concurs with the body, and mingles its sentiment with the exterior appetite.

Desire this passionate lover to give you a character of his mistress: He will tell you, that he is at a loss for words to describe her charms, and will ask you very seriously if ever you were acquainted with a goddess or an angel? If you answer that you never were: He will then say, that it is impossible for you to form a conception of such divine beauties as those which his charmer possesses; so complete a shape; such well-proportioned features; so engaging an air; such sweetness of disposition; such gaiety of humour. You can infer nothing, however, from all this discourse, but that the poor man is in love; and that the general appetite between the sexes, which nature has infused into all animals, is in him determined to a particular object by some qualities, which give him pleasure. The same divine creature, not only to a different animal, but also to a different man, appears a mere mortal being, and is beheld with the utmost indifference.

Nature has given all animals a like prejudice in favour of their offspring. As soon as the helpless infant sees the light, though in every other eye it appears a despicable and a miserable creature, it is regarded by its fond parent with the utmost affection, and is preferred to every other object, however perfect and accomplished. The passion alone, arising from the original structure and formation of human nature, bestows a value on the most insignificant object.

We may push the same observation further, and may conclude, that, even when the mind operates alone, and feeling the sentiment of blame or approbation, pronounces one object deformed and odious, another beautiful and amiable; I say, that, even in this case, those qualities are not really in the objects, but belong entirely to the sentiment of that mind which blames or praises. I grant, that it will be more difficult to make this proposition evident, and as it were, palpable, to negligent thinkers; because nature is more uniform in the sentiments of the mind than in most feelings of the body, and produces a nearer resemblance in the inward than in the outward part of human kind. There is something approaching to principles in mental tastes; and critics can reason and dispute more plausibly than cooks or perfumers. We may observe, however, that this uniformity among human kind, hinders not, but that there is a considerable diversity in the sentiments of beauty and worth, and that education, custom, prejudice, caprice, and humour, frequently vary our taste of this kind. You will never convince a man, who is not accustomed to ITALIAN music, and has not an ear to follow its intricacies, that a SCOTCH tune is not preferable. You have not even any single argument, beyond your own taste, which you can employ in your behalf: And to your antagonist, his particular taste will always appear a more convincing argument to the contrary. If you be wise, each of you will allow, that the other may be in the right; and having many other instances of this diversity of taste, you will both confess, that beauty and worth are merely of a relative nature, and consist in an agreeable sentiment, produced by an object in a particular mind, according to the peculiar structure and constitution of that mind.

By this diversity of sentiment, observable in human kind, nature has, perhaps, intended to make us sensible of her authority, and let us see what surprizing changes she could produce on the passions and desires of mankind, merely by the change of their inward fabric, without any alteration on the objects. The vulgar may even be convinced by this argument: But men, accustomed to thinking, may draw a more convincing, at least a more general argument, from the very nature of the subject.

In the operation of reasoning, the mind does nothing but run over its objects, as they are supposed to stand in reality, without adding any thing to them, or diminishing any thing from them. If I examine the PTOLOMAIC and COPERNICAN systems, I endeavour only, by my enquiries, to know the real situation of the planets; that is, in other words, I endeavour to give them, in my conception, the same relations, that they bear towards each other in the heavens. To this operation of the mind, therefore, there seems to be always a real, though often an unknown standard, in the nature of things; nor is truth or falsehood variable by the various apprehensions of mankind. Though all human race should for ever conclude, that the sun moves, and the earth remains at rest, the sun stirs not an inch from his place for all these reasonings; and such conclusions are eternally false and erroneous.

But the case is not the same with the qualities of *beautiful and deformed, desirable and odious,* as with truth and falsehood. In the former case, the mind is not content with merely surveying its objects, as they stand in themselves: It also feels a sentiment of delight or uneasiness, approbation or blame, consequent to that survey; and this sentiment determines it to affix the epithet *beautiful or deformed, desirable or odious.* Now, it is evident, that this sentiment must depend upon the particular fabric or structure of the mind, which enables such particular forms to operate in such a particular manner, and produces a sympathy or conformity between the mind and its objects. Vary the structure of the mind or inward organs, the sentiment no longer follows, though the form remains the same. The sentiment being different from the object, and arising from its operations upon the organs of the mind, an alteration upon the latter must vary the effect, nor can the same object, presented to a mind totally different, produce the same sentiment.

This conclusion every one is apt to draw of himself, without much philosophy, where the sentiment is evidently distinguishable from the object. Who is not sensible, that power, and glory, and vengeance, are not desirable of themselves, but derive all their value from the structure of human passions, which begets a desire towards such particular pursuits? But with regard to beauty, either natural or moral, the case is commonly supposed to be different. The agreeable quality is thought to lie in the object, not in the sentiment; and that merely because the sentiment is not so turbulent and violent as to distinguish itself, in an evident manner, from the perception of the object.

But a little reflection suffices to distinguish them. A man may know exactly all the circles and ellipses of the COPERNICAN system, and all the irregular spirals of the PTOLOMAIC, without perceiving that the former is more beautiful than the latter. EUCLID has fully explained every quality of the circle, but has not, in any proposition, said a word of its beauty. The reason is evident. Beauty is not a quality of the circle. It lies not in any part of the line *whose* parts are all equally distant from a common center. It is only the effect, which that figure produces upon a mind, whose particular fabric or structure renders it susceptible of such sentiments. In vain would you look for it in the circle, or seek it, either by your senses, or by mathematical reasonings, in all the properties of that figure.

The mathematician, who took no other pleasure in reading VIRGIL, but that of examining ENEAS'S voyage by the map, might perfectly understand the meaning of every Latin word, employed by that divine author; and consequently, might have a distinct idea of the whole narration. He would even have a more distinct idea of it, than they could attain who had not studied so exactly the geography of the poem. He knew, therefore, every thing in the poem: But he was ignorant of its beauty; because the beauty, properly speaking, lies not in the poem, but in the sentiment or taste of the reader. And where a man has no such delicacy of temper, as to make him feel this sentiment, he must be ignorant of the beauty, though possessed of the science and understanding of an angel.[32]

[32] Were I not afraid of appearing too philosophical, I should remind my reader of that famous doctrine, supposed to be fully proved in modern times, "That tastes and colours, and all other sensible qualities, lie not in the bodies, but merely in the senses." The case is the same with beauty and deformity, virtue and vice. This doctrine, however, takes off no more from the reality of the latter qualities, than from that of the former; nor need it give any umbrage either to critics or moralists. Tho' colours were allowed to lie only in the eye, would dyers or painters ever be less regarded or esteemed? There is a sufficient uniformity in the senses and feelings of mankind, to make all these qualities the objects of art and reasoning, and to have the greatest influence on life and manners. And as 'tis certain, that the discovery above-mentioned in natural philosophy, makes no alteration on action and conduct; why should a like discovery in moral philosophy make any alteration?

The inference upon the whole is, that it is not from the value or worth of the object, which any person pursues, that we can determine his enjoyment, but merely from the passion with which he pursues it, and the success which he meets with in his pursuit. Objects have absolutely no worth or value in themselves. They drive their worth merely from the passion. . . .

Alexander Gerard

1728–1795

A. Life

On their way to the Hebrides, Dr. Samuel Johnson and James Boswell visited Aberdeen and dined there with various professors of Marischal College, among whom was Dr. Alexander Gerard. As insatiably curious in the north as he was in London, Boswell "talked of the difference of genius, to try if I could engage Dr. Gerard in a disquisition with Dr. Johnson." Johnson had already expressed himself vigorously on the subjects of rules, invention, and imagination and Gerard had published *An Essay on Taste* in 1759, the latter portion of which expressed views concerning genius. Boswell's efforts to start a disputation failed: " . . . I did not succeed," he writes, and it is likely that he failed because Gerard's *An Essay on Genius* was to appear in 1774 and Johnson and Boswell were in Aberdeen September 23, 1773.

Both *An Essay on Taste* and *An Essay on Genius* are among the most significant writings in the eighteenth-century literature of Philosophy of Art. Coleridge possessed copies of Gerard's books, and Kant wrote of Gerard that he was the ablest of the English writers on genius.

Gerard was a minister. He became Professor of Natural Philosophy at Marischal College, Aberdeen, in 1752. In 1760, he was appointed Professor of Divinity at that College and in 1771 accepted the chair of divinity at King's College, Aberdeen, a position he occupied until his death in 1795. Gerard was awarded the gold medal of the Aberdeen Society and served as president of that Society, of which David Hume and Adam Smith were members. Both Hume and Smith served on the committee that made the award to Gerard.

B. Philosophy of Art

On Taste

I

A fine taste [33] is neither wholly the gift of *nature,* nor wholly the effect *of art.* It derives its origin from certain powers natural to the mind; but these powers cannot attain their full perfection, unless they be assisted by proper

[33] Alexander Gerard, *An Essay on Taste,* p. 1, London, 1759. A. Millar, A. Kincaid, and J. Bell. Edinburgh.

culture. Taste consists chiefly in the improvement of those principles, which are commonly called *the powers of imagination,* and are considered by modern philosophers as *internal* or *reflex senses,* supplying us with finer and more delicate perceptions, than any which can be properly referred to our external organs. These are reducible to the following principles; the senses of novelty, of sublimity, of beauty, of imitation, of harmony, of ridicule, and of virtue. With the explication of these, we must, therefore, begin our enquiry into the nature of *taste.* We shall next endeavour to discover, how these senses co-operate in forming *taste* what other powers of the mind are combined with them in their exertions, what constitutes that refinement and perfection of them, which we term *good taste,* and by what means it is obtained. And last of all, we shall, by a review of the principles, operation, and subjects of *taste,* determine its genuine rank among our faculties, its proper province, and real importance.

PART I

TASTE RESOLVED INTO ITS SIMPLE PRINCIPLES

Sect. I

Of the sense or taste of novelty

The mind receives pleasure or pain, not only from the impulse of external objects, but also from the consciousness of its own operations and dispositions. When these are produced by external objects, the pleasure or the pain, which arises immediately from the exertions of the mind, is ascribed to those things, which give occasion to them. We have a pleasant sensation, whenever the mind is in a lively and elevated temper. It attains this temper, when it is forced to exert its activity, and put forth its strength, in order to surmount any difficulty: and if its efforts prove successful, consciousness of the success inspires new joy. Hence moderate difficulty, such as exercises the mind, without fatiguing it, is pleasant, and renders the object by which it is produced agreeable. Even plainness and perspicuity becomes displeasing in an Author, when it is carried to excess, and leaves no room for exercising the reader's thought: and though great obscurity disgusts us, yet we are highly gratified by delicacy of sentiment, which always includes some degree of it, occasions a suspense of thought, and leaves the full meaning to be guessed at, and comprehended only on attention. The exercise of thought, which moderate difficulty produces, is a principal source of the pleasure we take in study and investigation of every kind; for though the utility of many subjects enhances our satisfaction, yet the former principle, without any aid from this, often renders very great labour, not only supportable, but agreeable. Witness the delight, with which antiquaries bestow indefatigable pains on recovering or illustrating ancient fragments, recommended only by their age, and obscurity, and scarce apprehended to be, on any other account, of great importance. This is in general the cause of our pleasure in all enquiries of mere curiosity.

Not only the performance of actions, but also the conception of most objects, to which we have not been accustomed, is attended with difficulty. On this account, when new objects are in themselves indifferent, the efforts that are necessary for conceiving them, exalt and enliven the frame of the mind, make it receive a strong impression from them, and thus render them in some measure agreeable. When the objects are in themselves agreeable, these efforts heighten our satisfaction. A fine country or an agreeable prospect is doubly beautiful to a stranger. It gives considerable exercise to the mind, to observe every part of it, and to conceive the situation of the several objects, which it includes. A fresh discovery in science, or a new performance in the arts gives greater satisfaction, when we become first acquainted with it, than ever after. The first time that we study a philosophical theory, the mind runs through it with eagerness, that it may get a view of all its parts, is constantly engaged in tracing the connection of the arguments, in examining their force, in conceiving what objections can be formed against them, and is by this means affected with an agreeable agitation, which ceases, after repeated perusals have rendered the theory familiar to us. A poem or a picture is examined, with a similar ardour and unremitted exertion of mind, by a person who has not seen it formerly. . . .

PART II

Sect. I

Of the union of the internal senses. . . .

. . . Now as all the objects of the same internal sense, however various, have their common qualities; so all these senses are analogous in their principles and feeling. The same turn of mind is, on this account, congruous to them all. The prevalence and exercise, of any one of them disposes and attunes the mind to all the rest. And this previous disposition to them bestows strength and vigour on all their exertions. In fact, the kindred powers of taste are seldom disunited. Where all of them have considerable vigour, one may be, in comparison with the rest, predominant; either by the natural construction of the mind, or by peculiar culture. But where one of them is remarkably dull, or altogether wanting, the others scarce ever appear in full perfection.

The union of these powers has a farther influence in forming taste, as that union opens a new field, in which taste may exercise itself and gather flowers to adorn the native beauty of its objects. As the fine arts are truly sisters, derived from the same common parent *Nature,* they bear to one another, and to their original various similitudes, relations, and analogies. These one, who possesses all the internal senses vigorous, and has employed them all about their various objects, is able to trace out. They have charmed every genuine critic; and every reader of taste is delighted with the metaphors and comparisons, which are founded on the perception of them. In observing them we find a noble and exquisite entertainment. They continually occur to an extensive taste; and, mingling with the more immediate and confined gratification of each power of imagination, increase its delightfulness. As one *science,* by supplying illustrations, makes another better *understood;* so one *art,* by throwing lustre on another, makes it more exquisitely *relished.* This enlargement of taste, places one as it were upon an eminence, and not only enables him to take in a wider prospect; but also improves all the parts of it, by comparing or contrasting them together. . . .

We may here take occasion to mention a principle, distinct from all the internal senses, from which taste will, in many instances, receive assistance. It is such a *sensibility of heart,* as fits a man for being easily moved, and for readily catching, as by infection, any passion, that a work is fitted to excite. The souls of men are far from being alike susceptible of impressions of this kind. A hard hearted man can be a spectator of very great distress, without feeling any emotion: A man of a cruel temper has a malignant joy in producing misery. On the other hand, many are composed of so delicate materials, that the smallest uneasiness of their fellow creatures excites their pity. A similar variety may be observed, in respect of the other passions.

Persons of the former cast will be little affected by the most moving tragedy; those of the latter turn will be interested by a very indifferent one. A performance, which can infuse the keenest passions into the breast of an *Italian,* will affect a *Frenchman* very little, and leave an *Englishman* perfectly unconcerned. We are apt to be astonished, when we read of the prodigious force, with which eloquence wrought upon the delicate spirits of the *Athenians,* and feel so little of any thing analogous to it, that nothing but the most unexceptionable evidence could make it credible. This diversity in the formation of the heart will produce a considerable diversity in the sentiments, which men receive from works of taste, and in the judgment, which they form concerning them. . . .

Sect. II

Of the influence of judgment upon taste

The compleatest *union* of the internal *senses,* is not of itself sufficient to form good taste, even though they be attended with the greatest delicacy of passion. They must be aided with *Judgment,* the faculty which distinguishes things different, separates truth from falsehood, and compares together objects and their qualities. Judgment must indeed accompany even their most *imperfect* exertions. They do not operate, till certain qualities in objects have been perceived, discriminated from others similar, compared and compounded. In all this judgment is employed: it bears a part in the discernment and production of every form that strikes them, But in assisting their *perfect* energies, it has a still more extensive influence. Good sense is an indispensable ingredient in true taste, which always implies a quick and accurate perception of things as they really are.

That judgment may compleatly exhibit to the internal senses, the beauties and excellencies of *nature,* it measures the amplitude of things, determines their proportions, and traces out their wise construction and beneficial tendency. It uses all the methods, which art and science indicate for discovering those qualities that lie too deep spontaneously to strike the eye. It investigates the laws and causes of the works of *nature*: it compares and contrasts them with the more imperfect works of *art;* and thus supplies materials, from which fancy may produce ideas and form combinations, that will strongly affect the mental taste.

Judgment finds out the general characters of *each art,* and, by comparing them, draws conclusions concerning the relations, which subsist between *different* arts. Till it has discovered these, none of them can acquire that additional power of pleasing, which is imparted to them by their reciprocal connection.

In every art, a just performance consists of various parts, combined into one system, and subservient to one design. But without the exercise of judgment, we cannot know whether the design is skillfully prosecuted, whether the means are well adjusted to the end, whether every member, which is introduced, has a tendency to promote it.

In *music* the *ear* immediately perceives the pleasure resulting from each principle: But *judgment,* assuming the perceptions of that organ, compares them, and by comparison determines their respective merit and due proportion. It enables the ear, from its discovery of the general relations, to distinguish with precision between invention and extravagance, to discern the suitableness or unsuitableness of the parts, and their fitness or unfitness to sustain the main subject.

In *painting* judgment discovers the meaning of the piece, not only remotely, as it is the instrument of that previous knowledge, which is necessary for understanding it; but also more immediately, as from the structure and relation of the parts it infers the general design, and explains their subserviency to the main end of the whole. It compares the imitation with its exemplar, and sees its likeness. It is judgment working on our experience, that puts it in our power to know, whether the painter has fixed upon the attitudes and airs in nature appropriated to the passions, characters, and actions he would represent; and, when these attitudes are various, whether he has chosen those, which most perfectly correspond with the unity and propriety of his design. Painting being circumscribed to an instant of time, judgment alone can perceive, whether that instant is properly selected, whether the artist has pitched on that moment which comprehends the circumstances most essential to the grand event, and best allows, without a deviation from simplicity, the indication of the other requisite circumstances. It estimates the due proportion of all the figures, in dignity, elegance, and lustre, and their due subordination to the principal. In fine, it is necessarily employed in that exhibition of the object of the senses, which must be previous to the perception of it. . . .

But, though the reflex senses and judgment meet, yet, in a consistence with true taste, they may be united in very different proportions. In some, the acuteness of the *senses,* in others, the accuracy of *judgment* is the predominant ingredient. Both will determine justly, but they are guided by different lights; the former, by the perception of sense, the latter, by the conviction of the understanding. One *feels* what pleases or displeases; the other *knows* what ought to gratify or disgust. Sense has a kind of instinctive infallibility, by means of which, when it is vigorous, it can preserve from error, though judgment should not be perfect. Judgment, by contemplating the qualities that affect taste, by surveying its sentiments in their causes, often makes amends for dullness of imagination. Where *that* prevails, one's chief entertainment from Works of genius lies in what he feels: where *this* is predominant, one enjoys principally the intellectual pleasure, which results from discovering the causes of his feelings. This diversity in the form and constitution of taste is very observable in two of the greatest critics of antiquity. *Longinus* is justly characterized

An ardent judge, who, zealous in his trust,
With warmth gives sentence.

In him the internal senses were exquisitely delicate; but his judgment, though good, was not in proportion. On this account he delivers just sentiments, with rapture and enthusiasm, and, by a kind of contagion, infuses them into his readers, without always explaining to them the reason of their being affected. *Aristotle* on the contrary appears to examine his subject, perfectly cool and unaffected; he discovers no warmth of imagination, no such admiration or extacy, as can, without reflection, transport his readers into his opinion. He derives his decisions, not from the liveliness of feeling, but from the depth of penetration; and seldom pronounces them, without convincing us they are just. Some degree of the same diversity may be remarked in *Bouhours* and *Bossu* among the Moderns.

Sect. VI

Of correctness of taste

. . . The chief utility of criticism lies in promoting correctness of taste. In the most imperfect essays, the authority of the critic will, at least, excite our attention, and provoke our enquiry. But everyone who really merits the name conveys much more momentous instruction, and more effectually teaches justness of thinking, by explaining the kind and degree of every excellence and blemish, by teaching us what are the qualities of things, to which we owe our pleasure or disgust, and what the principles of human nature, by which they are produced. . . .

Sect. VII

. . . Of the principles of taste

. . . Thus we have explained the manner, in which the principles of taste must be combined, to form its just extent; and the finishing it must receive, in order to its perfection. As it necessarily includes both judgment and all the reflex senses; so it must by culture, be improved in sensibility, refinement, correctness, and the due proportion of all its parts. In whatever degree any of these qualities are wanting, in the same, taste must be imperfect. Could any critic unite them all in a great degree, to his sentiments we might appeal, as to an unerring standard of merit, in all the productions of the fine arts. The nearer one comes to a complete union, of these qualities of taste, the higher authority will his decision justly claim. But when none of them is wanting, a peculiar predominance of one will by no means vitiate taste. They are so analogous, that an eminent degree of one will supply the place of another, and in some measure produce the same effect: or rather, perhaps, one cannot exist in full perfection, without implying all the rest, at least in an inferior degree. *Longins,* (*sic.*) *Dionysius of Halicarnassus,* and *Aristotle,* all possessed fine taste. But it will scarce be denied, that the first peculiarly excelled in *sensibility,* the second in *refinement*, and the last in *correctness* and *enlargement*. There is none of the ancients, in whom all the four appear to have been more equally or in a higher degree, combined, than in *Quintilian.*

PART III

Sect. I

. . . Taste and Imagination

. . . Imagination is first of all employed in presenting such ideas, as are not attended with *remembrance,* or a perception of their having been formerly in the mind. This defect of remembrance, as it prevents our referring them to their original sensations, dissolves their natural connection. But when *memory* has lost their real bonds of union, *fancy*, by its associating power, confers upon them new ties, that they may not lie perfectly loose, ranges them in an endless variety of forms. Many of these being representations of nothing that exists in nature, whatever is fictitious or chimerical is acknowledged to be the offspring of this faculty, and is termed imaginary. But wild and lawless as this faculty appears to be, it commonly observes certain general rules, associating chiefly ideas which *resemble,* or are *contrary,* or those that are conjoined, either merely by *custom,* or by the connection of their objects in *vicinity, coexistence*, or *causation.* It sometimes *presumes* that ideas have these relations, when they have them not; but it generally discovers them, where they are; and by this means becomes the cause of many of our most important operations. . . .

All these are operations of imagination, which naturally proceed from its simplest exertions, and are the principles, from which the sentiments of taste arise. These sentiments are not fantastical, imaginary, or unsubstantial; but are universally produced by the energies of fancy, which are indeed of the utmost consequence, and have the most extensive influence on the operations of the mind. By being compounded with one another, or with other original qualities of human nature, they generate most of our compounded powers. In particular, they produce *affection*, and *taste* of every kind; the former, by operating in conjunction with those qualities of the mind, which fit us for action; the latter, by being combined with the general laws of sensation.

Immanuel Kant

1724–1804

A. Life

Immanuel Kant was born in 1724 in Koenigsberg, East Prussia. He attended the University of Koenigsberg, served as *privat docent,* and at the age of forty-one was appointed Professor of Logic and Metaphysics.

In his early years, Kant was much influenced by Wolffian philosophy and lectured on the Rationalist philosophy of Baumgarten. His writings in Aesthetics were principally influenced by Edmund Burke, Alexander Pope, Alexander Gerard, William Duff, Joseph Addison, Lord Shaftesbury, Henry Home, and David Hume. In 1770, Kant published the *Dissertation on Any Future Metaphysics;* in 1781, *The Critique of Pure Reason;* in 1788, *The Critique of Practical Reason;* and in 1790, *The Critique of Judgement,* from which the readings that follow are selected. In 1764, Kant had written *Observations on the Feelings of the Sublime and the Beautiful,* an essay comparable neither in power nor insight to *The Critique of Judgement.*

It should be pointed out that in spite of the originality Kant displays in the third Critique, there are dogmatic and traditional points of view incorporated as well. It is paradoxical that some of these more dogmatic portions stemmed from David Hume's conceptions of taste and criticism—paradoxical because it was Hume who, Kant pointed out, awakened him from his dogmatic slumber in metaphysics.

B. Aesthetics

The Critique of Judgment

Part I
Critique of aesthetic judgment

FIRST SECTION
ANALYTIC OF AESTHETIC JUDGMENT

FIRST BOOK
ANALYTIC OF THE BEAUTIFUL[34]

FIRST MOMENT
OF THE JUDGMENT OF TASTE[35]: MOMENT OF QUALITY

§ 1
The judgment of taste is aesthetic.

If we wish to discern whether anything is beautiful or not, we do not refer the representation of it to the Object by means of understanding with a view to cognition, but by means of the imagination (acting perhaps in conjunction with understanding) we refer the representation to the Subject and its feeling of pleasure or displeasure. The judgment of taste, therefore, is not a cognitive judgment, and so not logical, but is aesthetic—which means that it is one whose determining ground *cannot be other than subjective.* Every reference of representations is capable of being objective, even that of sensations (in which case it signifies the real in an empirical representation). The one exception to this is the feeling of pleasure or displeasure. This denotes nothing in the object, but is a feeling which the Subject has of itself and of the manner in which it is affected by the representation.

To apprehend a regular and appropriate building with one's cognitive faculties, be the mode of representation clear or confused, is quite a different thing from being conscious of this representation with an accompanying sensation of delight. Here the representation is referred wholly to the Subject, and what is more to its feeling of life—under the name of the feeling of pleasure or displeasure—and this forms the basis of a quite separate faculty of discriminating and estimating, that contributes nothing to knowledge. All it does is to compare the given representation in the Subject with the entire faculty of representations of which the mind is conscious in the feeling of its state. Given representations in a judgment may be empirical, and so aesthetic; but the judgment which is pronounced by their means is logical, provided it refers them to the Object. Conversely, be the given representations even rational, but referred in a judgment solely to the Subject (to its feeling), they are always to that extent aesthetic.

§ 2
The delight which determines the judgment of taste is independent of all interest.

The delight which we connect with the representation of the real existence of an

[34] *Kant's Critique of Aesthetic Judgement,* translated by James Creed Meredith. By permission of the Clarendon Press, Oxford, 1911. Additional selections are given below, p. 408.

[35] The definition of taste here relied upon is that it is the faculty of estimating the beautiful. But the discovery of what is required for calling an object beautiful must be reserved for the analysis of judgements of taste. In my search for the moments to which attention is paid by this judgment in its reflection, I have followed the guidance of the logical functions of judging (for a judgement of taste always involves a reference to understanding). I have brought the moment of quality first under review, because this is what the aesthetic judgment on the beautiful looks to in the first instance.

object is called interest. Such a delight, therefore, always involves a reference to the faculty of desire, either as its determining ground, or else as necessarily implicated with its determining ground. Now, where the question is whether something is beautiful, we do not want to know, whether we, or any one else, are, or even could be, concerned in the real existence of the thing, but rather what estimate we form of it on mere contemplation (intuition or reflection). If any one asks me whether I consider that the palace I see before me is beautiful, I may, perhaps, reply that I do not care for things of that sort that are merely made to be gaped at. Or I may reply in the same strain as that Iroquois *sachem* who said that nothing in Paris pleased him better than the eating-houses. I may even go a step further and inveigh with the vigour of a *Rousseau* against the vanity of the great who spend the sweat of the people on such superfluous things. Or, in fine, I may quite easily persuade myself that if I found myself on an uninhabited island, without hope of ever again coming among men, and could conjure such a palace into existence by a mere wish, I should still not trouble to do so, so long as I had a hut there that was comfortable enough for me. All this may be admitted and approved; only it is not the point now at issue. All one wants to know is whether the mere representation of the object is to my liking, no matter how indifferent I may be to the real existence of the object of this representation. It is quite plain that in order to say that the object *is beautiful*, and to show that I have taste, everything turns on the meaning which I can give to this representation, and not on any factor which makes me dependent on the real existence of the object. Every one must allow that a judgment on the beautiful which is tinged with the slightest interest, is very partial and not a pure judgment of taste. One must not be in the least prepossessed in favour of the real existence of the thing, but must preserve complete indifference in this respect, in order to play the part of judge in matters of taste.

This proposition, which is of the utmost importance, cannot be better explained than by contrasting the pure disinterested [36] delight which appears in the judgment of taste with that allied to an interest—especially if we can also assure ourselves that there are no other kinds of interest beyond those presently to be mentioned.

§ 3

Delight IN THE AGREEABLE *is coupled with interest.*

That is AGREEABLE *which the senses find pleasing in sensation.* This at once affords a convenient opportunity for condemning and directing particular attention to a prevalent confusion of the double meaning of which the word "sensation" is capable. All delight (as is said or thought) is itself sensation (of a pleasure). Consequently everything that pleases, and for the very reason that it pleases, is agreeable—and according to its different degrees, or its relations to other agreeable sensations, is attractive, charming, delicious, enjoyable, &c. But if this is conceded, then impressions of sense, which determine inclination, or principles of reason, which determine the will, or mere contemplated forms of intuition, which determine judgment, are all on a par in everything relevant to their effect upon the feeling of pleasure, for this would be agreeableness in the sensation of one's state; and since, in the last resort, all the elaborate work of our

[36] A judgment upon an object of our delight may be wholly *disinterested* but withal very *interesting* i.e., it relies on no interest, but it produces one. Of this kind are all pure moral judgments. But, of themselves, judgments of taste do not even set up any interest whatsoever. Only in society is it *interesting* to have taste—a point which will be explained in the sequel.

faculties must issue in and unite in the practical as its goal, we would credit our faculties with no other appreciation of things and the worth of things, than that consisting in the gratification which they promise. How this is attained is in the end immaterial; and, as the choice of the means is here the only thing that can make a difference, men might indeed blame one another for folly or imprudence, but never for baseness or wickedness; for they are all, each according to his own way of looking at things, pursuing one goal, which for each is the gratification in question.

When a modification of the feeling of pleasure or displeasure is termed sensation, this expression is given quite a different meaning to that which it bears when I call the representation of a thing (through sense as a receptivity pertaining to the faculty of knowledge) sensation. For in the latter case the representation is referred to the Object, but in the former it is referred solely to the Subject and is not available for any cognition, not even for that by which the Subject *cognizes* itself.

Now in the above definition the word sensation is used to denote an objective representation of sense; and, to avoid continually running the risk of misinterpretation, we shall call that which must always remain purely subjective, and is absolutely incapable of forming a representation of an object, by the familiar name of feeling. The green colour of the meadows belongs to *objective* sensation, as the perception of an object of sense; but its agreeableness to *subjective* sensation, by which no object is represented: i.e. to feeling, through which the object is regarded as an Object of delight (which involves no cognition of the object).

Now, that a judgment on an object by which its agreeableness is affirmed, expresses an interest in it, is evident from the fact that through sensation it provokes a desire for similar objects, consequently the delight presupposes, not the simple judgment about it, but the bearing its real existence has upon my state so far as affected by such an Object. Hence we do not merely say of the agreeable that it *pleases*, but that it *gratifies*. I do not accord it a simple approval, but inclination is aroused by it, and where agreeableness is of the liveliest type a judgment on the character of the Object is so entirely out of place, that those who are always intent only on enjoyment (for that is the word used to denote intensity of gratification) would fain dispense with all judgment.

§ 4

Delight IN THE GOOD *is coupled with interest.*

THAT is *good* which by means of reason commends itself by its mere concept. We call that *good for something* (useful) which only pleases as a means; but that which pleases on its own account we call *good in itself*. In both cases the concept of an end is implied, and consequently the relation of reason to (at least possible) willing, and thus a delight in the *existence* of an Object or action, i.e. some interest or other.

To deem something good, I must always know what sort of a thing the object is intended to be, i.e. I must have a concept of it. That is not necessary to enable me to see beauty in a thing. Flowers, free patterns, lines aimlessly intertwining—technically termed foliage,—have no signification, depend upon no definite concept, and yet please. Delight in the beautiful must depend upon the reflection on an object precursory to some (not definitely determined) concept. It is thus also differentiated from the agreeable, which rests entirely upon sensation.

In many cases, no doubt, the agreeable and the good seem convertible terms. Thus it is commonly said that all (especially lasting) gratification is of itself good; which is almost equivalent to saying that to be permanently agreeable and to be good are identical. But it is readily apparent that this is merely a vicious confusion of words, for the concepts appropriate to these expressions are far from interchangeable. The agreeable, which, as such, represents the object solely in relation to sense, must in the first instance be brought under principles of reason through the concept of an end, to be, as an object of will, called good. But that the reference to delight is wholly different where what gratifies is at the same called *good*, is evident from the fact that with the good the question always is whether it is mediately or immediately good, i.e. useful or good in itself; whereas with the agreeable this point can never arise, since the word always means what pleases immediately—and it is just the same with what I call beautiful.

Even in everyday parlance a distinction is drawn between the agreeable and the good. We do not scruple to say of a dish that stimulates the palate with spices and other condiments that it is agreeable—owning all the while that it is not good: because, while it immediately *satisfies* the senses, it is mediately displeasing, i.e. in the eye of reason that looks ahead to the consequences. Even in our estimate of health this same distinction may be traced. To all that possess it, it is immediately agreeable—at least negatively, i.e. as remoteness of all bodily pains. But, if we are to say that it is good, we must further apply to reason to direct it to ends, that is, we must regard it as a state that puts us in a congenial mood for all we have to do. Finally, in respect of happiness every one believes that the greatest aggregate of the pleasures of life, taking duration as well as number into account, merits the name of a true, nay even of the highest, good. But reason sets its face against this too. Agreeableness is enjoyment. But if this is all that we are bent on, it would be foolish to be scrupulous about the means that procure it for us—whether it be obtained passively by the beauty of nature or actively and by the work of our own hands. But that there is any intrinsic worth in the real existence of a man who merely lives for *enjoyment*, however busy he may be in this respect, even when in so doing he serves others—all equally with himself intent only on enjoyment—as an excellent means to that one end, and does so, moreover, because through sympathy he shares all their gratifications,—this is a view to which reason will never let itself be brought round. Only by what a man does heedless of enjoyment, in complete freedom and independently of what he can procure passively from the hand of nature, does he give to his existence, as the real existence of a person, an absolute worth. Happiness, with all its plethora of pleasures, is far from being an unconditioned good.[37]

But, despite all this difference between the agreeable and the good, they both agree in being invariably coupled with an interest in their object. This is true, not alone of the agreeable, §3, and of the mediately good, i.e. the useful, which pleases as a means to some pleasure, but also of that which is good absolutely and from every point of view, namely the moral good which carries with it the highest interest. For the good is the Object of will, i.e. of a rationally determined faculty of desire. But to will something, and to take a delight in its existence, i.e. to take an interest in it, are identical.

§ 5

Comparison of the three specifically different kinds of delight.

BOTH the Agreeable and the Good involve a reference to the faculty of desire, and are

[37] An obligation to enjoyment is a patent absurdity. And the same, then, must also be said of a supposed obligation to actions that have merely enjoyment for their aim, no matter how spiritually this enjoyment may be refined in thought (or embellished), and even if it be a mystical, so-called heavenly, enjoyment.

thus attended, the former with a delight pathologically conditioned (by stimuli), the latter with a pure practical delight. Such delight is determined not merely by the representation of the object, but also by the represented bond of connexion between the Subject and the real existence of the object. It is not merely the object, but also its real existence, that pleases. On the other hand the judgment of taste is simply *contemplative,* i.e. it is a judgment which is indifferent as to the existence of an object, and only decides how its character stands with the feeling of pleasure and displeasure. But not even is this contemplation itself directed to concepts; for the judgment of taste is not a cognitive judgment (neither a theoretical one nor a practical), and hence, also, is not *grounded* on concepts, nor yet *intentionally directed* to them.

The agreeable, the beautiful, and the good thus denote three different relations of representations to the feeling of pleasure and displeasure, as a feeling in respect of which we distinguish different objects or modes of representation. Also, the corresponding expressions which indicate our satisfaction in them are different. The *agreeable* is what GRATIFIES a man; the *beautiful* what simply PLEASES him; the *good* what is ESTEEMED (*approved*), i.e. that on which he sets an objective worth. Agreeableness is a significant factor even with irrational animals; beauty has purport and significance only for human beings, i.e. for beings at once animal and rational (but not merely for them as rational—intelligent beings—but only for them as at once animal and rational); whereas the good is good for every rational being in general;—a proposition which can only receive its complete justification and explanation in the sequel. Of all these three kinds of delight, that of taste in the beautiful may be said to be the one and only disinterested and *free* delight; for, with it, no interest, whether of sense or reason, extorts approval. And so we may say that delight, in the three cases mentioned, is related to *inclination,* to *favour,* or to *respect.* For FAVOUR is the only free liking. An object of inclination, and one which a law of reason imposes upon our desire, leaves us no freedom to turn anything into an object of pleasure. All interest presupposes a want, or calls one forth; and, being a ground determining approval, deprives the judgment on the object of its freedom.

So far as the interest of inclination in the case of the agreeable goes, every one says: Hunger is the best sauce; and people with a healthy appetite relish everything, so long as it is something they can eat. Such delight, consequently, gives no indication of taste having anything to say to the choice. Only when men have got all they want can we tell who among the crowd has taste or not. Similarly there may be correct habits (conduct) without virtue, politeness without good-will, propriety without honour, &c. For where the moral law dictates, there is, objectively, no room left for free choice as to what one has to do; and to show taste in the way one carries out these dictates, or in estimating the way others do so, is a totally different matter from displaying the moral frame of one's mind. For the latter involves a command and produces a need of something, whereas moral taste only plays with the objects of delight without devoting itself sincerely to any.

DEFINITION OF THE BEAUTIFUL DERIVED FROM THE FIRST MOMENT

Taste is the faculty of estimating an object or a mode of representation by means of a delight or aversion *apart from any interest.* The object of such a delight is called *beautiful.*

SECOND MOMENT OF THE JUDGMENT OF TASTE: MOMENT OF QUANTITY

§ 6

The beautiful is that which, apart from concepts, is represented as the Object of a UNIVERSAL *delight.*

THIS definition of the beautiful is deducible from the foregoing definition of it as an object of delight apart from any interest. For where any one is conscious that his delight in an object is with him independent of interest, it is inevitable that he should look on the object as one containing a ground of delight for all men. For, since the delight is not based on any inclination of the Subject (or on any other deliberate interest), but the Subject feels himself completely *free* in respect of the liking which he accords to the object, he can find as reason for his delight no personal conditions to which his own subjective self might alone be party. Hence he must regard it as resting on what he may also presuppose in every other person; and therefore he must believe that he has reason for demanding a similar delight from every one. Accordingly he will speak of the beautiful as if beauty were a quality of the object and the judgment logical (forming a cognition of the Object by concept of it); although it is only aesthetic, and contains merely a reference of the representation of the object to the Subject;—because it still bears this resemblance to the logical judgment, that it may be presupposed to be valid for all men. But this universality cannot spring from concepts. For from concepts there is no transition to the feeling of pleasure or displeasure (save in the case of pure practical laws, which, however, carry an interest with them; and such an interest does not attach to the pure judgment of taste). The result is that the judgment of taste, with its attendant consciousness of detachment from all interest, must involve a claim to validity for all men, and must do so apart from universality attached to Objects, i.e. there must be coupled with it a claim to subjective universality.

§ 7

Comparison of the beautiful with the agreeable and the good by means of the above characteristic.

As regards the *agreeable* every one concedes that his judgment, which he bases on a private feeling, and in which he declares that an object pleases him, is restricted merely to himself personally. Thus he does not take it amiss if, when he says that Canary-wine is agreeable, another corrects the expression and reminds him that he ought to say: It is agreeable *to me.* This applies not only to the taste of the tongue, the palate, and the throat, but to what may with any one be agreeable to eye or ear. A violet colour is to one soft and lovely: to another dull and faded. One man likes the tone of wind instruments, another prefers that of string instruments. To quarrel over such points with the idea of condemning another's judgment as incorrect when it differs from our own, as if the opposition between the two judgments were logical, would be folly. With the agreeable, therefore, the axiom holds good: *Every one has his own taste* (that of sense).

The beautiful stands on quite a different footing. It would, on the contrary, be ridiculous if any one who plumed himself on his taste were to think of justifying himself by saying: This object (the building we see, the dress that person has on, the concert we hear, the poem submitted to our criticism) is beautiful *for me.* For if it merely pleases *him,* he must not call it *beautiful.* Many things may for him possess charm and agreeableness—no one cares about that; but when he puts a thing on a pedestal and calls it beautiful, he demands the same delight from others. He judges not merely for himself, but for all men, and then speaks of beauty as if it were a property of things. Thus he says the *thing* is beautiful; and it is not as if he counted, on others agreeing in his judgment of liking owing to his having found them in such agreement on a number of occasions, but he *demands* this agreement of them. He blames them if they judge differently, and denies them taste, which he still requires of them as something they ought to have; and to this extent it is not open to men to say: Every one has his own taste. This would be equivalent to saying that there is no such thing at all as taste, i.e no aesthetic judgment capable of making a rightful claim upon the assent of all men.

Yet even in the case of the agreeable we find that the estimates men form do betray a prevalent agreement among them, which leads to our crediting some with taste and denying it to others, and that, too, not as an organic sense but as a critical faculty in respect of the agreeable generally. So of one who knows how to entertain his guests with pleasures (of enjoyment through all the senses) in such a way that one and all are pleased, we say that he has taste. But the universality here is only understood in a comparative sense; and the rules that apply are, like all empirical rules, *general* only, not *universal*,—the latter being what the judgment of taste upon the beautiful deals or claims to deal in. It is a judgment in respect of sociability so far as resting on empirical rules. In respect of the good it is true that judgments also rightly assert a claim to validity for every one; but the good is only represented as an Object of universal delight *by means of a concept*, which is the case neither with the agreeable nor the beautiful.

§ 8

In a judgment of taste the universality of delight is only represented as subjective.

THIS particular form of the universality of an aesthetic judgment, which is to be met with in a judgment of taste, is a significant feature, not for the logician certainly, but for the transcendental philosopher. It calls for no small effort on his part to discover its origin, but in return it brings to light a property of our cognitive faculty which, without this analysis, would have remained unknown.

First, one must get firmly into one's mind that by the judgment of taste (upon the beautiful) the delight in an object is imputed to *every one*, yet without being founded on a concept (for then it would be the good), and that this claim to universality is such an essential factor of a judgment by which we describe anything as *beautiful*, that were it not for its being present to the mind it would never enter into any one's head to use this expression, but everything that pleased without a concept would be ranked as agreeable. For in respect of the agreeable every one is allowed to have his own opinion, and no one insists upon others agreeing with his judgment of taste, which is what is invariably done in the judgment of taste about beauty. The first of these I may call the taste of sense, the second, the taste of reflection: the first laying down judgments merely private, the second, on the other hand, judgments ostensibly of general validity (public), but both alike being aesthetic (not practical) judgments about an object merely in respect of the bearings of its representation on the feeling of pleasure or displeasure. Now it does seem strange that while with the taste of sense it is not alone experience that shows that its judgment (of pleasure or displeasure in something) is not universally valid, but every one willingly refrains from imputing this agreement to others (despite the frequent actual prevalence of a considerable consensus of general opinion even in these judgments), the taste of reflection, which, as experience teaches, has often enough to put up with a rude dismissal of its claims to universal validity of its judgment (upon the beautiful), can (as it actually does) find it possible for all that, to formulate judgments capable of demanding this agreement in its universality. Such agreement it does in fact require from every one for each of its judgments of taste,—the persons who pass these judgments not quarrelling over the possibility of such a claim, but only failing in particular cases to come to terms as to the correct application of this faculty.

First of all we have here to note that a universality which does not rest upon concepts of the Object (even though these are only empirical) is in no way logical, but aesthetic, i.e. does not involve any objective quantity of the judgment, but only one that is subjective. For this universality I use the expression *general validity*, which denotes the validity of the reference of a representation, not to the cognitive faculties, but to the feeling of pleasure or displeasure for every Subject. (The same expression, however, may also be employed for the logical quantity of the judgment provided we add *objective* universal validity, to distinguish it from the merely subjective validity which is always aesthetic.)

Now a judgment that has *objective universal validity* has always got the subjective also, i.e. if the judgment is valid for everything which is contained under a given concept, it is valid also for all who represent an object by means of this concept. But from a *subjective universal validity,* i.e. the aesthetic, that does not rest on any concept, no conclusion can be drawn to the logical; because judgments of that kind have no bearing upon the Object. But for this very reason the aesthetic universality attributed to a judgment must also be of a special kind, seeing that it does not join the predicate of beauty to the concept of the *Object* taken in its entire logical sphere, and yet does extend this predicate over the whole sphere of *judging Subjects.*

In their logical quantity all judgments of taste are *singular* judgments. For, since I must present the object immediately to my feeling of pleasure or displeasure, and that, too, without the aid of concepts, such judgments cannot have the quantity of judgments with objective general validity. Yet by taking the singular representation of the Object of the judgment of taste, and by comparison converting it into a concept according to the conditions determining that judgment, we can arrive at a logically universal judgment. For instance, by a judgment of taste I describe the rose at which I am looking as beautiful. The judgment, on the other hand, resulting from the comparison of a number of singular representations: Roses in general are beautiful, is no longer pronounced as a purely aesthetic judgment, but as a logical judgment founded on one that is aesthetic. Now the judgment, "The rose is agreeable" (to smell) is also, no doubt, an aesthetic and singular judgment, but then it is not one of taste but of sense. For it has this point of difference from a judgment of taste, that the latter imports an *aesthetic quantity* of universality, i.e. of validity for every one which is not to be met with in a judgment upon the agreeable. It is only judgments upon the good which, while also determining the delight in an object, possess logical and not mere aesthetic universality; for it is as involving a cognition of the Object that they are valid of it, and on that account valid for every one.

In forming an estimate of Objects merely from concepts, all representation of beauty goes by the board. There can, therefore, be no rule according to which any one is to be compelled to recognize anything as beautiful. Whether a dress, a house, or a flower is beautiful is a matter upon which one declines to allow one's judgment to be swayed by any reasons or principles. We want to get a look at the Object with our own eyes, just as if our delight depended on sensation. And yet, if upon so doing, we call the object beautiful, we believe ourselves to be speaking with a universal voice, and lay claim to the concurrence of every one, whereas no private sensation would be decisive except for the observer alone and *his* liking.

Here, now, we may perceive that nothing is postulated in the judgment of taste but such a *universal voice* in respect of delight that is not mediated by concepts; consequently, only the *possibility* of an aesthetic judgment capable of being at the same time deemed valid for every one. The judgment of taste itself does not *postulate* the agreement of every one (for it is only competent for a logically universal judgment to do this, in that it is able to bring forward reasons); it only *imputes* this agreement to every one, as an instance of the rule in respect of which it looks for confirmation, not from concepts, but from the concurrence of others. The universal voice is, therefore, only an idea—resting upon grounds the investigation of which is here postponed. It may be a matter of uncertainty whether a person who thinks he is laying down a judgment of taste is, in fact, judging in conformity with that idea; but that this idea is what is contemplated in his judgment and that, consequently, it is meant to be a judgment of taste, is proclaimed by his use of the expression "beauty", For himself he can be certain on the point from his mere consciousness of the separation of everything belonging to the agreeable and the good from the delight remaining to him; and this is all for which he promises himself the agreement of every one—a claim which, under these conditions, he would also be warranted in making, were it not that he frequently sinned against them, and thus passed an erroneous judgment of taste.

§ 9

Investigation of the question of the relative priority in a judgment of taste of the feeling of pleasure and the estimating of the object.

THE solution of this problem is the key to the Critique of taste, and so is worthy of all attention.

Were the pleasure in a given object to be the antecedent, and were the universal communicability of this pleasure to be all that the judgment of taste is meant to allow to the representation of the object, such a sequence would be selfcontradictory. For a pleasure of that kind would be nothing but the feeling of mere agreeableness to the senses, and so, from its very nature, would possess no more than private validity, seeing that it would be immediately dependent on the representation through which the object *is given.*

Hence it is the universal capacity for being communicated incident to the mental state in the given representation which, as the subjective condition of the judgment of taste, must be fundamental, with the pleasure in the object as its consequent. Nothing, however, is capable of being universally communicated but cognition and representation so far as appurtenant to cognition. For it is only as thus appurtenant that the representation is objective, and it is this alone that gives it a universal point of reference with which the power of representation of every one is obliged to harmonize. If, then, the determining ground of the judgment as to this universal communicability of the representation is to be merely subjective, that is to say, is to be conceived independently of any concept of the object, it can be nothing else than the mental state that presents itself in the mutual relation of the powers of representation so far as they refer a given representation *to cognition in general.*

The cognitive powers brought into play by this representation are here engaged in a free play, since no definite concept restricts them to a particular rule of cognition. Hence the mental state in this representation must be one of a feeling of the free play of the powers of representation in a given representation for a cognition in general. Now a representation, whereby an object is given, involves, in order that it may become a source of cognition at all, *imagination* for bringing together the manifold of intuition, and *understanding* for the unity of the concept uniting the representations. This state of *free play* of the cognitive faculties attending a representation by which an object is given must admit of universal communication: because cognition, as a definition of the

Object with which given representations (in any Subject whatever) are to accord, is the one and only representation which is valid for every one.

As the subjective universal communicability of the mode of representation in a judgment of taste is to subsist apart from the presupposition of any definite concept, it can be nothing else than the mental state present in the free play of imagination and understanding (so far as these are in mutual accord, as is requisite for *cognition in general*): for we are conscious that this subjective relation suitable for a cognition in general must be just as valid for every one, and consequently as universally communicable, as is any determinate cognition, which always rests upon that relation as its subjective condition.

Now this purely subjective (aesthetic) estimating of the object, or of the representation through which it is given, is antecedent to the pleasure in it, and is the basis of this pleasure in the harmony of the cognitive faculties. Again, the above-described universality of the subjective conditions of estimating objects forms the sole foundation of this universal subjective validity of the delight which we connect with the representation of the object that we call beautiful.

That an ability to communicate one's mental state, even though it be only in respect of our cognitive faculties, is attended with a pleasure, is a fact which might easily be demonstrated from the natural propensity of mankind to social life, i.e. empirically and psychologically. But what we have here in view calls for something more than this. In a judgment of taste the pleasure felt by us is exacted from every one else as necessary, just as if, when we call something beautiful, beauty was to be regarded as a quality of the object forming part of its inherent determination according to concepts; although beauty is for itself, apart from any reference to the feeling of the Subject, nothing. But the discussion of this question must be reserved until we have answered the further one of whether, and how, aesthetic judgments are possible *a priori*.

At present we are exercised with the lesser question of the way in which we become conscious, in a judgment of taste, of a reciprocal subjective common accord of the powers of cognition. Is it aesthetically by sensation and our mere internal sense? Or is it intellectually by consciousness of our intentional activity in bringing these powers into play?

Now if the given representation occasioning the judgment of taste were a concept which united understanding and imagination in the estimate of the objective so as to give a cognition of the Object, the consciousness of this relation would be intellectual (as in the objective schematism of judgment dealt with in the Critique). But, then, in that case the judgment would not be laid down with respect to pleasure and displeasure, and so would not be a judgment of taste. But, now, the judgment of taste determines the Object, independently of concepts, in respect of delight and of the predicate of beauty. There is, therefore, no other way for the subjective unity of the relation in question to make itself known than by sensation. The quickening of both faculties (imagination and understanding) to an indefinite, but yet, thanks to the given representation, harmonious activity, such as belongs to cognition generally, is the sensation whose universal communicability is postulated by the judgment of taste. An objective relation can, of course, only be thought, yet in so far as, in respect of its conditions, it is subjective, it may be felt in its effect upon the mind, and, in the case of a relation (like that of the powers of representation to a faculty of cognition generally) which does not rest on any concept, no other consciousness of it is possible beyond that through sensation of its effect upon the mind—an effect consisting in the more facile play of both mental powers (imagination and understanding) as quickened by their mutual accord. A representation which is singular and independent of comparison with other representations, and, being such, yet accords with the conditions of the universality that is the general concern of understanding, is one that brings the cognitive faculties into that proportionate accord which we require for all cognition and which we therefore deem valid for every one who is so constituted as to judge by means of understanding and sense conjointly (i.e. for every man).

DEFINITION OF THE BEAUTIFUL DRAWN FROM THE SECOND MOMENT

The *beautiful* is that which, apart from a concept, pleases universally.

THIRD MOMENT OF JUDGMENTS OF TASTE: MOMENT OF THE *RELATION* OF THE ENDS BROUGHT UNDER REVIEW IN SUCH JUDGMENTS

§ 10
Finality in general.

LET us define the meaning of "an end" in transcendental terms (i.e. without presupposing anything empirical, such as the feeling of pleasure). An end is the object of a concept so far as this concept is regarded as the cause of the object (the real ground of its possibility); and the causality of a *concept* in respect of its *Object* is finality (*forma finalis*). Where, then, not the cognition of an object merely, but the object itself (its form or real existence) as an effect, is thought to be possible only through a concept of it, there we imagine an end. The representation of the effect is here the determining ground of its cause and takes the lead of it. The consciousness of the causality of a representation in respect of the state of the Subject as one tending *to preserve a continuance* of that state, may here be said to denote in a general way what is called pleasure; whereas displeasure is that representation which contains the ground for converting the state of the representations into their opposite (for hindering or removing them).

The faculty of desire, so far as determinable only through concepts, i.e. so as to act in conformity with the representation of an end, would be the will. But an Object, or state of mind, or even an action may, although its possibility does not necessarily presuppose the representation of an end, be called final simply on account of its possibility being only explicable and intelligible for us by virtue of an assumption on our part of a fundamental causality according to ends, i.e. a will that would have so ordained it according to a certain represented rule. Finality, therefore, may exist apart from an end, in so far as we do not locate the causes of this form in a will, but yet are able to render the explanation of its possibility intelligible to ourselves only by deriving it from a will. Now we are not always obliged to look with the eye of reason into what we observe (i.e. to consider it in its possibility). So we may at least observe a finality of form, and trace it in objects—though by reflection only—without resting it on an end (as the material of the *nexus finalis*).

§ 11
The sole foundation of the judgment of taste is the FORM OF FINALITY *of an object (or mode of representing it).*

WHENEVER an end is regarded as a source of delight it always imports an interest as determining ground of the judgment on the object of pleasure. Hence the judgment of taste cannot rest on any subjective end as its ground. But neither can any representation of an objective end, i.e. of the possibility of the object itself on principles of final connexion, determine the judgment of taste, and, consequently, neither can any concept of the good. For the judgment of taste is an aesthetic and not a cognitive judgment, and so does not deal with any *concept* of the nature or of the internal or external possibility, by this or that cause, of the object, but simply with the relative bearing of the representative powers so far as determined by a representation.

Now this relation, present when an object is characterized as beautiful, is coupled with the feeling of pleasure. This pleasure is by the judgment of taste pronounced valid for every one; hence an agreeableness attending the representation is just as incapable of containing the determining ground of the judgment as the representation of the perfection of the object or the concept of the good. We are thus left with the subjective finality in the representation of an object, exclusive of any end (objective or subjective)—consequently the bare form of finality in the representation whereby an object is *given* to us, so far as we are conscious of it—as that which is alone capable of constituting the delight which, apart from any concept, we estimate as universally communicable, and so of forming the determining ground of the judgment of taste.

§ 12
The judgment of taste rests upon a priori *grounds.*

To determine *a priori* the connexion of the feeling of pleasure or displeasure as an effect, with some representation or other (sensation or concept) as its cause, is utterly impossible; for that would be a causal relation which, (with objects of experience,) is always one that can only be cognized *a posteriori* and with the help of experience. True, in the Critique of Practical Reason we did actually derive *a priori* from universal moral concepts the feeling of respect (as a particular and peculiar modification of this feeling which does not strictly answer either to the pleasure or displeasure which we receive from empirical objects). But there we were further able to cross the border of experience and call in aid a causality resting on a supersensible attribute of the Subject, namely that of freedom. But even there it was not this *feeling* exactly that we deduced from the idea of the moral as cause, but from this was derived the determination of the will. But the mental state present in the determination of the will by any means is at once in itself a feeling of pleasure and identical with it, and so does not issue from it as an effect. Such an effect must only be assumed where the concept of the moral as a good precedes the determination of the will by the law; for in that case it would be futile to derive the pleasure combined with the concept from this concept as a mere cognition. . . .

§ 15
The judgment of taste is entirely independent of the concept of perfection.

Objective finality can only be cognized by means of a reference of the manifold to a definite end, and hence only through a concept. This alone makes it clear that the beautiful, which is estimated on the ground of a mere formal finality, i.e. a finality apart from an end, is wholly independent of the representation of the good. For the latter presupposes an objective finality, i.e. the reference of the object to a definite end.

Objective finality is either external, i.e. the *utility,* or internal, i.e. the *perfection,* of the object. That the delight in an object on account of which we call it beautiful is incapable of resting on the representation of its utility, is abundantly evident from the two preceding articles; for in that case, it would not be an immediate delight in the object, which latter is the essential condition of the judgment upon beauty. But in an objective, internal finality, i.e. perfection, we have what is more akin to the predicate of beauty, and so this has been held even by philosophers of reputation to be convertible with beauty, though subject to the qualification: *where it is thought in a confused way*. In a Critique of taste it is of the utmost importance to decide whether beauty is really reducible to the concept of perfection.

For estimating objective finality we always require the concept of an end, where such finality has to be, not an external one (utility), but an internal one, the concept of an internal end containing the ground of the internal possibility of the object. Now an end is in general that, the *concept* of which may be regarded as the ground of the possibility of the object itself. So in order to represent an objective finality in a thing we must first have a concept of *what sort of thing it is to be*. The agreement of the manifold in a thing with this concept (which supplies the rule of its synthesis) is the *qualitative perfection* of the thing. Quantitative perfection is entirely distinct from this. It consists in the completeness of anything after its kind, and is a mere concept of quantity (of totality). In its case the question of *what the thing is to be* is regarded as definitely disposed of, and we only ask whether it is possessed of *all* the requisites that go to make it such. What is formal in the representation of a thing, i.e. the agreement of its manifold with a unity (i.e. irrespective of what it is to be) does not, of itself, afford us any cognition whatsoever of objective finality. For since abstraction is made from this unity as *end* (what the thing is to be) nothing is left but the subjective finality of the representations in the mind of the Subject intuiting. This gives a certain finality of the representative state of the Subject, in which the Subject feels itself quite at home in its effort to grasp a given form in the imagination, but no perfection of any Object, the latter not being here thought through any concept. For instance, if in a forest I light upon a plot of grass, round which trees stand in a circle, and if I do not then form any representation of an end, as that it is meant to be used, say, for country dances, then not the least hint of a concept of perfection is given by the mere form. To suppose a formal *objective* finality that is yet devoid of an end, i.e. the mere form of a *perfection* (apart from any matter or *concept* of that to which the agreement relates, even though there was the mere general idea of a conformity to law) is a veritable contradiction.

Now the judgment of taste is an aesthetic judgment, i.e. one resting on subjective grounds. No concept can be its determining ground, and hence not one of a definite end. Beauty, therefore, as a formal subjective finality, involves no thought whatsoever of a perfection of the object, as a would-be formal finality which yet, for all that, is objective: and the distinction between the concepts of the beautiful and the good, which represents both as differing only in their logical form, the first being merely a confused, the second a clearly defined, concept of perfection, while otherwise alike in content and origin, all goes for nothing: for then there would be no *specific* difference between them, but the judgment of taste would be just as much a cognitive judgment as one by which something is described as good—just as the man in the street, when he says that deceit is wrong, bases his judgment on confused, but the philosopher on clear grounds, while both appeal in reality to identical principles of reason. But I have already stated that an aesthetic judgment is quite unique, and affords absolutely no, (not even a confused,) knowledge of the Object. It is only through a logical judgment that we get knowledge. The aesthetic judgment, on the other hand, refers the representation, by which an Object is given, solely to the Subject, and brings to our notice no quality of the object, but only the final form in the determination of the powers of representation engaged upon it. The judgment is called aesthetic for the very reason that its determining ground cannot be a concept, but is rather the feeling (of the internal sense) of the concert in the play of the mental powers as a thing only capable of being felt. If, on the other hand, confused concepts, and the objective judgment based on them, are going to be called aesthetic, we shall find ourselves with an understanding judging by sense, or a sense representing its objects by concepts—a mere choice of contradictions. The faculty of concepts, be they confused or be they clear, is understanding; and although understanding has (as in all judgments) its rôle in the judgment of taste, as an aesthetic judgment, its rôle there is not that of a faculty for cognizing an object, but of a faculty for determining that judgment and its representation (without a concept) according to its relation to the Subject and its internal feeling, and for doing so in so far as that judgment is possible according to a universal rule.

§ 16

A judgment of taste by which an object is described as beautiful under the condition of a definite concept is not pure.

THERE are two kinds of beauty: free beauty (*pulchritudo vaga*), or beauty which is merely dependent (*pulchritudo adhaerens*). The first presupposes no concept of what the object should be; the second does presuppose such a concept and, with it, an answering perfection of the object. Those of the first kind are said to be (self-subsisting) beauties of this thing or that thing; the other kind of beauty, being attached to a concept (conditioned beauty), is ascribed to Objects which come under the concept of a particular end.

Flowers are free beauties of nature. Hardly any one but a botanist knows the true nature of a flower, and even he, while recognizing in the flower the reproductive organ of the plant, pays no attention to this natural end when using his taste to judge of its beauty. Hence no perfection of any kind—no internal finality, as something to which the arrangement of the manifold is related—underlies this judgment. Many birds (the parrot, the humming-bird, the bird of paradise), and a number of crustacea, are self-subsisting beauties which are not appurtenant to any object defined with respect to its end, but please freely and on their own account. So designs *à la grecque,* foliage for framework or on wall-papers, &c., have no intrinsic meaning; they represent nothing—no Object under a definite concept—and are free beauties. We may also rank in the same class what in music are called fantasias (without a theme), and, indeed, all music that is not set to words.

In the estimate of a free beauty (according to mere form) we have the pure judgment of taste. No concept is here presupposed of any end for which the manifold should serve the given Object, and which the latter, therefore, should represent—an incumbrance which would only restrict the freedom of the imagination that, as it were, is at play in the contemplation of the outward form.

But the beauty of man (including under this head that of a man, woman, or child), the beauty of a horse, or of a building (such as a church, palace, arsenal, or summer-house), presupposes a concept of the end that defines what the thing has to be, and consequently a concept of its perfection; and is therefore merely appendant beauty. Now, just as it is a clog on the purity of the judgment of taste to have the agreeable (of sensation) joined with beauty to which properly only the form is relevant, so to combine the good with beauty, (the good, namely, of the manifold to the thing itself according to its end,) mars its purity.

Much might be added to a building that would immediately please the eye, were it not intended for a church. A figure might be beautified with all manner of flourishes and light but regular lines, as is done by the New Zealanders with their tattooing, were we dealing with anything but the figure of a human being. And here is one whose rugged features might be softened and given a more pleasing aspect, only he has got to be a man, or is, perhaps, a warrior that has to have a warlike appearance.

Now the delight in the manifold of a thing,

in reference to the internal end that determines its possibility, is a delight based on a concept, whereas delight in the beautiful is such as does not presuppose any concept, but is immediately coupled with the representation through which the object is given (not through which it is thought). If, now, the judgment of taste in respect of the latter delight is made dependent upon the end involved in the former delight as a judgment of reason, and is thus placed under a restriction, then it is no longer a free and pure judgment of taste.

Taste, it is true, stands to gain by this combination of intellectual delight with the aesthetic. For it becomes fixed, and while not universal, it enables rules to be prescribed for it in respect of certain definite final Objects. But these rules are then not rules of taste, but merely rules for establishing a union of taste with reason, i.e. of the beautiful with the good—rules by which the former becomes available as an intentional instrument in respect of the latter, for the purpose of bringing that temper of the mind which is self-sustaining and of subjective universal validity to the support and maintenance of that mode of thought which, while possessing objective universal validity, can only be preserved by a resolute effort. But, strictly speaking, perfection neither gains by beauty, nor beauty by perfection. The truth is rather this, when we compare the representation through which an object is given to us with the Object (in respect of what it is meant to be) by means of a concept, we cannot help reviewing it also in respect of the sensation in the Subject. Hence there results a gain to the *entire faculty* of our representative power when harmony prevails between both states of mind.

In respect of an object with a definite end, a judgment of taste would only be pure where the person judging either has no concept of this end, or else makes abstraction from it in his judgment. But in cases like this, although such a person should lay down a correct judgment of taste, since he would be estimating the object as a free beauty, he would still be found fault with by another who saw nothing in its beauty but a dependent quality (i.e. who looked to the end of the object) and would be accused by him of false taste, though both would, in their own way, be judging correctly: the one according to what he had present to his senses, the other according to what was present in his thoughts. This distinction enables us to settle many disputes about beauty on the part of critics; for we may show them how one side is dealing with free beauty, and the other with that which is dependent: the former passing a pure judgment of taste, the latter one that is applied intentionally.

§ 17
The Ideal of Beauty.

THERE can be no objective rule of taste by which what is beautiful may be defined by means of concepts. For every judgment from that source is aesthetic, i.e. its determining ground is the feeling of the Subject, and not any concept of an Object. It is only throwing away labour to look for a principle of taste that affords a universal criterion of the beautiful by definite concepts; because what is sought is a thing impossible and inherently contradictory. But in the universal communicability of the sensation (of delight or aversion)—a communicability, too, that exists apart from any concept—in the accord, so far as possible, of all ages and nations as to this feeling in the representation of certain objects, we have the empirical criterion, weak indeed and scarce sufficient to raise a presumption, of the derivation of a taste, thus confirmed by examples, from grounds deep-seated and shared alike by all men, underlying their agreement in estimating the forms under which objects are given to them.

For this reason some products of taste are looked on as *exemplary*—not meaning thereby that by imitating others taste may be acquired.

For taste must be an original faculty; whereas one who imitates a model, while showing skill commensurate with his success, only displays taste as himself a critic of this model.[38] Hence it follows that the highest model, the archetype of taste, is a mere idea, which each person must beget in his own consciousness, and according to which he must form his estimate of everything that is an Object of taste, or that is an example of critical taste, and even of universal taste itself. Properly speaking, an *idea* signifies a concept of reason, and an *ideal* the representation of an individual existence as adequate to an idea. Hence this archetype of taste—which rests, indeed, upon reason's indeterminate idea of a maximum, but is not, however, capable of being represented by means of concepts, but only in an individual presentation—may more appropriately be called the ideal of the beautiful. While not having this ideal in our possession, we still strive to beget it within us. But it is bound to be merely an ideal of the imagination, seeing that it rests, not upon concepts, but upon the presentation—the faculty of presentation being the imagination.—Now, how do we arrive at such an ideal of beauty? Is it *a priori* or empirically? Further, what species of the beautiful admits of an ideal?

First of all, we do well to observe that the beauty for which an ideal has to be sought cannot be a beauty that is *free and at large*, but must be one *fixed* by a concept of objective finality. Hence it cannot belong to the Object of an altogether pure judgement of taste, but must attach to one that is partly intellectual. In other words, where an ideal is to have place among the grounds upon which any estimate is formed, then beneath grounds of that kind there must lie some idea of reason according to determinate concepts, by which the end underlying the internal possibility of the object is determined *a priori*. An ideal of beautiful flowers, of a beautiful suite of furniture, or of a beautiful view, is unthinkable. But, it may also be impossible to represent an ideal of a beauty dependent on definite ends, e.g. a beautiful residence, a beautiful tree, a beautiful garden, &c., presumably because their ends are not sufficiently defined and fixed by their concept, with the result that their finality is nearly as free as with beauty that is quite *at large*. Only what has in itself the end of its real existence—only *man* that is able himself to determine his ends by reason, or, where he has to derive them from external perception, can still compare them with essential and universal ends, and then further pronounce aesthetically upon their accord with such ends, only he, among all objects in the world, admits, therefore, of an ideal of *beauty*, just as humanity in his person, as intelligence, alone admits of the ideal of *perfection*.

Two factors are here involved. *First*, there is the aesthetic *normal idea*, which is an individual intuition (of the imagination). This represents the norm by which we judge of a man as a member of a particular animal species. *Secondly*, there is the *rational idea*. This deals with the ends of humanity so far as capable of sensuous representation, and converts them into a principle for estimating his outward form, through which these ends are revealed in their phenomenal effect. The normal idea must draw from experience the constituents which it requires for the form of an animal of a particular kind. But the greatest finality in the construction of this form—that which would serve as a universal norm for forming an estimate of each individual of the species in question—the image that, as it were, forms an intentional basis underlying the

[38] Models of taste with respect to the arts of speech must be composed in a dead and learned language; the first, to prevent their having to suffer the changes that inevitably overtake living ones, making dignified expressions become degraded, common ones antiquated, and ones newly coined after a short currency obsolete; the second to ensure its having a grammar that is not subject to the caprices of fashion, but has fixed rules of its own.

technic of nature, to which no separate individual, but only the race as a whole, is adequate, has its seat merely in the idea of the judging Subject. Yet it is, with all its proportions, an aesthetic idea, and, as such, capable of being fully presented *in concreto* in a model image. Now, how is this effected? In order to render the process to some extent intelligible (for who can wrest nature's whole secret from her?), let us attempt a psychological explanation.

It is of note that the imagination, in a manner quite incomprehensible to us, is able on occasion, even after a long lapse of time, not alone to recall the signs for concepts, but also to reproduce the image and shape of an object out of a countless number of others of a different, or even of the very same, kind. And, further, if the mind is engaged upon comparisons, we may well suppose that it can in actual fact, though the process is unconscious, superimpose as it were one image upon another, and from the coincidence of a number of the same kind arrive at a mean contour which serves as a common standard for all. Say, for instance, a person has seen a thousand full-grown men. Now if he wishes to judge normal size determined upon a comparative estimate, then imagination (to my mind) allows a great number of these images (perhaps the whole thousand) to fall one upon the other, and, if I may be allowed to extend to the case the analogy of optical presentation, in the space where they come most together, and within the contour where the place is illuminated by the greatest concentration of colour, one gets a perception of the *average size*, which alike in height and breath is equally removed from the extreme limits of the greatest and smallest statures, and this is the stature of a beautiful man. (The same result could be obtained in a mechanical way, by taking the measures of all the thousand, and adding together their heights, and their breadths (and thicknesses), and dividing the sum in each case by a thousand.) But the power of imagination does all this by means of a dynamical effect upon the organ of internal sense, arising from the frequent apprehension of such forms. If, again, for our average man we seek on similar lines for the average head, and for this the average nose, and so on, then we get the figure that underlies the normal idea of a beautiful man in the country where the comparison is instituted. For this reason a negro must necessarily (under these empirical conditions) have a different normal idea of the beauty of forms from what a white man has, and the Chinaman one different from the European. And the process would be just the same with the *model* of a beautiful horse or dog (of a particular breed).—This *normal idea* is not derived from proportions taken from experience as *definite rules*: rather is it according to this idea that rules for forming estimates first become possible. It is an intermediate between all singular intuitions of individuals, with their manifold variations—a floating image for the whole genus, which nature has set as an archetype underlying those of her products that belong to the same species, but which in no single case she seems to have completely attained. But the normal idea is far from giving the complete *archetype* of *beauty* in the genus. It only gives the form that constitutes the indispensable condition of all beauty, and, consequently, only *correctness* in the presentation of the genus. It is, as the famous *Doryphorus* of *Polycletus* was called, the *rule* (and *Myron's* Cow might be similarly employed for its kind). It cannot, for that very reason, contain anything specifically characteristic; for otherwise it would not be the *normal idea* for the genus. Further, it is not by beauty that its presentation pleases, but merely because it does not contradict any of the conditions under which alone a thing belonging to this genus can be beautiful. The presentation is merely academically correct.[39]

But the *ideal* of the beautiful is still something different from its *normal idea.* For reasons already stated it is only to be sought in the *human figure.* Here the ideal consists in the expression of the *moral*, apart from which the object would not please at once universally and positively (not merely negatively in a presentation academically correct). The visible expression of moral ideas that govern men inwardly can, of course, only be drawn from experience; but their combination with all that our reason connects with the morally good in the idea of the highest finality—benevolence, purity, strength, or equanimity, &c.—may be made, as it were, visible in bodily manifestation (as effect of what is internal), and this embodiment involves a union of pure ideas of reason and great imaginative power, in one who would even form an estimate of it, not to speak of being the author of its presentation. The correctness of such an ideal of beauty is evidenced by its not permitting any sensuous charm to mingle with the delight in its Object, in which it still allows us to take a great interest. This fact in turn shows that an estimate formed according to such a standard can never be purely aesthetic, and that one formed according to an ideal of beauty cannot be a simple judgment of taste.

DEFINITION OF THE BEAUTIFUL DERIVED FROM THIS THIRD MOMENT

Beauty is the form of *finality* in an object, so far as perceived in it *apart from the representation of an end.*[40]

FOURTH MOMENT OF THE JUDGMENT OF TASTE: MOMENT OF THE MODALITY OF THE DELIGHT IN THE OBJECT

§ 18

Nature of the modality in a judgement of taste.

I MAY assert in the case of every representation that the synthesis of a pleasure with the representation (as a cognition) is at least *possible.* Of what I call *agreeable* I assert that it *actually* causes pleasure in me. But what we have in mind in the case of the *beautiful* is a *necessary* reference on its part to delight. However, this necessity is of a special kind. It is not a theoretical objective necessity—such as would let us cognize *a priori* that every one

[39] It will be found that a perfectly regular face—one that a painter might fix his eye on for a model—ordinarily conveys nothing. This is because it is devoid of anything characteristic, and so the idea of the race is expressed in it rather than the specific qualities of a person. The exaggeration of what is characteristic in this way, i.e., exaggeration violating the normal idea (the finality of the race), is called *caricature.* Also experience shows that these quite regular faces indicate as a rule internally only a mediocre type of man; presumably—if one may assume that nature in its external form expresses the proportions of the internal—because, where none of the mental qualities exceed the proportion requisite to constitute a man free from faults, nothing can be expected in the way of what is called *genius,* in which nature seems to make a departure from its wonted relations of the mental powers in favour of some special one.

[40] As telling against this explanation, the instance may be adduced, that there are things in which we see a form suggesting adaptation to an end, without any end being cognized in them—as, for example, the stone implements frequently obtained from sepulchral tumuli and supplied with a hole, as if for [inserting] a handle; and although these by their shape manifestly indicate a finality, the end of which is unknown, they are not on that account described as beautiful. But the very fact of their being regarded as art-products involves an immediate recognition that their shape is attributed to some purpose or other and to a definite end. For this reason there is no immediate delight whatever in their contemplation. A flower, on the other hand, such as a tulip, is regarded as beautiful, because we meet with a certain finality in its perception, which, in our estimate of it, is not referred to any end whatever.

will feel this delight in the object that is called beautiful by me. Nor yet is it a practical necessity, in which case, thanks to concepts of a pure rational will in which free agents are supplied with a rule, this delight is the necessary consequence of an objective law, and simply means that one ought absolutely (without ulterior object) to act in a certain way. Rather, being such a necessity as is thought in an aesthetic judgment, it can only be termed *exemplary*. In other words it is a necessity of the assent of *all* to a judgment regarded as exemplifying a universal rule incapable of formulation. Since an aesthetic judgment is not an objective or cognitive judgment, this necessity is not derivable from definite concepts, and so is not apodictic. Much less is it inferable from universality of experience (of a thorough-going agreement of judgments about the beauty of a certain object). For, apart from the fact that experience would hardly furnish evidences sufficiently numerous for this purpose, empirical judgments do not afford any foundation for a concept of the necessity of these judgments.

§ 19

The subjective necessity attributed to a judgment of taste is conditioned.

THE judgment of taste exacts agreement from every one; and a person who describes something as beautiful insists that every one *ought* to give the object in question his approval and follow suit in describing it as beautiful. The *ought* in aesthetic judgments, therefore, despite an accordance with all the requisite data for passing judgment, is still only pronounced conditionally. We are suitors for agreement from every one else, because we are fortified with a ground common to all. Further, we would be able to count on this agreement, provided we were always assured of the correct subsumption of the case under that ground as the rule of approval.

§ 20

The condition of the necessity advanced by a judgment of taste is the idea of a common sense.

WERE judgments of taste (like cognitive judgments) in possession of a definite objective principle, then one who in his judgment followed such a principle would claim unconditioned necessity for it. Again, were they devoid of any principle, as are those of the mere taste of sense, then no thought of any necessity on their part would enter one's head. Therefore they must have a subjective principle, and one which determines what pleases or displeases, by means of feeling only and not through concepts, but yet with universal validity. Such a principle, however, could only be regarded as a *common sense*. This differs essentially from common understanding, which is also sometimes called common sense (*sensus communis*): for the judgment of the latter is not one by feeling, but always one by concepts, though usually only in the shape of obscurely represented principles.

The judgment of taste, therefore, depends on our presupposing the existence of a common sense. (But this is not to be taken to mean some external sense, but the effect arising from the free play of our powers of cognition.) Only under the presupposition, I repeat, of such a common sense, are we able to lay down a judgment of taste.

§ 21

Have we reason for presupposing a common sense?

COGNITIONS and judgment must, together with their attendant conviction, admit of being universally communicated; for otherwise a correspondence with the Object would not be due to them. They would be a conglomerate constituting a mere subjective play of the powers of representation, just as scepticism would have it. But if cognitions are to admit of communication, then our mental state, i.e. the way the cognitive powers are attuned for cognition generally, and, in fact, the relative proportion suitable for a representation (by which an object is given to us) from which cognition is to result, must also admit of being universally communicated, as, without this, which is the subjective condition of the act of knowing, knowledge, as an effect, would not arise. And this is always what actually happens where a given object, through the intervention of sense, sets the imagination at work in arranging the manifold, and the imagination, in turn, the understanding in giving to this arrangement the unity of concepts. But this disposition of the cognitive powers has a relative proportion differing with the diversity of the Objects that are given. However, there must be one in which this internal ratio suitable for quickening (one faculty by the other) is best adapted for both mental powers in respect of cognition (of given objects) generally; and this disposition can only be determined through feeling (and not by concepts). Since, now, this disposition itself must admit of being universally communicated, and hence also the feeling of it (in the case of a given representation), while again, the universal communicability of a feeling presupposes a common sense: it follows that our assumption of it is well founded. And here, too, we do not have to take our stand on psychological observations, but we assume a common sense as the necessary condition of the universal communicability of our knowledge, which is presupposed in every logic and every principle of knowledge that is not one of scepticism.

§ 22

The necessity of the universal assent that is thought in a judgment of taste, is a subjective necessity which, under the presupposition of a common sense, is represented as objective.

In all judgments by which we describe anything as beautiful we tolerate no one else being of a different opinion, and in taking up this position we do not rest our judgment upon concepts, but only on our feeling. Accordingly we introduce this fundamental feeling not as a private feeling, but as a public sense. Now, for this purpose, experience cannot be made the ground of this common sense, for the latter is invoked to justify judgments containing an 'ought'. The assertion is not that every one *will* fall in with our judgment, but rather that every one *ought* to agree with it. Here I put forward my judgment of taste as an example of the judgment of common sense, and attribute to it on that account *exemplary* validity. Hence common sense is a mere ideal norm. With this as presupposition, a judgment that accords with it, as well as the delight in an Object expressed in that judgment, is rightly converted into a rule for every one. For the principle, while it is only subjective, being yet assumed as subjectively universal (a necessary idea for every one), could, in what concerns the consensus of different judging Subjects, demand universal assent like an objective principle, provided we were assured of our subsumption under it being correct.

This indeterminate norm of a common sense is, as a matter of fact, presupposed by us; as is shown by our presuming to lay down judgments of taste. But does such a common sense in fact exist as a constitutive principle of the possibility of experience, or is it formed for us as a regulative principle by a still higher principle of reason, that for higher ends first seeks to beget in us a common sense? Is taste, in other words, a natural and original faculty, or is it only the idea of one that is artificial and to be acquired by us, so that a judgment of taste, with its demand for universal assent, is but a requirement of reason for generating such a con*sensus,* and does the 'ought,' i.e. the objective necessity of the coincidence of the feeling of all with the particular feeling of each, only betoken the possibility of arriving at some sort of unanimity in these matters, and the judgment of taste only adduce an example of the application of this principle? These are questions which as yet we are neither willing nor in a position to investigate. For the present we have only to resolve the faculty of taste into its elements, and to unite these ultimately in the idea of a common sense.

DEFINITION OF THE BEAUTIFUL DRAWN FROM THE FOURTH MOMENT

The beautiful is that which, apart from a concept, is cognized as object of a *necessary* delight.

§ 33
Second peculiarity of the judgment of taste.

PROOFS are of no avail whatever for determining the judgment of taste, and in this connexion matters stand just as they would were that judgment simply *subjective.*

If any one does not think a building, view, or poem beautiful, then, *in the first place* he refuses, so far as his inmost conviction goes, to allow approval to be wrung from him by a hundred voices all lauding it to the skies. Of course he may affect to be pleased with it, so as not to be considered as wanting in taste. He may even begin to harbour doubts as to whether he has formed his taste upon an acquaintance with a sufficient number of objects of a particular kind (just as one who in the distance recognizes, as he believes, something as a wood, which every one else regards as a town, becomes doubtful of the judgment of his own eyesight). But, for all that, he clearly perceives that the approval of others affords no valid proof, available for the estimate of beauty. He recognizes that others, perchance, may see and observe for him, and that, what many have seen in one and the same way may, for the purpose of a theoretical, and therefore logical judgment, serve as an adequate ground of proof for him, albeit he believes he saw otherwise, but that what has pleased others can never serve him as the ground of an aesthetic judgment. The judgment of others, where unfavourable to ours, may, no doubt, rightly make us suspicious in respect of our own, but convince us that it is wrong it never can. Hence there is no empirical *ground of proof* that can coerce any one's judgment of taste.

In the second place, a proof *a priori* according to definite rules is still less capable of determining the judgment as to beauty. If any one reads me his poem, or brings me to a play, which, all said and done, fails to commend itself to my taste, then let him adduce *Batteux* or *Lessing,* or still older and more famous critics of taste, with all the host of rules laid down by them, as a proof of the beauty of his poem; let certain passages particularly displeasing to me accord completely with the rules of beauty, (as set out by these critics and universally recognized): I stop my ears: I do not want to hear any reasons or any arguing about the matter. I would prefer to suppose that those rules of the critics were at fault, or at least have no application, than to allow my judgment to be determined by *a priori* proofs: I take my stand on the ground that my judgment is to be one of taste, and not one of understanding or reason.

This would appear to be one of the chief reasons why this faculty of aesthetic judgment has been given the name of taste. For a man may recount to me all the ingredients of a dish, and observe of each and every one of them that it is just what I like, and, in addition, rightly commend the wholesomeness of the food; yet I am deaf to all these arguments. I try the dish with *my own* tongue and palate, and I pass judgment according to their verdict (not according to universal principles).

As a matter of fact the judgment of taste is invariably laid down as a singular judgment upon the Object. The understanding can, from the comparison of the Object, in point of delight, with the judgments of others, form a universal judgment, e.g. "All tulips are beautiful." But that judgment is then not one of taste, but is a logical judgment which converts the reference of an Object to our taste into a predicate belonging to things of a certain kind. But it is only the judgment whereby I regard an individual given tulip as beautiful, i.e. regard my delight in it as of universal validity, that is a judgment of taste. Its peculiarity, however, consists in the fact that, although it has merely subjective validity, still it extends its claims to *all* Subjects, as unreservedly as it would if it were an objective judgment, resting on grounds of cognition and capable of being proved to demonstration.

§ 34

An objective principle of taste is not possible.

A PRINCIPLE of taste would mean a fundamental premiss under the condition of which one might subsume the concept of an object, and then, by a syllogism, draw the inference that it is beautiful. That, however, is absolutely impossible. For I must feel the pleasure immediately in the representation of the object, and I cannot be talked into it by any grounds of proof. Thus although critics, as Hume says, are able to reason more plausibly than cooks, they must still share the same fate. For the determining ground of their judgment they are not able to look to the force of demonstrations, but only to the reflection of the Subject upon his own state (of pleasure or displeasure), to the exclusion of precepts and rules.

There is, however, a matter upon which it is competent for critics to exercise their subtlety, and upon which they ought to do so, so long as it tends to the rectification and extension of our judgment of taste. But that matter is not one of exhibiting the determining ground of aesthetic judgment of this kind in a universally applicable formula—which is impossible. Rather is it the investigation of the faculties of cognition and their function in these judgments, and the illustration, by the analysis of examples, of their mutual subjective finality, the form of which in a given representation has been shown above to constitute the beauty of their object. Hence with regard to the representation whereby an Object is given, the Critique of Taste itself is only subjective; viz. it is the art or science of reducing the mutual relation of the understanding and the imagination in the given representation (without reference to antecedent sensation or concept), consequently their accordance or discordance, to rules, and of determining them with regard to their conditions. It is *art* if it only illustrates this by examples; it is *science* if it deduces the possibility of such an estimate from the nature of these faculties as faculties of knowledge in general. It is only with the latter, as Transcendental Critique, that we have here any concern. Its proper scope is the development and justification of the subjective principle of taste, as an *a priori* principle of judgment. As an art, Critique merely looks to the physiological (here psychological), and, consequently, empirical rules, according to which in actual fact taste proceeds, (passing by the question of their possibility,) and seeks to apply them in estimating its objects. The latter Critique criticizes the products of fine art, just as the former does the faculty of estimating them.

§ 35

The principle of taste is the subjective principle of the general power of judgment

THE judgment of taste is differentiated from logical judgment by the fact that, whereas the latter subsumes a representation under a concept of the Object, the judgment of taste does not subsume under a concept at all—for, if it did, necessary and universal approval would be capable of being enforced by proofs. And yet it does bear this resemblance to the logical judgment, that it asserts a universality and necessity, not, however, according to concepts of the Object, but a universality and necessity that are, consequently, merely subjective. Now the concepts in a judgment constitute its content (what belongs to the cognition of the Object). But the judgment of taste is not determinable by means of concepts. Hence it can only have its ground in the subjective formal condition of a judgment in general. The subjective condition of all judgments is the judging faculty itself, or judgment. Employed in respect of a representation whereby an object is given, this requires the harmonious accordance of two powers of representation. These are, the imagination (for the intuition and the arrangement of the manifold of intuition), and the understanding (for the concept as a representation of the unity of this arrangement). Now, since no concept of the Object underlies the judgment here, it can consist only in the subsumption of the imagination itself (in the case of a representation whereby an object is given) under the conditions enabling the understanding in general to advance from the intuition to concepts. That is to say, since the freedom of the imagination consists precisely in the fact that it schematizes without a concept, the judgment of taste must found upon a mere sensation of the mutually quickening activity of the imagination in its *freedom,* and of the understanding with its *conformity to law.* It must therefore rest upon a feeling that allows the object to be estimated by the finality of the representation (by which an object is given) for the furtherance of the cognitive faculties in their free play. Taste, then, as a subjective power of judgment, contains a principle of subsumption, not of intuitions under *concepts,* but of the *faculty* of intuitions or presentations, i.e. of the imagination, under the *faculty* of concepts, i.e. the understanding, so far as the former *in its freedom* accords with the latter *in its conformity to law.* . . .

Chapter 10

The Eighteenth Century: The Genius—Inspiration and Imagination

In examining some aspects of the conflicting theories of taste and the efforts of its proponents to preempt for taste the place of criticism in Philosophy of Art and Aesthetics, it becomes clear that the primary problems arise in the areas of judgment and in aesthetic experience. It remains for Benedetto Croce [1] and his twentieth century followers to declare that taste and genius are identical in creativity, an identity with which writers in the eighteenth century who addressed themselves to the problem of genius were rather little concerned. Still, there is one point at which the philosophies of art of genius and taste meet, and it is an important one. Precisely as the writers on taste in the eighteenth century were coping with the "I know not what" of the experience of art, so the essayists and philosophers of the period were caught up in the "I know not what" that marked off, for them, the original artist from the technicians and works of fine art from those bearing no aesthetic value. The identical reaction against Aristotelianism and its interpretation of art as "a rational state of capacity to make" which led to the denial to criticism of a place in Aesthetics led men to reassert the Platonic–Longinean theory of an art of such evocative power or such display of technical ability as to transcend the rules of art.

Plato's theory of the inspired artist,[2] out of his senses but a vehicle for the words of the gods, is buttressed throughout the centuries by those portions of Longinus *de Sublimitate* [3] in which the writer on great poetry asserts that what we call sublime art has little to do with minute correctness. But neither Plato nor Longinus offers more than sparse evidence of the means by which the artist brings inspiration to bear on the works of art through technique. Plato in the *Laws*,[4] does rather vaguely remark that although the poet is not in his right mind, still his art is imitative and he must represent men. That he does so without necessarily representing them accurately implies that, as he is both inspired and an imitator, he often contradicts himself. Longinus' remarks on the subject of the makers of great art that such men use technique, although it is clear that Longinus himself prefers creativity to correctness in art.

One of the interesting suggestions made in the Renaissance concerning the relation of

[1] See below, pp. 536 et seq.; and 556 et seq.

[2] See above, pp. 33 and pp. 45 for earlier Greek theory.

[3] See above, pp. 216, 217.

[4] Plato, *Laws* 719B. See above, for example, pp. 45 et seq.

inspiration and art appears in Boccaccio's examination of poetry.[5] Poetry, the author argues, "is a sort of fervid and exquisite invention, with fervid expression, in speech and writing, of that which the mind has invented." It derives from God and it is a rare gift with which some men are born. It is sublime in its effects and "impels the soul to a longing for utterance," but, most notably, "it brings forth strange and unheard-of creations of the mind." Not only is inspiration creative, however, but it also arranges these meditations in a fixed order and adorns the whole composition. More to the point, "however deeply the poetic impulse stirs the mind to which it is granted, it very rarely accomplishes anything commendable if the instruments by which its concepts are to be wrought are wanting. . . ." Moreover, Boccaccio emphasises the point that poetry is an art, "since nothing proceeds from this poetic fervour, which sharpens and illuminates the powers of the mind, except what is wrought by art. . . ." And, as if further to emphasize the point, Boccaccio traces the origin of the word "poetry" in order to indicate that the important issue concerning inspiration is the effect of the poetry rather than the process the writer undergoes in producing it.

It is clear that for Boccaccio the process of inspiration is not completed in a single instant of prophetic vision but that whatever the process may be it is one that affects, if it does not permeate, the entire process of making. Inspiration and technique would appear to be related integrally and in the entire process of producing the work of art. In speculation in the eighteenth century, this suggestion was largely ignored if, indeed, the specific instance we have cited influenced philosophers of art at all. Men speculated upon the wholly original "genius," believed to possess unlimited freedom and unlimited and unconditioned powers to create. Many essayists believed that the genius created what is wholly novel. By the '70s and '80s of the eighteenth century, the reaction against the Aristotelian conception that the "maker" was one who made actual what is potential in a medium had come under vigorous attack. As Katherine Gilbert wrote,[6] ". . . the artist's invention has subtly shifted from finding what is already there, though hidden, to selecting or creating or fashioning a mental image by human strength alone."

The emphasis in this quotation should be on the word "creating." The tool for the "creating" was long ago suggested by Philostratus[7] in his argument concerning the superiority of imagination over imitation. The speculative ground was Platonic and Augustinean philosophy. The artist comes to be conceived by analogy to God as Creator and God as Maker. The issue comes eventually to produce a sound statement concerning the conditions under which imagination may be curbed to insure the intelligibility of the work of art and at the same time to substitute "I know what" for the puzzling "I know not what" that had been presumed by many to be ingredient to both genius and creativity.

Two writers, George Puttenham, who wrote in an earlier century, and Edward Young provide adequate material for a beginning of what we need to know. Their writings serve as an introduction to the selections that follow. Puttenham is Epimethean and looks back to St. Augustine. Young is Promethean and gives a clue to much of the speculation of the century, including Kant's systematic Aesthetic.

In Puttenham's *The Arte of English Poesie*, we have perhaps the classic literary instance of the influence of the theological problem of God's power and knowledge as it affected the image of the creative artist. For Plato, as we

[5] Boccaccio, *Genealogia deorum gentilium* XIV, VI., trans. by Charles G. Osgood, *Boccaccio on Poetry*, pp. 39 et seq.

[6] See Gilbert and Kuhn, *A History of Esthetics*, p. 186.

[7] See above, pp. 206 et seq.

have observed,[8] the *Demiurgos* or cosmic architect makes the world after the model of the Ideas and out of a something that later philosophers called "matter." Plato's *Demiurgos* creates neither Ideas nor "matter." His freedom is the freedom to choose within limits. Man is made as a microcosm of the macrocosm. His freedom to make is similarly freedom within and under conditions imposed upon him. We have observed also the various usages of the "architect" of the universe.[9] In the Hebraic–Christian tradition, God is not a maker but a creator. He creates the world *ex nihilo* and He creates matter. His creativity is unconditioned. Man, made after God's image, is endowed with free will. It is true, as we have noted,[10] that the Platonist St. Augustine limits man's freedom in contrast to God's omnipotence and omniscience. Man does not create the material he forms. But, as regards Puttenham, the more important point is that the Augustinean conception of God provides a locus for the Platonic Ideas in God's mind and that matter is created. And so Puttenham says[11] of the poet that he resembles God "who without any trauell to his divine imagination, made all the world of nought, nor also by any paterne or mould as the Platonicks with their Ideas do phantastically suppose." Puttenham thus brings into Philosophy of Art of the eighteenth century—although he is himself a writer of an earlier period—St. Augustine's conception[12] of an unconditioned God who "was not fixing His gaze upon anything located outside Himself to serve as a model when He made the things He created. . . ."

It should be pointed out that Puttenham argues that "our maker or Poet" is one "holpen by a clear and bright phantasie and imagination," yet one also of "sounde iudgement and discourse." It is no less interesting, in view of the development of speculation that the imagination or "phantasie" is helped "as by a glasse or mirrour," which represents "vnto the soul all maner of bewtifull visions. . . ." To this it should be added that these visions help the "inuentive parts of the mynde . . . as without it no man could deuise any new or rare thing."

We are left by Puttenham with some rather general remarks concerning the curbs on phantastical imagination and its necessary relation to judgment. There is, however, nothing to compare to the close analysis of the process by which imagination produces or is aided by making, such as we find in Boccaccio's writing on poetry or Fracastoro's on music.[13]

As Puttenham looks back to the Platonism of St. Augustine, altered as it is so radically by the conception of a creative God in *Genesis*, Edward Young may be said to look forward to the paeans his successors were to sing concerning the original genius. Young[14] published his *Conjectures on Original Composition* in 1774. It is not so much a profound book as a seminal one that exerted an influence on Kant and many others. It may be said of Young, despite his incapacity to argue profoundly, that he made more specific than Puttenham the most extreme implications of a statement concerning the original poet. There are in poetry, the poet writes, "mysteries not to be explained but admired." He puts forward the theory that a genius "differs from a good understanding as a magician from a good architect" and explains this by asserting that the architect raises his structure by "the skillful use of common tools," whereas the genius "raises his structure by means invisible." To use "common tools" is to proceed according to the rules of art. To use "means invisible" implies that something may

[8] See above, pp. 12 et seq. and 93 et seq.

[9] See above, pp. 203 et seq.

[10] See above, pp. 232 et seq.

[11] See below for Puttenham's life and a selection from his writing, pp. 391 et seq.

[12] Augustine, *De Diversis Quaestionibus* LXXXIII, Q. 46 *de ideis* (30). See above, pp. 233 et seq.

[13] See Girolamo Fracastoro, *Naugerius, sive de Poetica Dialogus.*

[14] See below, pp. 393 et seq., for life and selection from Young's writings.

be produced by nontechnical and nonrational means. Nor is the end of art freed in Young's writings from this pervasive nonrationality: The inspired genius can accomplish great things "without the means reputed necessary to that end."

It is clear that no theory of imitation will fulfil the requirements laid down for such a theory of creativity. Even Plato, who had disdained mimetic art and despised the mimetic artist, had granted to both some, if rather diminished, value. It is in imagination that the writers of the eighteenth century seek the solution to the problems of the artistic originality. However, precisely as they interpret artistic originality in two ways, so they formulate or accept the formulations of others concerning imagination in two ways: To the original genius of a Puttenham or a Young, able to create without regard for conditions, we find the addition in the writings of the eighteenth century of the influence of the demiurgic analogue, of Plato's cosmic artisan. Here it will suffice to illustrate the point from Shaftesbury's "Soliloquy or Advice to an Author" by his well-known remark that "a poet is indeed a second *Maker*, a just Prometheus under Jove." Shaftesbury believes that the poet is "a real master, or architect in the kind," one who employs means to ends. In his *Characteristics of Men, Manners, Opinions, Times*, he compares the poet to "that sovereign artist or universal plastic nature," who "forms a whole, coherent and proportioned in itself, with due subjection and subordinacy of parts. . . ." It is essential for authors to consider a model or plan and attain to knowledge of a whole and parts. The ancient notion of the genius as a tutelary power appeals to him and it does so for a precise reason: "Tis on themselves that all depends." To assert that man is free to create is to assert that a man "has undoubtedly surpassed himself." To urge that men differ from themselves means that they "are in reality transformed and lost." Men should act "like themselves and suitably to their own geniuses and character." The artist must make his piece "as great and comprehensible as he can make it. . . ."

Shaftesbury's "just Prometheus under Jove" is scarcely the suitable model for many of the writers of the century, nor is his comprehensible product of art what they are in search of. What many philosophers of art demand from a theory of genius is an explanation of novelty, precisely as a creative God makes a unique individual soul. Edmund Burke denied that novelty would please for long, but Home believed as did Addison, that original genius could produce what has no correlative in nature. Home remarks of imagination that it has the ability to "fabricate ideas of fine visible objects, of more noble and heroic actions, of greater wickedness, of more surprising events, than ever in fact existed."

There are evident in the latter half of the eighteenth century many signs of a growing realization of the need to reconcile the extreme and conflicting estimates of the artistic genius. The word "genius" itself becomes an *omnium gatherum* term for a problem—the problem of accounting for creativity, originality or, at the least, inventiveness within a context in which technique and Art have their roles. Alexander Gerard, to whose writing on genius we shall shortly come,[15] uses a figure of speech that Kant repeats. Gerard remarks that original genius is displayed as the artist strikes out a "new path" and produces novelty; but, although the first property of genius is invention and the vigor of imagination carries the genius forward to invention, "understanding must always conduct it and regulate its motions." Gerard writes[16] that "A horse of high mettle ranging at liberty, will run with great swiftness and spirit, but in an irregular track and without any fixt direction: a skilful rider makes him

[15] See below, pp. 404 et seq. and above, pp. 352 et seq.

[16] Alexander Gerard. *An Essay on Genius*, pp. 72–73.

move straight in a road, with equal spirit and swiftness." Gerard draws the obvious inferences [17] concerning the uncurbed imagination. Kant, in the same vein, remarks [18] of the genius that, although originality is an essential element in the character of genius, "shallow minds" fancy that they can show themselves "fullblown geniuses" by throwing off the constraint of all rules: they believe, he adds, ". . . that one cuts a finer figure on the back of an ill-tempered horse than on the back of a trained animal. . . ."

Gerard, beginning with the theory of the association of ideas, produces, in this writer's own opinion, the most fruitful theory of criticism of his times. Kant, abandoning the theory of association as a means of accounting for aesthetic experience and eventually offering a theory of originality for the genius by relating imagination to understanding, provides the ablest, yet most divergent, efforts to reconcile the claims of judgment and imagination, of law and originality, in the Aesthetic of the time. Still, notice should be taken of the writings of one writer who, despite the fact that his interests were basically literary and not philosophical, made an extraordinary contribution to speculation on art and the artist. In Joseph Addison's essays in *The Spectator,* there is evident not only an attempt to reconcile the divergent ingredients of genius and imagination, but there is also a reinterpretation of Longinus' ancient theory of the kinds of genius.

In the essays in *The Spectator*, three points are of considerable interest for the philosopher of art. It is evident, first, that for Addison, imagination operates under constraint. In discussing the "pleasures of the imagination,"—visible objects—the pleasure arises from the direct experience of the object or images recalled in memory and arranged in new combinations. Sublimity, novelty, and beauty produce the pleasurable activities of the imagination. Secondly, Addison recalls a distinction made by Longinus between the great geniuses, the "Prodigies of Mankind," "who by the meer Strength of Natural Parts, and without any Assistance of Arts or Learning, have produced works that were the Delight of their own Times, and the Wonder of Posterity" and those geniuses who possess "nothing of that divine Impulse which raises the mind above its self and makes the Sounds more than human."

Thirdly, it is, for Addison [19] no deity or muse, or indeed any external stimulus, which is the source of the "divine Impulse" as he miscalls it. ". . . This talent of affecting the imagination has something in it like creation." Indeed, this power of affecting the imagination is such that it "might suffice to make up the whole of heaven or hell of any finite being." Addison believes that Milton's *Paradise Lost* is the noblest work of genius in the English language. But he takes care in his essay on genius to point out that great geniuses are sometimes thrown away upon trifles.[20]

In essays No. 412 and No. 413 of the *Spectator,* Addison writes of the delights of novelty and in No. 419 of the world of imagination and fancy. In the latter, for example, he expatiates on that "noble extravagance of fancy" in Shakespeare that permitted him to write of ghosts, fairies, witches "and the like imaginary persons" in such wise that we cannot "forbear thinking them natural, though we have no rule by which to judge them. . . ." "If there were such beings in the world," Addison adds, "it looks highly probably that they should talk and act as he had represented them."

The same capacity Addison displays here for taking the abstract notion of imagination and applying it to art leads to what is perhaps

[17] Ibid.

[18] I. Kant, *The Critique of Judgement,* Sect. 47. See below, pp. 413.

[19] See below, pp. 399 et seq., for life of Addison and for *Spectator* No. 160 and No. 421.

[20] See concluding paragraph to *Spectator,* No. 160. below, pp. 401.

the most valuable and interesting—for an aesthetician—contribution this essayist makes. In essay No. 160, we come upon Addison in process of making concrete the abstract notion of originality and novelty. He does so in terms of the individual: ". . . Very few Writers make an extraordinary Figure in the world," he writes, "who have not something in the Way of thinking or expressing themselves that is peculiar to them, and entirely their own."

For Addison, the individual artist's expression of his genius must be guarded against the temptation to produce what clearly is the result of mere dexterity in the making of what is trivial. The skill of the man who could keep four eggs in the air at the same time is *not* what Addison means by genius, although it might conceivably fall under that classification for those who maintained that, according to William Duff, the genius' imagination sketches out a creation of its own.

Addison's conception of genius is balanced, although it tends to move towards the extreme of creativity. He makes little use of his own division of genius into two kinds. Addison is perceptive and experienced in the ways of art, but his account of originality in terms of genius lacks the profundity and the power that the more systematic accounts of the creative genius constructed by Alexander Gerard and Immanuel Kant possess. The basis for Gerard's theory is the association of ideas and Kant's is based upon an a priori theory of judgment and the interrelation of understanding and imagination. That the problem of genius is the key to the explanation of originality in art is a point that comes clear in both Gerard's and Kant's systematic accounts of taste and genius. For Gerard, in *An Essay on Genius,*[21] we are informed that genius is properly the faculty of invention, "by means of which a man is qualified in making new discoveries in science, or for producing original works of art." The echoes of Longinus and Addison are heard, for the invention may be "irregular, wild, undisciplined; but still it is regarded an infallible mark of real natural genius." The phenomena of genius are "almost universally regarded as anomalous and inexplicable." Nor does Gerard neglect the experience of the genius' products. Genius is the power of expression "so far as it differs both from mechanical dexterity and from knowledge acquired by study. . . ." Its principal function is "the capacity of setting objects in such a light that they may affect others with the same ideas, associations, and feelings with which the artist is affected." [22]

Where Gerard extends the word "genius" to apply to science as well as art, Kant limits the word genius to the artist. He agrees with Gerard that artistic skill is communicated to the artist by "the hand of nature." The rules for the production of beautiful art cannot be reduced to a formula nor serve as a precept. The power of the genius cannot be taught.

Gerard's and Kant's theories strongly resemble each other, in addition, in the most important aspect of their authors' efforts to reconcile in genius originality and intelligibility. For Gerard, although he introduces and emphasizes the role of invention, it is clear that he fears that his own theory of genius will fail to account for the production of what is new. Quite unlike Edward Young,[23] who denies that the genius needs tools in the ordinary sense, Gerard insists that the "real genius" must execute his inventions by means of instruments and in manners well known and long in use.[24] Still, invention remains the faculty of genius, for precisely the same reason that Gerard subjects fancy or imagination in its power "to the same limitation as our power over the natural

[21] Alexander Gerard, *An Essay on Genius,* pp. 4–9. See below, pp. 404 et seq. for a selection from Gerard's writing, as well as above, pp. 352 et seq.

[22] James Beattie differed from Gerard on this point: "Taste and genius are kindred powers . . .! Taste is passive genius, genius active taste."

[23] See above, pp. 385 et seq.

[24] Gerard, *An Essay on Genius,* p. 423.

world."[25] It can produce "an endless variety of complex notions" from a stock of simple ideas. But we can create no new substance, nor can we "imagine the idea of a single quality which we have never had access to observe." [26] Similarly, the boldest fictions of the poets are composed of parts that exist in nature. The work of art, the product of genius, is for Gerard intelligible.[27]

It should be added at once that the work of art is intelligible within the limits of the theory of the association of ideas. Gerard urges that the principles of association are "never perhaps entirely dormant or impotent" [28] and do not exert themselves with the same ease or with the same force all of the time. Genius is "extensive and vigorous" and can with ease, he holds, "perfect inventions," when the principles are active "and ready to run from any idea that occurs, through a long train of other ideas related to it, without a possibility of our resisting their influence, or cooling their ardour which their activity inspires." Yet, the ability of the imagination to "perfect inventions" is like "a lucky and unaccountable hit, in pursuing which it has formerly toiled in vain." In a word, fancy or imagination do not create.

The most radical systematic difference between Gerard's and Kant's theories of genius and originality lies in Gerard's acceptance and Kant's rejection of the theory of the association of ideas as the ground for the explanation of genius and creativity.[29] Kant rids his theory of the genius of the associative principle by his distinction of productive and reproductive imagination. Imagination in its empirical employment is reproductive. To it are attached such associating powers as do not ensure originality. It is quite otherwise with imagination in its productive function. It is very powerful "for creating . . . a second nature . . . out of the material supplied to it by actual nature. . . ." [30]

By means of productive imagination we "remould experience." But we remould it under law. We have come to the fundamental meaning of genius in Kant's Aesthetic. He means by it freedom in terms of originality and creativity. Originality, Kant argues, is the first property of the beautiful art [31] and beautiful art is the product of genius. For Kant, imitating is aping. Equally, however, the genius does not create, if we mean that he produces either what is wholly novel or what emerges *ex nihilo.*

It is clear that for Kant, the genius is free because what he produces is original. The product is not merely "not commonplace"; it is "new." The genius is not productive, however, of what is original by means of a "lucky hit" such as Gerard mentions. This is true even though Kant's genius is, in some sense, inspired. Despite the fact that the genius does not learn or teach by rule, that he does not know himself how he has come to his idea,[32] and that originality must be the first property of beautiful art,[33] Kant insists that the freedom to create beautiful art is freedom under law. Some of Kant's arguments for this freedom to create are not particularly fruitful. For example, he writes that genius is "the exemplary originality" of the natural gifts of a subject in "the *free* employment of his cognitive faculties." But what Kant intends to do systematically is essential. He proposes to subsume the imagination under the rule of the understanding, so that imagination is not capricious, its freedom is not unintelligible, and its operations are under the guidance of the faculty of rules. He is insistent that the originality of genius which produces what is ineffable is nonsense unless it

25 Ibid., p. 101.
26 Ibid., p. 101.
27 Ibid., pp. 104–106.
28 Ibid., pp. 237–238.
29 Kant, *The Critique of Judgement,* Sect. 22 and Sect. 49. See above, pp. 360 et seq. and below, pp. 415 et seq.

30 Ibid., Sect. 49. See below, p. 415.
31 Ibid., Sect. 46. See below, pp. 411 et seq.
32 Ibid., Sect. 46, below, p. 411.
33 Ibid., Sect. 46, below, pp. 411 et seq.

is associated with the something of a compulsory character called mechanism.

It is evident that with Kant the conception of the genius as the artist who is free unconditionally is brought within the scope of intelligibility. What remains for his successors is to assay in detail such works of fine art as are evidence of the genius' superiority, both in originality and in the control of techniques which, along with symbols, provide the grounds for intelligibility. What Kant seeks is sound: Art is called free, he believes, but it is "not amiss, however, to remind the reader . . . that in all free arts something of a compulsory character is still required. . . ." [34] Clearly, for him, "Freedom . . . from the laws of nature is no doubt a liberation from compulsion, but also from the guidance of all rules." Some, at any rate, of the Post-Kantian Idealists sought for guidance under the rules of art in their explanations of the fine artist and the products of "fine" or "free" or "freeing" art.

[34] Ibid., Sect. 43, below, p. 409.

George Puttenham

1529?–1590

A. Life

It is generally assumed that the author of *The Arte of English Poesie* was George Puttenham, the son of Robert and Margery Puttenham, who entered Cambridge University in 1546 and the Middle Temple in 1556. In 1560, George Puttenham married Lady Elizabeth Windsor. In 1563, he was in Flanders. Various complaints brought him before the Privy Council.

The Arte of English Poesie was published in 1589.

B. Philosophy of Art

The First Booke of Poets and Poesie

CHAP. I.

WHAT A POET AND POESIE IS, AND WHO MAY BE WORTHILY SAYD THE MOST EXCELLENT POET OF OUR TIME

A poet [35] is as much to say as a maker. And our English name well conformes with the Greeke word, for of ποιεῖν, to make, they call a maker *Poeta.* Such as (by way of resemblance and reuerently) we may say of God; who without any trauell to his diuine imagination made all the world of nought, nor also by any paterne or mould, as the Platonicks with their Idees do phantastically suppose. Euen so the very Poet makes and contriues out of his owne braine both the verse and matter of his poeme, and not by any foreine copie or example, as doth the translator, who therefore may well be sayd a versifier, but not a Poet. The premises considered, it giueth to the name and profession no smal dignitie and preheminence, aboue all other artificers, Scientificke or Mechanicall. And neuerthelesse, without any repugnancie at all, a Poet may in some sort be said a follower or imitator, because he can expresse the true

[35] George Puttenham, *The Art of English Poesie,* Chapter I, pp. 3–5. In G. Gregory-Smith, *Elizabethan Critical Essays,* pp. 3–5. Oxford University Press (London, 1904).

and liuely of euery thing is set before him, and which he taketh in hand to describe: and so in that respect is both a maker and a counterfaitor: and Poesie an art not only of making, but also of imitation. And this science in his perfection can not grow but by some diuine instinct—the Platonicks call it *furor*; or by excellencie of nature and complexion; or by great subtiltie of the spirits & wit; or by much experience and obseruation of the world, and course of kinde; or, peraduenture, by all or most part of them. Otherwise, how was it possible that *Homer*, being but a poore priuate man, and, as some say, in his later age blind, should so exactly set foorth and describe, as if he had bene a most excellent Captaine or Generall, the order and array of battels, the conduct of whole armies, the sieges and assaults of cities and townes? or, as some great Princes maiordome and perfect Surueyour in Court, the order, sumptuousnesse, and magnificence of royal banket, feasts, weddings, and enteruewes? or, as a Polititian very prudent and much inured with the priuat and publique affaires, so grauely examine the lawes and ordinances Ciuill, or so profoundly discourse in matters of estate and formes of all politique regiment? Finally, how could he so naturally paint out the speeches, countenance, and maners of Princely persons and priuate, to wit, the wrath of *Achilles*, the magnanimitie of *Agamemnon*, the prudence of *Menelaus*, the prowesse of *Hector*, the maiestie of king *Priamus*, the grauitie of *Nestor*, the pollicies and eloquence of *Vlysses*, the calamities of the distressed *Queenes*, and valiance of all the Captaines and aduenturous knights in those lamentable warres of Troy? It is therefore of Poets thus to be conceiued, that if they be able to deuise and make all these things of them selues, without any subject of veritie, that they be (by maner of speech) as creating gods. If they do it by instinct diuine or naturall, then surely much fauoured from aboue; if by their experience, then no doubt very wise men; if by any president or paterne layd before them, then truly the most excellent imitators & counterfaitors of all others. But you (Madame) my most Honored and Gracious, if I should seeme to offer you this my deuise for a discipline and not a delight, I might well be reputed of all others the most arrogant and iniurious, your selfe being alreadie, of any that I know in our time, the most excellent Poet; forsooth by your Princely purse, fauours, and countenance, making in maner what ye list, the poore man rich, the lewd well learned, the coward couragious, and vile both noble and valiant: then for imitation no lesse, your person as a most cunning counterfaitor liuely representing *Venus* in countenance, in life *Diana*, *Pallas* for gouernement, and *Iuno* in all honour and regall magnificence.

Edward Young

1683–1765

A. Life

Edward Young is best known for his *Night Thoughts* (1742–1745), but his *Conjectures on Original Composition,* published in 1759, exerted an enormous influence on critics and speculative philosophers both in Great Britain and on the Continent.

Young was a satirist, dramatist, poet, and essayist. Alexander Pope maintained that he had "more genius than commonsense," but Dr. Johnson, while admitting Young's defects, remarked that he was "a man of genius and a poet." Young was born in Upham, near Winchester. His father was rector of Upham. The future author of *Conjectures* was educated at Winchester and New College, Oxford, and in 1708 was made Fellow at Law in All Souls College, Oxford. He became chaplain to George II in 1728 and in 1730 received the living at Welwyn, where he died in 1765.

B. Philosophy of Art

Conjectures on Original Composition

Dear Sir,

. . . You remember [36] that your worthy patron, and our common friend, put some questions on the serious drama, at the same time when he desired our sentiments on original and moral composition. Though I despair of breaking through the frozen obstructions of age, and care's incumbent cloud, into that flow of thought and brightness of expression which such polite subjects require, yet will I hazard some conjectures on them.

. . . I begin with original composition; but, first, a few thoughts on composition in general. Some are of opinion that its growth, at present, is too luxuriant, and that the press is overcharged. Overcharged, I think, it could never be, if none were admitted but such as brought their *imprimatur* from sound understanding and

[36] *Conjectures on Original Composition,* pp. 1 seq., *Edward Young's Conjectures on Original Composition in England and Germany; A Study in Literary Relations,* ed. M. W. Steinke (New York, 1917). *Conjectures* was addressed to "The Author of Sir Charles Grandison."

the public good. Wit, indeed, however brilliant, should not be permitted to gaze self-enamoured on its useless charms in that fountain of fame, (if so I may call the press,) if beauty is all that it has to boast; but, like the first Brutus, it should sacrifice its most darling offspring to the sacred interests of virtue, and real service of mankind.

This restriction allowed, the more composition the better. To men of letters and leisure, it is not only a noble amusement, but a sweet refuge; it improves their parts and promotes their peace; it opens a back-door out of the bustle of this busy and idle world into a delicious garden of moral and intellectual fruits and flowers, the key of which is denied to the rest of mankind. When stung with idle anxieties, or teazed with fruitless impertinence, or yawning over insipid diversions, then we perceive the blessing of a lettered recess. With what a gust do we retire to our disinterested and immortal friends in our closet and find our minds, when applied to some favorite theme, as naturally and as easily quieted and refreshed as a peevish child (and peevish children are we all till we fall asleep) when laid to the breast! Our happiness no longer lives on charity; nor bids fair for a fall by leaning on that most precarious and thorny pillow, another's pleasure, for our repose. How independent of the world is he who can daily find new acquaintance that at once entertain and improve him, in the little world, the minute but fruitful creation of his own mind!

These advantages composition affords us, whether we write ourselves, or in more humble amusement peruse the works of others. While we bustle through the thronged walks of public life, it gives us a respite, at least, from care; a pleasing pause of refreshing recollection. If the country is our choice or fate, there it rescues us from sloth and sensuality, which, like obscene vermin, are apt gradually to creep unperceived into the delightful bowers of our retirement and to poison all its sweets. Conscious guilt robs the rose of its scent, the lily of its lustre; and makes an Eden a deflowered and dismal scene. . . .

But there are who write with vigor and success to the world's delight and their own renown. These are the glorious fruits where genius prevails. The mind of a man of genius is a fertile and pleasant field; pleasant as Elysium, and fertile as Tempe; it enjoys a perpetual spring. Of that spring originals are the fairest flowers: imitations are of quicker growth, but fainter bloom. Imitations are of two kinds; one of nature, one of authors: the first we call "originals," and confine the term "imitation" to the second. I shall not enter into the curious inquiry of what is, or is not, strictly speaking, original, content with what all must allow, that some compositions are more so than others; and the more they are so, I say, the better. Originals are, and ought to be, great favorites, for they are great benefactors; they extend the republic of letters, and add a new province to its dominion: imitators only give us a sort of duplicates of what we had, possibly much better, before; increasing the mere drug of books, while all that makes them valuable, knowledge and genius, are at a stand. The pen of an original writer, like Armida's wand, out of a barren waste calls a blooming spring: out of that blooming spring an imitator is a transplanter of laurels, which sometimes die on removal, always languish in a foreign soil.

But suppose an imitator to be most excellent, (and such there are,) yet still he but nobly builds on another's foundation; his debt is, at least, equal to his glory; which, therefore, on the balance, cannot be very great. On the contrary, an original, though but indifferent (its originality being set aside,) yet has something to boast; it is something to say with him in Horace,

> Meo sum pauper in aere;

and to share ambition with no less than Caesar, who declared he had rather be the first in a village than the second at Rome.

Still farther: an imitator shares his crown, if he has one, with the chosen object of his imitation; an original enjoys an undivided applause. An original may be said to be of a vegetable nature: it rises spontaneously from the vital root of genius; it grows, it is not made; imitations are often a sort of manufacture wrought up by those mechanics, art and labor out of pre-existent materials not their own.

Again: we read imitation with somewhat of his languor who listens to a twice-told tale: our spirits rouse at an original: that is a perfect stranger and all throng to learn what news from a foreign land and though it comes, like an Indian prince, adorned with feathers only, having little of weight, yet of our attention it will rob the more solid, if not equally new. Thus every telescope is lifted at a new discovered star: it makes a hundred astronomers in a moment, and denies equal notice to the sun. But if an original, by being as excellent as new, adds admiration to surprise, then are we at the writer's mercy; on the strong wing of his imagination we are snatched from Britain to Italy, from climate to climate, from pleasure to pleasure; we have no home, no thought, of our own, till the magician drops his pen; and then, falling down into ourselves, we awake to flat realities, lamenting the change, like the beggar who dreamt himself a prince.

It is with thoughts as it is with words, and with both as with men: they may grow old and die. Words tarnished by passing through the mouths of the vulgar, are laid aside as inelegant and obsolete. So thoughts, when become too common, should lose their currency; and we should send new metal to the mint, that is, new meaning to the press. The division of tongues at Babel did not more effectually debar men from "making themselves a name" (as the Scripture speaks) than the too great concurrence or union of tongues will do for ever. We may as well grow good by another's virtue, or fat by another's food, as famous by another's thought. The world will pay its debt of praise but once, and, instead of applauding, explode a second demand as a cheat. . . .

. . . But why are originals so few? Not because the writer's harvest is over, the great reapers of antiquity having left nothing to be gleaned after them; nor because the human mind's teeming time is past, or because it is incapable of putting forth unprecedented births; but because illustrious examples engross, prejudice, and intimidate. They *engross* our attention, and so prevent a due inspection of ourselves; they *prejudice* our judgment in favor of their renown, and thus under diffidence own; and they *intimidate* us with the splendor of their own renown, and thus under diffiidence bury our strength. Nature's impossibilities, and those of diffidence, lie wide asunder.

Let it not be suspected that I would weakly insinuate anything in favor of the moderns, as compared with ancient authors; no, I am lamenting their great inferiority. But I think it is no necessary inferiority; that it is not from Divine destination, but from some cause far beneath the moon. I think that human souls, through all periods, are equal; that due care and exertion would set us nearer our immortal predecessors than we are at present; and he who questions and confutes this, will show abilities not a little tending toward a proof of that equality which he denies.

After all, the first ancients had no merit in being originals: they could not be imitators. Modern writers have a choice to make, and therefore have a merit in their power. They may soar in the regions of liberty, or move in the soft fetters of easy imitation; and imitation has as many plausible reasons to urge as pleasure had to offer to Hercules. Hercules made the choice of a hero and so became immortal.

Yet let not assertors of classic excellence imagine that I deny the tribute it so well deserves. He that admires not ancient authors, betrays a secret he would conceal, and tells the world that he does not understand them. Let us be as far from neglecting, as from copying, their admirable compositions: sacred by their rights, and inviolable their fame. Let our understanding feed on theirs; they afford the noblest nourishment; but let them nourish, not annihilate, our own. When we read, let our imagination kindle at their charms; when we write, let our judgment shut them out of our thoughts; treat even Homer himself as his royal admirer was treated by the cynic,—bid him stand aside, nor shade our composition from the beams of our own genius; for nothing original can rise, nothing immortal can ripen, in any other sun.

"Must we then," you say, "not imitate ancient authors?" Imitate them by all means; but imitate aright. He that imitates the divine Iliad does not imitate Homer; but he who takes the same method which Homer took for arriving at a capacity of accomplishing a work so great. Tread in his steps to the sole fountain of immortality; drink where he drank, at the true Helicon, that is, at the breast of nature. Imitate; but imitate not the composition, but the man. For may not this paradox pass into a maxim?—namely, "The less we copy the renowned ancients, we shall resemble them the more."

But possibly you may reply that you must either imitate Homer, or depart from nature. Not so: for suppose you were to change place, in time, with Homer, then, if you write naturally, you might as well charge Homer with an imitation of you. Can you be said to imitate Homer for writing so as you would have written, if Homer had never been? As far as a regard to nature and sound sense will permit a departure from your great predecessors, so far ambitiously depart from them; the farther from them in similitude, the nearer are you to them in excellence; you rise by it into an original; become a noble collateral, not an humble descendant from them. Let us build our compositions with the spirit and in the taste of the ancients; but not with their materials: thus will they resemble the structures of Pericles at Athens, which Plutarch commends for having had an air of antiquity as soon as they were built. All eminence and distinction lies out of the beaten road; excursion and deviation are necessary to find it; and the more remote your path from the highway, the more reputable, if, like poor Gulliver, (of whom anon,) you fall not into a ditch in your way to glory. . . .

Rome was a powerful ally to many states; ancient authors are our powerful allies; but we must take heed that they do not succor till they enslave, after the manner of Rome. Too formidable an idea of their superiority, like a spectre, would fright us out of a proper use of our wits, and dwarf our understanding, by making a giant of theirs. Too great awe for them lays genius under restraint and denies it that free scope, that full elbow-room, which is a requisite for striking its most masterly strokes. Genius is a master-workman, learning is but an instrument; and an instrument, though most valuable, yet not always indispensable. Heaven will not admit of a partner in the accomplishment of some favorite spirits; but rejecting all human means, assumes the whole glory to itself. Have not some, though not famed for erudition, so written as almost to persuade us that they shone brighter and soared higher for escaping the boasted aid of that proud ally?

Nor is it strange; for what, for the most part, mean we by genius but the power of accomplishing great things without the means generally reputed necessary to that end? A genius differs from a good understanding, as a magician from a good architect; that raises his structure by means invisible, this by the skilful use of common tools. Hence genius has ever been supposed to partake of something Divine. *Nemo unquam vir magnus fuit, sine aliquo afflatu divino.*

Learning, destitute of this superior aid, is fond and proud of what has cost it much pains; is a great lover of rules, and boaster of famed examples. As beauties less perfect, who owe half their charms to cautious art, she inveighs against natural, unstudied graces and small, harmless indecorums, and sets rigid bounds to that liberty to which genius often owes its supreme glory, but the non-genius its frequent ruin. For unprescribed beauties and unexampled excellence, which are characteristics of genius, lie without the pale of learning's authorities and laws; which pale, genius must leap to come at them; but by that leap, if genius is wanting, we break our necks: we lose that little credit which possibly we might have enjoyed before. For rules, like crutches, are a needful aid to the lame, though an impediment to the strong. A Homer casts them away and, like Achilles,

> Jura negat sibi nata, nihil non arrogat,

by native force of mind. There is something in poetry beyond prose reason; there are mysteries in it not to be explained, but admired, which render mere prose-men infidels to their divinity. And here pardon a second paradox: namely, "Genius often then deserves most to be praised when it is most sure to be condemned; that is, when its excellence, from mounting high, to weak eyes is quite out of sight."

If I might speak farther of learning and genius, I would compare genius to virtue, and learning to riches. As riches are most wanted where there is least virtue, so learning where there is least genius. As virtue without much riches can give happiness, so genius without much learning can give renown. As it is said in Terence, *Pecuniam negligere interdum maximum est lucrum,* so to neglect of learning genius sometimes owes its greater glory. Genius, therefore, leaves but the second place, among men of letters, to the learned. It is their merit and ambition to fling light on the works of genius, and point out its charms. We most justly reverence their informing radius for that favor; but we must much more admire the radiant stars pointed out by them.

A star of the first magnitude among the moderns was Shakespeare; among the ancients, Pindar; who, as Vossius tells us, boasted of his no-learning, calling himself the eagle, for his flight above it. And such genii as these may, indeed, have much reliance on their own native powers. For genius may be compared to the body's natural strength; learning to the superinduced accoutrements of arms. If the first is equal to the proposed exploit, the latter rather encumbers than assists; rather retards, than promotes, the victory. *Sacer nobis inest* Deus, says Seneca. With regard to the moral world, conscience—with regard to the intellectual, genius—is that god within. Genius can set us right in composition without the rules of the learned, as conscience sets us right in life without the laws of the land; this, singly, can make us good, as men; that, singly, as writers, can sometimes make us great.

I say "sometimes," because there is a genius which stands in need of learning to make it shine. Of genius there are two species, an earlier and a later; or call them infantine and adult. An adult genius comes out of nature's hand, as Pallas out of Jove's head, at full growth and mature: Shakespeare's genius was of this kind: on the contrary, Swift stumbled at the threshold, and set out for distinction on feeble knees. His was an infantine genius; a genius, which, like other infants, must be nursed and educated, or it will come to nought. Learning is its nurse and tutor; but this nurse may overlay with an indigested load, which smothers common sense; and this tutor may mislead with pedantic prejudice, which vitiates the best understanding. As too great admirers of the fathers of the church have sometimes set up their authority against the true sense of Scripture, so too great admirers of the classical fathers have sometimes set up their authority, or example, against reason.

> *Neve minor, neu sit quinto productior actu fabula.*

So says Horace, so says ancient example. But

reason has not subscribed. I know but one book that can justify our implicit acquiescence in it. . . .

. . . In the fairyland of fancy, genius may wander wild; there it has a creative power, and may reign arbitrarily over its own empire of chimeras. The wide field of nature also lies open before it, where it may range unconfined, make what discoveries it can, and sport with its infinite objects uncontrolled, as far as visible nature extends, painting them as wantonly as it will. But what painter of the most unbounded and exalted genius can give us the true portrait of a seraph? He can give us only what by his own, or other's eyes, has been seen; though that indeed infinitely compounded, raised, burlesqued, dishonored, or adorned. In like manner, who can give us Divine truth unrevealed? Much less should any presume to set aside Divine truth when revealed, as incongruous to their own sagacities. . . .

Moreover, so boundless are the bold excursions of the human mind, that, in the vast void beyond real existence, it can call forth shadowy beings and unknown worlds, as numerous, as bright, and, perhaps as lasting, as the stars: such quite-original beauties we may call paradisaical,—

Natos sine semine flores. Ovid.

When such an ample area for renowned adventure in original attempts lies before us, shall we be as mere leaden pipes, conveying to the present age small streams of excellence from its grand reservoir in antiquity, and those, too, perhaps, mudded in the pass? Originals shine like comets, have no peer in their path, are rivalled by none, and the gaze of all. All other compositions, if they shine at all, shine in clusters, like the stars in the galaxy; where, like bad neighbors, all suffer from all each particular being diminished, and almost lost in the throng. . . .

Joseph Addison

1672–1719

A. Life

Joseph Addison is principally known for his tragedy, *Cato*, and for the writings that appeared in *The Tatler* and *The Spectator*. In the latter publications, his name is usually associated with that of Richard Steele, but Addison's own diverse and interesting contributions exerted a very considerable influence upon philosophical speculation as well as upon literary men. This is principally true of his essays on imagination, his studies of John Milton's *Paradise Lost*, and his writing on genius and creative imagination. The last two articles from *The Spectator*, Numbers 160 and 421, are reproduced below.

Addison was born in Milston, in Wiltshire, the son of Lancelot Addison who became Dean of Lichfield. He attended Charterhouse and St. John's College, Oxford and travelled for four years in France, Italy and Germany. He gained his first fame as the author of *The Campaign*, which celebrated Marlborough's victory at Blenheim. Addison occupied various political positions, serving as a Commissioner of Excise and later as a member of Parliament.

B. Philosophy of Art

Spectator No. 160

Monday, September 3

> ——— *Cui mens divinior, atque os*
> *Magna sonaturum, des nominis hujus honorem.*
> HOR.

THERE[37] is no character more frequently given to a writer, than that of being a genius. I have heard many a little sonnetteer called a fine Genius. There is not an heroic scribbler in the nation, that has not his admirers, who think him a great Genius; and as for your smatterers in tragedy, there is scarce a man among them who is not cried up by one or other for a prodigious Genius.

My design in this paper is to consider what is properly a great genius, and to throw some thoughts together on so uncommon a subject.

Among great geniuses, those few draw the admiration of all the world upon them, and

[37] *The Works of the Right Honorable Joseph Addison, Collected by Mr. (Thomas) Tickell Vernor & Hood, etc.,* 1804. Vol. 1, pp. 344–347, Vol. 2, pp. 394–397.

stand up as the prodigies of mankind, who, by the mere strength of natural parts, and without any assistance of art or learning, have produced works that were the delight of their own times, and the wonder of posterity. There appears something nobly wild and extravagant in these great natural geniuses, that is infinitely more beautiful than all the turn and polishing of what the French call a *Bel Esprit*, by which they would express a genius refined by conversation, reflection, and the reading of the most polite authors. The greatest genius which runs through the arts, and sciences, takes a kind of tincture from them, and falls unavoidably into imitation.

Many of these great natural geniuses, that were never disciplined and broken by rules of art, are to be found among the ancients, and, in particular, among those of the more eastern parts of the world. Homer has innumerable flights that Virgil was not able to reach; and in the Old Testament we find several passages more elevated and sublime than any in Homer. At the same time that we allow a greater and more daring genius to the ancients, we must own that the greatest of them very much failed in, or, if you will, that they were much above, the nicety and correctness of the moderns. In their similitudes and allusions, provided there was a likeness, they did not much trouble themselves about the decency of the comparison: Thus Solomon resembles the nose of his beloved to the tower of Lebanon which looketh towards Damascus; as the coming of a thief in the night, is a similitude of the same kind in the New Testament. It would be endless to make collections of this nature: Homer illustrates one of his heroes encompassed with the enemy, by an ass in a field of corn, that has his sides belaboured by all the boys of the village without stirring a foot for it; and another of them tossing to and fro in his bed, and burning with resentment, to a piece of flesh broiled on the coals. This particular failure in the ancients, opens a large field of raillery to the little wits, who can laugh at an indecency, but not relish the sublime in these sorts of writings. The present emperor of Persia, conformable to this eastern way of thinking, amidst a great many pompous titles, denominates himself the Sun of Glory, and the Nutmeg of Delight. In short, to cut off all cavilling against the ancients, and particularly those of the warmer climates, who had most heat and life in their imaginations, we are to consider that the rule of observing what the French call the *Bienseance* in an allusion, has been found out of latter years, and in the colder regions of the world; where we would make some amends for our want of force and spirit, by a scrupulous nicety and exactness in our compositions. Our countryman Shakespear was a remarkable instance of this first kind of great geniuses.

I cannot quit this head, without observing that Pindar was a great ginus of the first class, who was hurried on by a natural fire and impetuosity to vast conceptions of things, and noble sallies of imagination. At the same time, can any thing be more ridiculous than for men of a sober and moderate fancy, to imitate this poet's way of writing in those monstrous compositions which go among us under the name of Pindarics? When I see people copying works, which, as Horace has represented them, are singular in their kind, and inimitable; when I see men following irregularities by rule, and by the little tricks of art, straining after the most unbounded flights of nature; I cannot but apply to them that passage in Terence:

> ————*incerta haec si tu postules*
> *Ratione certa facere, nihilo plus agas,*
> *Quàm si des operam, ut cum ratione insanias.*

In short, a modern pindaric writer compared with Pindar, is like a sister among the Camisars compared with Virgil's Sibyl: there is the distortion, grimace, and outward figure, but nothing of that divine impulse which raises the mind above itself, and makes the sounds more than human.

There is another kind of great geniuses which I shall place in a second class; not as I think them inferior to the first, but only for distinction's sake, as they are of a different kind. This second class of great geniuses are those that have formed themselves by rules, and submitted the greatness of their natural talents to the corrections and restraints of art. Such among the Greeks were Plato and Aristotle; among the Romans, Virgil and Tully; among the English, Milton and Sir Francis Bacon.

The genius in both these classes of authors may be equally great, but shews itself after a different manner. In the first it is like a rich soil in a happy climate, that produces a whole wilderness of noble plants, rising in a thousand beautiful landscapes, without any certain order or irregularity. In the other it is the same rich soil under the same happy climate, that has been laid out in walks and parterres, and cut into shape and beauty by the skill of the gardener.

The great danger in these latter kind of geniuses, is, lest they cramp their own abilities too much by imitation, and form themselves altogether upon models, without giving the full play to their own natural parts. An imitation of the best authors is not to compare with a good original; and I believe we may observe that very few writers make an extraordinary figure in the world, who have not something in their way of thinking, or expressing themselves, that is peculiar to them, and entirely their own.

It is odd to consider what great geniuses are sometimes thrown away upon trifles.

I once saw a shepherd, says a famous Italian author, who used to divert himself in his solitudes with tossing up eggs, and catching them again, without breaking them: in which he had arrived to so great a degree of perfection, that he would keep up four at a time for several minutes together, playing in the air, and falling into his hand by turns. I think, says the author, I never saw a greater severity than this man's face; for by his wonderful perseverance and application, he had contracted the seriousness and gravity of a privy counsellor: I could not but reflect with myself, that the same assiduity and attention, had they been rightly applied, might have made him a greater mathematician than Archimedes. . . .

Spectator No. 421

Thursday, July 3

Ignotis errare locis, ignota videre
Flumina gaudebat; studio minuente laborem.
OVID.

THE pleasures of the imagination are not wholly confined to such particular authors as are conversant in material objects, but are often to be met with among the polite masters of morality, criticism, and other speculations abstracted from matter, who, though they do not directly treat of the visible parts of nature, often draw from them their similitudes, metaphors, and allegories. By these allusions a truth in the understanding is as it were reflected by the imagination; we are able to see something like colour and shape in a notion, and to discover a scheme of thoughts traced out upon matter. And here the mind receives a great deal of satisfaction, and has two of its faculties gratified at the same time, while the fancy is busy in copying after the understanding, and transcribing ideas out of the intellectual world into the material.

The great art of a writer shews itself in the choice of pleasing allusions, which are generally to be taken from the great or beautiful works of art or nature; for though whatever is new or uncommon is apt to delight the imagination, the chief design of an allusion being to illustrate and explain the passages of an author, it should be always borrowed from what is more known and common, than the passages which are to be explained.

Allegories, when well chosen, are like so many tracks of light in a discourse, that make every thing about them clear and beautiful. A noble metaphor, when it is placed to an advantage, casts a kind of glory round it, and darts a lustre through a whole sentence: these different kinds of allusion are but so many different manners of similitude, and, that they may please the imagination, the likeness ought to be very exact, or very agreeable, as we love to see a picture where the resemblance is just, or the posture and air graceful. But we often find eminent writers very faulty in this respect; great scholars are apt to fetch their comparisons and allusions from the sciences in which they are most conversant, so that a man may see the compass of their learning in a treatise on the most indifferent subject. I have read a discourse upon love, which none but a profound chemist could understand; and have heard many a sermon that should only have been preached before a congregation of Cartesians. On the contrary, your men of business usually have recourse to such instances as are too mean and familiar. They are for drawing the reader into a game of chess or tennis, or for leading him from shop to shop, in the cant of particular trades and employments. It is certain, there may be found an infinite variety of very agreeable allusions in both these kinds, but for the generality, the most entertaining ones lie in the works of nature, which are obvious to all capacities, and more delightful than what is to be found in arts and sciences.

It is this talent of affecting the imagination, that gives an embellishment to good sense, and makes one man's compositions more agreeable than another's. It sets off all writings in general, but is the very life and highest perfection of poetry. Where it shines in an eminent degree, it has preserved several poems for many ages, that have nothing else to recommend them; and where all the other beauties are present, the work appears dry and insipid, if this single one be wanting. It has something in it like creation; it bestows a kind of existence, and draws up to the reader's view several objects which are not to be found in being. It makes additions to nature, and gives greater variety to God's works. In a word, it is able to beautify and adorn the most illustrious scenes in the universe, or to fill the mind with more glorious shows and apparitions, than can be found in any part of it.

We have now discovered the several originals of those pleasures that gratify the fancy; and here, perhaps, it would not be very difficult to cast under their proper heads, those contrary objects which are apt to fill it with distaste and terror; for the imagination is as liable to pain as pleasure. When the brain is hurt by any accident, or the mind disordered by dreams or sickness, the fancy is over-run with wild dismal ideas, and terrified with a thousand hideous monsters of its own framing.

Eumenidum veluti demens videt agmina Pentheus,
Et solem geminum, et duplices se ostendere Thebas:
Aut Agamemnonius scenis agitatus Orestes,
Armatam facibus matrem et serpentibus atris
Cum fugit, ultricesque sedent in limine dirae.

VIRG.

There is not a sight in nature so mortifying as that of a distracted person, when his imagination is troubled, and his whole soul disordered and confused: Babylon in ruins is not so melancholy a spectacle. But to quit so disagreeable a subject, I shall only consider, by way of conclusion, what an infinite advantage this faculty gives an Almighty Being over the soul of man, and how great a measure of happiness or misery we are capable of receiving from the imagination only.

We have already seen the influence that one man has over the fancy of another, and with what ease he conveys into it a variety of imagery; how great a power then may we suppose lodged in Him, who knows all the ways of affecting the imagination, who can infuse what ideas he pleases, and fill those ideas with terror or delight to what degree he thinks fit! He can excite images in the mind, without the help of words, and make scenes rise up before us, and seem present to the eye, without the assistance of bodies or exterior objects. He can transport the imagination with such beautiful and glorious visions, as cannot possibly enter into our present conceptions; or haunt it with such ghastly spectres and apparitions, as would make us hope for annihilation, and think existence no better than a curse. In short, he can so exquisitely ravish or torture the soul through this single faculty, as might suffice to make up the whole heaven or hell of any finite being.

Alexander Gerard

1728–1795 [38]

Philosophy of Art

On Genius

OF THE CONNEXION OF TASTE WITH GENIUS

Taste [39] may be considered either as an essential *Part*, or as a necessary *attendant* of genius; according as we consider genius in a more or less extensive manner. Every one acknowledges that they have a very near connexion. It is so evident, that it has almost past into a maxim, that the ablest performers are also the best judges in every art. How far the maxim is just will best appear, by briefly determining the nature and principles of genius.

The first and leading quality of genius is *invention*, which consists in an extensive comprehensiveness of imagination, in a readiness of associating the remotest ideas, that are any way related. In a man of genius the uniting principles are so vigorous and quick, that whenever any idea is present to the mind, they bring into view at once all others, that have the least connection with it. As the magnet selects from a quantity of matter the ferruginous particles, which happen to be scattered through it, without making an impression on other substances; so imagination, by a similar sympathy, equally inexplicable, draws out from the whole compass of nature such ideas as we have occasion for, without attending to any others; and yet presents them with as great propriety, as if all possible conceptions had been explicitly exposed to our view, and subjected to our choice.

At first these Materials may lie in a rude and indigested chaos: but when we attentively review them, the same associating power, which formerly made us sensible of their connection, leads us to perceive the different degrees of that connection; by it's magical force ranges them into different species, according to these degrees; disposes the most strongly related into the same member; and sets all the members in that position, which it points out as the

[38] See above, p. 352 et seq., for a brief biography of Alexander Gerard. This precedes selections from Gerard's examination of taste.

[39] Alexander Gerard, *An Essay on Taste,* Part III, Sect. II, p. 173, London, 1759. A. Millar, A. Kincaid and J. Bell, Edinburgh. I have quoted Gerard's *An Essay on Genius* (1774) in the Introduction but I have given selections from the earlier *An Essay on Taste* in the readings that follow. I have done this because of the close relation in the analysis between taste and genius in the earlier writing and because of the extraordinarily illuminating remarks Gerard makes concerning the relation not only of genius and taste but of taste and criticism, as well.

most natural. Thus from a confused heap of materials, collected by fancy, genius, after repeated reviews and transpositions, designs a regular and well proportioned whole.

This brightness and force of imagination throws a lustre on its effects, which will for ever distinguish them from the lifeless and insipid productions of inanimated industry. Diligence and acquired abilities may assist or improve genius; but a fine imagination alone can produce it. Hence is derived its inventive power in all the subjects to which it can be applied. This is possessed in common by the musician, the painter, the poet, the philosopher, and even the mathematician. In each indeed, its form has something peculiar arising either from the degree of extent and comprehension of fancy; or from the peculiar prevalence of some one of the associating qualities; or from the mind being, by original constitution, education, example, or study, more strongly turned to one kind than the others.

A genius for the fine arts implies, not only the power of invention or design, but likewise a capacity to express its designs in apt materials. Without this, it would not only be imperfect, but would for ever lie latent, undiscovered, and useless. It is chiefly the peculiar modification of this capacity, which adapts a genius to one art rather than another. To form a painter, the ideas assembled by fancy must give him a view of their correspondent objects, in such order and proportion, as will enable him to exhibit the original to the eye, by an imitation of its figure and colour. To form a poet, they must lead the thoughts, not to the corporeal forms of things, but to the signs, with which by the common use of language, they are connected; so that he may employ them with propriety, force, and harmony, in exciting strong ideas of his subject.

Culture may strengthen invention; knowledge is necessary for supplying a fund from which it may collect its materials; but improvement chiefly affects the capacity of expression. Painting requires a mechanical skill, produced by exercise: music a knowledge of the power of sounds, derived from experience: poetry and eloquence an acquaintance with all the force of words and instituted signs, an advantage which can be obtained only by careful study.

Thus genius is the grand architect, which not only chooses the materials, but disposes them into a regular structure. But it is not able to finish it by itself. It needs the assistance of taste, to guide and moderate its exertions. Though the different relations of the parts, in some measure, determine the form and position of each, we acquire much ampler assurance of its rectitude, when taste has reviewed and examined both the design and execution. It serves as a check on mere fancy; it interposes its judgment, either approving or condemning; and rejects many things, which unassisted genius would have allowed.

The distinct provinces of genius and taste being thus marked out, it will be easy to discover how far they are connected. They must be connected in a considerable degree, since they both spring from imagination: but as it is differently exerted in each, their connection will not be perfectly accurate and uniform.

Genius is not always attended with taste precisely equal and proportioned. It is sometimes incorrect, though copious and extensive. It is sometimes bold, yet can transfuse no delicacy or grace into its productions. But it is never found where taste is altogether wanting. The same vigour of the associating principles, which renders genius quick and comprehensive, must bestow such strength on the several dependent operations of fancy, which generate taste, as shall make that faculty considerably active and perceptive. The genius of the greatest masters in every kind has not been more perfect than their taste. The models they have given are so finished and correct, that the general rules and precepts of the art, afterwards established by critics, are deduced from their practice, and the very same which they observed, though uninstructed. The epos was not subjected to rules, when *Homer* composed the *Iliad*. *Aristotle* did not write his *Art of poetry*, till after the greatest tragic poets of antiquity had flourished. These great originals possessed, not only an excellent genius, but equal taste. The vigour of their imaginations led them into unexplored tracts; and they had such light and discernment, as, without danger of error, directed their course in this untrodden wilderness. Taste united with genius renders the effects of the latter like to diamonds, which have as great solidity as splendour.

But taste often prevails where genius is wanting; they may judge, who cannot themselves perform. The operations, that depend on the imagination, may be vigorous enough to form a high relish, though it be destitute of that brightness and extension, which is necessary for a comprehensive genius. The associating principles may be strong and active within their bounds, though these bounds be narrow. And soundness and strength of judgment may be possessed without considerable genius; but must always, if joined with any degree of the internal senses, produce acuteness and justness of taste. This rendered *Aristotle* the greatest of critics, tho he was not, like *Longinus, blest with a poet's fire*.

It must however be acknowledged, that genius will always throw a peculiar brightness upon taste, as it enables one, by a kind of contagion, to catch the spirit of an author, to judge with the same disposition, in which he composed, and by this means to feel every beauty with a delight and transport, of which a colder critic can form no idea. The fine genius of *Longinus* catches fire, as it were, from the mentioning of a sublime passage, and hurries him on to emulate its sublimity in his explication of it. *Quintilian*, by the same union of genius with taste, delivers his sentiments with the utmost elegance, and enlivens the abstractness of precept by the most beautiful and apposite figures and images.

SECT. III

ON THE INFLUENCE OF TASTE ON CRITICISM

As taste gives the last finishing to genius in the *author* or performer, so is it the fundamental ingredient in the character of the *critic*. The greatest refinement and justness of taste is necessary, but not alone sufficient, to qualify one for this office. A critic must not only *feel*, but possess that accuracy of discernment, which enables a person to *reflect* upon his feelings with distinctness, and to explain them to others.

Taste perceives the particular beauties and faults, and thus supplies the facts, for which we are to account; and the experiments, from which our conclusions cannot be formed without a vigorous abstracting faculty, the greatest force of reason, a capacity for the most careful and correct induction, and a deep knowledge of the principles of human nature. One does not merit the name of a critic, merely by being able to make a collection of beauties and faults from performances in the fine arts; to tell in general that those please, these displease; some more, some less. Such particular observations fall as much short of genuine criticism, as a collection of facts and experiments does of philosophy; or a series of news papers of a system of politicks. They are its rude materials, and nothing more. And to exhibit them is the whole that taste can do.

In order therefore to form an able critic, taste must be attended with a philosophical genius, which may subject these materials to a regular induction, reduce them into classes, and determine the general rules which govern them. In all this operation respect must be had to the subjects in which the excellencies or blemishes reside, and to the similitude of the qualities themselves, or of the sentiments which they excite. These are the circumstances common to a variety of particular phaenomena, which must regulate our distribution of them. It is not enough to discover that we are pleased or displeased; we must ascertain the precise species of either; and refer it to the sentiment or the expression; to the design or the execution; to sublimity or beauty; to wit or humour . . . .

Immanuel Kant

1724–1804 [40]

Philosophy of Art

On Art, Fine Art, and Genius

§ 43

ART IN GENERAL

1. *Art* [41] is distinguished from *nature* as making (*facere*) is from acting or operating in general (*agere*), and the product of the result of the former is distinguished from that of the latter as *work* (*opus*) from operation (*effectus*).

By right it is only production through freedom, i.e. through an act of will that places reason at the basis of its action, that should be termed art. For, although we are pleased to call what bees produce (their regularly constructed cells) a work of art, we only do so on the strength of an analogy with art; that is to say, as soon as we call to mind that no rational deliberation forms the basis of their labour, we say at once that it is a product of their nature (of instinct), and it is only to their Creator that we ascribe it as art.

If, as sometimes happens, in a search through a bog, we light on a piece of hewn wood, we do not say it is a product of nature but of art. Its producing cause had an end in view to which the object owes its form. Apart from such cases, we recognize an art in everything formed in such a way that its actuality must have been preceded by a representation of the thing in its cause (as even in the case of the bees), although the effect could not have been *thought* by the cause. But where anything is called absolutely a work of art, to distinguish it from a natural product, then some work of man is always understood.

2. *Art,* as human skill, is distinguished also from *science* (as *ability* from *knowledge*), as a practical from a theoretical faculty, as technic from theory (as the art of surveying from geometry). For this reason, also, what one *can* do the moment one only *knows* what is to be done, hence without anything more than sufficient knowledge of the desired result, is not called art. To art that alone belongs for which the possession of the most complete knowledge does not involve one's having then

[40] For a brief biography of Kant, see above, p. 359. Selections from the earlier part of *The Critique of Judgement* begin above, p. 360.

[41] Immanuel Kant, *Kant's Critique of Aesthetic Judgement*, translated by J. C. Meredith. By permission of the Clarendon Press, Oxford. 1911.

and there the skill to do it. *Camper* describes very exactly how the best shoe must be made, but he, doubtless, was not able to turn one out himself.[42]

3. *Art* is further distinguished from *handicraft.* The first is called *free,* the other may be called *industrial art.* We look on the former as something which could only prove final (be a success) as play, i.e. an occupation which is agreeable on its own account; but on the second as labour, i.e. a business, which on its own account is disagreeable (drudgery), and is only attractive by means of what it results in (e.g. the pay), and which is consequently capable of being a compulsory imposition. Whether in the list of arts and crafts we are to rank watchmakers as artists, and smiths on the contrary as craftsmen, requires a standpoint different from that here adopted—one, that is to say, taking account of the proportion of the talents which the business undertaken in either case must necessarily involve. Whether, also, among the so-called seven free arts some may not have been included which should be reckoned as sciences, and many, too, that resemble handicraft, is a matter I will not discuss here. It is not amiss, however, to remind the reader of this: that in all free arts something of a compulsory character is still required, or, as it is called, a *mechanism,* without which the *soul,* which in art must be *free,* and which alone gives life to the work, would be bodyless and evanescent (e.g. in the poetic art there must be correctness and wealth of language, likewise prosody and metre). For not a few leaders of a newer school believe that the best way to promote a free art is to sweep away all restraint, and convert it from labour into mere play.

[42] In my part of the country, if you set a common man a problem like that of Columbus and his egg, he says, "There is no art in that, it is only science": i.e., you *can* do it if you know *how*; and he says just the same of all the would-be arts of jugglers. To that of the tight-rope dancer, on the other hand, he has not the least compunction in giving the name of art.

§ 44

FINE ART

THERE is no science of the beautiful, but only a Critique. Nor, again, is there an elegant (*schöne*) science, but only a fine (*schöne*) art. For a science of the beautiful would have to determine scientifically, i.e. by means of proofs, whether a thing was to be considered beautiful or not; and the judgment upon beauty, consequently, would, if belonging to science, fail to be a judgment of taste. As for a beautiful science—a science which, as such, is to be beautiful, is a nonentity. For if, treating it as a science, we were to ask for reasons and proofs, we would be put off with elegant phrases (*bons mots*). What has given rise to the current expression *elegant sciences* is, doubtless, no more than this, that common observation has, quite accurately, noted the fact that for fine art, in the fulness of its perfection, a large store of science is required, as, for example, knowledge of ancient languages, acquaintance with classical authors, history, antiquarian learning, &c. Hence these historical sciences, owing to the fact that they form the necessary preparation and groundwork for fine art, and partly also owing to the fact that they are taken to comprise even the knowledge of the products of fine art (rhetoric and poetry), have by a confusion of words, actually got the name of elegant sciences.

Where art, merely seeking to actualize a possible object to the *cognition* of which it is adequate, does whatever acts are required for that purpose, then it is *mechanical.* But should the feeling of pleasure be what it has immediately in view it is then termed *aesthetic* art. As such it may be either *agreeable* or *fine* art. The description 'agreeable art' applies where the end of the art is that the pleasure should accompany the representations considered as mere *sensations,* the description 'fine art' where it is to accompany them considered as *modes of cognition.*

Agreeable arts are those which have mere enjoyment for their object. Such are all the charms that can gratify a dinner party: entertaining narrative, the art of starting the whole table in unrestrained and sprightly conversation, or with jest and laughter inducing a certain air of gaiety. Here, as the saying goes, there may be much loose talk over the glasses, without a person wishing to be brought to book for all he utters, because it is only given out for the entertainment of the moment, and not as a lasting matter to be made the subject of reflection or repetition. (Of the same sort is also the art of arranging the table for enjoyment, or, at large banquets, the music of the orchestra—a quaint idea intended to act on the mind merely as an agreeable noise fostering a genial spirit, which, without any one paying the smallest attention to the composition, promotes the free flow of conversation between guest and guest). In addition must be included play of every kind which is attained with no further interest than that of making the time pass by unheeded.

Fine art, on the other hand, is a mode of representation which is intrinsically final, and which, although devoid of an end, has the effect of advancing the culture of the mental powers in the interests of social communication.

The universal communicability of a pleasure involves in its very concept that the pleasure is not one of enjoyment arising out of mere sensation, but must be one of reflection. Hence aesthetic art, as art which is beautiful, is one having for its standard the reflective judgment and not organic sensation.

§ 45

FINE ART IS AN ART, SO FAR AS IT HAS AT THE SAME TIME THE APPEARANCE OF BEING NATURE

A PRODUCT of fine art must be recognized to be art and not nature. Nevertheless the finality in its form must appear just as free from the constraint of arbitrary rules as if it were a product of mere nature. Upon this feeling of freedom in the play of our cognitive faculties—which play has at the same time to be final—rests that pleasure which alone is universally communicable without being based on concepts. Nature proved beautiful when it wore the appearance of art; and art can only be termed beautiful, where we are conscious of its being art, while yet it has the appearance of nature.

For, whether we are dealing with beauty of nature or beauty of art, we may make the universal statement: *that is beautiful which pleases in the mere estimate of it* (not in sensation or by means of a concept). Now art has always got a definite intention of producing something. Were this "something," however, to be mere sensation (something merely subjective), intended to be accompanied with pleasure, then such product would, in our estimation of it, only please through the agency of the feeling of the senses. On the other hand, were the intention one directed to the production of a definite object, then, supposing this were attained by art, the object would only please by means of a concept. But in both cases the art would please, not in *the mere estimate of it,* i.e. not as fine art, but rather as mechanical art.

Hence the finality in the product of fine art, intentional though it be, must not have the appearance of being intentional; i.e. fine art must be clothed *with the aspect* of nature, although we recognize it to be art. But the way in which a product of art seems like nature, is by the presence of perfect *exactness* in the agreement with rules prescribing how alone the product can be what it is intended to be, but with an absence of *laboured effect,* (without academic form betraying itself,) i.e. with-without a trace appearing of the artist having always had the rule present to him and of its having fettered his mental powers.

§ 46

FINE ART IS THE ART OF GENIUS

Genius is the talent (natural endowment) which gives the rule to art. Since talent, as an innate productive faculty of the artist, belongs itself to nature, we may put it this way: *Genius* is the innate mental aptitude (*ingenium*) *through which* nature gives the rule to art.

Whatever may be the merits of this definition, and whether it is merely arbitrary, or whether it is adequate or not to the concept usually associated with the word *genius* (a point which the following sections have to clear up), it may still be shown at the outset that, according to this acception of the word, fine arts must necessarily be regarded as arts of *genius.*

For every art presupposes rules which are laid down as the foundation which first enables a product, if it is to be called one of art, to be represented as possible. The concept of fine art, however, does not permit of the judgment upon the beauty of its product being derived from any rule that has a *concept* for its determining ground, and that depends, consequently, on a concept of the way in which the product is possible. Consequently fine art cannot of its own self excogitate the rule according to which it is to effectuate its product. But since, for all that, a product can never be called art unless there is a preceding rule, it follows that nature in the individual (and by virtue of the harmony of his faculties) must give the rule to art, i.e. fine art is only possible as a product of genius.

From this it may be seen that genius (1) is a *talent* for producing that for which no definite rule can be given: and not an aptitude in the way of cleverness for what can be learned according to some rule; and that consequently *originality* must be its primary property. (2) Since there may also be original nonsense, its products must at the same time be models, i.e. be *exemplary*; and, consequently though not themselves derived from imitation, they must serve that purpose for others, i.e. as a standard or rule of estimating. (3) It cannot indicate scientifically how it brings about its product, but rather gives the rule as *nature*. Hence, where an author owes a product to his genius, he does not himself know how the *ideas* for it have entered into his head, nor has he it in his power to invent the like at pleasure, or methodically, and communicate the same to others in such precepts as would put them in a position to produce similar products. (Hence, presumably, our word *Genie* is derived from *genius*, as the peculiar guardian and guiding spirit given to a man at his birth, by the inspiration of which those original ideas were obtained). (4) Nature prescribes the rule through genius not to science but to art, and this also only in so far as it is to be fine art.

§ 47

ELUCIDATION AND CONFIRMATION OF THE ABOVE EXPLANATION OF GENIUS

EVERY one is agreed on the point of the complete opposition between genius and the *spirit of imitation*. Now since learning is nothing but imitation, the greatest ability, or aptness as a pupil (capacity), is still, as such, not equivalent to genius. Even though a man weaves his own thoughts or fancies, instead of merely taking in what others have thought, and even though he go so far as to bring fresh gains to art and science, this does not afford a valid reason for calling such a man of *brains*, and often great brains, a *genius*, in contradistinction to one who goes by the name of *shallow-pate*, because he can never do more than merely learn and follow a lead. For what is accomplished in this way is something that *could* have been learned. Hence it all lies in the natural path of investigation and reflection according to rules, and so is not specifically distinguishable from what may be acquired as the result of industry backed up by imitation. So all that *Newton* has set forth in his immortal work on the Principles of Natural Philosophy may well be learned, however great a mind it took to find it all out, but we cannot learn to write in a true poetic vein, no matter how complete all the precepts of the poetic art may be, or however excellent its models. The reason is that all the steps that Newton had to take from the first elements of geometry to his greatest and most profound discoveries were such as he could make intuitively evident and plain to follow, not only for himself but for every one else. On the other hand no *Homer* or *Wieland* can show how his ideas, so rich at once in fancy and in thought, enter and assemble themselves in his brain, for the good reason that he does not himself know, and so cannot teach others. In matters of science, therefore, the greatest inventor differs only in degree from the most laborious imitator and apprentice, whereas he differs specifically from one endowed by nature for fine art. No disparagement, however, of those great men, to whom the human race is so deeply indebted, is involved in this comparison of them with those who on the score of their talent for fine art are the elect of nature. The talent for science is formed for the continued advances of greater perfection in knowledge, with all its dependent practical advantages, as also for imparting the same to others. Hence scientists can boast a ground of considerable superiority over those who merit the honour of being called geniuses, since genius reaches a point at which art must make a halt, as there is a limit imposed upon it which it cannot transcend. This limit has in all probability been long since attained. In addition, such skill cannot be communicated, but requires to be bestowed directly from the hand of nature upon each individual, and so with him it dies, awaiting the day when nature once again endows another in the same way—one who needs no more than an example to set the talent of which he is conscious at work on similar lines.

Seeing, then, that the natural endowment of art (as fine art) must furnish the rule, what kind of rule must this be? It cannot be one set down in a formula and serving as a precept—for then the judgment upon the beautiful would be determinable according to concepts. Rather must the rule be gathered from the performance, i.e. from the product, which others may use to put their own talent to the test, so as to let it serve as a model not for *imitation*, but for *following*. The possibility of this is difficult to explain. The artist's ideas arouse like ideas on the part of the pupil, presuming nature to have visited him with a like proportion of the mental powers. For this reason the models of fine art are the only means of handing down this art to posterity. This is something which cannot be done by mere descriptions (especially not in the line of the arts of speech), and in these arts, furthermore, only those models can become classical of which the ancient, dead languages, preserved as learned, are the medium.

Despite the marked difference that distinguishes mechanical art, as an art merely depending upon industry and learning, from fine art, as that of genius, there is still no fine art in which something mechanical, capable of being at once comprehended and followed in obedience to rules, and consequently something *academic* does not constitute the essential condition of the art. For the thought of something as end must be present, or else its product would not be ascribed to an art at all, but would be a mere product of chance. But the effectuation of an end necessitates determinate rules which we cannot venture to dispense with. Now, seeing that originality of talent is one (though not the sole) essential factor that goes to make up the character of genius, shallow minds fancy that the best evidence they can give of their being full-blown geniuses is by emancipating themselves from all academic constraint of rules, in the belief that one cuts a finer figure on the back of an ill-tempered than of a trained horse. Genius can do no more than furnish rich *material* for products of fine art; its elaboration and its *form* require a talent academically trained, so that it may be employed in such a way as to stand the test of judgment. But, for a person to hold forth and pass sentence like a genius in matters that fall to the province of the most patient rational investigation, is ridiculous in the extreme. One is at a loss to know whether to laugh more at the impostor who envelops himself in such a cloud—in which we are given fuller scope to our imagination at the expense of all use of our critical faculty—or at the simple-minded public which imagines that its inability clearly to cognize and comprehend this masterpiece of penetration is due to its being invaded by new truths *en masse*, in comparison with which, detail, due to carefully weighed exposition and an academic examination of root-principles, seems to it only the work of a tyro.

§ 48

THE RELATION OF GENIUS TO TASTE

FOR *estimating* beautiful objects, as such, what is required is *taste*; but for fine art, i.e. the *production* of such objects, one needs *genius*.

If we consider genius as the talent for fine art (which the proper signification of the world imports), and if we would analyse it from this point of view into the faculties which must concur to constitute such a talent, it is imperative at the outset accurately to determine the difference between beauty of nature, which it only requires taste to estimate, and beauty of art, which requires genius for its possibility (a possibility to which regard must also be paid in estimating such an object).

A beauty of nature is a *beautiful thing*; beauty of art is a *beautiful representation* of a thing.

To enable me to estimate a beauty of nature, as such, I do not need to be previously possessed of a concept of what sort of a thing the object is intended to be, i.e. I am not obliged to know its material finality (the end), but, rather, in forming an estimate of it apart from any knowledge of the end, the mere form pleases on its own account. If, however, the object is presented as a product of art, and is as such to be declared beautiful, then, seeing that art always presupposes an end in the cause (and its causality), a concept of what the thing is intended to be must first of all be laid at its basis. And, since the agreement of the manifold in a thing with an inner character belonging to it as its end constitutes the perfection of the thing, it follows that in estimating beauty of art the perfection of the thing must be also taken into account—a matter which in estimating a beauty of nature, as beautiful, is quite irrelevant.—It is true that in forming an estimate, especially of animate objects of nature, e.g. of a man or a horse, objective finality is also commonly taken into account with a view to judgment upon their beauty; but then the judgment also ceases to be purely aesthetic, i.e. a mere judgment of taste. Nature is no longer estimated as it appears like art, but rather in so far as it actually *is* art, though superhuman art; and the teleological judgment serves as basis and condition of the aesthetic, and one which the latter must regard. In such a case, where one says, for example, "that is a beautiful woman," what one in fact thinks is only this, that in her form nature excellently portrays the ends present in the female figure. For one has to extend one's view beyond the mere form to a concept, to enable the object to be thought in such manner by means of an aesthetic judgment logically conditioned.

Where fine art evidences its superiority is in the beautiful descriptions it gives of things that in nature would be ugly or displeasing. The Furies, diseases, devastations of war, and the like, can (as evils) be very beautifully described, nay even represented in pictures. One kind of ugliness alone is incapable of being represented conformably to nature without destroying all aesthetic delight, and consequently artistic beauty, namely, that which excites *disgust*. For, as in this strange sensation, which depends purely on the imagination, the object is represented as insisting, as it were, upon our enjoying it, while we still set our face against it, the artificial representation of the object is no longer distinguishable from the nature of the object itself in our sensation, and so it cannot possibly be regarded as beautiful. The art of sculpture, again, since in its products art is almost confused with nature, has excluded from its creations the direct representation of ugly objects, and, instead, only sanctions, for example, the representation of death (in a beautiful genius), or of the warlike spirit (in Mars), by means of an allegory, or attributes which wear a pleasant guise, and so only indirectly, through an interpretation on the part of reason, and not for the pure aesthetic judgment.

So much for the beautiful representation of an object, which is properly only the form of the presentation of a concept, and the means by which the latter is universally communicated. To give this form, however, to the product of fine art, taste merely is required. By this the artist, having practised and corrected his taste by a variety of examples from nature or art, controls his work and, after many, and often laborious, attempts to satisfy taste, finds the form which commends itself to him. Hence this form is not, as it were, a matter of inspiration, or of a free swing of the mental powers, but rather of a slow and even painful process of improvement, directed to making the form adequate to his thought without prejudice to the freedom in the play of those powers.

Taste is, however, merely a critical, not a productive faculty; and what conforms to it is not, merely on that account, a work of fine art. It may belong to useful and mechanical art, of even to science, as a product following definite rules which are capable of being learned and which must be closely followed. But the pleasing form imparted to the work is only the vehicle of communication and a mode, as it were, of execution, in respect of which one remains to a certain extent free, notwithstanding being otherwise tied down to a definite end. So we demand that table appointments, or even a moral dissertation, and, indeed, a sermon, must bear this form of fine art, yet without its appearing *studied*. But one would not call them on this account works of fine art. A poem, a musical composition, a picture-gallery, and so forth, would, however, be placed under this head; and so in a would-be work of fine art we may frequently recognize genius without taste, and in another taste without genius.

§ 49

THE FACULTIES OF THE MIND WHICH CONSTITUTE GENIUS

OF certain products which are expected partly at least, to stand on the footing of fine art, we say they are *soul*less; and this, although we find nothing to censure in them as far as taste goes. A poem may be very pretty and elegant, but is soulless. A narrative has precision and method, but is soulless. A speech on some festive occasion may be good in substance and ornate withal, but may be soulless. Conversation frequently is not devoid of entertainment, but yet soulless. Even of a woman we may well say, she is pretty, affable, and refined, but soulless. Now what do we here mean by "soul"?

"Soul" (*Geist*) in an aesthetical sense, signifies the animating principle in the mind. But that whereby this principle animates the psychic substance (*Seele*)—the material which it employs for that purpose—is that which sets the mental powers into a swing that is final, i.e. into a play which is self-maintaining and which strengthens those powers for such activity.

Now my proposition is that this principle is nothing else than the faculty of presenting *aesthetic ideas.* But, by an aesthetic idea I mean that representation of the imagination which induces much thought, yet without the possibility of any definite thought whatever, i.e. *concept*, being adequate to it, and which language, consequently, can never get quite on level terms with or render completely intelligible. —it is easily seen, that an aesthetic idea is the counterpart (pendant) of a *rational idea*, which, conversely, is a concept, to which no *intuition* (representation of the imagination) can be adequate.

The imagination (as a productive faculty of cognition) is a powerful agent for creating, as it were, a second nature out of the material supplied to it by actual nature. It affords us entertainment where experience proves too commonplace; and we even use it to remodel experience, always following, no doubt, laws that are based on analogy, but still also following principles which have a higher seat in reason (and which are every whit as natural to us as those followed by the understanding in laying hold of empirical nature). By this means we get a sense of our freedom from the law of association (which attaches to the empirical employment of the imagination), with the result that the material can be borrowed by us from nature in accordance with that law, but be worked up by us into something else—namely, what surpasses nature.

Such representations of the imagination may be termed *ideas.* This is partly because they at least strain after something lying out beyond the confines of experience, and so seek to approximate to a presentation of rational concepts (i.e. intellectual ideas), thus giving to these concepts the semblance of an objective reality. But, on the other hand, there is this most important reason, that no concept can be wholly adequate to them as internal intuitions. The poet essays the task of interpreting to sense the rational ideas of invisible beings, the kingdom of the blessed, hell, eternity, creation, &c. Or, again, as to things of which examples occur in experience, e.g. death, envy, and all vices, as also love, fame, and the like, transgressing the limits of experience he attempts with the aid of an imagination which emulates the display of reason in its attainment of a maximum, to body them forth to sense with a completeness of which nature affords no parallel; and it is in fact precisely in the poetic art that the faculty of aesthetic ideas can show itself to full advantage. This faculty, however, regarded solely on its own account, is properly no more than a talent (of the imagination).

If, now, we attach to a concept a representation of the imagination belonging to its presentation, but inducing solely on its own account such a wealth of thought as would never admit of comprehension in a definite concept, and, as a consequence, giving aesthetically an unbounded expansion to the concept itself, then the imagination here displays a creative activity, and it puts the faculty of intellectual ideas (reason) into motion—a motion, at the instance of a representation, towards an extension of thought, that, while germane, no doubt, to the concept of the object, exceeds what can be laid hold of in that representation or clearly expressed.

Those forms which do not constitute the presentation of a given concept itself, but which, as secondary representations of the imagination, express the derivatives connected with it, and its kinship with other concepts, are called (aesthetic) *attributes* of an object, the concept of which, as an idea of reason, cannot be adequately presented. In this way Jupiter's eagle, with the lightning in its claws, is an attribute of the mighty king of heaven, and the peacock of its stately queen. They do not, like *logical attributes,* represent what lies in our concepts of the sublimity and majesty of creation, but rather something else—something that gives the imagination an incentive to spread its flight over a whole host of kindred representations that provoke more thought than admits of expression in a concept determined by words. They furnish an *aesthetic idea,* which serves the above rational idea as a substitute for logical presentation, but with the proper function, however, of animating the mind by opening out for it a prospect into a field of kindred representations stretching beyond its ken. But it is not alone in the arts of painting or sculpture, where the name of attribute is customarily employed, that fine art acts in this way; poetry and rhetoric also derive the soul that animates their works wholly from the aesthetic attributes of the objects—attributes which go hand in hand with the logical, and give the imagination an impetus to bring more thought into play in the matter, though in an undeveloped manner, than allows of being brought within the embrace of a concept, or, therefore, of being definitely formulated in language.—For the sake of brevity I must confine myself to a few examples only. When the great king expresses himself in one of his poems by saying:

Oui, finissons sans trouble, et mourons sans regrets,
En laissant l'Univers comblé de nos bienfaits.
Ainsi l'Astre du jour, au bout de sa carrière,
Répand sur l'horizon une douce lumière,
Et les derniers rayons qu'il darde dans les airs
Sont les derniers soupirs qu'il donne à l'Univers;

he kindles in this way his rational idea of a cosmopolitan sentiment even at the close of life, with the help of an attribute which the imagination (in remembering all the pleasures of a fair summer's day that is over and gone—a memory of which pleasures is suggested by a serene evening) annexes to that representation, and which stirs up a crowd of sensations and secondary representations for which no expression can be found. On the other hand, even an intellectual concept may serve, conversely, as attribute for a representation of sense, and so animate the latter with the idea of the supersensible; but only by the aesthetic factor subjectively attaching to the consciousness of the supersensible being employed for the purpose. So, for example, a certain poet says in his description of a beautiful morning: "The sun arose, as out of virtue rises peace." The consciousness of virtue, even where we put ourselves only in thought in the position of a virtuous man, diffuses in the mind a multitude of sublime and tranquillizing feelings, and gives a boundless outlook into a happy future, such as no expression within the compass of a definite concept completely attains.[43]

In a word, the aesthetic idea is a representation of the imagination, annexed to a given concept, with which, in the free employment of imagination, such a multiplicity of partial representations are bound up, that no expression indicating a definite concept can be found for it—one which on that account allows a concept to be supplemented in thought by much that is indefinable in words, and the feeling of which quickens the cognitive faculties, and with language, as a mere thing of the letter, binds up the spirit (soul) also.

The mental powers whose union in a certain relation constitutes *genius* are imagination and understanding. Now, since the imagination, in its employment on behalf of cognition, is subjected to the constraint of the understanding and the restriction of having to be conformable to the concept of belonging thereto, whereas aesthetically it is free to furnish of its own accord, over and above that agreement with the concept, a wealth of undeveloped material for the understanding, to which the latter paid no regard in its concept, but which it can make use of, not so much objectively for cognition, as subjectively for quickening the cognitive faculties, and hence also indirectly for cognitions, it may be seen that genius properly consists in the happy relation, which science cannot teach nor industry learn, enabling one to find out ideas for a given concept, and, besides, to hit upon the *expression* for them—the expression by means of which the subjective mental condition induced by the ideas as the concomitant of a concept may be communicated to others. This latter talent is properly that which is termed soul. For to get an expression for what is indefinable in the mental state accompanying a particular representation and to make it universally communicable—be the expression in language or painting or statuary—is a thing requiring a faculty for laying hold of the rapid and transient play of the imagination, and for unifying it in a concept (which for that very reason is original, and reveals a new rule which could not have been inferred from any preceding principles or examples) that admits of communication without any constraint of rules.

If, after this analysis, we cast a glance back upon the above definition of what is called *genius*, we find: *First*, that it is a talent for art—not one for science, in which clearly known rules must take the lead and determine the procedure. *Secondly*, being a talent in the line of art, it presupposes a definite concept of the product—as its end. Hence it presupposes understanding, but, in addition, a representation, indefinite though it be, of the material, i.e. of the intuition, required for the presentation of that concept, and so a relation of the imagination to the understanding. *Thirdly*, it displays itself, not so much in the working out of the projected end in the presentation of a definite concept, as rather in the portrayal, or expression of *aesthetic* ideas containing a wealth of material for effecting that intention. Consequently the imagination is represented by it in its freedom from all guidance of rules, but still as final for the presentation of the given concept. *Fourthly*, and lastly, the unsought and undesigned subjective finality in the free harmonizing of the imagination with the understanding's conformity to law presupposes a proportion and

[43] Perhaps there has never been a more sublime utterance, or a thought more sublimely expressed, than the well-known inscription upon the Temple of *Isis* (Mother *Nature*): "I am all that is, and that was, and that shall be, and no mortal hath raised the veil from before my face." *Segner* made use of this idea in a suggestive vignette on the frontispiece of his Natural Philosophy, in order to inspire his pupil at the threshold of that temple into which he was about to lead him, with such a holy awe as would dispose his mind to serious attention.

accord between these faculties such as cannot be brought about by any observance of rules, whether of science or mechanical imitation, but can only be produced by the nature of the individual.

Genius, according to these presuppositions, is the exemplary originality of the natural endowments of an individual in the *free* employment of his cognitive faculties. On this showing, the product of genius (in respect of so much in this product as is attributable to genius, and not to possible learning or academic instruction,) is an example, not for imitation (for that would mean the loss of the element of genius, and just the very soul of the work), but to be followed by another genius—one whom it arouses to a sense of his own originality in putting freedom from the constraint of rules so into force in his art, that for art itself a new rule is won—which is what shows a talent to be exemplary. Yet, since the genius is one of nature's elect—a type that must be regarded as but a rare phenomenon—for other clever minds his example gives rise to a school, that is to say a methodical instruction according to rules, collected, so far as the circumstances admit, from such products of genius and their peculiarities. And, to that extent, fine art is for such persons a matter of imitation, for which nature, through the medium of a genius, gave the rule.

But this imitation becomes *aping* when the pupil *copies* everything down to the deformities which the genius only of necessity suffered to remain, because they could hardly be removed without loss of force to the idea. This courage has merit only in the case of a genius. A certain *boldness* of expression, and, in general, many a deviation from the common rule becomes him well, but in no sense is it a thing worthy of imitation. On the contrary it remains all through intrinsically a blemish, which one is bound to try to remove, but for which the genius is, as it were, allowed to plead a privilege, on the ground that a scrupulous carefulness would spoil what is inimitable in the impetuous ardour of his soul. *Mannerism* is another kind of aping—an aping of *peculiarity* (originality) in general, for the sake of removing oneself as far as possible from imitators, while the talent requisite to enable one to be at the same time *exemplary* is absent.—There are, in fact, two modes (*modi*) in general of arranging one's thoughts for utterance. The one is called a *manner* (*modus aestheticus*), the other a *method* (*modus logicus*). The distinction between them is this: the former possesses no standard other than the *feeling* of unity in the presentation, whereas the latter here follows definite *principles*. As a consequence the former is alone admissible for fine art. It is only, however, where the manner of carrying the idea into execution in a product of art is *aimed at* singularity of being made appropriate to the idea, that *mannerism* is properly ascribed to such a product. The ostentatious (*précieux*), forced, and affected styles, intended to mark one out from the common herd (though soul is wanting), resemble the behaviour of a man who, as we say, hears himself talk, or who stands and moves about as if he were on a stage to be gaped at—action which invariably betrays a tyro.

§ 50

THE COMBINATION OF TASTE AND GENIUS IN PRODUCTS OF FINE ART

To ask whether more stress should be laid in matters of fine art upon the presence of genius or upon that of taste, is equivalent to asking whether more turns upon imagination or upon judgment. Now, imagination rather entitles an art to be called an *inspired* (*geistreiche*) than a *fine* art. It is only in respect of judgment that the name of fine art is deserved. Hence it follows that judgment, being the indispensable condition (*condito sine qua non*), is at least what one must look to as of capital importance in forming an estimate of art as fine art. So far as beauty is concerned, to be fertile and original in ideas is not such an imperative requirement as it is that the imagination in its freedom should be in accordance with the understanding's conformity to law. For in lawless freedom imagination, with all its wealth, produces nothing but nonsense; the power of judgment, on the other hand, is the faculty that makes it consonant with understanding.

Taste, like judgment in general, is the discipline (or corrective) of genius. It severely clips its wings, and makes it orderly or polished; but at the same time it gives it guidance, directing and controlling its flight, so that it may preserve its character of finality. It introduces a clearness and order into the plenitude of thought, and in so doing gives stability to the ideas, and qualifies them at once for permanent and universal approval, for being followed by others, and for a continually progressive culture. And so, where the interests of both these qualities clash in a product, and there has to be a sacrifice of something, then it should rather be on the side of genius; and judgment, which in matters of fine art bases its decision on its own proper principles, will more readily endure an abatement of the freedom and wealth of the imagination, than that the understanding should be compromised.

The requisites for fine art are, therefore, *imagination, understanding, soul,* and *taste.*[44]

[44] The first three faculties are first *brought into union* by means of the fourth. *Hume,* in his history, informs the English that although they are second in their works to no other people in the world in respect of the evidences they afford of the three first qualities *separately* considered, still in what unites them they must yield to their neighbours, the French.

PART SIX

SOME POST-KANTIAN AESTHETICIANS

Chapter 11

Schiller, Hegel, Schopenhauer and Nietzsche

As we shall observe, the influence of Kant's aesthetic theory is evident throughout the writings of Hegel, Schiller, Schopenhauer and, derivatively, in Nietzsche's Schopenhauerian and unsystematic but brilliant statements concerning art and creativity. We shall indicate some of the more specific points made by Kant which led his successors to elaborate upon his speculation in Aesthetics and the Philosophy of Fine Art. It should be noted, however, that despite marked divergences in their interpretations of Kantian aesthetic theory, the aestheticians to whom we now turn concentrated considerable attention upon the central issue of freedom and creativity. It might be said, indeed, that in the writings of these late eighteenth and nineteenth century philosophers the ancient and conflicting interpretations of freedom as the creative power to produce what is original and freedom as the creative power to produce what is intelligible moved towards the reconciliation presaged in Kant's theory of taste and of genius. In any case, it is clear that the abstract analogy of the artist to God becomes less evident in the naturalization of the theory of human freedom as creativity in the world of art.

This naturalization or implementation of freedom to Aesthetics and to the arts takes a variety of forms in the philosophies of the writers with whom we are immediately concerned. For Schiller, the experience of art is free play and, ultimately, free play of the imagination. More significantly, Schiller asserts human freedom in the form of creativity with the important statement that beauty is our second creator. For both Hegel and Schopenhauer, art is freed from relations to external and non-aesthetic subjects and ends. For Schopenhauer, art frees men from service to the will and, more specifically, from the province in which the principle of sufficient reason operates. For Hegel, the Philosophy of Art is limited to the analysis of fine art, rather than of nature. Hegel takes this step because fine art is free art, which mind generates out of itself and so creates.

It is important to note that for Hegel and Schopenhauer the issue of judgment and criticism assumes importance, with a consequent problem for the conception of artistic creativity and freedom. For Kant, the judgment of taste is disinterested and free and so it is for Hegel and Schopenhauer. But for Kant, taste is not creative, whereas genius is. For Hegel, the genius is wholly rational and the fine arts may be classified not only in terms of art-stages but in terms of the specific arts as well. For

Schopenhauer, the arts may be classified rationally, but it is noticeable that music is the direct expression of the Will and escapes the confines of language. It is upon this aspect of Schopenhauer's Philosophy of Art that Nietzsche seizes, arguing that valuing is creating. And this leads, as we shall observe in the next chapter, to the assertion by Croce that the work of art as image is beyond criticism. This is a working out of the implication in Kant's Aesthetic that the core of the subject is taste, not criticism. Moreover, integral to Croce's view is the identification of genius and taste, an identification that raises both artistic creation and aesthetic experience to the status of inspired creativity.

We turn now to a more detailed introduction to the Post-Kantian aestheticians and their relation to Kant.

The imprints of Kant's philosophy of taste in the *Critique of Judgment* are as deeply inscribed on aesthetic theory in the nineteenth century as were those of Plato's and Aristotle's philosophies of art upon Hellenist, Mediaeval, and Renaissance speculation. Nowhere is the Kantian influence more evident than in the writings upon art and the arts in Friedrich Schiller's *On the Aesthetic Education of Man*, G. W. F. Hegel's *The Philosophy of Fine Art*, and in the third part of Arthur Schopenhauer's *The World as Will and Idea*. In each instance, the Kantian assumption that the experience of fine art is disinterested is basic to an elaboration of Kant's abstract and somewhat negative theory in the rich world of fine art and natural beauty. Schiller's *Letters* manifest at every turn the riches of a poet's mind. Hegel enunciates one of the most profoundly influential theories of the classification of arts and one of the classic theories of tragedy. Schopenhauer offers to combine Platonic and Kantian philosophies in art and in the course of his argument formulates a theory of music that has had a considerable vogue. In spite of an identical source in Kant's speculation, each philosopher of art has remained an individual in his writing off of aesthetic experience and the evaluation of art and fine art. In the writings of Friedrich Nietzsche the Kantian influence is less direct and, indeed, it is in some instances negative. Nietzsche is radically influenced by Schopenhauer, but his own contribution lies principally in the unique conceptions of valuing and in his interpretation of tragedy in terms of conflict between Apollonian and Dionysian forces.

In this Introduction to some of the Post-Kantian philosophers of art, we begin in each instance with the indebtedness to Kant, as well as the grounds for criticism that are expressed. For Schiller and Hegel, the task is made easier by turning to Hegel's comments on Schiller's aesthetic writings. Hegel takes care to show how Schiller moved beyond Kant in aesthetic theory and in so doing suggests much concerning his own debt to Kant and the differences between his own theory and the critical philosophy. We quote the passage, but it is well to note what for Hegel is the importance of the Kantian philosophy as part of the "Historical Deduction of the True Idea of Art in Modern Philosophy." [1] Hegel argues that *The Critique of Judgement* is "instructive and remarkable." He calls attention to the "free play of the understanding and of the imagination," as well as the freedom grounded on the relation of these faculties in the appetitive. Hegel provides a concise summary of Kant's judgment of taste—in his own terminology. He then proceeds to criticism, but holds that the criticism he offers provides the starting-point for "the true conception of artistic beauty." The defects he finds at once in the abstractness of Kant's system and in the fact that Kant's theory states the aesthetic problem primarily in negative terms.

In the light of this, Hegel suggests that "the artistic sense of a profound, and, at the

[1] See below, pp. 451 et seq. for Hegel's philosophy of fine art.

same time, philosophic mind was beforehand with philosophy as such in the reconciliation of extremes." The reference is to Schiller, the poet with "the profound and philosophic mind." As Hegel sees it, Kant's critique is the starting-point for "the true conception of the beauty of art." Such a conception, however, could only make itself effective "as the higher comprehension of the true union of necessity and freedom, particular and universal, sensuous and rational, and by overcoming the defects still latent in the previous standpoint." Hegel believes that Schiller broke through the Kantian subjectivity and abstractness of thought, and commends the poet for "having ventured the attempt to pass beyond the same by comprehending in thought the principles of unity and reconciliation as the truth, and giving artistic realization to that truth. . . ."

Schopenhauer accepts the Kantian assumption that beauty is neither scientific nor the object of desire. For the author of *The World as Will and Idea,* however, these are negative statements and it is, in his view, necessary to frame a positive definition of beauty. "Beauty" for Schopenhauer, "comes from pure pleasure of contemplation." [2] Aesthetic experience is, in fact, the only form of disinterested contemplation, which is a kind of foreshadowing of freedom from the will to live. Such freedom, essentially an escape from the lust of living, is present in every moment of aesthetic contemplation. "Will to live" is at once the root of things and the explanation of the world. It is irrational and nonmoral. Nothing good can come out of the will to live except escape from it. Schopenhauer's is basically a theory of "art for art's sake" intended to justify such an escape. Peace comes in pure contemplation.[3] Everything, Schopenhauer implies, may be beautiful, if only we regard it in the proper way, and he suggests, moreover, that what makes things beautiful in fact is something in them akin to our own heart and will and being.

Let us now turn to the specific aesthetic theories of these post-Kantian philosophers and observe how each deals with such classic problems in Philosophy of Art as creativity, inspiration, play-theory, the work of art, the classification of the arts, the genius, and aesthetic experience. Let us first turn to Schiller.

Kant is the immediate source of Schiller's [4] theory that art is play; Plato is its more remote ancestor. The Kantian influence is evident not only in the assumption that both play and artistic activity are disinterested but in more specific suggestions as well. Kant writes of the judgment of taste in terms of the free interplay of the faculties.[5] He had written that art, compared to labor, may be considered as play. He had remarked upon the changing free play of sensations and had in fact classified the kinds of play.[6] He had written that many of the new school believe that the best way to promote a free art is to sweep away all restraints and convert it from labor into mere play.

Plato, whose dialogues are Schiller's other principal source, is more sophisticated than is Kant in his theory of play. He relates it to art and discusses play itself as propaedeutic to more serious activities. As for the first, play is an activity specifically associated with discipline of pleasure and pain,[7] and in its primitive manifestations is common to man and animals: ". . . The young of all creatures cannot be quiet in their bodies or in their voices; they are always wanting to move and cry out; some leaping and skipping, and overflowing with

[2] *The World as Will and Idea,* 34, 36. See below, pp. 508, 509. For Schopenhauer's life see below, p. 507.

[3] *Ibid.,* 38; below, pp. 515 et seq.

[4] Friedrich Schiller, *On the Aesthetic Education of Man* in a Series of Letters translated by Reginald Snell. Yale University Press, New Haven, Conn., 1954. For Schiller's life, see below, p. 434.

[5] *Critique of Judgement,* Sect. 9. See above, pp. 368 et seq.

[6] *Ibid.,* Sect. 54. Compare Sect. 43, 44. See above, pp. 410 et seq.

[7] Plato, *Laws* 653–4. See above, pp. 119 et seq.

sportiveness and delight at something, others uttering all sorts of cries. . . ." Plato writes in detail of play as preparation for serious activity:[8]

> According to my view, any one who would be good at anything must practise that thing from his youth upwards, both in sport and earnest, in its several branches: for example, he who is to be a good builder, should play at building children's houses; he who is to be a good husbandman, at tilling the ground; and those who have the care of their education should provide them when young with mimic tools. They should learn beforehand the knowledge which they will afterwards require for their art. For example, the future carpenter should learn to measure or apply the line in play; and the future warrior should learn riding, or some other exercise, for amusement . . . The most important part of education is right training in the nursery. The soul of the child in his play should be guided to the love of that sort of excellence in which when he grows up to manhood he will have to be perfected. . . .

It would appear that the higher forms of activities and of such arts as dancing and music have their origin in the aimless instinct for movement and sound. The actual emergence of the arts presupposes, however, a capacity discoverable only in man. To man is possible the pleasurable sense of rhythm and harmony. All other creatures are devoid of any perception of the various kinds of order or disorder in movement.

For Schiller, similarly, play rests upon the formal instinct (*Formtrieb*) and the sensuous instinct (*Stofftrieb*) but when it emerges as *Spieltrieb*, the ideal union of the two instincts, it is regarded by the poet as freedom in phenomenal appearance. Beauty becomes for Schiller "our second Creator." Man need not submit to the extreme abstracting power of the instinct for form, nor to the compulsions to passion implicit in the drive of the instinct for sensuousness. "The sense impulse excludes from its subject all spontaneity and freedom, the form impulse excludes all dependence, all passivity."[9] Man is neither exclusively matter nor exclusively spirit; Beauty—"the consummation of his humanity"—is neither mere life nor mere form. The common object of both impulses of sense and form is beauty, and this means the play impulse. Consequently, in his famous phrase,[10] Schiller concludes that man only plays when in the full sense of the word he is a man, and he is only wholly man when he is playing. Exclusive rationality divests appearance of its richness, exclusive sensuality deprives experience of its reality. Playful experience, which is aesthetic experience, mediates in beauty between reason and feeling. Man shall *only play* with Beauty, and with *Beauty* he *shall only play.*[11] In aesthetic experience men enjoy simultaneously the consciousness of freedom and the feeling of existence. In play, perception receives and form produces its object without conflict.

In play, i.e., in aesthetic experience, man is freed from serious nonaesthetic ends. It is notable, however, that in the most important examination of freedom in Schiller's *Letters,* the brunt is borne not so much by play or the play-impulse but by the imagination.[12] Schiller abandons the strict identification of all art with play and treats as aesthetic objects those that appeal to a cultured imagination.[13] In aesthetic experience, imagination has its origin in play, play which is propaedeutic but which ultimately is the ground for aesthetic imagination. The

[8] *Ibid.,* 643 B et seq. See above, pp. 123 et seq.

[9] Schiller, *On the Aesthetic Education of Man,* Letter 14.

[10] *Ibid.,* Letter 15. See below, p. 436.

[11] *Ibid.,* Letter 15. See below, p. 436.

[12] *See* Letter 27, below, pp. 446 et seq., particularly p. 447.

[13] The issue becomes one of freedom in imagination or "aesthetic play." In this developed stage, "Beauty for her own sake" becomes the object of the freer play-impulse and "even weapons may now be objects not simply of terror but also of delight. . . ." Ibid., p. 448.

correlative to the play-impulse may be diverse and it may simulate serious activity but in fact once we speak of aesthetic "image" or "living shape"[14] it becomes the object of Schiller's argument. Schiller eventually holds that the imagination has its own freedom of play, in which there is an "inherent power and freedom without reference to form."[15]

As we turn from Schiller's brilliant theory of art as play to Hegel's *The Philosophy of Fine Art,* we leave the realm of Philosophical poetry for that of one of the most complex and, indeed, profound studies of nature, art and fine art. It would be as difficult to measure accurately Hegel's influence on art history or art theory as it would be to measure the influence of Platonism or Aristotelianism. One finds it in Iconology, in the theory of historians of art such as Wölfflin, and in innumerable theories of tragedy. Max Schasler said of Hegel's aesthetic theory that it was not only the first complete system of a Philosophy of Art but that "by the profound vitality of its conception, by the richness and variety of the ideas contained, superseding whatever Hegel's predecessors and contemporaries had attempted, but which until the present, in spite of all that has been accomplished to complete it and better to distribute its major portions, it has not yet been superseded."

Hegel strikes out beyond the Kantian foundations from which he begins, precisely as he goes beyond the implications of Schiller's approach to the Philosophy of Art. His initial aim is to overcome the formalism and negativism of Kant's Aesthetic, precisely as he wants to systematize the Philosophy of Fine Art implicit in Schiller's *Letters*. His own speculation on fine art is an integral part of his philosophy: "What is rational is real and what is real is rational. . . . Nothing is real except the idea." The rational is real and is synonymous with the idea because "in realizing itself it passes into external existence. It thus appears in an endless wealth of forms, figures and phenomena. . . . The conscious identity of form and content is the philosophical idea. . . ."

Nowhere in Hegel's system more than in the analysis of art is it evident how profoundly this philosopher believes that "If a theory transgresses its time, and builds up a world as it ought to be, it has an existence merely in the unstable element of opinion." Nature and the arts are examined in *The Philosophy of Fine Art* as manifestations of *Geist* or Spirit. Kant had limited the objects of the judgment of taste to natural forms of the most abstract kind and to the products of genius, which are, in fact, scarcely richer in content than are the natural forms. Hegel's aesthetic theory opens the subject to make possible the inclusion of every phase of natural beauty and fine art. Kant goes so far as to eliminate objects and events regarded by many writers in the eighteenth century as sublime. For Hegel, on the other hand, the nature of the work of art is not limited by the failure of the artist to produce what is beautiful for all men; rather, Hegel considers works of art to be relative to men's attainments in technique and the grasp they attain of the Idea in their given culture. Unlike Schiller, whose Philosophy of Art is at least ostensibly a play-theory, although in fact it attributes to art the most serious purposes, Hegel examines art as a most serious activity and as a mode of the realization of the truth.

We may take in order[16] Hegel's writings on genius, on the medium of art, the relation of art to the feelings, the classification of the arts, and the theory of tragedy.

[14] *Ibid.,* Letter 15. See below, pp. 436 et seq. The object of the form impulse is shape, that of the sense-impulse is life. For Schiller, the object of the play-impulse is "living-shape."

[15] Schiller calls it a "new force." There is "a leap to aesthetic play," with its *"free sequence of images"* which attain a *"free form."* (Letter 27. See below, p. 447).

[16] See below, pp. 451 et seq. for a brief life of Hegel and for selections from his writings.

Hegel's genius[17] is integral to the tradition of the artist free under rules. His interpretation derives, ultimately, from the rational tradition of art which has its source in the analogy of the fine artist to God as an artisan. Hegel specifically criticizes the notion of the genius as one with "a mind endowed with wholly peculiar gifts" and with nothing more to do than give free play to that gift. Hegel believes that artistic excellence is not a specific force of nature, and he inveighs against the notion that artistic production is a state of inspiration. There is, he grants, a natural talent in the artist, but, it requires thought and cultivation, as well as "practice and skill in producing." "Goethe's and Schiller's first productions," he writes, "are of an immaturity, and even of a rudeness and barbarism, that are absolutely terrifying." Abandoning the critical mood, Hegel states his own position concerning the genius clearly:[18] ". . . True originality is . . . identical with true objectivity."

The argument that the original genius is original in his objectivity leads to the main contention of *The Philosophy of Fine Art,* namely, that true artistic freedom consists in the objectification of imagination in suitable media and its relation by technical means to the end of art.[19] ". . . In a kind of inspired state personal to the artist" the particular subject matter, which is essentially rational, is "seized hold of" and the "inspired state . . . reclothes the same as from within the artist himself. . . ."

Hegel maintains, in sharp contrast to Kant and in a view intended both to show the appeal of art to the feelings and imagination and to widen the boundaries of the subject of fine art, that the artist works in sensuous media. Nonetheless he argues that both in the making and in the experiencing of art in such media there is a freeing from the sunkenness of feeling.[20] More than that, however, spirit is objectified in the sensuous in art or, to put it otherwise, the life of *spirit* comes to dwell in it under sensuous guise. The artist's creative imagination is that of "a great mind and a big heart; it is the grasp and excogitation of ideas and shapes, and, in fact, nothing less than this grasp of the profoundest and most embracing human interests in the wholly definite presentation of imagery borrowed from objective experience."

For Hegel, the work of art is not merely a useful instrument. The function of art is to reveal truth under the mode of art's sensuous or material configuration. But art, as revelatory of truth in sensuous media, displays truth as spirit in sensuous guise in radically different ways and in considerably divergent degrees of adequacy. In Hegel's highly complex Philosophy of Art, the detail and comprehensiveness of his theory make it difficult to generalize concerning his method. It is perhaps safe to say, however, that art becomes a symbol not only of Spirit but of the culture in which Spirit manifests itself in more or less adequate ways in sensuous media. One important point is that in general ". . . the defects of a work of art are not to be regarded simply as always due, for instance to individual unskilfulness. *Defectiveness of form* arises from *defectiveness of content.*" The content is defective because the Idea is not clearly objectified. There are, for Hegel, three stages of art: Symbolical, Classical, and Romantic.[21] They would appear to be stages basic to any criticism or evaluation of art, but they are also stages in the objectification of Spirit in that manifestation or objectification of it called Art. Such objectification is examined by Hegel in terms of a double process. As conceptual progress is made, there occurs an

[17] See below, p. 428 and p. 459. Cf. below, p. 456.

[18] *The Philosophy of Fine Art,* I. p. 400, translation by F. P. B. Osmaston, London, G. Bell and Sons, 1920. Contrast Hegel's interpretation with above, pp. 45 et seq., and 83 et seq., and below, Chapt. II.

[19] *Ibid.,* p. 391.

[20] See below, pp. 470 et seq. Cf. pp. 458 et seq.

[21] See below, pp. 492 et seq.

evolution of art from Symbolical, through Classical, to Romantic. Within each of these stages of the evolution of Art, a single art or certain arts best manifest Spirit in the stage. Most characteristically, architecture is primarily symbolical, sculpture classical, painting, poetry, and music romantic. In the Symbolical stage, the objectification in sensuous media of Spirit in a culture occurs in such symbols of power as the Pyramids. Tremendous size is conceived as a sign for temporal power, as in a different culture but the same art-stage power is conceived in terms of Siva's many arms. In the Symbolical stage, the Idea is both obscure and ill-understood. Both the content and form of art are defective and the material cannot embody the Idea. Hegel believes that the symbol is some form of external existence, immediately presented to the senses. The perceiver is unable to rest content in the image made by the artist, because a certain defect of meaning indicates the defect in the symbol. Hegel argues that the sublime results because the Idea is united to *measureless dimension*, i.e., there is the expression of the infinite with no adequate phenomena to fit the representation.

In the Classical stage of art, Idea and technique are co-ordinated in the perfection of Greek sculpture of the human figure. Form and content are suited to each other. Hegel believes that only the human form is capable of revealing adequately the spiritual in sensuous guise. Classical art reveals no more than this and consequently content and form are adequate to each other. Hegel argues, however, that the conception of deity portrayed in sculpture is too anthropomorphic and narrow fully to serve men's spiritual needs. There is no conflict portrayed, for on Hegel's view sculpture shows men in repose. The Classical stage is that of beauty, but the Gods portrayed do not appeal to men's hearts and minds.

In Romantic art, Hegel provides increasing evidence of his thesis that Spirit may not be adequately objectified in sensuous media. The true principle of Romantic art is inventive and the function of works of art is to make the consciousness of the divine mind visible to the subject of consciousness. In contrast to Classical art, Romantic art expresses itself throughout the entire range of humanity, and the artist's concern is not solely with the production of formal beauty. Rather, he is interested in the ordinary sphere of human life and can produce what is ugly in art and, indeed, can adopt any subject matter to his art. His task is to portray the human as the senses perceive it. For Hegel, in the Romantic stage, Spirit makes itself at home in an external world where one object is like another.

In the Romantic stage, there is an increase of interest in individuality, in adventure, in chivalry, in martyrdom. But with the development of the Romantic stage, the necessity for any particular form to embody the content disappears. "No content, no form is any longer identical directly with the inmost soul of the artist." The artist stands supreme over the material and over his creations and chooses what he will, without restriction. Spirit transcends sensuous form in the Romantic stage. Painting, music, and poetry best express the Romantic stage but they are in fact the forecourt to Spirit as it transcends art to the realms of Religion and Philosophy.

The power and influence of Hegel's theory of tragedy is comparable to the power and influence of Aristotle's theory of tragedy.[22] To put the matter concisely, it may be said that Hegel is rather little concerned with the implications of Dante's suggestion [23] that "Tragedy in its beginning is admirable and quiet, in its ending or catastrophe foul and horrible. . . ." Nor is he particularly interested in tragedy as a conflict of good and evil. The core of his theory is that tragedy is in fact the conflict of goods

[22] For Aristotle, see above, pp. 169 et seq. For Hegel, see below, pp. 430 et seq. Compare Plato, above, pp. 109 et seq., 125 et seq.

[23] For Dante, see above, pp. 249–50.

at different levels. For him, *Antigone* is the tragedy *par excellence*—"the supreme and absolute example of tragedy." *Antigone* is among the "immortal productions of moral understanding and comprehension," which Hegel believes classical tragedy to be. In it, family love, which belongs to the inner life and to feeling, comes into conflict with the law of the state. Creon, the king, is not a tyrant but a moral power, and he is not in the wrong. For Antigone, however, the ethical principle is that of love for her brother and this exercises equal authority with the law. The conflict arises because Antigone's brother has proved to be an enemy of the state by bringing an army against Thebes. Creon forbids the burial of the brother's corpse; Antigone finds it impossible to leave her brother's corpse as prey to carrion birds. She violates Creon's decree.

Hegel maintains that each side in tragedy realizes only one side of the moral powers involved. Eternal justice opposes both claims and the principal cause of the tragedy is that good is pitted against good. "It is only the one-sidedness in their claims which justice comes forward to oppose."

One of the most revealing studies in Arthur Schopenhauer's *The World as Will and Idea* is likewise aimed at explaining tragedy. No less significant for an understanding of his Aesthetics and its relation to his metaphysical theory is his writing on music. What both tragedy and music tell us is the relation of art to the Will.[24] Tragedy, Schopenhauer writes, "is to be regarded, and is recognized as the summit of poetical art. . . ." It is also regarded by him as making both tragic hero and spectators at the drama aware of the quieting effect on the Will, an effect which produces resignation and surrender "not merely of life, but of the very will to live." Music, for Schopenhauer, differs from the other arts. Whereas the latter are interpreted in terms of Platonic ideas, music is the direct expression of the Will. Music ". . . never expresses the phenomenon, but only the inner nature, the in-itself of all phenomena, the will itself."

What Schopenhauer says concerning tragedy and music is to be understood in terms of an Aesthetic theory which is essentially one of the experience of art as an escape from life, a theory which has its foundations not only in Kant's Aesthetic but in Plato's philosophy of ideas and which, in the course of development, touches upon the problem of genius.

Schopenhauer, as we have seen, accepted Kant's assumption that beauty is not the object of desire. He is not satisfied, however, with such merely negative criteria. "Beauty," he believes,[25] "comes from pure pleasure of contemplation" and aesthetic experience is the only form of disinterested contemplation. This statement can best be understood by realizing that for Schopenhauer the "will to live" is the root of things and the explanation of the world. The will is irrational and nonmoral. Reason and morality are merely chance products of the will.[26] There is, however, not only Will but Idea. The archetype expresses itself in many individuals. The release from the world of Will occurs when the subject ceases to be mere individual and becomes pure will-less subject of knowledge. He contemplates and no longer seeks relations and so separates an object from other objects. He replaces *what* for where and *when* and is a creature of perception alone. He thus loses himself in the object of his contemplation and in this contemplation experiences one single sensuous picture. Freed from particularity, he is able to contemplate the ideal.

The importance of art as contemplative experience and as an escape from Will is everywhere evident in Schopenhauer's writing.

[24] For a brief life of Schopenhauer and for selections from his writings, see below, pp. 507 et seq.

[25] Arthur Schopenhauer, *The World as Will and Idea,* Book III, Sects. 34, 36. See below, pp. 508 et seq., 509 et seq.

[26] *Ibid.,* Sect. 38. See below, pp. 515 et seq.

The Will manifests itself in unsatisfied desire, yearning, and endless striving. "Every goal attained is merely the starting point of a new race and so on to infinity." [27] "Everywhere in nature we see combat, struggle and varying fortunes of war. . . . The universal struggle is most readily seen in the animal world which lives on the vegetable world, and in which every animal becomes the prey of another. . . . Thus the will to live forever devours itself."

The will, as ultimate reality, objectifies itself at various levels of development, and these levels are Platonic ideas or types. The ideas are a fixed pattern, glimpsed only by aesthetic contemplation. The Will is insatiable and cruel. Moral reason is too weak to conquer will. Man, however, not only desires and wills; he also knows. All abstract knowledge is, however, at the service of the will. Only disinterested knowledge, aesthetic contemplation, is free of will, for it has no ultimate aim or purpose, either in space or time, in phenomena, or in such essential reality as music:

> If ceasing to consider the when, why, and whither of things we concentrate ourselves on the what, not allowing abstract thought with its concepts to possess our consciousness, but sinking ourselves wholly in perception of the object; then we escape our individuality and will, and continue to exist only in the pure mirror of the object, with which we become identified; so that what is known is no longer the particular thing, but the idea, and the knower is no longer an individual but the pure knowing subject.

The disposition to contemplate is, Schopenhauer says, "facilitated by the attractiveness of natural objects for our contemplation." The issue for science is that it "follows the stream of reason and consequence, and with each attainment sees further, and never attains a satisfying goal. . . ." Art, on the contrary, "is always at its goal."

Art as contemplative knowledge is direct, intuitive, and immediate experience. To subject it to analysis is to distort it. For Schopenhauer, the maker of such art is the genius, who has direct and immediate knowledge. He is precocious. Perhaps most significantly, he is like the madman. For the madman "has a true knowledge of what is actually present, and also of certain particulars of the past, but . . . he mistakes the connection, the relations, and therefore falls into error and talks nonsense. . . ." The genius "also leaves out of sight the knowledge of the connection of things, since he neglects that knowledge of relations which conforms to the principle of sufficient reason." Genius, for Schopenhauer, "is the power of leaving one's interest, wishes, and aims entirely out of sight, then of entirely recovering one's personality for a time, so as to remain *pure knowing subject* . . . for a sufficient length of time, and with sufficient consciousness to enable one to reproduce by deliberate art what has thus been apprehended." The genius, however, must have not only a capacity for deliberate art, he must also have the essential element, imagination. The objects of genius are the eternal ideas. Perception is not sufficient for genius —his imagination "must extend his horizon far beyond the limits of his actual personal existence . . . and so to let almost all scenes of life pass before him in his own consciousness." Schopenhauer concludes that extraordinary strength of imagination is a necessary condition for genius.

As we turn from the abstract to the highest form of art man can produce, we encounter tragedy. It is difficult to determine precisely what might be gained by adopting Schopenhauer's theory of tragedy.[28] The repose gained by realizing the power of the will in the experience of this "highest form of poetry" scarcely accounts for the value of the experience itself.

[27] *Ibid.*, Sect. 29.

[28] See below, pp. 517 et seq. for Schopenhauer on tragedy and music. For contrasting theories of tragedy, see above, p. 250. See also, below, Nietzsche, p. 527.

Nor is it clear precisely how music as the direct expression of the will—the will made audible—is compatible with the remainder of Schopenhauer's argument. There is, however, in that theory something perhaps more important than inconsistency. Music is not imitative but expressive, and it would appear indeed that the effect of music is to create in the hearer a creativity of the imagination: ". . . Our imagination is . . . easily excited by music, and now seeks to give form to that invisible yet actively moving spirit-world which moves us directly, and clothes it with flesh and blood, *i.e.* to embody it in an analogous example. . . ."

We may proceed immediately from Schopenhauer's theory of art as an escape from the driving force of the Will to Friedrich Nietzsche's brilliant, if unsystematic writings upon art.[29] As is well known, Nietzsche once followed Schopenhauer—as he followed Wagner—in his approach to Philosophy of Art and no doubt the traces of his discipleship are of interest. But of primary significance in Nietzsche's writings is the individual interpretation of artistic creativity, expressed in his theory of genius, in his description of his own inspired state in producing, and in the pronounced difference between his own theory of the relation of the dithyramb to tragedy and that formulated by Aristotle.

We may best begin with Nietzsche's clear conception of what is implied in Schopenhauer's assertion that music, in contrast to the other arts, is the direct expression of the Will. What Nietzsche says is implicit in Plato's theory of the inspired artist,[30] as well as Kant's assertion [31] that there remains something ineffable in the fine arts. "Only in so far as the genius in the act of artistic production coalesces with this primordial artist of the world does he catch a glimpse of the eternal essence of art." The inference is drawn immedately: "By no means is it possible for language adequately to render the cosmic symbolism of music for the very reason that music . . . symbolizes a sphere which is above all appearance and beyond all phenomena." Nietzsche generalizes the inference in a view that is basic to Croce's argument [32] that all classifications of the arts are meaningless: For Nietzsche, all knowledge of art is "basically illusory."

In a sense, artistic creativity evades intelligibility as linguistic classification. This also holds for the process of artistic productivity, which Nietzsche believes is subjective to the degree that he describes it as beyond choice and volition, that is, free of rules and wholly subjective:[33] ". . . A thought suddenly flashes up like lightning, it comes without necessity, without faltering—I have never had any choice in the matter. . . . Everything happens quite involuntarily, as if in a tempestuous outburst of freedom. . . ."

It is important to observe that while Nietzsche—like Schopenhauer—argues that language and therefore classification do not penetrate to the essence of music, what they suggest runs counter to what Hegel writes concerning that particular art but not counter to all criticism. Hegel [34] holds that music may be classified because it "has within itself, like architecture, a relation of quantity, conformable to the understanding. . . ." Nietzsche is far from denying, however, the possibility of classifying arts, and to a brief statement concerning his conception of Dionysian and Apollonian arts we shall shortly come. But what is of immediate interest is that in brilliant insight into the grounds for aesthetic criticism, Nietzsche asserts [35] that "Valuing is creating. . . . Valuation is itself the treasure and jewel of valued things. Through valuing alone can value arise; and without valuing, the nut of existence would be hollow. . . ."

To this, Nietzsche adds the basic aesthetic

[29] See below, pp. 526 et seq. for a brief life of Nietzsche and a selection from his writings.

[30] See above, pp. 83 et seq.

[31] Cf. *The Critique of Judgement*, Sect. 47.

[32] See below, pp. 547 et seq.

[33] F. Nietzsche, *Ecce Homo,* I, IX., pp. 101–103.

[34] G. W. F. Hegel, *The Philosophy of Fine Art,* Introduction, p. 207.

[35] Nietzsche, *Thus Spake Zarathustra,* I. XI.

inference: "Change of values—that is, change of creators."

Men are freed, that is, created in the process of valuing. The artist creates the creator, precisely as Plato suggests [36] in the *Symposium* (209) and Kant [37] in *The Critique of Judgement*. At the conclusion to *The Birth of Tragedy*,[38] Nietzsche hints that the creativity of the Greeks derives from what they had suffered. Certainly, for him the birth and development of tragedy are themselves envisaged as conflict and struggle between opposed and opposing forces. Basically, what Nietzsche tells us concerning Greek tragedy begins, as does Aristotle's account, with the relation between dithyramb and tragedy. But the two views are radically different. For Aristotle,[39] the dithyramb is the potentiality for the tragedy, which is actualized by the tragic artist's technique, reaches its goal, and develops no farther. Here is a theory of artistic choice, in which potentialities are made actual but in which nothing is created *ex nihilo*. Moreover, the artistic process forms what in the material is the same as what appears in the finished product. In addition, the dithyramb is temporally prior to the tragedy, which is logically prior to the dithyramb. For Nietzsche, the conflict endures. Hellenic tragedy emerges from the conflict of these "two hostile forces." For Aristotle, tragedy is produced by the imposition of a form upon a matter. For Nietzsche, "the esthetic phenomenon is simple: if a man merely has the faculty of seeing perpetual vitality around him, of living continually surrounded by hosts of spirits, he will be a poet. If he but feels the impulse to transform himself and to speak from out the bodies and souls of others, he will be a dramatist." The inspiration that Nietzsche describes as his own experience is provided for the audience by the tragic chorus: "to see yourself transformed before your own eyes, and then to act as if you had actually taken possession of another body and another character." The individual surrenders himself by entering an alien body, not, clearly, for the sake of alienating himself from himself but for that superbly intuited reason which lies at the basis of aesthetic experience: Under the spell of this enchantment, in which we regard ourselves "as transformed among one another," the Dionysian reveler ". . . in his transformation . . . sees a new vision outside him as the Apollonian consummation of his own state. With this new vision the drama completes itself . . . ." The spectator is "transformed" and a "new vision" follows. Nietzsche sums it up in *The Will to Power in Art*:[40] it is "the greatest stimulus of life . . . it does more than imagine, it actually transposes values. . . ." Moreover, as we have observed in Nietzsche's statements concerning the incapacity of language to define music, beauty, in general, is "something which is above all order of rank. . . ."

The question for Nietzsche is not whether art is "half-medicinal," "half-moral" as he interprets Aristotle to mean,[41] but whether man can "acknowledge the terrible and questionable character of things," in order to transfigure them and to transvalue values.

Nietzsche takes the radical and significant step of bringing valuing under the aegis of creating. Moreover, he glimpses—even if only fleetingly—the fact that the principal function of artistic creativity is the creation of creativity, a fact Kant had stated,[42] as we have observed, in his suggestion that the genius creates another nature out of the actual materials nature provides. The full implications of this movement in Aesthetics from the ancient theory that art is imitation, that it is a discovering of what is potential in the material, to a view that it is originating, are made explicit in the philosophy of expression.[43]

36 See above, p. 86.
37 See above, p. 417.
38 See below, p. 530.
39 See above, p. 150, Aristotle, *Poetics* 1449a 12.

40 Compare below, p. 433.
41 See above, Chapter 4, for various interpretations of Aristotle's theory of catharsis.
42 See above, p. 417.
43 See next chapter, pp 537 et seq. for Croce's version.

Johann Christoph Friedrich von Schiller

1759–1805

A. Life

Schiller, one of the outstanding poets and dramatists Germany has produced, turned his attention to philosophy of art and problems in Aesthetics with no less success. His letters on the aesthetic education of man exerted influence on many philosophers, the most notable instance probably being Hegel.

Schiller was born in Marbach on the Neckar on Nov. 10, 1759. His father was a baker, his mother an innkeeper's daughter. He attended military school near Ludwigsburg and later was trained in medicine. In 1777–1778 he completed *Die Räuber,* in 1786 the *Philosophische Briefe* and in 1787, *Don Carlos.* He was welcomed to Weimar in 1787 by Herder and in 1789 was made Professor at Jena on Goethe's recommendation. In 1790, Schiller married Charlotte von Lengefeld.

In 1792, appeared *Uber tragische Kunst* and in 1795 the letters, *On the Aesthetic Education of Man.* Among his dramas are *Wallenstein, Die Piccolomini, Mary Stuart, Die Jungfrau von Orleans, The Bride of Messina* and *William Tell.* Schiller died on May 9, 1805.

B. Aesthetics

On the Aesthetic Education of Man

FIRST LETTER

. . . I will,[44] to be sure, not conceal from you the fact that it is Kantian principles upon which the propositions that follow will for the most part be based; but you must attribute it to my incapacity, not to those principles, if in the course of these enquiries you should be reminded of any particular school of philosophy. No, I shall regard the freedom of your mind as inviolable. Your own sensibility will furnish the facts upon which I build; your own free intellectual power will dictate the laws by which we shall proceed.

Concerning those ideas which predominate in the practical part of the Kantian

[44] *On the Aesthetic Education of Man* by Friedrich Schiller; translated by Reginald Snell (London: Routledge and Kegan Paul Ltd., 1954; New Haven: Yale University Press, 1954).

system it is only the philosphers who are at variance; I am confident of shewing that mankind as a whole has from the remotest times been in agreement about them. You have only to free them from their technical formulation, and they will emerge as the time-honoured utterances of common reason, and as data of that moral instinct which Nature in her wisdom appointed as Man's guardian until clear insight should bring him to maturity. But it is just this technical formulation which reveals the truth to our understanding, that conceals it once again from our feeling; for unfortunately the understanding must first destroy the objects of the inner sense before it can appropriate them. Like the chemist, the philosopher finds combination only through dissolution, and the work of spontaneous Nature only through the torture of Art. In order to seize the fleeting appearance he must bind it in the fetters of rule, dissect its fair body into abstract notions, and preserve its living spirit in a sorry skeleton of words. Is it any wonder if natural feeling does not recognize itself in such a likeness, and if truth appears in the analyst's report as paradox?

I too must therefore crave some measure of forbearance if the following enquiries should remove their object from the sphere of sense in attempting to approximate it to the understanding. What is true of moral experience must be true, in a still higher degree, of the manifestation of Beauty. Its whole enchantment lies in its mystery, and its very essence is extinguished with the extinction of the necessary combination of its elements.

TWELFTH LETTER

To the fulfilment of this twofold task, of bringing what is necessary *within us* to reality, and subjecting what is real *outside us* to the law of necessity, we are urged by two contrary forces which, because they impel us to realize their object, are very properly called impulses. The first of these impulses, which I shall name the *sensuous*, proceeds from the physical existence of Man or from his sensuous nature, and is concerned with setting him within the bounds of time and turning him into matter; not with giving him matter, since that is the province of a free activity of the person, which matter receives and distinguishes from the persisting self. By matter I here mean nothing but alteration, or reality which occupies time; consequently this impulse demands that there should be alteration, that time should have content. This condition of merely occupied time is called sensation, and it is this alone through which physical existence proclaims itself.

As everything in time is *successive*, so the fact that a thing exists excludes everything else. When we touch a note upon an instrument, only this single note among all those which it is capable of emitting is realized; when Man perceives what is present, the whole infinite possibility of his disposition is confined to this single form of existence. So wherever this impulse acts exclusively, there is necessarily present the highest degree of limitation; Man in this condition is nothing but a unit of magnitude, an occupied moment of time—or rather, *he* is not, for his personality is extinguished so long as sense perception governs him and time whirls him along with itself.[45]

[45] Everyday language has for this condition of absence-of-self under the domination of sense-perception the very appropriate expression *to be beside oneself*—that is, to be outside one's ego. Although this phrase only occurs where the perception becomes a passion, and the condition grows more noticeable by reason of its longer duration, yet everyone is beside himself as long as he only perceives. To return from this condition to self-possession is called, equally correctly, *coming to oneself*—that is, returning to one's ego, re-establishing the personality. We do not say of a man who lies in a swoon, *he is beside himself,* but *he has passed out*—that is, he has been deprived of his ego, since he is no longer inside it. Hence a man who recovers from a swoon is only *his own self again,* which is quite compatible with the condition of being beside himself.

The sphere of this impulse is coextensive with the finiteness of Man; and as every form appears only in some material, everything absolute only through the medium of limitations, it is of course the sense impulse in which the whole phenomenon of mankind is ultimately rooted. But although this alone arouses and develops the potentialities of mankind, it is this alone that makes their perfection impossible. It fetters the upward striving spirit with indestructible bonds to the world of sense, and summons abstraction from its freest excursions into the infinite, back into the boundaries of the present. Thought may indeed elude it for the moment, and a firm will may triumphantly oppose its demands; but Nature once rebuffed soon returns to claim her rights, to press for reality of existence, for some content in our perceptions and for purpose in our actions.

The second of these impulses, which we may call the *formal* impulse, proceeds from Man's absolute existence or from his rational nature, and strives to set him at liberty, to bring harmony into the diversity of his manifestation, and to maintain his person throughout every change of circumstance. As this person, being an absolute indivisible unity, can never be at variance with itself, since we are ourselves to all eternity, that impulse which insists on affirming the personality can never demand anything other than what it must demand to all eternity; it therefore decides for ever as it decides for the moment, and enjoins for the moment what it enjoins for ever. Consequently it embraces the whole time series, which is as much as to say it annuls time and change; it wishes the actual to be necessary and eternal, and the eternal and necessary to be actual; in other words, it aims at truth and right.

If the first impulse only furnishes *cases*, the other gives *laws*: laws for every judgment where knowledge is concerned, laws for every volition where it is a question of action. Whether we recognize an object, and lend objective validity to a subjective condition in ourselves, or whether we act from knowledge, and make something objective the determining principle of our condition, in both cases we snatch this condition away from the jurisdiction of time and endow it with reality for all men and all times—that is, with universality and necessity. Feeling can only say: this is true *for this person* and *at this moment,* and another moment, another person may come to withdraw the assertion of the present sensation. But when once thought pronounces: *that is,* it decides for ever and aye, and the validity of its pronouncement is vouched for by the personality itself, which defies all change. Inclination can only say: that is good *for your individuality* and *for your present need*, but your individuality and your present need will be swept away by change, and what you now ardently desire will one day become the object of your abhorrence. But when the moral feeling says: *this shall be*, it decides for ever and aye—when you acknowledge truth because it is Truth and practise justice because it is Justice, you have turned a single case into a law for all cases, and treated one moment of your life as eternity.

When therefore the formal impulse holds sway, and the pure object acts within us, there is the highest expansion of being, all barriers disappear, and from being the unit of magnitude to which the needy sense confined him, Man has risen to a *unit of idea* embracing the whole realm of phenomena. By this operation we are no more in time, but time, with its complete and infinite succession, is in us. We are no longer individuals, but species; the judgment of all spirits is expressed by our own, the choice of all hearts is represented by our action.

FIFTEENTH LETTER

I am drawing ever nearer the goal to which I am leading you, along a not very exhilarating path. If you will consent to follow me a few steps further, a much wider field of view will be displayed, and a cheerful prospect will perhaps reward the exertions of the road.

The object of the sense impulse, expressed in a general concept, may be called *life* in the widest sense of the word; a concept which expresses all material being and all that is immediately present in the senses. The object of the form impulse, expressed generally may be called *shape*, both in the figurative and in the literal sense; a concept which includes all formal qualities of things and all their relations to the intellectual faculties. The object of the play impulse, conceived in a general notion, can therefore be called *living shape*, a concept which serves to denote all aesthetic qualities of phenomena and—in a word—what we call *Beauty* in the widest sense of the term.

According to this explanation, if it is such, Beauty is neither extended to cover the whole realm of living things, nor merely confined within this realm. A block of marble, therefore, although it is and remains lifeless, can nevertheless become living shape through the architect and sculptor; a human being, although he lives and has shape, is far from being on that account a living shape. That would require his shape to be life, and his life shape. So long as we only think about his shape, it is lifeless, mere abstraction; so long as we only feel his life, it is shapeless, mere impression. Only as the form of something lives in our sensation, and its life takes form in our understanding, is it living shape, and this will everywhere be the case where we judge it to be beautiful.

But by our knowing how to specify the ingredients which combine to produce Beauty, its genesis is by no means yet explained; for that would require that we ourselves grasped that combination which, like all reciprocal action between the finite and the infinite, remains inscrutable to us. Reason demands, on transcendental grounds, that there shall be a partnership between the formal and the material impulse, that is to say a play impulse, because it is only the union of reality with form, of contingency with necessity, of passivity with freedom, that fulfils the conception of humanity. It is obliged to make this demand because it is Reason, because its nature impels it to seek fulfilment and the removal of all barriers, while every exclusive activity of one or other of the impulses leaves human nature unfulfilled and establishes a barrier within it. Consequently, as soon as it issues the command: a humanity shall exist, it has thereby proclaimed the law: there shall be a Beauty. Experience can give us answer *whether* there is a Beauty, and we shall know that as soon as it has taught us whether there is a humanity. But *how* there can be a Beauty, and how a humanity is possible, neither reason nor experience can teach us.

We know that Man is neither exclusively matter nor exclusively spirit. Beauty, therefore, as the consummation of his humanity, can be neither exclusively mere life, as has been maintained by acute observers who adhered too closely to the evidence of experience, a course to which the taste of the age would fain reduce them; nor can it be exclusively mere form, as has been judged by speculative philosophers who strayed too far from experience, and by philosophizing artists who allowed themselves to be influenced overmuch in their explanation of Beauty, by the requirements of Art;[46] it is the common object of both impulses, that is to say of the play impulse. The term is fully warranted by the usage of speech, which is accustomed to

[46] Burke, in his *Philosophical Enquiry into the Origin of our Ideas of the Sublime and Beautiful*, turns Beauty into mere life. It is turned into mere form, so far as I am aware, by every adherent of the *dogmatic* system who ever gave testimony upon this subject; among artists, by Raphael Mengs in his *Thoughts on Taste in Painting*. In this department, as in every other, *critical* philosophy has disclosed the way to lead empiricism back to principles and speculation to experience.

denote by the word play everything that is neither outward nor inward necessity. As our nature finds itself, in the contemplation of the Beautiful, in a happy midway point between law and exigency, so, just because it is divided between the two, it is withdrawn from the constraint of both alike. The material impulse and the formal are equally earnest in their demands, since the former relates in its cognition to the actuality, the latter to the necessity, of things; while in its action the first is directed towards the maintenance of life, the second towards the preservation of dignity—both, that is to say, towards truth and perfection. But life becomes more indifferent as dignity blends with it, and duty compels no longer when inclination begins to attract; in like manner the mind entertains the actuality of things, material truth, more freely and calmly as soon as the latter encounters formal truth, the law of necessity; and it feels itself no longer strained by abstraction as soon as direct contemplation can accompany that truth. In a word, as it comes into association with ideas, everything actual loses its seriousness, because it grows *small*; and as it meets with perception, necessity puts aside its seriousness, because it grows *light*.

But surely, you must long have been tempted to object, surely the Beautiful is degraded by being turned into mere play, and reduced to the level of the frivolous objects which have at all times owned this title? Does it not contradict the rational conception and the dignity of Beauty, which is after all regarded as an instrument of culture, if we limit it to a mere game, and does it not contradict the empirical idea of play, which can co-exist with the exclusion of all taste, to confine it merely to Beauty?

But why call it a *mere* game, when we consider that in every condition of humanity it is precisely play, and play alone, that makes man complete and displays at once his twofold nature? What you call limitation, according to your conception of the matter, I call extension according to mine, which I have justified by proofs. I should therefore prefer to put it in exactly the opposite way: Man is only serious with the agreeable, the good, the perfect; but with Beauty he plays. Certainly we must not here call to mind those games which are in vogue in actual life, and which are commonly concerned only with very material objects; but in actual life we should also seek in vain for the Beauty of which we are now speaking. The Beauty we actually meet with is worthy of the play impulse we actually meet with; but with the ideal of Beauty which Reason sets up, an ideal of the play impulse is also presented which Man should have before him in all his games.

We shall never be wrong in seeking a man's ideal of Beauty along the selfsame path in which he satisfies his play impulse. If the peoples of Greece, in their athletic sports at Olympia, delighted in the bloodless combats of strength, of speed, of agility, and in the nobler combat of talents; and if the Roman people enjoyed the death throes of a vanquished gladiator or of his Libyan antagonist, we can comprehend from this single propensity of theirs why we have to look for the ideal forms of a Venus, a Juno or an Apollo not in Rome but in Greece.[47] But now Reason says: the Beautiful is not to be mere life, nor mere shape, but living shape—that is, Beauty—as it dictates to mankind the twofold law of absolute formality and absolute reality. Consequently it also pronounces the sentence:

[47] To confine ourselves to the modern world, if we compare the horse races in London, the bull fights in Madrid, the spectacles of former days in Paris, the gondola races in Venice, the animal baiting in Vienna and the gay, attractive life of the Corso at Rome, it cannot be difficult to differentiate subtly between the tastes of these several peoples. Yet we find among the popular games of the different countries far less uniformity than among the games of the upper classes in these same countries, a fact which is easily accounted for.

Man shall *only play* with Beauty, and he shall play *only with Beauty*.

For, to declare it once and for all, Man plays only when he is in the full sense of the word a man, and *he is only wholly Man when he is playing*. This proposition, which at the moment perhaps seems paradoxical, will assume great and deep significance when we have once reached the point of applying it to the twofold seriousness of duty and of destiny; it will, I promise you, support the whole fabric of aesthetic art, and the still more difficult art of living. But it is only in science that this statement is unexpected; it has long since been alive and operative in Art, and in the feeling of the Greeks, its most distinguished exponents; only they transferred to Olympus what should have been realized on earth. Guided by its truth, they caused not only the seriousness and the toil which furrow the cheeks of mortals, but also the futile pleasure that smooths the empty face, to vanish from the brows of the blessed gods, and they released these perpetually happy beings from the fetters of every aim, every duty, every care, and made idleness and indifference the enviable portion of divinity; merely a more human name for the freest and sublimest state of being. Not only the material sanction of natural laws, but also the spiritual sanction of moral laws, became lost in their higher conception of necessity, which embraced both worlds at once, and out of the unity of these two necessities they derived true freedom for the first time. Inspired by this spirit, they effaced from the features of their ideal, together with inclination, every trace of volition as well; or rather, they made both unrecognizable because they knew how to unite them both in the closest alliance. It is neither charm, nor is it dignity, that speaks to us from the superb countenance of a Juno Ludovici; it is neither of them, because it is both at once. While the womanly god demands our veneration, the godlike woman kindles our love; but while we allow ourselves to melt in the celestial loveliness, the celestial self-sufficiency holds us back in awe. The whole form reposes and dwells within itself, a completely closed creation, and—as though it were beyond space—without yielding, without resistance; there is no force to contend with force, no unprotected part where temporality might break in. Irresistibly seized and attracted by the one quality, and held at a distance by the other, we find ourselves at the same time in the condition of utter rest and extreme movement, and the result is that wonderful emotion for which reason has no conception and language no name.

EIGHTEENTH LETTER

THROUGH Beauty the sensuous man is led to form and to thought; through Beauty the spiritual man is brought back to matter and restored to the world of sense.

It appears to follow from this that a condition must exist midway between matter and form, between passivity and activity, and that Beauty transports us into this intermediate condition. This is the conception of Beauty that the majority of people actually form for themselves, as soon as they begin to reflect upon her workings, and all experiences do point that way. But on the other hand nothing is more inconsistent and contradictory than such a conception, since the distance between matter and form, between passivity and activity, between sensation and thought, is infinite, and the two cannot conceivably be reconciled. How are we to remove this contradiction? Beauty combines the two opposite conditions of perceiving and thinking, and yet there is no possible mean between the two of them. The one is made certain through experience, the other directly through reason.

This is the precise point to which the

whole question concerning Beauty is leading; and if we succeed in solving this problem satisfactorily we have at the same time the clue which will lead us through the whole labyrinth of aesthetics.

It is really a question of two utterly different operations, which in this enquiry must necessarily support each other, Beauty, it is said, links together two conditions which are *opposed to each other* and can never become one. It is from this opposition that we must start; we must comprehend and recognize it in its whole purity and strictness, so that the two conditions are separated in the most definite way; otherwise we are mixing but not uniting them. Secondly, it is said that Beauty *combines* those two opposite conditions, and thus removes the opposition. But since both conditions remain eternally opposed to one another, they can only be combined by cancellation.[48] Our second business, then, is to make this combination perfect, to accomplish it so purely and completely that both conditions entirely disappear in a third, and no trace of the division remains behind in the whole; otherwise we are isolating but not uniting them. All the disputes that have ever prevailed in the philosophical world, and still prevail to some extent nowadays, about the conception of Beauty, have the single origin that people either began the enquiry without the requisite strictness of discrimination, or else did not carry it through to a completely pure combination. Those philosophers who blindly trust the guidance of their feelings in considering the subject can arrive at no *concept* of Beauty, because they distinguish nothing individual in the totality of the sensuous impression. The others, who take the intellect as their exclusive guide, can never arrive at a concept of *Beauty*, because they never see in its totality anything but the parts, and spirit and matter remain, even in completest union, for ever separate to them. The first are afraid of invalidating Beauty *dynamically*—that is, as an operative power by separating what is yet combined in the feeling; the others are afraid of invalidating Beauty *logically*—that is, as a concept—by bringing together what is yet separate in the understanding. The former want to think of Beauty as it operates; the latter want to have it operate as it is thought. Both must therefore miss the truth, the former because they seek to rival infinite Nature with their limited intellectual capacity, the latter because they are trying to restrict infinite Nature to their own intellectual laws. The first are afraid of robbing Beauty of its freedom by analysing it too closely; the others are afraid of destroying the definiteness of its conception by combining it too boldly. But the former do not reflect that the freedom in which they quite rightly place the essence of Beauty is not lawlessness but harmony of laws, not arbitrariness but the utmost inner necessity; the latter do not reflect that the definiteness which they equally rightly demand of Beauty consists not in the *exclusion of certain realities* but in the *absolute inclusion of them all*, so that it is therefore not restriction but infinity. We shall avoid the rocks upon which they both of them founder if we start from the two elements into which Beauty is divided for the intellect, and then later ascend to the pure aesthetic unity through which she

[48] The German word thus inadequately translated is *aufgehoben*, which is here used, possibly for the first time, to mean *preserved by destruction* in the dialectical sense. It was to have a long, important and occasionally sinister career in the history of German philosophy. Goethe, indeed, sometimes uses *Aufhebung* to mean *disappearance in a higher import* in a very similar sense; but the peculiar logical context of this passage makes it probable that it was from these Letters that Hegel derived the characteristic technical term of his philosophical system. This whole Letter reveals a logical clarity of thought and expression, and an understanding of the nature of synthesis, which are not usually to be found in Schiller.—*Trans.*

works upon the perceptions, and in which both those conditions completely disappear.[49]

NINETEENTH LETTER

WE may distinguish in mankind in general two different conditions of passive and active determinability, and as many conditions of passive and active determination. The explanation of this statement will be the shortest way to our goal.

The condition of the human spirit *before* any determination, the one that is given it through impressions of the senses, is an unlimited capacity for being determined. The boundlessness of space and time is presented to Man's imagination for its free employment, and since *ex hypothesi* nothing in this wide realm of the possible is ordained, and consequently nothing is yet excluded, we may call this condition of indeterminability an *empty infinity*, which is by no means to be confused with an infinite emptiness.

And now his sense is to be touched, and out of the infinite number of possible determinations one single one is to attain actuality. A conception is to arise within him. What in the previous condition of mere determinability was nothing but an empty capacity now becomes an operative power that acquires a content; but at the same time it receives, as operative power, a limit, after being as mere capacity unlimited. So reality is there; but infinity is lost. In order to describe a shape in space, we must *set limits* to infinite space; in order to represent to ourselves an alteration in time, we must *divide* the totality of time. So we arrive at reality only through limitation, at the *positive*, or actually established, only through *negation* or exclusion, at determination only through the surrender of our free determinability.

But no reality would arise to all eternity from mere exclusion, and no idea would arise to all eternity from mere sense perception, unless there were something there *from which* the exclusion could be made, unless by an absolute act of the mind the negation were related to something positive, and from nonentity some entity arose; this activity of the mind is called judging or thinking, and its result is called *thought.*

Before we determine a position in space, there simply is no space for us; but without absolute space we should never be able to determine a position at all. It is the same with time. Before we have the instant, there simply is no time for us; but without everlasting time we should never have a manifestation of the instant. Thus we arrive, to be sure, at the whole only through the part, at the unlimited only through limitation; but we also arrive at the part only through the whole, at limitation only through the unlimited.

So when it is asserted of the Beautiful, that it paves the way for mankind to a transition from sensation to thought, we are by no

[49] The attentive reader will have observed, in the foregoing comparison, that the sensuous aestheticians, who attach greater importance to the testimony of sensation than to that of ratiocination, are *in practice* less far removed from the truth than their opponents, although they are no match for them in *discernment;* and this is the relationship which we find everywhere between Nature and Science. Nature (sensation) everywhere combines, intellect everywhere separates; but Reason combines again; before he begins to philosophize, therefore, Man is nearer truth than the philosopher who has not yet completed his enquiry. We can consequently, without further examination, declare a philosophical conclusion to be erroneous as soon as it has common observation against it in the actual result; but we are equally justified in holding it in suspicion if it has common observation on its side in the matter of form and method. The latter consideration may console every writer who cannot, as many readers apparently expect him to do, propound a philosophical conclusion in the manner of a fireside chat. The former may reduce to silence anyone who wishes to found new systems at the expense of ordinary common sense.

means to suppose by this that the Beautiful can fill up the gulf which separates sensation from thought, passivity from activity; this gulf is infinite, and without the intervention of a new and autonomous faculty nothing universal can to all eternity arise from the particular, nothing necessary from the fortuitous. Thought is the immediate operation of this absolute capacity, which must indeed be induced by the senses to declare itself, but in its actual declaration depends so little on sense perception that it rather reveals itself only through opposition to it. The self-dependence with which it acts excludes every outside influence; and it is not insofar as she helps reflection (which contains an obvious contradiction), but only insofar as she secures for the intellectual faculties the freedom to express themselves according to their own laws, that Beauty can become a means of leading Man from matter to form, from perception to principles, from a limited to an absolute existence.

But this presupposes that the freedom of the intellectual faculties can be restricted, which seems to conflict with the idea of an autonomous faculty. Because a faculty which receives from outside nothing but the material of its operation, can be hampered in its operation only by the withdrawal of the material, only negatively, and we misconstrue the nature of a human spirit if we attribute to the sensuous passions the power of positively suppressing the freedom of the mind. Experience certainly affords plenty of examples where the rational powers appear to be suppressed in proportion to the violence of the sensuous powers; but instead of deducing this weakness of mind from the strength of the emotion, we should rather explain this overwhelming strength of emotion by the weakness of the mind; for the senses cannot represent an authority over a man except insofar as the mind has of its own free will neglected to establish itself as such.

But while I seek by means of this explanation to meet one objection, I have, it appears, become involved in another, and have secured the self-dependence of the mind only at the expense of its unity. For how can the mind find in itself at the same time the principles of inactivity and of activity, if it is not itself divided, if it is not in opposition to itself?

At this point we must recall that we are considering the finite, not the infinite mind. The finite mind is that which only becomes active through passivity, only attains the absolute by means of limitations, only works and fashions insofar as it receives material. Such a mind will accordingly associate with the impulse towards form, or towards the absolute, an impulse towards the material, or towards limitation, as being the condition without which it could neither possess nor satisfy the first impulse. To decide how two such opposite tendencies can subsist together side by side in the same being, is a task that might indeed set the metaphysician—though not the transcendental philosopher—in sore perplexity. The latter does not presume to explain the possibility of things, but contents himself with establishing the knowledge from which the possibility of experience is apprehended. And as experience could as little exist without that opposition in the mind, as it could without the mind's absolute unity, he maintains both concepts with complete justification as equally necessary conditions of experience, without troubling himself further about their compatibility. Moreover, this indwelling of two fundamental impulses in no way contradicts the absolute unity of the mind, as soon as we distinguish the latter itself from both the impulses. Certainly each impulse exists and operates within the mind, but the mind itself is neither matter nor form, neither sensuousness nor reason, a fact which does not always seem to have been considered by those who only allow the human mind to be active when it proceeds according to reason, and where it contradicts reason declare it to be merely passive.

Each of these two fundamental impulses,

as soon as it has developed, strives by its nature and by necessity towards satisfaction; but just because both are necessary and both are yet striving towards opposite objectives, this twofold constraint naturally cancels itself, and the will preserves complete freedom between them both. It is therefore the will that maintains itself toward both impulses as an authority (a basis of actuality), but neither of the two can of its own accord, act as an authority against the other. By the most positive inclination to justice, which he by no means lacks, the violent man is not withheld from injustice, and the strong-minded man is not led to a breach of his principles by the keenest temptation to enjoyment. There is in Man no other authority than his will, and only something that annuls the man himself—death, or some deprivation of his consciousness—can annul his inner freedom.

A necessity *outside ourselves* determines our condition, our existence in time, by means of sense perception. This is quite involuntary, and as it acts upon us so we must abide it. Similarly a necessity *inside ourselves* reveals our personality, at the direction of that sense perception and through opposition to it; for consciousness of self cannot depend upon the will, which presupposes it. This primitive manifestation of the personality is no more a merit than the absence of it is a defect in us. Reason —that is to say absolute consistency and universality of consciousness—is required only from the man who is conscious of himself; before that he is not a man, nor can any act of humanity be expected from him. The *metaphysician* can no more account for the limits which the free and autonomous mind meets within sensation, than the *physicist* can comprehend the infinity which is revealed in the personality through these limits. Neither abstraction nor experience will lead us back to the source from which our concepts of universality and necessity derive; its early appearance in time hides it from the observer, and its suprasensible origin from the metaphysical enquirer. It is sufficient that the consciousness of self is there, and together with its own unalterable unity the law of unity for everything that is *for* man, and for everything that is to come about *through* him, is established for his apprehension and his activity. Inescapable, incorruptible, inconceivable, the concepts of truth and right present themselves even in the age of sensuousness, and without being able to say whence and how it arose we are aware of the eternal in time and the necessary in the train of chance. So sensation and the consciousness of self arise, entirely without the assistance of the personality, and the origin of them both lies as much beyond our will as it lies beyond the sphere of our knowledge.

But if both are real, and if Man has had by means of sensation the experience of a definite existence, and through apperception the experience of his own absolute existence, both his fundamental impulses will be aroused directly their objects are present. The sensuous impulse awakens with the experience of life (with the beginning of the individual), the rational with the experience of law (with the beginning of the personality), and only at this point, after both of them have come into existence, is his humanity established. Until this has happened, everything in him has proceeded according to the law of necessity; but now Nature's hand abandons him, and it is his own business to assert the humanity which she planned and disclosed in him. As soon, that is to say, as both the opposite fundamental impulses are active in him, they both lose their sanction, and the opposition of two necessities gives rise to *freedom*.[50]

[50] To avoid any misconception I would observe that whenever I speak of freedom I do not mean the sort which necessarily attaches to Man in his capacity as intelligent being, and can neither be given to him nor taken from him, but the sort which is based upon his composite nature. By only acting, in general, in a rational manner, Man displays a freedom of the first kind; by acting rationally within the limits of his material and materially within the laws of actuality, he displays a freedom of the second kind. We might explain the latter simply as a natural possibility of the former.

TWENTY-FIFTH LETTER

So long as Man in his first physical condition accepts the world of sense merely passively, merely perceives, he is still completely identified with it, and just because he himself is simply world, there is no world yet for him. Not until he sets it outside himself or *contemplates* it, in his aesthetic status, does his personality become distinct from it, and a world appears to him because he has ceased to identify himself with it.[51]

Contemplation (reflection) is Man's first free relation to the universe which surrounds him. If desire directly apprehends its object, contemplation thrusts its object into the distance thereby turning it into its true and inalienable possession and thus securing it from passion. The necessity of Nature which governed him with undivided power in the condition of mere sensation, abandons him when reflection begins; an instantaneous calm ensues in the senses; time itself, the eternally moving, stands still while the dispersed rays of consciousness are gathered together, and *form*, an image of the infinite, is reflected upon the transient foundation. As soon as it becomes light inside Man, there is also no longer any night outside him; as soon as it is calm within him, the storm in the universe is also lulled, and the contending forces of Nature find rest between abiding boundaries. No wonder, therefore, that ancient poetry tells of this great occurrence in the inner Man as of a revolution in the world outside him, and embodies the thought which triumphs over the laws of time in the figure of Zeus who brings the reign of Saturn to an end.

From being a slave of Nature, so long as he merely perceives her, Man becomes her lawgiver as soon as she becomes his thought. She who had formerly ruled him only as *force*, now stands as *object* before the judgment of his glance. What is object to him has no longer power over him; for in order to be object it must experience his own power. Insofar as he gives form to matter, and so long as he gives it, he is invulnerable to her influences; for nothing can injure a spirit except what deprives it of freedom, and Man proves his freedom by his very forming of the formless. Only where substance holds its ponderous and shapeless sway, and the dim outlines fluctuate between uncertain boundaries, does fear have its abode; Man is superior to every terror of Nature so long as he knows how to give form to it, and to turn it into his object. Just as he begins to assert his self-dependence in the face of Nature as phenomenon, so he also asserts his dignity in the face of Nature as power, and with noble freedom he rises up against his deities. They throw off the ghastly masks with which they had frightened his infancy, and in becoming his own conception they surprise him with his own image. The divine monster of the Oriental, that governs the world with the blind strength of a beast of prey, dwindles in the Grecian fantasy into the friendly outlines of humanity; the empire of the Titans falls, and infinite force is mastered by infinite form.

But while I have been merely looking for a way out of the material world and a passage into the world of spirit, the free range of my

[51] I recall once more that both these periods, though they are indeed necessarily to be distinguished from each other in idea, are in experience more or less intermingled. We are also not to think that there has ever been a time when Man has been situated only in this physical status, or a time when he has shaken himself quite free from it. As soon as a man *sees an object,* he is already no longer in a merely physical condition, and so long as he continues to see an object, he will also not escape from that physical situation, since he can only see insofar as he perceives. Those three moments, therefore, which I specified at the beginning of my twenty-fourth letter are indeed, regarded in general, three different ages for the development of a whole humanity and for the whole development of individual man, but they may also be distinguished in every particular awareness of an object, and they are, in a word, the necessary conditions of every cognition which we receive through the senses.

imagination has already led me into the midst of the latter. The Beauty that we seek lies already behind us, and we have leapt over her as we passed directly from mere life to pure shape and to pure object. Such a leap is not in human nature, and to keep pace with it we shall have to return to the world of sense.

Beauty is, to be sure, the work of free contemplation, and we step with her into the world of ideas—but, it must be observed, without thereby leaving the world of sense, as is the case with cognition of truth. This latter is the pure product of abstraction from everything that is material and contingent, pure object in which no barrier of subjectivity may remain behind, pure spontaneity without any admixture of passivity. There is, certainly, a way back to sense even from the utmost abstraction; for thought stirs the inner sensation, and the conception of logical and moral unity passes into a feeling of sensuous accord. But when we take delight in cognition, we distinguish very precisely our conception from our sensation, and look upon the latter as something accidental which might very well be omitted without the cognition thereby vanishing, or truth not being truth. But it would be a wholly fruitless undertaking to try to sever this relation to the perceptive faculty from the notion of Beauty; therefore it is not sufficient for us to think of one as the effect of the other, but we must look upon both jointly and reciprocally as effect and as cause. In our pleasure in cognitions we distinguish without difficulty the passage from activity to passivity, and observe distinctly that the first ends when the second begins. In our pleasure in Beauty, on the other hand, no such succession between activity and passivity can be distinguished, and reflection is so completely intermingled with feeling that we believe ourselves to perceive form immediately. Beauty is therefore certainly an *object* for us, since reflection is the condition under which we have a sensation of it; but it is at the same time a *state of our personality*, since feeling is the condition under which we have a conception of it. It is then certainly form, because we contemplate it; but it is at the same time life, because we feel it. In a word, it is at once our state and our act.

And just because it is both these things together, it affords a triumphant proof that passivity by no means excludes activity, any more than matter does form, or limitation infinity—that consequently Man's moral freedom is by no means abolished by his necessary physical dependence. It proves this, and I must add, it is the *only* thing that can prove this to us. For as in the enjoyment of truth or of logical unity, perception is not necessarily one with thought, but follows the latter accidentally so it can only prove to us that a rational nature can be followed by a sensuous one, and *vice versa*, not that both of them subsist together, not that they mutually influence each other, not that they are to be absolutely and necessarily combined. Rather, I would have to conclude the exact contrary from this exclusion of feeling so long as there is thought, and of thought, so long as there is sensation—that is, the *incompatibility* of the two natures; and indeed the analytical thinkers are actually capable of adducing no better proof of the practicability of pure reason in human beings than that it is enjoined upon them. But as with the enjoyment of Beauty, or aesthetic unity, there occurs a real union and interchange of matter with form, and of passivity with activity, by this very ocurrence the *compatibility* of both natures is proved, the practicability of the infinite in finiteness, and consequently the possibility of a sublime humanity.

We must therefore be no longer at a loss to find a passage from sensuous dependence to moral freedom, after we have seen in the case of Beauty, that the two can prefectly well subsist together, and that in order to shew himself a spirit Man does not need to eschew matter. But if he is already free in association with sensuousness, as the fact of Beauty teaches us, and if freedom is something absolute and suprasensible, as its very concept necessarily implies, there can no longer be any question how he came to rise from the limited to the absolute, to oppose sensuousness in his thought and will, since this has already occurred in Beauty. There can, in a word, no longer be any question how he passes from Beauty to Truth, since the latter by its very nature lies within the former; the question is rather how he makes his way from an ordinary actuality to an aesthetic one, from a sense of mere life to a sense of Beauty.

TWENTY-SEVENTH LETTER

You need fear nothing for reality and truth if the lofty concept which I put before you in the last letter about aesthetic appearance should become universal. It will not become universal so long as mankind is still uncultivated enough to be able to abuse it; and if it were universal, this could only be effected by means of a culture which would at the same time make every such abuse impossible. To strive after absolute appearance demands greater capacity for abstraction, more freedom of heart, more vigour of will than Man needs if he confines himself to reality, and he must already have put the latter behind him if he wishes to arrive at appearance. How ill advised he would be, therefore, if he sought to follow the path to the ideal in order to spare himself the path to actuality! From appearance as we are here conceiving it, then, we should not have much to apprehend on behalf of actuality; all the more reason, therefore, to be apprehensive about actuality on behalf of appearance. Chained as he is to the material, Man has long since allowed appearance merely to serve his ends, before he has conceded it a personality of its own in the art of the ideal. For this purpose a total revolution is needed in the whole mode of perception, without which he would not find himself even on the right road towards the ideal. When therefore we discover traces of a disinterested free appreciation of pure appearance, we can infer some such revolution of his nature and the real beginnings in him of humanity. But traces of this sort are actually to be found already in the earliest crude attempts which he makes to *embellish* his existence—makes even at the risk of impairing it thereby in regard to its sensuous contents. As soon as he begins at all to prefer shape to material and to hazard reality for appearance (which however, he must recognize as such), his animal sphere is opened and he finds himself upon a track that has no end.

Not content with what simply satisfies Nature and meets his need, he demands superfluity; to begin with, certainly, merely a superfluity *of* material, in order to conceal from his desires their boundaries, in order to assure his enjoyment beyond the existing need, but soon a superfluity *in* the material, an aesthetic supplement, in order to be able to satisfy his formal impulse also, in order to extend his enjoyment beyond every need. When he is simply collecting provisions for future use, and relishing them in advance in imagination, he is certainly trespassing beyond the present moment, but without altogether trespassing beyond time; he is enjoying *more*, not enjoying *differently*. But when at the same time he brings shape into his enjoyment, and becomes aware of the forms of the objects which satisfy his desires, he has not merely enhanced his enjoyment in scope and in degree, but also exalted it in kind.

Certainly Nature has given even to the creatures without reason more than the bare necessities of life, and cast a gleam of freedom over the darkness of animal existence. When the lion is not gnawed by hunger and no beast of prey is challenging him to battle, his idle energy creates for itself an object; he fills the echoing desert with his high-spirited roaring, and his exuberant power enjoys itself in purposeless display. The insect swarms with joyous life in the sunbeam; and it is assuredly not the cry of desire which we hear in the melodious warbling of the song-bird. Undeniably there is freedom in these movements, but not freedom from need in general, simply from a definite external need. The animal *works* when deprivation is the mainspring of its activity, and it *plays* when the fullness of its strength is this mainspring, when superabundant life is its own stimulus to activity. Even in mindless Nature there is revealed a similar luxury of powers and a laxity of determination which in that natural context might well be called play. The tree puts forth innumerable buds which perish without developing, and stretches out for nourishment many more roots, branches and leaves than are used for the maintenance of itself and its species. What the tree returns from its lavish profusion unused and unenjoyed to the kingdom of the elements, the living creature may squander in joyous movements. So Nature gives us even in her material realm a prelude to the infinite, and even here partly removes the chains which she casts away entirely in the realm of form. From the sanction of need, or *physical seriousness*, she makes her way through the sanction of superfluity, or *physical play*, to aesthetic play; and before she soars in the lofty freedom of the Beautiful above the fetters of every purposed end, she is already approaching this independence, at least from a distance, in the *free movement* which is itself end and means.

Man's imagination has, like his bodily organs, its free movement and its material play, in which, without any reference to shape, it simply delights in its absolute and unfettered power. Insofar as nothing of form is yet interfering with this play of fancy, and an unconstrained sequence of images constitutes its whole attraction, it belongs—though it is peculiar to Man alone—purely to his animal life, and only points to his liberation from every external sensuous constraint, without connoting as yet any independent creative power in him.[52]

From this play of the *free sequence of images*, which is still of a quite material kind and declares itself by simple natural laws, the imagination finally makes, in its attempt at a *free form*, the leap to aesthetic play. A leap we must call it, since a wholly new force now comes into play; for here, for the first time, the legislative faculty interferes with the operations of a blind instinct, subjects the arbitrary process of the imagination to its immutable and eternal unity, imposes its own self-dependence upon the variable and its infiniteness upon the sensuous. But so long as crude Nature which knows no other law than hurrying restlessly from variation to variation, is still too powerful, it will oppose that necessity by its fitful lawlessness, that stability by its unrest, that self-dependence by its indigence, that sublime simplicity by its insatiability. The aesthetic play impulse will then be hardly recognizable yet in its first attempts, as the sensuous impulse is incessantly interfering with its headstrong caprice and its savage appetite. Hence we see crude taste first seizing on what is new and startling, gaudy, fantastic and bizarre, what is

[52] The majority of games which are in vogue in ordinary life either depend entirely on this feeling of the free sequence of ideas, or at any rate derive their chief attraction from it. But little as it may point, in itself, to a higher nature, and readily as the most indolent souls are accustomed to yield themselves up to this free flow of images, yet this very independence of the fancy from external impressions is at least the negative condition of its creative capacity. Only as it turns away from actuality does plastic power rise to the ideal, and before the imagination can act according to its own law in its productive quality, it must already have liberated itself from extraneous law in its reproductive process. Certainly there is still a big step to be taken from mere lawlessness to a self-dependent internal system of law, and an entirely new power—the capacity for ideas—must at this point be brought into play; but this power can now develop with greater facility, since the senses are not working counter to it, and the indeterminate is bordering, at least negatively, on the infinite.

violent and wild, and avoiding nothing so much as simplicity and quiet. It fashions grotesque shapes, loves swift transitions, exuberant forms, striking contrasts, glaring shades, pathetic songs. In this age beautiful means simply what excites a man, what gives him material—but excites him to spontaneous resistance, gives him material for possible fashioning; for otherwise it would not be the Beautiful, even for him. Thus a remarkable alteration has taken place in the form of his judgments; he seeks these objects not because they give him something to bear, but because they give him something to deal with; things please him not because they meet a need, but because they satisfy a law which speaks, albeit softly, in his breast.

Soon he is not content that things should please him, he wants to give pleasure himself, at first indeed only through what *belongs* to him, finally through what *he* is. What he possesses, what he produces, may no longer wear upon it simply the marks of servitude, the uneasy form of its purpose; besides the service which it renders, it must at the same time reflect the genial intellect which conceived it, the loving hand which executed it, the serene and free spirit which chose and established it. Now the ancient German goes in search of glossier animals' skins, statelier antlers, more elegant drinking horns, and the Caledonian selects the choicest shells for his festivals. Even weapons may now be objects not simply of terror but also of delight, and the ornamented baldrick tries to attract as much attention as the deadly blade of the sword. Not content with bringing an aesthetic surplus into the necessary, the freer play impulse finally breaks completely away from the fetters of exigency, and Beauty for her own sake becomes the object of its endeavour. Man *adorns* himself. Free delight takes a place among his wants, and the superfluous is soon the chief part of his pleasures.

And just as form gradually approaches him from without, in his dwelling, his furniture, his clothing, it begins finally to take possession of Man himself, to transform at first only the outward but ultimately the inward man. The lawless leap of joy becomes a dance, the shapeless gesture a graceful and harmonius miming speech; the confused noises of perception unfold themselves, begin to obey a rhythm and weld themselves into song. While the Trojan host with shrill cries storms like a flight of cranes across the battlefield, the Greek army approaches quietly, with noble tread.[53] There we see only the arrogance of blind strength, here the triumph of form and the simple majesty of law.

A lovelier necessity now links the sexes together, and the sympathy of hearts helps to maintain the bond which was knitted only capriciously and inconstantly by desire. Released from its sullen chains, the quieter eye apprehends form, soul gazes into soul, and out of a selfish exchange of lust there grows a generous interplay of affection. Desire extends and exalts itself into love as mankind arises in its object, and the base advantage over sense is disdained for the sake of a nobler victory over the will. The need to please subjects the man of force to the gentle tribunal of taste; lust can be robbery, but love must be a gift. For this loftier prize he can contend through form alone, not through matter. He must cease to approach feeling as force, and to confront the intellect as a phenomenon; in order to please liberty, he must concede it. And just as Beauty resolves the conflict of natures in its simplest and purest example, in the eternal opposition of the sexes, so does she resolve it —or at least aims at resolving it—in the intricate totality of society, and reconciles every thing gentle and violent in the moral world after the pattern of the free union which she there contrives between masculine strength and feminine gentleness. Weakness now becomes sacred, and unbridled strength disgraceful; the

[53] Iliad, III, 1–9—*Trans.*

injustice of Nature is rectified by the generosity of the chivalric code. The man whom no force may confound is disarmed by the tender blush of modesty, and tears stifle a revenge which no blood could slake. Even hatred pays heed to the gentle voice of honour, the victor's sword spares the disarmed foe, and a hospitable hearth smokes for the fugitive on the dreaded shore where of old only murder awaited him.

In the midst of the awful realm of powers, and of the sacred realm of laws, the aesthetic creative impulse is building unawares a third joyous realm of play and of appearance, in which it releases mankind from all the shackles of circumstance and frees him from everything that may be called constraint, whether physical or moral.

If in the *dynamic* state of rights man encounters man as force and restricts his activity, if in the *ethical* state of duties he opposes him with the majesty of law and fetters his will, in the sphere of cultivated society, in the *aesthetic* state, he need appear to him only as shape, confront him only as an object of free play. *To grant freedom by means of freedom* is the fundamental law of this kingdom.

The dynamic state can only make society possible, by curbing Nature through Nature; the ethical State can only make it (morally) necessary by subjecting the individual to the general will; the aesthetic State alone can make it actual, since it carries out the will of the whole through the nature of the individual. Though need may drive Man into society, and Reason implant social principles in him, Beauty alone can confer on him a *social character*. Taste alone brings harmony into society, because it establishes harmony in the individual. All other forms of perception divide a man, because they are exclusively based either on the sensuous or on the intellectual part of his being; only the perception of the Beautiful makes something whole of him, because both his natures must accord with it. All other forms of communication divide society, because they relate exclusively either to the private sensibility or to the private skilfulness of its individual members, that is, to what distinguishes between one man and another; only the communication of the Beautiful unites society, because it relates to what is common to them all. We enjoy the pleasures of the senses simply as individuals, and the race which lives within us has no share in them; hence we cannot extend our sensuous pleasures into being universal, because we cannot make our own individuality universal. We enjoy the pleasures of knowledge simply as race, and by carefully removing every trace of individuality from our judgment; hence we cannot make our intellectual pleasures universal, because we cannot exclude the traces of individuality from the judgment of others as we do from our own. It is only the Beautiful that we enjoy at the same time as individual and as race, that is, as *representatives* of the race. Sensuous good can make only *one* happy man, since it is based on appropriation, which always implies exclusions; it can also make this one man only partially happy, because the personality does not share in it. Absolute good can bring happiness only under conditions which are not to be universally assumed; for truth is only the reward of renunciation, and only a pure heart believes in the pure will. Beauty alone makes all the world happy, and every being forgets its limitations as long as it experiences her enchantment.

No pre-eminence, no rival dominion is tolerated as far as taste rules and the realm of the Beautiful extends. This realm stretches upward to the point where Reason governs with unconditional necessity and all matter ceases; it stretches downwards to the point where natural impulse holds sway with blind compulsion and form has not yet begun; indeed, even on these outermost boundaries, where its legislative power has been taken from it, taste still does not allow its executive power to be wrested away. Unsocial desire must renounce its selfishness, and the agreeable, which otherwise allures only the senses, must cast the toils of charm over spirits too. Necessity's stern voice, Duty, must alter its reproachful formula, which resistance alone can justify, and honour willing Nature with a nobler confidence. Taste leads knowledge out of the mysteries of science under the open sky of common sense, and transforms the perquisite of the schools into a common property of the whole of human society. In its territory even the mightiest genius must resign its grandeur and descend familiarly to the comprehension of a child. Strength must let itself be bound by the Graces, and the haughty lion yield to the bridle of a Cupid. In return, taste spreads out its soothing veil over physical need, which in its naked shape affronts the dignity of free spirits, and conceals from us the degrading relationship with matter by a delightful illusion of freedom. Given wings by it, even cringing mercenary art rises from the dust, and at the touch of its wand the chains of thraldom drop away from the lifeless and the living alike. Everything in the aesthetic State, even the subservient tool, is a free citizen having equal rights with the noblest; and the intellect, which forcibly moulds the passive multitude to its designs, must here ask for its assent. Here, then, in the realm of aesthetic appearance, is fulfilled the ideal of equality which the visionary would fain see realized in actuality also; and if it is true that fine breeding matures earliest and most completely near the throne, we are bound to recognize here too the bountiful dispensation which seems often to restrict mankind in the actual, only in order to incite him into the ideal world.

But does such a State of Beauty in Appearance really exist, and where is it to be found? As a need, it exists in every finely tuned soul; as an achievement we might perhaps find it, like the pure Church, or the pure Republic, only in a few select circles where it is not the spiritless imitation of foreign manners but people's own lovely nature that governs conduct, where mankind passes through the most complex situations with eager simplicity and tranquil innocence, and has no need either to encroach upon another's freedom in order to assert his own, or to display gracefulness at the cost of dignity.

Georg Wilhelm Friedrich Hegel

1770–1831

A. Life

Georg Wilhelm Friedrich Hegel was born in Stuttgart in 1770. From 1788 until 1793 he studied Philosophy and Theology at the University of Tübingen. He was a tutor at the University of Frankfurt from 1796 until 1800. He taught at the Universities of Tübingen, Jena, Heidelberg and, finally, at Berlin. He published the *Phenomenology of Spirit* in 1807, *Logic* in 1812–1813, and the *Encyclopaedia* in 1816–1817. In 1818, Hegel succeeded Fichte to the Chair of Philosophy in Berlin. He died of cholera in 1831.

Hegel's *The Philosophy of Fine Art* was published in 1835. Few writings have been more influential in Aesthetics, not only among philosophers of art but among historians of art and students of art in its relation to culture as well.

B. Aesthetics

The Philosophy of Fine Art

Introduction [54]

I

The present inquiry [55] has for its subject-matter *Aesthetic*. It is a subject co-extensive with the entire *realm of the beautiful*; more specifically described, its province is that of *Art*, or rather, we should say, of *Fine Art*.

For a subject-matter such as this the term "Aesthetic" is no doubt not entirely appropriate, for "Aesthetic" denotes more accurately the science of the senses or emotion. It came by its origins as a science, or rather as something that to start with purported to be a branch of philosophy, during the period of the school of Wolff, in other words when works

[54] From Hegel: *The Philosophy of Fine Art*, translated, with notes, by F. P. B. Osmaston, B.A., published by G. Bell & Sons, Ltd., London, 1920. [*Editor's note*: I have omitted one or two of Mr. Osmaston's notes, primarily because they were directed to a clarification of Bernard Bosanquet's translation of the *Introduction of Hegel's Philosophy of Fine Art* rather than to Hegel's own text.]

[55] The introduction begins as an introduction of lectures. But as the work is merely based to a large extent on notes for lectures, or on a manuscript which did not preserve the lectures as they were delivered, it will be found most convenient to ignore this fact, and in references to regard it simply as a written treatise.

of art were generally regarded in Germany with reference to the feelings they were calculated to evoke, as, for example, the feelings of pleasure, admiration, fear, pity, and so forth. It is owing to the unsuitability or, more strictly speaking, the superficiality of this term that the attempt has been made by some to apply the name "Callistic" to this science. Yet this also is clearly insufficient inasmuch as the science here referred to does not investigate beauty in its general signification, but the beauty of art pure and simple. For this reason we shall accommodate ourselves to the term Aesthetic, all the more so as the mere question of nomenclature is for ourselves a matter of indifference. It has as such been provisionally accepted in ordinary speech, and we cannot do better than retain it. The *term,* however, which fully expresses our science is "Philosophy of Art," and, with still more precision, "Philosophy of Fine Art."

(*a*) In virtue of this expression we at once exclude the beauty of Nature from the scientific exposition of Fine Art. Such a limitation of our subject may very well appear from a certain point of view as an arbitrary boundary line, similar to that which every science is entitled to fix in the demarcation of its subject-matter. We must not, however, understand the limitation of "Aesthetic" to the beauty of art in this sense. We are accustomed, no doubt, in ordinary life to speak of a beautiful colour, a beautiful heaven, a beautiful stream, to say nothing of beautiful flowers, animals, and, above all, of beautiful human beings. Without entering now into the disputed question how far the quality of beauty can justly be predicted of such objects, and consequently the beauty of Nature comes generally into competition with that of art, we are justified in maintaining categorically that the beauty of art stands *higher* than Nature. For the beauty of art is a beauty begotten, a new birth of mind; [56] and to the extent that Spirit and its creations stand higher than Nature and its phenomena, to that extent the beauty of art is more exalted than the beauty of Nature. Indeed, if we regard the matter in its formal aspect, that is to say, according to the way it is there, any chance fancy that passes through any one's head,[57] is of higher rank than any product of Nature. For in every case intellectual conception and freedom are inseparable from such a conceit. In respect to *content* the sun appears to us an absolutely necessary constituent of actual fact, while the perverse fancy passes away as something accidental and evanescent. None the less in its own independent being a natural existence such as the sun possesses no power of self-differentiation; it is neither essentially free nor self-aware; and, if we regard it in its necessary cohesion with other things, we do not regard it independently for its own sake, and consequently not as beautiful.

Merely to maintain, in a general way, that mind and the beauty of art which originates therefrom stand *higher* than the beauty of Nature is no doubt to establish next to nothing. The expression *higher* is obviously entirely indefinite; it still indicates the beauty of Nature and art as standing juxtaposed in the field of conception, and emphasizes the difference as a quantitative and accordingly external difference. But in predicating of mind and its artistic beauty a higher place in contrast to Nature, we do not denote a distinction which is merely relative. Mind, and mind alone, is pervious to truth, comprehending all in itself, so that all which is beautiful can only be veritably beautiful as partaking in this higher sphere and as begotten of the same. Regarded under this point of view it is only a reflection of the beauty appertinent to mind, that is, we have

[56] Hegel, alluding no doubt to the words of the Gospel, puts it "born and born again from mind (spirit)."

[57] It is assumed that such a fancy is seized and defined as such in separation from other experience.

it under an imperfect and incomplete mode, and one whose substantive being is already contained in the mind itself.

And apart from this we shall find the restriction to the beauty of art only natural, for in so far as the beauties of Nature may have come under discussion—a rarer occurrence among ancient writers than among ourselves—yet at least it has occurred to no one to insist emphatically on the beauty of natural objects to the extent of proposing a science, or systematic exposition of such beauties. It is true that the point of view of *utility* has been selected for such exclusive treatment. We have, for example, the conception of a science of natural objects in so far as they are useful in the conflict with diseases, in other words a description of minerals, chemical products, plants, animals, which subserve the art of healing. We do not find any analogous exploitation and consideration of the realm of Nature in its aspect of beauty. In the case of natural beauty we are too keenly conscious that we are dealing with an indefinite subject-matter destitute of any real criterion. It is for this reason that such an effort of comparison would carry with it too little interest to justify the attempt.

These preliminary observations over beauty in Nature and art, over the relation of both, and the exclusion of the first-mentioned from the province of our real subject-matter are intended to disabuse us of the notion that the limitation of our science is simply a question of capricious selection. We have, however, not reached the point where a *demonstration* of this fact is feasible for the reason that such an investigation falls within the limits of our science itself, and it is therefore only at a later stage that we can either discuss or prove the same.

Assuming however, that we have, by way of prelude, limited our inquiry to the beauty of art, we are merely by this first step involved in fresh difficulties.

(*b*) What must first of all occur to us is the question whether Fine Art in itself is truly susceptible to a scientific treatment. It is a simple fact that beauty and art pervade all the affairs of life like some friendly genius, and embellish with their cheer all our surroundings, mental no less than material. They alleviate the strenuousness of such relations, the varied changes of actual life; they banish the tedium of our existence with their entertainment; and where nothing really worth having is actually achieved, it is at least an advantage that they occupy the place of actual vice. Yet while art prevails on all sides with its pleasing shapes, from the crude decorations of savage tribes up to the splendours of the sacred shrine adorned with every conceivable beauty of design, none the less such shapes themselves appear to fall outside the real purposes of life, and even where the imaginative work of art is not impervious to such serious objects, nay, rather at times even appear to assist them, to the extent at least of removing what is evil to a distance, yet for all that art essentially belongs to the *relaxation* and *recreation* of spiritual life, whereas its substantive interests rather make a call upon its strained energy. On such grounds an attempt to treat that which on its own account is not of a serious character with all the gravity of scientific exposition may very possibly appear to be unsuitable and pedantic. In any case from such a point of view art appears a *superfluity* if contrasted with the essential needs and interests of life, even assuming that the *softening* of the soul which a preoccupation with the beauty of objects is capable of producing, does not actually prove injurious in its effeminate influence upon the serious quality of those *practical* interests. Owing to this fundamental assumption that they are a luxury it has often appeared necessary to undertake the defence of the fine arts relatively to the necessities of practical life, and in particular relatively to morality and piety; and inasmuch as this harmlessness is incapable of demonstrating, the idea has been at least to make it appear credible, that this luxury of human experience contributes a larger proportion of *advantages* than *disadvantages.* In this respect serious aims have been attributed to art, and in many quarters it has been commended as a mediator between reason and sensuous associations, between private inclinations and duty, personified in short as a reconciler of these forces in the strenuous conconflict and opposition which this antagonism generates. But it is just conceivable[58] that, even assuming the presence of such aims with all their indubitably greater seriousness, neither reason nor duty come by much profit from such mediation, for the simple reason that they are incapable by their very nature of any such interfusion or compromise, demanding throughout the same purity which they intrinsically possess. And we might add that art does not become in any respect more worthy thereby of scientific discussion, inasmuch as it remains still on two sides a menial, that is, subservient to idleness and frivolity, if also to objects of more elevated character. In such service, moreover, it can at most merely appear as a means instead of being an object for its own sake. And, in conclusion, assuming that art is a means, it still invariably labours under the formal defect, that so far as it in fact is subservient to more serious objects, and produces results of like nature, the means which actually brings this about is *deception.* For beauty is made vital in the *appearance.*[59] Now it can hardly be denied that aims which are true and serious ought not to be achieved by deception; and though such an effect is here and there secured by this means, such ought only to be the case in a restricted degree; and even in the exceptional case we are not justified in regarding deception as the right means. For the means ought to correspond with the dignity of the aim. Neither semblance nor deception, but only what is itself real and true, possesses a title to create what is real and true. Just in the same way science has to investigate the true interests of the mind in accordance with the actual process of the real world and the manner of conceiving it as we actually find it.

We may possibly conclude from the above grounds that the art of beauty is unworthy of philosophical examination. It is after all, it may be said, only a pleasant pastime, and, though we may admit more serious aims are also in its purview, nevertheless it is essentially opposed to such aims in their seriousness. It is at the most merely the servant of specific amusements no less than the exceptional serious objects, and for the medium of its existence as also for the means of its operations can merely avail itself of deception and show.

But yet further in the *second* place, it is a still more plausible contention that even supposing fine art to be compatible generally with philosophical disquisition, none the less it would form no really adequate subject-matter for scientific enquiry in the strict sense. For the beauty of art is presented to sense, feeling, perception, and imagination: its field is not that of thought, and the comprehension of its activity and its creations demands another faculty than that of the scientific intelligence. Furthermore, what we enjoy in artistic beauty is just the *freedom* of its creative and plastic activity. In the production and contemplation of these we appear to escape the principle of rule and system. In the creations of art we seek for an atmosphere of repose and animation as some counterpoise to the austerity of the realm of law and the sombre self-concentration of thought; we seek for blithe and powerful reality in exchange for the shadow-world of the Idea. And, last of all, the free activity of the imagination is the source of the fair works of art, which in this world of the mind are even more free than Nature is herself. Not only has art at its service the entire wealth of natural form in all their superabundant variety, but the

[58] The sentence is slightly ironical.
[59] *Dem Scheine.*

creative imagination is able inexhaustibly to extend the realm of form by its *own* productions and modifications. In the presence of such an immeasurable depth of inspired creation and its free products, it may not unreasonably be supposed that thought will lose the courage to apprehend such in their apparent *range*, to pronounce its verdict thereon, and to appropriate such beneath its universal formulae.

Science, on the other hand, everyone must admit, is formally bound to occupy itself with thinking which abstracts from the mass of particulars: and for this very reason, from one point of view, the imagination and its contingency and caprice, in other words the organ of artistic activity and enjoyment, is excluded from it. On the other hand, when art gives joyous animation to just this gloomy and arid dryness of the notion, bringing its abstractions and divisions into reconciliation with concrete fact, supplementing with its detail what is wanting to the notion in this respect, even in that case a *purely* contemplative reflection simply removes once more all that has been added, does away with it, conducting the notion once again to that simplicity denuded of positive reality which belongs to it and its shadowland of abstraction. It is also a possible contention that science in respect to consent is concerned with what is essentially *necessary*. If our science of Aesthetic places on one side natural beauty, not merely have we apparently made no advance, but rather separated ourselves yet further from what is necessary. The expression *Nature* implies from the first the ideas of *necessity* and *uniformity*, that is to say a constitution which gives every expectation of its proximity and adaptability to scientific inquiry. In mental operations generally, and most of all in the imagination, if contrasted in this respect with Nature, caprice and superiority to every kind of formal restriction, caprice, it is here assumed, is uniquely in its right place and these at once put out of court the basis of a scientific inquiry.

From each and all these points of view consequently, in its origin, that is to say, in its effect and in its range, fine art, so far from proving itself fitted for scientific effort, rather appears fundamentally to resist the regulative principle of thought, and to be ill-adapted for exact scientific discussion.

Difficulties of this kind, and others like them, which have been raised in respect to a thoroughly scientific treatment of fine art have been borrowed from current ideas, points of view, and reflection, the more systematic expansion of which we may read *ad nauseam* in previous literature, in particular French literature, upon the subject of beauty and the fine arts. Such contain to some extent facts which have their justification; in fact, elaborate arguments [60] are deduced therefrom, which also are not without their tincture of apparent plausibility. In this way, for instance, there is the fact that the configuration of beauty is as multifold as the phenomenon of beauty is of universal extension; from which we may conclude, if we care to do so, that a universal impulse towards beauty is enclosed in our common nature, and may yet further conceivably infer, that because the conceptions of beauty are so countless in their variety and withal are obviously something *particular*, it is impossible to secure laws of *universal* validity either relatively to beauty or our taste for it.

Before turning away from such theories to the subject, as we ourselves conceive it, it will be a necessary and preliminary task to discuss the questions and objections raised above.

First, as to the *worthiness* of art to form the object of scientific inquiry, it is no doubt the case that art can be utilized as a mere pastime in the service of pleasure and entertainment, either in the embellishment of our surroundings, the imprinting of a delight-giving surface to the external conditions of life, or the emphasis placed by decoration on other ob-

[60] *Raisonnements*: a disparaging expression.

jects. In these respects it is unquestionably no independent or free art, but an art subservient to certain objects. The kind of art, however, which *we* ourselves propose to examine is one which is *free* in its aim and its means. That art in general can serve other objects, and even be merely a pastime, is a relation which it possesses in common with thought itself. From one point of view thought likewise, as science subservient to other ends, can be used in just the same way for finite purposes and means as they chance to crop up, and as such serviceable faculty of science is not self-determined, but determined by something alien to it. But, further, as distinct from such subservience to particular objects, science is raised of its own essential resources in free independence to truth, and exclusively united with its own aims in discovering the true fulfilment in that truth.

Fine art is not art in the true sense of the term until it is also thus free, and its *highest* function is only then satified when it has established itself in a sphere which it shares with religion and philosophy, becoming thereby merely one mode and form through which the *Divine,* the profoundest interests of mankind, and spiritual truths of widest range, art brought home to consciousness and expressed. It is in works of art that nations have deposited the richest intuitions and ideas they possess; and not infrequently fine art supplies a key of intepretation to the wisdom and religion of peoples; in the case of many it is the only one. This is an attribute which art shares in common with religion and philosophy, the peculiar distinction in the case of art being that its presentation of the most exalted subject-matter is in sensuous form, thereby bringing them nearer to Nature and her mode of envisagement, that is closer to our sensitive and emotional life. The world, into the profundity of which thought penetrates, is a supersensuous one, a world which to start with is posited as a Beyond in contrast to the immediacy of ordinary conscious life and present sensation. It is the freedom of reflecting consciousness which disengages itself from this immersion in the *"this side,"* or immediacy, in other words sensuous reality and finitude. But the mind is able, too, to heal the *fracture* which is thus created in its progression. From the wealth of its own resources it brings into being the works of fine art as the primary bond of mediation between that which is exclusively external, sensuous and transitory, and the medium of pure thought, between Nature and its finite reality, and the infinite freedom of a reason which comprehends. Now it was objected that the *element* [61] *of art* was, if we view it as a whole of an *unworthy* character, inasmuch as it consisted of appearance and deceptions inseparable from such. Such a contention would of course be justifiable, if we were entitled to assume that appearance had no *locus standi* [62] at all. An appearance or show is, however, essential to actuality. There could be no such thing as truth if it did not appear, or, rather, let itself appear,[63] were it not further true for some *one* thing or person, *for* itself as also *for* spirit. Consequently it cannot be appearance in general against which such an objection can be raised, but the particular mode of its manifestation under which art makes actual what is essentially real and true. If, then, the appearance, in the medium of which art gives determinate existence to its creations, be defined as *deception,* such an objection is in the first instance intelligible if we compare it with the *external world* of a phenomena, and its *immediate* relation to ourselves as material substance, or view it relatively to our own world of emotions, that is our inward sensuous life. Both these are worlds to which in our everyday life, the life, that is, of visible experience, we are accustomed to attach the worth

[61] Hegel here means the formal character, not the material on which it is imposed in the several arts.

[62] Hegel says, "as that which has no right to be," *das Nichtseyn sollende.*

[63] *Erscheine* as contrasted with *scheine.*

and name of reality, actuality and truth as contrasted with that of art, which fails to possess such reality as we suppose. Now it is just this entire sphere of the empirical world, whether on its personal side or its objective side, which we ought rather to call in a stricter sense than when we apply the term to the world of art, merely to a show of appearance, and an even more unyielding form of deception. It is only beyond the immediacy of emotional life and that world of external objects that we shall discover reality in any true sense of the term. Nothing is actually real but that which is actual in its own independent right and substance,[64] that which is at once of the substance of Nature and of mind, which, while it is actually *here* in present and determinate existence, yet retains under such limitation an essential and self-concentred being, and only in virtue of such is truly real. The predominance of these universal powers is precisely that which art accentuates and manifests. In the external and soul-world of ordinary experience we have also no doubt this essence of actuality, but in the chaotic congeries of particular detail, encumbered by the immediacy of sensuous envisagement, and every kind of caprice of condition, event, character, and so forth. Now it is just the show and deception of this false and evanescent world which art disengages from the veritable significance of phenomena to which we have referred, implanting in the same a reality of more exalted rank born of mind. The phenomena of art therefore are not merely not appearance and nothing more; we are justified in ascribing to them, as contrasted with the realities of our ordinary life, an actually higher reality and more veritable existence. To as little extent are the representations of art a deceptive appearance as compared with the assumed truer delineations of historical writing. For immediate existence also does not belong to historical writing. It only possesses the intellectual appearance of the same as the medium of its delineations, and its content remains charged with the entire contingent *materia* of ordinary reality and its events, developments and personalities, whereas the work of art brings us face to face with the eternal powers paramount in history with this incidental association of the immediate sensuous present and its unstable appearance expunged.

If, however, it is in contrast with philosophic thought and religious and ethical principles, that the mode of appearance of the shapes of art, is described as a deception, there is certainly this in support of the view that the mode of revelation attained by a content in the realm of thought is the truest reality. In comparison, nevertheless, with the appearance of immediate sensuous existence and that of historical narration, the show of art possesses the advantage that, in its own virtue, it points beyond itself, directing us to a somewhat spiritual, which it seeks to envisage to the conceptive mind. Immediate appearance, on the contrary, does not give itself out to be thus illusive, but rather to be the true and real, though as a matter of fact such truth is contaminated and obstructed by the immediately sensuous medium. The hard rind of Nature and the everyday world offer more difficulty to the mind in breaking through to the Idea than do the products of art.

But if from this particular point of view we place art thus highly, we must not, on the other hand, fail to remember that neither in respect to content or form is art either the highest or most absolute mode of bringing the true interests of our spiritual life to consciousness. The very form of art itself is sufficient to limit it to a definite content. It is only a particular sphere and grade of truth which is capable of being reproduced in the form of a work of art. Such truth must have the power

[64] *Das An-und-Fürsichseyende.* That which is explicitly to itself self-determinate being, no less than essentially such in its substantive right.

in its own determinate character to go out freely into sensuous shape and remain adequate to itself therein, if it is to be the genuine content of art, as is the case, for example, with the gods of Greece. On the other hand there is a profounder grasp of truth, in which the form is no longer on such easy and friendly terms with the sensuous material as to be adequately accepted and expressed by that medium. Of such a type is the Christian conception of truth; and above all it is the prevailing spirit of our modern world, or, more strictly, of our religion and our intellectual culture, which have passed beyond the point at which art is the highest mode under which the absolute is brought home to human consciousness. The type peculiar to art-production and its products fails any longer to satisfy man's highest need. We are beyond the stage of reverence for works of art as divine and objects deserving our worship. The impression they produce is one of a more reflective[65] kind, and the emotions which they arouse require a higher test and a further verification. Thought and reflection have taken their flight above fine art. To those who are fond of complaint and grumbling such a condition of things may be held as a form of decadence; it may be ascribed to the obsession of passion and selfish interests, which scare away the seriousness of art no less than its blithesomeness. Or we may find the fault to lie in the exigencies of the present day, the complex conditions of social and political life, which prevent the soul, entangled as it is in microscopic interests, from securing its freedom in the nobler objects of art, a condition, too, in which the intelligence itself becomes a menial to such trifling wants and the interests they excite in sciences, which subserve objects of a like nature, and are seduced into the voluntary exile of such a wilderness.

[65] *Besonnener Art.* Possibly Hegel means "one more compatible with common sense."

But however we may explain the fact it certainly is the case that Art is no longer able to discover that satisfaction of spiritual wants, which previous epochs and nations have sought for in it and exclusively found in it, a satisfaction which, at least on the religious side, was associated with art in the most intimate way. The fair days of Greek art, as also the golden time of the later middle ages, are over. The reflective culture of our life of to-day makes it inevitable, both relatively to our volitional power and our judgment, that we adhere strictly to general points of view, and regulate particular matters in consonance with them, so that universal forms, laws, duties, rights, and maxims hold valid as the determining basis of our life and the force within of main importance. What is demanded for artistic interest as also for artistic creation is, speaking in general terms, a vital energy, in which the universal is not present as law and maxim, but is operative in union with the soul and emotions, just as also, in the imagination, what is universal and rational is enclosed only as brought into unity with a concrete sensuous phenomenon. For this reason the present time is not, if we review the conditions in their widest range, favourable to art. And with regard to the executive artist himself it is not merely that reflection on every side, which *will* insist on utterance, owing to the universal habit of critical opinion and judgment, leads him astray from his art and infects his mind with a like desire to accumulate abstract thought in his creations; rather the entire spiritual culture of the times is of such a nature that he himself stands within a world thus disposed to reflection and the conditions it presupposes, and, do what he may, he cannot release himself either by his wish or his power of decision from their influence, neither can he by means of exceptional education, or a removal from the ordinary conditions of life, conjure up for himself and secure a solitude capable of replacing all that is lost.

In all these respects art is and remains for us, on the side of its highest possibilities, a thing of the past. Herein it has further lost its genuine truth and life, and is rather transported to our world of *ideas* than is able to maintain its former necessity and its superior place in reality. What is now stimulated in us by works of art is, in addition to the fact of immediate enjoyment, our judgment. In other words we subject the content, and the means of presentation of the work of art, and the suitability and usuitability of both, to the contemplation of our thought. A *science* of art is therefore a far more urgent necessity in our own days in times in which art as art sufficed by itself alone to give complete satisfaction. We are invited by art to contemplate it reflectively, not, that is to say, with the object of recreating such art,[66] but in order to ascertain scientifically its nature.

In doing our best to accept such an invitation we are confronted with the objection already adverted to, that even assuming that art is a subject adapted for philosophical investigation in a general way, yet it unquestionably is not so adapted to the systematic procedure of science. Such an objection, however, implies to start with the false notion that we can have a philosophical inquiry which is at the same time unscientific. In reply to such a point I can only here state summarily my opinion, that whatever ideas other people may have of philosophy and philosophizing, I myself conceive philosophical inquiry of any sort or kind to be inseparable from the methods of science. The function of philosophy is to examine subject-matter in the light of the principle of necessity, not, it is true, merely in accordance with its subjective[67] necessity or external co-ordination, classification, and so forth; it has rather to unfold and demonstrate the object under review out of the necessity of its own intimate nature. Until this essential process is made explicit the scientific quality of such an inquiry is absent. In so far, however, as the objective necessity of an object subsists essentially in its logical and metaphysical nature the isolated examination of art may in such a case, at any rate, or rather inevitably, must be carried forward with a certain relaxation of scientific stringency. For art is based upon many assumptions, part of which relate to its content, part to its material or conceptive[68] medium, in virtue of which art is never far from the borders of contingency and caprice. Consequently it is only relatively to the essential and ideal progression of its content and its means of expression that we are able to recall with advantage the formative principles of its necessity.[69]

The objection that works of fine art defy the examination of scientific thought, because they originate in the unregulated world of imagination and temperament, and assert their effect exclusively on the emotions and the fancy with a complexity and variety which defies exact analysis, raises a difficulty which still carries genuine weight behind it. As a matter of fact the beauty of art does appear in a form which is expressly to be contrasted with abstract thought, a form which it is compelled to disturb in order to exercise its own activity in its own way. Such a result is simply a corollary of the thesis that reality anywhere and everywhere, whether the life of Nature

[66] I think by the words *kunst wieder hervorzurufen* Hegel rather means to call up art as it was previously cultivated than merely to "stimulate art production." The latter is, however, Professor Bosanquet's translation.

[67] *Subjective* apparently in the sense of being wholly personal to the writer or philosopher in so far as the form of his treatise deals in classification and arrangement peculiar to himself and so *external*, if not entirely arbitrary.

[68] I agree with the note of Professor Bosanquet (Trans., p. 21) that the word *element* refers here to the mental constituents of art, as contrasted with the sensuous medium.

[69] That is to say, the essential formative process involved in its necessity.

or mind, is defaced and slain by its comprehension; that so far from being brought more close to us by the comprehension of thinking, it is only by this means that it is in the complete sense removed apart from us, so that in his attempt to grasp through thought as a *means* the nature of life, man rather renders nugatory this very aim. An exhaustive discussion of the subject is here impossible; we propose merely to indicate the point of view from which the removal of this difficulty or impossibility and incompatibility might be effected. It will at least be readily admitted that mind is capable of self-contemplation, and of possessing a consciousness, and indeed, one that implies a power of thought co-extensive with itself and everything which originates from itself. It is, in fact, precisely *thought,* the process of thinking, which constitutes the most intimate and essential nature of mind. It is in this thinking-consciousness over itself and its products, despite all the freedom and caprice such may otherwise and indeed must invariably possess—assuming only mind or spirit to be veritably pregnant therein—that mind exhibits the activity congenial to its essential nature. Art and the creations of art, being works which originate in and are begotten of the spirit, are themselves stamped with the hall-mark of spirit, even though the mode of its presentation accept for its own the phenomenal guise of sensuous reality, permeating as it does the sensuous substance with intelligence. Viewed in this light art is placed from the first nearer to spirit and its thought than the purely external and unintelligent Nature. In the products of art mind is exclusively dealing with that which is its own. And although works of art are not thought and notion simply as such, but an evolution of the notion out of itself, an alienation of the same in the direction of sensuous being, yet for all that the might of the thinking spirit is discovered *not merely* in its ability to grasp *itself* in its most native form as pure thinking, but also, and as completely, to recognize itself in its self-divestment in the medium of emotion and the sensuous, to retain the grasp of itself in that "other" which it transforms but is not, transmuting the alien factor into thought-expression, and by so doing recovering it to itself. And moreover in this active and frequent relation to that "other" than itself the reflective mind is not in any way untrue to itself. We have here no oblivion or surrender of itself; neither is it so impotent as to be unable to comprehend what is differentiated from that other;[70] what it actually does is to grasp in the notion *both* itself and its opposite. For the notion is the universal, which maintains itself in its particularizations, which covers in its grasp both itself and its "other," and consequently contains the power and energy to cancel the very alienation into which it passes. For this reason the work of art, in which thought divests itself of itself,[71] belongs to the realm of comprehending thought; and mind, by subjecting it[72] to scientific contemplation, thereby simply satisfies its most essential nature. For inasmuch as thought is its essence and notion, it can only ultimately find such a satisfaction after passing all the products of its activity through the alembic of rational thought, and in this way making them for the first time in very truth part of its own substance. But though art, as we shall eventually see with yet more distinctness, is far indeed from being the highest form of mind, it is only in the philosophy of art that it comes into all that it may justly claim.

In the same way art is not debarred from a philosophical inquiry by reason of its unregulated caprice As already intimated, it is its true function to bring to consciousness the highest interests of mind. An immediate consequence

[70] *Von ihm.* The pronoun, I take it, must refer here to *das Andere* rather than the subject of the verb.

[71] "Makes itself an alien to itself" perhaps expresses the German better.

[72] That is, the work of art.

of this is that, so far as the *content* of fine art is concerned, it cannot range about in all the wildness of an unbridled fancy; these interests of spirit posit categorically for the content that embodies them definite points of attachment'[73] however multifold and inexhaustible may be the forms and shapes they assume. The same may be said of the forms themselves. They too do not remain unaffected by constraining principles. It is not every chance form which is capable of expressing and presenting these interests, capable of assimilating them and reproducing them. It is only through one determinate content that the form adequate to its embodiment is defined.

It is upon grounds such as these that we are also able to discover a track adapted to critical reflection through the apparently endless vistas of artistic creations and shapes.

We have now, I trust, by way of prelude, succeeded in restricting the content of our science on the lines of definition proposed. We have made it clear that neither is fine art unworthy of philosophical study, nor is such a philosophical study incapable of accepting as an object of its cognition the essense of fine art.

II

If we now investigate the required *mode* of such scientific investigation, we are here again face to face with two contradictory modes of handling the subject, each of which appears to exclude the other and to permit us to arrive at no satisfactory result.

On the one hand we *observe* the science of art, merely so to speak, from an external point of view busying itself with actual works of art, cataloguing them in a history of art, drawing up a sort of commentary upon extant works, or propounding theories which are intended to supply the general points of view for artistic criticism no less than artistic production.

On the other hand we find science wholly giving itself up in its independence and self-assured to the contemplation of the beautiful, offering generalizations which do not concern the specific characteristics of a work of art, producing in short an abstract philosophy of the beautiful.

1. With regard to the first mentioned method of study, the starting-point of which is the *empirical* study of definite *facts*, such is the path everyone must tread who means to study art at all. And just as everyone nowadays, even though he does not actually concern himself with physical science, yet deems it indispensable to his intellectual equipment to have some kind of knowledge of the principles of that science,[74] so too it is generally considered more or less essential to any man of real cultivation, that he should possess some general knowledge of art; and indeed the pretension to be ranked as dilletante, or even as genuine *connoisseur*, meets with comparatively few exceptions.

(a) If however knowledge of this kind is really to claim the rank of *connoisseurship* of the first class it must be both varied in its character and of the widest range. It is an indispensible condition to such that it should possess an accurate knowledge of the wellnigh limitless field of particular works of art both of ancient and modern times, some of which have already disappeared, while others are only to be found in distant countries or portions of the globe, and which it is the misfortune of our situation to be unable to inspect. Add to this that every work of art belongs to *one* age, *one* nationality, and depends upon particular historical or other ends and ideas. On account of this

[73] *Haltpunkte.* Points of arrest in essential ideas necessary which restrain this tendency to purely arbitrary caprice.

[74] I do not think the first part of this sentence ironical. Hegel admits that a general knowledge is a legitimate feature of modern culture. But he points out that people are only too ready to confuse such a general knowledge with real art scholarship. To bring out this I have translated rather freely.

it is indispensable that the finest type of art-scholarship should have at its command not merely historical knowledge of a wide range, but knowledge that is highly specialized. In other words, a work of art is associated with particular[75] detail in a peculiar sense, and a specific treatment, is imperative to the comprehension and interpretation of it. And in conclusion this connoisseurship of the finest class does not merely imply like every other a retentive memory, but also a keen imaginative sense, in order to hold clearly before the mind the images of such artistic representations in all their characteristic lines, and above all, to have them ready for comparison with other works of art.

(*b*) Within the limits of such a method of study which is primarily historical,[76] distinct points of view will soon assert themselves which in the contemplation of such works we are not suffered to lose sight of, inasmuch as they are indispensable to a critical verdict. Such points of view, as is the case with other sciences the commencement of which is empirical, are summarized, after their due collection as separate units and comparison, in general criteria and propositions, emerging in a yet further stage of formal generalization in "*Theories* of the arts." This is not the place to dwell at length upon literature of this kind; we will merely recall a few specimens of such work in the most general way. There is, for instance, the "Poetics" of Aristotle, which contains a theory of tragedy still of real interest. With still more pertinency among the ancients the "Ars Poetica" of Horace and the Essay on the "Sublime" by Longinus will exemplify generally the manner in which this type of theorizing is carried out. The general theses which are therein formulated are intended to stand as premises and rules, in accordance with which works of art ought to be produced, their necessity being above all insisted on in times of the decadence of poetry and art. They are, in short, prescriptions to the practitioner. The prescriptions, however, of these physicians of art were even less successful in their curative effect on art than are the ordinary ones in the restoration of bodily health.

As to such theories I will merely remark that although in the *detail* they contain much that is instructive, yet what they have to say is based on a very limited range of artistic production, which passed no doubt for *the* superlatively beautiful ones, but for all that occupied but a very restricted portion of the entire field of survey. From a further point of view such generalizations are in part very trivial reflections, which in their generality led up to no secure grasp of actual detail, though that is above all the matter of most importance. The epistle of Horace already cited is full of such general theses, and consequently a book for everyone, but one which for this very reason contains much of no importance at all. Take the lines:

> Omne tulit punctum qui miscuit utile dulci
> Lectorum delectando pariterque monendo—

"He carries all votes who has interfused the useful and the pleasant, by at the same time charming and instructing his reader." This is no better than copybook headings such as "Stay where you are and earn an honest six-pence"—which are good enough as generalization, but are defective in the concrete determinacy upon which action depends. An interest of another kind deducible from this type of artistic study does not so much consist in the expressed object to promote the production of genuine works of art: the intention appears to be rather that of influencing the judgment of others upon artistic works by such theories,

[75] Detail of historical fact and artistic observation.

[76] It is historical, first, regarded as a survey of historical condition, and, secondly, because facts are collected whether in relation to ancient or modern art as a historian collects his facts.

creating, in short, a *standard of taste*. It is for an object of this kind that Home's "Elements of Criticism," the writings of Batteux, and Ramler's "Introduction to the Fine Arts" have found many readers in their day. Taste, in this sense, has to do with co-ordination and artistic treatment, the thing in its right place, and all that concerns the finish of that which belongs to the external embodiment of a work of art. Add to this that to the principles of such a taste views were attached which belonged to the psychology in fashion at the time, views which had been discovered by empirical observations of capacities and activities of the soul, or of passions and their potential aggrandizement, succession, and so forth. It is, however, an invariable fact that every one forms his opinion of works of art, or characters, actions and events according to the measure of his insight and his perceptive temperament; and inasmuch as the formation of taste to which we have referred merely touched what was external and therefore jejune, and apart from this deduced its prescriptions entirely from a limited circle of artistic works and an intellectual culture and emotional discipline equally restricted, its sphere of influence was ineffective, and it had neither the power to comprehend the profounder significance[77] and the true, nor to make the vision more keen for their apprehension.

Such theories proceed through generalization as do the rest of the non-philosophic sciences. The content which they submit to examination is accepted from ordinary ideas as something final and received as such. Questions are then asked about the constitution of such a concept, the need for more distinct specification making itself apparent, and this too is borrowed from current ideas, and forthwith finally established from it in definitions. But in such a procedure we at once find ourselves on an insecure basis exposed to controversy. It might in the first instance no doubt appear that the beautiful was quite a simple idea. But we soon discover it combines several aspects; one writer will emphasize one of these, another some other one; or, even assuming the same point of view are considered, the question for dispute still remains which aspect is to be regarded as essential.

With regard to such questions it is generally reckoned as inseparable from scientific completeness, that the various definitions of the beautiful should be enumerated and criticized. For ourselves we do not propose to attempt this with such historical *exhaustiveness* as would unfold all the many refinements of such essays at definition, nor indeed on account of their *historical* interest. We simply, by way of illustration, shall offer a few specimens of the more recent and more interesting ways of regarding the matter which do in fact hit off pretty nearly what is actually implied in the idea of the beautiful. With this in view it is of first importance to recall Goethe's definition of the beautiful, which Meyer has incorporated in his "History of the Creative Arts in Greece," in which work he also brings forward the views of Hirt, though he does not actually mention his name.

Hirt, one of the greatest among connoisseurs of the first class in our time, in his "Essay upon Fine Art" (*Horen*, 1797, seventh number), after considering the beautiful in the several arts, summarizes his conclusions in the statement that the basis of a just criticism of fine art and cultivation of taste is the idea of the *Characteristic*. In other words he defines the beautiful ultimately as the "Consummate[78] which is or can be an object of eye, ear, or imagination." He then proceeds to define this "consummate" as "that which is adequate to its aim, which nature or art aimed at producing

[77] Lit., the inmost or most ideal (meaning).

[78] *Vollkommen.* Complete or rather completely articulate and rounded in itself. It is not easy to select the English word that exactly corresponds.

in the constitution of the object—after its generic kind and specific type." For which reason it is necessary that, in order to instruct our critical sense of beauty, we should direct our attention, so far as possible, to the specific indications of the object's essential constitution. It is, in fact, these *insignia* of individuality which are its characteristic. Consequently under the term *character* as a principle of art he understands "that definite individual characterization,[79] whereby forms, movement and gesture, mien and expression, local colouring, light and shadow, chiaroscuro and pose are severally distinguished in due relation of course to the requirements of the object previously selected." This formula is more significant in its actual terms than other definitions in vogue. If we proceed to ask what the "characteristic" is we find that it implies, first a *content*, as, for instance, a definite emotion, situation, event, action, individual person or thing; secondly, the specific *manner* in accordance with which such a content is represented. It is to this mode or manner of presentation that the artistic principle of the "characteristic" is related. It requires that every aspect of detail in the mode of expression shall subserve the clearer expression's content, and become a vital member of such expression.

The abstract determination of the characteristic emphasizes therefore the pertinency with which particular detail ought to bring into prominence the content which it is intended to reproduce. Attempting an elucidation of this conception apart from technical phrase we may state the limitation implied in it as follows: In the drama, for instance, it is an action which constitutes the content. That is to say, the drama has to represent how this or that action takes place. Now men do all kinds of different things. They speak to each other, take their meals, sleep, put on their clothes, say this and that, and all the rest of it. But in all this business of life what does not lie in immediate relation with the particular action selected as the real dramatic content, must be excluded in order that relatively to it everything shall be significant. In the same way in a picture which only includes one moment of that action, and it is possible to accumulate—such are the countless vistas into which the objective world draws us—a mass of circumstances, persons, situations or other occurrences, which stand in no relation to the specific action as it actually occurs, nor subserve in any way the clearer characterization of the same. But according to the definition given of the characteristic only that ought to enter into a work of art, which is appertinent to the manifestation and essential expression of precisely this one content and no other. Nothing must declare itself as idle or superfluous.

This definition is no doubt of real importance, and from a certain point of view admits of justification. Meyer, however, in the work cited, is of opinion that the view propounded has vanished, every vestige of it, and in his opinion only to the advantage of art. Such a conception he thinks would in all probability lead to caricature. This judgment is based on the previous idea that an attempt of this kind to define the beautiful once and for all is associated with the notion of *prescription*. The philosophy of art has absolutely nothing to do with precepts for artists. The object is to unfold the essential nature of the beautiful, and—apart from any intention to propound rules for the executant—how it is illustrated in actual work, that is works of art. To such a criticism we may observe that the definition of Hirt no doubt includes what is capable of being caricature, for caricature may also be characteristic. The obvious point to make, however, against it is this, that in caricature character in its definition is emphasized to the point of exaggeration, and is, if we may say

[79] *Bestimmte Individualität.* The definition may, as Hegel says, be more significant, but it is for all that not very clearly expressed. Professor Bosanquet translates the words "determinate individual modification."

so, a superfluity of the characteristic. But a surfeit of this kind is no longer appropriate to the characteristic, but a burdensome reiteration whereby the characteristic may itself be ousted from what it ought to be. Moreover, what is of the nature of caricature is displayed as the characteristic presentment of what is ugly, which is of course a mode of distortion. *Ugliness* is in its own right in this way more closely related to the content,[80] so that it may be actually asserted that the principle of the characteristic includes also ugliness and the presentment of the same as a part of its essential determination. The definition of Hirt, of course, gives us no further account of the content of the beautiful. It merely supplies us in this respect with a purely formal statement, which, however, contains real truth in it although formulated in abstract terms.

There is, however, the further question—what Meyer would substitute for the artistic principle of Hirt, what he proposes himself? He deals in the first instance exclusively with the principle as we have it in ancient works of art, which, however, must contain in the widest connotation of the term the essential determinant [81] of beauty.[82] In doing so he finds occasion to refer to Mengs and to Winckelmann's definition of the Ideal, and expresses himself to the effect that he does not wish either to reject or wholly to accept this principle of beauty, but on the other hand that he feels no hesitation in subscribing to the opinion of an enlightened judge of art (that is Goethe), inasmuch as its meaning is distinct and it appears to solve the problem with more accuracy. Now what Goethe says is this: "The highest principle of the ancients was the *significant*; the highest result of successful artistic *handling* is the *beautiful*."

If we look more closely at what this dictum implies we have again once more two aspects, that is to say a content or subject matter, and the mode of its presentation. In our consideration of a work of art we begin with that which is directly presented to us, and after seeing it we proceed to inquire what its significance or content is. That external husk possesses no value to us simply as such. We assume that there is an inward, an ideality or a significance behind it, in virtue of which the external appearance is made alive with mind or spirit. It is to this, its soul, that the external appearance points and attests. For an appearance which is significant of something does not present itself to us, and merely that which it is *quá* externality, but something other than this; as also does the symbol for example and with yet more clarity the fable, the significance of which is simply the moral and teaching of the same. In fact there is no word which does not point to a meaning, possessing no value by itself. In the same way the human eye, the face, flesh, skin, the entire presence are a revelation of spirit, intelligence and soul; and in such a case the significance is without exception something beyond that which is offered in the bare appearance. In this way too the work of art must possess significance; it must not appear to have told its tale simply in the fact of particular lines, curves, surfaces, indentations, reliefs of stone-work, in particular colours, tones, sounds of words, whatever medium in fact art may employ. Its function is to unveil an inward or ideal vitality, emotion, soul, a content and mind, which is precisely what we mean by the significance of a work of art.

80 My view is that what Hegel means to say is that in caricature ugliness is emphasized and made more (*näher*) a part of the content that belongs to the true nature of the characteristic of which it is (in Hegel's opinion) no essential determinant or property. The view stated in the sentence is therefore a kind of *reductio ad absurdum*. Professor Bosanquet's translation appears to me to leave it doubtful whether the view stated is a just one or not. He translates *näher* by "closely," not the comparative. In my view Hegel agrees that caricature may be characteristic, but he does not agree that it is a genuine property of the characteristic where it is pressed to the excess ot ugliness.

81 *Bestimmung.*

82 That is, in Hegel's View.

This demand, therefore, for significance in a work of art is to all intents, and in its embrace much the same thing as Hirt's principle of the characteristic.

According to this conception we find as characteristic constituents of the beautiful an inward somewhat, a content, and an external rind which possesses that content as its significance. The inner or ideal constituent appears in the external and thus enables itself to be recognized, that which is external pointing away from itself to the inward.

We cannot, however, pursue the matter here into further detail.

(*c*) But the earlier fashion of this "theory-spinning," no less than the laying down of rules for the executant already adverted to, has already been thrust on one side despotically in Germany—mainly owing to the appearance of genuine living poetry—and the right of genius, its work and effects, have had their full independence insisted upon as against the pretensions of such rules of thumb and the broad water-ducts of theory. From this foundation of an art which is itself of truly spiritual rank, as also of a sympathy and absorption of the same, have arisen the receptivity and freedom which make it possible for us to enjoy and appreciate great works of art which have long since been within our reach, whether it be those of the modern world, of the Middle Ages, or of wholly foreign peoples of the Past, the works of India for example; works, which, in virtue of their antiquity or the remoteness of their nationality, possess unquestionably for ourselves a side alien to ourselves; but which, if we consider the way in which their content passes over and beyond such national limits, and the matter in it of common appeal to all mankind, can only be hall-marked by the prejudice of theory among the products of a barbarous or corrupt taste. This recognition of works of art anywhere and everywhere, works which depart from the specific circle and forms of those upon which in the main the abstractions of theory were based, has, as a primary consequence, led to the recognition of a peculiar type of art—*the romantic art*. It became necessary to apprehend the notion and the nature of the beautiful in a profounder way than these theories attempted. With this fact another, too, co-operated, viz., that the notions in its form of apperception, the mind as pure thought on its part reached in philosophy a point of profounder self-cognition, and was thereby compelled forthwith to grasp the essence of art too on profounder lines. In this way, even in virtue of the point in the process reached of this general evolution of human thought, the type of theorizing upon art we have described, both relatively to its principles no less than their elaboration, has become obsolete. It is only the *scholarship* of the history of art which retains an abiding value, and must continue to retain it in proportion as the boundaries of its survey have enlarged in every direction by means of the advance made in man's powers of receptivity already noticed. Its business and function consists in the aesthetic appreciation of particular works of art and the knowledge of the historical, in other words the external conditions from which the work of art originates. It is an attitude of the mind, which, if assisted with sound sense and critical insight, supported too with historical knowledge, is an indispensable condition to the complete penetration into the individuality of a given work of art. The many writings of Goethe upon art and works of art are an excellent illustration. Theorising, in the specific sense noticed, is not the aim of this type of examination, although no doubt it not unfrequently also busies itself with abstract principles and categories, and may drop into such a style unconsciously. If, however, without letting such deviations on our route detain us, we keep before our vision these concrete illustrations of artistic works, such at least, whatever else they may do, supply a philosophy of art with the visible warrant and confirmation of actual work, into the historical detail of which, in each particular case, philosophy is not permitted to enter.

This then may be accepted as the first method of art study. It starts from the particular work which we have before us.

2. The method or point of view to be contrasted with this, in other words an entirely theoretical reflection, which is concerned to cognize the beautiful as such from its own intrinsic wealth, and to penetrate to the idea of it, is essentially distinct from the first method. As is well known, Plato was the first to demand of philosophical inquiry in a profounder sense, that objects should not be cognized in their *particularity,* but in their *universality,* in their generic type, their essential being and its explicit manifestation. He maintained that this true essence[83] did not consist in *particular* actions which were good, in particular true opinions, handsome men or beautiful works of art, but in *goodness, beauty,* and *truth* in their universality. Now if in fact the beautiful ought to be cognized according to its essence and notion, this can only be effected by means of the thinking notion,[84] by means of which the logical and metaphysical nature of the *Idea as such,* as also of that of the particular *Idea of the beautiful* enters into the thinking consciousness. But the consideration of the beautiful in its self-independence and its idea may readily once more become an abstract metaphysic; and even though Plato is accepted as founder and pioneer, the Platonic abstraction no longer supplies all we require, not even for the logical Idea of the beautiful. We are bound to grasp this idea more profoundly and more in the concrete. The emptiness of content which clings to the Platonic Idea, no longer satisfies the richer philosophical requirements of the mind to-day. It is no doubt the case that we also in the philosophy of art must make the Idea of the beautiful our starting point; but it is by no means inevitable that we should adhere to the Platonic ideas in their abstraction, ideas from which the philosophy of the beautiful merely dates its origins.

3. The philosophical idea of the beautiful to indicate at any rate its true nature provisionally, must contain both extremes which we have described mediated in itself. It must combine, that is to say, metaphysical universality with the determinate content of real particularity. It is only by this means that it is grasped in its essential no less than explicit truth. For on the one hand it is then, as contrasted with the sterility of one-sided reflection, fruit-bearing out of its own wealth. It is its function, in consonance with its own notion, to develop into a totality of definite qualities, and this essential conception itself, no less than its detailed explication, comprises the necessary coherence of its particular features as also of the progress and transition of one phase thereof into another. On the other hand, these particulars into which the passage is made essentially carry the universality and essentiality of the fundamental notion as the particulars of which they appear. The modes of inquiry hitherto discussed lack both these aspects, and for this reason it is only the notion, as above formulated, in its completeness, which conducts us to definitive principles which are substantive, necessary, and self-contained in their completeness.

[83] *Das Wahre.*

[84] *Den denkenden Begriff.* It is possible that the "notion of thought" would express Hegel's meaning, as it would be a less strange expression. But I have retained the more literal translation as the reference may be to the self-evolution of Thought in its own dialectical process, thought or the Idea thinking out itself in the Hegelian sense. Professor Bosanquet seems to assume this, as he translates "the thinking Idea."

III

After these preliminaries we come to closer quarters with our actual subject-matter, namely, the philosophy of Fine Art; [85] and for the reason that we are undertaking to treat it scientifically, our commencement must be with the notional concept of the same. It is only after we have definitely ascertained this that we can map out the division of its parts, and with it the plan of the science as a whole. A division of this kind, if it is not to be, as is the case with non-philosophical inquiry, undertaken in a purely external way, must discover its principle in the notion of the subject treated itself.

Face to face with such a demand we are at once met by the question: "Whence do we arrive at such a conception?" If we begin with the notional concept of Fine Art itself the same at once becomes a *pre-supposition* and mere assumption. Mere assumptions, however, are excluded from the philosophical method; whatever here is allowed as valid must have its truth demonstrated, in other words must be established in its necessity.

We will endeavour to arrive at an understanding in a few words in the presence of this difficulty which invariably recurs in the introduction to every course of philosophical study if treated independently. The subject-matter of every science presents in the first instance two aspects for consideration: first, the fact that a given object *is*; secondly, the question *what* it is.

Upon the question of fact in ordinary scientific inquiry little difficulty is experienced. Indeed it might on a cursory view even appear ridiculous if the demand were made that we had to prove in geometry, for instance, that there were such objects as space, and geometrical figures, or in astronomy and physics that there was a sun, stars, and magnetic phenomena. In these sciences, which are concerned with what is actually presented to sense perception, objects are accepted from objective experience, and so far from it being regarded necessary to demonstrate (*beweisen*) them, it is deemed sufficient to point to (*weisen*) the bare facts. Yet even within the limits of non-philosophical instruction doubts may arise as to the existence of certain objects. In psychology, for example, the science of mind, the doubt is possible whether there *is* a soul, an intelligence, *i.e.,* something distinct from material conditions, something immaterial,[86] independent and self-substantive, or in the theology whether a God actually *exists*. Moreover, assuming the objects of the science to be thus immaterial, in other words, merely present in the mind, and not a part of the objective world we perceive, we have to face the possible conviction that there is nothing in the mind, but that which it has evoked in virtue of its own activity. This brings up incidentally the question whether men have produced this idea or intuition which is inward to their minds or not, and even if we do actually accept the first alternative, whether they have not made such an idea once more to vanish, or depreciated the same at any rate to an idea of wholly *subjective* validity, whose content possesses no independent or self-contained existence.[87] In this way, for example, the beautiful has been frequently regarded as possessing no necessarily essential and independent stability in the world of our ideas;

[85] *Kunstschönen.* I have translated this by the expression "fine art" because Hegel in the opening of the introduction makes the expression interchangeable with *schöne kunst.* At the same time it must be recollected that the emphasis here is even more on "beauty" than the fact that it is the beauty of human art. And it is for this reason, I presume, that Professor Bosanquet translates it here "artistic beauty." The only objection I have to make to this, apart from Hegel's words I have referred to, is that the expression "artistic beauty" is sometimes used to signify beauty that is capable of being expressed by art. Of course that is excluded from Hegel's use of the term; he means the beauty of artistic work.

[86] *Subjektiven.*

[87] Independent, that is, of the consciousness of any particular individual. Hegel does not necessarily mean independent of consciousness altogether. He has, no doubt, generally in his mind the kind of scepticism which received its most logical exposition in Hume.

rather it is accepted as a pleasure purely personal to ourselves, due to the caprice of our senses.[88] Even our external intuitions, observations and perceptions frequently deceive and lead us astray; but still more is this the case with those ideas that do not arise from sense-perception, even though they possess in themselves the greatest vitality, and are able to transport us into passion, we are powerless to resist.

This doubt, then, whether an object of the inward world of our ideas and intuitions actually exists as an independent fact or not, as also that further incidental problem, whether the particular consciousness in question has produced it in itself, and whether the particular mode or process, in which it objectified it to itself, is also adequate to the object thus envisaged in its essential and independent nature—these are precisely the kind of questions which have awakened in men the higher demand of philosophy, which is that, even if there is every appearance that an object is, or that we have before us such an object, yet none the less that object must be expounded or demonstrated on the basis of its necessity. A demonstration of this kind, if developed on truly philosophical lines, ought at the same time to supply a sufficient answer to the question: *What* a given object is. To work this out fully would, however, carry us further than is now possible. We propose to limit ourselves to the following general remarks.

If we are to propound the necessity of our subject-matter, in other words the beauty of art, we are bound to prove that art, or the beautiful, is a result of antecedents such as, when regarded relatively to their true notional concept, conduct us with scientific necessity to the similar notion of fine art itself. Inasmuch as, however, we propose to make art the point of departure, and its idea and the objective presence of the same, and do *not* propose to deal with the antecedent conditions which are essential to the necessary exposition of its notional concept, for this reason art, in our treatment of it as a particular object of scientific inquiry, involves a pre-assumption, which lies outside the boundary of our investigation; which, implying as it does a different content, belongs, as scientifically treated, to another course of philosophical inquiry. We have therefore now no other alternative than frankly to accept the notional idea of art, so to speak, provisionally,[89] which is inevitable with every one of the *particular* philosophical sciences, if regarded in their abstract isolation. For it is the entire body of philosophy, and that alone, which either is or can be the comprehension of the universe as one essentially *single* organic totality; and which, as such a totality, self-evolved from its own notional Idea, and returning into itself so as to form a whole in virtue of the necessary principle in which it is placed relatively to itself, encloses itself, and all that is itself, into one single world of truth. In the coronal of this scientific necessity is every particular member thereof a self-complete circle which returns into itself, while, at the same time, and as imperatively, it possesses a necessary bond of connection with other parts. This bond of coherence is a backward from which it is self-derived, no less than a forward to which it is self-impelled onward, in so far as it fruitfully begets fresh material from its own resources, and renders the same open and

[88] This appears to me the meaning of *zufälliger Sinn.* Professor Bosanquet translates it "accidental sense." By that I presume he understands the meaning to be "a sense of beauty that is entirely personal to the recipient," *i.e.,* it may be possessed by one man, but not by another. Hegel's illustration hardly supports this, so it seems to me.

[89] I do not know the exact translation of *lemmatisch,* and by a curious slip the sentence is omitted from Professor Bosanquet's translation. The general sense is plain enough. Every particular science accepts its subject-matter as a *datum.* It starts from the empirical fact. Whether it admits the assumption or not, it does assume such facts. It is obvious that Hegel's adoption of this standpoint is only relatively true.

pervious to scientific cognition. It is not therefore our purpose to demonstrate the Idea of the beautiful, which is our point of departure, or, in other words, to deduce it in all its necessity from the assumptions which are its antecedents in philosophy, and from the womb of which it is born. This is the object appropriate to an encyclopaedic development of philosophy as a whole and in its specific branches. For ourselves the notional concept of the beautiful and art is a pre-supposition supplied us by the system of philosophy. Inasmuch, however, as we are not prepared to discuss this system, and the association of art with it in the present context,[90] we have not as yet the idea of the beautiful before us in a *scientific form*: what we have and are able to deal with are simply the phases and aspects of the same as we find them in the various conceptions of beauty and art of our everyday conscious life, or as they have been conceived by previous writers. Having made our start at this point we shall then at a later stage pass on to the more fundamental investigation of those views, in order thereby to secure the advantage of, in the first instance, working out a general idea of our subject-matter no less than obtaining a provisional acquaintance, as a result of our necessarily brief criticism, with its higher principles, which will occupy our thoughts in the inquiry which follows.[91] By this means our final introduction [92] will supply a sort of overture to the exposition of the subject itself, and will aim at being a general concatenation and direction of our reflection on the real subject-matter before us. What in the first instance is known to us under current conceptions of a work of art may be subsumed under the three following determinations:

(1) A work of art is no product of Nature. It is brought into being through the agency of man.

(2) It is created essentially *for* man; and, what is more, it is to a greater or less degree delivered from a sensuous medium, and addressed to his *senses*.[93]

(3) It contains an *end* bound up with it.

1. With regard to the first point, that a work of art is a product of human activity, an inference has been drawn from this (*a*) that such an activity, being the conscious production of an external object also be *known* and *divulged*, and learned and reproduced by others. For that which one is able to effect, another—such is the notion—is able to effect or to imitate,[94] when he has once simply mastered the way of doing it. In short we have merely to assume an acquaintance with the rules of art-production universally shared, and anybody may then, if he cares to do so, give effect to executive ability of the same type, and produce works of art. It is out of reasoning of this kind that the above-mentioned theories, with their provision of rules, and their prescriptions formulated for practical acceptance, have arisen. Unfortunately that which is capable of being brought into effect in accordance with suggestions of this description can only be something formally regular and mechanical. For only that which is mechanical is of so exterior a type that only an entirely empty effort of will and dexterity is required to accept it among our working conceptions, and forthwith to carry it out; an effort, in fact, which

[90] Hegel means, I presume, mainly in the introduction. After that he does in a qualified degree discuss the profounder import of the Idea of Fine Art. His statements are not perhaps wholly free from inconsistency, because he has previously said that apart from an encyclopaedic consideration of all the sciences, it was not possible to do so, and also some of his statements seem to imply that he does not intend to do so.

[91] That is, in the first Part of the entire treatise.

[92] What Hegel means by the *die letzte einleitende Betrachtung* I am not quite sure. I presume he means the introduction to the first Part. The whole of this paragraph is not very clear.

[93] By *Sinn* man's sensitive life in its widest sense is, I think, intended.

[94] The German words are *machen* and *nachmachen.* We have no exact equivalents.

is not under the necessity to contribute out of its own resources anything concrete such as is quite outside the prescriptive power of such general rules.

This is apparent with most vividness when percepts of this kind are not limited to what is purely external and mechanical, but extend their pretensions to the activity of the artist in the sense that implies wealth of significance and intelligence. In this field our rules pass off to purely indefinite generalities, such as "the theme ought to be interesting, and each individual person must speak as is appropriate to his status, age, sex and situation." But if rules are really to suffice for such a purpose their directions ought to be formulated with such directness of detail that, without any further co-operation of mind, they could be executed precisely in the manner they are prescribed. Such rules being, in respect to this content, abstract, clearly and entirely fall short of their pretension of being able to complete [95] the artistic consciousness. Artistic production is not a formal activity in accordance with a series of definitions; it is, as an activity of soul, constrained to work out of its own wealth, and to bring before the mind's eye a wholly other and far richer content, and a more embracing and unique [96] creation than ever can be thus prescribed. In particular cases such rules may prove of assistance, in so far, that is, as they contain something really definite and consequently useful for practice. But even here their guidance will only apply to conditions wholly external.

(*b*) This above indicated tendency has consequently been wholly given up; but writers in doing so have only fallen as unreservedly into the opposite extreme. A work of art came to be looked upon, and so far rightly, as no longer the product of an activity *shared by all men,* but rather as a creation of a mind gifted in an extraordinary degree. A mind of this type has in this view *merely* to give free vent to its peculiar endowment, regarded as a specific natural power. It has to free itself absolutely from a pursuit of rules of universal application, as also from any admixture of conscious reflection with its creative and, as thus viewed, wholly instinctive powers, or rather it should be on its guard therefrom, the assumption being that such an exercise of conscious thought can only act on its creations as an infection and a taint. Agreeably to such a view the work of art has been heralded as the product of *talent* and *genius*; and it is mainly the aspect of natural gift inseparable from the ordinary conception of talent and genius, which has been emphasized. There is to some extent real truth in this. Talent is specific, genius universal capacity. With neither [97] of these can a man endow himself *simply* by the exercise of his self-conscious activity. We shall consider this at greater length in a subsequent chapter.[98]

In the present context we would merely draw attention to the false assumption in this view that in artistic production every kind of self-reflection upon the artist's own activity was regarded as not merely superfluous, but actually injurious. In such a view the process of creation by talent or genius simply is taken to be a general *state*; or we may define it more precisely as a condition of inspiration. To such a condition, it is said, genius is in some measure exalted by the subject-matter itself; it is also to some extent voluntarily able to place itself under such a condition, a process of self-inhibition in which the genial service of the

[95] *Lit.,* "to fill out (*ausfullen*) in complete equipment."

[96] *Individuelle.*

[97] The German will admit of the interpretation that the reference is merely to genius, but I think Hegel clearly means that neither one nor the other can be thus conjured up.

[98] At the end of the first main division of the work.

champagne bottle is not forgotten.[99] An idea of this kind was in vogue during the so-called "Epoch of Genius," which originated with the early poetical work of Goethe, receiving subsequent illustration in those of Schiller. These poets by their rejection of all rules hitherto fabricated made as it were an entirely new start; with deliberate intention they ran counter to such rules, and while doing so distanced all competitors by many lengths. I do not, however, propose to discuss with more detail the confusions which have prevailed over the conception of inspiration and genius, and the notion, which even at the present day finds advocates, that inspiration simply by itself can effect anything and everything. The real and indeed sole point to maintain as essential is the thesis that although artistic talent and genius essentially implies an element of natural power, yet it is equally indispensable that it should be thoughtfully cultivated, that reflection should be brought to bear on the particular way it is exercised, and that it should be also kept alive with use and practice in actual work. The fact is that an important aspect of the creating process is merely facility in the use of a medium;[100] that is to say, a work of art possesses a purely technical side, which extends to the borders of mere handicraft. This is most obviously the case in architecture and sculpture, less so in painting and music, least of all in poetry. A facility here is not assisted at all by inspiration; what solely indispensable is reflection, industry, and practice. Such technical skill an artist simply *must* possess in order that he may be master over the external material, and not be thwarted by its obstinacy.

Add to this that the more exalted the rank of an artist the more profoundly ought he to portray depths of soul and mind; and these are not to be known by flashlight, but are exclusively to be sounded, if at all, by the direction of the man's own intelligence on the world of souls and the objective world. In this respect, therefore, once more *study* is the means whereby the artist brings to consciousness such a content, and appropriates the material and structure of his conceptions. At the same time no doubt one art will require such a conscious reception and cognitive mastery of the content in question more than another. Music, for example, which has exclusively to deal with the entirely undefined motion of the soul within, with the musical tones of that which is, relatively, feeling denuded of positive thought, has little or no need to bring home to consciousness the substance of intellectual conception. For this very reason musical talent declares itself as a rule in very early youth, when the head is still empty and the emotions have barely had a flutter; it has, in fact, attained real distinction at a time in the artist's life when both intelligence and life are practically without experience. And for the matter of that we often enough see very great accomplishment in musical composition and execution hung together with considerable indigence of mind and character. It is quite another matter in the case of poetry. What is of main importance here is a presentation of our humanity rich in subject-matter and reflective power, of its profounder interests, and of the forces which move it. Here at least mind and heart must themselves be richly and profoundly disciplined by life, experience, and thought before genius itself can bring into being the fruit that is ripe, the content that has

[99] One of Meredith's correspondents has put the question with all gravity whether he considered inspiration could be assisted by wine drinking. With equal gravity our humourist replied that though wine might be something of a restorative after mental effort it was not his experience that it contributed to first-rate artistic work. He actually mentions the case of Schiller. Though I have read somewhere that this poet used to be inspired by the smell of rotten apples I do not recollect reading that he favoured the champagne bottle. Meredith also mentions the case of Hoffman, and adds that the type of his work does not increase our respect for the precedent.

[100] *Eine äusserliche Arbeit.* A craftsmanship which has to deal with the outside surface. We may translate "external craftsmanship"; but the translation in the text gives the meaning best, I think.

substance, and is essentially consummate. The early productions of Goethe and Schiller are characterized by an immaturity, we may even call it a rawness and barbarity, which really are appalling. This phenomenon, that in the majority of those experiments we find a preponderating mass of features which are absolutely prosaic, or at least uninspired and commonplace, is a main objection to the ordinary notion that inspiration is inseparable from youth and its sirocco season. These two men of genius were the first beyond question to give our nation true works of poetry, are, in fact, our national poets; but for all that it was only their mature manhood, which made it a present of creations profound, sterling of their kind, creations of genuine inspiration, and no less technically complete in their artistic form.[101] We naturally recall the case of the veteran Homer, who only composed and uttered his immortal songs in his old age. . . .

(*c*) A third view, held relatively to the idea of a work of art as a product of human activity, concerns the position of such towards the phenomena of Nature. The natural tendency of ordinary thinking in this respect is to assume that the product of human art is of *subordinate* rank to the works of Nature. The work of art possesses no feeling of its own; it is not through and through a living thing, but, regarded as an external object, is a dead thing. It is usual to regard that which is alive of higher worth than what is dead. We may admit, of course, that the work of art is not in itself capable of movement and alive. The living, natural thing is, whether looked at within or without, an organization with the life-purpose of such worked out into the minutest detail. The work of art merely attains to the show of animation on its surface. Below this it is ordinary stone, wood, or canvas,[102] or in the case of poetry idea, the medium of such being speech and letters. But this element of external existence is not that which makes a work a creation of fine art. A work of art is only truly such in so far as originating in the human spirit it continues to belong to the soil from which it sprang, has received, in short, the baptism of the mind and soul of man, and only presents that which is fashioned in consonance with such a sacrament. An interest vital to man, the spiritual values which the single event, one individual character, one action possesses in its devolution and final issue, is seized in the work of art and emphasized with greater purity[103] and clarity than is possible on the ground of ordinary reality where human art is not. And for this reason the work of art is of higher rank than any product of Nature whatever, which has not submitted to this passage through the mind. In virtue of the emotion and insight, for example, in the atmosphere of which a landscape is portrayed by the art of painting, this creation of the human spirit assumes a higher rank than the purely natural landscape. Everything which partakes of spirit is better than anything begotten of mere Nature. However this may be, the fact remains that no purely natural existence is able, as art is, to represent divine ideals.

And further, all that the mind borrows from its own ideal content it is able, even in the direction of external existence, to endow with *permanence.* The individual living thing on the contrary is transitory; it vanishes and is unstable in its external aspect. The work of art persists. At the same time it is not mere continuation, but rather the form and pressure thereon of the mintage of soul-life which con-

[101] The "Iphigenie" was completed in Goethe's thirty-eighth year, fourteen years later than "Götz." The bulk of his more important works are of the same date or later. Schiller's "Wallenstein" was completed after his thirty-fifth year.

[102] This is surely not quite accurate. The medium of painting in the sense that speech or writing is the medium of poetry is not canvas or panel but oil or other colour. Canvas would correspond with the blank pages of a book.

[103] Free, that is, from accidental and irrelevant matter.

stitutes its true pre-eminence as contrasted with Nature's reality.

But this higher position we have thus assigned to the work of art is yet further contested by another prevalent conception of ordinary ideas. It is contended that Nature and all that proceeds from her are a work of God, created by His goodness and wisdom. The work of art is on the contrary *merely* a human product fashioned by human hands according to human design. The fallacy implied in this contrast between the products of Nature viewed as a divine creation and human activity as of wholly finite energy consists in the apparent assumption that God is not operative in and through man, but limits the sphere of His activity to Nature alone. We must place this false conception entirely on one side if we are desirous of penetrating to the true idea of art; or rather, as opposed to such a conception we ought to accept the extreme opposite thereto, namely, that God is more honoured by that which mind makes and creates than by everything brought into being and fashioned in the natural process. For not only is there a divinity in man, but it is actually effective in him in a form which is adequate to the essential nature of God in a far higher degree than in the work of Nature. God is a Spirit, and it is only in man that the medium, through which the Divine passes, possesses the form of spirit fully conscious of the activity in which it manifests its ideal presence. In Nature the medium correspondent to this is the unconscious [104] and external *materia,* which is by many degrees inferior to consciousness in its worth. In the products of art God works precisely as He works through the phenomena of Nature. The divine substance, however, as it is asserted in the work of art has secured, being begotten of spirit life itself, a highway commensurable to its existence; determinate existence in the unconscious sensuousness of Nature is not a mode of appearance adequate to the Divine Being.

(*d*) Assuming, then, that the work of art is a creation of man in the sense that it is the offspring of mind or spirit we have still a further question in conclusion, which will help us to draw a more profound inference still from our previous discussion. That question is, "What is the human *need* which stimulates art-production?" On the one hand the artistic activity may be regarded as the mere play of accident, or human conceits, which might just as well be left alone as attempted. For, it may be urged, there are other and better means for carrying into effect the aims of art, and man bears within himself higher and more weighty interests, than art is capable of satisfying. In contrast to such a view art appears to originate in a higher impulse, and to satisfy more elevated needs, nay, at certain times the highest and most absolute of all, being, as it has been, united to the most embracing views of entire epochs and nations upon the constitution of the world and the nature of their religion.

This inquiry, however, concerning a necessity for art which shall not be merely contingent, but absolute, we are not as yet able to answer with completeness; it demands, in fact, a concreter mode of exposition than is compatible with the form of this introduction. We must accordingly deem it sufficient for the present merely to establish the following points.

The universal and absolute want from which art on its side of essential form [105] arises

[104] Professor Bosanquet translates *sinnliche* here as "sensitive." I am inclined to think that Hegel here rather leaves out of sight the fact that in the process of Nature we have sensitive organic life no less than unconscious inorganic. His contrast is rather between the conscious life of man and unconscious nature, the conscious life that is not self-unconscious being for the object of the contrast treated as equivalent to unconscious. He would also apparently ignore the fact that man himself and the higher beauty which attaches to him is also from one point of view a part of the natural process.

[105] That is, apart from purely personal ends in its pursuit, which are accidental to its essential notion.

originates in the fact that man is a *thinking* consciousness, in other words that he renders explicit *to himself,* and from his own substance,[106] what he is and all in fact that exists. The objects of Nature exist exclusively in immediacy and *once for all.*[107] Man, on the contrary, as mind *reduplicates* himself. He is, to start with, an object of Nature as other objects; but in addition to this, and no less truly, he exists *for himself*; he observes himself, makes himself present to his imagination and thought, and only in virtue of this active power of self-realization is he actually mind or spirit. This consciousness of himself man acquires in a twofold way; in the *first* instance *theoretically.* This is so in so far as he is under a constraint to bring himself in his own inner life to consciousness—all which moves in the human heart, all that surges up and strives therein—and generally, so far as he is impelled to make himself an object of perception and conception, to fix for himself definitively that which thought discovers as essential being, and in all that he summons out of himself, no less than in that which is received from without, to recognize only himself. And *secondly,* this realization is effected through a *practical* activity. In other words man possesses an impulse to assert himself in that which is presented him in immediacy, in that which is at hand as an external something to himself, and by doing so at the same time once more to recognize himself therein. This purpose he achieved by the alteration he effects in such external objects, upon which he imprints the seal of his inner life, rediscovering in them thereby the features of his own determinate nature. And man does all this, in order that he may as a free agent divest the external world of its stubborn alienation from himself—and in order that he may enjoy in the configuration of objective fact an external reality simply of himself. The very first impulse of the child implies in essentials this practical process of deliberate change in external fact. A boy throws stones into the stream, and then looks with wonder at the circles which follow in the water, regarding them as a result in which he sees something of his own doing. This human need runs through the most varied phenomena up to that particular form of self-reproduction in the external fact which is presented us in human art. And it is not merely in relation to external objects that man acts thus. He treats himself, that is, his natural form, in a similar manner: he will not permit it to remain as he finds it; he alters it deliberately. This is the rational ground of all ornament and decoration, though it may be as barbarous, tasteless, entirely disfiguring, nay, as injurious as the crushing of the feet of Chinese ladies, or the slitting of ears and lips. For it is among the really cultured alone that a change of figure, behaviour, and every mode and manner of self-expression will issue in harmony with the dictates of mental elevation.[108]

This universal demand for artistic expression [109] is based on the rational impulse in man's nature to exalt both the world of his soul experience and that of Nature for himself into the conscious embrace of mind as an object in which he rediscovers himself. He satisfies the demand of his spiritual freedom by making explicit to his *inner* life all that exists, no less than from the further point of view giving a realized *external* embodiment to the self made thus explicit. And by this reduplication of what is his own he places before the vision and within the cognition of himself and others what is within him. This is the free rationality of man, in which art as also all

[106] That is, in the medium of conscious life.

[107] *Einmal.* They are there, but they do not know they are there.

[108] *Aus geistiger Bildung, i.e.,* a high level of mental culture is necessary before the advent of civilized manners and customs in which spiritual life is reflected with real refinement and directness.

[109] *Bedurfniss zur Kunst.*

action and knowledge originates. We shall investigate at a later stage the specific need for art as compared with that for other political and ethical action, or that for religious ideas and scientific knowledge.

2. We have hitherto considered the work of art under the aspect that it is fashioned by man; we will now pass over to the second part of our definition, that it is produced for his *sense-apprehension,* and consequently is to a more or less degree under obligations to a sensuous medium.

(*a*) This reflection has been responsible for the inference that the function of fine art is to arouse feeling, more precisely the feeling which suits us—that is, pleasant feeling. From such a point of view writers have converted the investigation of fine art into a treatise on the emotions and asked what kind of feelings art ought to excite—take fear, for example, and compassion—with the further question how such can be regarded as pleasant, how, in short, the contemplation of a misfortune can bring satisfaction. This tendency of reflection dates for the most part from the times of Moses Mendelssohn, and many such trains of reasoning may be found in his writings. A discussion of this kind, however, did not carry the problem far. Feeling is the undefined obscure region of spiritual life. What is felt remains cloaked in the form of the separate personal experience under its most abstract persistence; [110] and for this reason the distinctions of feeling are wholly abstract; they are not distinctions which apply to the subject-matter itself. To take examples—fear, anxiety, care, dread, are of course one type of emotion under various modifications; but in part they are purely quantitative degrees of intensity, and in part forms which reflect no light on their content itself, but are indifferent to it. In the case of fear, for instance, an existence is assumed, for which the individual in question possesses an interest, but sees at the same time the negative approach which threatens to destroy this existence, and thereupon discovers in immediate fusion within himself the above interest and the approach of that negative as a contradictory affection of his personal life. A fear of this sort, however, does not on its own account condition any particular content; it may associate with itself subject-matter of the most opposed and varied character. The feeling merely as such is in short a wholly empty form of a subjective state. Such a form may no doubt in certain cases itself be essentially complex, as we find it is with hope, pain, joy, and pleasure; it may also in this very complexity appropriate various modes of content, as, for example, we have a feeling of justice, an ethical feeling, a sublime religious feeling, and so forth; but despite the fact that a content of this kind is present in different modes of feeling, no light whatever is thereby thrown on such content which will disclose its essential and definite character. The feeling throughout remains a purely subjective state which belongs to me, one in which the concrete fact vanishes, as though contracted to a vanishing point in the most abstract of all spheres.[111] For this reason an inquiry over the nature of the emotions which art ought or ought not to arouse, comes simply to a standstill in the undefined; it is an investigation which deliberately abstracts from genuine content and its concrete substance and notion. Reflection upon feeling is satisfied with the observation of the personal

[110] *Lit.,* "In the form of the most abstract single subjectivity." That is to say, that the main fact about it is that it is felt; but, except in respect to intensity, it cannot be described as an object of thought with defining attributes. It is abstract individual sensation.

[111] By the expression *Kreis* Hegel would mean rather an indefinite sphere than a definite circle. The simile is perhaps not very apt. The idea, apparently, is of a sphere of feeling, that is, such as being self-complete, but is so abstract or indefinable that the introduction into it of positive ideas such as justice, etc., are the mere entrance of spectral forms which vanish in such an indefinable medium, without disclosing their nature. They are felt but not cognized for what they really are.

emotional state and its singularity, instead of penetrating and sounding the matter for study, in other words the work of art, and in doing so bidding good-bye to the wholly subjective state and its conditions. In feeling, however, it is just this subjective state void of content which is not merely accepted, but becomes the main thing; and that is precisely why people are so proud of having emotions. And for no other reason that is why such an investigation is tedious owing to its indefinite nature and emptiness, and even repellent in its attention to trivial personal idiosyncrasies.

(*b*) Inasmuch, however, as the work of art is not merely concerned with exciting some kind of emotion or other—for this is an object it would share without any valid distinction with eloquence, historical composition, religious edification and much else—but is only a work of art in so far as it is beautiful, it occurred to reflective minds to discover a *specific feeling for beauty,* and a distinct *sense-faculty* correspondent with it. In such an inquiry it soon became clear that a sense of this kind was no definite and mere [112] instinct rigidly fixed by Nature, which was able by itself and independently to distinguish the beautiful. As a consequence the demand was made for *culture* as a condition precedent to such a sense, and the sense of beauty as thus cultivated was called *taste,* which, albeit an instructed apprehension and discovery of the beautiful, was none the less assumed to persist in the character of immediate feeling. We have already discussed the way in which abstract theory attempted to form such a sense of taste, and how external and one-sided that sense remained. While the critical sense generally of the time when such ideas were in currency was lacking in the *universality* of its principles, as a *specfic* critique of particular works of art it was less concerned to substantiate a judgment *more decisive* than hitherto—indeed the material to effectuate this was not as yet forthcoming—than to promote in a general way the *cultivation* of such a taste.[113] Consequently this educative process also came to a halt in the region of the more indefinite, and merely busied itself by its reflections in the fitting out of feeling as a sense of beauty in such a way that beauty could immediately be discovered whenever and wherever it might chance to appear. The real depth of the subject-matter remained notwithstanding a closed book to such a taste. Profundity of this kind demands not merely sensitive reception and abstract thought, but the reason in its concrete grasp and the most sterling qualities of soul-life. Taste on the contrary is merely directed to the outside surfaces, which are the playground of the feelings, and upon which one-sided principles may very well pass as currency. But for this very reason our so-called good taste is scared by every kind of profounder artistic effect, and is dumb where the ideal significance [114] is in question, and all mere externalities and accessories vanish. For when great passions and the movements of a profound

[112] *Blinder,* blind in the sense that it is not guided by deliberate and self-conscious reason, *i.e.,* mere animal instinct.

[113] A difficult sentence to translate. I have followed Professor Bosanquet in assuming that the substantive with which *mangelhaft* agrees must be borrowed from the following sentence, though it seems also to be carried on in a loose kind of way from the previous sentence (*Geschmacksinn*). The entire sentence is built, as we have it, on the further confusion that there are two parallels which before the sentence ends are regarded as one! That is to say, the general critical sense is contrasted with the critique of particular works of art and further the defect of that general sense in its neglect of *universal* principles is further contrasted with the way the specific critique deals with *particular* works. I hardly think, however, that my admirable predecessor is justified in ignoring the comparative degree of *bestimmteres,* or in his translation of *Zéug* as "power." I take it to mean the material of actual works of art. The sentence is a good example of some of the difficulties of Hegel translation.

[114] *Die Sache.* The subject-matter in its most real sense as "content."

soul assert themselves, we do not bother ourselves any more with the finer distinctions of taste and its retail traffic in trifles. It is[115] conscious that genius leaves such ground far behind it in its stride; and shrinking before that power feels on its part far from comfortable, not knowing very well which way to turn.

(*c*) Thus it is the further change has come about that critics of art-production no longer have an eye simply to the education of taste, or are intent upon the illustration of such a sense. The *connoisseur*, or art-scholar, has taken the place of the man, or judge of artistic taste. The positive side of art-scholarship, in so far as it implies a sound and exhaustive acquaintance with the entire embrace of what is distinctive and peculiar in a given work of art, we have already maintained to be a necessary condition of artistic research. A work of art, owing to its nature, which, if it is material from one point of view, is also related to a particular person, originates from specific conditions of the most varied kind, among which as exceptionally important we may mention the date and place of its origins, the characteristic personality of the artist, and, above all, the degree of executive accomplishment secured by the art. All these points of view have to be taken into consideration if we wish to obtain a view and knowledge of such a work which is clear in its outlines, and founded on a true basis, nay, even wish to enjoy it rightly. It is with these that our art-scholarship is mainly occupied; and all that it can do for us in this way should be gratefully accepted. Though it is quite true such art-scholarship must be reckoned as of essential importance, it ought not to be regarded as the sole, or indeed the highest, constituent in the relation of the contemplative spirit to a work of art and art generally. Such art-scholarship (this is the defective tendency) may restrict itself wholly to a knowledge of purely external characteristics, either on the side of technique or historical condition, or in other directions; it may continue to possess the barest inkling of the true nature of a given work, or simply no knowledge at all. It may even form a depreciatory verdict on the value of profounder inquiries as compared with purely matter of fact, technical, and historical knowledge. Yet even so an art-scholarship, assuming it to be really genuine and thorough, at least proceeds upon grounds and knowledge which are definite, and an intelligent judgment; and it is association with such that our more accurate review of the distinct, if also to some extent exterior, aspects of a work of art, and our estimate of their relative significance is secured.

(*d*) Following the above observations upon the modes of inquiry which were suggested by that aspect of a work of art in which as itself an object with a material medium, it possessed an essential relation to man as himself receptive through sense, we will now examine this point of view in its more essential connection with art itself. We propose to do this partly (α) in respect to the art-product viewed as an object, partly (β) as regards the personal characteristics of the artist, his genius, talent, and so forth. We do not, however, propose to enter into matter which can in this connection exclusively proceed from the knowledge of art according to its universal concept.[116] The truth is we are not as yet in the full sense on scientific ground; we have merely reached the province of external reflection.

(α) There is no question, then, that a work of art is presented to sensuous apprehension. It is submitted to the emotional sense, whether outer or inner, to sensuous perception and the imaged sense, precisely as the objective world is so presented around us, or as is our own inward sensitive nature. Even a speech, for example, may be addressed to the sensuous imagination and feeling. Notwithstanding this fact, however, the work of art is not exclus-

[115] That is, the so-called "good taste."

[116] *Begriff*. Concrete notional Idea.

ively directed to the *sensuous* apprehension, viewed, that is, as an object materially conditioned. Its position is of the nature, that along with its sensuous presentation it is fundamentally addressed to the *mind*. The mind is intended to be affected by it and to receive some kind of satisfaction in it.

This function of the work of art at once makes it clear how it is that it is in no way intended to be a natural product or, on the side where it impinges on Nature, to possess the living principle of Nature. This, at least, is a fact whether the natural product is ranked lower or higher than a *mere* work of art, as people are accustomed to express themselves in the tone of depreciation.

In other words the sensuous aspect of a work of art has a right to determine existence only in so far as it exists for the human mind, not, however, in so far as itself, as a material object, exists for itself independently.

If we examine more closely in what way the sensuous *materia* is presented to man we find that what is so can be placed under various relations to the mind.

(*aa*) The lowest in grade and that least compatible with relation to intelligence is purely sensuous sensation. It consists primarily in mere looking, listening, just as in times of mental overstrain it may often be a relaxation to go about without thought, and merely listen and have a look round. The mind, however, does not rest in the mere apprehension of external objects through sight and hearing; it makes them objective to its own inward nature, which thereupon is impelled itself to give effect to itself in these things as a further step under a sensuous mode, in other words, it relates itself to them as *desire*. In this appetitive relation to the external world man, as a sensuous[117] particular thing, stands in a relation of opposition to things in general as in the same way particulars. He does not address himself to them with open mind and the universal ideas of thought; he retains an isolated position, with its personal impulse and interests, relatively to objects as fixed in their obduracy as himself, and makes himself at home in them by using them, or eating them up altogether, and, in short, gives effect to his self-satisfaction by the sacrifice he makes of them. In this negative relation desire requires for itself not merely the superficial show of eternal objects, but the actual things themselves in their material concrete existence. Mere pictures of the wood, which it seeks to make use of, or of the animals, which it hopes to eat up, would be of no service to desire. Just as little is it possible for desire to suffer the object to remain in its freedom; its craving is just this to force it to annihilate this self-subsistency and freedom of external facts, and to demonstrate that these things are only there to be destroyed and devoured. But at the same time the particular person is neither himself free, begirt as he is by the particular limited and transitory interests of his desires, for his definite acts do not proceed from the essential universality and rationality of his will, neither is he free relatively to the external world, for desire[118] remains essentially determined by things and related to them.

This relation, then, of desire is not that in which man is related to the work of art. He suffers it to exist in its free independence as an object; he associates himself with it without any craving of this kind, rather as with an object reflective of himself,[119] which exists solely for the contemplative faculty of mind. For this reason, as we have said, the work of art, although it possesses sensuous existence, does not require sensuous concrete existence,

[117] That is, in his physical form.

[118] Hegel is here considering desire abstractedly, that is, on its own account (*als solche*). It may of course in its turn subserve a rational purpose, such as the preservation of health or life. But the contrast here is between the relation of appetite, and that of the theoretic faculty to objects.

[119] *Sein Objekt.* The object in which he finds himself; rather this, I think, than that which he has created.

nor yet the animated life of such objects. Or, rather, we should add, it *ought* not to remain on such a level, in so far as its true function is exclusively to satisfy spiritual interests, and to shut the door on all approach to mere desire. Hence we can understand how it is that practical desire rates the particular works of Nature in the organic or inorganic world, which are at its service, more highly than works of art, which are obviously useless in this sense, and only contribute enjoyment to other capacities of man's spirit.

(ßß) A second mode under which the externally present comes before the conscious subject is, as contrasted with the single sensuous perception and active desire, the purely theoretical relation to the *intelligence.* The theoretic contemplation of objects has no interest in consuming the same in their particularity and satisfying or maintaining itself through the sense by their means; its object is to attain a knowledge of them in their *universality,* to seek out their ideal nature and principle, to comprehend them according to their notional idea. Consequently this contemplative interest is content to leave the particular things as they are, and stands aloof from them in their objective singularity, which is not the object of such a faculty's investigation. For the rational intelligence is not a property of the particular person in the sense that desire is so; it appertains to his singularity as being itself likewise essentially universal. So long as it persists in this relation of universality to the objects in question, it is his reason in its universal potency which is attempting to discover *itself* in Nature, and thereby the inward or essential being of the natural objects, which his sensuous existence does not present under its mode of immediacy, although such existence is founded therein. This interest of contemplation, the satisfaction of which is the task of *science,* is, however, shared in this scientific form just as little by art as it shared in the common table of those impulses of the purely practical desire. Science can, it is true, take as its point of departure the sensuous thing in its singularity, and possess itself of some conception, how this individual thing is present in its specific colour or form. But for all that this isolated thing of sense as such posesses no further relation to mind, inasmuch as the interest of intelligence makes for the universal, the law, the thought and notion of the object, and consequently not only does it forsake it in its immediate singularity, but it actually transforms it within the region of idea,[120] converting a concrete object of sense into an abstract subject-matter of thought, that is converting it into something other than the same object of its sensuous perception actually was. The artistic interest does not follow such a process, and is distinct from that of science for this reason. The contemplation of art restricts its interests simply in the way in which the work of art, as external object, in the directness of its definition, and in the singularity wherein it appears to sense, is manifested in all features of colour, form, and sound, or as a single isolated vision of the whole; it does not go far beyond the immediately received objective character as to propose, as is the case with science, the ideal or conceptive thinking of this particular objectivity under the terms of the rational and universal notion which underlies it.

The interest of art, therefore, is distinguishable from the practical interest of desire in virtue of the fact that it suffers its object to remain in its free independence, whereas desire applies it, even to the point of destruction, to its own uses. The contemplation of art, on the other hand, differs from that of a scientific intelligence in an analogous way[121] in virtue of the fact that it cherishes an interest for the object in its isolated existence, and is not con-

[120] *Innerlich, i.e.,* in the world of mind as contrasted with that of the sensuous *vorhandene.*

[121] Hegel or his editors have "in a converse way." This is obviously a mistake. In both examples the point is that the object is *preserved* as against *desire* with its destruction, and the *contemplative intelligence* with its ideal transformation.

cerned to transform the same into terms of universal thought and notion.

($\gamma\gamma$) It follows, then, that, though the sensuous *materia* is unquestionably present in a work of art, it is only as surface or *show* of the sensuous that it is under any necessity to appear. In the sensuous appearance of the work of art it is neither the concrete material stuff, the empirically perceived completeness and extension of the internal organism which is the object of desire, nor is it the universal thought of pure ideality, which in either case the mind seeks for. Its aim is the sensuous presence, which, albeit suffered to persist in its sensuousness, is equally entitled to be delivered from the framework of its purely material substance. Consequently, as compared with the immediately envisaged and incorporated object of Nature, the sensuous presence in the work of art is transmuted to mere semblance or *show*, and the work of art occupies a midway ground, with the directly perceived objective world on one side and the ideality of pure thought on the other. It is not as yet, pure thought, but, despite the element of sensuousness which adheres to it, it is no longer purely material existence, in the sense at least that stones, plants, and organic life are such. The sensuous element in a work of art is rather itself somewhat of ideal intension,[122] which, however, as not being actually the ideal medium of thought, is still externally presented at the same time as an object. This semblance of the sensuous presents itself to the mind externally as the form, visible appearance, and harmonious vibration of things. This is always assuming that it suffers the objects to remain in their freedom as objective facts, and does not seek to penetrate into their inward essence by abstract thought, for by doing so they would (as above explained) entirely cease to exist for it in their external singularity.

For this reason the sensuous aspect of art is only related to the two *theoretical*[123] senses of *sight* and *hearing;* smell, on the other hand, taste, and the feeling of touch are excluded from the springs of art's enjoyment. Smell, taste, and touch come into contact with matter simply as such,[124] and with the immediate sensuous qualitites of the same; smell with the material volatization through the air; taste with the material dissolution of substance, and touch or mere bodily feeling with qualities such as heat, coldness, smoothness, and so forth. On

[122] *Ein ideelles.* The meaning is, I think, that the *materia* is stamped with the hall-mark of deliberate artistic purpose. The ideality, though relatively jejune on such a work as the pyramids, in the higher reaches of art such as poetry and music affects of course the medium itself, the musical chord being pure ideality. Professor Bosanquet's translation omits this and the previous sentence, probably by an oversight. But it is also possible that this thinker conceived the statement *as here expressed* to be misleading, or at least open to misconception. In architecture and even painting it is obvious, from a certain point of view, the sensuous *materia,* if directed to an artistic end, remains none the less the material borrowed from natural fact though the fact as natural may be modified in its form. Painting may *represent* the semblance, but it employs a medium simply sensuous. Hegel has mainly before his attention here obviously the arts of painting, poetry, and music.

[123] They are *theoretical* because as applied to a work of art they imply the presence of the contemplative faculty. In a later section of the work Hegel makes a more complete analysis of what is implied in the sense of hearing as applied to musical composition and in the colour sense. In both cases it is obvious the mind contributes to the facts cognized. Hearing is, however, from Hegel's point of view the most *ideal* of the two, and he conceives the position of the ears itself points to this distinction.

[124] It may at least be questioned whether the ground given here of this distinction, or part of it, is strictly accurate. It may be said that our sense of sight and hearing are both in contact with the waves of the medium, the vibration of which produces the impression we call sound or light. The most obvious distinction then appears to be that the natural object is left as it is by hearing and sight. This at least holds good as against taste. But at least it may be questioned, I think, whether the sense of touch may not be the source of artistic enjoyment, certainly in the case of the blind. And the sense of smell at least leaves objects as they are, and some may contend that it is a source of enjoyment of the beauty of Nature. Hegel would reply, of course, that no works of human art are enjoyed by such means. The main ground is, however, that sight and hearing are the senses closest to intelligence.

this account these senses cannot have to do with the objects of art, which ought to subsist in their actual and very independence, admitting of no purely sensuous or rather physical relation. The pleasant for such senses is not the beauty of art. Thus art on its sensuous side brings before us deliberately merely a shadow-world of shapes, tones, and imaged conceptions,[125] and it is quite beside the point to maintain that it is simply a proof of the impotence and limitations of man that he can only present us with the surface of the physical world, mere *schemata*, when he calls into being his creative works. In art these sensuous shapes and tones are not offered as exclusively for themselves and their form to our direct vision. They are presented with the intent to secure in such shape satisfaction for higher and more spiritual interests, inasmuch as they are mighty to summon an echo and response in the human spirit evoked from all depths of its conscious life. In this way the sensuous is *spiritualized* in art, or, in other words, the life of *spirit* comes to dwell in it under sensuous guise.

(β) For this reason, however, a product of art is only possible in so far as it has received its passage through the mind, and has originated from the productive activity of mind. This brings us to another question we have to answer, and it is this: "How is the sensuous or material aspect, which is imperative as a condition of art, operative in the artist as conjoined to his personal productive activity?" [126] Now this mode or manner of artistic production contains, as an activity personal to the artist, in essentials just the same determinants which we found posited in the work of art. It must be a spiritual activity, which, however, at the same time possesses in itself the element of sensuousness and immediacy. It is neither, on the one hand, purely mechanical work, such as is purely unconscious facility in sleight of hand upon physical objects, or a stereotyped activity according to teachable rule of thumb; nor, on the other hand, is it a productive process of science, which tends to pass from sensuous things to abstract ideas and thoughts, or is active exclusively in the medium of pure thought. In contrast to these the two aspects of mental idea and sensuous material must in the artistic product be united. For example, it would be possible in the case of poetical compositions to attempt to embody what was the subject-matter in the form of prosaic thought in the first instance, and only after doing so to attach to the same imaginative ideas rhymes and so on, so that as a net result such imagery would be appendent to the abstract reflections as so much ornament and decoration. An attempt of this kind, however, could only lead us to a poor sort of poetry, for in it we should have operative a twofold kind of activity in its *separation*, which in the activity of genuine artistic work only holds good in inseparable unity. It is this true kind of creative activity which forms what is generally described as the artistic *imagination*. It is the rational element, which in its import as spirit only exists, in so far as it actively forces its way into the presence of consciousness, yet likewise, and only subject to this condition, displays all its content to itself under a sensuous form. This activity possesses therefore a spiritual content, but it clothes the same in sensuous image, and for this reason that it is only able to come to a knowledge of the same under this sensuous garb. We may compare such a process with that of a man of experience in life, a man, shall we add, of real geniality and wit, who—while at the same time being fully conscious in what

[125] By *Anschauungen* Hegel apparently has in mind all the ideas of poetry. We should certainly rather have expected the word *Vorstellungen*, the word used being rather "visible perceptions." But the three words here seem generally to denote the subject-matter of painting, music, and poetry.

[126] Lit., "Operative in the artist viewed (*i.e.*, the artist) as the personal energy (*Subjektivität*) which creates." Professor Bosanquet's translation "as a productive state of the person" would appear to make "the sensuous side" a subjective state of the artist. But apart from construction, can we speak of this as a "state"? It is modified by his energy—but it can hardly be regarded as a part of it.

the main importance of life consists, what are the things which essentially bind men together, what moves them and is the mainspring of their lives—nevertheless has neither brought home this content in universal maxims, nor indeed is able to unfold it to others in the generalities of the reflective process, but makes these mature results of his intelligence without exception clear to himself and others in particular cases, whether real or invented, or by examples and such like which hit the mark. For in the ideas of such a man everything shapes itself into the concrete image determinate in its time and place, to which therefore the addition of names and any other detail of external condition causes no difficulty. Yet such a kind of imagination rather rests on the recollection of conditions, he has lived through, actual experience, than it is a creative power of itself. Memory preserves and renews the particularity and external fashion of such previous events with all their more distinct circumstances, but on the other hand does not suffer the universal to appear independently. The creative imagination of an artist is the imagination of a great mind and a big heart; it is the grasp and excogitation of ideas and shapes, and, in fact, nothing less than this grasp of the profoundest and most embracing human interests in the wholly definite presentation of imagery borrowed from objective experience. A consequence of this is, that imagination of this type [127] is based in a certain sense on a natural gift, a general talent for it, as we say, because its creative power essentially implies an aspect of sense presentation. It is no doubt not unusual to speak in the same way of scientific "talent." The sciences, however, merely presuppose the general capacity for thought, which does not possess, as imagination does, together with its intellectual activity, a reference to the concrete testimony of Nature, but rather precisely abstracts from the activity that form in which we find it in Nature. It would be, therefore, truer to the mark if we said there is no specific scientific talent in the sense of a purely natural endowment. Imagination,[128] on the other hand, combines within it a mode of instinct-like creativeness. In other words the essential plasticity and material element in a work of art is subjectively present in the artist as part of his native disposition and impulse,[129] and as his

[127] I find it impossible to fix any one English equivalent to Hegel's use of the words *Einbildungskraft, Phantasie,* or *Vorstellung,* in the sense at least that fancy, imagination, or phantasy have been used and defined by famous English writers. Generally speaking, I should say that *Phantasie,* or as it is called sometimes "artistic" or "creative" *Phantasie,* stands for the most intellectual faculty, though *Vorstellung* is also used in much the same sense. But it is impossible to arrive at any clear distinction such as was originally made so profoundly by Ruskin between fancy, the instrument of poetical talent, the surface gift, and imagination or, as he called it *penetrative* imagination, which summarizes all the powers of a genius and personality and enters into the heart of the subject-matter by an illuminating flash which *reveals* reality rather than illustrates by means of image. The present passage appears to me even more unsatisfactory than the more carefully digested analysis at the end of Part I, when Hegel discusses the artist. It not merely ignores the indispensable presence of imagination in the pioneers of science, but appears to myself to confuse talent as the natural gift of a man with the mode in which it is exercised in presenting ideas in sensuous imagery, or at least makes the former depend on the latter. Professor Bosanquet translates *Phantasie* here by "fancy." But "fancy" is, in our way of looking at it, precisely not the faculty which *distinctively* belongs to "the great mind and the big heart or soul," though other parts of the description are more applicable. And in short, as I say, to fix definite English equivalents to Hegel's phraseology appears to me impossible.

[128] *Die Phantasie.*

[129] This is, I presume, Hegel's way of putting the simple fact, that much of the process of artistic production is unconscious. One man instinctively draws, or picks up his notes on the piano, another cannot. I think Hegel rather refers to this *original* talent than the much more important one in which genius, right into maturity, rides over difficulties without knowing how it does so. Such happy or even miraculous effects—such as artists sometimes playfully call them—are obviously in part, if only in part, the result of profound artistic experience. He is dealing almost exclusively with the natural bias, which makes one man naturally an artist, whether creative or executant, and is absent from another. He hardly approaches the question what constitutes the artist of genius as contrasted with the man of natural talent.

unconscious activity belongs in part to that which man receives straight from Nature. No doubt the entire talent and genius of an individual is not wholly exhausted by that we describe as natural capability. The creation of art is quite as much a spiritual and self-cognized process; but for all that we affirm that its spirituality contains an element of plastic or configurative facility which Nature confers on it. For this reason, though almost anybody can reach a certain point in art, yet, in order to pass beyond this—and it is here that the art in question really begins—a talent for art which is inborn and of a higher order altogether is indispensable.

Considered simply as a natural basis a talent of this kind asserts itself for the most part in early youth, and is manifested in the restless persistency, ever intent with vivacity and alertness, to create artistic shapes in some particular sensuous medium, and to make this mode of expression and utterance the unique one or the one of main importance and most suitable. And thus also a virtuosity up to a certain point in the technique of art which is arrived at with ease is a sign of inborn talent. A sculptor finds everything convertible into plastic shape, and from early days takes to modelling clay; and so on generally whatever men of such innate powers have in their minds, whatever excites and moves their souls, becomes forthwith a plastic figure, a drawing, a melody, or a poem. . . .

(*d*) When discussing moral improvement as the ultimate end accepted for art it was found that its principle pointed to a higher standpoint. It will be necessary also to vindicate this standpoint for art.

Thereby the false position to which we have already directed attention vanishes, namely that art has to serve as a means for moral ends and the moral end of the world generally by means of its didactive and ameliorating influence, and by doing so has its essential aim not in itself, but in something else. If we therefore continue still to speak of an end or goal of art, we must at once remove the perverse idea, which in the question, "What is the end?" will still make it include the supplemental query, "What is the use?" The perverseness consists in this that the work of art would then have to be regarded as related to something else, which is presented us as what is essential and ought to be. A work of art would in that case be merely a useful instrument in the realization of an end which possessed real and independent importance outside the realm of art. As opposed to this we must maintain that it is art's function to reveal *truth* under the mode of art's sensuous or material configuration, to display the reconciled antithesis previously described, and by this means to prove that it possesses its final aim in itself, in this representation in short and self-revelation. For other ends such as instruction, purification, improvement, procuring of wealth, struggle after fame and honour have nothing whatever to do with this work of art as such, still less do they determine the fundamental idea [130] of it.

It is then from this point of view, into which the reflective consideration of our subject-matter finally issues, that we have to grasp the fundamental idea of art in terms of its ideal or inward necessity, as it is also from this point of view that historically regarded the true appreciation and acquaintance with art took its origin. For that antithesis, to which we have drawn attention, did not merely assert its presence within the general thought of educated men, but equally in philosophy as such. It was only after philosophy was in a position to overcome this opposition absolutely that it grasped the fundamental notion of its own content, and, to the extent it did so, the idea of Nature and of art.

For this reason, as this point of view implies the re-awakening of philosophy in the

[130] *Begriff.* Notion, or concrete Idea of it.

widest connotation of the term, so also it is the re-awakening of the science of art. We may go further and affirm that aesthetic as a science is in a real sense primarily indebted to this re-awakening for its true origination, and art for its higher estimation.

IV

From this point of transition, I will briefly summarize the historical subject-matter that I have in my mind's eye ,partly on account of the historical importance itself, and in part because thereby the points of view are more clearly indicated to which importance is attached, and upon the basis of which we propose the superstructure. In its most general definition that basis consists in this, that the beauty of art has become recognized as one of the means which resolve and bring back to unity that antithesis and contradiction between the mind and Nature as they repose in abstract alienation from each other in themselves, whether this latter is regarded as external phenomena or the inward world of individual feeling and emotion.[131]

1. It was the philosophy of Kant which, in the first instance, not merely experienced the want of such a point of union, but secured definite knowledge of it and brought it clearly before the mind. Speaking generally, Kant accepted as his basis for intelligence no less than for the will the rationality which relates itself to itself or freedom, the self-consciousness that discovers and knows itself essentially as infinite. This knowledge of the absoluteness of reason in its essential substance, which has proved in more modern times the turning-point of philosophy, this absolute point of departure deserves recognition, and does not admit of refutation, even though in other respects the Kantian philosophy is inadequate. But at the same time it was Kant who through falling back upon the fixed opposition between subjective thought and objective things, between abstract universality and the sensuous individuality of the will, in a pre-eminent degree strained to the extremest limit the very antithesis of morality we have previously adverted to, inasmuch as over and above this he emphasized the practical operation of mind to the disadvantage of the contemplative. In virtue of this fixity of the antithesis as cognized by the faculty of the understanding he had no other alternative than to express the unity exclusively in the form of subjective ideas for which no adequate reality could be demonstrated as correspondent; or, on its practical side, as postulates, which it was no doubt possible to deduce from the practical reason, but whose essential being was not within the cognition of thought, and the practical fulfilment of which remained throughout a mere "ought" deferred to infinity. And for this reason, though Kant did actually bring the reconciled opposition within the compass of intelligible ideas, he was neither able to develop its essential truth scientifically, nor to assert the same as actual and exclusive reality. Unquestionably Kant did press beyond this point, in the sense, that is to say, that he discovered the unity demanded in what he called the *intuitive* understanding; but in this respect too he is held up by the opposition of subjectivity and objectivity, so that, while he no doubt offers us a resolution in an abstract sense of the antithesis between conception and reality, universality and particularity, understanding and sense-perception, and suggests the Idea, yet he once more conceives this resolution and reconciliation itself in a wholly *subjective* sense, not as being true and real both essentially and on its own independent account. In this respect the Critique of the power of judgment, in which he investigates the aesthetic and teleological power of the judgment is both instructive and remarkable.

[131] Of that world in its opposition to reason.

The beautiful objects of Nature and art, the products of Nature with their adaptations to ends, by means of which he approaches more closely the notion of the organic and the living, he considers wholly from the point of view of the reflection which judges them subjectively. And indeed Kant himself generally defines the power of judgment as "the capacity to think the particular as comprised under the universal," and calls the power of judgment *reflective* "when it has only the particular submitted to it, and has to discover the universal under which it is subsumed." To this end it requires a law, a principle, which it has to contribute to itself; and Kant affirms *teleology* to be this law. With regard to the conception of freedom which belongs to the practical reason the achievement of end or purpose gets no further than a mere "ought"; and in the teleological judgment, however, relatively to the living thing, Kant does manage to regard the living organism in such a way that the notional concept, the universal, succeeds in also including the particular, and as end does not determine the particular and external, the structure of the members from outside, but as an inward principle, and under the mode, that the particular conforms to the end spontaneously. Yet with such a judgment once more it is assumed that the objective nature of the thing is not known, but that it is only a mode of subjective reflection which is thereby expressed. In a similar way Kant so conceives the *aesthetic* judgment that it neither proceeds from the understanding, as such, in other words as the faculty of ideas, nor yet from the sensuous perception as such, and its varied manifold, but from the free play of the understanding and the imagination. In this common agreement of the faculties of knowledge the object finds its relation to the individual consciousness, and its feeling of pleasure and contentment.

(*a*) Now this general feeling of contentment is, in the first place, without any interest, that is to say, it is *devoid of relation* to our *appetitive faculty.* If we have an interest of curiosity, shall we say, or a sensuous interest excited for a physical want, a desire for possession and use, then the objects are not important for their own sake, but in virtue of our need of them. In a case such as this what exists merely possesses a value in relation to such a need, and the relation is of the kind, that the object is on the one side and on the other is an attribute distinct from the object to which we relate it none the less. As an illustration if I consume the object in order to nourish myself therewith, this interest rests exclusively in me, and remains alien to the object. Now, in Kant's view, our position relatively to the beautiful is not of this description. The aesthetic judgment suffers that which is externally presented to subsist in free independence, proceeding as it does from the desire to permit the object to persist on its own account and to retain its end unimpaired within itself. This is, as we have already observed, an important observation.

(*b*) In the second place, Kant maintains that the beautiful is definable as that which without a conception, *i.e.*, without a category of the understanding, is placed before us as the object of a *universal* satisfaction. To estimate the beautiful an educated mind is indispensable. The man in the street [132] has no judgment about the beautiful; this judgment, in fact, claims universal validity. The universal is no doubt in the first instance simply, *as such*, an abstraction, one which, however, is in its essential and on its independent account, true; and consequently carries essentially the property and demand to pass also as universally valid. In this sense, too, the beautiful ought to be universally recognized, although the mere concepts of the understanding are compatible with no judgment thereupon. The good—the right which enters into particular actions, for example

[132] *Der Mensch als er geht und steht.* The man in ordinary conditions—the *average* man, however, rather than the *natural* man, which carries slightly different associations

—is subsumed under universal concepts, and the action is accepted as good, if it is conformable to such concepts. The beautiful, on the contrary, ought, according to this view, to arouse a universal satisfaction without any such mediation of concept. This simply means that in the contemplation of the beautiful we are not conscious of the notional concept or any subsumption under it, and do not permit the independent passage of the separation between the particular object and the universal concept, which is present in all other cases of the judgment.

(*c*) Thirdly, in this view of Kant, the beautiful ought to have the *teleological* form to the extent that the teleological relation is apprehended in the object without the idea of an end. This is substantially a mere repetition of the view just discussed. Any natural product—take, for instance, a plant or an animal—is organized as adapted to an end, and is so immediately to us in this its teleological purpose, that we have no conception of the end on its own account as separate and distinct from the actual presence of the object. It is in this way that the beautiful also is presented us teleologically. In finite teleology end and means remain external to each other; the end stands in no essential inner relation to the material means of its execution.[133] In this case the idea of the end as recognized in apartness [134] is distinguishable from the object in which the end appears as realized. The beautiful, on the contrary, exists as teleological in the essential sense, without means and end appearing as disparate in aspects distinct from each other. For example, the purpose of the members of the organism is the principle of life which exists in the members as actual therein. In their separation [135] the parts cease to be members of a whole. For in the living thing the end and material medium of the end are so immediately united, that the existing being only exists in so far as the end remains indwelling. The beautiful as thus regarded and in Kant's view, does not carry its teleological purpose as an external form attached to it: but the teleological correspondence of the inner and outer is to be regarded as the immanent nature of the beautiful object.

(*d*) Fourthly and finally the view of Kant posits the beautiful under the mode that it is recognized without a universal concept as object of a *necessary* feeling of satisfaction. Necessity is an abstract category, and indicates an ideal and essential relation between two aspects or sides: if the one is, and because the one is, then, and for that reason, the other is also. The one likewise includes the other within its determinate nature. Cause is meaningless without effect. The pleasure which we obtain from beauty is necessary in this sense, and it is so wholly without a relation to conceptions, that is to say the categories of the understanding. Thus, no doubt, we derive pleasure from what is symmetrical, for this is constructed in accord with an idea of the understanding. Kant, however, demands more as a definition

[133] The difference between a material instrument, which is a mere means to an end conceived by the craftsman, such as a plough for ploughing, a rake for raking, and a purpose inseparable from the organic whole as a mouth for eating, for without life the organism collapses.

[134] *Für sich.*

[135] In his history of Aesthetic in Germany Lötze disputes this. It seems to some extent a question of definition. In Hegel's view a dead body is not a human body in the full sense, but the *corpse* of a man. A hand separated from the body, whether we call it a hand or not, is no longer, whatever it may be, a living member, its essential significance as a hand has disappeared. It was only a hand in its coherence as part of a larger whole. It may still for a time preserve the semblance of its life, but it is cut off as the withered leaf. These are facts at least that are undeniable, and the objection appears to me based on a misunderstanding. A hand is only *an und für sich* human when it is part of a living man. What is the organic reality in the complete sense is the man as a *whole.* The hand is merely the extremity of one of his arms. You may call a dead hand a hand if you like. The point is what was implied in the fact that you called it a hand at all whether alive or dead.

of delight in art than the unity and uniformity of such an idea as this.

Now what we find in all these theses of Kant is the non-seperation of that which otherwise is assumed to be distinct in consciousness. In the beautiful this separation is found to be abolished. The universal and particular, purpose and means, idea and object completely interpenetrate each other. Thus, too, Kant sees the beauty of *art* as a concurrence, in which the particular itself is conformable to the conception. Particulars, taken alone, are primarily, both as against each other and the universal, of a contingent nature; and this very contingent element, whether we find it in sense, feeling, susceptibility, or impulse, is now in the beauty of art not merely *subsumed* under the catagories of the understanding, and *dominated* by the notion of freedom in its abstract universality, but united to the universal in such a way that it appears inwardly and on its own merits as realized fact adequate thereto. By this means thought is incorporated in fine art, and the material is not externally defined by such thought, but continues to exist in its own freedom. In other words, what is natural—the senses, emotional temperament, and so forth—possess in themselves measure, end, and agreement. Perception and feeling, too, in the same way are raised to a power or spiritual universality; and thought no less not merely renounces its hostility to Nature, but is made blithe therein. Feeling, pleasure, and enjoyment are thereby justified and sanctified, and thus it is that Nature and freedom, sense and idea in *one* presence discover their just place and their satisfaction. Yet even this apparently complete reconciliation is ultimately still assumed to be merely subjective in respect to our judgment no less than our productive activity, and not to be essentially and on its own account either the true or real.

These may, I think, be taken to be the main results of the Critique of Kant so far as they affect our present inquiry. It constitutes the starting-point for the true conception of the beauty of art. Such a conception could, however, only make itself effective as the higher comprehension of the true union of necessity and freedom, particular and universal, sensuous and rational, by its overcoming the defects still latent in the previous standpoint.

It must in fact be admitted that the artistic sense of a profound and, at the same time, philosophical spirit anticipated philosophy in the stricter sense by its demand for and expression of the principle of totality and reconciliation in its opposition to that abstract finiteness of thought, that duty for duty's sake, that understanding faculty devoid of any substantive content, which one and all apprehend nature and reality, sense and feeling, merely as a *limit*, something downright alien or hostile. It is Schiller who must be credited with the important service of having broken through the Kantian subjectivity and abstractness of thought and of having ventured the attempt to pass beyond the same by comprehending in thought the principles of unity and reconciliation as the truth, and giving artistic realization to that truth. For Schiller, in his aesthetic investigations, did not merely adhere to art and its interest unaffected by their relation to philosophy proper, but he compared his own interest in the beauty of art in their due relation to philosophical principles; and it is only from the starting-point of these latter and by their aid that he penetrated the profounder nature and notional concept of Beauty. Thus we are conscious that it was a feature of a certain period of his productive activity that he was actively engaged with reflective thought, more perhaps than was wholly favourable to the simple and direct beauty of his work as an art product. The deliberate character of abstract reflections, and even the interest of the philosophical notion, arrest the attention in several of his poems. He has, in fact, been made the subject of stricture on this account; and especially his work has been blamed and depreciated in its contrast with the equable serenity and straightforward simplicity of Goethe's ideas and more objective naturalism. But in this respect Schiller as poet did but pay the debt of his century. A real ideal evolution was responsible, the recognition of which only redounds to the honour of this sublime soul and profound genius, as it has been no less of signal profit to science and knowledge. This stimulating movement of science during the same epoch also diverted Goethe from the sphere, most distinctively his own, as poet. But just as Schiller was absorbed in the study of the ideal depths of the *mind*, so the characteristic predilection of Goethe inclined to the *physical* aspect of art, to external nature, such as animal and vegetable organization, crystals, cloud-formation and colours. To such scientific inquiry Goethe applied his extraordinary powers of intuition, which in these provinces have driven off the field the theories of the mere understanding and their errors, just as Schiller, on the other side, succeeded in demonstrating the Idea of the free totality of Beauty as against the theory of the analytical understanding relative to volition and thinking. An entire series of Schiller's productions is devoted to this insight in the nature of art. Above all in importance come the "Letters upon aesthetic education." In these letters the main point of departure is that every individual man contains within himself the natural capacity of an ideal humanity. This genuine human being is represented in the State, which, in his view, is the objective, universal, and, in short, normal form, in which the separate individuals or subjects of such human consciousness aim at making all coalesce and concentrate in unity. There were then, in his view, two imaginable ways in which man in the temporal process could thus coalesce with the human being in the notional Idea.[136] On the one hand this could be effected in the suppression of individuality by the State under its generic idea of morality, law, and intelligence:[137] while, on the other, a similar result could be effected by the individual himself raising himself to the level of such a generic conception, in other words, by the man of the particular temporal condition ennobling himself to the level of the essential man of the Idea. Now, in this view, reason demands unity as such, the generic attribution; Nature, however, asks for variety and individuality, and both these legislatures make a simultaneous claim upon man. Confronted with the conflict of these antagonistic rivals, aesthetic education simply consists in giving actual effect to the demand for their mediation and reconcilement. The aim of such an education is, according to Schiller, to give vital form to inclination, the senses, impulse and emotional life in such a way that they become essentially permeated with mind; and, from the reverse point of view, that reason, freedom, and spirituality come forth from the grave-clothes of their abstractedness, are mated in union with the natural element thus essentially rationalized, and thus receive the substance of flesh and blood. Beauty is therefore affirmed to be the conformative unification[138] of the rational and the sensuous, and this union is pronounced the truly real.

This view of Schiller will in its general terms be all the more readily recognized in "Anmuth und Würde,"[139] as also in his poems for the reason that the praise of women is in such works more particularly the theme. It was pre-eminently in *their* character that he recognized and emphasized the spontaneously present conjunction of the spiritual and natural.

This unity of the universal and particular, of freedom and necessity, of spirituality and the natural element, which Schiller conceived with scientific thoroughness as the principle and

[136] That is, the concrete idea of humanity as a collective aggregate.

[137] That is, intelligence as asserted by a society of human beings as public opinion, etc.

[138] *Die Ineinsbildung.*

[139] "Grace and Dignity."

essence of art, and endeavoured indefatigably to call into actual life by means of art and aesthetic education, has received yet further recognition in *the Idea itself,* cognized as the supreme principle of knowledge and of existence, the Idea in this sense being apprehended as sole truth and reality. By means of this acknowledgment science, in the philosophy of Schelling, attained its absolute standpoint; and although art had already begun to assert its peculiar rights and dignity in their relation to the highest interests of man, it was only now that the *notion* itself and the scientific position of art were discovered. It was then that art was —even if, from a certain point of view, with a measure of perversity, which this is not the proper place to discuss—accepted with due reference to its exalted and true vocation. . . .

V[140]

1. After the above introductory observations we may now pass on to the consideration of our subject itself. We are, however, still within the introduction; and being so I do not propose to attempt anything more than indicate by way of sketch the main outlines of the general course of the scientific inquiry which is to follow it. Inasmuch, however, as we have referred to art as issuing from the absolute Idea itself, and, indeed, have assigned as its end the sensuous presentation of the Absolute itself, it will be incumbent on us to conduct this survey of the entire field in such a way, as at least to disclose generally, how the particular parts originate in the notional concept of the beauty of art. We must therefore attempt to awaken some idea of this notion in its broadest significance.

It has already been stated that the content of art is the Idea, and the form of its display the configuration of the sensuous or plastic image. It is further the function of art to mediate these two aspects under the reconciled mode of free totality. The *first* determinant implied by this is the demand that the content, which has to secure artistic representation, shall disclose an essential capacity for such display. If this is not so all that we possess is a defective combination. A content that, independently, is ill adapted to plastic form and external presentment is compelled to accept this form, or a matter that is to itself prosaic in its character is driven to make the best it can of a mode of presentation which is antagonistic to its nature.

The *second* requirement, which is deducible from the first is the demand that the content of art should be nothing essentially abstract. This does not mean, however, that it should be merely concrete in the sense that the sensuous object is such in its contrast to all that is spiritual and the content of thought, regarding these as the essentially simple and abstract. Everything that possesses truth for Spirit, no less than as part of Nature, is essentially concrete, and, despite its universality, possesses both ideality[141] and particularity essentially within it. When we state, for example, of God that He is simple One, the Supreme Being as such, we have thereby merely given utterance to a lifeless abstraction of the irrational understanding. Such a God, as He is thus not conceived in His concrete truth, can supply no content for art, least of all plastic art. Consequently neither the Jews nor the Turks have been able to represent their God, who is not even an abstraction of the understanding in the above sense, under the positive mode in which Christians have represented Him. For in Christianity God is conceived in His Truth, and as such essentially concrete, as personality, as the

[140] This final section is called the Division of the Subject.

[141] *Subjektivität.* That is, the ideality of consciousness, or thought.

subjective focus of conscious life, or, more accurately defined, as Spirit. And what He is as Spirit is made explicit to the religious apprehension as a trinity of persons, which at the same time are, in their independence, regarded as One. Here is essentially, universality, and particularity, no less than their reconciled unity, and it is only a unity such as this which gives us the concrete. And inasmuch as a content, in order to unveil truth at all, must be of this concrete character, art makes the demand for a like concreteness, and, for this reason, that a purely abstract universal does not in itself possess the property to proceed to particularity and external manifestation, and to unity with itself therein.

If, then, a sensuous form and configuration is to be correspondent with a true and therefore concrete content, such must in the third place likewise be as clearly individual, entirely concrete and a self-enclosed unity. This character of concreteness, predicable of both aspects of art, the content no less than the representation, is just the point in which both coalesce and fall in with one another. The natural form of the human body is, for example, such a sensuous concrete capable of displaying Spirit in its essential concreteness and of adapting itself wholly to such a presentment. For which reason we must quit ourselves of the idea that it is a matter of mere accident that an actual phenomenon of the objective world is accepted as the mode in which to embody such a form coalescent with truth. Art does not lay hold of this form either because it is simply there or because there is no other. The concrete content itself implies the presence of external and actual, we may even add the sensuous appearance. But to make this possible this sensuous concrete, which is essentially impressed with a content that is open to mind, is also essentially addressed to the inward conscious life, and the external mode of its configuration, whereby it is visible to perception and the world of idea, has for its aim the being there exclusively for the soul and mind of man. This is the sole reason that content and artistic conformation are dovetailed one into the other. The *purely* sensuous concrete, that is external Nature as such, does not exclusively originate in such an end. The variously coloured plumage of birds is resplendent unseen; the notes of this song are unheard. The Cereus,[142] which only blossoms for a night, withers away without any admiration from another in the wilderness of the southern forests; and these forests, receptacles themselves of the most beautiful and luxuriant vegetation, with the richest and most aromatic perfumes, perish and collapse in like manner unenjoyed. The work of art has no such naive and independent being. It is essentially a question, an address to the responding soul of man, an appeal to affections and intelligence.

Although the endowment by art of sensuous shape is not in this respect accidental, yet on the other hand it is not the highest mode of grasping the spiritually concrete. Thought is a higher mode of presentment than that of the sensuous concrete. Though abstract in a relative sense; yet it must not be one-sided, but concrete thinking, in order to be true and rational. The extent to which a definite content possesses for its appropriate form sensuous artistic representation, or essentially requires, in virtue of its nature, a higher and more spiritual embodiment is a question of difference exemplified at once if we compare the Greek gods with God as conceived under Christian ideas. The Greek god is not abstract, but individual, and is in close association with the natural human form. The Christian God is also, no doubt, a concrete personality, but under the mode of pure spiritual actuality, who is cognized as Spirit and in Spirit.[143] His medium of determinate existence is therefore essentially knowledge of the mind and not external natural shape, by means of

[142] *Fackeldistel.* "Torch thistle," a plant of the genus Cereus.

[143] Or, "as mind and in mind."

which His representation can only be imperfect, and not in the entire depths of His idea or notional concept.

Inasmuch, however, as it is the function of art to represent the Idea to immediate vision in sensuous shape and not in the form of thought and pure spirituality in the strict sense, and inasmuch as the value and intrinsic worth of this presentment consists in the correspondence and unity of the two aspects, that is the Idea and its sensuous shape, the supreme level and excellence of art and the reality, which is truly consonant with its notion, will depend upon the degree of intimacy and union with which idea and configuration appear together in elaborated fusion. The higher truth consequently is spiritual content which has received the shape adequate to the conception of its essence; and this it is which supplies the principle of division for the philosophy of art. For before the mind can attain to the true notion of its absolute essence, it is constrained to traverse a series of stages rooted in this very notional concept; and to this course of stages which it unfolds to itself, corresponds a coalescent series, immediately related therewith, of the plastic types of art, under the configuration whereof mind as art-spirit presents to itself the consciousness of itself.[144]

This evolution within the art-spirit has further itself two sides in virtue of its intrinsic nature. *First*, that is to say, the development is itself a spiritual and universal one; in other words there are the definite and comprehensive views of the world [145] in their series of gradations which give artistic embodiment to the specific but widely embracing consciousness of Nature, man, and God. *Secondly*, this ideal or *universal* art-development has to provide for itself immediate existence and sensuous configuration, and the definite modes of this art-actualization in the sensuous medium are themselves a totality of necessary distinctions in the realm of art—that is to say, they are the *particular types* of art. No doubt the types of artistic configuration on the one hand are, in respect to their spirituality, of a general character, and not restricted to any one material, and the sensuous existence is similarly itself of varied multiplicity of medium. Inasmuch, however, as this material potentially possesses precisely as the mind or spirit does, the Idea for its inward soul or significance, it follows that a definite sensuous involves with itself a closer relation and secret bond of association with the spiritual distinctions and specific types of artistic embodiment.[146]

Relatively to these points of view our philosophy will be divided into three fundamental parts.

First, we have a *general* part. It has for its content and object the universal Idea of fine art, conceived here as the Ideal, together with the more elaborated relation under which it is placed respectively to Nature and human artistic production.

Secondly, we have evolved from the notional concept of the beauty of art a *particular* part, in so far as the essential distinctions, which this idea contains in itself, are

[144] That is to say, presents to itself to conscious grasp of itself as such Art-spirit (*als künstlerischer*).

[145] The two evolutions here alluded to are (i) that of a particular way of regarding Nature, man, and God in a particular age and nation such as the Egyptian, Greek, and Christian viewed in express relation to art; (ii) The several arts—sculpture, music, poetry, etc., each on their own foundation and viewed relatively to the former evolution.

[146] The point, of course, is that the different media of the several arts are inherently, and in virtue of the fact that we have not here *mere* matter as opposed to that which is intellectual rather than sensuous, but matter in which the notional concept is already essentially present or pregnant (sound is, for instance, more ideal than the spatial matter of architecture), adapted to the particular arts in which they serve as the medium of expression.

unfolded in a graduated series of *particular* modes of configuration.[147]

Thirdly, there results a *final* part which has to consider the particularized content of fine art itself. It consists in the advance of art to the sensuous realization of its shapes and its consummation in a system of the several arts and their genera and species.

2. In respect to the first and second of these divisions it is important to recollect, in order to make all that follows intelligible, that the Idea, viewed as the beautiful in art, is not the Idea in the strict sense, that is as a metaphysical Logic apprehends it as the Absolute. It is rather the Idea as carried into concrete form in the direction of express realization, and as having entered into immediate and adequate unity with such reality. For the *Idea as such*, although it is both potentially and explicitly true, is only truth in its universality and not as yet presented in objective embodiment. The Idea as fine art, however, is the Idea with the more specific property of being essentially individual reality, in other words, an individual configuration of reality whose express function it is to manifest the Idea—in its appearance. This amounts to the demand that the Idea and its formative configuration as concrete realization must be brought together under a mode of complete adequacy. The Idea as so conceived, a reality, that is to say, moulded in conformity with the notional concept of the Idea, is the Ideal. The problem of such consonancy might, in the first instance, be understood in the wholly formal sense that the Idea might be any idea so long as the actual shape, it matters not what the shape might be, represented this particular Idea and no other. In that case, however, the required truth of the Ideal is a fact simply interchangeable with mere correctness, a correctness which consists in the expression of any significance in a manner adapted to it, provided that its meaning is thereby directly discoverable in the form. The Ideal, however, is not to be thus understood. According to the standard or test of its own nature any content whatever can receive adequate presentation, but it does not necessarily thereby possess a claim to be the fine art of the Ideal. Nay, more, in comparison with ideal beauty the presentation will even appear defective. And in this connection we may once for all observe—though actual proof is reserved to a later stage—that the defects of a work of art are not invariably to be attributed to defects of executive skill. *Defectiveness of form* arises also from *defectiveness of content*. The Chinese, Hindoos, and Egyptians, for example, in their artistic images, sculptured deities and idols, never passed beyond a formless condition, or a definition of shape that was vicious and false, and were unable to master true beauty. And this was so for the reason that their mythological conceptions, the content and thought of their works of art, were still essentially indeterminate in a false sense, did not, in fact, attain to a content which was absolute in itself. Viewed in this sense the excellence of works of art is so much the greater in the degree that their content and thought is ideal and profound. And in affirming this we have not merely in our mind the degree of executive mastery displayed in the grasp and imitation of natural form as we find it in the objective world. For in certain stages of the artistic

[147] Professor Bosanquet explains these "plastic forms" (*Gestaltungs formen*) as the various modifications of the subject-matter of art (Trans., p. 140 note). I am not quite sure of the meaning here intended. It would apparently identify the term with the *Gebilde* referred to in the third division. I should myself rather incline to think that Hegel had mainly in his mind the specific general types, that is, the three relations of the Idea itself to its external configuration, viewed as a historical evolution, which Hegel calls symbolic, classical, and romantic. Perhaps this is what Professor Bosanquet means. But in that case it does not appear to me so much the subject-matter as the generic forms in the shaping of that matter.

consciouness and its reproductive effects the desertion and distortion of the conformations of Nature is not so much due to unintentional technical inexperience or lack of ability, as it is to deliberate alteration, which originates in the mental content itself, and is demanded by the same. From this point of view there is therefore imperfect art, which, both in technical and other respects, may be quite consummate in its *own specific sphere*, yet if tested with the true notion of art and the Ideal can only appear as defective. Only in the highest art are the Idea and the artistic presentation truly consonant with one another in the sense that the objective embodiment of the Idea is in itself essentially and as realized the true configuration, because the content of the Idea thus expressed is itself in truth the genuine content. It is appertinent to this, as already noted, that the Idea must be defined in and through itself as concrete totality, thereby essentially possessing in itself the principle and standard of its particularization and definition as thus manifested objectively. For example, the Christian imagination will only be able to represent God in human form and with man's means of spiritual expression, because it is herein that God Himself is fully known in Himself as mind or Spirit. Determinacy is, as it were, the bridge to phenomenal presence. Where this determinacy is not totality derived from the Idea itself, where the Idea is not conceived as that which is self-definitive and self-differentiating, it remains abstract and possesses its definition, and with it the principle for the particular made of embodiment adapted to itself not within itself but as something outside it. And owing to this the Idea is also still abstract and the configuration it assumes is not as yet posited by itself. The Idea, however, which is essentially concrete, carries the principle of its manifestation in itself, and is thereby the means of its own free manifestation. Thus it is only the truly concrete Idea that is able to evoke the true embodiment, and this appropriate coalescence of both is the Ideal.

3. But inasmuch as in this way the Idea is concrete unity, this unity can only enter the artistic consciouness by the expansion and further mediation of the particular aspects of the Idea; and it is through this evolution that the beauty of art receives a *totality of particular stages and forms.* Therefore, after we have considered fine art in its essence and on its own account, we must see how the beautiful in its entirety breaks up into its particular determinations. This gives, as our second part, the *doctrine of the types of art*. The origin of these types is to be found in the varied ways under which the Idea is conceived as the content of art; it is by this means that a distinction in the mode of form under which it manifests itself is conditioned. These types are therefore simply the different modes of relation which obtain between the Idea and its configuration, relations which emanate from the Idea itself, and thereby present us with the general basis of division for this sphere. For the principle of division must always be found in the notional concept, the particularization and division of which it is.

We have here to consider *three* relations of the Idea to its external process of configuration.

(*a*) *First*, the origin of artistic creation proceeds from the Idea when, being itself still involved in defective definition and obscurity, or in vicious and untrue determinacy, it becomes embodied in the shapes of art. As indeterminate it does not as yet possess in itself that individuality which the Ideal demands. Its abstract character and one-sidedness leaves its objective presentment still defective and contingent. Consequently this first type of art is rather a mere search after plastic configuration than a power of genuine representation. The Idea has not as yet found the formative principle within itself, and therefore still continues to be the mere effort and strain to find it. We may in general terms describe this form as the *symbolic* type of art. The abstract Idea possesses in it its external shape outside itself in the purely material substance of Nature, from which the shaping process proceeds, and to which in its expression it is entirely yoked. Natural objects are thus in the first instance left just as they are, while, at the same time the substantive Idea is imposed upon them as their significance, so that their function is henceforth to express the same, and they claim to be interpreted, as though the Idea itself was present in them. A rationale of this is to be found in the fact that the external objects of reality do essentially possess an aspect in which they are qualified to express a universal import. But as a completely adequate coalescence is not yet possible, all that can be the outcome of such a relation is an *abstract attribute*, as when a lion is understood to symbolize strength.

On the other hand this abstractness of the relation makes present to consciousness no less markedly how the Idea stands relatively to natural phenomena as an alien; and albeit it expatiates in all these shapes, having no other means of expression among all that is real, and seeks after itself in their unrest and defects of genuine proportion, yet for all that it finds them inadequate to meet its needs. It consequently exaggerates natural shapes and the phenomena of Nature in every degree of indefinite and limitless extension; it flounders about in them like a drunkard, and seethes and ferments, doing violence to their truth with the distorted growth of unnatural shapes, and strives vainly by the contrast, hugeness, and splendour of the forms accepted to exalt the phenomena to the plane of the Idea. For the Idea is here still more or less indeterminate, and unadaptable, while the objects of Nature are wholly definite in their shape.

Hence, on account of the incompatibility of the two sides of ideality and objective form to one another, the relation of the Idea to the other becomes a *negative* one. The former, being in its nature ideal, is unsatisfied with such an embodiment, and posits itself as its inward or ideally universal substance under a relation of *sublimity* over and above all the inadequate superfluity of natural form. In virtue of this sublimity the natural phenomena, of course, and the human form and event are accepted and left simply as they are, but at the same time, recognized as unequal to their significance, which is exalted far above all earthly content.

These features constitute in general terms the character of the primitive artistic pantheism of the East, which, on the one hand, charges the meanest objects with the significance of the absolute Idea, or, on the other, compels natural form, by doing violence to its structure, to express its world-ideas. And, in consequence, it becomes bizarre, grotesque, and deficient in taste, or turns the infinite but abstract freedom of the substantive Idea contemptuously against all phenomenal existence as alike nugatory and evanescent. By such means the significance cannot be completely presented in the expression, and despite all straining and endeavour the final inadequacy of plastic configuration to Idea remains insuperable. Such may be accepted as the first type of art—symbolic art with its yearning, its fermentation, its mystery, and sublimity.

(*b*) In the *second* type of art, which we propose to call "*Classical*." the twofold defect of symbolic art is annulled. Now the symbolic configuration is imperfect, because, first, the Idea here only enters into consciousness in *abstract* determinacy or indeterminateness: and, secondly, by reason of the fact that the coalescence of import with embodiment can only throughout remain defective, and in its turn also wholly abstract. The classical art-type solves both these difficulties. It is, in fact, the free and adequate embodiment of the Idea in the shape which, according to its notional concept, is uniquely appropriate to the Idea itself. The Idea is consequently able to unite in free and completely assonant concord with it. For this reason the classical type of art is the first to present us with the creation and vision of the complete Ideal, and to establish the same as realized fact.

The conformability, however, of notion and reality in the classical type ought not to be taken in the purely *formal* sense of the coalescence of a content with its external form, any more than this was possible in the case of the Ideal. Otherwise every copy from Nature, and every kind of portrait, every landscape, flower, scene, and so forth, which form the aim of the presentment, would at once become classical in virtue of the fact of the agreement it offers between such content and form. In classical art, on the contrary, the characteristic feature of the content consists in this, that it is itself concrete Idea, and as such the concrete spiritual; for it is only that which pertains to Spirit which is veritable ideality.[148] To secure such a content we must find out that in Nature which on its own account is that which is essentially and explicitly appropriate to the spiritual. It must be the *original* notion itself,[149] which has invented the form for concrete spirituality, and now the *subjective* notion—in the present case the spirit of art—has merely *discovered* it, and made it, as an existence possessed of natural shape, concordant with free and individual spirituality. Such a configuration, which the Idea essentially possesses as spiritual, and indeed as individually determinate spirituality, when it must perforce appear as a temporal phenomenon, is the *human form.* Personification and anthropomorphism have frequently been abused as a degradation of the spiritual. But art, in so far as its function is to bring to vision the spiritual in sensuous guise, must advance to such anthropomorphism, inasmuch as Spirit is only adequately presented to perception in its bodily presence. The transmigration of souls in this respect an abstract conception,[150] and physiology ought to make it one of its fundamental principles, that life has necessarily, in the course of its evolution, to proceed to the human form, for the reason that it is alone the visible phenomenon adequate to the expression of intelligence.

The human bodily form, then, is employed in the classical type of art not as purely sensuous existence, but exclusively as the existence and natural shape appropriate to mind. It has therefore to be relieved of all the defective excrescences which adhere to it in its purely physical aspect, and from the contingent finiteness of its phenomenal appearance. The external shape must in this way be purified in order to express in itself the content adequate for such a purpose; and, furthermore, along with this, that the coalescence of import and embodiment may be complete, the spirituality which constitutes the content must be of such a character that it is completely able to express itself in the natural form of man, without projecting beyond the limits of such expression within the sensuous and purely physical sphere of existence. Under such a condition Spirit is at the same time defined as particular, the spirit or mind of man, not as simply absolute and eternal. In this latter case it is only capable of asserting and expressing itself as intellectual being.[151]

Out of this latter distinction arises, in its turn, the defect which brings about the dissolution of the classical type of art, and makes the demand for a third and higher form, namely the *romantic* type.

[148] *Das wahrhaft Innere.* That is, the inward of the truth of conscious life.

[149] Means apparently the notion in its absolute sense.

[150] Because it represents spirit as independent of an appropriate bodily form.

[151] What appears to be denoted by *Geistigkeit* is the generic term of intelligence—that activity of conscious life which does not necessarily make us think of a single individual—the common nature of all spirit.

(*c*) The romantic type of art annuls the completed union of the Idea and its reality, and occurs, if on a higher plane, to the difference and opposition of both sides, which remained unovercome in symbolic art. The classical type of art no doubt attained the highest excellence of which the sensuous embodiment of art is capable. The defect, such as it is, is due to the defect which obtains in art itself throughout, the limitations of its entire province, that is to say. The limitation consists in this, that art in general and, agreeably to its fundamental idea, accepts for its object Spirit, the notion of which is infinite concrete universality, under the guise of sensuously concrete form. In the classical type it sets up the perfected coalescence of spiritual and sensuous existence as adequate conformation of both. As a matter of fact, however, in this fusion mind itself is not represented agreeably to its *true notional concept*. Mind is the infinite subjectivity of the Idea, which as absolute inwardness,[152] is not capable of freely expanding in its entire independence, so long as it remains within the mould of the bodily shape, fused therein as in the existence wholly congenial to it.

To escape from such a condition the romantic type of art once more cancels that inseparable unity of the classical type, by securing a content which passes beyond the classical stage and its mode of expression. This content, if we may recall familiar ideas—is coincident with what Christianity affirms to be true of God as Spirit, in contrast to the Greek faith in gods which forms the essential and most fitting content of classical art. In Greek art the concrete ideal substance is potentially, but not as fully realized, the unity of the human and divine nature; a unity which for the very reason that it is purely *immediate* and not wholly explicit, is manifested without defect under an immediate and *sensuous* mode. The Greek god is the object of naive intuition and sensuous imagination. His shape is therefore the bodily form of man. The sphere of his power and his being is individual and individually limited; and in his opposition to the individual person[153] is an essence and a power with whom the inward life of soul[154] is merely potentially in unity, but does not itself possess this unity as inward subjective knowledge. The higher stage is the *knowledge* of this *implied* unity, which in its latency the classical art-type receives as its content and is able to perfectly represent in bodily shape. This elevation of mere potentiality into self-conscious knowledge constitutes an enormous difference. It is nothing less than the infinite difference which, for example, separates man generally from the animal creation. Man is animal; but even in his animal functions he is not restricted within the potential sphere as the animal is, but becomes conscious of them, learns to understand them, and raises them—as, for instance, the process of digestion—into self-conscious science. By this means man dissolves the boundaries of his merely potential immediacy; in virtue of the very fact that he knows himself to be animal he ceases to be merely animal, and as mind is endowed with self-knowledge.

If, then, in this way the unity of the human and divine nature, which in the previous stage was potential, is raised out of this immediate into a self-conscious unity, it follows that the genuine medium for the reality of this content is no longer the sensuous and immediate existence of what is spiritual, that is, the physical body of man, but the *self-aware* inner life of *soul itself*. Now it is Christianity —for the reason that it presents to mind God as *Spirit*, and not as the particular individual

[152] By *Innerlichkeit,* which might also be rendered as pure ideality, what is signified is that in a mental state there are no parts outside of each other.

[153] *Subjekt, i.e.,* the individual Ego of self-consciousness.

[154] *Das subjektive Innere,* lit., the subjective inner state.

spirit, but as absolute in spirit and in truth—which steps back from the sensuousness of imagination into the inward life of reason, and makes *this* rather than *bodily* form the medium and determinate existence of its content. So also, the unity of the human and divine nature is a conscious unity exclusively capable of realization by means of *spiritual* knowledge, and in *Spirit*. The new content secured thereby is consequently not indefeasibly bound up with the sensuous presentation, as the mode completely adequate, but is rather delivered from this immediate existence, which has to be hypostatized as a negative factor, overcome and reflected back into the spiritual unity. In this way romantic art must be regarded as art transcending itself, albeit within the boundary of its own province, and in the form of art itself.

We may therefore briefly summarize our conclusion that in this third stage the object of art consists in the free and concrete presence of spiritual activity,[155] whose vocation it is to appear as such a presence or activity for the inner world of conscious intelligence: In consonance with such an object art cannot merely work for sensuous perception. It must deliver itself to the inward life, which coalesces with its object simply as though this were none other than itself,[156] in other words, to the intimacy of soul, to the heart, the emotional life, which as the medium of Spirit itself essentially strives after freedom, and seeks and possesses its reconciliation only in the inner chamber of spirit. It is this inward or ideal world which constitutes the content of the romantic sphere: it will therefore necessarily discover its representation as such inner idea or feeling, and in the show or appearance of the same. The world of the soul and intelligence celebrates its triumph over the external world, and, actually in the medium of that outer world, makes that victory to appear, by reason of which the sensuous appearance sinks into worthlessness.

On the other hand, this type of art, like every other, needs an external vehicle of expression. As already stated, the spiritual content has here withdrawn from the external world and its immediate unity into its own world. The sensuous externality of form is consequently accepted and represented, as in the symbolic type, as unessential and transient; furthermore the subjective finite spirit and volition is treated in a similar way; a treatment which even includes the idiosyncracies or caprice of individuals, character, action, or the particular features of incident and plot. The aspect of external existence is committed to contingency and handed over to the adventurous action of imagination, whose caprice is just as able to reflect the facts given *as* they are,[157] as it can change the shapes of the external world into a medley of its own invention and distort them to mere caricature. For this external element has no longer its notion and significance in its own essential province, as in classical art. It is now discovered in the emotional realm, and this is manifested in the medium of that realm itself rather than in the external and *its* form of reality, and is able to secure or to recover again the condition of reconciliation with itself in every accident, in all the chance circumstance that falls into independent shape, in all misfortunes and sorrow, nay, in crime itself.

Hence it comes about that the characteristics of symbolic art, its indifference, incompatibility and severance of Idea from configurative expression, are here reproduced

[155] *Geistigkeit.* Professor Bosanquet translates it here "intellectual being."

[156] The distinction between a percipient and an external object falls away. The content displayed is part of the soul-life itself.

[157] Professor Bosanquet apparently assumes a negative has slipped out. But the text probably is correct in the rather awkward form in which it stands.

once more, if with essential difference. And this difference consists in the fact that in romantic art the Idea, whose defectiveness, in the case of the symbol, brought with it the defect of external form, has to display itself as Spirit and in the medium of soul-life as essentially self-complete. And it is to complete fundamentally this higher perfection that it withdraws itself from the external element. It can, in short, seek and consummate its true reality and manifestation nowhere but in its own domain.

This we may take to be in general terms the character of the symbolic, classical, and romantic types of art, which in fact constitute the three relations of the Idea to its embodiment in the realm of human art. They consist in the aspiration after, the attainment and transcendency of the Ideal, viewed as the true concrete notion of beauty.

4. In contrast to these two previous divisions of our subject the *third* part presupposes the notional concept of the Ideal, and the universal art-types. It in other words consists in their realization through specific sensuous media. We have consequently no longer to deal with the inner or ideal evolution of the beauty of art in conformity with its widest and most fundamental determinations. What we have now before us to consider is how these ideal determinants pass into actual existence, how they are distinguishable in their external aspect, and how they give an independent and a realized shape to every element implied in the evolution of this Idea of beauty as a *work of art*, and not merely as a *universal* type. Now it is the peculiar differences immanent in the Idea of beauty which are carried over by it into external existence. For this reason in this third fundamental division these general art-types must themselves supply the basic principle for the articulation and definition of the *particular arts*. Or, to put the same thing another way, the several species of art possess in themselves the same essential differences, which we have already become acquainted with as the universal art-types. *External* objectivity, however, to which these types are subjected in a sensuous and consequently *specific* material, necessitates the differentiation of these types into diverse and independent modes of realization, in other words, those of particular arts. Each general type discovers its determinate character in one determinate external material or medium, in which its adequate presentation is secured under the manner it prescribes. But, from another point of view, these types of art, inasmuch as their definition is none the less consistent with the fact of the *universality* of their typical import, break through the boundaries of their *specific* realization in some definite art-species, and achieve an existence in other arts no less, although their position in such is of subordinate importance. For this reason, albeit the particular arts belong specifically to one of these general art-types respectively, the *adequate* external embodiment whereof they severally constitute, yet this does not prevent them, each after its own mode of external configuration, from representing the totality of these art-types.[158] To summarize, then, in this third principal division we are dealing with the beauty of art, as it unveils itself in a world of realized beauty by means of the arts and their creations. The content of this world is the beautiful, and the true beautiful, as we have seen, is spiritual being in concrete form, the Ideal; or apprehended with still more intimacy it is the independent, free of divine Image,[159] which has completely appropriated the externality of form and medium, and now wears them simply

[158] Thus poetry is primarily a romantic art, but in the Epic it is affiliated with the objective character of classical art, or we may say that there is a romantic and classical type of architecture, though the art is primarily symbolic.

[159] *Gestalt.* Plastic power is perhaps a better translation.

as the means of its self-manifestation. Inasmuch, however, as the beautiful is unfolded here as *objective* reality, and in this process is differentiated into particular aspects and phases, this centre posits its extremes, as realized in their peculiar actuality, in antithetical relation to itself. Thus one of these extremes consists of an objectivity as yet devoid of mind, which we may call the natural environment of God. Here the external element, when it receives form, remains as it was, and does not possess its spiritual aim and content in itself, but in another.[160] The other extreme is the divine as inward, something known, as the manifold particularized *subjective* existence of Deity. It is the truth as operative and vital in sense, soul, and intelligence of particular persons, which does not persist as poured forth into its mould of external shape, but returns into the inward life of individuals. The Divine is under such a mode at once distinguishable from its pure manifestation as Godhead, and passes itself thereby into the variety of particularization which belongs to every kind of particular subjective knowledge, feeling, perception, and emotion. In the analogous province of religion with which art, at its highest elevation, is immediately connected, we conceive the same distinction as follows. First, we imagine the natural life on Earth in its finitude as standing on one side; but then, secondly, the human consciousness accepts God for its object, in which the distinction between objectivity and subjectivity falls away; then, finally, we advance from God as such to the devotion of the *community*, that is to God as He is alive and present in the subjective consciousness. These three fundamental modifications present themselves in the world of art in independent evolution.

(*a*) The *first* of the particular arts with which, according to their fundamental principle, we have to start is architecture considered as a fine art. Its function consists in so elaborating the external material of inorganic Nature that the same becomes intimately connected with Spirit as an artistic and external environment. Its medium is matter itself as an external object, a heavy mass that is subject to mechanical laws; and its forms persist as the forms of inorganic Nature coordinated with the relations of the abstract understanding such as symmetry and so forth. In this material and in these forms the Ideal is incapable of realization as concrete spirituality, and the reality thus presented remains confronting the Idea as an external fabric with which it enters into no fusion, or has only entered so far as to establish an abstract relation. And it is in consequence of this that the fundamental type of the art of building is that of *symbolism*. Architecture is in fact the first pioneer on the highway toward the adequate realization of Godhead. In this service it is put to severe labour with objective nature, that it may disengage it by its effort from the confused growth of finitude and the distortions of contingency. By this means it levels a space for the God, informs His external environment, and builds Him His temple, as a fit place for the concentration of Spirit, and its direction to the absolute objects of intelligent life. It raises an enclosure for the congregation of those assembled, as a defence against the threatening of the tempest, against rain, the hurricane, and savage animals. It in short reveals the will thus to assemble, and although under an external relation, yet in agreement with the principles of art. A significance such as this it can to a greater or less extent import into its material and its forms, in proportion as the determinate content of its fabric, which is the object of its operations and effort, is more or less significant, is more concrete or more abstract, more profound in penetrating its own essential depth, or more obscure and superficial. Indeed architecture may in this respect proceed so far in the

[160] He means that in architecture the building is merely a shrine or environment of the image of the god.

execution of such a purpose as to create an adequate artistic existence for such an ideal content in its very forms and material. In doing so, however, it has already passed beyond its peculiar province and is diverted into the stage immediately above it of sculpture. For the boundary of sculpture lies precisely in this that it retains the spiritual as an inward being which persists in direct contrast to the external embodiment of architecture. It can consequently merely point to that which is absorbed in soul-life as to something external to itself.

(*b*) Nevertheless, as above explained, the external and inorganic world is purified by architecture, it is coordinated under symmetrical laws, and made cognate with mind, and as a result the temple of God, the house of his community, stands before us. Into this temple, in the *second* place, the God himself enters in the lightning-flash of individuality which smites its way into the inert mass, permeating the same with its presence. In other words the infinite [161] and no longer purely symmetrical form belonging to intelligence brings as it were to a focus and informs the shape in which it is most at home. This is the task of *sculpture*. In so far as in it the inward life of Spirit, to which the art of architecture can merely point away to, makes its dwelling within the sensuous shape and its external material, and to the extent that these two sides come into plastic communion with one another in such a manner that neither is predominant, sculpture receives as its fundamental type the *classical* art-form.

For this reason the sensuous element on its own account admits of no expression here which is not affected by spiritual affinities,[162] just as, conversely, sculpture can reproduce with completeness no spiritual content, which does not maintain throughout adequate presentation to perception in bodily form. What sculpture, in short, has to do is to make the presence of Spirit stand before us in its bodily shape and in immediate union therewith at rest and in blessedness; and this form has to be made vital by means of the content of spiritual individuality. The external sensuous material is consequently no longer elaborated either in conformity with its mechanical quality alone, as a mass of weight, nor in shapes of the inorganic world simply, nor in entire indifference to colour, etc. It is carried into the ideal forms of the human figure, and, we may add, in the completeness of all three spatial dimensions. In other words and relatively to such a process we must maintain for sculpture that in it the inward or ideal content of Spirit are first revealed in their eternal repose and essential self-stability. To such repose and unity with itself there can only correspond that external shape which itself persists in such unity and repose. And this condition is satisfied by configuration viewed in its *abstract spatiality*.[163] The spirit which sculpture represents is that which is essentially sound, not broken up in the play of chance conceits and passions; and for this reason its external form also is not dissolved in the manifold variety of appearance, but exhibits itself under this one presentment only as the abstraction of space in the totality of its dimensions.

Assuming, then, that the art of architecture has executed its temple, and the hand of sculpture has placed therein the image of the god, we have in the *third* place to assume the *community* of the faithful as confronting the god thus presented to vision in the wide chambers of his dwelling-place. Now this community is the spiritual reflection into its own world of that sensuous presence, the subjective and inward animating life of soul, in its union with which, both for the artistic content and the

[161] Infinite, of course, in the concrete sense of rounded in itself, as the circle, or, still more, the living organism.

[162] Lit., "which is not also that of the spiritual sphere."

[163] That is, an object limited only in space.

external material which manifests it, the determining principle may be identified with particularization in varied shapes and qualities, individualization and the life of soul [164] which they imply. The downright and solid fact of unity the god possesses in sculpture breaks up into the multiplicity of a world of particular souls,[165] whose union is no longer sensuous but wholly ideal.

Here for the first time God Himself is revealed as veritably Spirit—viz., the Spirit revealed in His community. Here at last He is seen apprehended as this moving to-and-fro, as this alternation between His own essential unity and His realization in the knowledge of individual persons and that separation which it involves, as also in the universal spiritual being [166] and union of the many. In such a community God is disengaged from the abstraction of His unfolded self-seclusion and self-identity, no less than from the immediate absorption in bodily shape, in which He is presented by sculpture. He is, in a word, lifted into the actual sphere of spiritual existence and knowledge, into the reflected appearance, whose manifestation is essentially inward and the life of heart and soul. Thereby the higher content is now the nature of Spirit, and that in its ultimate or absolute shape. But at the same time the separation to which we have alluded displays this as *particular* spiritual being, a specific emotional life. Moreover, for the reason that the main thing here is not the untroubled repose of the God in himself,[167] but his manifestation simply, the Being which is *for another*, self-revealment in fact, it follows that, on the plane we have now reached, all the varied content of human subjectivity in its vital movement and activity, whether viewed as passion, action, or event, or more generally the wide realm of human feeling, volition and its discontinuance, become one and all for their sake objects of artistic representation.

Agreeably with such a content the sensuous element of art has likewise to show itself potentially adapted to such particularization and the display of such an inward content of heart and mind. Media of this description are supplied by colour, musical tones, and finally in sound as mere sign for ideal perceptions and conceptions; and we further obtain the means of realizing with the use of such media a content of this kind in the arts of painting, music, and poetry. Throughout this sphere the sensuous medium is found to be essentially disparate in itself and throughout posited [168] as ideal. In this way it responds in the highest degree to the fundamentally spiritual content of art, and the coalescence of spiritual significance and sensuous material attains a more intimate union than was possible either in architecture or sculpture. At the same time such a union is necessarily more near to soul-life, leaning exclusively to the subjective side of human experience; one which, in so far as form and content are thus constrained to particularization and to posit their result as ideal, can only be actually effected at the expense of the objective universality of the content as also of the fusion with the immediately sensuous medium.[169]

[164] *Subjektivität.* The particularization in romantic art implies the presence of an ideal element imported by the soul of the artist, which appeals directly to the soul in its emotional life. Compare a picture by an Italian master with a Greek statue.

[165] Lit., "A multiplicity of isolated examples of inwardness."

[166] That is, in the life shared by all as one community actuated by a common purpose.

[167] As in sculpture.

[168] Professor Bosanquet's note is here (Trans., p. 166) "Posited or laid down to be ideal. This almost is equal to made *to be* in the sense of *not being.* In other words musical sound is "ideal" as existing, *quâ* work of art, in memory only, the moment in which it is actually heard being fugitive. A picture is equally so in respect of the third dimension, which has to be read into it. Poetry is almost wholly ideal, *i.e.,* uses hardly any sensuous element, and appeals almost wholly to what exists in the *mind.*"

[169] By particularization is meant the variety in

The arts, then, which are lifted into a higher strain of ideality, abandoning as they do the symbolism of architecture and the classical Ideal of sculpture, accept their predominant type from the *romantic* art-form; and these are the arts most fitted to express its mode of configuration. They are, however, a totality of arts, because the romantic type is itself essentially the most concrete.

(*c*) The articulation of this *third sphere* of the particular arts may be fixed as follows:

(*d*) The *first* art which comes next to sculpture is that of painting. It avails itself for a medium of its content and the plastic configuration of the same of visibility as such, to the extent that it is differentiated in its own nature, in other words is defined in the continuity of colour. No doubt the material of architecture and sculpture is likewise both visible and coloured. It is, however, not, as in painting, visibility in its pure nature, not the essentially simple light, which by its differentiating of itself in its opposition to darkness, and in association with that darkness gives rise to colour.[170] This quality of visibility made essentially ideal[171] and treated as such no longer either requires, as in architecture, the abstractly mechanical qualities of mass as appropriate to materials of weight, nor, as is the case with sculpture, the complete dimensuration of spatial condition, even when concentrated into organic forms. The visibility and the making apparent, which belong to painting, possess differences of quality under a more ideal mode—that is, in the specific varieties of colour—which liberates art from the objective totality of spatial condition, by being limited to a plane surface.

On the other hand the content also attains the widest compass of particularity. Whatever can find a place in the human heart, as emotion, idea, and purpose, whatever it is capable of actually shaping—all such diversity may form part of the varied presentations of painting. The entire world of particular existence, from the most exalted embodiment of mind to the most insignificant natural fact, finds a place here. For it is possible even for finite Nature, in its particular scenes and phenomena, to form part of such artistic display, provided only that we have some reference to conscious life which makes it akin to human thought and emotion.[172]

(β) The *second* art which continues the further realization of the romantic type and forms a distinct contrast to painting is that of *music*. Its medium, albeit still sensuous, yet proceeds into still profounder subjectivity and particularization. We have here, too, the deliberate treatment of the sensuous medium as ideal, and it consists in the negation and idealization into the isolated unity of a single point,[173] the indifferent external collocation of space,[174] whose complete appearance is retained

the material of colours, musical tones, and ideas, which latter are really quite as much the medium of poetry as written language. The *sensuous* medium is here an abstract sign, and Hegel would contend, nothing more than this.

170 Reference, of course, to Hegel's unfortunate acceptance of Goethe's theory of colour.

171 The colour of art is not merely ideal as applied to only two dimensions of space, but also is "subjective" in the artistic treatment of it under a definite "scheme." It is not clear whether Hegel alludes also to this; apparently not, though it is the most important feature. In fact, even assuming his theory of light to be correct, it is difficult entirely to follow his distinction between the appearance of colour on a flat or a round surface. As *natural* colour the one would be as ideal as the other. Only regarded as a composition would painting present distinction.

172 It is obvious that the reference here is mainly to an intentional appeal to the human soul through the content of the composition. But the appeal may also be made through the technique and artistic treatment of the medium itself.

173 The parts of a chord are not in space, but are ideally cognized. Hegel describes this by saying that music idealizes space and concentrates it to a point. It would perhaps be more intelligible to say that it transmutes the positive effects of a material substance in motion into the positive and more ideal condition of time. The point which is continually negated is at least *quâ* music the point, or rather, moment of a temporal process.

174 By the indifferent externality of space is

by painting and deliberately feigned in its completeness. This isolated point, viewed as this process of negation, is an essentially concrete and active process of cancellation within the determinate substance of the material medium, viewed, that is, as motion and vibration of the material object within itself and in its relation to itself. Such an inchoate ideality of matter, which no longer appears under the form of space, but as temporal ideality,[175] is sound or tone. We have here the sensuous set down as negated, and its abstract visibility converted into audibility. In other words sound liberates the ideal content from its fetters in the material substance. This earliest [176] secured inwardness of matter and impregnation of it with soul-life supplies the medium for the intimacy and soul of Spirit —itself as yet indefinite—permitting, as it does, the echo and reverberation of man's emotional world through its entire range of feelings and passions. In this way music forms the centre of the romantic arts, just as sculpture represents the midway point of arrest between architecture and the arts of the romantic subjectivity. Thus, too, it forms the point of transition between the abstract, spatial sensuousness of painting and the abstract spirituality of poetry. Music carries within itself, like architecture, and in contrast to the emotional world simply and its inward self-seclusion, a relation of quantity conformable to the principles of the understanding and their modes of co-ordinated configuration.[177]

signified the fact that the parts of space, though external to each other, are not qualitatively distinguishable.

[175] Succession in time is "more ideal" then coexistence in space because it exists only as continuity in a conscious subject.

[176] Painting no doubt introduces ideal elements into the artistic composition of colour, but the colour still remains the appearance of a material thing or superficies.

[177] That is to say, music or harmony is based on a solid conformity to law on the part of its tones in their conjunction and succession, their structure and resolution.

(γ) We must look for our *third* and most spiritual type of artistic presentation among the romantic arts in that of *poetry*. The supreme characteristic of poetry consists in the power with which it brings into vassalage of the mind and its conceptions the sensuous element from which music and painting began to liberate art. For sound, the only remaining external material retained by poetry, is in it no longer the feeling of the sonorous itself, but is a mere sign without independent significance. And it is, moreover, a sign of idea which has become essentially concrete, and not merely [178] of indefinite feeling and its subtle modes and gradations. And this is how sound develops into the Word, as essentially articulate voice, whose intention it is to indicate ideas and thoughts. The purely negative moment to which music advanced now asserts itself as the wholly concrete point, the point which is mind itself, the self-conscious individual, which produces from itself the infinite expansion of its ideas and unites the same with the temporal condition of sound. Yet this sensuous element, which was still in music immediately united to emotion, is in poetry separated from the content of consciousness. Mind, in short, here determines this content for its own sake and apart from all else into the content of idea; to express such idea it no doubt avails itself of sound, but employs it merely as a sign without independent worth or substance. Thus viewed, the sound here may be just as well reproduced by the mere letter, for the audible, like the visible, is here reduced to a mere indication of mind.[179] For this reason,

[178] As in painting.

[179] The views here propounded suggest considerable criticism. It appears to me that the stress here laid upon the intelligible content of poetry as contrasted with the sensuous qualities of its form as modulated speech is certainly untenable. What we call the music of verse may unquestionably be most intimately associated with the ideal content expressed; but apart from the artistic collocation of language as sound no less than symbol we certainly do not get the art of poetry. Even where Hegel deals directly

the true medium of poetical representation is the poetical imagination and the intellectual presentation itself; and inasmuch as this element is common to all types of art it follows that poetry is a common thread through them all, and is developed independently in each. Poetry is, in short, the universal art of the mind, which has become essentially free, and which is not fettered in its realization to an externally sensuous material, but which is creatively active in the space and time belonging to the inner world of ideas and emotion. Yet it is precisely in this its highest phrase, that art terminates, by transcending itself; it is just here that it deserts the medium of a harmonious presentation of mind in sensuous shape and passes from the poetry of imaginative idea into the prose of thought.

Such we may accept as the articulate totality of the particular arts; they are the external art of architecture, the objective art of sculpture and the subjective arts of painting, music, and poetry. Many other classifications than these have been attempted, for a work of art presents such a wealth of aspects, that it is quite possible, as has frequently been the case, to make first one and then another the basis of division. For instance, you may take the sensuous medium simply. Architecture may then be viewed as a kind of crystallization; sculpture, as the organic configuration of material in its sensuous and spatial totality; painting as the coloured surface and line, while in music, space, as such, passes over into the point or moment of time replete with content in itself, until we come finally to poetry, where the external medium is wholly suppressed into insignificance. Or, again, these differences have been viewed with reference to their purely abstract conditions of space and time. Such abstract divisions of works of art may, as their medium also may be consequentially traced in their characteristic features. They cannot, however, be worked out as the final and fundamental principle, because such aspects themselves derive their origins from a higher principle, and must therefore fall into subordination thereto.

This higher principle we have discovered in the types of art—symbolic, classical, and romantic—which are the universal stages or phases of the Idea of beauty itself.

Their relation to the individual arts in their concrete manifestation as embodiment is of a kind that these arts constitute the real and positive existence of these general art-types. For *symbolic* art attains its most adequate realization and most pertinent application in *architecture*, in which it expatiates in the full import of its notion, and is not as yet depreciated, as it were, into the merely inorganic nature dealt with by some other art. The *classical* type of art finds its unfettered realization, on the other hand, in sculpture, treating architecture merely as the enclosure which surrounds it, and being unable to elaborate painting and music into the wholly adequate [180] forms of its content. Finally, the *romantic* art-type is supreme in the products of painting and music, and likewise in poetical composition, as their pre-eminent and unconditionally adequate modes of expression. Poetry is, however, conformable to all types of the

with rhythm and rhyme in the body of the treatise I think it is clear he underrates all that is implied in the difference between the musical expression of poetry as contrasted even with the sonorous language of mere prose. A further question upon which more doubt is permissible is how far the actual script in written or printed letters is not entitled to be regarded as at least in part the sensuous medium. No doubt the poem is not dependent upon it as a painting is upon colour, or the canvas which supports it, for it may be recited. But at least it is practically dependent upon it for its preservation. The point may very possibly appear, however, as nugatory or entirely unimportant, beside the question whether the medium of the art is not really imaginative idea rather than articulate speech.

[180] *Absolute Formen.* Adequate in the sense of being unconditionally so.

beautiful, and its embrace reaches them all for the reason that the poetic imagination is its own proper medium, and imagination is essential to every creation of beauty, whatever its type may be.

To sum up, then, what the particular arts realize in particular works of art, are according to their fundamental conception, simply the universal types which constitute the self-unfolding Idea of beauty. It is as the external realization of this Idea that the wide Pantheon of art is being raised; and the architect and builder thereof is the spirit of beauty as it gradually comes to self-cognition, and to complete which the history of the world will require its evolution of centuries.

Arthur Schopenhauer

1788–1860

A. Life

The author of *The World as Will and Idea* was born in Danzig in 1788 and entered the University of Göttingen in 1809. At the University his principal interest was the philosophies of Plato and Kant, the influence of which is most evident in the third book of *The World as Will and Idea,* which is primarily concerned with problems of art, its production and its experience. Schopenhauer heard Fichte and Schleiermacher lecture at the University of Berlin, where he spent two years and in 1808, attended lectures by Friedrich Schlegel and became interested in Eastern speculation. In 1819, *The World as Will and Idea* was published and Schopenhauer became a *privat docent* at the University of Berlin. He was a failure in academic life. In 1833 he came to Frankfurt to live. Only late in life was he recognized as an outstanding thinker.

B. Aesthetics

The Platonic Idea: The Object of Art

§ 30. In [181] the First Book the world was explained as mere *idea,* object for a subject. In the Second Book we considered it from its other side, and found that in this aspect it is *will,* which proved to be simply that which this world is besides being idea. In accordance with this knowledge we called the world as idea, both as a whole and in its parts, the *objectification of will,* which therefore means the will become object, *i.e.,* idea. Further, we remember that this objectification of will was found to have many definite grades, in which, with gradually increasing distinctness and completeness, the nature of will appears in the idea, that is to say, presents itself as object. In these grades we already recognised the

[181] Arthur Schopenhauer, *The World as Will and Idea,* Book III, translated by R. B. Haldane and J. Kemp, London, Routledge & Kegan Paul Ltd., 1883–1896; New York: Humanities Press Inc.

Platonic Ideas, for the grades are just the determined species, or the original unchanging forms and qualities of all natural bodies, both organised and unorganised, and also the general forces which reveal themselves according to natural laws. These Ideas, then, as a whole express themselves in innumerable individuals and particulars, and are related to these as archetypes to their copies. The multiplicity of such individuals is only conceivable through time and space, their appearing and passing away through causality, and in all these forms we recognise merely the different modes of the principle of sufficient reason, which is the ultimate principle of all that is finite, of all individual existence, and the universal form of the idea as it appears in the knowledge of the individual as such. The Platonic Idea, on the other hand, does not come under this principle, and has therefore neither multiplicity nor change. While the individuals in which it expresses itself are innumerable, and unceasingly come into being and pass away, it remains unchanged as one and the same, and the principle of sufficient reason has for it no meaning. As, however, this is the form under which all knowledge of the subject comes, so far as the subject knows as an *individual*, the Ideas lie quite outside the sphere of its knowledge. If, therefore, the Ideas are to become objects of knowledge, this can only happen by transcending the individuality of the knowing subject. The more exact and detailed explanation of this is what will now occupy our attention.

§ 31. First, however, the following very essential remark. I hope that in the preceding book I have succeeded in producing the conviction that what is called in the Kantian philosophy the *thing-in-itself*, and appears there as so significant, and yet so obscure and paradoxical a doctrine, and especially on account of the manner in which Kant introduced it as an inference from the caused to the cause, was considered a stumbling-stone, and, in fact, the weak side of his philosophy,—that this, I say, if it is reached by the entirely different way by which we have arrived at it, is nothing but the *will* when the sphere of that conception is extended and defined in the way I have shown. I hope, further, that after what has been said there will be no hesitation in recognising the definite grades of the objectification of the will, which is the inner reality of the world, to be what Plato called the *eternal Ideas* or unchangeable forms (ειδη̃); a doctrine which is regarded as the principal, but at the same time the most obscure and paradoxical dogma of his system, and has been the subject of reflection and controversy of ridicule and of reverence to so many and such differently endowed minds in the course of many centuries. . . .

§ 34. The transition which we have referred to as possible, but yet to be regarded as only exceptional, from the common knowledge of particular things to the knowledge of the Idea, takes place suddenly; for knowledge breaks free from the service of the will, by the subject ceasing to be merely individual, and thus becoming the pure will-less subject of knowledge, which no longer traces relations in accordance with the principle of sufficient reason, but rests in fixed contemplation of the object presented to it, out of its connection with all others, and rises into it.

A full explanation is necessary to make this clear, and the reader must suspend his surprise for a while, till he has grasped the whole thought expressed in this work, and then it will vanish of itself.

If, raised by the power of the mind, a man relinquishes the common way of looking at things, gives up tracing, under the guidance of the forms of the principle of sufficient reason, their relations to each other, the final goal of which is always a relation to his own will; if he thus ceases to consider the where, the when, the why, and the whither of things, and looks simply and solely at the *what*; if, further, he does not allow abstract thought, the concepts of the reason, to take possession of his consciousness, but, instead of all this, gives the whole power of his mind to perception, sinks himself entirely in this, and lets his whole consciousness be filled with the quiet contemplation of the natural object actually present, whether a landscape, a tree, a mountain, a building, or whatever it may be; inasmuch as he *loses* himself in this object (to use a pregnant German idiom), *i.e.,* forgets even his individuality, his will, and only continues to exist as the pure subject, the clear mirror of the object, so that it is as if the object alone were there, without any one to perceive it, and he can no longer separate the perceiver from the perception, but both have become one, because the whole consciousness is filled and occupied with one single sensuous picture; if thus the object has to such an extent passed out of all relation to something outside it, and the subject out of all relation to the will, then that which is so known is no longer the particular thing as such; but it is the *Idea*, the eternal form, the immediate objectivity of the will at this grade; and, therefore, he who is sunk in this perception is no longer individual, for in such perception the individual has lost himself; but he is *pure*, will-less, painless, timeless *subject of knowledge*. . . .

§ 36. History follows the thread of events; it is pragmatic so far as it deduces them in accordance with the law of motivation, a law that determines the self-manifesting will wherever it is enlightened by knowledge. At the lowest grades of its objectivity, where it still acts without knowledge, natural science, in the form of etiology, treats of the laws of the changes of its phenomena, and, in the form of morphology, of what is permanent in them. This almost endless task is lightened by the aid of concepts, which comprehend what is general in order that we may deduce what is particular from it. Lastly, mathematics treats of the mere forms, time and space, in which the Ideas, broken up into multiplicity, appear for the knowledge of the subject as individual. All these, of which the common name is science, proceed according to the principle of sufficient reason in its different forms, and their theme is always the phenomenon, its laws, connections, and the relations which result from them. But what kind of knowledge is concerned with that which is outside and independent of all relations, that which alone is really essential to the world, the true content of its phenomena, that which is subject to no change, and therefore is known with equal truth for all time, in a word, the *Ideas*, which are the direct and adequate objectivity of the thing in-itself, the will? We answer, *Art,* the work of genius. It repeats or reproduces the eternal Ideas grasped through pure contemplation, the essential and abiding in all the phenomena of the world; and according to what the material is in which it reproduces, it is sculpture or painting, poetry or music. Its one source is the knowledge of Ideas; its one aim the communication of this knowledge. While science, following the unresting and inconstant stream of the fourfold forms of reason and consequent, with each end attained sees further, and can never reach a final goal nor attain full satisfaction, any more than by running we can reach the place where the clouds touch the horizon; art, on the contrary, is everywhere at its goal. For it plucks the object of its contemplation out of the stream of the world's course, and has it isolated before it. And this particular thing, which in that stream was a small perishing part, becomes to art the representative of the whole, an equivalent of the endless multitude in space and time. It therefore pauses at this particular thing; the course of time stops; the relations vanish for it; only the essential, the Idea, is its object. We may, therefore, accurately define it as the *way of viewing things independent of the principle of sufficient reason*, in opposition to the way of viewing them which proceeds in accordance with that principle, and which is the method of experience and of science. This last method of considering things may be compared to a line infinitely extended in a horizontal direction, and the former to a vertical line which cuts it any any point. The method of viewing things which proceeds in accordance with the principle of sufficient reason is the rational method, and it alone is valid and of use in practical life and in science. The method which looks away from the content of this principle is the method of genius, which is only valid and of use in art. The first is the method of Aristotle; the second is, on the whole, that of Plato. The first is like the mighty storm, that rushes along without beginning and without aim, bending, agitating, and carrying away everything before it; the second is like the silent sunbeam, that pierces through the storm quite unaffected by it. The first is like the innumerable showering drops of the waterfall, which, constantly changing, never rest for an instant; the second is like the rainbow, quietly resting on this raging torrent. Only through the pure contemplation described above, which ends entirely in the object, can Ideas be comprehended; and the nature of *genius* consists in pre-eminent capacity for such contemplation. Now, as this requires that a man should entirely forget himself and the relations in which he stands, *genius* is simply the completest *objectivity, i.e.*, the objective tendency of the mind, as opposed to the subjective, which is directed to one's own self—in other words, to the will. Thus genius is the faculty of continuing in the state of pure perception, of losing oneself in perception, and of enlisting in this service the knowledge which originally existed only for the service of the will; that is to say, genius is the power of leaving one's own interests, wishes, and aims entirely out of sight, thus of entirely renouncing one's own personality for a time, so as to remain *pure knowing subject*, clear vision of the world; and this not merely at moments, but for the sufficient length of time, and with sufficient consciousness, to enable one to reproduce by deliberate art what has thus been apprehended, and "to fix in lasting thoughts the wavering images that float before the mind." It is as if, when genius appears in an individual, a far larger measure of the power of knowledge falls to his lot than is necessary for the service of an individual will; and this superfluity of knowledge, being free, now becomes subject purified from will, a clear mirror of the inner nature of the world. This explains the activity, amounting even to disquietude, of men of genius, for the present can seldom satisfy them, because it does not fill their consciousness. This gives them that restless aspiration, that unceasing desire for new things, and for the contemplation of lofty things, and also that longing that is hardly ever satisfied, for men of similar nature and of like stature, to whom they might communicate themselves; whilst the common mortal, entirely filled and satisfied by the common present, ends in it, and finding everywhere his like, enjoys that peculiar satisfaction in daily life that is denied to genius.

Imagination has rightly been recognised as an essential element of genius; it has sometimes even been regarded as identical with it; but this is a mistake. As the objects of genius are the eternal Ideas, the permanent, essential forms of the world and all its phenomena, and as the knowledge of the Idea is necessarily knowledge through perception, is not abstract, the knowledge of the genius would be limited to the Ideas of the objects actually present to his person, and dependent upon the chain of circumstances that brought these objects to him, if his imagination did not extend his horizon far beyond the limits of his actual personal existence, and thus enable him to construct the whole out of the little that comes into his own actual apperception, and so to let almost all possible scenes of life pass before him in his own consciousness. Further, the actual objects are almost always very imperfect copies of the Ideas expressed in them; therefore the man of genius requires imagination in order to see in things, not that which Nature has actually made, but that which she endeavoured to make, yet could not because of that conflict of her forms among themselves which we referred to in the last book. We shall return to this farther on in treating of sculpture. The imagination then extends the intellectual horizon of the man of genius beyond the objects which actually present themselves to him, both as regards quality and quantity. Therefore extraordinary strength of imagination accompanies, and is indeed a necessary condition of genius. But the converse does not hold, for strength of imagination does not indicate genius; on the contrary, men who have no touch of genius may have much imagination. For as it is possible to consider a real object in two opposite ways, purely objectively, the way of genius grasping its Idea, or in the common way, merely in the relations in which it stands to other objects and to one's own will, in accordance with the principle of sufficient reason, it is also possible to perceive an imaginary object in both of these ways. Regarded in the first way, it is a means to the knowledge of the Idea, the communication of which is the work of art; in the second case, the imaginary object is used to build castles in the air congenial to egotism and the individual humour, and which for the moment delude and gratify; thus only the relations of the phantasies so linked together are known. The man who indulges in such an amusement is a dreamer; he will easily mingle those fancies that delight his solitude with reality, and so unfit himself for real life: perhaps he will write them down, and then we shall have the ordinary novel of every description, which entertains those who are like him and the public at large, for the readers imagine themselves in the place of the hero, and then find the story very agreeable.

The common mortal, that manufacture of Nature which she produces by the thousand every day, is, as we have said, not capable, at least not continuously so, of observation that in every sense is wholly disinterested, as sensuous contemplation, strictly so called, is. He can turn his attention to things only so far as they have some relation to his will, however indirect it may be. Since in this respect, which never demands anything but the knowledge of relations, the abstract conception of the thing is sufficient, and for the most part even better adapted for use; the ordinary man does not linger long over the mere perception, does not fix his attention long on one object, but in all that presented to him hastily seeks merely the concept under which it is to be brought, as the lazy man seeks a chair, and then it interests him no further. This is why he is so soon done with everything, with works of art, objects of natural beauty, and indeed everywhere with the truly significant contemplation of all the scenes of life. He does not linger; only seeks to know his own way in life, togther with all that might at any time become his way. Thus he makes topographical notes in the widest sense; over the consideration of life itself as such he wastes no time. The man of genius, on the other hand, whose excessive power of knowledges frees it at times from the service of will, dwells on the consideration of life itself, strives to comprehend the Idea of each thing, not its relations to other things; and in doing this he often forgets to consider his own path in life, and therefore for the most part pursues it awkwardly enough. While to the ordinary man his faculty of knowledge is a lamp to lighten his path, to the man of genius it is the sun which reveals the world. This great diversity in their way of looking at life soon becomes visible in the outward appearance both of the man of genius and of the ordinary mortal. The man in whom genius lives and works is easily distinguished by his glance, which is both keen and steady, and bears the stamp of perception, of contemplation. This is easily seen from the likenesses of the few men of genius whom Nature has produced here and there among countless millions. On the other hand, in the case of an ordinary man, the true object of his contemplation, what he is prying into, can be easily seen from his glance, if indeed it is not quite stupid and vacant, as is generally the case. Therefore the expression of genius in a face consists in this, that in it a decided predominance of knowledge over will is visible, and consequently there also shows itself in it a knowledge that is entirely devoid of relation to will, *i.e., pure knowing.* On the contrary, in ordinary countenances there is a predominant expression of will; and we see that knowledge only comes into activity under the impulse of will, and thus is directed merely by motives.

Since the knowledge that pertains to genius, or the knowledge of Ideas, is that knowledge which does not follow the principle of sufficient reason, so, on the other hand, the knowledge which does follow that principle is that which gives us prudence and rationality in life, and which creates the sciences. Thus men of genius are affected with the deficiencies entailed in the neglect of this latter kind of knowledge. Yet what I say in this regard is subject to the limitation that it only concerns them in so far as and while they are actually engaged in that kind of knowledge which is peculiar to genius; and this is by no means at every moment of their lives, for the great though spontaneous exertion which is demanded for the comprehension of Ideas free from will must necessarily relax, and there are long intervals during which men of genius are placed in very much the same position as ordinary mortals, both as regards advantages and deficiencies. On this account the action of genius has always been regarded as an inspiration, as indeed the name indicates, as the action of a superhuman being distinct from the individual himself, and which takes possession of him only periodically. The disinclination of men of genius to direct their attention to the content of the principle of sufficient reason will first show itself, with regard to the ground of being, as dislike of mathematics; for its procedure is based upon the most universal forms of the phenomenon space and time, which are themselves merely modes of the principle of sufficient reason, and is consequently precisely the opposite of that method of thought which seeks merely the content of the phenomenon, the Idea which expresses itself in it apart from all relations. The logical method of mathematics is also antagonistic to genius, for it does not satisfy but obstructs true insight, and presents merely a chain of conclusions in accordance with the principle of the ground of knowing. The mental faculty upon which it makes the greatest claim is memory, for it is necessary to recollect all the earlier propositions which are referred to. Experience has also proved that men of great artistic genius have no faculty for mathematics; no man was ever very distinguished for both. Alfieri relates that he was never able to understand the fourth proposition of Euclid. Goethe was constantly reproached with his want of mathematical knowledge by the ignorant opponents of his theory of colours. Here certainly, where it was not a question of calculation and measurement upon hypothetical data, but of direct knowledge by the understanding of causes and effects, this reproach was so utterly absurd and inappropriate, that by making it they have exposed their entire want of judgment, just as much as by the rest of their ridiculous arguments. The fact that up to the present day, nearly half a century after the appearance of Goethe's theory of colours, even in Germany the Newtonian fallacies still have undisturbed possession of the professorial chair, and men continue to speak quite seriously of the seven homogeneous rays of light and their different refrangibility, will some day be numbered among the great intellectual peculiarities of men generally, and especially of Germans.

From the same cause as we have referred to above, may be explained the equally well-known fact that, conversely, admirable mathematicians have very little susceptibility for works of fine art. This is very naively expressed in the well-known anecdote of the French mathematician, who, after having read Racine's "Iphigenia," shrugged his shoulders and asked, *"Qu'est ce que cela prouve?"* Further, as quick comprehension of relations in accordance with the laws of causality and motivation is what specially constitutes prudence or sagacity, a prudent man, so far as and while he is so, will not be a genius, and a man of genius, so far as and while he is so, will not be a prudent man. Lastly, perceptive knowledge generally, in the province of which the Idea always lies, is directly opposed to rational or abstract knowledge, which is guided by the principle of the ground of knowing. It is also well known that we seldom find great genius united with pre-eminent reasonableness; on the contrary, persons of genius are often subject to violent emotions and irrational passions. But the ground of this is not weakness of reason, but partly unwanted energy of that whole phenomenon of will—the man of genius—which expresses itself through the violence of all his acts of will, and partly preponderance of the knowledge of perception through the senses and understanding over abstract knowledge, producing a decided tendency to the perceptible, the exceedingly lively impressions of which so far outshine colourless concepts, that they take their place in the guidance of action, which consequently becomes irrational. Accordingly the impression of the present moment is very strong with such persons, and carries them away into unconsidered action, violent emotions and passions. Moreover, since, in general, the knowledge of persons of genius has to some extent freed itself from the service of will, they will not in conversation think so much of the person they are addressing as of the thing they are speaking about, which is vividly present to them; and therefore they are likely to judge or narrate things too objectively for their own interests; they will not pass over in silence what would more prudently be concealed, and so forth. Finally, they are given to soliloquising, and in general may exhibit certain weaknesses which are actually akin to madness. It has often been remarked that there is a side at which genius and madness touch, and even pass over into each other, and indeed poetical inspiration has been called a kind of madness: *amabilis insania,* Horace calls it (Od. iii. 4), and Wieland in the introduction to "Oberon" speaks of it as "amiable madness." Even Aristotle, as quoted by Seneca (De Tranq. Animi, 17, 10), is reported to have said: *Nullum magnum ingenium sine mixtura dementiœ fuit.* Plato expresses it in the figure of the dark cave, referred to above (De Rep. 7), when he says: "Those who, outside the cave, have seen the true sunlight and the things that have true being (Ideas), cannot afterwards see properly down in the cave, because their eyes are not accustomed to the darkness; they cannot distinguish the shadows, and are jeered at for their mistakes by those who have never left the cave and its shadows." In the "Phædrus" also (p. 317), he distinctly says that there can be no true poet without a certain madness; in fact, (p. 327), that every one appears mad who recognises the eternal Ideas in fleeting things. Cicero also quotes: *Negat enim sine furore, Democritus, quemquam poetam magnum esse posse; quod idem dicit Plato* (De Divin., i. 37). And lastly, Pope says—

" Great wits to madness sure are near allied,
And thin partitions do their bounds divide . . ."

. . . We see, from what has been said, that the madman has a true knowledge of what is actually present, and also of certain particulars of the past, but that he mistakes the connection, the relations, and therefore falls into error and talks nonsense. Now this is exactly the point at which he comes into contact with the man of genius; for he also leaves out of sight the knowledge of the connection of things, since he neglects that knowledge of relations which conforms to the principle of sufficient reason, in order to see in things only their Ideas, and to seek to comprehend their true nature, which manifests itself to perception, and in regard to which *one thing* represents its whole species, in which way, as Goethe says, one case is valid for a thousand. The particular object of his contemplation, or the present which is perceived by him with extraordinary vividness, appear in so strong a light that the other links of the chain to which they belong are at once thrown into the shade, and this gives rise to phenomena which have long been recognised as resembling those of madness. That which in particular given things exists only incompletely and weakened by modifications, is raised by the man of genius, through his way of contemplating it, to the Idea of the thing, to completeness: he therefore sees everywhere extremes, and therefore his own action tends to extremes; he cannot hit the mean, he lacks soberness, and the result is what we have said. He knows the Ideas completely but not the individuals. Therefore it has been said that a poet may know mankind deeply and thoroughly, and may yet have a very imperfect knowledge of men. He is easily deceived, and is a tool in the hands of the crafty.

§ 37. Genius, then, consists, according to our explanation, in the capacity for knowing, independently of the principle of sufficient reason, not individual things, which have their existence only in their relations, but the Ideas of such things, and of being oneself the correlative of the Idea, and thus no longer an individual, but the pure subject of knowledge. Yet this faculty must exist in all men in a smaller and different degree; for if not, they would be just as incapable of enjoying works of art as of producing them; they would have no susceptibility for the beautiful or the sublime; indeed, these words could have no meaning for them. We must therefore assume that there exists in all men this power of knowing the Ideas in things, and consequently of transcending their personality for the moment, unless indeed there are some men who are capable of no æsthetic pleasure at all. The man of genius excels ordinary men only by possessing this kind of knowledge in a far higher degree and more continuously. Thus, while under its influence he retains the presence of mind which is necessary to enable him to repeat in a voluntary and intentional work what he has learned in this manner; and this repetition is the work of art. Through this he communicates to others the Idea he has grasped. This Idea remains unchanged and the same, so that æsthetic pleasure is one and the same whether it is called forth by a work of art or directly by the contemplation of nature and life. The work of art is only a means of facilitating the knowledge in which this pleasure consists. That the Idea comes to us more easily from the work of art than directly from nature and the real world, arises from the fact that the artist, who knew only the Idea, no longer the actual, has reproduced in his work the pure Idea, has abstracted it from the actual, omitting all disturbing accidents. The artist lets us see the world through his eyes. That he has these eyes, that he knows the inner nature of things apart from all their relations, is the gift of genius, is inborn; but that he is able to lend us this gift, to let us see with his eyes, is acquired, and is the technical side of art. Therefore, after the account which I have given in the preceding pages of the inner nature of æsthetical knowledge in its most general outlines, the following more exact philosophical treatment of the beautiful and the sublime will explain them both, in nature and in art, without separating them further. First of all we shall consider what takes place in a man when he is affected by the beautiful and the sublime; whether he derives this emotion directly from nature, from life, or partakes of it only through the medium of art, does not make any essential, but merely an external, difference.

§ 38. In the æsthetical mode of contemplation we have found *two inseparable constituent parts*—the knowledge of the object, not as individual thing but as Platonic Idea, that is, as the enduring form of this whole species of things; and the self-consciousness of the knowing person, not as individual, but as *pure will-less subject of knowledge*. The condition under which both these constituent parts appear always united was found to be the abandonment of the method of knowing which is bound to the principle of sufficient reason, and which, on the other hand, is the only kind of knowledge that is of value for the service of the will and also for science. Moreover we shall see that the pleasure which is produced by the contemplation of the beautiful arises from these two constituent parts, sometimes more from the one, sometimes more from the other, according to what the object of the æsthetical contemplation may be.

All *willing* arises from want, therefore from deficiency, and therefore from suffering. The satisfaction of a wish ends it; yet for one wish that is satisfied there remain at least ten which are denied. Further, the desire lasts long, the demands are infinite; the satisfaction is short and scantily measured out. But even the final satisfaction is itself only apparent; every satisfied wish at once makes room for a new one; both are illusions; the one is known to be so, the other not yet. No attained object of desire can give lasting satisfaction, but merely a fleeting gratification; it is like the alms thrown to the beggar, that keeps him alive to-day that his misery may be prolonged till the morrow. Therefore, so long as our consciousness is filled by our will, so long as we are given up to the throng of desires with their constant hopes and fears, so long as we are the subject of willing, we can never have lasting happiness nor peace. It is essentially all the same whether we pursue or flee, fear injury or seek enjoyment; the care for the constant demands of the will, in whatever form it may be, continually occupies and sways the consciousness; but without peace no true well-being is possible. The subject of willing is thus constantly stretched on the revolving wheel of Ixion, pours water into the sieve of the Danaids, is the ever-longing Tantalus.

But when some external cause or inward disposition lifts us suddenly out of the endless stream of willing, delivers knowledge from the slavery of the will, the attention is no longer directed to the motives of willing, but comprehends things free from their relation to the will, and thus observes them without personal interest, without subjectivity, purely objectively, gives itself entirely to them so far as they are ideas, but not in so far as they are motives. Then all at once the peace which we were always seeking, but which always fled from us on the former path of the desires, comes to us of its own accord, and it is well with us. It is the painless state which Epicurus prized as the highest good and as the state of the gods; for we are for the moment set free from the miserable striving of the will; we keep the Sabbath of the penal servitude of willing; the wheel of Ixion stands still.

But this is just the state which I described above as necessary for the knowledge of the Idea, as pure contemplation, as sinking oneself in perception, losing oneself in the object, forgetting all individuality, surrendering that kind of knowledge which follows the principle of sufficient reason, and comprehends only relations; the state by means of which at once and inseparably the perceived particular thing is raised to the Idea of its whole species, and the knowing individual to the pure subject of will-less knowledge, and as such they are both taken out of the stream of time and all other relations. It is then all one whether we see the sun set from the prison or from the palace.

Inward disposition, the predominance of knowing over willing, can produce this state under any circumstances. This is shown by those admirable Dutch artists who directed this purely objective perception to the most insignificant objects, and established a lasting monument of their objectivity and spiritual peace in their pictures of *still life*, which the æsthetic beholder does not look on without emotion; for they present to him the peaceful still, frame of mind of the artist, free from will, which was needed to contemplate such insignificant things so objectively, to observe them so attentively, and to repeat this perception so intelligently; and as the picture enables the onlooker to participate in this state, his emotion is often increased by the contrast between it and the unquiet frame of mind, disturbed by vehement willing, in which he finds himself. In the same spirit, landscape-painters, and particularly Ruisdael, have often painted very insignificant country scenes, which produce the same effect even more agreeably.

All this is accomplished by the inner power of an artistic nature alone; but that purely objective disposition is facilitated and assisted from without by suitable objects, by the abundance of natural beauty which invites contemplation, and even presses itself upon us. Whenever it discloses itself suddenly to our view, it almost always succeeds in delivering us, though it may be only for a moment, from subjectivity, from the slavery of the will, and in raising us to the state of pure knowing. This is why the man who is tormented by passion, or want, or care, is so suddenly revived, cheered, and restored by a single free glance into nature: the storm of passion, the pressure of desire and fear, and all the miseries of willing are then at once, and in a marvellous manner, calmed and appeased. For all the moment at which, freed from the will, we give ourselves up to pure will-less knowing, we pass into a world from which everything is absent that influenced our will and moved us so violently through it. This freeing of knowledge lifts us as wholly and entirely away from all that, as do sleep and dreams; happiness and unhappiness have disappeared; we are no longer individual; the individual is forgotten; we are only pure subject of knowledge; we are only that *one* eye of the world which looks out from all knowing creatures, but which can become perfectly free from the service of will in man alone. Thus all difference of individuality so entirely disappears, that it is all the same whether the perceiving eye belongs to a mighty king or to a wretched beggar; for neither joy nor complaining can pass that boundary with us. So near us always lies a sphere in which we escape from all our misery; but who has the strength to continue long in it? As soon as any single relation to our will, to our person, even of these objects of our pure contemplation, comes again into consciousness, the magic is at an end; we fall back into the knowledge which is governed by the principle of sufficient reason; we know no longer the Idea, but the particular thing, the link of a chain to which we also belong, and we are again abandoned to all our woe. Most men remain almost always at this standpoint because they entirely lack objectivity. *i.e.,* genius. Therefore they have no pleasure in being alone with nature; they need company, or at least a book. For their knowledge remains subject to their will; they seek, therefore, in objects, only some relation to their will, and whenever they see anything that has no such relation, there sounds within them, like a ground bass in music, the constant inconsolable cry, "It is of no use to me;" thus in solitude the most beautiful surroundings have for them a desolate, dark, strange, and hostile appearance.

Lastly, it is this blessedness of will-less perception which casts an enchanting glamour over the past and distant, and presents them to us in so fair a light by means of self-deception. For as we think of days long gone by, days in which we lived in a distant place, it is only the objects which our fancy recalls, not the subject of will, which bore about with it then its incurable sorrows just as it bears them now; but they are forgotten, because since then they have often given place to others. Now, objective perception acts with regard to what is remembered just as it would in what is present, if we let it have influence over us, if we surrendered ourselves to it free from will. Hence it arises that, especially when we are more than ordinarily disturbed by some want, the remembrance of past and distant scenes suddenly flits across our minds like a lost paradise. The fancy recalls only what was objective, not what was individually subjective, and we imagine that that objective stood before us then just as pure and undisturbed by any relation to the will as its image stands in our fancy now; while in reality the relation of the objects to our will gave us pain then just as it does now. We can deliver ourselves from all suffering just as well through present objects as through distant ones whenever we raise ourselves to a purely objective contemplation of them, and so are able to bring about the illusion that only the objects are present and not we ourselves. Then, as the pure subject of knowledge, freed from the miserable self, we become entirely one with these objects, and, for the moment, our wants are as foreign to us as they are to them. The world as idea alone remains, and the world as will has disappeared.

In all these reflections it has been my object to bring out clearly the nature and the scope of the subjective element in aesthetic pleasure; the deliverance of knowledge from the service of the will, the forgetting of self as an individual, and the raising of the consciousness to the pure will-less, timeless subject of knowledge, independent of all relations. With this subjective side of aesthetic contemplation, there must always appear as its necessary correlative the objective side, the intuitive comprehension of the Platonic Idea. But before we turn to the closer consideration of this, and to the achievements of art in relation to it, it is better that we should pause for a little at the subjective side of aesthetic pleasure, in order to complete our treatment of this by explaining the impression of the *sublime* which depends altogether upon it, and arises from a modification of it. After that we shall complete our investigation of aesthetic pleasure by considering its objective side. . . .

. . . Tragedy is to be regarded, and is recognized as the summit of poetical art, both on account of the greatness of its effect and the difficulty of its achievement. It is very significant for our whole system, and well worthy of observation, that the end of this highest poetical achievement is the representation of the terrible side of life. The unspeakable pain, the wail of humanity, the triumph of evil, the scornful mastery of chance, and the irretrievable fall of the just and innocent, is here presented to us; and in this lies a significant hint of the nature of the world and of existence. It is the strife of will with itself, which here, completely unfolded at the highest grade of its objectivity, comes into fearful prominence. It becomes visible in the suffering of men, which is now introduced, partly through chance and error, which appear as the rulers of the world, personified as fate, on account of their insidiousness, which even reaches the appearance of design; partly it proceeds from man himself, through the self-mortifying efforts of a few, through the wickedness and perversity of most. It is one and the same will that lives and appears in them all, but whose phenomena fight against each other and destroy each other. In one individual it appears powerfully, in another more weakly; in one more subject to reason, and softened by the light of knowledge, in another less so, till at last, in some single case, this knowledge, purified and heightened by suffering itself, reaches the point at which the phenomenon, the veil of Maya, no longer deceives it. It sees through the form of the phenomenon, the *principium individuationis.* The egoism which rests on this perishes with it, so that now the *motives* that were so powerful before have lost their might, and instead of them the complete knowledge of the nature of the world, which has a *quieting* effect on the will, produces resignation, the surrender not merely of life, but of the very will to live. . . .

§ 52. Now that we have considered all the fine arts in the general way that is suitable to our point of view, beginning with architecture, the peculiar end of which is to elucidate the objectification of will at the lowest grades of its visibility, in which it shows itself as the dumb unconscious tendency of the mass in accordance with laws, and yet already reveals a breach of the unity of will with itself in a conflict between gravity and rigidity—and ending with the consideration of tragedy, which presents to us at the highest grades of the objectification of will this very conflict with itself in terrible magnitude and distinctness; we find that there is still another fine art which has been excluded from our consideration, and had to be excluded, for in the systematic connection of our exposition there was no fitting place for it—I mean *music.* It stands alone, quite cut off from all the other arts. In it we do not recognise the copy or repetition of any Idea of existence in the world. Yet it is such a great and exceedingly noble art, its effect on the inmost nature of man is so powerful, and it is so entirely and deeply understood by him in his inmost consciousness as a perfect universal language, the distinctness of which surpasses even that of the perceptible world itself, that we certainly have more to look for in it than an *exercitum arithmeticæ occultum nescientis se numerare animi,*[182] which Leibnitz called it. Yet he was perfectly right, as he considered only its immediate external significance, its form. But if it were nothing more, the satisfaction which it affords would be like that which we feel when a sum in arithmetic comes out right, and could not be that intense pleasure with which we see the deepest recesses of our nature find utterance. From our standpoint, therefore, at which the aesthetic effect is the criterion, we must attribute to music a far more serious and deep significance, connected with the inmost nature of the world and our own self, and in reference to which the arithmetical proportions, to which it may be reduced, are related, not as the thing signified, but merely as the sign. That in some sense music must be related to the world as the representation to the thing represented, as the copy to the original, we may conclude from the analogy of the other arts, all of which possess this character, and affect us on the whole in the same way as it does, only that the effect of music is stronger, quicker, more necessary and infallible. Further, its representative relation to the world must be very deep, absolutely true, and strikingly accurate, because it is instantly understood by every one, and has the appearance of a certain infallibility, because its form may be reduced to perfectly definite rules expressed in numbers, from which it cannot free itself without entirely ceasing to be music. Yet the point of comparison between music and the world, the respect in which it stands to the world in the relation to a copy or repetition, is very obscure. Men have practised music in all ages without being able to account for this; content to understand it directly, they renounce all claim to an abstract conception of this direct understanding itself.

I gave my mind entirely up to the impression of music in all its forms, and then returned to reflection and the system of thought expressed in the present work, and thus I arrived at an explanation of the inner nature of its imitative relation to the world—which from analogy had necessarily to be presupposed—

[182] Leibnitii epistolae, collectio Kortholti, ep. 154.

an explanation which is quite sufficient for myself, and satisfactory to my investigation, and which will doubtless be equally evident to any one who has followed me thus far and has agreed with my view of the world. Yet I recognise the fact that it is essentially impossible to prove this explanation, for it assumes and establishes a relation of music, as idea, to that which from its nature can never be idea, and music will have to be regarded as the copy of an original which can never itself be directly presented as idea. . . .

The (Platonic) Ideas are the adequate objectification of will. To excite or suggest the knowledge of these by means of the representation of particular things (for works of art themselves are always representations of particular things) is the end of all the other arts, which can only be attained by a corresponding change in the knowing subject. Thus all these arts objectify the will indirectly only by means of the Ideas; and since our world is nothing but the manifestation of the Ideas in multiplicity, though their entrance into the *principium individuationis* (the form of the knowledge possible for the individual as such), music also, since it passes over the Ideas, is entirely independent of the phenomenal world, ignores it altogether, could to a certain extent exist if there was no world at all, which cannot be said of the other arts. Music is as *direct* an objectification and copy of the whole *will* as the world itself, nay, even as the Ideas, whose multiplied manifestation constitutes the world of individual things. Music is thus by no means like the other arts, the copy of the Ideas, but the *copy of the will itself*, whose objectivity the Ideas are. This is why the effect of music is so much more powerful and penetrating than that of the other arts, for they speak only of shadows, but it speaks of the thing itself. Since, however, it is the same will which objectifies itself both in the Ideas and in music, though in quite different ways, there must be, not indeed a direct likeness, but yet a parallel, an analogy, between music and the Ideas whose manifestation in multiplicity and incompleteness is the visible world. The establishing of this analogy will facilitate, as an illustration, the understanding of this exposition, which is so difficult on account of the obscurity of the subject.

I recognise in the deepest tones of harmony, in the bass, the lowest grades of the objectification of will, unorganised nature, the mass of the planet. It is well known that all the high notes which are easily sounded, and die away more quickly, are produced by the vibration in their vicinity of the deep bass-notes. When, also, the low notes sound, the high notes always sound faintly, and it is a law of harmony that only those high notes may accompany a bass-note which actually already sound along with it of themselves (its *sons harmoniques*) on account of its vibration. This is analogous to the fact that the whole of the bodies and organisations of nature must be regarded as having come into existence through gradual development out of the mass of the planet; this is both their supporter and their source, and the same relation subsists between the high notes and the bass. There is a limit of depth, below which no sound is audible. This corresponds to the fact that no matter can be perceived without form and quality, *i.e.*, without the manifestation of a force which cannot be further explained, in which an Idea expresses itself, and, more generally, that no matter can be entirely without will. Thus, as a certain pitch is inseparable from the note as such, so a certain grade of the manifestation of will is inseparable from matter. Bass is thus, for us, in harmony what unorganised nature, the crudest mass, upon which all rests, and from which everything originates and develops, is in the world. Now, further, in the whole of the complemental parts which make up the harmony between the bass and the leading voice singing the melody, I recognise the whole gradation of the Ideas in which the will objectifies itself. Those nearer to the bass are the lower of these grades, the still unorganised, but yet manifold phenomental things; the higher represent to me the world of plants and beasts. The definite intervals of the scale are parallel to the definite grades of the objectification of will, the definite species in nature. The departure from the arithmetical correctness of the intervals, through some temperament, or produced by the key selected, is analogous to the departure of the individual from the type of the species. Indeed, even the impure discords, which give no definite interval, may be compared to the monstrous abortions by beasts of two species, or by man and beast. But to all these bass and complemental parts which make up the *harmony* there is wanting that connected progress which belongs only to the high voice singing the melody, and it alone moves quickly and lightly in modulations and runs, while all these others have only a slower movement without a connection in each part for itself. The deep bass moves most slowly, the representative of the crudest mass. Its rising and falling occurs only by large intervals, in thirds, fourths, fifths, never by *one* tone, it is a base inverted by double counterpoint. This slow movement is also physically essential to it; a quick run or shake in the low notes cannot even be imagined. The higher complemental parts, which are parallel to animal life, move more quickly, but yet without melodious connection and significant progress. The disconnected course of all the complemental parts, and their regulation by definite laws, is analogous to the fact that in the whole irrational world, from the crystal to the most perfect animal, no being has a connected consciousness of its own which would make its life into a significant whole, and none experiences a succession of mental developments, none perfects itself by culture, but everything exists always in the same way according to its kind, determined by fixed law. Lastly, in the *melody*, in the high, singing, principal voice leading the whole and progressing with unrestrained freedom, in the unbroken significant connection of *one* thought from beginning to end representing a whole, I recognise the highest grade of the objectification of will, the intellectual life and effort of man. As he alone, because endowed with reason, constantly looks before and after on the path of his actual life and its innumerable possibilities, and so achieves a course of life which is intellectual, and therefore connected as a whole; corresponding to this, I say, the *melody* has significant intentional connection from beginning to end. It records, therefore, the history of the intellectually enlightened will. This will expresses itself in the actual world as the series of its deeds; but melody says more, it records the most secret history of this intellectually-enlightened will, pictures every excitement, every effort, every movement of it, all that which the reason collects under the wide and negative concept of feeling, and which it cannot apprehend further through its abstract concepts. Therefore it has always been said that music is the language of feeling and of passion, as words are the language of reason. Plato explains it as

ἡ των μελων κινησις μεμιμημενη, εν τοις παθημασιν ὁταν ψυχη γινηται

(*melodiarum motus, animi affectus imitans*), De Leg. vii.; and also Aristotle says:

δια τι οἱ ρυθμοι και τα μελη, φωνη ουσα, ηθεσιν εοικε

(*cur numeri musici et modi, qui voces sunt, moribus similes sese exhibent?*): Probl. c. 19.

Now the nature of man consists in this, that his will strives, is satisfied and strives anew, and so on for ever. Indeed, his happiness and well-being consist simply in the quick transition from wish to satisfaction, and from satisfaction to a new wish. For the absence of satisfaction is suffering, the empty longing for a new wish, languor, *ennui.* And corresponding to this the nature of melody is a constant digression and deviation from the key-note in a thousand ways, not only to the harmonious intervals to the third and dominant, but to every tone, to the dissonant sevenths and to the superfluous degrees; yet there always follows a constant return to the key-note. In all these deviations melody expresses the multifarious efforts of will, but always its satisfaction also by the final return to an harmonious interval, and still more, to the key-note. . . .

But it must never be forgotten, in the investigation of all these analogies I have pointed out, that music has no direct, but merely an indirect relation to them, for it never expresses the phenomenon, but only the inner nature, the in-itself of all phenomena, the will itself. It does not therefore express this or that particular and definite joy, this or that sorrow, or pain, or horror, or delight, or merriment, or peace of mind; but joy, sorrow, pain, horror, delight, merriment, peace of mind *themselves,* to a certain extent in the abstract, their essential nature, without accessories, and therefore without their motives. Yet we completely understand them in this extracted quintessence. Hence it arises that our imagination is so easily excited by music, and now seeks to give form to that invisible yet actively moved spirit-world which speaks to us directly, and clothe it with flesh and blood, *i.e.,* to embody it in an analogous example. This is the origin of the song with words, and finally of the opera, the text of which should therefore never forsake that subordinate position in order to make itself the chief thing and the music a mere means of expressing it, which is a great misconception and a piece of utter perversity; for music always expresses only the quintessence of life and its events, never these themselves, and therefore their differences do not always affect it. It is precisely this universality, which belongs exclusively to it, together with the greatest determinateness that gives music the high worth which it has as the panacea for all our woes. Thus, if music is too closely united to the words, and tries to form itself according to the events, it is striving to speak a language which is not its own. No one has kept so free from this mistake as Rossini; therefore his music speaks *its own language* so distinctly and purely that it requires no words, and produces its full effect when rendered by instruments alone.

According to all this, we may regard the phenomenal world, or nature, and music as two different expressions of the same thing, which is therefore itself the only medium of their analogy, so that a knowledge of it is demanded in order to understand that analogy. Music, therefore, if regarded as an expression of the world, is in the highest degree a universal language, which is related indeed to the universality of concepts, much as they are related to the particular things. Its universality, however, is by no means that empty universality of abstraction, but quite of a different kind, and is united with thorough and distinct definiteness. In this respect it resembles geometrical figures and numbers, which are universal forms of all possible objects of experience and applicable to them all *a priori,* and yet are not abstract but perceptible and thoroughly determined. All possible efforts, excitements, and manifestations of will, all that goes on in the heart of man and that reason includes in the wide, negative concept of feeling, may be expressed by the infinite number of possible melodies, but always in the universal, in the mere form, without the material, always according to the thing-in-itself, not the phenomenon, the inmost soul, as it were, of the phenomenon, without the body. This deep relation which music has to the true nature of all things also explains the fact that suitable music played to any scene, action, event, or surrounding seems to disclose to us its most secret meaning, and appears as the most accurate and distinct commentary upon it. This is so truly the case, that whoever gives himself up entirely to the impression of a symphony, seems to see all the possible events of life and the world take place in himself, yet if he reflects, he can find no likeness between the music and the things that passed before his mind. For, as we have said, music is distinguished from all the other arts by the fact that it is not a copy of the phenomenon, or, more accurately, the adequate objectivity of will, but is the direct copy of the will itself, and therefore exhibits itself as the metaphysical to everything physical in the world, and as the thing-in-itself to every phenomenon. We might, therefore, just as well call the world embodied music as embodied will; and this is the reason why music makes every picture, and indeed every scene of real life and of the world, at once appear with higher significance, certainly all the more in proportion as its melody is analogous to the inner spirit of the given phenomenon. It rests upon this that we are able to set a poem to music as a song, or a perceptible representation as a pantomime, or both as an opera. Such particular pictures of human life, set to the universal language of music, are never bound to it or correspond to it with stringent necessity; but they stand to it only in the relation of an example chosen at will to a general concept. In the determinateness of the real, they represent that which music expresses in the universality of mere form. For melodies are to a certain extent, like general concepts, an abstraction from the actual. This actual world, then, the world of particular things, affords the object of perception, the special and individual, the particular case, both to the universality of the concepts and to the universality of the melodies. But these two universalities are in a certain respect opposed to each other; for the concepts contain particulars only as the first forms abstracted from perception, as it were, the separated shell of things; thus they are, strictly speaking, *abstracta*; music, on the other hand, gives the inmost kernel which precedes all forms, or the heart of things. This relation may be very well expressed in the language of the schoolmen by saying the concepts are the *universalia post rem*, but music gives the *universalia ante rem*, and the real world the *universalia in re*. To the universal significance of a melody to which a poem has been set, it is quite possible to set other equally arbitrarily selected examples of the universal expressed in this poem corresponding to the significance of the melody in the same degree. This is why the same composition is suitable to many verses; and this is also what makes the *vaudeville* possible. But that in general a relation is possible between a composition and a perceptible representation rests, as we have said, upon the fact that both are simply different expressions of the same inner being of the world. When now, in the particular case, such a relation is actually given, that is to say, when the composer has been able to express in the universal language of music the emotions of will which constitute the heart of an event, then the melody of the song, the music of the opera, is expressive. But the analogy discovered by the composer between the two must have proceeded from the direct knowledge of the nature of the world unknown to his reason, and must not be an imitation produced with conscious intention by means of conceptions, otherwise the music does not express the inner nature of the will itself, but merely gives an inadequate imitation of its phenomenon. All specially imitative music does this; for example, "The Seasons," by Haydn; also many passages of his "Creation," in which phenomena of the external world are directly imitated; also all battle-pieces. Such music is entirely to be rejected.

The unutterable depth of all music by virtue of which it floats through our consciousness as the vision of a paradise firmly believed in yet ever distant from us, and by which also it is so fully understood and yet so inexplicable, rests on the fact that it restores to us all the emotions of our inmost nature, but entirely without reality and far removed from their pain. So also the seriousness which is essential to it, which excludes the absurd from its direct and peculiar province, is to be explained by the fact that its object is not the idea, with reference to which alone deception and absurdity are possible; but its object is directly the will, and this is essentially the most serious of all things, for it is that on which all depends. How rich in content and full of significance the language of music is, we see from the repetitions, as well as the *Da capo*, the like of which would be unbearable in works composed in a language of words, but in music are very appropriate and beneficial, for, in order to comprehend it fully, we must hear it twice.

In the whole of this exposition of music I have been trying to bring out clearly that it expresses in a perfectly universal language, in a homogeneous material, mere tones, and with the greatest determinateness and truth, the inner nature, the in-itself of the world, which we think under the concept of will, because will is its most distinct manifestation. Further, according to my view and contention, philosophy is nothing but a complete and accurate repetition or expression of the nature of the world in very general concepts, for only in such is it possible to get a view of that whole nature which will everywhere be adequate and applicable. Thus, whoever has followed me and entered into my mode of thought, will not think it so very paradoxical if I say, that supposing it were possible to give a perfectly accurate, complete explanation of music, extending even to particulars, that is to say, a detailed repetition in concepts of what it expresses, this would also be a sufficient repetition and explanation of the world in concepts, or at least entirely parallel to such an explanation, and thus it would be the true philosophy. Consequently the saying of Leibnitz quoted above, which is quite accurate from a lower standpoint, may be parodied in the following way to suit our higher view of music: *Musica est exercitium metaphysices occultum nescientis se philosophari animi;* for *scire,* to know, always means to have fixed in abstract concepts. But further, on account of the truth of the saying of Leibnitz, which is confirmed in various ways, music, regarded apart from its æsthetic or inner significance, and looked at merely externally and purely empirically, is simply the means of comprehending directly and in the concrete large numbers and complex relations of numbers, which otherwise we could only know indirectly by fixing them in concepts. Therefore by the union of these two very different but correct views of music we may arrive at a conception of the possibility of a philosophy of number, such as that of Pythagoras and of the Chinese in Y-King, and then interpret in this sense the saying of the Pythagoreans which Sextus Empiricus quotes (adv. Math., L. vii): *τῳ αριθμῳ δε τα παντ' επεοιπεν* (*numero cuncta assimilantur*). And if, finally, we apply this view to the interpretation of harmony and melody given above, we shall find that a mere moral philosophy without an explanation of Nature, such as Socrates wanted to introduce, is precisely analogous to a mere melody without harmony, which Rousseau exclusively desired; and, in opposition to this mere physics and metaphysics without ethics, will correspond to mere harmony without melody. Allow me to add to these cursory observations a few more remarks concerning the analogy of music with the phenomenal world. We found in the second book that the highest grade of the objectification of will, man, could not appear alone and isolated, but presupposed the grades below him, as these again presupposed the grades lower still. In the same way music, which directly objectifies the will, just as the world does, is complete only in full harmony. In order to achieve its full effect, the high leading voice of the melody requires the accompaniment of all the other voices, even to the lowest bass, which is to be regarded as the origin of all. The melody itself enters as an integral part into the harmony, as the harmony enters into it, and only thus, in the full harmonious whole, music expresses what it aims at expressing. Thus also the one will outside of time finds its full objectification only in the complete union of all the steps which reveal its nature in the innumerable ascending grades of distinctness. The following analogy is also very remarkable. We have seen in the preceding book that notwithstanding the self-adaptation of all the phenomena of will to each other as regards their species, which constitutes their teleological aspect, there yet remains an unceasing conflict between those phenomena as individuals, which is visible at every grade, and makes the world a constant battle-field of all those manifestations of one and the same will, whose inner contradiction with itself becomes visible through it. In music also there is something corresponding to this. A complete, pure, harmonious system of tones is not only physically but arithmetically impossible. The numbers themselves by which the tones are expressed have inextricable irrationality. There is no scale in which, when it is counted, every fifth will be related to the keynote as 2 to 3, every major third as 4 to 5, every minor third as 5 to 6, and so on. For if they are correctly related to the keynote, they can no longer be so to each other; because, for example, the fifth must be the minor third to the third, &c. For the notes of the scale may be compared to actors who must play now one part, now another. Therefore a perfectly accurate system of music cannot even be thought, far less worked out; and on this account all possible music deviates from perfect purity; it can only conceal the discords essential to it by dividing them among all the notes, *i.e.,* by temperament. On this see Chladni's "Akustik," § 30, and his "Kurze Uebersicht der Schall- und Klanglehre."

I might still have something to say about the way in which music is perceived, namely, in and through time alone, with absolute exclusion of space, and also apart from the influence of the knowledge of causality, thus without understanding; for the tones make the æsthetic impression as effect, and without obliging us to go back to their causes, as in the case of perception. I do not wish, however, to lengthen this discussion, as I have perhaps already gone too much into detail with regard to some things in this Third Book, or have dwelt too much on particulars. But my aim made it necessary, and it will be the less disapproved if the importance and high worth of art, which is seldom sufficiently recognised, be kept in mind. For if, according to our view, the whole visible world is just the objectification, the mirror, of the will, conducting it to knowledge of itself, and, indeed, as we shall soon see, to the possibility of its deliverance; and if, at the same time, the world as idea, if we regard it in isolation, and, freeing ourselves from all volition, allow it alone to take possession of our consciousness, is the most joy-giving and the only innocent side of life; we must regard art as the higher ascent, the more complete development of all this, for it achieves essentially just what is achieved by the visible world itself, only with greater concentration, more perfectly, with intention and intelligence, and therefore may be called, in the full significance of the word, the flower of life. If the whole world as idea is only the visibility of will, the work of art is to render this visibility more distinct. It is the *camera obscura* which shows the objects more purely, and enables us to survey them and comprehend them better. It is the play within the play, the stage upon the stage in "Hamlet."

The pleasure we receive from all beauty, the consolation which art affords, the enthusiasm of the artist, which enables him to forget the cares of life,—the latter an advantage of the man of genius over other men, which alone repays him for the suffering that increases in proportion to the clearness of consciousness, and for the desert loneliness among men of a different race,—all this rests on the fact that the in-itself of life, the will, existence itself, is, as we shall see farther on, a constant sorrow, partly miserable, partly terrible; while, on the contrary, as idea alone, purely contemplated, or copied by art, free from pain, it presents to us a drama full of significance. This purely knowable side of the world, and the copy of it in any art, is the element of the artist. He is chained to the contemplation of the play, the objectification of will; he remains beside it, does not get tired of contemplating it and representing it in copies; and meanwhile he bears himself the cost of the production of that play, *i.e.*, he himself is the will which objectifies itself, and remains in constant suffering. That pure, true, and deep, knowledge of the inner nature of the world becomes now for him an end in itself: he stops there. Therefore it does not become to him a quieter of the will, as, we shall see in the next book, it does in the case of the saint who has attained to resignation; it does not deliver him for ever from life, but only at moments, and is therefore not for him a path out of life, but only an occasional consolation in it, till his power, increased by this contemplation and at last tired of the play, lays hold on the real. The St. Cecilia of Raphael may be regarded as a representation of this transition. To the real, then, we now turn in the following book.

Friedrich Nietzsche

1844–1900

A. Life

The brilliant author of *The Birth of Tragedy* and *The Will to Power in Art* which provide the selections that appear below[183] was born in Rocken, Prussia. He was the son of a Lutheran minister. He studied theology and classical philology at the University of Bonn and in 1865 went to Leipzig. He studied the writings of Arthur Schopenhauer and Richard Wagner, wrote on Theognis, and produced a prize-winning essay on Diogenes Laertius in 1868–1869. Nietzsche was appointed associate professor of classical philosophy at the University of Basel when he was twenty-four years of age. His doctorate was granted by the University of Leipzig and Nietzsche was made full professor at Basel in 1870.

In 1872, Nietzsche published *The Birth of Tragedy. The Will to Power* appeared first in 1901 arranged by Nietzsche's sister from notes the philosopher accumulated between the years 1884 and 1888.

In 1889, Nietzsche fell mortally ill and died insane the following year.

B. Philosophy of Art

The Will to Power in Art[184]

801. . . . There are things with which we meet which already show us this transfiguration and fulness (states in which we transfigure things and make them fuller . . . until they reflect our own fulness and love of life. . . .) and the animal world's response thereto is a state of excitement in the spheres where these states of happiness originate. A blending of these very delicate shades of animal well-being and desires is the *æsthetic state*. . . .

803. Beauty therefore is, to the artist, something which is above all order of rank, because in beauty contrasts are overcome,

[183] See below, pp. 526 et seq.

[184] Friedrich Nietzsche, *The Will to Power*, translated by Anthony M. Ludovici, The Macmillan Co., New York, 1914. By permission of George Allen & Unwin Ltd.

the highest sign of power thus manifesting itself in the conquest of opposites. . . .

808. *Art* here acts as an organic function; we find it as the greatest stimulus of life . . . it does more than merely imagine, it actually transposes values. And it not only transposes the *feeling* for values: the lover actually *has* a greater value; he is stronger.

The Birth of Tragedy.[185]

. . . In contrast to all those who are intent on deriving the arts from one exclusive principle, as the necessary vital source of every work of art, I shall keep my eyes fixed on the two artistic deities of the Greeks, Apollo and Dionysus, and recognize in them the living and conspicuous representatives of *two* worlds of art differing in their intrinsic essence and in their highest aims. I see Apollo as the transfiguring genius of the *principium individuationis* through which alone the redemption in appearance is truly to be obtained; while by the mystical triumphant cry of Dionysus the spell of individuation is broken, and the way lies open to the Mothers of Being, to the innermost heart of things. This extraordinary antithesis, which stretches like a yawning gulf between plastic art as the Apollonian, and music as the Dionysian art, has revealed itself to only one of the great thinkers, to such an extent that, even without this clue to the symbolism of the Hellenic divinities, he conceded to music a character different from, and an origin anterior to, all the other arts, because, unlike them, it is not a copy of the phenomenon, but an immediate copy of the will itself, and therefore represents *the metaphysical of everything physical in the world*, the thing-in-itself of every phenomenon. (Schopenhauer, *Welt als Wille und Vorstellung,* I. 310). To this most important perception of esthetics (with which, in the most serious sense, esthetics properly begins), Richard Wagner, by way of confirmation of its eternal truth, affixed his seal, when he asserted in his *Beethoven* that music must be evaluated according to esthetic principles quite different from those which apply to all plastic arts, and not, in general, according to the category of beauty, although an erroneous esthetics inspired by a mistaken and degenerate art, has, by virtue of the concept of beauty obtaining in the plastic domain accustomed itself to demand of music an effect similar to that produced by works of plastic art, namely, the arousing of *delight in beautiful forms.* Upon perceiving this extraordinary antithesis, I felt a strong necessity to approach the essence of Greek tragedy and, with it, the profoundest revelation of the Hellenic genius: for I at last thought that I possessed a charm to enable me—far beyond the phraseology of our usual esthetics—to represent vividly to my mind the fundamental problem of tragedy: whereby I was granted such a surprising and unusual insight into the Hellenic character that it necessarily seemed to me as if our classical-Hellenic science that bears itself so proudly had thus far contrived to subsist mainly on phantasmagoria and externals.

Perhaps we may lead up to his fundamental problem by asking: what esthetic effect results when the essentially separate art-forces, the Apollonian and the Dionysian, enter into simultaneous activity? Or more briefly: how is music related to image and concept? Schopenhauer, whom Richard Wagner, with special reference to this point, praises for an unsurpassable clearness and perspicuity of exposition, expresses himself most thoroughly on the subject in the following passage which I shall cite here at full length (*Welt als Wille und Vorstellung*, I. p. 309): "According to all this, we may regard the phenomenal world, or nature, and music as two different expressions of the same thing, which is therefore itself the only medium of their analogy,

[185] Friedrich Nietzsche, *The Birth of Tragedy,* The Macmillan Co., 1909. By permission of George Allen & Unwin Ltd.

so that a knowledge of it is demanded in order to understand that analogy. Music, therefore, if regarded as an expression of the world, is in the highest degree a universal language, which is related indeed to the universality of concepts, much as they are related to the particular things. Its universality, however, is by no means that empty universality of abstraction, but quite of a different kind, and is united with thorough and distinct definiteness. In this respect it resembles geometrical figures and numbers, which are the universal forms of all possible objects of experience and applicable to them all *a priori*, and yet are not abstract but perceptible and thoroughly determinate. All possible efforts, excitements and manifestations of will, all that goes on in the heart of man and that reason includes in the wide, negative concept of feeling, may be expressed by the infinite number of possible melodies, but always in the universal, in the mere form, without the material, always according to the thing-in-itself, not the phenomenon, the inmost soul, as it were, of the phenomenon without the body. This deep relation which music has to the true nature of all things also explains the fact that suitable music played to any scene, action, event, or surrounding seems to disclose to us its most secret meaning, and appears as the most accurate and distinct commentary upon it. This is so truly the case, that whoever gives himself up entirely to the impression of a symphony, seems to see all the possible events of life and the world take place in himself, yet if he reflects, he can find no likeness between the music and the things that passed before his mind. For, as we have said, music is distinguished from all the other arts by the fact that it is not a copy of the phenomenon, or, more accurately, the adequate objectivity of the will, but is the direct copy of the will itself, and therefore exhibits itself as the metaphysical to everything physical in the world, and as the thing-in-itself to every phenomenon. We might, therefore, just as well call the world embodied music as embodied will; and this is the reason why music makes every picture, and indeed every scene of real life and of the world, at once appear with higher significance, certainly all the more, in proportion as its melody is analogous to the inner spirit of the given phenomenon. It rests upon this that we are able to set a poem to music as a song, or a perceptible representation as a pantomime, or both as an opera. Such particular pictures of human life, set to the universal language of music, are never bound to it or correspond to it with stringent necessity; but they stand to it only in the relation of an example chosen at will to a general concept. In the determinateness of the real, they represent that which music expresses in the universality of mere form. For melodies are to a certain extent, like general concepts, an abstraction from the actual. This actual world, then, the world of particular things, affords the object of perception, the special and individual, the particular case, both to the universality of the concepts and to the universality of the melodies. But these two universalities are in a certain respect opposed to each other; for the concepts contain particulars only as the first forms abstracted from perception, as it were, the separated shell of things; thus they are, strictly speaking, *abstracta*: music, on the other hand, gives the inmost kernel which precedes all forms, or the heart of things. This relation may be very well expressed in the language of the schoolmen, by saying, the concepts are the *universalia post rem*, but music gives the *universalia ante rem*, and the real world the *universalia in re*. But that in general a relation is possible between a composition and a perceptible representation rests, as we have said, upon the fact that both are simply different expressions of the same inner being of the world. When now, in the particular case, such a relation is actually given, that is to say, when the composer has been able to express in the universal language of music the emotions of will which constitute the heart of an event, then the melody of the song, the music of the opera, is expressive. But the analogy discovered by the composer between the two must have proceeded from the direct knowledge of the nature of the world unknown to his reason, and must not be an imitation produced with conscious intention by means of conceptions, otherwise the music does not express the inner nature of the will itself, but merely gives an inadequate imitation of its phenomenon. All specially imitative music does this."

According to the doctrine of Schopenhauer, therefore, we may understand music as the immediate language of the will, and we feel our fancy stimulated to give form to this invisible and yet so actively stirred spirit-world which speaks to us, and we feel prompted to embody it in an analogous example. On the other hand, image and concept, under the influence of a truly corresponding music, acquire a higher significance. Dionysian art therefore is wont to exercise two kinds of influences on the Apollonian art-faculty: music incites to the *symbolic-intuition* of Dionysian universality, and music allows the symbolic image to emerge *in its highest significance*. From these facts, intelligible in themselves and not inaccessible to a more penetrating examination, I infer the capacity of music to give birth to *myth* (the most significant exemplar), and particular the *tragic* myth: the myth which expresses Dionysian knowledge in symbols. In the phenomenon of the lyrist, I have shown how music strives to express its nature in Apollonian images. If now we reflect that music at its greatest intensity must seek to attain also to its highest symbolization, we must deem it possible that it also knows how to find the symbolic expression for its unique Dionysian wisdom; and where shall we seek for this expression if not in tragedy and, in general, in the conception of the tragic?

From the nature of art as it is usually conceived according to the single category of appearance and beauty, the tragic cannot honestly be deduced at all; it is only through the spirit of music that we can understand the joy involved in the annihilation of the individual. For only by the particular examples of such annihilation are we made clear as to the eternal phenomenon of Dionysian art, which gives expression to the will in its omnipotence, as it were, behind the *principium individuationis*, the eternal life beyond all phenomena, and despite all annihilation. The metaphysical joy in the tragic is a translation of the instinctive unconscious Dionysian wisdom into the language of the scene: the hero, the highest manifestation of the will, is disavowed for our pleasure, because he is only phenomenon, and because the eternal life of the will is not affected by his annihilation. "We believe in eternal life," exclaims tragedy; while music is the immediate idea of this life. Plastic art has an altogether different aim: here Apollo dispels the suffering of the individual by the radiant glorification of the *eternity of the phenomenon*: here beauty triumphs over the suffering inherent in life; pain is in a sense obliterated from the features of nature. In Dionysian art and its tragic symbolism the same nature cries to us with its true, undissembled voice: "Be as I am! Amidst the ceaseless flux of phenomena I am the eternally creative primordial mother, eternally impelling to existence, eternally self-sufficient amid this flux of phenomena!" . . .

25

Music and tragic myth are equally the expression of the Dionysian capacity of a people, and are inseparable from each other. Both originate in a sphere of art lying beneath and beyond the Apollonian; both transfigure a region in whose joyous harmony all dissonance, like the terrible picture of the world, dies charmingly away; both play with the sting of displeasure, relying on their most potent magic; both thereby justify the existence even of the "worst world." Here the Dionysian, as compared with the Apollonian, exhibits itself as the eternal and original artistic force, which in general calls into existence the entire world of phenomena; in the midst of which a new transfiguring appearance becomes necessary, in order to keep alive the animated world of individuation. If we could conceive of an incarnation of dissonance—and what else is man?—then, that it might live, this dissonance would need a glorious illusion to cover its features with a veil of beauty. This is the true artistic function of Apollo: in whose name we include all the countless manifestations of the fair realm of illusion, which at each moment render life in general worth living and impel one to the experience of the next moment.

At the same time, just as much of this basis of all existence—the Dionysian substratum of the world—is allowed to enter into the consciousness of human beings, as can be surmounted again by the Apollonian transfiguring power, so that these two art-impulses are compelled to develop their powers in strictly mutual proportion, according to the law of eternal justice. When the Dionysian powers rise with such strength as we are experiencing at present, there can be no doubt that, wrapped in a cloud, Apollo has already descended to us; whose fullest and most beautiful effects a coming generation may perhaps behold.

That this effect is necessary, however, each one would most surely perceive intuitively, if once he found himself carried back—even in a dream—into an Old-Hellenic existence. Walking under high Ionic colonnades, looking up towards a horizon defined by clear and noble lines, with reflections of his transfigured form by his side in shining marble, and around him solemnly marching or quietly moving men, with harmonious voices and rhythmical pantomime—in the presence of this perpetual influx of beauty would he not have to raise his hand to Apollo and exclaim: "Blessed race of Hellenes! How great Dionysus must be among you, when the Delian god deems such charms necessary to cure you of your dithyrambic madness!" To such a one, however, an aged Athenian, looking up to him with the sublime eyes of Æschylus, might answer: "Say also this, thou curious stranger: what must this people have suffered, that they might become thus beautiful! But now follow me to a tragic play, and sacrifice with me in the temple of both the deities!"

PART SEVEN

EXPRESSION, WORK OF ART, AND CRITICISM

Chapter 12

The Work of Art as Expressed Image and as "Concrete Significant Form"

In the last two chapters of this book of readings in Philosopy of Art and Aesthetics, our principal interest is to examine and illustrate various twentieth-century theories of the work of art, its experience, and the relation of criticism to the work of art as image, symbol, and object made. Insofar as it helps to illuminate the later theory, we shall place them in the context of the earlier speculation in this book.

In the present chapter, we are concerned principally with the work of art, in the next chapter with the relation of criticism to the work of art and to Aesthetics. Here the emphasis is on the work of art as an image or intuition, as the Expressionist interprets it, and upon various critical problems which arise if the work of art is treated solely as an image, an intuition, a symbol or an object made. In the portion of the chapter which takes the work of art to be a "concrete significant form," we shall observe some of the problems inherited by Aesthetics from Philosophy of Art, more particularly those which have as their ground the theory of the inspired artist. The opposing views in both chapters are those of Plato's conception of the genius—that "slight, wingéd, and holy thing" who is carried out of himself—and such a conception as Hegel's, in which genius is interpreted in essentially rational terms.

The Philosophy of Art called "Expression" is a more complicated theory of the work of art and its experience than might be inferred from the ordinary interpretation that Benedetto Croce [1] and his followers, R. G. Collingwood and E. F. Carritt, were engaged in speculation simply upon "image" and "imagination." Precisely how complicated the theory of art as expression is will be evident in the mere mention of some of the minor themes and some of the major subjects of speculation that have engaged the attention of philosophers of art and æstheticians over the past two-and-a-half millenia that enter into the modern theory. To that brief list we shall shortly come; but it is important to mention at the outset the major themes conjoined in Expressionist theory of

[1] For Croce's life and selections from his writings, see below, pp. 536 et seq. and 559 et seq.

imagination. They are the theme of inspiration and that of the creative genius, a concept derived from the "great analogy" [2] of the artist to God the Creator and now elaborated to include the man of taste.

The principal minor themes that appear in the Aesthetic of Expression are the following: The work of art is an image or intuition without external relations;[3] in the stage of art, truth and falsity, subject and predicate, are inappropriate;[4] works of art, that is, images, are neither accurate nor inaccurate because art is not imitation but expression;[5] expression is prior to all other forms of Spirit, and therefore is not open to judgment in terms of such later forms as practice, economics, science, action, etc.[6]

These and other historical antecedents add interest to Croce's version of the Philosophy of Art as expression. The theory's principal point, however, derives from the fact that it is basically an hypothesis that reflects the eighteenth century's main achievement, that of formulating cogent theories of creative imagination [7] as these are conjoined with the ancient theory of inspiration.[8] The two theories —that of creative imagination and of inspiration—are used to argue the artist's absolute and unconditioned freedom to create.

Croce's use of the theory of inspiration to free the artist to create parallels Plato's use of the same theory to free the artist from the rules of art. What is different is Croce's alliance of inspiration to imagination. Moreover, Croce's theory of inspiration is not only more systematically developed than is Plato's but it is also used more systematically than Plato's to establish the artist's freedom.[9]

In Croce's theory, the artist is not only freed from the burden of imitating the external world—and it will be recalled that for Plato the inspired man is still an imitator—but he is freed as well from the need to choose or select. In fact, he is freed from all implications of the Aristotelian supposition that Art is a rational state of capacity to make [10] as well as to produce a work of art as a stimulus for a specific response. With this argument is dismissed as well any requirement that the artist use means to ends.[11]

The artist expresses impressions and because no two impressions are identical, what is expressed is an individual. The analogy to God's creating of individual souls is striking, the more so inasmuch as Croce's artist, like the deity of the traditional theology of creativity, creates free of the conditions that he inform matter or use external ideas as patterns for making.[12] Croce's artist is in fact the genius [13] now wholly freed of traditional theological trappings.

[2] See above, pp. 10 et seq.

[3] See below, p. 537. Compare above, pp. 86–8, in the reference to Plato, where the issue is drawn between the idea of beauty that has its essence in itself and the imitation that has its essence in another; Kant, see above pp. 371–2, where the problem is one of purpose; and Schopenhauer, above, pp. 508 et seq., where the issue is the freedom of the object of art from the principle of sufficient reason.

[4] See above, Plato's *Laws,* pp. 128 et seq., where Plato maintains that the poet cannot differentiate the correctness or incorrectness of his imitation.

[5] See Kant, above, pp. 412 et seq.

[6] See below, pp. 545 et seq.

[7] See above, Chapters IX and X, for selections from the writings of Young, Addison, Hume and Kant.

[8] For the beginnings of the theory, see Democritus, above, p. 31; Plato, *Ion,* above, pp. 54 et seq.; and Plato's *Phaedrus,* above, pp. 88 et seq.

[9] See below, pp. 536–7, for Croce's statement concerning inspiration.

[10] See, for Aristotle, above, pp. 136 et seq. and below, p. 545.

[11] "The search for the *end of art* is ridiculous, when it is understood of art as art" and "Expression does not possess *means,* because it has not an *end.*" B. Croce, *Aesthetic,* pp. 51, 112 (Ainslie's translation.)

[12] See above, George Puttenham's *The Arte of English Poesie,* pp. 391 et seq., which in turn reflects St. Augustine's conception of creativity; see above, pp. 232–4.

[13] See above, Chapter 10, for the eighteenth-century theory of genius.

In terms of Aesthetics, Croce's theory is not only a denial that the work of art as image is made by art or technique but it is also a denial that the work of art is a symbol. "Structure and the Judgment of Art" by M. C. Nahm [14] is intended to show that the work of art is an object made and a symbol, as well as an image expressed in sensuous media.

[14] See below, pp. 573 et seq.

Benedetto Croce

1866–1952

A. Life

Benedetto Croce was born in Pescasseroli in the Abruzzi, Italy, and lived the greater part of his life in Naples. He attained eminence not only as a philosopher and historian, but also as a senator and adviser to the King of Italy. He was greatly influenced by Vico's philosophy, as well as by Hegel's Idealism, to which he later brought serious criticism. Croce's is a philosophy of "pure spirit," of which Aesthetic is the first moment. *Aesthetic as Science of Expression and General Linguistic* is the first part of *The Philosophy of Spirit*. The work on Aesthetics was published in 1902, the last volume of the *Philosophy of Spirit* in 1917; Croce's *What is Living and What is Dead in Hegel's Philosophy* was published in 1907, the *Breviary of Aesthetics* in 1913. Croce lived on the Island of Capri during the Second World War and helped to arrange the armistice between the Italian and the Allied armies. He died in Naples in 1952.

B. Aesthetics

On Inspiration

. . . The[15] search for the end of art is ridiculous, when it is understood of art as art. And since to fix an end is to choose, the theory that the content of art must be *selected* is another form of the same error. A selection among impressions and sensations implies that these are already expressions, otherwise how could a selection be made among the continuous and indistinct? To choose is to will: to will this and not to will that: and this and that must be before us, expressed. Practice follows, it does not precede theory; expression is free inspiration.

The true artist, in fact, finds himself big

[15] Benedetto Croce, *Aesthetic as Science of Expression and General Linguistic.* By permission of St. Martin's Press, Inc., New York, The Macmillan Company of Canada and Macmillan and Company, Ltd., London, 1929. Translated by Douglas Ainslie. Chapter 6, pp. 51–52.

with his theme, he knows not how; he feels the moment of birth drawing near, but he cannot will it or not will it. If he were to wish to act in opposition to his inspiration, to make an arbitrary choice, if, born Anacreon, he should wish to sing of Atreus and of Alcides, his lyre would warn him of his mistake, sounding only of Venus and of Love, notwithstanding his efforts to the contrary. . . . When critics of art remark that a theme is *badly selected*, in cases where that observation has a just foundation, it is a question of blaming, not the selection of the theme . . . but the manner in which the artist has treated it, the failure of the expression due to the contradictions which it contains. And when the same critics object to the theme or content of works which they proclaim to be artistically perfect as being unworthy of art and blameworthy; if these expressions really are perfect, there is nothing to be done but to advise the critics to leave the artists in peace, for they can only derive inspiration from what has moved their soul. . . .

Intuition and Expression

KNOWLEDGE [16] has two forms: it is either *intuitive* knowledge or *logical* knowledge; knowledge obtained through the *imagination* or knowledge obtained through the *intellect*; knowledge of the *individual* or knowledge of the *universal;* of *individual things* or of the *relations* between them: it is, in fact, productive either of *images* or of *concepts.*

In ordinary life, constant appeal is made to intuitive knowledge. It is said that we cannot give definitions of certain truths; that they are not demonstrable by syllogisms; that they must be learnt intuitively. The politician finds fault with the abstract reasoner, who possesses no lively intuition of actual conditions; the educational theorist insists upon the necessity of developing the intuitive faculty in the pupil before everything else; the critic in judging a work of art makes it a point of honour to set aside theory and abstractions, and to judge it by direct intuition; the practical man professes to live rather by intuition than by reason.

But this ample acknowledgment granted to intuitive knowledge in ordinary life, does not correspond to an equal and adequate acknowledgment in the field of theory and of philosophy. There exists a very ancient science of intellectual knowledge, admitted by all without discussion, namely, Logic; but a science of intuitive knowledge is timidly and with difficulty asserted by but a few. Logical knowledge has appropriated the lion's share; and if she does not slay and devour her companion outright, yet yields to her but grudgingly the humble place of maid-servant or doorkeeper.—What can intuitive knowledge be without the light of intellectual knowledge? It is a servant without a master; and though a master find a servant useful, the master is a necessity to the servant, since he enables him to gain his livelihood. Intuition is blind; intellect lends her eyes.

Now, the first point to be firmly fixed in the mind is that intuitive knowledge has no need of a master, nor to lean upon any one; she does not need to borrow the eyes of others, for she has excellent eyes of her own. Doubtless it is possible to find concepts mingled with intuitions. But in many other intuitions there is no trace of such a mixture, which proves that it is not necessary. The impression of a moonlight scene by a painter; the outline of a country drawn by a cartographer; a musical motive, tender or energetic; the words of a sighing lyric, or those with which we ask,

[16] Benedetto Croce, *Aesthetics as Science of Expression and General Linguistic.* By permission of St. Martin's Press, Inc., New York, The Macmillan Company of Canada and Macmillan and Co., Ltd., London, 1929. Translated by Douglas Ainslie. Chapters 1 and 2.

command and lament in ordinary life, may well all be intuitive facts without a shadow of intellectual relation. But, think what one may of these instances, and admitting further the contention that the greater part of the intuitions of civilized man are impregnated with concepts, there yet remains to be observed something more important and more conclusive. Those concepts which are found mingled and fused with the intuitions are no longer concepts, in so far as they are really mingled and fused, for they have lost all independence and autonomy. They have been concepts, but have now become simple elements of intuition. The philosophical maxims placed in the mouth of a personage of tragedy or of comedy, perform there the function, not of concepts, but of characteristics of such personage; in the same way as the red in a painted face does not there represent the red colour of the physicists, but is a characteristic element of the portrait. The whole is that which determines the quality of the parts. A work of art may be full of philosophical concepts; it may contain them in greater abundance and they may there be even more profound than in a philosophical dissertation, which in its turn may be rich to overflowing with descriptions and intuitions. But notwithstanding all these concepts the total effect of the work of art is an intuition; and notwithstanding all those intuitions, the total effect of the philosophical dissertation is a concept. The *Promessi Sposi* contains copious ethical observations and distinctions, but does not for that reason lose as a whole its character of simple story or intuition. In like manner the anecdotes and satirical effusions to be found in the works of a philosopher like Schopenhauer do not deprive those works of their character of intellectual treatises. The difference between a scientific work and a work of art, that is, between an intellectual fact and an intuitive fact, lies in the difference of the total effect aimed at by their respective authors. This it is that determines and rules over the several parts of each, not these parts separated and considered abstractly in themselves.

But to admit the independence of intuition as regards concept does not suffice to give a true and precise idea of intuition. Another error arises among those who recognize this, or who at any rate do not explicitly make intuition dependent upon the intellect, to obscure and confuse the real nature of intuition. By intuition is frequently understood *perception*, or the knowledge of actual reality, the apprehension of something as *real*.

Certainly perception is intuition: the perceptions of the room in which I am writing, of the ink-bottle and paper that are before me, of the pen I am using, of the objects that I touch and make use of as instruments of my person, which, if it write, therefore exists;—these are all intuitions. But the image that is now passing through my brain of a me writing in another room, in another town, with different paper, pen and ink, is also an intuition. This means that the distinction between reality and non-reality is extraneous, secondary, to the true nature of intuition. If we imagine a human mind having intuitions for the first time, it would seem that it could have intuitions of actual reality only, that is to say, that it could have perceptions of nothing but the real. But since knowledge of reality is based upon the distinction between real images and unreal images, and since this distinction does not at the first moment exist, these intuitions would in truth not be intuitions either of the real or of the unreal, not perceptions, but pure intuitions. Where all is real, nothing is real. The child, with its difficulty of distinguishing true from false, history from fable, which are all one to childhood, can furnish us with a sort of very vague and only remotely approximate idea of this ingenuous state. Intuition is the undifferentiated unity of the perception of the real and of the simple image of the possible. In our intuitions we do not oppose ourselves as empirical beings to external reality, but we simply objectify our impressions, whatever they be.

Those, therefore, who look upon intuition as sensation formed and arranged simply according to the categories of space and time, would seem to approximate more nearly to the truth. Space and time (they say) are the forms of intuition; to have an intuition is to place it in space and in temporal sequence. Intuitive activity would then consist in this double and concurrent function of spatiality and temporality. But for these two categories must be repeated what was said of intellectual distinctions, when found mingled with intuitions. We have intuitions without space and without time: the colour of a sky, the colour of a feeling, a cry of pain and an effort of will, objectified in consciousness: these are intuitions which we possess, and with their making space and time have nothing to do. In some intuitions, spatiality may be found without temporality, in others, *vice versa;* and even where both are found, they are perceived by later reflexion: they can be fused with the intuition in like manner with all its other elements: that is, they are in it *materialiter* and not *formaliter*, as ingredients and not as arrangement. Who, without an act of reflexion which for a moment breaks in upon his contemplation, can think of space while looking at a drawing or a view? Who is conscious of temporal sequence while listening to a story or a piece of music without breaking into it with a similar act of reflexion? What intuition reveals in a work of art is not space and time, but *character, individual physiognomy.* The view here maintained is confirmed in several quarters of modern philosophy. Space and time, far from being simple and primitive functions, are nowadays conceived as intellectual constructions of great complexity. And further, even in some of those who do not altogether deny to space and time the quality of formative principles, categories and functions, one observes an effort to unite them and to regard them in a different manner from that in which these categories are generally conceived. Some limit intuition to the sole category of spatiality, maintaining that even time can only be intuited in terms of space. Others abandon the three dimensions of space as not philosophically necessary and conceive the function of spatiality as void of all particular spatial determination. But what could such a spatial function be, a simple arrangement that should arrange even time? It represents, surely, all that criticism and refutation have left standing—the bare demand for the affirmation of some intuitive activity in general. And is not this activity truly determined, when one single function is attributed to it, not spatializing nor temporalizing, but characterizing? Or rather, when it is conceived as itself a category or function which gives us knowledge of things in their concreteness and individuality?

Having thus freed intuitive knowledge from any suggestion of intellectualism and from every later and external addition, we must now explain it and determine its limits from another side and defend it from a different kind of invasion and confusion. On the hither side of the lower limit is sensation, formless matter, which the spirit can never apprehend in itself as simple matter. This it can only possess with form and in form, but postulates the notion of it as a mere limit. Matter, in its abstraction, is mechanism, passivity; it is what the spirit of man suffers, but does not produce. Without it no human knowledge or activity is possible; but mere matter produces animality, whatever is brutal and impulsive in man, not the spiritual dominion, which is humanity. How often we strive to understand clearly what is passing within us! We do catch a glimpse of something, but this does not appear to the mind as objectified and formed. It is in such moments as these that we best perceive the profound difference between matter and form. These are not two acts of ours, opposed to one another; but the one is outside us and assaults and sweeps us off our feet, while the other inside us tends to absorb and identify itself with that which is outside. Matter, clothed and conquered by form, produces concrete form. It is the matter, the content, which differentiates one of our intuitions from another: the form is constant: it is spiritual activity, while matter is changeable. Without matter spiritual activity would not forsake its abstractness to become concrete and real activity, this or that spiritual content, this or that definite intuition.

It is a curious fact, characteristic of our times, that this very form, this very activity of the spirit, which is essentially ourselves is so often ignored or denied. Some confound the spiritual activity of man with the metaphorical and mythological activity of what is called nature, which is mechanism and has no resemblance to human activity, save when we imagine, with Æsop, that *"arbores loquuntur non tantum ferae."* Some affirm that they have never observed in themselves this "miraculous" activity, as though there were no difference, or only one of quantity, between sweating and thinking, feeling cold and the energy of the will. Others, certainly with greater reason, would unify activity and mechanism in a more general concept, though they are specifically distinct. Let us, however, refrain for the moment from examining if such a final unification be possible, and in what sense, but admitting that the attempt may be made, it is clear that to unify two concepts in a third implies to begin with the admission of a difference between the two first. Here it is this difference that concerns us and we set it in relief.

Intuition has sometimes been confused with simple sensation. But since this confusion ends by being offensive to common sense, it has more frequently been attenuated or concealed with a phraseology apparently designed at once to confuse and to distinguish them. Thus, it has been asserted that intuition is sensation, but not so much simple sensation as *association* of sensations. Here a double meaning is concealed in the word "association." Association is understood, either as memory, mnemonic association, conscious recollection, and in that case the claim to unite in memory elements which are not intuited, distinguished, possessed in some way by the spirit and produced by consciousness, seems inconceivable: or it is understood as association of unconscious elements, in which case we remain in the world of sensation and of nature. But if with certain associationists we speak of an association which is neither memory nor flux of sensations, but a *productive* association (formative, constructive, distinguishing); then our contention is admitted and only its name is denied to it. For productive association is no longer association in the sense of the sensationalists, but *synthesis*, that is to say, spiritual activity. Synthesis may be called association; but with the concept of productivity is already posited the distinction between passivity and activity, between sensation and intuition.

Other psychologists are disposed to distinguish from sensation something which is sensation no longer, but is not yet intellectual concept: the *representation* or *image*. What is the difference between their representation or image and our intuitive knowledge? Everything and nothing: for "representation" is a very equivocal word. If by representation be understood something cut off and standing out from the psychic basis of the sensations, then representation is intuition. If, on the other hand, it be conceived as complex sensation we are back once more in crude sensation, which does not vary in quality according to its richness or poverty, or according to whether the organism in which it appears is rudimentary or highly developed and full of traces of past sensations. Nor is the ambiguity remedied by defining representation as a psychic product of secondary degree in relation to sensation, defined as occupying the first place. What does secondary degree mean here? Does it mean a qualitative, formal difference? If so, representation is an elaboration of sensation and therefore intuition. Or does it mean greater complexity and complication, a quantitative, material difference? In that case intuition is once more confused with simple sensation.

And yet there is a sure method of distinguishing true intuition, true representation, from that which is inferior to it: the spiritual fact from the mechanical, passive, natural fact. Every true intuition or representation is also *expression*. That which does not objectify itself in expression is not intuition or representation, but sensation and mere natural fact. The spirit only intuites in making, forming, expressing. He who separates intuition from expression never succeeds in reuniting them.

Intuitive activity *possesses intuitions to the extent that it expresses them*. Should this proposition sound paradoxical, that is partly because, as a general rule, a too restricted meaning is given to the word "expression." It is generally restricted to what are called verbal expressions alone. But there exist also non-verbal expressions, such as those of line, colour and sound, and to all of these must be extended our affirmation, which embraces therefore every sort of manifestation of the man, as orator, musician, painter, or anything else. But be it pictorial, or verbal, or musical, or in whatever other form it appear, to no intuition can expression in one of its forms be wanting; it is, in fact, an inseparable part of intuition. How can we really possess an intuition of a geometrical figure, unless we possess so accurate an image of it as to be able to trace it immediately upon paper or on the blackboard? How can we really have an intuition of the contour of a region, for example of the island of Sicily, if we are not able to draw it as it is in all its meanderings? Every one can experience the internal illumination which follows upon his success in formulating to himself his impressions and feelings, but only so far as he is able to formulate them. Feelings or impressions, then, pass by means of words from the obscure region of the soul into the clarity of the contemplative spirit. It is impossible to distinguish intuition from expression in this cognitive process. The one appears with the other at the same instant, because they are not two, but one.

The principal reason which makes our view appear paradoxical as we maintain it, is the illusion or prejudice that we possess a more complete intuition of reality than we really do. One often hears people say that they have many great thoughts in their minds, but that they are not able to express them. But if they really had them, they would have coined them into just so many beautiful, sounding words, and thus have expressed them. If these thoughts seem to vanish or to become few and meagre in the act of expressing them, the reason is that they did not exist or really were few and meagre. People think that all of us ordinary men imagine and intuite countries, figures and scenes like painters, and bodies like sculptors; save that painters and sculptors know how to paint and carve such images, while we bear them unexpressed in our souls. They believe that any one could have imagined a Madonna of Raphael; but that Raphael was Raphael owing to his technical ability in putting the Madonna upon canvas. Nothing can be more false than this view. The world which as a rule we intuite is a small thing. It consists of little expressions, which gradually become greater and wider with the increasing spiritual concentration of certain moments. They are the words we say to ourselves, our silent judgments: "Here is a man, here is a horse, this is heavy, this is sharp, this pleases me," etc. It is a medley of light and colour, with no greater pictorial value than would be expressed by a haphazard splash of colours, from among which one could barely make out a few special, distinctive traits. This and nothing else is what we possess in our ordinary life; this is the basis of our ordinary action. It is the index of a book. The labels tied to things (it has been said) take the place of the things themselves. This index and these labels (themselves expressions) suffice for small needs and small actions. From time to time we pass from the index to the book, from the label to the thing, or from the slight to the greater intuitions, and from these to the greatest and most lofty. This passage is sometimes far from easy. It has been observed by those who have best studied the psychology of artists that when, after having given a rapid glance at any one, they attempt to obtain a real intuition of him, in order, for example, to paint his portrait, then this ordinary vision, that seemed so precise, so lively, reveals itself as little better than nothing. What remains is found to be at the most some superficial trait, which would not even suffice for a caricature. The person to be painted stands before the artist like a world to discover. Michael Angelo said, "One paints, not with the hands, but with the brain." Leonardo shocked the prior of the Convent of the Graces by standing for days together gazing at the "Last Supper," without touching it with the brush. He remarked of this attitude: "The minds of men of lofty genius are most active in invention when they are doing the least external work." The painter is a painter, because he sees what others only feel or catch a glimpse of, but do not see. We think we see a smile, but in reality we have only a vague impression of it, we do not perceive all the characteristic traits of which it is the sum, as the painter discovers them after he has worked upon them and is thus able to fix them on the canvas. We do not intuitively possess more even of our intimate friend, who is with us every day and at all hours, than at most certain traits of physiognomy which enable us to distinguish him from others. The illusion is less easy as regards musical expression; because it would seem strange to every one to say that the composer had added or attached notes to a motive which was already in the mind of him who is not the composer; as if Beethoven's Ninth Symphony were not his own intuition and his intuition the Ninth Symphony. Now, just as one who is deluded as to the amount of his material wealth is confuted by arithmetic, which states its exact amount, so he who nourishes delusions as to the wealth of his own thoughts and images is brought back to reality, when he is obliged to cross the *Pons Asinorum* of expression. Let us say to the former, count; to the latter, speak; or, here is a pencil, draw, express yourself.

Each of us, as a matter of fact, has in him a little of the poet, of the sculptor, of the musician, of the painter, of the prose writer: but how little, as compared with those who bear those names, just because they possess the most universal dispositions and energies of human nature in so lofty a degree! How little too does a painter possess of the intuitions of a poet! And how little does one painter possess those of another painter! Nevertheless, that little is all our actual patrimony of intuitions or representations. Beyond these are only impressions, sensations, feelings, impulses, emotions, or whatever else one may term what still falls short of the spirit and is not assimilated by man; something postulated for the convenience of exposition, while actually non-existent, since to exist also is a fact of the spirit.

We may thus add this to the various verbal descriptions of intuition, noted at the beginning: intuitive knowledge is expressive knowledge. Independent and autonomous in respect to intellectual function; indifferent to later empirical discriminations, to reality and to unreality, to formations and apperceptions of space and time, which are also later: intuition or representation is distinguished as *form* from what is felt and suffered, from the flux or wave of sensation, or from psychic matter; and this form, this taking possession, is expression. To intuite is to express; and nothing else (nothing more, but nothing less) than *to express.*

Intuition and Art

BEFORE proceeding further,[17] it may be well to draw certain consequences from what has been established and to add some explanations.

We have frankly identified intuitive or expressive knowledge with the æsthetic or artistic fact, taking works of art as examples of intuitive knowledge and attributing to them the characteristics of intuition, and *vice versa.* But our identification is combated by a view held even by many philosophers, who consider art to be an intuition of an altogether special sort. "Let us admit" (they say) "that art is intuition; but intuition is not always art: artistic intuition is a distinct species differing from intuition in general by something *more.*"

But no one has ever been able to indicate of what this something more consists. It has sometimes been thought that art is not a simple intuition, but an intuition of an intuition, in the same way as the concept of science has been defined, not as the ordinary concept, but as the concept of a concept. Thus man would attain to art by objectifying, not his sensations, as happens with ordinary intuition, but intuition itself. But this process of raising to a second power does not exist; and the comparison of it with the ordinary and scientific concept does not prove what is intended, for the good reason that it is not true that the scientific concept is the concept of a concept. If this comparison proves anything, it proves just the opposite. The ordinary concept, if it be really a concept and not a simple representation, is a perfect concept, however poor and limited. Science substitutes concepts for representations; for those concepts that are poor and limited it substitutes others, larger and more comprehensive; it is ever discovering new relations. But its method does not differ from that by which is formed the smallest universal in the brain of the humblest of men. What is generally called *par excellence* art, collects intuitions that are wider and more complex than those which we generally experience, but these intuitions are always of sensations and impressions.

Art is expression of impressions, not expression of expression.

For the same reason, it cannot be asserted that the intuition, which is generally called artistic, differs from ordinary intuition as intensive intuition. This would be the case if it were to operate differently on the same matter. But since the artistic function is extended to wider fields, yet does not differ in method from ordinary intuition, the difference between them is not intensive but extensive. The intuition of the simplest popular love-song, which says the same thing, or very nearly, as any declaration of love that issues at every moment from the lips of thousands of ordinary men, may be intensively perfect in its poor simplicity, although it be extensively so much more limited than the complex intuition of a love-song by Leopardi.

The whole difference, then is quantitative, and as such is indifferent to philosophy, *scientia qualitatum.* Certain men have a greater aptitude, a more frequent inclination fully to express certain complex states of the soul. These men are known in ordinary language as artists. Some very complicated and difficult expressions are not often achieved, and these are called works of art. The limits of the expression-intuitions that are called art, as opposed to those that are vulgarly called non-art, are empirical and impossible to define. If an epigram be art, why not a simple word? If a story, why not the news-jottings of the

[17] Ibid., Chapt. 2.

journalist? If a landscape, why not a topographical sketch? The teacher of philosophy in Molière's comedy was right: "whenever we speak, we create prose." But there will always be scholars like Monsieur Jourdain, astonished at having spoken prose for forty years without knowing it, who will have difficulty in persuading themselves that when they call their servant John to bring their slippers, they have spoken nothing less than—prose.

We must hold firmly to our indentification, because among the principal reasons which have prevented Æsthetic, the science of art, from revealing the true nature of art, its real roots in human nature, has been its separation from the general spiritual life, the having made of it a sort of special function or aristocratic club. No one is astonished when he learns from physiology that every cell is an organism and every organism a cell or synthesis of cells. No one is astonished at finding in a lofty mountain the same chemical elements that compose a small stone fragment. There is not one physiology of small animals and one of large animals; nor is there a special chemical theory of stones as distinct from mountains. In the same way, there is not a science of lesser intuition as distinct from a science of greater intuition, nor one of ordinary intuition as distinct from artistic intuition. There is but one Æsthetic, the science of intuitive or expressive knowledge, which is the æsthetic or artistic fact. And this Æsthetic is the true analogue of Logic, which includes, as facts of the same nature, the formation of the smallest and most ordinary concept and the most complicated scientific and philosophical system.

Nor can we admit that the word *genius* or artistic genius, as distinct from the non-genius of the ordinary man, possesses more than a quantitative signification. Great artists are said to reveal us to ourselves. But how could this be possible, unless there were identity of nature between their imagination and ours, and unless the difference were only one of quantity? It were better to change *poeta nascitur* into *homo nascitur poeta*: some men are born great poets, some small. The cult of the genius with all its attendant superstitions has arisen from this quantitative difference having been taken as a difference of quality. It has been forgotten that genius is not something that has fallen from heaven, but humanity itself. The man of genius who poses or is represented as remote from humanity finds his punishment in becoming or appearing somewhat ridiculous. Examples of this are the *genius* of the romantic period and the *superman* of our time.

But it is well to note here, that those who claim unconsciousness as the chief quality of an artistic genius, hurl him from an eminence far above humanity to a position far below it. Intuitive or artistic genius, like every form of human activity, is always conscious; otherwise it would be blind mechanism. The only thing that can be wanting to artistic genius is the *reflective* consciousness, the superadded consciousness of the historian or critic, which is not essential to it.

The relation between matter and form, or between *content* and *form*, as is generally said, is one of the most disputed questions in Æsthetic. Does the æsthetic fact consist of content alone, or of form alone, or of both together? This question has taken on various meanings, which we shall mention, each in its place. But when these words are taken as signifying what we have above defined, and matter is understood as emotionality not æsthetically elaborated, or impressions, and form as intellectual activity and expression, then our view cannot be in doubt. We must, that is to say, reject both the thesis that makes the æsthetic fact to consist of the content alone (that is, the simple impressions), and the thesis which makes it to consist of a junction between form and content, that is, of impressions plus expressions. In the æsthetic fact, expressive activity is not added to the fact of the impressions, but these latter are formed and elaborated by it. The impressions reappear as it were in expression, like water put into a filter, which reappears the same and yet different on the other side. The æsthetic fact, therefore, is form, and nothing but form.

From this was inferred not that the content is something superfluous (it is, on the contrary, the necessary point of departure for the expressive fact); but that *there is no passage* from the qualities of the content to those of the form. It has sometimes been thought that the content, in order to be æsthetic, that is to say, transformable into form, should possess some determined or determinable qualities. But were that so, then form and content, expression and impression, would be the same thing. It is true that the content is that which is convertible into form, but it has no determinable qualities until this transformation takes place. We know nothing about it. It does not become æsthetic content before, but only after it has been actually transformed. The æsthetic content has also been defined as the *interesting*. That is not an untrue statement; it is merely void of meaning. Interesting to what? To the expressive activity? Certainly the expressive activity would not have raised the content to the dignity of form, had it not been interested in it. Being interested is precisely the raising of the content to the dignity of form. But the word "interesting" has also been employed in another and a illegitimate sense, which we shall explain further on.

The proposition that art is *imitation of nature* has also several meanings. Sometimes truths have been expressed or at least shadowed forth in these words, sometimes errors have been promulgated. More frequently, no definite thought has been expressed at all. One of the scientifically legitimate meanings occurs when "imitation" is understood as representation or intuition of nature, a form of knowledge. And when the phrase is used with this intention, and in order to emphasize the spiritual character of the process, another proposition becomes legitimate also: namely, that art is the *idealization* or *idealizing* imitation of nature. But if by imitation of nature be understood that art gives mechanical reproductions, more or less perfect duplicates of natural objects, in the presence of which is renewed the same tumult of impressions as that caused by natural objects, then the proposition is evidently false. The coloured waxen effigies that imitate the life, before which we stand astonished in the museums where such things are shown, do not give æsthetic intuitions. Illusion and hallucination have nothing to do with the calm domain of artistic intuition. But on the other hand if an artist paint the interior of a wax-work museum, or if an actor give a burlesque portrait of a man-statue on the stage, we have work of the spirit and artistic intuition. Finally, if photography have in it anything artistic, it will be to the extent that it transmits the intuition of the photographer, his point of view, the pose and grouping which he has striven to attain. And if photography be not quite an art, that is precisely because the element of nature in it remains more or less unconquered and ineradicable. Do we ever, indeed, feel complete satisfaction before even the best of photographs? Would not an artist vary and touch up much or little, remove or add something to all of them?

The statements repeated so often, that art is not knowledge, that it does not tell the truth, that it does not belong to the world of theory, but to the world of feeling, and so forth, arise from the failure to realize exactly the theoretic character of simple intuition. This simple intuition is quite distinct from intellectual knowledge, as it is distinct from perception of the real; and the statements quoted above arise from the belief that only intellectual cognition is knowledge. We have seen that intuition is knowledge, free from concepts and more simple than the so-called perception of the real. Therefore art is knowledge, form; it does not belong to the world of feeling or to psychic matter. The reason why so many æstheticians have so often insisted that art is *appearance* (*Schein*), is precisely that they have felt the necessity of distinguishing it from the more complex fact of perception, by maintaining its pure intuitiveness. And if for the same reason it has been claimed that art is *feeling* the reason is the same. For if the concept as content of art, and historical reality as such, be excluded from the sphere of art, there remains no other content than reality apprehended in all its ingenuousness and immediacy in the vital impulse, in its *feeling*, that is to say again, pure intuition.

The theory of the *æsthetic senses* has also arisen from the failure to establish, or from having lost to view, the character of expression as distinct from impression, of form as distinct from matter.

This theory can be reduced to the error just indicated of wishing to find a passage from the qualities of the content to those of the form. To ask, in fact, what the æsthetic senses are, implies asking what sensible impressions are able to enter into æsthetic expressions, and which must of necessity do so. To this we must at once reply, that all impressions can enter into æsthetic expressions or formations, but that none are bound to do so of necessity. Dante raised to the dignity of form not only the "sweet colour of the oriental sapphire" (visual impressions), but also tactual or thermic impressions, such as the "dense air" and the "fresh rivulets" which "parch the more" the throat of the thirsty. The belief that a picture yields only visual impressions is a curious illusion. The bloom on a cheek, the warmth of a youthful body, the sweetness and freshness of a fruit, the edge of a sharp knife, are not these, too, impressions obtainable from a picture? Are they visual? What would a picture mean to an imaginary man, lacking all or many of his senses, who should in an instant acquire the organ of sight alone? The picture we are looking at and believe we see only with our eyes would seem to his eyes to be little more than an artist's paint-smeared palette.

Some who hold firmly to the æsthetic character of certain groups of impressions (for example, the visual and auditive), and exclude others, are nevertheless ready to admit that if visual and auditive impressions enter *directly* into the æsthetic fact, those of the other senses also enter into it, but only as *associated*. But this distinction is altogether arbitary. Æsthetic expression is synthesis, in which it is impossible to distinguish direct and indirect. All impressions are placed by it on a level, in so far as they are æstheticized. A man who absorbs the subject of a picture or poem does not have it before him as a series of impressions, some of which have prerogatives and precedence over the others. He knows nothing as to what has happened prior to having absorbed it, just as, on the other hand, distinctions made after reflexion have nothing whatever to do with art as such.

The theory of the æsthetic senses has also been presented in another way; as an attempt to establish what physiological organs are necessary for the æsthetic fact. The physiological organ or apparatus is nothing but a group of cells, constituted and disposed in a particular manner; that is to say, it is a merely physical and natural fact or concept. But expression does not know physiological facts. Expression has its point of departure in the impressions, and the physiological path by which these have found their way to the mind is to it altogether indifferent. One way or another comes to the same thing: it suffices that they should be impressions.

It is true that the want of given organs, that is, of certain groups of cells, prevents the formation of certain impressions (when these are not otherwise obtained through a kind of organic compensation). The man born blind cannot intuite and express light. But the impressions are not conditioned solely by the organ, but also by the stimuli which operate upon the organ. One who has never had the impression of the sea will never be able to express it, in the same way as one who has never had the impression of the life of high society or of the political arena will never express either. This, however, does not prove the dependence of the expressive function on the stimulus or on the organ. It merely repeats what we know already: expression presupposes impression, and particular expressions particular impressions. For the rest, every impression excludes other impressions during the moment in which it dominates; and so does every expression.

Another corollary of the conception of expression as activity is the *indivisibility* of the work of art. Every expression is a single expression. Activity is a fusion of the impressions in an organic whole. A desire to express this has always prompted the affirmation that the work of art should have *unity*, or, what amounts to the same thing, *unity in variety*. Expression is a synthesis of the various, or multiple, in the one.

The fact that we divide a work of art into parts, a poem into scenes, episodes, similes, sentences, or a picture into single figures and objects, background, foreground, etc., may seem opposed to this affirmation. But such division annihilates the work, as dividing the organism into heart, brain, nerves, muscles and so on, turns the living being into a corpse. It is true that there exist organisms in which division gives rise to other living beings, but in such a case we must conclude, maintaining the analogy between the organism and the work of art, that in the latter case too there are numerous germs of life each ready to grow, in a moment, into a single complete expression.

It may be said that expression sometimes arises from other expressions. There are simple and there are *compound* expressions. One must surely admit some difference between the *eureka*, with which Archimedes expressed all his joy at his discovery, and the expressive act (indeed all the five acts) of a regular tragedy.—Not in the least: expression always arises directly from impressions. He who conceives a tragedy puts into a crucible a great quantity, so to say, of impressions: expressions themselves, conceived on other occasions, are fused together with the new in a single mass, in the same way as we can cast into a melting furnace formless pieces of bronze and choicest statuettes. Those choicest statuettes must be melted just like the pieces of bronze, before there can be a new statue. The old expressions must descend again to the level of impressions, in order to be synthesized in a new single expression.

By elaborating his impressions, man *frees* himself from them. By objectifying them, he removes them from him and makes himself their superior. The liberating and purifying function of art is another aspect and another formula of its character as activity. Activity is the deliverer, just because it drives away passivity.

This also explains why it is usual to attribute to artists both the maximum of sensibility or *passion*, and the maximum of insensibility or Olympian *serenity*. The two characters are compatible, for they do not refer to the same object. The sensibility or passion relates to the rich material which the artist absorbs into his psychic organism; the insensibility or serenity to the form with which he subdues and dominates the tumult of the sensations and passions.

Milton C. Nahm

1903–

Structure and the Judgment of Art

It is [18] the primary purpose of this paper to examine the implications of three traditional philosophies of art concerning the "real," i.e., concerning the structure of the work of art as object of esthetic judgment. The theories under consideration, those of making, of symbolizing, and of expression, respectively, take the work of art to be object made, sign symbolized, and image expressed. It will be maintained that these theories are complementary, rather than autonomous. It will be argued, in addition, that the work of art, describable in terms of these complementary relations, is properly designated as a "concrete significant form." It will be urged, finally, that the structure of the work of art derived by analysis of these complementary theories is object of sound judgments of fact, which are necessary but insufficient grounds for esthetic or valuational judgments.

The basis for the claim that making provides a sound ground for the judgment of art is twofold: making may be differentiated from acting [19] and the structure produced by tools and techniques, a structure ordinarily called an artifact, is an object or event separated from the maker. It is inferred that, because of its spatial and temporal independence, the work of art is an object for objective judgment. The recurrent claim that this artifact is likewise a work of fine art is persuasively put by Rhys Carpenter: "Out of materials which—artistically—are nothing at all, the artist creates the work of art. . . . Style is all that structure and articulation by which a painted picture or carved marble becomes emotionally intelli-

[18] Milton C. Nahm, "Structure and the Judgment of Art," *The Journal of Philosophy,* Vol. XLV, No. 25, Dec. 2, 1948, pp. 684–694.

[19] Aristotle, *E.N.* 1140 a 1 sq. [See above, pp. 136 et seq.]

gible." [20] Style it is, therefore, which in [21] "that broader discipline" converts the "layman's ordinary world of vision into the painted world of pigment, the cast world of bronze, the carved world of wood and stone," and which is central to the mature theory of making.

The "real," as object of our judgment, is on this view the object made and stylized. But that the theory of making does in fact need reinforcement from the theory of expression is evident the moment one inquires into the problem of judgment of the work of art as made. This is well illustrated by Samuel Alexander's writing on esthetic. Alexander assumes, in tracing the development of the "instinct for constructiveness" into "object of contemplation," that he has offered a sufficient analysis of the emergence and character of fine art. The account,[22] however, does go beyond the author's initial postulates, which are that the ultimate basis for the esthetic sense is this "instinct for constructiveness," and that the esthetic impulse and the esthetic emotion which goes with the impulse are an outgrowth of that instinct "when it has become first human, and next, contemplative." [23] For, in order to relate the making of the work of fine art and the experience of making, i.e., the judgment upon it, Alexander converts the *process*, making, into the object of judgment. In esthetic experience, however, no external object or event corresponding to that made by the artist is in fact made. The contemplation of the process, that is, our judgment or esthetic experience,[24] must therefore be regarded as an event, meaningful in large part as the perceiver's reconstruction in imagination of the maker's original and succesive mental and physical processes as these were directed to the production of the work of art.[25]

It would be an error to conclude, however, that the "real" as object of judgment in Alexander's theory is the imagined event alone and to the exclusion of the object or event made. By "the simple process of imputation," Alexander contends,[26] the object brought before the mind "forms part of the whole perceived external object because the conation to which it corresponds is linked into a unity with the conations evoked by the presented external thing."

There are significant reasons for retaining, even by "imputation," the "presented external thing" in an examination of the judgment of the "real". [27] Of more immediate interest, however, is the fact that it is precisely upon the issue of the "reality" of the external object that the expressionist denies the relevance to esthetic of "making." For the expressionist, the image and the object made are not complementary but, rather, mutually exclusive.[28] In the theory of expression, the "real" is the imaginative re-forming of the artist's expression or imaginative process. "How could we judge," asks Croce,[29] "what remained external to us?"

The reasons for Croce's exclusion of the "external" work of art are various and complex, but none is more compelling than his intention of formulating in expressionism an esthetic of complete and free creativity. "If by art be understood the externalization of art," he holds,[30] "then utility and morality have a

[20] *The Bases of Artistic Creation*, pp. 30–31.

[21] *Ibid.*, p. 41.

[22] As given in *Art and Instinct*.

[23] *Art and Instinct*, p. 6.

[24] Alexander appears to identify the two. See, for example, his statement concerning evaluation, *Beauty and Other Forms of Value*, p. 7, and his agreement with Croce, *ibid.*, p. 29.

[25] *Ibid.*, pp. 29–30: "The work of art throws the spectator back into the frame of mind in which the artist produced it."

[26] *Ibid.*, p. 26.

[27] [See below, pp. 553–4.]

[28] See Collingwood, R., *The Principles of Art*, p. 149.

[29] *Aesthetic* (Ainslie's translation), p. 121. Compare Collingwood, *The Principles of Art*, pp. 150–151. [For Croce, see above, pp. 537 et seq. and below, pp. 559 et seq.]

[30] *Aesthetic*, p. 116.

perfect right to enter into it; that is to say, the right to be master in one's own house." For Croce, the structure of the work of art, the "image," "intuition," or "expression," is precisely the "form" which permits us to distinguish freedom from that which the "spirit can never apprehend in itself as simple matter . . . ," from "mechanism" and "passivity" which the spirit of man "suffers but does not produce." [31] The complete creativity of the imagination produces the "indivisible" and individual intuition, "image," or "work of art." Each "image" is novel and therefore, incomparable. And, as I have indicated elsewhere,[32] Croce's identification of the artist with the free creator, implies, inasmuch as he likewise identifies "taste" with "what produces it," that judgment is likewise absolutely free: "The sublime (or comic, tragic, humorous, etc.) is *everything* that is or shall be *called* by those who have employed or shall employ these *words.*" [33]

It may be urged, in the face of this acceptance of nominalism for esthetic judgment, that the most evident implication of expression without "matter," and to the exclusion of making, would appear to be that judgments are absolutely free because they are absolutely meaningless.[34] One might, indeed, yield to the temptation to conclude that the "image" as the structure of the work of art would necessarily be precluded as ground for objective judgment. Yet, it would appear, such a conclusion would be incompatible with another level of Croce's argument, since he argues [35] that "we find our own impressions fully determined and realized in the expression of the poet." More specifically,[36] "we are not Dante, nor Dante we," but, "in that moment of contemplation and judgment, our spirit is one with that of the poet, and in that moment we and he are one thing." Such suggestions, in view of the asserted individuality of expressions, are the more confusing because Croce denies that the work of art produced by the artist is a "symbol" for our experience: "if the symbol be conceived as separable—if the symbol can be on one side, and on the other the thing symbolized . . . the so-called . . . symbol is science,[37] or art aping science."

It is significant that, to account for the identity of spirit of which he has written, Croce introduces into the theory of expression the analogue to Alexander's "presented external thing" in order to provide for the "reproduction" induced by "physical beauty" or "stimulus" [38] Moreover, he proposes to answer what would appear to be the crucial question, "How are we to succeed in causing the expression to be reproduced by means of the physical object?" That such "reproduction" does occur is taken to be the fact and we are assured [39] that it "always occurs when we can replace ourselves in the conditions in which the stimulus (physical beauty) was produced." Moreover, we are told how this reproductive experience is to be induced: "with the help of memory we surround the physical stimulus with all the facts among which it arose; and thus we enable it to act upon us as it acted upon him who produced it." [40]

This, however, is certainly to admit that by means of paleography, philology, and history we can and do separate off from the "physical stimulus" that "symbol on the one

[31] *Ibid.*, pp. 5–6. [See above, pp. 539–40.]

[32] "The Theological Background of the Theory of the Artist as Creator," *Journal of the History of Ideas,* Vol. VIII (1947), pp. 363–372 [See above, pp. 11 et seq.] See, also, "The One and the Many in Croce's Aesthetic," by Katherine Gilbert in *Studies in Recent Aesthetic,* pp. 111 ff.

[33] *Aesthetic,* p. 90.

[34] *Aesthetic,* p. 90.

[35] *Ibid.*, p. 34.

[36] *Ibid.*, p. 121.

[37] *Ibid.*, p. 34.

[38] *Ibid.*, p. 125.

[39] *Ibid.*, p. 125.

[40] *Ibid.*, p. 126. Compare Collingwood, op. cit., pp. 147–151.

side" from "the thing symbolized," i.e., the expression from the "facts among which" the stimulus arose. This must be the case, inasmuch as the facts which memory and science relate to the "physical stimulus" in the reproduction of the artist's expression do in fact relate to it and it, as physical stimulus, must therefore be a sign for the facts which it signifies and which we relate to it. It is thus significant that Croce's identification of esthetic and artistic processes implies that the "physical stimulus" is no isolated "image," but a sign for the artist's, for tradition's, and for history's meanings. It may be inferred that the theory of expression, in its introduction of the "physical stimulus," shows its need for the traditional theory of making as a necessary complement. For the latter theory has traditionally been used to explain the intelligible individual in terms of a theory of symbols. The theory of making implies that a form has been imposed upon material, that the material embodies this form, and that what the artificer takes to be the end of his art the perceiver knows as an intelligible form. This embodied form is, it is true, separated from the maker by the act of making.[41] Yet, the fact that the work of art is intelligible in terms of the artist's intention, has rightly come to be regarded by the history of esthetic as ground for judgment that the work of art is a symbol.

We turn from "form" to the "meaning" of the work of art as we investigate the third of the great traditions of the structure of art. And it is in iconology that we discover that the judgment of the "real" is the judgment of precisely those paleographical, philological, and historical aspects of the work of art which, Croce hints, are of avail in our "reproduction" of "all the facts" among which the "physical stimulus" arose. For it is the iconologists who explicitly urge their concern with those classes of 'intrinsic meanings" which Professor Panofsky so carefully lists[42] as "political, poetical, religious, philosophical, and social." Do we, in these extensive studies of signs and symbols, in iconography which explicitly marks out its field as "subject matter or meaning of works of art, as opposed to their form," do we here come upon the structure which is the "real" object of judgment?

It should be noted, in an effort to answer this question, that Professor Panofsky remarks of the *"three strata of subject matter or meaning"* in the work of art that they are not merely "neatly differentiated categories" which seem "to indicate three independent spheres of meaning." On the contrary, the strata "refer in reality to aspects of one phenomenon, namely, the work of art as a whole," while the methods of approach "which here appear as three unrelated operations of research merge with each other in one organic and individual process."[43]

It is this statement which raises the significant problem. It may be that Professor Panofsky does not mean by 'the work of art as a whole," the whole work of art. His distinction between "form" and "subject matter or meaning" suggests that he does not; his inclusion[44] of the "expressional" as one of the two factors in the *"primary* or *natural"* class of meanings suggests that he does. And the general tone of his writing—as well as the puzzle concerning the object of judgment—makes the latter possibility the more likely one. The puzzling aspect of Professor Panofsky's account of the work of art derives from his inclusion of "empathic" and "psychological nuances" within the general description of the strata of meaning. The controlling principle of the "expressional" is said to be the history of style.[45] And it may be assumed

[41] See above, p. 548.

[42] *Studies in Iconology,* p. 16.

[43] *Ibid.,* pp. 16–17.

[44] *Ibid.,* pp. 3–4.

[45] *Ibid.,* pp. 14–15.

that by "empathic" and "psychological" as parts of the "expressional" are meant the individual and creative aspects of the work of art. But how, by way of illustration, may either factor be assumed to be compatible with such categorical statements concerning the meaning of icons as appear in Professor Panofsky's argument[46] that a painting by Maffei represents Judith rather than Salome? We are told that there are "several sixteenth-century paintings depicting Judith with a charger; there was a *type* of 'Judith with a charger,' but there was no *type* of 'Salome with a sword.'" But what, on this argument, has become of the "expressional" meanings included[47] in the synoptical table?

There is no logical contradiction in assuming that an individual artist associated both Salome and Judith with a sword, or, indeed, that the structure of the made work of art may have suggested its inclusion. What, then, of the empathic or psychological nuances? The sword as symbol of Salome would scarcely require an inventiveness on the part of artists such as that which gave sea-coasts to Bohemia or "blind mouths" to ecclesiasts. And what of the general set of "expressional" meanings? One searches in vain for mention of style as "structure and articulation," of the light and shade which, as Carpenter rightly insists, are essential to the work of art.[48]

The iconologist would appear to give us the genus of the work of art at the expense of esthetic criteria, which must take into account—as Croce rightly insists—both individuality and beauty. His contribution to the meaning of the work of art is made at a sacrifice, presumed to be necessary because the iconologist would appear to regard his art as a science in which the goal is set at certainty of judgment. It must be urged, however, that if "expressional" or stylistic and individual factors are to be considered, as they must be in fact as well as in theory, the "scientist of symbols" must rest content with probability rather than certainty. If pretensions to absolute exactitude are abandoned, individual techniques may be attended, as well as "intrinsic meanings." And it may be, also, that historians of art will become sufficiently reflective to concentrate their fine scholarship upon the history of ideas, signs, and symbols as the latter are incorporated in works of fine art. Estheticians are correct in their assumption that some communicable meanings are also esthetically valuable and that not all judgments of fine art are judgments of non-esthetic meanings. Not all judgments of fine art are judgments of fact; not all symbols are necessarily replicas of other symbols; not all meanings are merely generic. Iconology, as a theory of the structure of art as symbol, needs, as its complements, expression and making, as expression similarly needs making and iconology, and making needs iconology and expression.

The three major traditions of the work of art as a structure which serves as the "real" object of judgment do in fact complement each other. The task still remains, however, to formulate a theory which, having recourse to the contributions of the three theories taken together, relates to the morphology of art. A mere aggregate of theories will leave us with judgments upon art which are evaluative, but not meaningful; meaningful, but not evaluative; objective, but merely generic; or subjective, but only nominal. To meet these difficulties and to make a beginning of a sound theory which will serve as a basis for agreement among estheticians, I should suggest the following:

(1) The work of art may be characterized in morphological terms as a "concrete significant form"; "concrete," as made in material; "significant," as embodying a sign; "form," as

[46] *Ibid.*, pp. 12 ff.

[47] *Ibid.*, pp. 14–15.

[48] *The Bases of Artistic Creation*, pp. 31–32 and 36.

expressed. In the structure of art, the relations of the three processes may be characterized briefly as follows: Symbolization brings into fine art signs derived from human experience. In their passage through the mind, the signs are imaged and expressed as possible modes of making in a potential material. This subjective process is objectified and embodied in the actual material of art by means of making.

(2) Croce is correct in his insistence that the unique individual is central to esthetic theory. In his own interpretations, however, the isolation of the individual as the datum for judgment does not permit the consideration of the individual as a member of a class. The Crocean error is the consequence of regarding the individual "image" as the artist's expression.[49] The artist, in fact, expresses neither the work of art alone nor a symbol of esthetic experience. What he does express is the potential esthetic experience. The work of art is not a static creation. It is an event in the total structure of the work of fine art, a structure which relates artist and esthetic perceiver and which as an event is made actual by the creative powers of the esthetic perceiver.

(3) The grounds for comparison and contrast, lacking in Croce's theory, are thus provided at two levels. Generically, there is possible a comparison and contrast between work of art and work of fine art, between judgments of fact and judgments of taste. Specifically, the *differentiae* for judgments of fact are supplied by the three functions of the structure of art, i.e., making, expressing, and symbolizing.

(4) The direction of the analysis within the bounds of judgment of fact is toward the work of fine art as a novel and individual event, i.e., as that which is not wholly definable in terms of the demonstrable fact. The "work of fine art," i.e., Croce's completely expressed beauty, is a term indicating a limiting conception, progressively approachable in judgment as a unique individual but never the object of an absolute and final judgment. The three processes, making, expression, and symbolization, lead into the work of art, contributing to it as a "concrete significant form." As directed by the artist and by us toward this limited structure, they provide us with "what the work of art has been and is not." In conjunction, as "concrete significant form" and as directed from the limited structure of the work of art toward the "work of fine art," the three processes provide us with the ground from which we postulate the work of art as what "ought to be" but "is not." The first direction provides us with grounds for judgments of fact; the second, for judgments of value.

(5) The movements of the analysis toward the work of art and from the work of art toward the work of fine art provide us with the correction necessary to avoid the nominalism of the theory of expression. Meaningful judgments are meaningful only if they are, as Singer asserts,[50] "capable of confirmation or refutation from an indefinite series of points of view." In contrast to the meaningless judgments which result from Croce's conception of the free creation of images, we now seek wholly meaningful judgments, judgments which are absolutely limited, i.e., ideally considered as wholly restricted to the artistic experience, the work of art, the esthetic experience, and the end of art. Such judgments are approached after fullest comparison and contrast of the interrelated structure in the various levels of meaning through which our science and reflection inform us that the work of art has passed in its emergence as a work of fine art.

(6) As regards judgments of fact, we

[49] It also results, in my opinion, from a confusion between the "individual" as an evaluative and as a logical term.

[50] E. A. Singer, Jr., *Mind as Behavior*, pp. 196–197.

ascertain the levels through which the generic expression, generic symbol and generic making are carried in the direction of individualization. Each instance of such ascertainment is a comparison and contrast of "what is" with its prior and posterior stage. This provides us with judgment as the subsumption of the particular level under the general morphological level; and it also provides grounds for comparison and contrast of one stage of the emerging process within the works of art with the other two stages. And, inasmuch as some artists can feel but not think, while others can make but not feel, and still others can make but neither feel nor think, such "horizontal" judgments are as valuable for our purposes as are the "vertical" ones.

Each of the individual processes, making, expression, and symbolization, can be set with some accuracy within various general levels of individualization and in relation to the other two processes as our analysis approaches "concrete significant form." Implicit in this phrase, in fact, are the three processes which serve as "series" for meaningful judgments. The general levels of fact are, for symbolization, the philosophical science of logic; for making, the philosophical analysis of teleology, in which means and ends are related; and, for expression, the philosophy of feeling, for man is not interested solely in connotations and in the construction of instruments but also in the emotions and moods aroused by signs and configurations. Within the more specific field of judgments of fact called philosophy of art, wherein the meanings of "concrete," "significant," and "form" are separately and collectively describable as "concrete significant form," similar processes of individualization may be indicated. That of "making" provides concreteness, as the instinct for construction moves successively from making, through craft, skill, technique, and, finally, to Alexander's "object of contemplation." Croce's "expression" as "form" is materialized by "making" into "concrete form," as expression itself moves from feeling into apperception, conation and imagination. Making, however, not only affects expression, but it likewise externalizes signs as symbols which have been expressed in the feeling and imagination of the artist. The need for making is evident, once we consider the status of Croce's "physical stimulus," which corresponds to Alexander's "imputed" and "externally presented object." For if, from the "physical stimulus," we may wholly reconstruct the artist's expression, the adequacy with which the technically produced structure can embody the "image" depends wholly upon the skill with which the "image" is imposed upon the material by the artist.

Logic becomes iconology in the province of art and this specification of the science corresponds to the individualization in art of signs into symbols. Unique symbols emerge from generic signs as expression becomes more fully productive and while making becomes object of contemplation. In this conjunction of processes is provided "concrete significant form," the ground for sound judgments of fact in philosophy of art.

However complete may be our analyses of the structure of the work of art as "concrete significant form"—whether our concern be the emergence of styles and modes or the morphological intricacies resulting from the uses of repetition, harmony, or rhythm [51]—we shall discover their incompetence to serve as more than a factual ground for judgments of value. Judgments upon the "concrete significant form" are to a considerable degree recreative. But, as Nietzsche succinctly expresses it, "valuing is creating."[52] Nietzsche is, none the less, in error in implying that the power of evaluation is "a prodigy." Judgments of value do differ from judgments of fact, but they do

[51] See M. C. Nahm, *Aesthetic Experience and its Presuppositions,* Ch. XVIII.

[52] *Thus Spake Zarathustra,* I, XV. [See above, pp. 527 et seq.]

not differ in kind. Both are forms of subsumption, of which those concerning fact are logically prior to and presupposed by those of value. Difficulties of judgment arise in part by our confusion of the two species and by our frequent assumption that one may perform the task of the other.[53]

To the philosopher of art, the work of art is a complex unity produced by the techniques of making as these operate in materials to embody expressed symbols. To the esthetician, it is this, but it is also a work of fine art, a complex unity toward which, as a limit, we extrapolate. We extrapolate from the synthesis of the various methods by which the work of art was produced. We extrapolate to a new class of value, rather than to such combination of the three factors of "concrete significant form" as provides objectivity, intelligibility, and individuality. The new class of value is a new event under which the whole event called the work of art is subsumed and by means of which it is judged. In this judgment of a single instrument understood in terms of an end, we are concerned no longer with the components of the "concrete significant form" as comprising what that form either "used to be" or "is." We are concerned with what the work of art "ought to be" as a whole. It does not follow that in such evaluational judgments the work of fine art, the "whole," may not be analyzed into parts. It does mean that, once the value has been discerned, the parts of the whole are invested with that value. As regards the work of fine art, as a whole, we judge by comparing or contrasting it as an expressed and made symbol with what it "ought to be" in the ideal technique, completely expressed, and in its most comprehensive meaning.

The new class of value extends the range of meaning to include another series, that of creativity. Within this added "series of points of view," confirmation or refutation of meaningful judgments turns on the stirring of imagination to creativity through the instrumentality of the work of fine art. Esthetic judgments are probable and in this are to be contrasted to the certainty of factual analyses of "concrete significant form." Some judgments of fine art, it is true, may be invalidated by reference to the negative criterion that the event has been analyzed in terms of too limited a set of rules as object made, or expressed, or symbolized. For the most part, however, the validation or invalidation of esthetic judgments depends upon criteria such as recurrence of interest, traditions emerging from and renewed by techniques, attitudes, and ideas of artists and schools of artists, critical clarifications of meanings and crafts, and diverging interpretations of works of art. These criteria are presupposed by attitudes and opinions of groups, rather than of individuals, and, in addition, ordinarily need for their formulation and clarification considerable periods of time. But the necessary, if insufficient, bases for such judgments of value are the complementary theories of the structure of art which describe the work of art as a "concrete significant form."[54]

[53] Compare Kant, *K.d.U.*, Section 33. [See above, pp. 380 et seq.]

[54] See next Chapter, pp. 573 et seq., for an elaboration of this argument.

Chapter 13

Expression, Inspiration, and Criticism

The most important implication of the denial by the expressionists that the work of art is the product of technique or that it is a symbol is the denial to the work of art of intelligibility or definability. As we have observed, the initial conflict in theories of Philosophy of Art arose out of the claims of originality and intelligibility. In the course of millenia of speculation, the issue of intelligibility became that of the possibility of accurate criticism, with results we have observed in the complexity of such systematic classifications of art as Hegel's. We have observed as well the increased tendency to substitute taste for criticism, the principal point of Croce's aesthetic, of Hume's speculation on art, and of Kant's *The Critique of Judgment.*

Croce proposes to make short work of classifications. He attacks Hegel[1] in *What Is Living and What Is Dead in Hegel's Philosophy* because, he believes, the German philosopher deals with art as "practically reduced to a philosophical error." The free creativity of Croce's artist produces individuals and, in consequence, classifications of art are held by the Italian philosopher to be meaningless. Classificatory schemes for the arts succeed intuitions or images and are science, not art or imagination. So valueless are classifications that, Croce holds, they might all be burned without loss. The point is made the stronger by the assumption that expressions are individual images and have no external relations. There can be, therefore, neither comparisons nor contrasts of such individuals.

Other philosophers have exiled criticism from Aesthetic—notably Kant as he followed Hume—but no Philosophy of Art does so and at the same time makes so evident as does Croce the presumed grounds for the procedure. The issue is drawn sharply between, on the one side, the creative artist, the genius and man of taste, the man of delicate sensibilities —and on the other, the presumably non-creative critic; between those who assert that what the artist produces is original and those who state that the critic dare not be creative.

[1] See below, pp. 559 et seq. Compare J. Spingarn, above, pp. 326 et seq.

As we shall see, what Croce asserts on the basis of inspiration and what Plato first asserted[2] in the *Timaeus* 71E and the *Laws* 670 has had an enormous influence and it is with the issue and its consequences that we are concerned both in this introduction and the readings that follow.

The main points, the presumed originality of the artist and the presumed noncreative nature of criticism, as well as the assumption that the work of art is a stimulus for a response, appear clearly in E. M. Forster's "The Raison d'Etre of Criticism."[3] The novelist argues that the artistic and critical states are "grotesquely remote" from one another if what is under consideration is the possible "spiritual parity between them on grounds of creativity." Forster's analysis of the competence and incompetence of criticism is interesting but his conclusion is the cliché: "Think before you speak is criticism's motto, speak before you think is creation's."

In spite of other values to be found in Mr. Forster's essay, it is clear that he "justified" criticism on the wrong grounds, that is, by denying that the critic may be creative. That the remark, "Think before you speak is criticism's motto, speak before you think is creation's," is initially plausible but eventually in error is evident if we compare, for example, John Milton's preface to *Samson Agonistes*, to the lines that begin "Nothing is here for tears. . . . " If we do so, it is difficult to believe that the prose and the poetry, the criticism and the creation, could conceivably be distinguished one from the other on the grounds of priority or posteriority of thinking.[4] The fact is that the problem of the relation of works of art to aesthetic value and criticism presents not so much a literary, or even a critical, as a philosophical issue, which turns in part upon the validity or invalidity of assertions made concerning artistic inspiration.

It is of value to have before us some of the many reasons which explain the recurrence of inspiration and the persistence of theory in the history of a subject in which elsewhere dependence upon explanation in supranatural terms has given way to explanation in natural terms. We are not here concerned with invocations to the muse or to the gods but with the hard fact that many speculative aestheticians are still convinced that inspiration is the ground for creativity. To use the word "explanation" here is in error. What is implied is that the creative process is beyond explanation and that the core of originality is inaccessible to analysis. It should be noted that men like Nietzsche[5] have written vividly of their creative experiences in terms of inspiration. But it is often assumed that only what is inspired is of value. Nonetheless, it remains to be proved, as Paul Valéry remarks,[6] that "this miraculous method of production . . . ensures the worth of what is produced." As Valéry adds, "The spirit blows where it will, one sees it blow on fools, and it whispers to them what they are able to hear."

This suggests, however, the first issue, the worth of the "special ray, which lights up simultaneously ideas hitherto unconnected," as well as the value of the ideas themselves. The second issue is, however, more central to

[2] See above, pp. 92 and 124–6. For the crucial Kantian acceptance of Hume's evaluation of critics, see above, pp. 349, 380–1. Kant denied aesthetic value to criticism and assumed the centrality of taste principally because he wanted to affirm the importance of the subject's feelings in aesthetic experience. He also wanted to deny the importance of criticism on the grounds that, as authoritative and conceptual, it is unfree.

[3] See below, pp. 561 et seq.

[4] See M. C. Nahm, "The Relation of Aesthetics and Criticism," below, pp. 575 et seq. See below, p. 569 for Katherine E. Gilbert's "The Relation between Aesthetics and Art-Criticism." See above, pp. 174 et seq. for Milton's interpretation of Aristotle's theory of catharsis.

[5] See above, pp. 432 and 527.

[6] Paul Valéry, "Memoirs of a Poem," *The Art of Poetry*, pp. 130–131.

the problem of criticism. A great critic and poet, Coleridge, believed that poetry is " . . . a dim analogue to creation." He insisted nonetheless that "It is the prerogative of poetic genius to distinguish by parental instinct its proper offspring from the changelings. . . ." And this means—and Coleridge is correct—that the creative and the critical are reciprocal processes and that criticism begins simultaneously with the originating process. At the critical level, "The heart doth need a language," and the language is that of criticism.

The issue is no less fundamental in the area of the experience of fine art than in that of the inspiration of the artist. Here the issue again is two-fold. The first obstacle to the acceptance of criticism as adequate to the explanation of the experience of fine art is the assumption that taste or aesthetic experience is immediate judgment and unanalyzable. The second obstacle is encountered even if it be granted that criticism is adequate to explain the work of art in terms similar to "concrete significant form,"[7] simply because, it is argued, any kind of criticism is inadequate to discriminate or describe the aesthetic qualifications of the work of fine art.

The counterattack is mounted by assuming that in fact the issues of aesthetic value and of criticism of fine art have primarily to do with Aesthetics, rather than with criticism alone or with the analysis by artists of aesthetic experence.[8] The readings that follow concern inspiration, criticism, and the relation of criticism to Aesthetics and are drawn from the writings of Croce,[9] Forster,[10] Gilbert,[11] and Nahm.[12]

[7] See above, preceding Chapter, pp. 548 et seq.

[8] See below, pp. 575 et seq., M. C. Nahm, "The Relation of Aesthetics and Criticism."

[9] See below, pp. 559 et seq.

[10] See below, pp. 561 et seq.

[11] See below, pp. 569 et seq.

[12] See below, pp. 575 et seq.

Benedetto Croce

1866–1952

Philosophy of Criticism

The Metamorphosis of Particular Concepts into Philosophical Errors[13]

I. ART AND LANGUAGE (ÆSTHETIC)

. . . Hegel deprived himself of the means of recognizing the autonomy and of attributing their just and proper value to the various forms of the spirit. Error was confused with particular truth, and, as philosophical errors had become for Hegel particular truths, so particular truths were bound to be associated with errors and to become philosophical errors, to lose all intrinsic measure, to be brought to the level of speculative truth, and to be treated as nothing but *imperfect forms of philosophy.*

For this reason, Hegel did not completely succeed in recognizing the nature of the aesthetic, or of the historical, or of the naturalistic activity; that is to say, of art, or of history, or of the physical and natural sciences.

[13] Benedetto Croce, *What is Living and What is Dead in the Philosophy of Hegel.* By permission of St. Martin's Press, Inc., New York, The Macmillan Company of Canada and Macmillan and Company Ltd., London, 1915. Translated by Douglas Ainslie, chapter 6, pp. 120 et seq. For Hegel, see above, pp. 428 et seq. and 451 et seq.

Without doubt, the pages of Hegel concerning aesthetic are animated with great artistic feeling; and on the whole there prevails in them the tendency to make art a primary element in human life, a mode of knowledge and of spiritual elevation. We are carried by these pages far beyond and far above the vulgar view, for which art is a superfluous accident of real life, a pleasure, a game, a pastime; or a simple mode of instruction, empirical and relative. The constant contact of Hegelian speculation with taste and with works of art, and the dignity which is assigned to the artistic activity, gave it an effective influence over men's minds and made it a powerful stimulus to the study of aesthetic problems. This is a merit, which, in part, is common to all the aesthetic theories of the Romantic period (the great period of the fermentation and the renewal of the philosophy of art and of literary and artistic criticism and history), and which, in part, is peculiar to the Hegelian aesthetic, in virtue of its wealth of ideas, of judgments and of problems.

But the elements of truth, scattered in plenty in the Hegelian aesthetic, are either too general, or merely incidental, and are, in principle, divergent from the fundamental concept of art, which Hegel accepts, and which is erroneous.

It is erroneous, because Hegel, firm in his belief that every form of spirit (save the ultimate and supreme form) is nothing but a provisional and contradictory way of conceiving the Absolute, could not discover that first ingenuous theoretic form, which is the lyric or the music of spirit, and in which there is nothing philosophically contradictory, because the philosophic problem has not yet emerged. This first form is its condition. It is the region of the intuition, of pure fancy, of language, in its essential character, as painting, music or song: in a word, it is the region of art. When Hegel begins his meditation upon the phases of spirit, he is already at a point where that region is behind him, and yet he does not recognize that he has passed it. . . .

When philosophy is completely developed, art must disappear, because it is superflous: art must die, and indeed it is already quite dead. If it is an error, it is not necessary and eternal. The history of art, which Hegel traces is directed to shewing the gradual dissolution of the artistic form, which has no place, in modern times, in our true and highest interests. It is a past, or the survival of the past. This grandiose paradox illuminates everywhere the aesthetic error of Hegel, and better perhaps than any other example makes clear the error of his logical assumption. In defence of Hegel, it has been said that the death of art, of which he speaks, is that eternal death, which is an eternal rebirth: such as we observe in the spirit of man, when he passes from poetry to philosophy, rising from the intuition to the universal, so that in his eyes, the world of intuition loses its colour. But against this interpretation, there is the fact that Hegel speaks of the death of art, not in the sense of perpetually renewing itself, but as actually about to happen and as having happened, of a *death of art in the historical world.* This is in complete agreement with his treatment of the degrees of reality as a series of opposites, difficult to abstract and to separate from one another. Once he had assumed this application of the dialect, Hegel had no other choice than one of two ways, either to suppress art by means of that grandiose paradox, or to preserve it with a not less grandiose inconsistency.

For this reason, it is not altogether wrongly that the system of Hegel (whose twin principles of the concrete concept and the dialectic, are of frankly aesthetic inspiration) has appeared to be a cold intellectualism, irreconcilable to the artistic consciousness. And the misunderstanding of art leaves its traces in his treatment of all the problems into which the concept of art enters as a necessary and proximate premiss. . . .

Edward Morgan Forster

1879–1970

A. Life

E. M. Forster, one of England's most distinguished novelists, was educated at King's College, Cambridge University. He is principally known for the novels, *A Room With a View*, *Howard's End*, and *A Passage to India*. "The Raison d'Etre of Criticism," a portion of which follows, was printed in *Two Cheers for Democracy* and was originally delivered as a lecture by Mr. Forster at Harvard University.

B. Philosophy of Criticism

The Raison d'Etre of Criticism in the Arts

An address at a Symposium on Music at Harvard University

Believing[14] as I do that music is the deepest of the arts and deep beneath the arts, I venture to emphasise music in this brief survey of the raison d'être of criticism in the arts. I have no authority here. I am an amateur whose inadequacy will become all too obvious as he proceeds. Perhaps, though, you will remember in your charity that the word amateur implies love. I love music. Just to love it, or just to love anything or anybody is not enough. Love has to be clarified and controlled to give full value, and here is where criticism may help. But one has to start with love; one has, in the case of music, to want to hear the notes. If one has no initial desire to listen and no sympathy after listening, the notes will signify nothing, sound and fury, whatever their intellectual content.

The case *against* criticism is alarmingly strong, and much of my paper is bound to be a brief drawn up by the Devil's Advocate. I will postpone the evil day, and begin by indicating the case *for* criticism.

Most of us will agree that previous training is desirable before we approach the arts. We mistrust untrained appreciation, believing that it often defeats its own ends. Appreciation

[14] E. M. Forster, *Two Cheers for Democracy*, pp. 117 sq. London, Edward Arnold and Co., 1951. By permission of Edward Arnold (Publishers) Ltd.

ought to be enough. But unless we learn by example and by failure and by comparison, appreciation will not bite. We shall tend to slip about on the surface of masterpieces, exclaiming with joy, but never penetrating. "Oh, I do like Bach," cries one appreciator, and the other cries, "Do you? I don't. I like Chopin." Exit in opposite directions chanting Bach and Chopin respectively, and hearing less the composers than their own voices. They resemble investors who proclaim the soundness of their financial assets. The Bach shares must not fall, the Chopin not fall further, or one would have been proved a fool on the aesthetic stock exchange. The objection to untrained appreciation is not its naïveté but its tendency to lead to the appreciation of no one but oneself. Against such fatuity the critical spirit is a valuable corrective.

Except at the actual moment of contact—and I shall have much to say on the subject of that difficult moment—it is desirable to know why we like a work, and to be able to defend our preferences by argument. Our judgment has been strengthened and if all goes well the contacts will be intensified and increased and become more valuable.

I add the proviso "if all goes well" because success lies on the knees of an unknown God. There is always the contrary danger; the danger that training may sterilise the sensitiveness that is being trained; that education may lead to knowledge instead of wisdom, and criticism to nothing but criticism; that spontaneous enjoyment, like the Progress of Poesy in Matthew Arnold's poem, may be checked because too much care has been taken to direct it into the right channel. Still it is a risk to be faced, and if no care had been taken the stream might have vanished even sooner. We hope criticism will help. We have faith in it as a respectable human activity, as an item in the larger heritage which differentiates us from the beasts.

How best can this activity be employed? One must allow it to construct aesthetic theories, though to the irreverent eyes of some of us they appear as travelling laboratories, beds of Procrustes whereon Milton is too long and Keats too short. In an age which is respectful to theory—as for instance the seventeenth century was respectful to Aristotle's theory of the dramatic unities—a theory may be helpful and stimulating, particularly to the sense of form. French tragedy could culminate in Racine because certain leading strings had been so willingly accepted that they were scarcely felt. Corneille and Tasso were less happy. Corneille, having produced the *Cid,* wasted much time trying to justify its deviations from Aristotle's rules; and Tasso wasted even more, for he published his theory of Christian Epic Poetry before he wrote the *Gerusalemme Liberata* which was to illustrate it. His epic was attacked by the critics because it deviated from what Aristotle said and also from what Tasso thought he might have said. Tasso was upset, became involved in three volumes of controversy, tried to write a second epic which should not deviate, failed, and went mad. Except perhaps in Russia, where the deviations of Shostakovitch invite a parallel, a theory in the modern world has little power over the fine arts, for good or evil. We have no atmosphere where it can flourish, and the attempts of certain governments to generate such an atmosphere in bureaus are unlikely to succeed. The construction of aesthetic theories and their comparison are desirable cultural exercises: the theories themselves are unlikely to spread far or to hinder or help.

A more practical activity for criticism is the sensitive dissection of particular works of art. What did the artist hope to do? What means did he employ, subconscious or conscious? Did he succeed, and if his success was partial where did he fail? In such a dissection the tools should break as soon as they encounter any living tissue. The apparatus is nothing, the specimen all. Whether expert critics will agree with so extreme a statement is doubtful, but I do enjoy following particular examinations so far as an amateur can. It is delightful and profitable to enter into technicalities to the limit of one's poor ability, to continue as far as one can in the wake of an expert mind, to pursue an argument till it passes out of one's grasp. And to have, while this is going on, a particular work of art before one can be a great help. Besides learning about the work one increases one's powers. Criticism's central job seems to be education through precision.

A third activity, less important, remains to be listed, and since it lies more within my sphere than precision I will discuss it at greater length. Criticism can stimulate. Few of us are sufficiently awake to the beauty and wonder of the world, and when art intervenes to reveal them it sometimes acts in reverse, and lowers a veil instead of raising it. This deadening effect can often be dispersed by a well-chosen word. We can be awakened by a remark which need not be profound or even true, and can be sent scurrying after the beauties and wonders we were ignoring. Journalism and broadcasting have their big opportunity here. Unsuited for synthesis or analysis, they can send out the winged word that carries us off to examine the original. . . .

. . . We can readily agree that criticism has educational and cultural value; the artist helps to civilise the community, builds up standards, forms theories, stimulates, dissects, encourages the individual to enjoy the world into which he has been born; and on its destructive side criticism exposes fraud and pretentiousness and checks conceit. These are substantial achievements. But I would like if I could to establish its raison d'être on a higher basis than that of public utility. I would like to discover some spiritual parity between it and the objects it criticises, and this is going to be difficult. The difficulty has been variously expressed. One writer—Mr. F. L. Lucas—has called criticism a charming parasite; another—Chekhov—complains it is a gadfly which hinders the oxen from ploughing; a third—the eighteenth-century philosopher Lord Kames—compares it to an imp which distracts critics from their objective and incites them to criticise each other. My own trouble is not so much that it is a parasite, a gadfly or an imp, but that there is a basic difference between the critical and creative states of mind, and to the consideration of that difference I would now invite your attention.

What about the creative state? In it a man is taken out of himself. He lets down as it were a bucket into his subconscious, and draws up something which is normally beyond his reach. He mixes this thing with his normal experiences, and out of the mixture he makes a work of art. It may be a good work of art or a bad one—we are not here examining the question of quality—but whether it is good or bad it will have been compounded in this unusual way, and he will wonder afterwards how he did it. Such seems to be the creative process. It may employ much technical ingenuity and worldly knowledge, it may profit by critical standards, but mixed up with it is this stuff from the bucket, this subconscious stuff, which is not procurable on demand. And when the process is over, when the picture or symphony or lyric or novel (or whatever it is) is complete, the artist, looking back on it, will wonder how on earth he did it. And indeed he did not do it on earth.

A perfect example of the creative process is to be found in Kubla Khan. Assisted by opium, Coleridge had his famous dream, and dipped deep into the subconscious. Waking up, he started to transcribe it, and was proceeding successfully when that person from Porlock unfortunately called on business.

> Weave a circle round him thrice
>   And close your eyes with holy dread,
>   For he on honeydew hath fed
> And drunk the milk of Paradise—

and in came the person from Porlock. Coleridge could not resume. His connection with the subconscious had snapped. He had created and did not know how he had done it. As Professor John Livingstone Lowes has shown, many fragments of Coleridge's day-to-day reading are embedded in Kubla Khan, but the poem itself belongs to another world, which he was seldom to record.

The creative state of mind is akin to a dream. In Coleridge's case it was a dream. In other cases—Jane Austen's for instance—the dream is remote or sedate. But even Jane Austen, looking back upon *Emma,* could have thought "Dear me, how came I to write that? It is not ill-contrived." There is always, even with the most realistic artist, the sense of withdrawal from his own creation, the sense of surprise.

The French writer, Paul Claudel, gives the best description known to me of the creative state. It occurrs in *La Ville.* A poet is speaking. He has been asked whence his inspiration comes, and how is it that when he speaks everything becomes explicable although he explains nothing. He replies:

I do not speak what I wish, but I conceive in sleep,
And I cannot explain whence I draw my breath, for it is my breath which is drawn out of me.
I expand the emptiness within me, I open my mouth, I breathe in the air, I breathe it out.
I restore it in the form of an intelligible word,
And having spoken I know what I have said.

There is a further idea in the passage, which my brief English paraphrase has not attempted to convey: the idea that if the breathing in is *in*spiration the breathing out is *ex*piration, a prefiguring of death, when the life of a man will be drawn out of him by the unknown force for the last time. Creation and death are closely connected for Claudel. I'm confining myself, though, to his description of the creative act, and ask you to observe how precisely it describes what happened in Kubla Khan. There is conception in sleep, there is the connection between the subconscious and the conscious, which has to be effected before the work of art can be born, and there is the surprise of the creator at his own creation.

Je restitue une parole intelligible,
Et l'ayant dite, je sais ce que j'ai dit.

Which is exactly what happened to Coleridge. He knew what he had said, but as soon as inspiration was interrupted he could not say any more.

After this glance at the creative state, let us glance at the critical. The critical state has many merits, and employs some of the highest and subtlest faculties of man. But it is grotesquely remote from the state responsible for the works it affects to expound. It does not let down buckets into the subconscious. It does not conceive in sleep, or know what it has said after it has said it. Think before you speak is criticism's motto; speak before you think creation's. Nor is criticism disconcerted by people arriving from Porlock; in fact it sometimes comes from Porlock itself. While not excluding imagination and sympathy, it keeps them and all the faculties under control, and only employs them when they promise to be helpful.

Thus equipped, it advances on its object. It has two aims. The first and the more important is aesthetic. It considers the object in itself, as an entity, and tells us what it can about its life. The second aim is subsidiary: the relation of the object to the rest of the world. Problems of less relevance are considered, such as the conditions under which the work of art was composed, the influences which formed it (criticism adores influences), the influence it has exercised on subsequent works, the artist's life, the lives of the artist's father and mother, prenatal possibilities and so on, straying this way into psychology and that way into history. Much of the above is valuable, but what meanwhile has become of Monteverdi's Vespers, or the Great Mosque at Delhi, or the Frogs of Aristophanes, or any other work which you happen to have in mind? I throw these three objects at you because they happen to be in my own mind. I have been hearing the Vespers, seeing the Frogs, and thinking about the Delhi Mosque. If we wheel up an aesthetic theory—the best attainable, and there are some excellent ones—if we wheel it up and apply it with its measuring rods and pliers and forceps, its calipers and catheters, to Vespers, Mosque, and Frogs, we are visited at once by a sense of the grotesque. It doesn't work, two universes have not even collided, they have been juxtaposed. There is no spiritual parity. And if criticism strays from her central aesthetic quest to influences and psychological and historical considerations, something does happen then, contact is established. But no longer with a work of art.

A work of art is a curious object. Isn't it infectious? Unlike machinery, hasn't it the power of transforming the person who encounters it towards the condition of the person who created it? (I use the clumsy phrase "towards the condition" on purpose.) We—we the beholders or listeners or whatever we are—undergo a change analogous to creation. We are rapt into a region near to that where the artist worked, and like him when we return to earth we feel surprised. To claim we actually entered his state and became co-creators with him there is presumptuous. However much excited I am by Brahms' Fourth Symphony I cannot suppose I feel Brahms' excitement, and probably what he felt is not what I understand as excitement. But there has been an infection from Brahms through his music to myself. Something has passed. I have been transformed towards his condition, he has called me out of myself, he has thrown me into a subsidiary dream; and when the passacaglia is trodden out, and the transformation closed, I too feel surprise.

Unfortunately this infection, this sense of co-operation with a creator, which is the supremely important step in our pilgrimage through the fine arts, is the one step over which criticism cannot help. She can prepare us for it generally, and educate us to keep our senses open, but she has to withdraw when reality approaches, like Virgil from Dante on the summit of Purgatory. With the coming of love, we have to rely on Beatrice, whom we have loved all along, and if we have never loved Beatrice we are lost. We shall remain pottering about with theories and influence and psychological and historical considerations—supports useful in their time, but they must be left behind at the entry of Heaven. I would not suggest that our comprehension of the fine arts is or should be of a nature of a mystic union. But, as in mysticism, we enter an unusual state, and we can only enter it through love. Putting it more prosaically, we cannot understand music unless we desire to hear it. And so we return to the earth.

Let us reconsider that troublesome object, the work of art, and observe another way in which it is recalcitrant to criticism. I am thinking of its freshness. So far as it is authentic, it presents itself as eternally virgin. It expects always to be heard or read or seen for the first time, always to cause surprise. It does not expect to be studied, still less does it present itself as a crossword puzzle, only to be solved after much re-examination. If it does that, if it parades a mystifying element, it is, to that extent not a work of art, nor an immortal Muse but a Sphinx who dies as soon as her riddles are answered. The work of art assumes the existence of the perfect spectator, and is indifferent to the fact that no such person exists. It does not allow for our ignorance and it does not cater for our knowledge.

This eternal freshness in creation presents a difficulty to the critic, who when he hears or reads or sees a work a second time rightly profits by what he has heard or read or seen of it the first time, and studies and compares, remembers and analyses, and often has to reject his original impressions as trivial. He may thus in the end gain a just and true opinion of the work, but he ought to remain startled, and this is usually beyond him. Take Beethoven's Ninth Symphony, the one in A. Isn't it in A? The opening bars announce the key as explicitly as fifths can, leaving us only in doubt as to whether the movement will decide on the major or minor mode. In the fifteenth bar comes the terrifying surprise, the pounce into D minor, which tethers the music, however far it wanders, right down to the ineluctable close. Can one hope to feel that terror and surprise twice? Can one avoid hearing the opening bars as a preparation for the pounce—and thus miss the life of the pounce? Can we combine experience and innocence? I think we can. The willing suspension of experience is possible, it is possible to become like a child who says "Oh!" each time the ball bounces, although he has seen it bounce before and knows it must bounce.

It is possible but it is rare. The critic who is thoroughly versed in the score of the Ninth Symphony and can yet hear the opening bars as a trembling introduction in A to the unknown has reached the highest rank in his profession. Most of us are content to remain well-informed. It is so restful to be well-informed. We forget that Beethoven intended his Symphony to be heard always for the first time. We forget with still greater ease that Tchaikovsky intended the same for his Piano Concerto in B flat minor. Dubious for good reasons of that thumping affair, we sometimes scold it for being "stale"—a ridiculous accusation, for it too was created as an eternal virgin, it too should startle each time it galumphs down the waltz. No doubt the Concerto, and much music, has been too often performed, just as some pictures have been too often looked at. Freshness of reception is exhausted more rapidly by a small or imperfect object than by a great one. Nevertheless the objects themselves are eternally new, it is the recipient who may wither. You remember how at the opening of Goethe's *Faust,* Mephistopheles, being stale himself, found the world stale, and reported it as such to the Almighty. The archangels took no notice of him and continued to sing of eternal freshness. The critic ought to combine Mephistopheles with the archangels, experience and innocence. He ought to know everything inside out, and yet be surprised. Virginia Woolf—who was born a creative artist and a critic—believed in reading a book twice. The first time she abandoned herself to the author unreservedly. The second time she treated him with severity and allowed him to get away with nothing he could not justify. After these two readings she felt qualified to discuss the book. Here is a good rule of thumb advice. But it does not take us to the heart of our problem, which is superrational. For we ought really to read the book in two ways at once (And we ought to look at a picture in two ways at once, and to listen to music similarly.) We ought to perform a miracle the nature of which was hinted at by the Almighty when he said he was always glad to receive Mephistopheles in Heaven and hear him chat.

I would speak tentatively in the presence of an expert audience, but it seems to me that we are most likely to perform that miracle in the case of music. Music, more than the other arts, postulates a double existence. It exists in time, and also exists outside time, instantaneously. With no philosophic training, I cannot put my belief clearly, but I can conceive myself hearing a piece as it goes by and also when it has finished. In the latter case I should hear it as an entity, as a piece of sound-architecture, not as a sound-sequence, not as something divisible into bars. Yet it would be organically connected with the concert-hall performance. Architecture and sequence would, in my apprehension, be more closely fused than the two separate readings of a book in Virginia Woolf's.

The claim of criticism to take us to the heart of the Arts must therefore be disallowed. Another claim has been made for it, a more precise one. It has been suggested that criticism can help an artist to improve his work. If that be true, a raison d'être is established at once. Criticism becomes an important figure, a handmaid to beauty, holding out the sacred lamp in whose light creation proceeds, feeding the lamp with oil, trimming the wick when it flares or smokes. There must be many artists, musicians and others here, and it would be interesting to know whether criticism has helped them in their work, and if so how. Has she held up the lamp? No doubt she illuminates past mistakes or merits, that certainly is within her power, but has the better knowledge of them any practical value?

A remark of Mr. C. Day Lewis is interesting in this connection. It comes at the opening of *The Poetic Image.*

> There is something formidable for the poet in the idea of criticism—something, dare I say it? almost unreal. He writes a poem, then he moves on to a new experience, the next poem: and when a critic comes along and tells him what is right or wrong about the first poem, he has a feeling of irrelevance.

Something almost unreal. That is a just remark. The poet is always developing and moving on, and when his creative state is broken into by comments on something he has just put behind him, he feels bewildered. His reaction is "What are you talking about? Must you?" Once again, and in its purest form, the division between the critical and creative states, the absence of spiritual parity, becomes manifest. In its purest form because poetry is an extreme form of art, and is a convenient field for experiment. My own art, the mixed art of fiction, is less suitable, yet I can truly say with Mr. Day Lewis that I have nearly always found criticism irrelevant. When I am praised, I am pleased; when I am blamed, I am displeased; when I am told I am elusive, I am surprised—but neither the pleasure nor the sorrow nor the astonishment makes any difference when next I enter the creative state. One can eliminate a particular defect perhaps; to substitute merit is the difficulty. I remember that in one of my earlier novels I was blamed for the number of sudden deaths in it, which were said to amount to forty-four per cent of the fictional population. I took heed, and arranged that characters in subsequent novels should die less frequently and give previous notice where possible by means of illness or some other acceptable device. But I was not inspired to put anything vital in the place of the sudden deaths. The only remedy for a defect is inspiration, the subconscious stuff that comes up in the bucket. A piece of contemporary music, to my ear, has a good many sudden deaths in it; the phrases expire as rapidly as the characters in my novel, the chords cut each other's throats, the arpeggio has a heart attack, the fugue gets into a nose-dive. But these defects—if defects they be—are vital to the general conception. They are not to be remedied by substituting sweetness. And the musician would do well to ignore the critic even when he admits the justice of the particular criticism.

Only in two ways can criticism help the artist a little with his work. The first is general. He ought—if he keeps company at all—to keep good company. To be alone may be best—to be alone was that Fate reserved for Beethoven. But if he wishes to consort with ideas and standards and the works of his fellows—and he usually has to in the modern world—he must beware of the second-rate. It means a relaxation of fibre, a temptation to rest on his own superiority. I do not desire to use the words "superior" and "inferior" about human individuals; in an individual so many factors are present that one cannot grade him. But one can legitimately apply them to cultural standards, and the artist should be critical here, and alive in particular to the risks of the clique. The clique is a valuable social device, which only a fanatic would condemn; it can protest and encourage the artist. It is the artist's duty, if he wants to be in a clique, to choose a good one, and to take care it doesn't make him bumptious or sterile or silly. The lowering of critical standards in what one may call daily-studio life, their corruption by adulation or jealousy, may lead to inferior work. Good standards may lead to good work. That is all that there seems to be to say about this vague assistance, and maybe it was not worth saying.

The second way in which criticism can help the artist is more specific. It can help him over details, niggling details, minutiae of style. To refer to my own work again, I have certainly benefited by being advised not to use the word "but" so often. I have had a university education, you see, and it disposes one to overwork that particular conjunction. It is the strength of the academic mind to be fair and see both sides of a question. It is its weakness to be timid and to suffer from that fear-of-giving-oneself-away disease of which Samuel Butler speaks. Both its strength and its weakness incline it to the immoderate use of "but." A good many "buts" have occurred to-day, but not as many as if I had not been warned. The writer of the opposed type, the extrovert, the man who knows what he knows, and likes what he likes, and doesn't care who knows it—he should doubtless be subject to the opposite discipline; he should be criticised because he never uses "but," he should be tempted to employ the qualifying clause. The man who has a legal mind should probably go easy on his "if's." Fiddling little matters. Yes, I know. The sort of trifling help which criticism can give the artist. She cannot help him in great matters.

With these random considerations my paper must close. The latter part of it has been overshadowed and perhaps obsessed by my consciousness of the gulf between the creative and critical states. Perhaps the gulf does not exist, perhaps it does not signify, perhaps I have been making a gulf out of a molehill. But in my view it does not prevent the establishment of a first class raison d'être for criticism in the arts. The only activity which can establish such a raison d'être is love. However cautiously, with whatever reservations, after whatsoever purifications, we must come back to love. That alone raises us to the co-operation with the artist which is the sole reason for our aesthetic pilgrimage. That alone promises spiritual parity. My main conclusion on criticism has therefore to be unfavourable, nor have I succeeded in finding that it has given substantial help to the artists.

[1947]

Katherine E. Gilbert

1886–1952

A. Life

Katherine E. Gilbert was born in Newport, Rhode Island. She studied at Brown and Cornell Universities. She was Professor of Philosophy at Duke University from 1930 until 1941 and was appointed Chairman of the Department of Aesthetics, Art and Music in 1942 at Duke University. She remained head of the Department until her death in 1952.

Mrs. Gilbert's principal writings are in Aesthetics and include the article on "Aesthetics" in *Collier's Encyclopaedia* (1949); "The One and the Many in Croce's Aesthetic," in *The Philosophical Review,* Vol. XXXIV; *Studies in Recent Aesthetics* (1927); *A History of Esthetics* (with Helmut Kuhn) (1939); and *Aesthetic Studies*: *Architecture and Poetry* (1952), in which was published "The Relation between Aesthetics and Art-Criticism," the essay printed below.

B. Aesthetic

The Relation between Aesthetics and Art-Criticism

It has been peculiarly difficult [15] to avoid the too much and the too little in distinguishing the art-critic from the philosopher of art. Loose thought has lumped them together as intellectually concerned with art. Precise thought and jealousy for the cultural compartment have erected high barriers between them. Our chief historian of literary criticism had an unerring scent for the metaphysical taint in criticism, and by the very thoroughness of his exclusion of aesthetic seemed to verge on making, on his own part, a metaphysical pronouncement. Morelli in the last century became the father of a school in the criticism of painting that repudiated before all else "any bump of philosophy." Wilenski has recently taken a

[15] Katherine Gilbert, "Relation between Aesthetics and Art-Criticism," *The Journal of Philosophy,* Vol. XXXV, No. 11.

firm step forward in this same partitioning tradition by proposing that any overstepping of boundaries in the various concerns with art shall automatically mean forfeiture of a degree for a candidate in a specific subject.[16] Aesthetics has not failed to reciprocate these amenities. For Croce the first business of an aesthetician is to determine the concept "art," and that determination rests upon a speculative and ideal history of spirit. Franz Böhm, speaking from the point of view of the Heidelberg school, cleaves sharply the empirical concern with the facts of art and the derivation of style concepts from the philosophical deduction of the "value-moment," questions of fact from questions of worth.[17] Grudin insists that aesthetics is a form of logic, that it manipulates verbal symbols, and that any other concern with art in respect to it assumes the role of datum.[18]

Whatever one thinks ultimately about the relation of art-criticism and aesthetics, one must agree with the incisive captains of the two camps that alliances, blendings, and compromises ought to follow and not precede the best possible discrimination of territory and aim. What, then, should be the preliminary statement of the distinction of function between these two disciplines? The critic aims to *sharpen an image*; the philosopher to *define a sphere.*

In sharpening the image a critic tries to set in relief both the detail and the gross contour of the work. Just as improved methods of making and adjusting lantern slides have made possible increased visibility of the images on the screen, so the devices of the good critic intensify for the beholder both the sensuous qualities, the intellectual "bonds and tyes," and the individual physiognomy of the whole. From Dionysius of Halicarnassus to Lascelles Abercrombie critics have isolated the simplest elements of verbal music and of spoken rhythm in order to make manifest the contribution of these musical atoms to the final poetical effect. We are aware of "tactile values" in Giotto and Masaccio as we were not before Berenson pointed them out. The symbolism of Dürer's *Melencolia I* has been richly documented for us by Panofsky so that we respond to the image as a whole with new eyes. Ruskin taught his own generation to notice the light values in Turner and the connotation of Milton's words. Today we are made aware of the feeling value of the thirds and sixths in Brahms's waltzes, the "poignant, lacerating ninths" in Wolf's songs by Ernest Newman; the *Helligkeit* of organ tones by J. Biehle. Whether the critic lingers longest with the isolable qualities, with the logical intervals and relations, or with the total "habit," his aim throughout is to impress upon us more vividly the stamp of the image's form.

This definition of a critic holds, whatever the disagreements within the profession about the number of planes in a work of art. Whether the poem "refers to" or "reveals" a reality outside itself or not, whether there is or is not a layer that has conceptual significance underneath the layers composing the decorative schema, there is always at least the artistic essence that lies within the frame. This essence the uninstructed always need to be taught to contemplate more penetratingly. It is not only the great traditional critics, for example, Winckelmann and Lessing, that have given us new aesthetic organs. Any successful critic to the degree that he is successful adds to the sensitivity of our responding mechanism. The end of the critic, says Mr. T. S. Eliot, is simply to enable us to perceive; that is, to return to

[16] "The Organization of the Study of Art History," *Deuxième Congrès International d'Esthétique et de Science de l'Art,* II, 73–76.

[17] *Die Logik der Asthetik* (Tübingen, 1930), p. 57.

[18] *A Primer of Æsthetics* (New York, 1930), p. 241.

the work of art with improved perception and with intensified, because more conscious, enjoyment.[19] M. Mauron says in almost the same words that the critic's aim is to heighten our pleasure by clarifying our consciousness; Ernest Newman, that it is to intensify our experience. This conception is not new. Even certain good Victorian critics with a moralistic bias said after all much the same thing. For Matthew Arnold the end of criticism is to see the object as in itself it really is; for Ruskin, to induce energy of contemplation. The sum of the sayings is that criticism works to illuminate the matter in hand and to lighten the beholder's darkness so that the picture or poem before him shines into his consciousness as an intelligible and shapely individuality.

But this unanimity of opinion regarding the perfect critic presupposes something. It presupposes that there is an object there; that it has shape and unity; that it has matter that is logical and fitted to intellectual illumination. Suppose when the critic enters into the alleged "object" in order to stamp it out more clearly, it refuses to be one. Suppose the firm contour, the logical texture, the definite qualities will not answer to the critical summons. Conceivably that upon which the critic feels moved to operate sympathetically may not be altogether an *object*, a one.

Perhaps the expression "a one" may frighten the reader, as if Plotinus were approaching. The critic, we say with that reader, ought not to approach the work of art with preconceived ideas of what the work of art ought to be. It is his business to let the work operate on him and tell him—he lying wisely passive—what it is. But that the work should be a one would seem to be such an elementary condition of his ability to function that he is scarcely conscious of it. For, suppose that the matter before him tells him conflicting stories that will not be reconciled even in his wisely passive head. Suppose part of it does not speak at all, but is dumb or drones. Is it, or is it not, his function to report this unsuccess in bringing alive to his own consciousness the logic and the individuality of the piece before him? Presumably no one would insist that every alleged art object to which the critic exposes his sensitive plate has actually "come through."

Reflection on these possibilities shows us that the work of the critic can hardly be summed up as simply aiding the perception of what is given. He has corrective as well as contemplative offices. Even from Aristotle himself, the perfect critic according to Mr. Eliot, derives the canon which enables critics to mend what is wrong as well as see what is right. Aristotle said that a good tragedy must be in such a sense one that the addition or withdrawal or alteration of any part would spoil the whole. The reference to these irreconcilable parts that are excrescenes or deficiencies or misplacements implies that the critic is aware of alleged cases of art that cannot be perceived as single objects. In such a case his business is not to be wisely passive, but to be wisely active. A musical critic has suggested that this part of the critic's work is ideally compared to plastic surgery. The critic can say of the finished product

> . . . where it is clumsily worked, where it is muddled, where it fails in that steady procession from premises to conclusion that all good art ought to show . . . [He] might have told Bach that now and then his piano works were not so much finished as merely terminated . . .; Beethoven or Brahms when he was becoming too mechanical, too text-bookish, in his "working-out"—in that always awkward moment, for example, of transition from the exposition section to the development section . . .; Wagner that he was weakening a passage by gross excess of

[19] *The Sacred Wood* (New York, 1930), pp. 11–15.

sequential repetition . . .; Debussy when the whole-tone scale had exhausted its welcome . . .; this English composer that piety was a poor substitute for inspiration, even in the British oratorio; another, that he was in danger of exploiting to death a certain sequence of descending chromatic harmonies; another that a certain sort of bogus polyphony was beginning to reveal all too plainly its complete absence of a secret.[20]

This indication of needed aesthetic surgery presupposes that the critic may be baffled in his effort to see and set in relief a long series of ones. Without any arrogance of a priori ideals, the course of his beholding may run other than smoothly. On the basis of what, then, does the passive labor cease and the active labor come in? "Out of the fund of a richer experience of art,"[21] we are told. If this be true, the critic beholds his alleged object not with a nice one-to-one correspondence, but with a mind constituted for the time being by the energies incorporated in it from many experienced objects. The thing is looked at by the hardly acknowledged light of almost innumerable examples that have distilled into essence of critical mind. And in this sense the critic measures his object by something external to the object. In so doing, he does not stretch it on a Procrustean bed, but—so we must allow him—still measures it by a standard relevant, and on a properly liberal interpretation, immanent. He measures it by what he conceives the thing itself wants to be but has failed to be.

This wider something that measures artistic success and that sometimes artificially produces artistic unity by surgery; this regulative principle that both stays inside the object and travels freely beyond it, is the critic's matured sense of *kind*. In building up his sense of *kind* the critic develops what the old psychologists used to call "wit." Wit characteristically seeks out the similarities and associations between things, whereas judgment characteristically seeks out the differences and unlikenesses between things. The critic with his strong native wit, then, passes constantly and sensitively from poem to poem, fugue to fugue, picture to picture, building up a sense of a style. This sense of style is at once an awareness of the defining marks and relations in kindred works and an operating norm in respect to them.

Now philosophers of art also deal with *kinds*. But with them, the sense of kind is primary and at the focus of attention rather than a half-acknowledged organ dimly felt to be functioning. As the philosophical temperament is on the whole rather discriminative than associative, the aesthetician from the very beginnings of his experiencing of art objects lingers by preference on the borderline between art and nonart. He often takes over what generations of critics have pronounced good and have set in relief as good and tries to match the nature of this as a whole with some adequate definition, a definition that both tells what it is and what it is not. Our philosopher savours, then, preferentially the special quality of what is within the contour of a product as over against the special quality of what is outside. And when he lingers within the art object he gravitates towards the place of problematic interpretation. He likes to stay by the swaying barrier between matter shaped and matter recalcitrant. Since his forte is judgment rather than wit, he tends to take over the volume of others' labor as a whole, to perceive it as a qualified totality, and to make intelligible to himself and others, the series or system of qualified totalities. Thus will he get a maximum sense of precise differentiation. He builds up not a sense of style, but of the universe of discourses; he distinguishes spheres.

The whole history of aesthetics illustrates

[20] Ernest Newman, "On Musical Surgery," *A Musical Motley* (New York, 1925), pp. 96, 97.

[21] *Ibid.*

this interpretation of the aesthetician. For example, Plato defended the thesis that poetry is not theology, and that Homer is not a military manual but imagery; Aristotle asserted that poetry is not history; Bruno that it is not the application of rules; Kant that what taste approves is not logical, yet, again, not dissimilar to logic. The philosopher of art is interested primarily not quite in the place where two roads meet, but in the area where two fields have a tendency to overlap. He would distinguish the sphere of practical persuasion from that of the ranging fancy; the sphere of the recipe from that of plastic creation; the sphere of philosophical theory from that of unattached form; the sphere of profitable lesson from that of nontendential emotional fulfilment. That rich fund of experience upon the basis of which the philosopher of art "places" a phenomenon is experience in the refining attributes of the major fields of human interest. When a literary critic would surgically cleanse Galsworthy or George Eliot of the moral fallacy, he might well take counsel of the philosopher who knows by profession the differentiating property of morality. His life is spent in tracing and sorting universals.

Since the art-critic, however modestly he holds himself to his primary business of seeing the object for what it really is, cannot do even this without comparing and relating the given with the many kindred objects that make up his sense of style and his empirical norm; and since the philosopher of art cannot define a sphere nor identify with sure tact the nature of a universal, without having apprehended it innumerable times in the concrete, we are driven in the end, I think, to consider these two functions, however distinguishable, as abstractions from a total ideal concern with art. The philosopher should be the critic's expert consultant on the precise meaning of the predicate terms "art," "beautiful," "ugly," "moral," "religious," "end," "means," "matter," "form," etc. In adjusting his definition exactly to the proposed sphere, the philosopher needs the constant aid of the richer experience and finer analysis of detail of the critic. If the needy critic or philosopher can find the required brother laborer within his own organism, the more speedily and amicably is the total task completed.

The union of the two functions within one personal substance is not so unrealizable an ideal as one is at first prone to think. Mr. T. S. Eliot has recently crowned Aristotle as the ideal critic. But I suppose Aristotle did not cease to be a philosopher at the coronation. Mr. Eliot says that Aristotle does not treat of any critical matter in poetry which he does not illuminate. But all the special points in poetry which he illuminates are illuminated largely because they are bathed in the light of logical and metaphysical distinctions worked out patiently elsewhere in the Aristotelian corpus: the four causes; potentiality and actuality; telescoping forms; the relation of pleasure to action. I would venture the assertion that no more satisfactory basis for criticism could be found than some variant of Aristotle's metaphysics. It is such a framework that gives support and cogency to Santayana's essay on the nature of poetry and Lascelles Abercrombie's theory of poetry; and these discourses seem to me successful both as criticism and as philosophy. Of Coleridge's rank as a critic no encomium is ever needed; and A. C. Bradley has on occasion been rated even higher. If A. C. Bradley competes with Coleridge, it is no less true that his criticism stands firmly fixed in Hegel as Coleridge's did in Kant. No more distinguished critic of Italian Renaissance painting is active today than Sig. Lionello Venturi, and he writes: "It is obvious, then, that a critical history of art should benefit from aesthetics as well as from historical facts."[22]

[22] *History of Art Criticism* (New York, 1936), p. 29.

My conclusion is that it is the function of criticism, *qua* abstract ideal method, to sharpen the image; of the philosophy of art, *qua* ideal abstract method, to define spheres; but that the ideal trafficker with art is like Diotima's *δαίμων* who "conveys and takes across" the definitions of universals to the critics, and the clarified images and norms of the critic to the philosopher, and so "spans the chasm which divides them."

Milton C. Nahm

1903–

Philosophy of Criticism

The Relation of Aesthetics and Criticism

I propose to examine[23] the relation of Aesthetics and criticism. I assume that criticism is integral to Aesthetics and not merely externally related to that subject. In my opinion, it is on this assumption and perhaps only on this assumption that we may determine what criticism is as an autonomous art. I call such an autonomous art "aesthetic criticism" and it is this art which the aesthetic critic—the "man of taste," as he is designated by philosophers of art who deny that criticism is integral to Aesthetics—uses to produce aesthetic values. Aesthetic criticism is distinct from the fine art of criticism. It is by means of fine art that the artistically gifted critic may produce works of criticism which are also works of fine or freeing art. Finally, I offer the present discussion of the relation of Aesthetics to criticism as a necessary preliminary to the construction of an architectonic of criticism. I believe that such a systematization of criticism is needed and that among the "aggregates" of criticism which must not only be brought into an architectonic but must serve as its core is "aesthetic criticism."

[23] Milton C. Nahm, "The Relation of Aesthetics and Criticism." *The Personalist,* Vol. 45, No. 3, 1964, pp. 362 et seq. The School of Philosophy, University of Southern California.

I turn to Katherine E. Gilbert's "The Relation Between Aesthetics and Art-Criticism" for the starting point of my argument. Mrs. Gilbert's essay was first published in *The Journal of Philosophy* in 1938. In 1952, it was one of a sheaf of essays, *Aesthetic Studies: Architecture and Poetry,* presented to Mrs. Gilbert shortly before her death. "The Relation Between Aesthetics and Art-Criticism" is remarkable for many reasons but for none more so than that it is the work of a philosopher who approaches Aesthetics in the footsteps of Plato and Croce. Mrs. Gilbert is one of the few writers in this speculative tradition who entertains the possibility that the relation of criticism to the work of art, or of the artist to either the critic or the aesthetician, is an intelligible one and that its details may be set forth in comprehensible language.

Mrs. Gilbert approaches her subject after a close consideration of critical writings. This leads me to a remark concerning one aspect of Aesthetics which should be, but too often is not obvious in speculation in that subject. The basic problems in Aesthetics confront us because the phenomena—artistic productivity and the data which relate to the work of art and to works in criticism—are wholly explicable only in aesthetic terms. We are led to doubt this on occasion simply because there is no aesthetically definable object or event which is not also in part explicable in non-aesthetic terms. It is because we so frequently are offered adequate critical interpretations that many theorists conclude of criticism that it is externally related to Aesthetics and integrally related to other arts and sciences. My point is that the phenomena of art and criticism present the conditions which require us to relate Aesthetics and criticism.

I may most easily suggest where the core of the problem of relating Aesthetics and criticism is to be found by quoting a passage from Mrs. Gilbert's essay and then discussing two words in one of its sentences:

> "The critic aims to *sharpen an image* . . . In sharpening an image a critic tries to set in relief the detail and gross contour of the work . . . The devices of the good critic intensify for the beholder both the sensuous qualities, the 'intellectual bonds and tyes,' and the individual physiognomy of the whole . . . We are aware of 'tactile values' in Giotto and Masaccio as we were not before Berenson pointed them out. The symbolism of Dürer's *Melencolia I* has been richly documented for us by Panofsky so that we respond to the image as a whole with new eyes . . . Today we are aware of the feeling value of the thirds and sixths in Brahms' waltzes, the 'poignant, lacerating ninths' in Wolf's songs by Ernest Newman, the *Helligkeit* of organ tones by J. Biehle . . ."

This passage is of interest for many reasons. It shows the kinds of criticism upon which Mrs. Gilbert makes her judgments and from which she draws her general conclusions. It suggests the degree to which she depends upon terms familiar to all aestheticians, upon phrases like "sensuous qualities," "individual physiognomy of the whole," and "feeling value." In my present argument, I attach particular importance to one sentence and to two words in that sentence. The sentence is, "The symbolism of Dürer's *Melencolia I* has been richly documented for us by Panofsky so that we respond to the image as a whole with new eyes." The words are "documented" and "new."

Perhaps, for the philosopher, the most interesting documentation in Panofsky's study of *Melencolia I* reveals Dürer's debt to Aristotle. In the *Physical Problems,* Aristotle remarks that "all men who are outstanding in philosophy, poetry or the arts are melancholic, and some to such an extent that they are infected by diseases arising from black bile." He refers to Plato, Socrates, Empedocles and "most of those who have handled poetry" among men who have suffered in this way. For the aesthetician, the passage in the *Problems* is of special interest because in it Aristotle substitutes a naturalist explanation of genius and inspiration for the Platonic notion of divine afflatus.

Such criticism as Panofsky's illustrates the use of documentation as part of an art, as a "right procedure." It is usually assumed that criticism of this kind is the correlative in language to the artist's intelligible technique. It is clear, as well, that a critic who has so "richly documented" his criticism has made choices of a particular art from among many arts and from among the many possible aspects to be criticised in the work of art. The critic is free to choose. He may choose to interpret signs or symbols, to explain the particular work of art in terms of styles or the history of media, to judge the skill or lack of skill with which a specific technique is used, or to interpret the work of art in relation to the artist's life or temperament. He may choose to interpret the art of poetry, of architecture, the dance, painting, or sculpture. In any case, the critic in choosing would appear to have accepted accuracy as the primary requisite of his art and the excellence to be attained by the perfection of technical means as a goal of his critical activities.

For many philosophers of art and critics, as well as for many aestheticians, the problems of criticism end with the completion of the task of documenting or of some other aspect of "right procedure" and with the subjection of the results to evaluation in terms of precision and perfection. Critics of this kind deny that the second word in Mrs. Gilbert's sentence, "new," is relevant to the art of criticism or to works of criticism. It may be of value, before we examine the grounds for Mrs. Gilbert's use of the word, to ask why "new" has been taken to be inapplicable to criticism and to consider some of the consequences of excluding originality as a tool available to the critic.

In the present vigorous state of criticism, it is clear that the historian of art, the archæologist, and the iconologist have usually agreed that only factual judgments come within the scope of their arts. Indeed, these critics and interpreters have frequently—and correctly, in my opinion,—asserted that their task is completed once the facts obtained by measuring and documenting have been verified. They maintain that if there are legitimate questions concerning the aesthetic value of the objects men have made it is the aesthetician who must ask them or provide sound grounds for such judgments of value as the specialist may wish to make in the diverse areas of art. It is clearly understood that judgments of value are not judgments of fact. It is believed that judgments of value are subjective and inaccurate. It is recognized that "taste" does not provide a scientific ground for criticism. But what may occur to an aesthetician is that precisely the kinds of problems the technician leaves unanswered are those which lead to an examination of the claim that there is no "aesthetic criticism" or that if there is no such criticism there clearly should be. It is perhaps less clearly understood that if there is such criticism it means that there is a freedom in criticism which differs from that of choice. It is precisely such freedom as is manifest in art of a special kind that is the presupposition of value-judgments.

The more immediate issue is a simpler one. Neither the critic who describes his task as that of documentation of some sort, nor the aesthetician who defers to the philosopher of art and acquiesces in the received notion that originality need not play a part in criticism can declare any longer and in a categorical fashion that there is no problem here or assume that if there is a problem it is one easily disposed of. We encounter phenomena which present an issue we cannot evade and we come upon it in an area of human endeavor in which men have set store by precision and excellence.

The fact is that the critic has recently experienced no little difficulty in coping with the products of the physicist's brain-children. A good illustration is provided by word that the Hinman Collator, at work on texts of Hawthorne's writings at the Ohio State University, will collate in two years what it would otherwise take one man fifty years to complete without the machine. If accuracy and intelligibility are, respectively, the criteria and end of criticism, a machine of this kind could well replace many critical minds whose powers and procedures would appear to be primarily reproductive in character.

As one examines the situation in contemporary criticism more closely, it is interesting and valuable to realize that its problems are in fact of a familiar kind, whatever their present guise. I have used the word "reproductive" to characterize what the Hinman and other machines appear to be engaged in, but a more precise term is "imitative." It is extraordinary, indeed, that the evidences of our astonishing advances in science should lead in criticism to a reversion to a Platonism which reached the height of its influence in the 18th century. What I suggest is illustrated in *Remarks on the Beauties of Poetry,* published in 1762. The author, Daniel Webb, wrote that the critic is ". . . a dependent, a sort of planet to his original," one who may do no more than "receive and reflect that light of which the poet is a fountain." Not the least interesting point in this sentence is that Webb, too, has taken into account the advances of science. His critic works in a Copernican cosmos, but the theory of criticism he voices is of another universe. Plato writes in the *Laws* that "The poet, according to the tradition which has ever prevailed among us, and is accepted of all men, when he sits down on the tripod of the muse, is not in his right mind; like a fountain, he allows to flow out freely whatever comes in, and . . . he is often compelled . . . to contradict himself; neither can he tell whether there is more truth in one thing that he has said than in another . . ."

Webb's poet is Plato's, pictured by the Athenian philosopher as one divinely inspired but also as one bereft of his wits and with no comprehension of what he produces. Plato's poet is, however, creative. On the other hand, the critic is, for both Plato and Webb, uninspired and unfree. In fact, the majority of Plato's followers dispose of interpreters of literature and art according to the letter of the passage in *Timaeus* in which Plato tells us that "no man in his wits . . . attains inspiration, and for this reason it is customary to appoint interpreters to be judges of true inspiration."

I do not maintain that our present-day advances in sciences have led only to a meek submission to the tyranny of Plato's dogma concerning the critic. In fact, the most vigorous defenses of the various arts on grounds of autonomy and creativity have followed the mechanization of art. It is ironical, however, that these have tended to bolster the argument in which not only the creative artist but the critic is reduced in status to an imitative mechanism. It is because this paradox has emerged that we do well to examine Mrs. Gilbert's use of the word "new" in her essay on the relation of Aesthetics to art-criticism. But we shall understand her argument more fully if we pause to glance at one such declaration of the independence of art before we return to Mrs. Gilbert's essay.

The instance I shall cite concerns not only the Hinman Collator but the Collator's cousins, the "sound track" and "electronic instruments," as they have been used in the production of "music." It is in fact to the "music" produced by such instruments that one musicologist, Paul Henry Lang, has turned his critical ear. Lang's conclusions are of especial interest because music, from Pythagorean times, has been the art upon which scientists, mathematicians, and philosophers have focussed their attention. They have done so in the expectation that it will yield all its secrets to the critical mind using the precise terms of scientific disciplines.

Lang is convinced that the venture is footless. In an editorial in *The Musical Quarterly,* he asserts that "The creative process in music is subject neither to physics, physiology, nor mathematics." "There is," he believes, "a decisive difference between mathematical-physical hypotheses and the actual effects of music as an art."

I doubt that many aestheticians would disagree with Mr. Lang on this point. It is, rather, the inferences he draws from his assertions in order to establish the autonomy of the musical art that are likely to produce doubts. The difficulties arise precisely when the issue of the relation of Aesthetics and criticism and of these arts to musical compositions is examined. As it turns out, the crucial issue is not whether there is or is not a "decisive difference" between "mathematical-physical hypotheses and the actual effects of music." Rather, it is whether it is valid to interpret, as Mr. Lang does, such scientific statements about music and to explain music in terms of mathematics as translations or criticisms of works in that art and then proceed to deny validity to each such statement or interpretation because it is expressed in a language other than music. This is the argument Mr. Lang offers us. He writes of Aesthetic in his *Music in Western Civilization* and tells us that the aesthetic of music is "created by composers." He holds that so long as Aesthetics "is *practised*, that is translated into actual works of art, it is not difficult to follow." He adds, however, that "once there is an attempt to make deductions and abstractions, to formulate into concrete statements the theories hidden in them, the task becomes all but insurmountable."

This theory concerning the aesthetic of music provides the framework of reference for Lang's theory of criticism. It is obvious that the main point thus far put forward is that the aesthetic of music is essentially expression of music. What this means for criticism is evident as the musicologist turns to an examination of the musical criticism of the "romantics," Carl Maria von Weber and E. T. A. Hoffman:

> All these men . . . were endowed with literary gifts and represented—in varying degree—the romantic ideal of the union of arts which would abolish the difference between poetry and music. For the expression of so lofty a purpose the ordinary technical equipment and language of musical writing did not suffice, so they drew on poetry and philosophy, a course which inevitably carried some of them far afield . . . With delightful aphorisms and poetic similes, but also with penetrating and dramatic strength, they achieved the impossible . . .

We may interrupt the quotation to ask, What is "the impossible" these critics achieved? We learn the answer once we are told that the romantic critics were able "to talk about music so that the impression such talk leaves does not pale hopelessly in comparison with the music it discusses."

It is clear to me, at any rate, that Mr. Lang in this last quotation, lays down a requirement which is pertinent to criticism. He stipulates that the critic produce what "does not pale hopelessly in comparison with the music" the author discusses, and this means that the critic is challenged to establish his adequacy as a critic by showing that he can make a work of fine art comparable to the work of fine art he is criticizing. I shall come to this point shortly. But the principal error is that Mr. Lang in fact is not describing criticism in the major portion of his account of what the romantics do. He identifies criticism with the experiencing of a work of art. Mr. Lang suggests that critics and aestheticians practise their "arts" correctly only if they make the work of criticism in the same medium as that in which the artist originally produced the work of art.

The tacit assumption that the experience of a work of art is its criticism is a point which the musicologist does not argue. The more immediate issue is that if Mr. Lang identifies the interpretation and criticism with "practice" or translation into "actual works of art," he implies that the critic must be an imitator. It is curious, indeed, that what Mr. Lang requires of his aesthetician and his critic, in a theory which assumes that music is creative, should parallel so closely as to be almost indistinguishable from them the stipulations Plato lays down in the *Laws* for the critics or judges of imitative arts. He who is to be a competent judge "in everything to be imitated, whether in drawing, music, or any other art," writes Plato, "must possess three things;—he must know, in the first place, of what the imitation is; secondly, he must know that it is true; and thirdly, that it is well executed in words and melodies and rhythms."

Mr. Lang differs from Plato in this, that the philosopher asks that the judge of music *know* that a work is well executed, whereas the musicologist requires that the critic *be able* to execute it. Lang's critic must be able to produce a work of art which does not "pale hopelessly" in comparison with the work it criticizes. Mr. Lang is not alone in requiring that the critic be an artist. The point is startling here because it is related to a new problem, that of machine-made music. But what Mr. Lang says repeats the recurrent protests made by artists who feel that they have been dealt with unjustly. The artist often challenges his critic to produce a work of art equal or superior in value to what the artist has made. But this is the artist's statement concerning the critic's qualifications and it is interesting only because it is pervasive, not because it is persuasive. I cite a few examples. W. C. Fields, in the face of adverse criticism of his juggling act on the vaudeville stage, defended his own skill: "Jugglers," he remarked, "can out-juggle non-jugglers." Kant thought along much the same lines. "Camper," he writes," could no doubt describe very exactly how the best shoes are made, but he was not able to turn one out himself." We may add the poet to the musicologist, the juggler, and the philosopher. In *The Testament of Beauty,* Robert Bridges tells us

How in its naked self
Reason wer powerless showeth when philosophers
will treat of Art . . .
But since they must lack vision of Art,
(for elsewise they had been artists, not
philosophers) they miss the way.

Only if we adopt the theory that art is imitation does it follow that the critic must duplicate the work of art he criticizes and then only if we are prepared to argue that the aesthetician or the critic must use the identical medium for his criticism as the artist does for the original. What, in fact, may the artist require of the critic? Surely, he has the right to ask only that the critic produce a work of criticism comparable in value as criticism to the work of art as work of art. Dr. Samuel Johnson, in his forthright and commonsensical fashion, gave the reason: "You *may* abuse a tragedy, though you cannot write one. You may scold a carpenter who has made you a bad table. It is not your trade to make tables."

What Johnson holds, namely, that the critic practises his own trade or art and not that of the tragic poet, is in my opinion also the core of Mrs. Gilbert's argument at the philosophical level. But as we return to "The Relation Between Aesthetics and Art-Criticism," our immediate concern is with the word, "new," used in addition to "documented" in Mrs. Gilbert's remark concerning Panofsky. She suggests that the critic produces in the "image as a whole" a new combination, a work of art and a work of criticism. One may infer that the critic discovers, selects, and chooses. But he also may make a "new" work of art and it is this which serves to free the perceiver's imagination. In this way, one might interpret Mrs. Gilbert to mean that the critic is free to create a creator and in this sense produce what is original or new.

It would be imprudent in the extreme to rest the weight of even a brief study of the complex relation of Aesthetics and criticism upon two words, "documented" and "new." I have used them thus far only to locate the principal problems in the context of a quotation which suggests the importance of the phenomena of criticism. The quotation from "The Relation Between Aesthetics and Art-Criticism" has a context of its own, however, in one of the most extraordinary statements concerning creativity ever made by a speculative philosopher. Plato's *Symposium* provides this context for Mrs. Gilbert's entire essay. Here Plato refers to the passage of non-being into being, called poetry or making. Plato writes in *Symposium* of "birth in beauty," of men who are creative in their souls, and of poets and all artists "who are deserving of the name inventors."

Mrs. Gilbert extends the context of the creative process to criticism, treating it not as a servile but as an originating art. This is significant. No less so is the fact that Mrs. Gilbert does not suggest that inspiration is necessary for creation or invention. This permits her to speak of the relation between the artist and the critic or aesthetician in intelligible terms, in contrast to more literal interpreters of Plato's theory who recall the fact that Plato's own theory of the inspired genius offers evidence of its origin in the mythology of demonic agents. It is true that Mrs. Gilbert likens her ideal critic, her "Ideal Trafficker with Art," to Diotima's δαίμων in *Symposium.* She makes it clear, however, that she intends this as a figure of speech. How different Mrs. Gilbert's Platonism is from that of more literal followers of Plato's philosophy will be clear if we turn to E. M. Forster's "justification" of criticism. Forster tells us, in an essay called "The *Raison d'Etre* of Criticism," that the artist and the critic are "grotesquely remote" from each other, if what is under consideration is the possible "spiritual parity between them on grounds of creativity." Forster describes the artistic process as one in which the artist "lets down as it were a bucket into his subconsciousness, and draws up something which is normally beyond his reach . . . and when the process is over, when the picture or symphony or lyric or novel (or whatever it is) is complete, the artist looking back on it, will wonder how on earth he did it." "And indeed," concludes Mr. Forster, "he did not do it on earth." Mr. Forster believes that criticism does not "let down buckets into the subconscious." We await the cliché and are not disappointed: "Think before you speak is criticism's motto," says the novelist, "speak before you think is creation's"

Forster's is a restatement of an ancient demonic theory in modern psychological terms, Mrs. Gilbert's a use of an analogy between the critic as "this Ideal Trafficker with Art" and Plato's Eros. Mrs. Gilbert is intent upon what the ideal critic "conveys and takes across the chasm." In Mrs. Gilbert's essay, the δαίμων is translated into a "Trafficker" who performs an intelligible task, that of relating the artist, the critic, and the aesthetician.

In the course of her essay, Mrs. Gilbert readily grants that some criticism may perform only "corrective" or "contemplative" offices. No doubt, the critic may perform mimetic functions as well but it is clear that corrective, contemplative and mimetic tasks do not wholly account for all critical activities. As Mrs. Gilbert sees it, we may respond to "the image as a whole with new eyes," if the critic be successful in the degree that he "adds to the sensitivity of our responding mechanism." The "Ideal Trafficker with Art" is then creative and he is so "by human strength alone." I use the latter phrase because we may now place Mrs. Gilbert's critic in the context of a statement she makes in *A History of Aesthetics* and another which appears in her *Studies in Recent Aesthetic.* In the first book, she describes the change that has taken place from classical times to the present in the conception of the artist: "The artist's invention has subtly shifted from finding what is already there, though hidden, to selecting or creating or fashioning a mental image by human strength alone." In "The One and the Many in Croce's Philosophy," Mrs. Gilbert has written of the experience of the work of art that it is "freed from dissection or generalization about realities." She commends the theory of expression. She believes that it permits "each work of art or experience of beauty" to remain *sui generis.*

For Mrs. Gilbert, criticism, too, is an autonomous art. Here we encounter at least the appearance of paradox. It will be asked at once, if the critic is free to create and if what he creates is new, on what grounds may his "criticism" be called "criticism"?

To the question concerning the "original critic," one may add a problem of more metaphysical character. Some theorists argue that in the nature of the case the critic is a dependent because criticism follows in time upon the object criticized. I shall do no more here than suggest that this argument is of importance only if it leads to a confusion between temporal and causal relations, i.e., if it be argued that the work of art is the cause of the work of criticism as its effect. Even if the work of art is prior to the work of criticism, it does not follow that the art of criticism is posterior to the art of producing what is criticized.

I shall not argue these matters in detail. My principal point is, rather, to suggest that I find no systematic reason for assuming that the critic is dependent upon the artist to the degree that he may not be creative or that his art may not be aesthetic. It is quite evident to me that the presumed paradox suggested by the phrase, "aesthetic criticism," with its implication that the critic may not produce what is "new," is no paradox at all. What has led us to believe that the critic may not produce what is novel or original is an historical controversy.

Precisely what occurred in the history of criticism which leads to a conception like Mrs. Gilbert's "Ideal Trafficker with Art" is best understood if we observe what theorists in the 18th century believed the Platonic figure, and the theory associated with it, achieved. We come upon the answer to this question once we realize that Plato's *Symposium, Ion,* and *Phaedrus,* together with Longinus' *de Sublimitate,* provided the arguments by which an entrenched Aristotelian theory of art and criticism was displaced from the center of the aesthetic stage. The Platonists of the period were in rebellion against a critical theory which had converted the rules of art and criticism into laws. The grounds for the laws were taken to be reason, art, right procedure, and correctness. The Platonists employed a non-rationalist and basically demonic doctrine to counter the rational dogma and emphasized inspiration and original genius.

The impact of the Platonic theory of genius and inspiration was profound. It produced the conception of the artist possessed of inexplicable creative powers, employing techniques no longer describable in terms of "rational procedures" but of magic gifts, and producing not "beautiful" works of art, intelligible to a rational being, but sublime objects or works of beautiful art which were assumed to be unique, incomparable, and ineffable.

It is important for our present purposes to notice that the influence of the theory of the natural and original genius and of sublime or beautiful objects which were believed to be not wholly intelligible, also affected theories concerning the experience of art and the criticism of works of art. It is evident that the non-rational theory influenced many writers to the degree that they were prepared to submit criticism to explanations not unlike those which had been used to discuss the genius, his powers, and the greatness of the products of his activities. Various writers began to entertain the notion that what had been accepted as a logical correlative to a rational technique for the production of art could be reinterpreted as a function of the same creative energy which permitted the genius to produce great art. This line of speculation is suggested by Alexander Pope in his *Essay on Criticism*:

> Both must alike from Heaven derive their light,
> These born to judge, as well as those to write.

As the ancient theory of inspiration is naturalized to art and criticism, the mythology of the demonic genius disappears. The problem then becomes one of determining whether the critic may introduce into his criticism statements which reflect his feelings. Thus, as Mrs. Gilbert uses the words "feeling-states," "the sensitivity of our responding mechanisms," and refers to the "sensuous qualities" of the work of art, her writing shows the influence of well-defined tradition. For example, the historian, Gibbon, describes a fundamental alteration in his own view concerning criticism. He comments on *de Sublimate,* and writes that until he had read Longinus' writing he had believed criticism to be "an exact anatomy of the distinct beauties of a passage" and "whence they had sprung." But, as Gibbon continues in his *Memoirs of My Life,* Longinus taught him another form of criticism: "He tells me his own feelings upon reading and he tells them with such energy that he communicates them."

Men are affected, not only by Longinus'

capacity to make us feel that he, the critic, is "blest by the poet's fire," but, also, as Alexander Gerard in *An Essay on Genius* adds, they came to realize what Longinus means when he writes that great art makes us feel "as if we had ourselves produced the very thing we had heard." More significantly, Gerard holds that "the greatest refinement and justness of taste is necessary" for criticism, but that this is "not alone sufficient to qualify for this office" of the critic: "A critic must not only *feel*, but possess that accuracy of discernment, which enables a person to *reflect* upon his feelings with distinctness, and to explain them to others."

It is clear that there was a strong tendency in the latter part of the 18th century to judge the critic to be a man of original genius, endowed with creative powers and possessed not only of a capacity for deep feeling but also of the ability to reflect upon his emotions and express what he feels. In the long run, however, the contrary view prevails. Thomas Warton, writing in *An Essay on the Genius and Writings of Pope*, shows us the limitations which conservative and rationalist critics discover in Longinus' qualifications. Warton grants that Longinus possesses "exquisite taste" and "sensibility," but he insists that his "observations are too general, and his method too loose. The precision of the true philosophical critic is lost in the declamation of the florid rhetorician . . . Instead of discovering the secret power by which the sentiments and images affect the reader with pleasure, he is ever intent on producing something SUBLIME himself, and strokes of his own eloquence."

Judgments of this kind lead to the substitution of taste for criticism as a factor to be taken into account in Aesthetics. Kant's speculation serves both to illustrate what happened and why, once it occurred, taste continued to perform the function of criticism. The *Critique of Judgment* exerted an enormous influence upon the Aesthetic and the criticism which followed, as is evident as we read Hegel and Coleridge. The influence of Pope and Gerard, among others, is passed on to readers of Kant but it is the passages in their writings which deny that criticism is an integral part of the subject which affect Kant. Kant turns to the Gerard of the early *Talks on Education*, in which the Scottish philosopher writes that "Logic is precisely the same to philosophy that works of criticism are to poetry. The rules of criticism are formed by an accurate scrutiny and examination of the best works of poetry." Likewise, it is the spirit in which Pope wrote the following lines which influences Kant's speculation upon taste and criticism:

> In Poets as true genius is but rare
> True taste as seldom is the Critic's share.

Kant is clear in his own attitude towards critical criteria. He tells us that he is "deaf to all arguments" and remains unconvinced even by critics as eminent as Lessing and Batteux. Criticism, for Kant, is devoid of feeling. It proceeds rationally from premises to conclusions. Judgments of taste are not demonstrable but, although Kant admits that they are subjective, he also argues that they are none the less universally valid. One of Kant's major tasks is to show precisely what place the feelings play in the judgment of taste. But I believe it is the fact that criticism proceeds rationally which leads him to deny the art a place in Aesthetics. The claims of taste are analogous to those of experience when someone tells "me all the ingredients of a dish" and observes "of each and everyone that it is just what I like. I try the dish with *my own* tongue and palate, and I pass judgment according to their verdict (not according to universal principles.)"

In contrast, Mrs. Gilbert's is a theory of criticism which returns to the older tradition of men radically influenced by Plato's and Longinus's theory of the creative genius. But she treats criticism as though the critic could cope with both the problems of taste and criticism without difficulty because they belong to the same order of speculation.

It is here, I believe, that we encounter difficulties. In my opinion, Mrs. Gilbert ignores a necessary distinction. She describes what the "Ideal Trafficker with Art" does and in this shows us why her own ideal critic fails to span "the chasm" between artist and critic and between critic and aesthetician. Specifically, the critic's initial task is to "sharpen the image." The philosopher "defines spheres." The "Ideal Trafficker" moves between critic and philosopher. In discussing what this ideal critic does, it is implied that the relation between the critic and the philosopher varies. It has one significance as we move from critic to philosopher, another as we go from philosopher to critic. The first movement relates the work of art or criticism to the universal, the second relates the universal to the specific work or art. What occurs within the area of these relations and what they relate, Mrs. Gilbert calls the "total concern of art." Mrs. Gilbert tells us that "The philosopher should be the critic's expert consultant on the precise meaning of the predicate terms, 'art,' 'beautiful,' 'ugly,' 'moral,' 'religious,' 'end,' 'means,' 'matter,' 'form,' etc. In adjusting his definition exactly to the proposed sphere, the philosopher needs the constant aid of the richer experience and finer analysis of detail of the critic. . . ."

We know in general, then, what both critic and philosopher do. If, however, we ask what the ideal critic carries across the "chasm," we receive two distinct answers. On the one hand, Mrs. Gilbert's critic must relate the "given with the many kindred objects that make up his sense of style and his empirical norms." The significant word in this answer is the "given." The alternative is complex. Mrs. Gilbert first remarks that the critic presents us with the image, together with its sensuous qualities, of what the artist has produced. We later learn that the critic makes "the image as a whole." This implies that the critic has incorporated the critical data in sensuous media to produce the "new" work of art. Finally, we are informed that the critic has produced a work of criticism which may evoke originating powers in the perceiver.

The "given," in this theory provides the datum for immediate experience. If, however, we ignore the originating of a new perceiver, the "given" is the only factor in this theory which can be "new." In the form in which Mrs. Gilbert presents the argument for the "given," we come to the most clearly marked evidence of Plato's and Croce's influence on her thinking in Aesthetics. Both Plato and Croce hold that beauty has no external relations. For Plato, this is argued both for the form of beauty in *Symposium* and for the absolutely beautiful mathematical forms in *Philebus.* Beauty has its essence in itself, whereas mimetic art has its essence in another. For Croce, expressions or intuitions are beautiful. They have no external relations. Croce divides knowledge into the intuitive or expressive and the logical. Intuitive knowledge is knowledge of the perceptions of individuals. What Croce means is made explicit by R. G. Collingwood in *The Principles of Art*· "Everything which imagination presents to itself is a here and now; something complete in itself, absolutely self-contained, unconnected with anything else by the relations between what it is and what it is not, what it is and that because of which it is what it is, what it is and what it might have been, what it is and what it ought to be."

If we recall for a moment the conflict between philosophers of art who advance the claims of taste and those who assert the primacy of criticism in Aesthetics, we recognize in Mrs. Gilbert's two descriptions of the work of art which the critic must carry across the chasm both the object of taste and the object of criticism. The "given" is the traditional object of taste, the object without external relations. The "object as a whole" is the traditional object of criticism. Alexander Gerard, whom I have already mentioned, makes a clear distinction between them: "Taste is . . . a power which receives its perception immediately, as soon as the object is exhibited previous to any reason concerning the qualities of the object or the cause of the perception." Gerard believes that criticism requires philosophical genius: "Without such genius," he writes, "our observations will be unconnected."

Mrs. Gilbert fails to make the distinction noted by Gerard. Her knowledge of history serves her well as she traces the speculative changes in analyses of creativity from classical to modern times. She is fully aware that Aesthetic has no place for the genius, inspired and bereft of his wits. But this does not guard her theory against a survival of that form of non-rational explanation which is also a survival of Platonic philosophy and of the theory of the object of taste as the "given."

As a result of her failure to distinguish the object of taste from the object of criticism, Mrs. Gilbert requires her ideal critic to perform incompatible tasks. He experiences the "given" as a datum. The object of this experience is "unconnected" or "unrelated." The critic must relate this "given" to "many kindred objects." It is the 'new" and, as a "given," has no external relations. But if we attempt to classify it, this classical object of taste must be related to other "kindred" objects. The process of classification requires such relations because Mrs. Gilbert's "ideal trafficker" must classify the "given" under definitions provided by the philosopher. But the "new," the "given," is unique and beyond classification.

To argue that the critic must simultaneously experience the "given" and classify "the object as a whole" is to suppose that criticism and aesthetic theory may proceed even though the line of communication between the work of art and the act of criticism has been cut. It is impossible to relate the critic and the philosopher on these grounds, precisely as it is impossible to relate the artist and the critic.

If I am correct in what I have argued here, the difficulty of relating Aesthetics and criticism is owing to a traditional interpretation of what the work of art is, rather than to an intrinsic incompatibility between the two subjects. The solution to the problem requires an inquiry into the relations of a work of art to its various contexts. For this, we first take into account relations to external contexts similar to those which documentation requires. We begin, therefore, on the assumption that there is no aesthetic object without external relations. Coleridge, rather than either Plato or Croce, is correct: "It is the prerogative of poetic genius to distinguish by parental instinct its proper offspring from the changelings. . . ." By making these relations explicit, we clarify the meanings of symbols, media, and styles. This process is one of abstracting from the work of art to non-aesthetic contexts and it informs us not only what right procedure will discover but also what excellence the artist seeks to attain.

Right procedure means accuracy and excellence in criticism as documentation; but there is another "right procedure" for the critic at another level. This is why I mentioned the fact that Mrs. Gilbert's theory implies that there is a difference to be noted between going toward Aesthetics from criticism and going from Aesthetics to criticism. The aesthetician creates aesthetic values; the aesthetic critic applies these value to works of fine art. The aesthetician creates aesthetic values from ultimate values, i.e., he originates such values as the beautiful, the sublime, the ugly in the area of Aesthetics from the systematic values produced by the search for perfection and originality. The critic, as aesthetic critic, creates from the systematic values of individuality and intelligibility the values of the tragic and the comic. But there is also the task of specifying these general aesthetic values and making them his own, as an individual critic must do. This, it seems to me, is precisely what Mrs. Gilbert's remark concerning Panofsky means. Not only does Panofsky "document" Dürer's work but he permits us to see it with "new eyes." Other aesthetic critics have done the same. When Charles Lamb writes *On the Artificial Comedy of the Last Century,* what we are presented with is not "documentation," but what is "new," i.e., the plays of Wycherley and Congreve in a new context and with a new imprint upon them. Lamb confesses that he "could never connect those sports of a witty fancy in any shape with any result to be drawn from them to imitation in real life." He draws up a new formula, a new evaluation: "They are a world of themselves almost as much as fairy land." Similarly, Malraux interprets El Greco, not in terms of the history of Venetian and Spanish painting, but in the context of "voices of silence." Hegel is similarly creative in arguing his theory of tragedy as a conflict between values at different levels. Focillon makes us see paintings "with new eyes," once he argues his theory of the "life of forms in painting."

We proceed in this way from "empirical norms" to "aesthetic values," from documentation to Aesthetics and on to aesthetic criticism. We begin, also, to observe that there are additional "aggregates" of criticism which must be submitted to an architectonic if we are to understand more fully what the meaning of "aesthetic criticism" is. Some of these aggregates are already before us: criticism as documentation; philosophical criticism, such as appears in Plato's *Symposium* and is concerned with the metaphysical problems of art—with the nature of the processes of becoming and making or creating—or in Aristotle's theory of art as right procedure or Hegel's influential theory of the stages of art as expressions of *Geist* or Spirit; and aesthetic criticism, internal to the aesthetic universe of discourse and presenting the issues of artistic and aesthetic freedom.

I should include among the "aggregates" to be systematized in an architectonic one aspect of criticism ordinarily excluded. This is the fine art of criticism. It is evident in interpretations of aesthetics and criticism like Mr. Lang's that it is necessary to insist upon a distinction between expression and criticism. It is essential, too, to recognize not only that there is an art of criticism which is not to be confused with imitation or duplication but that there is a fine art of criticism, as well.

My claim that there is a fine art of criticism is supported by an examination of phenomena. I shall be content here to offer two passages from the same literary work, with the suggestion that both are works of fine art. The first is in the preface to *Samson Agonistes.* John Milton writes

> Tragedy, as it was anciently composed, hath been ever held the gravest, moralest, and most profitable of all other poems: therefore said by Aristotle to be of power, by raising pity and fear, or terror, to purge the mind of those and such-like passions; that is, to temper and reduce them to just measure with a kind of delight, stirred up by reading or seeing those passions well imitated. Nor is Nature wanting in her own effects to make good his assertion; for so, in physic, things of melancholic hue and quality are used against melancholy, sour against sour, salt to remove salt humours . . .

In the second passage are the lines

> "Nothing is here for tears, nothing to wail
> Or knock the breast; no weakness, no contempt,
> Dispraise, or blame; nothing but well and fair,
> And what may quiet us in a death so noble . . ."

I do not find the prose to be "grotesquely remote" from the poetry as regards "creativity." Both passages have their own source in Aristotle's theory of *catharsis.* I am, therefore, not convinced that one is the result of Milton having thought before he spoke and the other of his having spoken before he thought. Both are products of the same mind. I should not agree that Milton's mind is inferior in its task of criticizing to Milton's mind in its task of writing the tragedy. I should not agree that the passages differ in originality simply because one is written in prose, the other in poetry. I judge both to be works of fine art produced by means of fine art.

I believe that Mrs. Gilbert's essay, "The Relation Between Aesthetics and Art-Criticism," clears the way for the construction of a needed architectonic. If I have been overly critical of her essay, it is because I have approached her argument and her "Ideal Trafficker with Art" with the seriousness they deserve.